International Accounting

Timothy Doupnik
University of South Carolina

Hector Perera
Massey University

Boston   Burr Ridge, IL   Dubuque, IA   Madison, WI   New York   San Francisco   St. Louis
Bangkok   Bogotá   Caracas   Kuala Lumpur   Lisbon   London   Madrid   Mexico City
Milan   Montreal   New Delhi   Santiago   Seoul   Singapore   Sydney   Taipei   Toronto

McGraw-Hill
Irwin

INTERNATIONAL ACCOUNTING
Published by McGraw-Hill/Irwin, a business unit of The McGraw-Hill Companies, Inc., 1221
Avenue of the Americas, New York, NY, 10020. Copyright © 2007 by The McGraw-Hill Companies,
Inc. All rights reserved. No part of this publication may be reproduced or distributed in any form
or by any means, or stored in a database or retrieval system, without the prior written consent of
The McGraw-Hill Companies, Inc., including, but not limited to, in any network or other electronic
storage or transmission, or broadcast for distance learning.

Some ancillaries, including electronic and print components, may not be available to customers
outside the United States.

This book is printed on acid-free paper.

1 2 3 4 5 6 7 8 9 0 QPD/QPD 0 9 8 7 6 5

ISBN-13: 978-0-07-250775-1
ISBN-10: 0-07-250775-6

Editorial director: *Brent Gordon*
Publisher: *Stewart Mattson*
Executive editor: *Tim Vertovec*
Editorial coordinator: *Andy C. Set*
Marketing manager: *Melissa Larmon*
Media producer: *Greg Bates*
Project manager: *Marlena Pechan*
Senior production supervisor: *Rose Hepburn*
Designer: *Kami Carter*
Media project manager: *Brian Nacik*
Cover design: *Chris Bowyer*
Typeface: *10/12 Palatino*
Compositor: *Interactive Composition Corporation*
Printer: *Quebecor World Dubuque Inc.*

Library of Congress Cataloging-in-Publication Data

Doupnik, Timothy S.
    International accounting / Timothy Doupnik, Hector Perera.—1st ed.
        p. cm.
    Includes index.
    ISBN-13: 978-0-07-250775-1 (alk. paper)
    ISBN-10: 0-07-250775-6 (alk. paper)
        1. International business enterprises—Accounting. I. Perera, Hector. II. Title.

HF5686.I56D68 2007
657'.96—dc22   2005049602

To my wife Birgit and children, Stephanie and Alexander

—TSD

To my daughter Hasanka

—HBP

About the Authors

Timothy S. Doupnik   *University of South Carolina*

Timothy S. Doupnik is a Professor of Accounting at the University of South Carolina, where he has been on the faculty since 1982. He became director of the School of Accounting in August 2003. He has an undergraduate degree from California State University, Fullerton, and received his Master's and Ph.D. from the University of Illinois.

Professor Doupnik's research has dealt exclusively with international accounting issues and has been published in various journals, including *Accounting, Organizations, and Society; Journal of International Accounting Research; Journal of Accounting Literature; International Journal of Accounting; Journal of International Accounting, Auditing, and Taxation;* and *Journal of International Business Studies.* In an article appearing in a 1999 issue of the *International Journal of Accounting,* he was ranked first in authorship of international accounting research in U.S. journals over the period 1980–1996.

Professor Doupnik is a past president of the International Accounting Section of the American Accounting Association and served as editor of *Advances in International Accounting* from 1995 to 1997. He currently serves as an associate editor for the *Journal of International Accounting Research* and on the editorial board of several other journals.

Professor Doupnik has been a visiting professor teaching international and financial accounting at a number of universities around the world, including Xiamen University, China; Potsdam University and Marburg University, Germany; Helsinki School of Economics, Finland; and Barna Escuela de Alta Direccion, Dominican Republic. He was a visiting researcher at the University of São Paulo, Brazil in 1981.

Hector B. Perera   *Massey University*

Hector Perera is a Professor of Accounting at Massey University, where he has been on the faculty since 1986. He has an undergraduate degree from University of Sri Lanka, Peradeniya, and received his Ph.D. from the University of Sydney, Australia.

Professor Perera's research has dealt mainly with international accounting issues and has been published in various journals, including *Journal of International Accounting Research; Journal of Accounting Literature; International Journal of Accounting; Advances in International Accounting; Journal of International Financial Management and Accounting; Abacus; Accounting and Business Research; Accounting, Auditing and Accountability Journal; Accounting Education; Australian Accounting Review;* and *Pacific Accounting Review.* In an article appearing in a 1999 issue of the *International Journal of Accounting,* he was ranked fourth equal in authorship of international accounting research in U.S. journals over the period 1980–1996.

Professor Perera served as Chair of International Relations Committee of the American Accounting Association's International Accounting Section in 2003 and 2004. He is currently an associate editor for the *Journal of International Accounting Research* and on the editorial boards of several other journals.

Professor Perera has been a visiting professor at a number of universities, including the University of Glasgow in Scotland; New South Wales University, Wollongong University, and Northern Territory University in Australia; and Turku School of Economics and Business Administration, and Åbo Akademi University in Finland.

Preface

ORIENTATION AND UNIQUE FEATURES

International accounting can be viewed in terms of the accounting issues uniquely confronted by companies involved in international business. It also can be viewed more broadly as the study of how accounting is practiced in each and every country around the world, learning about and comparing the differences in financial reporting, taxation, and other accounting practices that exist across countries. This book is designed to be used in a course that attempts to provide an overview of the broadly defined area of international accounting, but that focuses on the accounting issues related to international business activities and foreign operations.

The unique benefits of this textbook include its up-to-date coverage of relevant material, extensive numerical examples provided in most chapters, a separate chapter devoted to the application of International Financial Reporting Standards (IFRSs), and coverage of nontraditional but important topics such as strategic accounting issues of multinational companies and international corporate governance. This book contains several important distinguishing features:

- Numerous excerpts from recent annual reports to demonstrate differences in financial reporting practices across countries and to demonstrate financial reporting issues especially relevant for multinational corporations.
- Incorporation of research findings into the discussion on many issues.
- End-of-chapter assignments that help students develop their analytical, communication, and research skills.
- Detailed discussion on the most recent developments in the area of international harmonization/convergence of financial reporting standards.
- A separate chapter on International Financial Reporting Standards that provides detailed information on selected standards. (Most other IFRSs are covered in other chapters.) The chapter also includes numerical examples demonstrating major differences between IFRSs and U.S. GAAP and their implications for financial statements.
- Separate chapters for (1) foreign currency transactions and hedging foreign exchange risk and (2) translation of foreign currency financial statements. Detailed examples demonstrating the accounting for foreign currency derivatives used to hedge a variety of types of foreign currency exposure.
- Separate chapters for (1) international taxation and (2) international transfer pricing, with detailed examples based on provisions in U.S. tax law.
- A chapter devoted to a discussion of the strategic accounting issues facing multinational corporations, with a focus on the role accounting plays in strategy formulation and implementation.
- Use of a corporate governance framework to cover external and internal auditing issues in an international context, with substantial coverage of the Sarbanes-Oxley Act of 2002.
- A well-organized Web index provided at the end of the book.

CHAPTER-BY-CHAPTER CONTENT

Chapter 1 introduces the accounting issues related to international business by following the evolution of a fictional company as it grows from a domestic company to a global enterprise. This chapter provides the context into which the topics covered in the remaining chapters can be placed.

Chapters 2–5 focus on differences in financial reporting across countries and the international harmonization of accounting standards.

- Chapter 2 presents evidence of the diversity in financial reporting that exists around the world, explores the reasons for that diversity, and describes the problems that are created by differences in accounting practice across countries. In this chapter, we also describe and compare several major models of accounting used internationally. We discuss the potential impact that culture has on the development of national accounting systems and present a simplified model of the reasons for international differences in financial reporting. The final section of this chapter uses excerpts from recent annual reports to present additional examples of some of the differences in accounting that exist across countries.

- Chapter 3 focuses on the major efforts worldwide to harmonize financial reporting practices with an emphasis on the activities of the International Accounting Standards Board (IASB). We explain the meaning of harmonization, identify the arguments for and against harmonization, and discuss the use of the IASB's International Financial Reporting Standards (IFRSs), including national efforts to converge with those standards.

- The growing international recognition of IFRSs is arguably the most important development in the world of international accounting. More than 30 countries now use IFRSs for financial reporting purposes, with the United States being the economically most important country not to do so. Chapter 4 summarizes the major types of differences between IFRSs and U.S. GAAP. It provides detailed information on selected IFRSs, concentrating on standards that relate to the recognition and measurement of assets. (Standards related to liabilities and some other issues are covered in an appendix to this chapter.) Chapter 4 also includes numerical examples demonstrating major differences between IFRSs and U.S. GAAP and their implications for financial statements.

- Chapter 5 describes the accounting environment in five economically significant countries—China, Germany, Japan, Mexico, and the United Kingdom—that are representative of major clusters of accounting system. The discussion related to each country's accounting system is organized into four parts: background, accounting profession, accounting regulation, and accounting principles and practices. Exhibits throughout the chapter provide detailed information on differences between each country's GAAP and IFRSs, as well as reconciliations from local GAAP to U.S. GAAP.

Chapters 6–8 deal with financial reporting issues that are of particular importance to multinational corporations. Two different surveys of business executives indicate that the most important topics that should be covered in an international accounting course are related to the accounting for foreign currency.[1] Because of its

---

[1] T. Conover, S. Salter, and J. Price, "International Accounting Education: A Comparison of Course Syllabi and CFO Preferences," *Issues in Accounting Education,* Fall 1994, and T. Foroughi and B. Reed, "A Survey of the Present and Desirable International Accounting Topics in Accounting Education," *International Journal of Accounting,* Fall 1987, pp. 64–82.

importance, this topic is covered in two separate chapters (Chapters 6 and 7). Chapter 8 covers three additional financial reporting topics of particular importance to multinational corporations—inflation accounting, business combinations and consolidated financial statements, and segment reporting.

- Chapter 6 begins with a description of the foreign exchange market and then demonstrates the accounting for foreign currency transactions. Much of this chapter deals with the accounting for derivatives used in foreign currency hedging activities. We first describe how foreign currency forward contracts and foreign currency options can be used to hedge foreign exchange risk. We then explain the concepts of cash flow hedges, fair value hedges, and hedge accounting. Finally, we demonstrate the accounting for forward contracts and options used as cash flow hedges and fair value hedges to hedge foreign currency assets and liabilities, foreign currency firm commitments, and forecasted foreign currency transactions.

- Chapter 7 focuses on the translation of foreign currency financial statements for the purpose of preparing consolidated financial statements. We begin by examining the conceptual issues related to translation, focusing on the concept of balance sheet exposure and the economic interpretability of the translation adjustment. Only after a thorough discussion of the concepts and issues do we then describe the manner in which these issues have been addressed by the IASB and by the U.S. FASB. We then illustrate application of the two methods prescribed by both standard setters and compare the results. We discuss hedging the net investment in foreign, and highlight some of the international differences in translation procedures.

- Chapter 8 covers three additional financial reporting issues. The section on inflation accounting begins with a conceptual discussion of asset valuation and capital maintenance through the use of a simple numerical example, and then summarizes the inflation accounting methods used in different countries. The second section focuses on International Financial Reporting Standards related to business combinations and consolidations, covering issues such as the purchase method, accounting for goodwill, proportionate consolidation, and the equity method. We also describe the extent to which accounting practices in selected economically significant countries are consistent with IFRSs. The final section of this chapter focuses on International Accounting Standard 14, *Segment Reporting*.

Chapter 9 introduces issues related to the analysis of foreign financial statements. We explore potential problems (and possible solutions to those problems) associated with using the financial statements of foreign companies for decision-making purposes. This chapter also provides an example of how an analyst would reformat and restate financial statements from one set of GAAP to another.

Business executives rank international taxation second only to foreign currency in importance as a topic to be covered in an international accounting course.[2] International taxation and tax issues related to international transfer pricing are covered in Chapters 10 and 11.

- Chapter 10 focuses on the taxation of foreign operation income by the home country government. Much of this chapter deals with foreign tax credits, the most important mechanism available to companies to reduce double taxation.

---

[2] Ibid.

This chapter provides a comprehensive example demonstrating the major issues involved in U.S. taxation of foreign operation income. It also describes recent changes in U.S. tax law brought about by the American Jobs Creation Act of 2004.

- Chapter 11 covers the topic of international transfer pricing, focusing on tax implications. We explain how discretionary transfer pricing can be used to achieve specific cost minimization objectives and how the objectives of performance evaluation and cost minimization can conflict in determining international transfer prices. We also describe government reactions to the use of discretionary transfer pricing by multinational companies, focusing on the U.S. rules governing intercompany pricing.

Chapter 12 covers strategic accounting issues of particular relevance to multinational corporations. This chapter discusses multinational capital budgeting as a vital component of strategy formulation and operational budgeting as a key ingredient in strategy implementation. Chapter 12 also deals with issues that must be addressed in designing a process for evaluating the performance of foreign operations.

Chapter 13 covers comparative international auditing and corporate governance. This chapter discusses both external and internal auditing issues as they relate to corporate governance in an international context. Chapter 13 also describes international diversity in external auditing and the international harmonization of auditing standards.

SUPPLEMENTARY MATERIAL

International Accounting is accompanied by supplementary items for both students and instructors. The Online Learning Center (www.mhhe.com/doupnik) is a book-specific Web site that includes the following:

- Chapter summaries.
- Learning objectives.
- Links to relevant sites.
- Online quizzing.

The Instructor's Resource CD-ROM (ISBN-13: 978-0-07-250775-1, ISBN-10: 0-07-250775-6) is a comprehensive resource for instructors combining several teaching supplements into one easy-to-use format. The IRCD includes the following:

- *Instructor's Manual:* Contains teaching notes and suggested course outlines.
- *Solutions Manual:* Contains detailed solutions for all problem material.
- *PowerPoint Slides:* Provides PowerPoint lecture outlines for all chapters.
- *EZ test Computerized Test Bank:* Contains approximately 50 multiple-choice questions.

Acknowledgments

We want to thank the many people who participated in the review process and offered their helpful comments and suggestions:

Wagdy Abdallah
Seton Hall University

Randon C. Otte
Clarion University

Teresa Conover
University of North Texas

Obeua Persons
Rider University

Orapin Duangploy
University of Houston–Downtown

Felix Pomeranz
Florida International University

Emmanuel Emmenyonu
Southern Connecticut State University

Grace Pownall
Emory University

Paul Foote
California State University–Fullerton

Juan Rivera
University of Notre Dame

Mohamed Gaber
State University of New York at Plattsburgh

Kurt Schulzke
Kennesaw State University

We also are thankful to Gary P. Braun of the University of Texas at El Paso for developing PowerPoint slides to accompany the text and Timothy A. Farmer of the University of Missouri—St. Louis, for the Test Bank.

We also pass along many thanks to all the people at McGraw-Hill/Irwin who participated in the creation of this book. In particular, Executive Editor Timothy Vertovec, Editorial Coordinator Andy Set, Project Manager Marlena Pechan, Designer Kami Carter, Media Project Manager Brian Nacik, Media Producer Greg Bates, and Marketing Manager Melissa Larmon all contributed significantly, and we thank them for their hard work and professionalism.

Professor Perera would like to acknowledge with thanks the support and encouragement received for this project from the School of Accountancy, Massey University, and the Department of Business Administration, Åbo Akademi University in Turku (while on sabbatical leave in 2004).

Brief Contents

Contents

Chapter 6
Foreign Currency Transactions and Hedging Foreign Exchange Risk   233

Chapter 7
Translation of Foreign Currency Financial Statements   295

Chapter 8
Additional Financial Reporting Issues   341

Chapter 9
Analysis of Foreign Financial Statements   385

Chapter 13
Comparative International Auditing and Corporate Governance   574

Chapter **One**

Introduction to International Accounting

Learning Objectives

After reading this chapter, you should be able to

- Discuss the nature and scope of international accounting.
- Describe accounting issues confronted by companies involved in international trade (import and export transactions).
- Explain reasons for, and accounting issues associated with, foreign direct investment.
- Describe the practice of cross-listing on foreign stock exchanges.
- Explain the notion of international harmonization of accounting standards.
- Examine the importance of international trade, foreign direct investment, and multinational corporations in the global economy.

WHAT IS INTERNATIONAL ACCOUNTING?

Most accounting students are familiar with financial accounting and managerial accounting, but many have only a vague idea of what international accounting is. Defined broadly, the *accounting* in international accounting encompasses the functional areas of financial accounting, managerial accounting, auditing, taxation, and accounting information systems.

The word *international* in international accounting can be defined at three different levels.[1] The first level is supranational accounting, which denotes standards, guidelines, and rules of accounting, auditing, and taxation issued by supranational organizations. Such organizations include the United Nations, the Organization for Economic Cooperation and Development, and the International Federation of Accountants.

[1] This framework for defining international accounting was developed by Professor Konrad Kubin in the preface to *International Accounting Bibliography 1982–1994*, distributed by the International Accounting Section of the American Accounting Association (Sarasota, FL: AAA, 1997).

At the second level, the company level, international accounting can be viewed in terms of the standards, guidelines, and practices that a company follows related to its international business activities and foreign investments. These would include standards for accounting for transactions denominated in a foreign currency and techniques for evaluating the performance of foreign operations.

At the third and broadest level, international accounting can be viewed as the study of the standards, guidelines, and rules of accounting, auditing, and taxation that exist within each country as well as comparison of those items across countries. Examples would be cross-country comparisons of (1) rules related to the financial reporting of plant, property, and equipment; (2) income and other tax rates; and (3) the requirements for becoming a member of the national accounting profession.

Clearly, international accounting encompasses an enormous amount of territory—both geographically and topically. It is not feasible or desirable to cover the entire discipline in one course, so an instructor must determine the scope of an international accounting course. This book is designed to be used in a course that attempts to provide an overview of the broadly defined area of international accounting but that also focuses on the accounting issues related to international business activities and foreign operations.

EVOLUTION OF A MULTINATIONAL CORPORATION

To gain an appreciation for the accounting issues related to international business, let us follow the evolution of Magnum Corporation, a fictional auto parts manufacturer headquartered in Detroit, Michigan.[2] Magnum was founded in the early 1950s to produce and sell rearview mirrors to automakers in the United States. For the first several decades, all of Magnum's transactions occurred in the United States. Raw materials and machinery and equipment were purchased from suppliers located across the United States, finished products were sold to U.S. automakers, loans were obtained from banks in Michigan and Illinois, and the common stock was sold on the New York Stock Exchange. At this stage, all of Magnum's business activities were carried out in U.S. dollars, its financial reporting was done in compliance with U.S. generally accepted accounting principles (GAAP), and taxes were paid to the U.S. federal government and the state of Michigan.

Sales to Foreign Customers

In the 1980s, one of Magnum's major customers, Normal Motors Inc., acquired a production facility in the United Kingdom, and Magnum was asked to supply this operation with rearview mirrors. The most feasible means of supplying Normal Motors UK (NMUK) was to manufacture the mirrors in Michigan and then ship them to the United Kingdom, thus making export sales to a foreign customer. If the sales had been invoiced in U.S. dollars, accounting for the export sales would have been no different from accounting for domestic sales. However, Normal Motors required Magnum to bill the sales to NMUK in British pounds (£), thus creating foreign currency sales for Magnum. The first shipment of mirrors to NMUK was

---

[2] The description of Magnum's evolution is developed from a U.S. perspective. However, the international accounting issues that Magnum is forced to address would be equally applicable to a company headquartered in any other country in the world.

invoiced at £100,000 with credit terms of 2/10, net 30. If Magnum were a British company, the journal entry to record this sale would have been:

Dr. Accounts receivable (+ Assets) £100,000
      Cr. Sales revenue (+ Equity) £100,000

However, Magnum is a U.S.-based company that keeps its accounting records in U.S. dollars (US$). To account for this export sale, the British pound sale and receivable must be translated into US$. Assuming that the exchange rate between the £ and US$ at the time of this transaction was £1 = US$1.60, the journal entry would have been:

Dr. Accounts receivable (£) (+ Assets) . . . . US$160,000
      Cr. Sales revenue (+ Equity) . . . . US$160,000

This is the first time since its formation that Magnum found it necessary to account for a transaction denominated (invoiced) in a currency other than the U.S. dollar. The company added to its chart of accounts a new account indicating that the receivable was in a foreign currency, "Accounts receivable (£)," and the accountant had to determine the appropriate exchange rate to translate £ into US$.

As luck would have it, by the time NMUK paid its account to Magnum, the value of the £ had fallen to £1 = US$1.50, and the £100,000 received by Magnum was converted into US$150,000. The partial journal entry to record this would have been:

Dr. Cash (+ Asset) . . . . US$150,000
      Cr. Accounts receivable (£) (− Asset) . . . . US$160,000

This journal entry is obviously incomplete because the debit and credit are not equal and the balance sheet will be out of balance. A question arises: How should the difference of US$10,000 between the original US$ value of the receivable and the actual number of US$ received be reflected in the accounting records? Two possible answers would be (1) to treat the difference as a reduction in sales revenue or (2) to record the difference as a separate loss resulting from a change in the foreign exchange rate. This is an accounting issue that Magnum was not required to deal with until it became involved in export sales. Specific rules for accounting for foreign currency transactions exist in the United States, and Magnum's accountants had to develop an ability to apply those rules.

Through the British-pound account receivable, Magnum became exposed to foreign exchange risk—the risk that the foreign currency will decrease in US$ value over the life of the receivable. The obvious way to avoid this risk is to require foreign customers to pay for their purchases in US$. Sometimes foreign customers will not or cannot pay in the seller's currency, and to make the sale, the seller will be obliged to accept payment in the foreign currency. Thus, foreign exchange risk will arise.

Hedges of Foreign Exchange Risk

Companies can use a variety of techniques to manage, or hedge, their exposure to foreign exchange risk. A popular way to hedge foreign exchange risk is through the purchase of a foreign currency option that gives the option owner the right, but not the obligation, to sell foreign currency at a predetermined exchange rate known as the strike price. Magnum purchased such an option for US$200 and was able to sell the £100,000 it received for a total of US$155,000 because of the option's strike price. The foreign currency option was an asset that Magnum was required to account for over its 30-day life. Options are a type of derivative financial instrument,[3] the accounting for which can be quite complicated. Foreign currency forward contracts are another example of derivative financial instruments commonly used to hedge foreign exchange risk. Magnum never had to worry about how to account for hedging instruments such as options and forward contracts until it became involved in international trade.

Foreign Direct Investment

Although the managers at Magnum at first were apprehensive about international business transactions, they soon discovered that foreign sales were a good way to grow revenues and, with careful management of foreign currency risk, would allow the company to earn adequate profit. Over time, Magnum became known throughout Europe for its quality products. The company entered into negotiations and eventually landed supplier contracts with several European automakers, filling orders through export sales from its factory in the United States. Because of the combination of increased shipping costs and its European customers' desire to move toward just-in-time inventory systems, Magnum began thinking about investing in a production facility somewhere in Europe. The ownership and control of foreign assets, such as a manufacturing plant, is known as foreign direct investment. Exhibit 1.1 summarizes some of the major reasons for foreign direct investment.

Two ways for Magnum to establish a manufacturing presence in Europe were to purchase an existing mirror manufacturer (acquisition) or to construct a brand-new plant (greenfield investment). In either case, the company needed to calculate the net present value (NPV) from the potential investment to make sure that the return on investment would be adequate. Determination of NPV involves forecasting future profits and cash flows, discounting those cash flows back to their present value, and comparing this with the amount of the investment. NPV calculations inherently involve a great deal of uncertainty.

In the early 1990s, Magnum identified a company in Portugal (Espelho Ltda.) as a potential acquisition candidate. In determining NPV, Magnum needed to forecast future cash flows and determine a fair price to pay for Espelho. Magnum had to deal with several complications in making a foreign investment decision that would not have come into play in a domestic situation.

First, to assist in determining a fair price to offer for the company, Magnum asked for Espelho's financial statements for the past five years. The financial statements had been prepared in accordance with Portuguese accounting rules, which were much different from the accounting rules Magnum's managers were familiar with. The balance sheet did not provide a clear picture of the company's assets,

---

[3] A derivative is a financial instrument whose value is based on (or derived from) a traditional security (such as a stock or bond), an asset (such as foreign currency or a commodity like gold), or a market index (such as the S&P 500 index). In this example, the value of the British-pound option is based on the price of the British pound.

EXHIBIT 1.1
Reasons for Foreign Direct Investment

Source: Alan M. Rugman and Richard M. Hodgetts, *International Business: A Strategic Management Approach* (New York: McGraw-Hill, 1995), pp. 64–69.

Increase Sales and Profits

International sales may be a source of higher profit margins or of additional profits through additional sales. Unique products or technological advantages may provide a comparative advantage that a company wishes to exploit by expanding sales in foreign countries.

Enter Rapidly Growing or Emerging Markets

Some international markets are growing much faster than others. Foreign direct investment is a means for gaining a foothold in a rapidly growing or emerging market. The ultimate objective is to increase sales and profits.

Reduce Costs

A company sometimes can reduce the cost of providing goods and services to its customers through foreign direct investment. Significantly lower labor costs in some countries provide an opportunity to reduce the cost of production. If materials are in short supply or must be moved a long distance, it might be less expensive to locate production close to the source of supply rather than to import the materials. Transportation costs associated with making export sales to foreign customers can be reduced by locating production close to the customer.

Protect Domestic Markets

To weaken a potential international competitor and protect its domestic market, a company might enter the competitor's home market. The rationale is that a potential competitor is less likely to enter a foreign market if it is preoccupied protecting its own domestic market.

Protect Foreign Markets

Additional investment in a foreign country is sometimes motivated by a need to protect that market from local competitors. Companies generating sales through exports to a particular country sometimes find it necessary to establish a stronger presence in that country over time to protect their market.

Acquire Technological and Managerial Know-How

In addition to conducting research and development at home, another way to acquire technological and managerial know-how is to set up an operation close to leading competitors. Through geographical proximity, companies find it easier to more closely monitor and learn from industry leaders and even hire experienced employees from the competition.

and many liabilities appeared to be kept off-balance-sheet. Footnote disclosure was limited, and cash flow information was not provided. This was the first time that Magnum's management became aware of the significant differences in accounting between countries. Magnum's accountants spent much time and effort restating Espelho's financial statements to a basis that Magnum felt it could use for valuing the company.

Second, in determining NPV, cash flows should be measured on an after-tax basis. To adequately incorporate tax effects into the analysis, Magnum's management had to learn a great deal about the Portuguese income tax system and the taxes and restrictions imposed on dividend payments made to foreign parent companies. These and other complications make the analysis of a foreign investment much more challenging than the analysis of a domestic investment.

Magnum determined that the purchase of Espelho Ltda. would satisfy its European production needs and also generate an adequate return on investment.

Magnum acquired all of the company's outstanding common stock, and Espelho Ltda. continued as a Portuguese corporation. The investment in a subsidiary located in a foreign country created several new accounting challenges that Magnum previously had not been required to address.

Financial Reporting for Foreign Operations

As a publicly traded company in the United States, Magnum Corporation is required to prepare consolidated financial statements in which the assets, liabilities, and income of its subsidiaries (domestic and foreign) are combined with those of the parent company. The consolidated financial statements must be presented in U.S. dollars and prepared using U.S. GAAP. Espelho Ltda., being a Portuguese corporation, keeps its accounting records in euros (€) in accordance with Portuguese GAAP. To consolidate the results of its Portuguese subsidiary, two procedures must be completed.

First, for all those accounting issues in which Portuguese accounting rules differ from U.S. GAAP, amounts calculated under Portuguese GAAP must be converted to a U.S. GAAP basis. To do this, Magnum needs someone who has expertise in both U.S. and Portuguese GAAP and can reconcile the differences between them. Magnum's financial reporting system was altered to accommodate this conversion process. Magnum relied heavily on its external auditing firm (one of the so-called Big Four firms) in developing procedures to restate Espelho's financial statements to U.S. GAAP.

Second, after the account balances have been converted to a U.S. GAAP basis, they then must be translated from the foreign currency (€) into US$. Several methods exist for translating foreign currency financial statements into the parent's reporting currency. All the methods involve the use of both the current exchange rate at the balance sheet date and historical exchange rates. By translating some financial statement items at the current exchange rate and other items at historical exchange rates, the resulting translated balance sheet no longer balances, as can be seen in the following example:

Assets	€1,000	×	$1.05	US$1,050
Liabilities	600	×	1.05	630
Stockholders' equity	400	×	1.00	400
	€1,000			US$1,030

To get the US$ financial statements back into balance, a translation adjustment of US$20 must be added to stockholders' equity. One of the major debates in translating foreign currency financial statements is whether the translation adjustment should be reported in consolidated net income as a gain or whether it should simply be added to equity with no effect on income. Each country has developed rules regarding the appropriate exchange rate to be used for the various financial statement items and the disposition of the translation adjustment. Magnum's accountants needed to learn and be able to apply the rules in force in the United States.

International Income Taxation

The existence of a foreign subsidiary raises two kinds of questions with respect to taxation:

1. What are the income taxes that Espelho Ltda. has to pay in Portugal, and how can those taxes legally be minimized?

2. What are the taxes, if any, that Magnum Corporation has to pay in the United States related to the income earned by Espelho in Portugal, and how can those taxes legally be minimized?

All else being equal, Magnum wants to minimize the total amount of taxes it pays worldwide because doing so will maximize its after-tax cash flows. To achieve this objective, Magnum must have expertise in the tax systems in each of the countries in which it operates. Just as every country has its own unique set of financial accounting rules, each country also has a unique set of tax regulations.

As a Portuguese corporation doing business in Portugal, Espelho Ltda. will have to pay income tax to the Portuguese government on its Portuguese source income. Magnum's management began to understand the Portuguese tax system in the process of determining after-tax net present value when deciding to acquire Espelho. The United States taxes corporate profits on a worldwide basis, which means that Magnum will also have to pay tax to the U.S. government on the income earned by its Portuguese subsidiary. However, because Espelho is legally incorporated in Portugal (as a subsidiary), U.S. tax generally is not owed until Espelho's income is repatriated to the parent in the United States as a dividend. (If Espelho were registered with the Portuguese government as a branch, its income would be taxed currently in the United States regardless of when the income is remitted to Magnum.) Thus, income earned by the foreign operations of U.S. companies is subject to double taxation.

Most countries, including the United States, provide companies relief from double taxation through a credit for the amount of taxes already paid to the foreign government. Tax treaties between two countries might also provide some relief from double taxation. Magnum's tax accountants must be very conversant in U.S. tax law as it pertains to foreign source income to make sure that the company is not paying more taxes to the U.S. government than is necessary.

International Transfer Pricing

Some companies with foreign operations attempt to minimize the amount of worldwide taxes they pay through the use of discretionary transfer pricing. Auto mirrors consist of three major components: mirrored glass, a plastic housing, and a steel bracket. The injection-molding machinery for producing the plastic housing is expensive, and Espelho Ltda. does not own such equipment. The plastic parts that Espelho requires are produced by Magnum in the United States and then shipped to Espelho as an intercompany sale. Prices must be established for these intercompany transfers. The transfer price generates sales revenue for Magnum and is a component of cost of goods sold for Espelho. If the transfer were being made within the United States, Magnum's management would allow the buyer and seller to negotiate a price that both would be willing to accept.

This intercompany sale is being made from one country to another. Because the income tax rate in Portugal is higher than that in the United States, Magnum requires these parts to be sold to Espelho at as high a price as possible. Transferring parts to Portugal at high prices shifts gross profit to the United States that otherwise would be earned in Portugal, thus reducing the total taxes paid to both countries. Most governments are aware that multinational companies have the ability to shift profits between countries through discretionary transfer pricing. To make sure that companies pay their fair share of local taxes, most countries have laws that regulate international transfer pricing. Magnum Corporation must be careful that, in transferring parts from the United States to Portugal, the transfer price is acceptable to tax authorities in both countries. The United States, especially, has become aggressive in enforcing its transfer pricing regulations.

Performance Evaluation of Foreign Operations

To ensure that operations in both the United States and Portugal are achieving their objectives, Magnum's top management requests that the managers of the various operating units submit periodic reports to headquarters detailing their unit's performance. Headquarters management is interested in evaluating the performance of the operating unit as well as the performance of the individuals responsible for managing those units. The process for evaluating performance that Magnum has used in the past for its U.S. operations is not directly transferable in evaluating the performance of Espelho Ltda. Several issues unique to foreign operations must be considered in designing the evaluation system. For example, Magnum has to decide whether to evaluate Espelho's performance on the basis of euros or U.S. dollars. Translation from one currency to another can affect return-on-investment ratios that are often used as performance measures. Magnum must also decide whether reported results should be adjusted to factor out those items over which Espelho's managers had no control, such as the inflated price paid for plastic parts imported from Magnum. There is no universally correct solution to the various issues that Magnum must address, and the company is likely to find it necessary to make periodic adjustments to its evaluation process for foreign operations.

International Auditing

The primary objective of Magnum's performance evaluation system is to maintain control over its decentralized operations. Another important component of the management control process is internal auditing. The internal auditor must (1) make sure that the company's policies and procedures are being followed, and (2) uncover errors, inefficiencies, and, unfortunately at times, fraud. There are several issues that make the internal audit of a foreign operation more complicated than domestic audits.

Perhaps the most obvious obstacle to performing an effective internal audit is language. To be able to communicate with Espelho's managers and employees—asking the questions that need to be asked and understanding the answers—Magnum's internal auditors need to speak Portuguese. The auditors also need to be familiar with the local culture and customs, because these may affect the amount of work necessary in the audit. This familiarity can help to explain some of the behavior encountered and perhaps can be useful in planning the audit. Another important function of the internal auditor is to make sure that the company is in compliance with the Foreign Corrupt Practices Act, which prohibits a U.S. company from paying bribes to foreign government officials to obtain business. Magnum needs to make sure that internal controls are in place to provide reasonable assurance that illegal payments are not made.

External auditors encounter the same problems as internal auditors in dealing with the foreign operations of their clients. External auditors with multinational company clients must have an expertise in the various sets of financial accounting rules as well as the auditing standards in the various jurisdictions in which their clients operate. Magnum's external auditors, for example, must be capable of applying Portuguese auditing standards to attest that Espelho's financial statements present a true and fair view in accordance with Portuguese GAAP. In addition, they must apply U.S. auditing standards to verify that the reconciliation of Espelho's financial statements for consolidation purposes brings the financial statements in compliance with U.S. GAAP.

EXHIBIT 1.2
The History of KPMG

Source: KPMG International, www.kpmg.com/about/history.asp.

KPMG was formed in 1987 through the merger of Peat Marwick International (PMI) and Klynveld Main Goerdeler (KMG). KPMG's history can be traced through the names of its principal founding members—whose initials form the name "K.P.M.G."

- **K** stands for Klynveld. Piet Klynveld founded the accounting firm Klynveld Kraayenhof & Co. in Amsterdam in 1917.
- **P** is for Peat. William Barclay Peat founded the accounting firm William Barclay Peat & Co. in London in 1870.
- **M** stands for Marwick. James Marwick founded the accounting firm Marwick, Mitchell & Co. with Roger Mitchell in New York City in 1897.
- **G** is for Goerdeler. Dr. Reinhard Goerdeler was for many years chairman of the German accounting firm Deutsche Treuhand-Gesellschaft.

In 1911, William Barclay Peat & Co. and Marwick Mitchell & Co. joined forces to form what would later be known as Peat Marwick International (PMI), a worldwide network of accounting and consulting firms.

In 1979, Klynveld joined forces with Deutsche Treuhand-Gesellschaft and the international professional services firm McLintock Main Lafrentz to form Klynveld Main Goerdeler (KMG).

In 1987, PMI and KMG and their member firms joined forces. Today, all member firms throughout the world carry the KPMG name exclusively or include it in their national firm names.

As firms have become more multinational, so have their external auditors. Today, the Big Four international accounting firms are among the most multinational organizations in the world. Indeed, one of the Big Four accounting firms, KPMG, is the result of a merger of four different accounting firms that originated in four different countries (see Exhibit 1.2) and currently has offices in more than 150 jurisdictions around the world.

Cross-Listing on Foreign Stock Exchanges

Magnum's investment in Portugal turned out to be extremely profitable, and over time the company established operations in other countries around the world. As each new country was added to the increasingly international company, Magnum had to address new problems associated with foreign GAAP conversion, foreign currency translation, international taxation and transfer pricing, and management control.

By the beginning of the 21st century, Magnum had become a truly global enterprise with more than 10,000 employees spread across 16 different countries. Although the United States remained its major market, the company generated less than half of its revenues in its home country. Magnum eventually decided that in addition to its stock being listed on the New York Stock Exchange (NYSE), there would be advantages to having the stock listed and traded on several foreign stock exchanges. Most stock exchanges require companies to file an annual report and specify the accounting rules that must be followed in preparing financial statements. Regulations pertaining to foreign companies often differ from those for domestic companies. For example, in the United States, the Securities and Exchange Commission requires all U.S. companies to use U.S. GAAP in preparing their financial statements. Foreign companies listed on U.S. stock exchanges may use foreign GAAP in preparing their financial statements but must provide a reconciliation of net income and stockholders' equity to U.S. GAAP.

Many stock exchanges around the world now allow foreign companies to be listed on those exchanges by using standards developed by the International Accounting Standards Board (IASB). Magnum determined that by preparing a set of financial statements based on the IASB's International Financial Reporting Standards (IFRSs), it could gain access to most of the stock exchanges it might possibly want to, including London's and Frankfurt's. With the help of its external auditing firm, Magnum's accountants developed a second set of financial statements prepared in accordance with IFRSs and the company was able to obtain stock exchange listings in several foreign countries.

International Harmonization of Accounting Standards

Through their experiences in analyzing the financial statements of potential acquisitions and in cross-listing the company's stock, Magnum's managers began to wonder whether the differences that exist in GAAP across countries were really necessary. There would be significant advantages if all countries, including the United States, were to adopt a common set of accounting rules. In that case, Magnum could use one set of accounting standards as the local GAAP in each of the countries in which it has operations and thus avoid the GAAP conversion that it currently must perform in preparing consolidated financial statements. A single set of accounting rules used worldwide also would significantly reduce the problems the company had experienced over the years in evaluating foreign investment opportunities based on financial statements prepared in compliance with a variety of local GAAP. Magnum Corporation became a strong proponent of the international harmonization of accounting standards.

THE GLOBAL ECONOMY

Although Magnum is a fictitious company, its evolution into a multinational corporation is not unrealistic. Most companies begin by selling their products in the domestic market. As foreign demand for the company's product arises, this demand is met initially through making export sales. Exporting is the entry point for most companies into the world of international business.

International Trade

International trade (imports and exports) constitutes a significant portion of the world economy. In 2003, companies worldwide exported over $7.5 trillion worth of merchandise.[4] The three largest exporters were Germany, the United States, and Japan, in that order. The United States, Germany, and China were the three largest importers. Although international trade has existed for thousands of years, recent growth in trade has been phenomenal. Over the period 1991–2003, U.S. exports increased from $422 billion to $724 billion per year, a 72 percent increase. During the same period, Chinese exports increased sixfold to $438 billion in 2003. From 1990 to 2001, global gross domestic product increased by 27 percent while during the same period total global exports increased by 75 percent. Exhibit 1.3 shows the composition of world merchandise trade and suggests the importance of manufactured products.

---

[4] World Trade Organization, *International Trade Statistics 2004,* Table I.5, Leading Exporters and Importers in World Merchandise Trade, 2004.

EXHIBIT 1.3
Composition of World Merchandise Trade, 2003

Source: World Trade Organization, *International Trade Statistics 2004,* Table A.2.

Agricultural products		9.3%
Mining products		13.2
Fuels	10.3%	
All other	2.9	
Manufactured products		74.6
Chemicals	10.9%	
Machinery and transportation equipment	39.7	
Automotive products	9.9%	
Office machines and telecom equipment	12.8	
Other machinery and transportation equipment	17.0	
All other	24.0	
Nonspecified other		2.9
Total		100.0%

The number of companies involved in trade also has grown substantially. The number of U.S. companies making export sales rose by 233 percent from 1987 to 1999, when the number stood at 231,420.[5] Boeing is a U.S.-based company with billions of dollars of annual export sales. In 2002, 33 percent of the company's sales were outside of the United States. In addition, some of the company's key suppliers and subcontractors are located in Europe and Japan. However, not only large companies are involved in exporting. Companies with fewer than 500 workers comprise 97 percent of U.S. exporters.

Foreign Direct Investment

The product cycle theory suggests that, as time passes, exporters may feel the only way to retain their advantage over competition in foreign markets is to produce locally, thereby reducing transportation costs. Companies often acquire existing operations in foreign countries as a way to establish a local production capability. Alternatively, companies can establish a local presence by founding a new company specifically tailored to the company's needs. Sometimes this is done through a joint venture with a local partner.

The acquisition of existing foreign companies and the creation of new foreign subsidiaries are the two most common forms of what is known as foreign direct investment (FDI). The growth in FDI can be seen in Exhibit 1.4. The tremendous increase in the flow of FDI from 1982 to 2003 is partially attributable to the liberalization of investment laws in many countries specifically aimed at attracting FDI. Of 244 changes in national FDI laws in 2003, 220 were more favorable for foreign investors.[6]

FDI is playing a larger and more important role in the world economy. Global sales of foreign affiliates were about twice as high as global exports in 2003, compared to almost parity about two decades earlier. Global sales of foreign affiliates comprises about 10 percent of worldwide gross domestic product.

In 2003, there were 56 cross-border acquisitions of existing companies in which the purchase price exceeded $1 billion. The largest deal was the acquisition of the U.S. firm Household International Inc. by HSBC Holdings PLC, a UK-based company, for a reported $15.3 billion. More than 9,000 FDI greenfield and expansion

---

[5] U.S. Department of Commerce, International Trade Administration, "Small and Medium-Sized Enterprises Play an Important Role," *Export America,* September 2001, pp. 26–29.

[6] United Nations, *World Investment Report 2004,* p. xvii.

EXHIBIT 1.4
Growth in Foreign
Direct Investment,
1982–2003

Source: United Nations,
World Investment Report 2004,
Table I.3.

Item	Value ($ billions)		
	1982	1990	2003
FDI inflows	$ 58	$ 209	$ 560
FDI outflows	37	245	612
FDI inward stock	594	1,761	8,245
FDI outward stock	567	1,716	8,197
Sales of foreign affiliates	2,462	5,503	17,580
Assets of foreign affiliates	1,886	5,706	30,362
Employment of foreign affiliates (thousands)	17,433	23,605	54,170

projects were announced in 2003 at an estimated cost of $440 billion.[7] China was the leading location of these projects, followed by the United States, India, Russia, the United Kingdom, and Brazil.

After years of steady increases, inflows of FDI within the countries of the Organization for Economic Cooperation and Development (OECD) reached a peak of $1.2 trillion in 2000, dropping to 384 billion in 2003.[8] The most popular locations for inbound FDI in 2003 among OECD countries were, in order of importance, Luxembourg, France, the United States, Belgium, and Spain. The countries with the largest dollar amount of outbound FDI in 2003 were the United States, Luxembourg, France, the United Kingdom, and Belgium.

The extent of foreign corporate presence in a country can be viewed by looking at the cumulative amount of inward FDI. Over the period 1994–2003, the United States received more FDI ($1.35 trillion) than any other country—almost three times as much as the second-place United Kingdom.[9] However, in relation to the size of the economy, New Zealand had the greatest amount of inward FDI, exceeding more than 50 percent of the country's gross domestic product (GDP).

Multinational Corporations

A multinational corporation is a company that is headquartered in one country but has operations in other countries.[10] The United Nations estimates that there are over 61,000 multinational companies in the world, with more than 900,000 foreign affiliates.[11] These companies account for approximately 10 percent of the world's GDP.[12]

Companies located in a relatively small number of countries conduct a large proportion of international trade and investment. These countries—collectively

[7] Ibid., p. 6.

[8] Organization for Economic Cooperation and Development, "Trends and Recent Developments in Foreign Direct Investment," *International Investment Perspectives,* 2004, p. 1.

[9] Ibid., p. 4.

[10] There is no universally accepted definition of a multinational corporation. The definition used here comes from Alan M. Rugman and Richard M. Hodgetts, *International Business: A Strategic Management Approach* (New York: McGraw-Hill, 1995, p. 3). Similarly, the United Nations defines *multinational corporations* as "enterprises which own or control production or service facilities outside the country in which they are based" (United Nations, *Multinational Corporations in World Development,* 1973, p. 23), and defines *transnational corporations* as "enterprises comprising parent companies and their foreign affiliates" (United Nations, *World Investment Report 2001,* p. 275).

[11] United Nations, *World Investment Report 2004,* p. xiii.

[12] Ibid., p. 3.

EXHIBIT 1.5
Home Country
of Largest 100
Companies by Sales

Source: *Fortune,* "The 2004
Global 500," July 22, 2004.

United States	35	Japan	14
European Union		**Other**	
Germany	15	Switzerland	4
France	10	China	3
Italy	3	Mexico	1
Netherlands	2	Venezuela	1
United Kingdom	6	South Korea	2
Spain	1		11
Netherlands/United Kingdom	2		
Belgium/Netherlands	1		
	40		

EXHIBIT 1.6   The World's Top 10 Companies in Terms of Multinationality, 1998

Source: United Nations, *World Investment Report 2000*, p. 79.

Corporation	Country	Industry	MNI[*]
Seagram Company	Canada	Beverages/media	94.8
Thomson Corporation	Canada	Media/publishing	94.6
Nestlé SA	Switzerland	Food/beverages	94.2
Electrolux AB	Sweden	Electrical equipment/electronics	92.7
British American Tobacco PLC	United Kingdom	Food/tobacco	91.0
Holderbank Financiere Glarus	Switzerland	Construction materials	90.5
Unilever	Netherlands/United Kingdom	Food/beverages	90.1
ABB	Switzerland	Electrical equipment	89.1
SmithKline Beecham PLC	United Kingdom	Pharmaceuticals	82.3
SCA	Sweden	Paper	80.8

[*]Multinationality index (MNI) is calculated as the average of three ratios: foreign assets/total assets, foreign sales/total sales, and foreign employment/total employment.

known as the triad—are the United States, Japan, and members of the European Union. As Exhibit 1.5 shows, 89 of the 100 largest companies in the world are located in the triad.

The largest companies are not necessarily the most multinational. Of the 500 largest companies in the United States, for example, 36 percent have no foreign operations.[13] In 1998, the United Nations measured the multinationality of companies by averaging three factors: the ratio of foreign sales to total sales, the ratio of foreign assets to total assets, and the ratio of foreign employees to total employees. Exhibit 1.6 lists the top 10 companies according to this measure. Seagram Company was the most multinational company in the world, with more than 90 percent of its assets, sales, and employees located outside of its home country of Canada. Most of the companies on this list come from countries with relatively small domestic markets. The three most multinational U.S. companies in 1998, in order, were Exxon, Coca-Cola, and McDonald's.

Many companies have established a worldwide presence. Wm. Wrigley Jr. Company, the world's largest manufacturer of chewing gum, has production

---

[13] T. Doupnik and L. Seese, "Geographic Area Disclosures under SFAS 131: Materiality and Fineness," *Journal of International Accounting, Auditing & Taxation*, 2001, pp. 117–38.

facilities in 12 countries, has offices in 34 countries, sells products in over 180 countries, and has more than 14,000 employees around the globe. Wrigley generates approximately 65 percent of its sales outside of the United States.[14]

Nokia, the Finnish cellular telephone manufacturer, has 16 manufacturing facilities in nine different countries around the world, including Korea, Brazil, China, and the United States. Because these subsidiaries are outside of the euro zone, Nokia must translate the financial statements from these operations into euros for consolidation purposes. Nokia's management states that, from time to time, it uses forward contracts and foreign currency loans to hedge the foreign exchange risk created by foreign net investments.[15]

International Capital Markets

Many multinational corporations have found it necessary, for one reason or another, to have their stock cross-listed on foreign stock exchanges. Large companies in small countries, such as Finland's Nokia, might find this necessary to obtain sufficient capital at a reasonable cost. Nokia's shares are listed on the Helsinki, Stockholm, Frankfurt, Paris, and New York stock exchanges. Other companies obtain a listing on a foreign exchange to have an "acquisition currency" for acquiring firms in that country through stock swaps. Not long after obtaining a New York Stock Exchange (NYSE) listing, Germany's Daimler-Benz acquired Chrysler in the United States in an exchange of shares.

In 2003, there were 467 foreign companies from 51 countries cross-listed on the NYSE.[16] During 2003, 34.8 billion shares of stock in these companies were traded. The total market value of these companies' NYSE shares at the end of 2003 was $680 billion. Each of these companies was required to reconcile its local GAAP financial statements to a U.S. GAAP basis.

Many U.S. companies are similarly cross-listed on non-U.S. stock exchanges. For example, more than 60 U.S. companies are listed on the London Stock Exchange, including Abbott Labs, Boeing, and Xerox. U.S. companies such as Altria, Caterpillar, and Merrill Lynch are listed on Euronext, a merger of the Amsterdam, Brussels, and Paris stock exchanges. In addition to being listed on the NYSE, shares in General Motors' common stock are listed on the Toronto, London, Frankfurt, Paris, and Brussels exchanges.

OUTLINE OF THE BOOK

The evolution of the fictitious Magnum Corporation presented earlier in this chapter highlights many of the major accounting issues that a multinational corporation must address and that form the focus for this book. The remainder of this book is organized in 12 chapters.

Chapters 2–5 focus on differences in financial reporting across countries and the international harmonization of accounting standards. Chapter 2 provides evidence of the diversity in financial reporting that exists internationally, explores the reasons for that diversity, and describes the various attempts to classify countries by accounting system. Chapter 3 describes and evaluates the major efforts to harmonize accounting internationally. The most important player in global

---

[14] Wm. Wrigley Jr. Company, 2004 annual report, various pages.

[15] Nokia Corporation, 2003 Form 20-F, various pages.

[16] New York Stock Exchange, *Factbook Online,* www.nysedata.com/factbook.

harmonization has been the International Accounting Standards Board (IASB). Chapter 4 summarizes the IASB's International Financial Reporting Standards. Chapter 5 describes the accounting environment in five economically significant countries—China, Germany, Japan, Mexico, and the United Kingdom—that are representative of major clusters of accounting system.

Chapters 6–8 focus on financial reporting issues that are of international significance either because they relate to international business operations or because there is considerable diversity in how they are handled worldwide. Chapters 6 and 7 deal with issues related to foreign currency translation. Chapter 6 covers the accounting for foreign currency transactions and hedging activities, and Chapter 7 demonstrates the translation of foreign currency financial statements. Chapter 8 covers several other important financial reporting issues, specifically inflation accounting, business combinations and consolidated financial statements, and segment reporting.

Chapter 9 introduces issues related to the analysis of foreign financial statements and explores potential problems (and potential solutions) associated with using the financial statements of foreign companies in decision making. This chapter also provides an example of how an analyst would reformat and restate financial statements from one set of GAAP to another.

International taxation and international transfer pricing are covered in Chapters 10 and 11. Chapter 10 focuses on the taxation of foreign operation income by the home country government. Much of this chapter deals with foreign tax credits, the most important mechanism available to companies to reduce double taxation. Chapter 11 covers the topic of international transfer pricing, focusing on tax implications.

Strategic accounting issues of particular relevance to multinational corporations are covered in Chapter 12. This chapter covers multinational capital budgeting as a vital component of strategy formulation and operational budgeting a key ingredient in strategy implementation. Chapter 12 also deals with issues that must be addressed in designing a process for evaluating the performance of foreign operations.

Chapter 13 covers comparative international auditing and corporate governance. This chapter discusses both external and internal auditing issues as they relate to corporate governance in an international context. Chapter 13 also describes international diversity in external auditing and the international harmonization of auditing standards.

Summary

1. International accounting is an extremely broad topic. At a minimum, it focuses on the accounting issues unique to multinational corporations. At the other extreme, it includes the study of the various functional areas of accounting (financial, managerial, auditing, tax, information systems) in all countries of the world, as well as a comparison across countries. This book provides an overview of the broadly defined area of international accounting, with a focus on the accounting issues encountered by multinational companies engaged in international trade and making foreign direct investments.

2. The world economy is becoming increasingly more integrated. International trade (imports and exports) has grown substantially in recent years and is even becoming a normal part of business for relatively small companies. The number of U.S. exporting companies more than doubled in the 1990s.

3. The tremendous growth in foreign direct investment (FDI) over the last two decades is partially attributable to the liberalization of investment laws in many

countries specifically aimed at attracting FDI. The aggregate revenues generated by foreign operations outstrip the revenues generated through exporting by a two-to-one margin.

4. There are more than 60,000 multinational companies in the world, and their 900,000 foreign subsidiaries generate approximately 10 percent of global gross domestic product (GDP). A disproportionate number of multinational corporations are headquartered in the triad: the United States, Japan, and the European Union.

5. The largest companies in the world are not necessarily the most multinational. Indeed, many large U.S. companies have no foreign operations. According to the United Nations, the two most multinational companies in the world in 1998 were Canadian.

6. In addition to establishing operations overseas, many companies also cross-list their shares on stock exchanges outside of their home country. There are a number of reasons for doing this, including gaining access to a larger pool of capital.

7. The remainder of this book consists of 12 chapters. Eight chapters (Chapters 2–9) deal primarily with financial accounting and reporting issues, including the analysis of foreign financial statements. Chapters 10 and 11 focus on international taxation and transfer pricing. Chapter 12 deals with the management accounting issues relevant to multinational corporations in formulating and implementing strategy. The final chapter, Chapter 13, covers comparative international auditing and corporate governance.

Questions

1. How important is international trade (imports and exports) to the world economy?
2. What accounting issues arise for a company as a result of engaging in international trade (imports and exports)?
3. Why might a company be interested in investing in an operation in a foreign country (foreign direct investment)?
4. How important is foreign direct investment to the world economy?
5. What financial reporting issues arise as a result of making a foreign direct investment?
6. What taxation issues arise as a result of making a foreign direct investment?
7. What are some of the issues that arise in evaluating and maintaining control over foreign operations?
8. Why might a company want its stock listed on a stock exchange outside of its home country?
9. Where might one find information that could be used to measure the "multi-nationality" of a company?
10. What would be the advantages of having a single set of accounting standards used worldwide?

Exercises and Problems

1. Sony Corporation reported the following in the summary of Significant Accounting Policies included in the company's 2004 annual report on Form 20-F (p. F-18):

Translation of Foreign Currencies

All asset and liability accounts of foreign subsidiaries and affiliates are translated into Japanese yen at approximate year-end current rates and all income and expense accounts are translated at rates that approximate those rates prevailing at the time of the transactions. The resulting translation adjustments are accumulated as a component of accumulated other comprehensive income.

Foreign currency receivables and payables are translated at appropriate year-end current rates and the resulting translation gains or losses are taken into income.

Required:

Explain in your own words the policies that Sony uses in reflecting in the financial statements the impact of changes in foreign exchange rates.

2. Sony Corporation reported the following in the Notes to Consolidated Financial Statements included in the company's 2004 annual report on Form 20-F (p. F-38):

Foreign Exchange Forward Contracts and Foreign Currency Option Contracts

Sony enters into foreign exchange forward contracts and purchased and written foreign currency option contracts primarily to fix the cash flows from intercompany accounts receivable and payable and forecasted transactions denominated in functional currencies (Japanese yen, U.S. dollars and euros) of Sony's major operating units.

Sony also enters into foreign exchange forward contracts, which effectively fix the cash flows from foreign currency denominated debt.

Required:

Explain in your own words why Sony has entered into foreign exchange forward contracts and foreign currency option contracts.

3. Cooper Grant is the president of Acme Brush of Brazil the wholly owned Brazilian subsidiary of U.S.-based Acme Brush Inc. Cooper Grant's compensation package consists of a combination of salary and bonus. His annual bonus is calculated as a predetermined percentage of the pretax annual income earned by Acme Brush of Brazil. A condensed income statement for Acme Brush of Brazil for the most recent year is as follows (amounts in thousands of Brazilian reals [BRL]):

Sales	BRL10,000
Expenses	9,500
Pretax income	BRL 500

After translating the Brazilian real income statement into U.S. dollars, the condensed income statement for Acme Brush of Brazil appears as follows (amounts in thousands of U.S. dollars [US$]):

Sales	US$3,000
Expenses	3,300
Pretax income (loss)	US$ (300)

Required:

a. Explain how Acme Brush of Brazil's pretax income (in BRL) became a U.S.-dollar pretax loss.

b. Discuss whether Cooper Grant should be paid a bonus or not.

4. The New York Stock Exchange (NYSE) provides a list of non-U.S. companies listed on the exchange on its home page (www.nyse.com) under the heading "International."

Required:

a. Determine the number of foreign companies listed on the NYSE and the number of countries they represent.

b. Determine the five countries with the largest number of foreign companies listed on the NYSE.

c. Speculate as to why non-U.S. companies have gone to the effort to have their shares listed on the NYSE.

5. The London Stock Exchange (LSE) provides a list of non-UK companies listed on the exchange on its home page (www.londonstockexchange.com) under "Prices and News," "Statistics," "List of Companies," "Overseas Companies."

Required:

a. Determine the number of foreign companies listed on the LSE and the number of countries they represent.

b. Determine the number of companies listed on the LSE from these countries: Australia, Brazil, Canada, France, Germany, Mexico, and the United States. Speculate as to why there are more companies listed on the LSE from Australia and Canada than from France and Germany.

c. After completing Exercise 4 above, identify five non-U.S., non-UK companies that are listed on both the NYSE and the LSE.

6. UK-based Astra-Zeneca PLC and Swiss-based Roche Group are two of the largest pharmaceutical companies in Europe. The following information was provided in each company's 2002 annual report.

ASTRA-ZENECA
Annual Report 2002

Geographic Areas	Turnover* ($ million)	Net Operating Assets ($ million)	Employees
United Kingdom	$ 3,964	3,101	10,700
Continental Europe	6,674	4,805	22,600
The Americas	10,464	1,004	17,800
Asia, Africa, and Australia	1,742	958	6,400

*Turnover = Sales.

ROCHE GROUP
Annual Report 2002

Geographical Information	Sales (CHF million)	Segment Assets (CHF million)	Headcount
Switzerland	532	5,272	8,569
European Union	9,067	11,872	
Rest of Europe	1,439	494	23,982*
North America	11,297	16,194	17,988
Latin America	2,393	1,493	5,816
Japan	2,243	4,229	6,381
Rest of Asia	1,805	679	5,169
Africa, Australia, and Oceania	949	273	1,754

*Roche does not split Headcount in Europe other than Switzerland into European Union and Rest of Europe.

Required:

Use the United Nations formula to determine which of these two companies is more multinational.

Case 1-1

Besserbrau AG

Besserbrau AG is a German beer producer headquartered in Ergersheim, Bavaria. The company, which was founded in 1842 by brothers Hans and Franz Besser, is publicly traded with shares listed on the Frankfurt Stock Exchange. Manufacturing in strict accordance with the almost 500-year-old German Beer Purity Law, Besserbrau uses only four ingredients in making its products: malt, hops, yeast, and water. While the other ingredients are obtained locally, Besserbrau imports hops from a company located in the Czech Republic. Czech hops are considered to be among the world's finest. Historically, Besserbrau's products were marketed exclusively in Germany. To take advantage of a potentially enormous market for its products and expand sales, Besserbrau began making sales in the People's Republic of China three years ago. The company established a wholly owned subsidiary in China (BB Pijio) to handle the distribution of Besserbrau products in that country. In the most recent year, sales to BB Pijio accounted for 20 percent of Besserbrau's sales, and BB Pijio's sales to customers in China accounted for 10 percent of the Besserbrau Group's total profits. In fact, sales of Besserbrau products in China have expanded so rapidly and the potential for continued sales growth is so great that the company recently broke ground on the construction of a brewery in Shanghai, China. To finance construction of the new facility, Besserbrau negotiated a listing of its shares on the London Stock Exchange to facilitate an initial public offering of new shares of stock.

Required:

Discuss the various international accounting issues confronted by Besserbrau AG.

Case 1-2

Vanguard International Growth Fund

The Vanguard Group is an investment firm with over 50 different mutual funds in which the public may invest. Among these funds are 10 international funds that concentrate on investments in non-U.S. stocks and bonds. One of these is the International Growth Fund. The following information about this fund was provided in the fund's prospectus, dated December 31, 2004.

VANGUARD INTERNATIONAL GROWTH FUND
Excerpts from Prospectus
December 31, 2004

Fund Profile

Investment Objective

The Fund seeks to provide long-term capital appreciation.

Primary Investment Strategies

The Fund invests in the stocks of companies located outside the United States. In selecting stocks, the Fund's advisors evaluate foreign markets around the world and choose companies considered to have above-average growth potential. The Fund uses multiple investment advisors to manage its portfolio.

Market Exposure

The Fund invests mainly in common stocks of non-U.S. companies that are considered to have above-average potential for growth. About two-thirds of the Fund's assets are invested in long-term growth stocks; the remainder may be invested in stocks of companies that represent shorter-term opportunities. The asset-weighted median market capitalization of the Fund as of August 31, 2004, was $16.7 billion.

The Fund is subject to investment style risk, which is the chance that returns from non-U.S. growth stocks and, to the extent that the Fund is invested in them, small- and mid-cap stocks, will trail returns from the overall domestic stock market. Specific types of stocks tend to go through cycles of doing better—or worse—than the stock market in general. These periods have, in the past, lasted for as long as several years. Historically, small- and mid-cap stocks have been more volatile in price than the large-cap stocks that dominate the overall market, and they often perform quite differently.

The Fund is subject to stock market risk, which is the chance that stock prices overall will decline. Stock markets tend to move in cycles, with periods of rising prices and periods of falling prices. In addition, investments in foreign stock markets can be riskier than U.S. stock investments. The prices of foreign stocks and the prices of U.S. stocks have, at times, moved in opposite directions.

The Fund is subject to country risk and currency risk. *Country risk* is the chance that domestic events—such as political upheaval, financial troubles, or natural disasters—will weaken a country's securities market. *Currency risk* is the chance that the value of a foreign investment, measured in U.S. dollars, will decrease because of unfavorable changes in currency exchange rates.

The Fund is subject to manager risk, which is the chance that poor security selection will cause the Fund to underperform relevant benchmarks or other funds with a similar investment objective.

Plain Talk About
International Investing

U.S. investors who invest abroad will encounter risks not typically associated with U.S. companies, because foreign stock and bond markets operate differently from the U.S. markets. For instance, foreign companies are not subject to the same accounting, auditing, and financial-reporting standards and practices as U.S. companies, and their stocks may not be as liquid as those of similar U.S. firms. In addition, foreign stock exchanges, brokers, and companies generally have less government supervision and regulation than their counterparts in the United States. These factors, among others, could negatively affect the returns U.S. investors receive from foreign investments.

Source: Vanguard International Growth Fund Prospectus, pp. 1–8.

The International Growth Fund's annual report for the year ended August 31, 2004, indicated that 98 percent of the fund's portfolio was invested in 198 non-U.S. stocks and 2 percent was in short-term reserves of cash. The allocation of fund net assets by region was as follows: Europe 60 percent, Pacific 28 percent, and Emerging Markets 10 percent. The sectors and individual countries in which the fund was invested are presented in the following tables:

Sector Diversification (% of portfolio)	
Consumer discretionary	17%
Consumer staples	13
Energy	8
Financials	19
Health care	4
Industrials	14
Information technology	10
Materials	3
Telecommunication services	7
Utilities	3
Short-term reserves	2

Source: Annual report, p. 10.

Country Diversification (% of portfolio)			
Europe		**Pacific**	
United Kingdom	28%	Japan	24%
France	11	Australia	2
Switzerland	5	Hong Kong	2
Italy	4	Subtotal	28%
Ireland	3	**Emerging Markets**	
Netherlands	2		
Sweden	2	South Korea	4%
Germany	2	China	2
Spain	1	India	1
Finland	1	Brazil	1
Denmark	1	Taiwan	1
Subtotal	60%	Indonesia	1
		Subtotal	10%
		Short-term reserves	2%
		Total	100%

Source: Annual report, p. 11.

Required:

1. Explain why an individual investor might want to invest in an international growth fund.
2. Describe the risks associated with making an investment in an international growth fund. Identify the risks that would be common to domestic and international funds, and those risks that would be unique to an international fund.
3. Discuss how the fact that foreign companies are not subject to the same accounting, auditing, and financial reporting standards and practices as U.S. companies poses a risk not typically encountered when investing in the stock of U.S. companies.
4. Consider the allocation of fund assets by region. Speculate as to why the proportions of fund assets are distributed in this manner.
5. Consider the country diversification of fund assets. Identify the countries in which the fund is most heavily invested. Speculate as to why this might be the case. Are there any countries in which you would have expected the fund to be more heavily invested than it is? Are there any countries in which you would have expected the fund to be invested and it is not?
6. Consider the sector diversification of funds assets. Identify the sectors in which the fund is most heavily invested. Speculate as to why this might be the case.

Case 1-3

Nestlé Group

Nestlé is the largest food and beverage company in the world. Founded in 1866 on the shore of Lake Geneva, the company is headquartered in Vevey, Switzerland, but has operations in many countries. Nestlé has more than 500 manufacturing facilities and employs 250,000 people worldwide. The company generates over half its revenue from two major lines of business—beverages and milk products—each with more than 25 percent of 2004 sales. Some of Nestlé's better-known brands are Nescafé (coffee), Perrier (water), Libby's (other beverages), Carnation (dairy), PowerBar (health care nutrition), Stouffer's (frozen foods), KitKat (chocolate), and Alpo (pet food).

Nestlé's corporate Web site contains a section titled "Global Commitment." The company supports the principles of the United Nations Global Compact and is "committed to reflecting these in its business principles and practices. . . . The Global Compact is based on the recognition that development and poverty reduction depend on prosperity, which can only come from efficient and profitable business. International trade and investment create new employment, raise skill levels and increase local economic activity." As an example of Nestlé's global commitment, the company is the founding corporate sponsor of the Red Cross/Red Crescent Africa Health Initiative, whose primary aim is to prevent the spread of HIV/AIDS.

Nestlé's 2004 annual report includes a section titled "Companies of the Nestlé Group." In accordance with a directive of the Swiss Stock Exchange, Nestlé separately discloses the name, location, percent ownership, and capital investment in each operating company that has sales exceeding 10 million Swiss francs (CHF) and each financial company with equity exceeding CHF 10 million or total assets exceeding CHF 50 million. A summary of the companies included in Nestlé's consolidated financial statements is presented in the following table:

Country	Number of Companies	% Capital Shareholdings	Currency
1. Affiliated Companies for Which Full Consolidation Treatment Is Applied			
Europe			
Germany	12	70.00–100.00	EUR
Austria	4	75.33–100.00	EUR
Belgium	6	75.33–100.00	EUR
Bulgaria	1	99.97	BGN
Denmark	3	75.33–100.00	DKK
Spain	10	75.33–100.00	EUR
Finland	3	100.00	EUR
France	17	75.33–100.00	EUR
Greece	2	75.33–100.00	EUR
Hungary	5	75.33–100.00	EUR
Italy	6	75.33–100.00	HUF
Lithuania	1	100.00	LTL
Malta	1	100.00	MTL
Norway	3	75.33–100.00	NOK
Netherlands	6	75.33–100.00	EUR
Poland	5	75.33–100.00	PLN
Portugal	7	75.33–100.00	EUR
Ireland	1	100.00	EUR
Czech Republic	3	100.00	CZK
Romania	1	100.00	ROL
United Kingdom	9	75.33–100.00	GBP
Russia	12	75.33–100.00	RUB
Slovakia	2	100.00	SKK
Sweden	5	75.33–100.00	SEK
Switzerland	7	75.33–100.00	CHF
Turkey	3	75.33– 99.94	TRL
Ukraine	3	94.46–100.00	UAK
Africa			
South Africa	3	75.33–100.00	ZAR
Cameroon	1	99.80	XAF
Côte d'Ivoire	2	86.30–100.00	XOF
Egypt	3	99.16–100.00	EGP
Gabon	1	90.00	XAF
Ghana	1	70.00	GHC
Guinea	1	99.00	GNF
Kenya	1	100.00	KES
Mauritius	2	100.00	BSD
Morocco	1	94.50	MAD
Mozambique	1	100.00	MZM
Niger	1	75.00	XOF
Nigeria	1	62.32	NGN
Senegal	1	100.00	XOF
Tunisia	1	59.20	TND
Zimbabwe	1	100.00	ZWD

Country	Number of Companies	% Capital Shareholdings	Currency
Americas			
Argentina	3	50.89–100.00	ARS
Bolivia	1	100.00	BOB
Brazil	6	75.33–100.00	BRL
Canada	3	50.00–100.00	CAD
Chile	2	75.33– 99.50	CLP
Colombia	3	75.33–100.00	COP
Costa Rica	1	100.00	USD
Cuba	1	50.02	USD
El Salvador	2	100.00	SVC
Ecuador	2	100.00	USD
United States	9	75.33–100.00	USD
Guatemala	2	100.00	GTQ
Honduras	1	100.00	PAB
Jamaica	1	100.00	JMD
Mexico	5	75.33–100.00	MXN
Nicaragua	1	100.00	USD
Panama	2	100.00	PAB
Paraguay	1	100.00	PYG
Peru	1	97.38	PEN
Puerto Rico	1	100.00	USD
Dominican Republic	1	97.00	DOP
Trinidad & Tobago	2	100.00	TTD, USD
Uruguay	1	100.00	UYP
Venezuela	3	75.33–100.00	VEB
Asia			
Saudi Arabia	3	51.00– 75.00	SAR
Bangladesh	1	100.00	BDT
Cambodia	1	80.00	USD
United Arab Emirates	1	49.00–100.00	AED, USD
India	1	61.85	INR
Indonesia	1	90.24	IDR
Israel	1	51.86	ILS
Japan	19	75.33–100.00	JPY
Jordan	1	87.00	JDD
Kuwait	1	49.00	KWD
Lebanon	3	100.00	LBP, CHF
Malaysia	5	72.18	MYR
Oman	1	49.00	OMR
Pakistan	1	59.00	PKR
Philippines	4	99.80–100.00	PHP
Republic of Korea	4	51.00–100.00	KRW
Greater China Region	19	60.00–100.00	CNY, HKD, TWD, USD, CHF
Kingdom of Bahrain	1	49.00	BHD
Singapore	1	100.00	SGD
Sri Lanka	3	90.20– 96.32	LKR
Syria	2	100.00	SYP, CHF
Thailand	9	49.00–100.00	THB, USD
Vietnam	2	65.00–100.00	USD
Oceania			
Australia	4	75.33–100.00	AUD
Fiji	1	74.00	FJD

Continued

Country	Number of Companies	% Capital Shareholdings	Currency
New Zealand	1	100.00	NZD
Papua-New Guinea	1	100.00	PGK
French Polynesia	1	100.00	XPF
New Caledonia	1	100.00	XPF

2. Affiliated Companies for Which the Method of Proportionate Consolidation Is Used

Europe			
Germany	2	50.00	EUR
Austria	1	50.00	EUR
Spain	2	50.00	EUR
France	2	50.00	EUR
Greece	1	50.00	EUR
Hungary	1	50.00	EUR
Italy	1	50.00	EUR
Poland	1	50.00	PLN
Portugal	1	50.00	EUR
Czech Republic	1	50.00	CZK
Russia	1	50.00	RUB
Sweden	1	50.00	SEK
United Kingdom	2	50.00	GBP
Switzerland	5	50.00	CHF
Americas			
Argentina	2	50.00	ARS
Brazil	4	50.00	BRL
Canada	1	50.00	CAD
Chile	1	50.00	CLP
United States	2	50.00	USD
Mexico	2	50.00	MXN
Puerto Rico	1	50.00	PRD
Venezuela	1	50.00	VEB
Asia			
Dubai	1	50.00	AED
Malaysia	1	50.00	MYR
Greater China Region	1	50.00	HKD
Philippines	1	50.00	PHP
Republic of Korea	2	50.00	KRW
Thailand	1	49.00	THB
Oceania			
Australia	2	50.00	AUD

3. Principal Associated Companies for Which the Equity Method Is Used

Germany	2	25.00–49.00	EUR
France	2	26.90–50.00	EUR
Saudi Arabia	1	43.50	SAR
Malaysia	1	25.00	MYR

Subholding, Financial, and Property Companies Are Located in:

Europe: Germany, Belgium, France, Italy, Luxemburg, Netherlands, Switzerland
Americas: Bahamas, Bermuda, Canada, Ecuador, United States, Panama
Asia: Philippines, Singapore

Technical Assistance, Research, and Development Companies Are Located in:

Switzerland, France, Germany, Greater China Region, United States, United Kingdom, Israel, and Singapore

Source: P. Brabeck-Letmathe, CEO, Nestlé S.A., at www.nestle.com//html/about/global.asp.

Required:

1. Identify five countries in which Nestlé does not have an equity interest in a company.
2. Identify the top five countries for Nestlé in terms of the number of companies located in those countries.
3. Identify the different accounting methods used by Nestlé to include its companies in the consolidated financial statements.
4. Determine the number of different currencies in which Nestlé conducts business worldwide. Determine the number of different currencies in which Nestlé conducts business in Europe alone.
5. Discuss the complexity Nestlé faces in preparing consolidated financial statements.
6. Discuss the risks Nestlé faces with respect to its worldwide operations. Discuss possible reasons why Nestlé has operations in as many countries as it does.
7. Describe the ways in which Nestlé might be able to fulfill its commitment to the United Nations Global Compact.

References

Doupnik, T., and L. Seese. "Geographic Area Disclosures under SFAS 131: Materiality and Fineness." *Journal of International Accounting, Auditing & Taxation 2001*, pp. 117–38.

Kubin, Konrad. *Preface, International Accounting Bibliography 1982–1994*. Sarasota, FL: International Accounting Section of the American Accounting Association, 1997.

New York Stock Exchange. *Factbook Online*, www.nysedata.com/factbook.

Organization for Economic Cooperation and Development. "Trends and Recent Developments in Foreign Direct Investment." *International Investment Perspectives*, 2004.

Alan M. Rugman and Richard M. Hodgetts. *International Business: A Strategic Management Approach*. New York: McGraw-Hill, 1995.

"The 2004 Global 500." *Fortune*, July 22, 2004.

United Nations. *Multinational Corporations in World Development*, 1973.

———. *World Investment Report 2000*.

———. *World Investment Report 2004*.

U.S. Department of Commerce. "Small and Medium-Sized Enterprises Play an Important Role." *Export America*, September 2001.

World Trade Organization. *International Trade Statistics 2004*.

Chapter Two

Worldwide Accounting Diversity

Learning Objectives

After reading this chapter, you should be able to

- Provide evidence of the diversity that exists in accounting internationally.
- Explain the problems caused by accounting diversity.
- Describe the major environmental factors that influence national accounting systems and lead to accounting diversity.
- Describe a judgmental classification of countries by financial reporting system.
- Discuss the influence that culture is thought to have on financial reporting.
- Describe a simplified model of the reasons for international differences in financial reporting.
- Categorize accounting differences internationally and provide examples of each type of difference.

INTRODUCTION

Considerable differences exist across countries in the accounting treatment of many items. For example, U.S. companies are not allowed to report property, plant, and equipment at amounts greater than historical cost. In contrast, companies in Chile write up their assets to inflation-adjusted amounts, and Dutch companies are allowed to report their assets on the balance sheet at replacement costs. Research and development costs must be expensed as incurred in Mexico, but development costs may be capitalized as an asset in Canada and France. British companies are required to provide segment information in the notes to financial statements; the same is not true for companies in Bulgaria, Romania, and Slovenia. Numerous other differences in financial reporting exist across countries.

Differences in accounting can result in significantly different amounts being reported on the balance sheet and income statement. In its 2003 annual report, the Korean telecommunications firm SK Telecom Company Ltd. described 15 significant differences between Korean and U.S. accounting rules. Under Korean generally accepted accounting principles (GAAP), SK Telecom reported 2003 net income of 1,966 billion Korean won (KRW). If SK Telecom had used U.S. GAAP in 2003, its net income would have been KRW 2,063 billion, approximately 5 percent larger.[1]

[1] The largest adjustments related to "cancellation of amortization of goodwill" and the recognition of revenue for "nonrefundable activation fees."

Shareholders' equity as stated under Korean GAAP was KRW 6,094 billion but would have been KRW 7,015 billion under U.S. GAAP, a 15 percent difference. Braskem SA, a Brazilian chemical company, made 12 adjustments in 2003 to its Brazilian GAAP net income to report net income on a U.S. GAAP basis. These adjustments caused Brazilian GAAP income of 215.1 million Brazilian reais to increase by 76 percent, to 378.1 million reais under U.S. GAAP. Conversely, stockholders' equity of 2,112.6 million reais on a Brazilian GAAP basis decreased to only 7.8 million reais under U.S. GAAP.[2]

This chapter presents evidence of accounting diversity, explores the reasons for that diversity, and describes the problems that are created by differences in accounting practice across countries. Several major models of accounting have been used internationally, with clusters of countries following them. These are also described and compared in this chapter. We describe the potential impact that culture has on the development of national accounting systems and present a simplified model of the reasons for international differences in financial reporting. The final section of this chapter uses excerpts from annual reports to present additional examples of some of the differences in accounting that exist across countries.

EVIDENCE OF ACCOUNTING DIVERSITY

Exhibits 2.1 and 2.2 present balance sheets for the British company AstraZeneca PLC and its U.S. competitor Johnson & Johnson Company. A quick examination of these statements shows several differences in format and terminology between the United Kingdom and the United States. Perhaps the most obvious difference is the order in which assets are presented. Whereas Johnson & Johnson presents assets in order of liquidity, beginning with cash and cash equivalents, AstraZeneca presents assets in reverse order of liquidity, starting with fixed assets. *Fixed assets* in the United Kingdom encompasses all assets classified as noncurrent in the United States, whereas property, plant, and equipment is referred to as *tangible fixed assets.* Liabilities are called *creditors*, and accounts receivable are *debtors*. Unless one is fluent in the language of British accounting, *stocks* might be thought to be marketable securities, when in actuality *stocks* are inventories. *Called-up share capital* is the equivalent of the common stock account on a U.S. balance sheet, and *share premium capital* is the additional paid-in capital in excess of par value. Unappropriated retained earnings on a U.S. balance sheet are reflected in the item labeled *Profit and loss account* on a UK balance sheet. Several *reserve* accounts are used to indicate appropriations of retained earnings.

From the perspective of U.S. financial reporting, the UK balance sheet has an unusual structure. Rather than the U.S. norm of Assets = Liabilities + Shareholders' equity, AstraZeneca's balance sheet is presented as Assets − Liabilities = Shareholders' equity. Closer inspection shows that the balance sheet presents the left-hand side of the equation as Noncurrent assets + Working capital − Noncurrent liabilities = Net assets.

Johnson & Johnson includes only consolidated financial statements in its annual report. In addition to consolidated (group) financial statements, AstraZeneca also includes the parent company's separate balance sheet (not shown) in the notes to the

---

[2] Most of the difference in stockholder's equity is attributable to an amount treated as goodwill under Brazilian GAAP that would be treated as a distribution to stockholders (reduction in equity) under U.S. GAAP.

EXHIBIT 2.1

ASTRAZENECA PLC
Balance Sheet

Group Balance Sheet at 31 December

	Notes	2003 $m	2002 $m
Fixed assets			
Tangible fixed assets	9	**7,536**	6,597
Goodwill and intangible assets	10	**2,884**	2,807
Fixed asset investments	11	**220**	46
		10,640	9,450
Current assets			
Stocks	12	**3,022**	2,593
Debtors	13	**5,960**	4,845
Short-term investments	14	**3,218**	3,962
Cash		**733**	726
		12,933	12,126
Total assets		**23,573**	21,576
Creditors due within one year			
Short-term borrowings and overdrafts	15	**(152)**	(202)
Current instalments of loans	17	**—**	(314)
Other creditors	16	**(7,543)**	(7,699)
		(7,695)	(8,215)
Net current assets		**5,238**	3,911
Total assets less current liabilities		**15,878**	13,361
Creditors due after more than one year			
Loans	17	**(303)**	(328)
Other creditors	16	**(52)**	(34)
		(355)	(362)
Provisions for liabilities and charges	19	**2,266**	(1,773)
Net assets		**13,257**	11,226
Capital and reserves			
Called-up share capital	35	**423**	429
Share premium capital	21	**449**	403
Capital redemption reserve	21	**23**	16
Merger reserve	21	**433**	433
Other reserves	21	**1,401**	1,440
Profit and loss account	21	**10,449**	8,451
Shareholders' funds—equity interests	20	**13,176**	11,172
Minority equity interests		**79**	54
Shareholders' funds and minority interests		**13,257**	11,226

financial statements. In the parent company balance sheet, investments in subsidiaries are not consolidated but instead are reported in the *Fixed asset investments* line item.

All of these superficial differences would probably cause a financial analyst no problem in analyzing the company's financial statements. More important

EXHIBIT 2.2

JOHNSON & JOHNSON AND SUBSIDIARIES COMPANY
Consolidated Balance Sheets

At December 28, 2003, and December 29, 2002 (Dollars in Millions
Except Share and Per Share Data) (Note 1)

Assets	2003	2002
Current assets		
Cash and cash equivalents (Notes 1, 14 and 15)	$ 5,377	2,894
Marketable securities (Notes 1, 14 and 15)	4,146	4,581
Accounts receivable trade, less allowances for doubtful accounts $192 (2002, $191)	6,574	5,399
Inventories (Notes 1 and 2)	3,588	3,303
Deferred taxes on income (Note 8)	1,526	1,419
Prepaid expenses and other receivables	1,784	1,670
Total current assets	22,995	19,266
Marketable securities, noncurrent (Notes 1, 14 and 15)	84	121
Property, plant, and equipment, net (Notes 1 and 3)	9,846	8,710
Intangible assets, net (Notes 1 and 7)	11,539	9,246
Deferred taxes on income (Note 8)	692	236
Other assets (Note 5)	3,107	2,977
Total assets	$48,263	40,556
Liabilities and Shareholders' Equity		
Current liabilities		
Loans and notes payable (Note 6)	$ 1,139	2,117
Accounts payable	4,966	3,621
Accrued liabilities	2,639	2,059
Accrued rebates, returns and promotions	2,308	1,761
Accrued salaries, wages and commissions	1,452	1,181
Accrued taxes on income	944	710
Total current liabilities	13,449	11,449
Long-term debt (Note 6)	2,955	2,022
Deferred tax liability (Note 8)	780	643
Employee related obligations (Notes 5 and 13)	2,262	1,967
Other liabilities	1,949	1,778
Shareholders' equity		
Preferred stock—without par value (authorized and unissued 2,000,000 shares)	—	—
Common stock—par value $1.00 per share (Note 20) (authorized 4,320,000,000 shares; issued 3,119,842,000 shares)	3,120	3,120
Notes receivable from employee stock ownership plan (Note 16)	(18)	(25)
Accumulated other comprehensive income (Note 12)	(590)	(842)
Retained earnings	30,503	26,571
	33,015	28,824
Less: common stock held in treasury, at cost (Note 20) (151,869,000 and 151,547,000)	6,146	6,127
Total shareholders' equity	26,869	22,697
Total liabilities and shareholders' equity	$48,263	40,556

EXHIBIT 2.3

ASTRAZENECA PLC
Reconciliation to U.S. GAAP

Net income	2003 $m	2002 $m	2001 $m
Net income, as shown in the consolidated statements of income before exceptional items....................	**3,036**	3,186	3,044
Exceptional items after tax	—	(350)	(138)
Net income for the period under UK GAAP................	**3,036**	2,836	2,906
Adjustments to conform with US GAAP			
Purchase accounting adjustments (including goodwill and intangibles)			
Deemed acquisition of Astra			
Amortisation and other acquisition adjustments	**(952)**	(864)	(1,514)
Others...........................	**59**	55	—
Capitalisation, less disposals and amortisation of interest	**17**	46	57
Deferred taxation			
On fair values of Astra............................	**266**	239	249
Others...........................	**(91)**	(99)	(198)
Pension and other post-retirement benefits expense	**(43)**	(46)	(29)
Software costs	**(18)**	(46)	(10)
Restructuring costs	—	—	(22)
Share based compensation	**(12)**	33	(7)
Fair value of derivative financial instruments	**10**	93	18
Deferred income recognition.........................	**14**	61	(75)
Unrealised losses on foreign exchange and others...........	**(18)**	(1)	(10)
Net income before cumulative effect of change in accounting policy	**2,268**	2,307	1,365
Cumulative effect of change in accounting policy, net of tax, on adoption of SFAS No. 133.................	—	—	32
Net income in accordance with US GAAP	**2,268**	2,307	1,397

Shareholders' equity	2003 $m	2002 $m
Total shareholders' equity under UK GAAP	**13,178**	11,172
Adjustments to conform to US GAAP		
Purchase accounting adjustments (including goodwill and intangibles)		
Deemed acquisition of Astra		
Goodwill..................................	**14,311**	12,692
Tangible and intangible fixed assets	**7,661**	7,707
Others..................................	**145**	86
Capitalisation, less disposals and amortisation of interest	**255**	238
Deferred taxation		
On fair value of Astra	**(2,313)**	(2,305)
Others..................................	**(207)**	(159)
Dividend..................................	**914**	808
Pension and other post-retirement benefits expense	**(534)**	(295)
Software costs capitalized............................	**46**	64
Fair value of derivative financial instruments	**109**	99
Deferred income recognition.........................	—	(14)
Others..................................	**89**	90
Shareholders' equity in accordance with US GAAP........	**33,654**	30,183

than the format and terminology differences are the differences in measurement rules employed to value assets and liabilities and to calculate income. Because AstraZeneca's common stock is listed on the New York Stock Exchange, the company is required to be registered and file financial statements with the U.S. Securities and Exchange Commission (SEC). For foreign registrants, the SEC requires income and stockholders' equity reported under foreign GAAP to be reconciled with U.S. GAAP. AstraZeneca's 2003 reconciliation to U.S. GAAP is presented in Exhibit 2.3. This reconciliation provides insight into some of the major differences in accounting principles between the United States and the United Kingdom. Note that although only 11 items required adjustment in 2003, the aggregate effect on income and stockholders' equity was highly significant. Net income in accordance with U.S. GAAP in 2003 was only 75 percent the amount of UK GAAP net income. Stockholders' equity in 2003 under U.S. GAAP was 2.5 times larger than under UK GAAP. In 2003, return on average total stockholders' equity is 25 percent under British GAAP, but only 7 percent under U.S. GAAP; this ratio is 3.5 times larger under British accounting rules!

MAGNITUDE OF ACCOUNTING DIVERSITY

Although it is generally assumed that accounting diversity results in significant differences in the measurement of income and equity across countries, there is little systematic documentation of the effect these differences have on published financial statements. In 1993, the SEC published a survey that examines the U.S. GAAP reconciliations made by 444 foreign entities from 36 countries.[3] The results of that survey indicate that approximately two-thirds of the foreign companies showed material differences between net income and stockholders' equity reported on the basis of home GAAP and U.S. GAAP. Of those with material differences, net income would have been lower under U.S. GAAP for about two-thirds of the companies (higher using U.S. GAAP for about one-third). This indicates that, for the majority of foreign entities with stock listings in the United States, U.S. GAAP is more conservative than their home country GAAP. Similar results were found with regard to stockholders' equity. At the extremes, income was 29 times higher under U.S. GAAP for one foreign entity, and 178 times higher using British GAAP for another entity. In addition, the study found that significant differences are spread relatively evenly across countries. In other words, material differences are as likely to exist for a British or Canadian company as for a company located in South America, Asia, or Continental Europe.

Focusing on the U.S. GAAP reconciliations of British companies, a separate study found that all 39 companies examined reported material differences in income or equity. Over 90 percent reported lower income under U.S. GAAP and approximately 60 percent reported higher equity. The average difference in income, even after including those with higher U.S. GAAP income, was a 42 percent reduction in income when reconciling to U.S. GAAP.[4] It is clear that differences in accounting principles can have a material impact on amounts reported in financial statements.

---

[3] U.S. Securities and Exchange Commission, *Survey of Financial Statement Reconciliations by Foreign Registrants,* Washington, DC, 1993.

[4] Vivian Periar, Ron Paterson, and Allister Wilson, *UK/US GAAP Comparison,* 2nd ed. (London: Kogan Page, 1992).

REASONS FOR ACCOUNTING DIVERSITY

Why does each country have its own set of financial reporting practices? Accounting scholars have hypothesized numerous influences on a country's accounting system, including factors as varied as the nature of the political system, the stage of economic development, and the state of accounting education and research. A survey of the relevant literature has identified the following five items as being commonly accepted as factors influencing a country's financial reporting practices: (1) legal system, (2) taxation, (3) providers of financing, (4) inflation, and (5) political and economic ties.[5]

Legal System

There are two major types of legal systems used around the world: common law and codified Roman law. Common law began in England and is primarily found in the English-speaking countries of the world. Common law countries rely on a limited amount of statute law, which is then interpreted by the courts. Court decisions establish precedents, thereby developing case law that supplements the statutes. A system of code law, followed in most non-English-speaking countries, originated in the Roman *jus civile* and was developed further in European universities during the Middle Ages. Code law countries tend to have relatively more statute or codified law governing a wider range of human activity.

What does a country's legal system have to do with accounting? Code law countries generally have corporation law (sometimes called a commercial code or companies act), which establishes the basic legal parameters governing business enterprises. The corporation law often stipulates which financial statements must be published in accordance with a prescribed format. Additional accounting measurement and disclosure rules are included in an accounting law debated and passed by the national legislature. In countries where accounting rules are legislated, the accounting profession tends to have little influence on the development of accounting standards. In countries with a tradition of common law, although a corporation law laying the basic framework for accounting might exist (such as in the United Kingdom), specific accounting rules are established by the profession or by an independent nongovernmental body representing a variety of constituencies. Thus, the type of legal system in a country tends to determine whether the primary source of accounting rules is the government or a nongovernmental organization.

In *code law* countries, the accounting law tends to be rather general and does not provide much detail regarding specific accounting practices and may provide no guidance at all in certain areas. Germany is a good example of this type of country. The German accounting law passed in 1985 is only 47 pages long and is silent with regard to issues such as leases, foreign currency translation, and cash flow statements.[6] When no guidance is provided in the law, German companies refer to other sources, including tax law, opinions of the German auditing profession, and standards issued by the German Accounting Standards Committee, to decide how to do their accounting. Interestingly enough, important sources of accounting practice in Germany have been textbooks and commentaries written by accounting academicians.

---

[5] Gary K. Meek and Sharokh M. Saudagaran, "A Survey of Research on Financial Reporting in a Transnational Context," *Journal of Accounting Literature*, 1990, pp. 145–82.

[6] Jermyn Paul Brooks and Dietz Mertin, *Neues Deutsches Bilanzrecht*. (Düsseldorf: IDW-Verlag, 1986).

In *common law* countries, where there is likely to be a nonlegislative organization developing accounting standards, much more detailed rules are developed. The extreme case might be the Financial Accounting Standards Board (FASB) in the United States, which specifically details in its Statements of Financial Accounting Standards (SFASs) how to apply the rules and has been accused of producing a "standards overload."

To illustrate this point, consider the rules related to accounting for leases established by the FASB in the United States and in German accounting law. In the United States, SFAS 13 requires leases to be capitalized if any one of four very specific criteria is met. Subsequent FASB statements establish rules for specific situations such as sales with leasebacks, sales-type leases of real estate, and changes in leases resulting from refundings of tax-exempt debt. In contrast, the German accounting law is silent with regard to leases. The only guidance in the law can be found in paragraph 285, which simply states that all liabilities must be recorded.

Taxation

In some countries, published financial statements form the basis for taxation, whereas in other countries, financial statements are adjusted for tax purposes and submitted to the government separately from the reports sent to stockholders. Continuing to focus on Germany, the so-called congruency principle (*Massgeblichkeitsprinzip*) in that country stipulates that the published financial statements serve as the basis for taxable income.[7] In most cases, for an expense to be deductible for tax purposes it must also be used in the calculation of financial statement income. Well-managed German companies attempt to minimize income for tax purposes, for example, through the use of accelerated depreciation, so as to reduce their tax liability. As a result of the congruency principle, accelerated depreciation must also be taken in the calculation of accounting income.

In the United States, in contrast, conformity between the tax statement and financial statements is required only with regard to the use of the last-in, first-out (LIFO) inventory cost flow assumption. U.S. companies are allowed to use accelerated depreciation for tax purposes and straight-line depreciation in the financial statements. All else being equal, because of the influence of the congruency principle, a German company is likely to report lower income than its U.S. counterpart.

The difference between tax and accounting income gives rise to the necessity to account for deferred income taxes, a major issue in the United States in recent years. Deferred income taxes are much less of an issue in Germany; for many German companies, they do not exist at all. This is also true in other code law countries such as France and Japan.

Providers of Financing

The major providers of financing for business enterprises are family members, banks, governments, and shareholders. In those countries in which company financing is dominated by families, banks, or the state, there will be less pressure for public accountability and information disclosure. Banks and the state will often be represented on the board of directors and will therefore be able to obtain

---

[7] German taxable income is computed by comparing an opening and closing tax balance sheet, the *Steuerbilanz*. The tax balance sheet is based on the published balance sheet, the *Handelsbilanz*.

information necessary for decision making from inside the company. As companies become more dependent on financing from the general populace through the public offering of shares of stock, the demand for more information made available outside the company becomes greater. It simply is not feasible for the company to allow the hundreds, thousands, or hundreds of thousands of shareholders access to internal accounting records. The information needs of those financial statement users can be satisfied only through extensive disclosures in accounting reports.

There can also be a difference in financial statement orientation, with stockholders more interested in profit (emphasis on the income statement) and banks more interested in solvency and liquidity (emphasis on the balance sheet). Bankers tend to prefer companies to practice rather conservative accounting with regard to assets and liabilities.

Inflation

Countries with chronic high rates of inflation have been forced to adopt accounting rules that require the inflation adjustment of historical cost amounts. This has been especially true in Latin America, which as a region has had more inflation than any other part of the world. For example, throughout the 1980s and 1990s, the average annual rate of inflation rate in Mexico was approximately 50 percent, with a high of 159 percent in 1987.[8] Double- and triple-digit inflation rates render historical costs meaningless. This factor primarily distinguishes Latin America from the rest of the world with regard to accounting.

Adjusting accounting records for inflation results in a write-up of assets and therefore related expenses. Adjusting income for inflation is especially important in those countries in which accounting statements serve as the basis for taxation; otherwise, companies will be paying taxes on fictitious profits.

Political and Economic Ties

Accounting is a technology that can be relatively easily borrowed from or imposed on another country. Through political and economic links, accounting rules have been conveyed from one country to another. For example, through previous colonialism, both England and France have transferred their accounting frameworks to a variety of countries around the world. British-style accounting systems can be found in countries as far-flung as Australia and Zimbabwe. French accounting is prevalent in the former French colonies of western Africa. More recently, it is thought that economic ties with the United States have had an impact on accounting in Canada, Mexico, and Israel.

Correlation of Factors

Whether by coincidence or not, there is a high degree of correlation between legal system, tax conformity, and source of financing. As Exhibit 2.4 shows, common law countries tend to have greater numbers of publicly traded companies, relying more heavily on equity as a source of capital. Code law countries tend to link taxation to accounting statements and rely less on financing provided by shareholders.

[8] Joseph B. Lipscomb and Harold Hunt, "Mexican Mortgages: Structure and Default Incentives, Historical Simulation 1982–1998," *Journal of Housing Research* 10, no. 2 (1999), pp. 235–65.

EXHIBIT 2.4
Relationship
between Several
Factors Influencing
Accounting
Diversity

Sources: Number of publicly
traded companies obtained
from Christopher W. Nobes
and Robert H. Parker, eds.,
*Comparative International
Accounting,* 5th ed. (Harlow,
Eng.: Pearson Education,
2002), p. 12. Country
populations obtained from
CIA World Fact Book (2001).

| Country | Legal System | Publicly Traded Companies | | Tax Conformity |
		Number	Per Million of Population	
Germany	Code	933	11.23	Yes
Japan	Code	1,894	14.94	Yes
France	Code	980	16.46	Yes
Spain	Code	718	17.93	Yes
United States	Common	7,019	25.24	No
United Kingdom	Common	2,292	38.42	No
Canada	Common	1,409	44.60	No
Australia	Common	1,217	62.87	No

PROBLEMS CAUSED BY ACCOUNTING DIVERSITY

Preparation of Consolidated Financial Statements

The diversity in accounting practice across countries causes problems that can be quite serious for some parties. One problem relates to the preparation of consolidated financial statements by companies with foreign operations. Consider General Motors Corporation, which has subsidiaries in more than 50 countries around the world. Each subsidiary incorporated in the country in which it is located is required to prepare financial statements in accordance with local regulations. These regulations usually require companies to keep books in local currency using local accounting principles. Thus, General Motors de Mexico prepares financial statements in Mexican pesos using Mexican accounting rules and General Motors Japan Ltd. prepares financial statements in Japanese yen using Japanese standards. To prepare consolidated financial statements in the United States, in addition to translating the foreign currency financial statements into U.S. dollars, the parent company must also convert the financial statements of its foreign operations into U.S. GAAP. Each foreign operation must either maintain two sets of books prepared in accordance with both local and U.S. GAAP or, as is more common, reconciliations from local GAAP to U.S. GAAP must be made at the balance sheet date. In either case, considerable effort and cost are involved; company personnel must develop an expertise in more than one country's accounting standards.

Access to Foreign Capital Markets

A second problem caused by accounting diversity relates to companies gaining access to foreign capital markets. If a company desires to obtain capital by selling stock or borrowing money in a foreign country, it might be required to present a set of financial statements prepared in accordance with the accounting standards in the country in which the capital is being obtained. Consider the case of the Swedish appliance manufacturer AB Electrolux. The equity market in Sweden is so small (there are fewer than 9 million Swedes) and Electrolux's capital needs are so great that the company has found it necessary to have its common shares listed on stock exchanges in London and on the NASDAQ in the United States, in addition to its home exchange in Stockholm. To have stock traded in the United States, foreign companies must either prepare financial statements using U.S. accounting standards or provide a reconciliation of local GAAP net income and stockholders' equity to U.S. GAAP. This can be quite costly. In preparing for a New York Stock

Exchange (NYSE) listing in 1993, the German automaker Daimler-Benz estimated it spent $60 million to initially prepare U.S. GAAP financial statements; it expected to spend $15 to $20 million each year thereafter.[9] The appendix to this chapter describes the case of Daimler-Benz in becoming the first German company to list on the NYSE.

Comparability of Financial Statements

A third problem relates to the lack of comparability of financial statements between companies from different countries. This can significantly affect the analysis of foreign financial statements for making investment and lending decisions. In 2003 alone, U.S. investors bought and sold nearly $3 trillion worth of foreign stocks while foreign investors traded over $6 trillion in U.S. equity securities.[10] In recent years there has been an explosion in mutual funds that invest in the stock of foreign companies: from 123 in 1989 to 534 at the end of 1995.[11] T. Rowe Price's New Asia Fund, for example, invests exclusively in stocks and bonds of companies located in Asian countries other than Japan. The job of deciding which foreign company to invest in is complicated by the fact that foreign companies use accounting rules different from those used in the United States and those rules differ from country to country. It is very difficult if not impossible for a potential investor to directly compare the financial position and performance of an automobile manufacturer in Germany (Volkswagen), Japan (Nissan), and the United States (Ford) because these three countries have different financial accounting and reporting standards. According to Ralph E. Walters, former chairman of the steering committee of the International Accounting Standards Committee, "either international investors have to be extremely knowledgeable about multiple reporting methods or they have to be willing to take greater risk."[12]

A lack of comparability of financial statements also can have an adverse effect on corporations when making foreign acquisition decisions. As a case in point, consider the experience of foreign investors in Eastern Europe. After the fall of the Berlin Wall in 1989, Western companies were invited to acquire newly privatized companies in Poland, Hungary, and other countries in the former communist bloc. The concept of profit and accounting for assets in those countries under communism was so different from accounting practice in the West that most Western investors found financial statements useless in helping to determine which enterprises were the most attractive acquisition targets. In many cases, the international public accounting firms were called on to convert financial statements to a Western basis before acquisition of a company could be seriously considered.

There was a very good reason why accounting in the communist countries of Eastern Europe and the Soviet Union was so much different from accounting in capitalist countries. Financial statements were not prepared for the benefit of investors and creditors to be used in making investment and lending decisions. Instead, financial statements were prepared to provide the government with information to determine whether the central economic plan was being fulfilled.

---

[9] Allan B. Afterman, *International Accounting, Financial Reporting, and Analysis* (New York: Warren, Gorham & Lamont, 1995), pp. C1-17, C1-22.

[10] U.S. Department of Commerce, Bureau of Economic Analysis, "U.S. International Transactions," *Survey of Current Business,* January 2005, pp. 45–76, Table 7a.

[11] James L. Cochrane, James E. Shapiro, and Jean E. Tobin, "Foreign Equities and U.S. Investors: Breaking Down the Barriers Separating Supply and Demand," NYSE Working Paper 95-04, 1995.

[12] Stephen H. Collins, "The Move to Globalization," *Journal of Accountancy,* March 1989, p. 82.

Financial statements prepared for central planning purposes have limited value in making investment decisions.

Lack of High-Quality Accounting Information

A fourth problem associated with accounting diversity is the lack of high-quality accounting standards in some parts of the world. There is general agreement that the failure of many banks in the 1997 East Asian financial crisis was due to three factors: a highly leveraged corporate sector, the private sector's reliance on foreign currency debt, and a lack of accounting transparency.[13] To be sure, inadequate disclosure did not create the East Asian meltdown, but it did contribute to the depth and breadth of the crisis. As Rahman explains: "It is a known fact that the very threat of disclosure influences behavior and improves management, particularly risk management. It seems that the lack of appropriate disclosure requirements indirectly contributed to the deficient internal controls and imprudent risk management practices of the corporations and banks in the crisis-hit countries."[14] International investors and creditors were unable to adequately assess risk because financial statements did not reflect the extent of risk exposure due to the following disclosure deficiencies:

- The actual magnitude of debt was hidden by undisclosed related-party transactions and off-balance-sheet financing.
- High levels of exposure to foreign exchange risk were not evident.
- Information on the extent to which investments and loans were made in highly speculative assets (such as real estate) was not available.
- Contingent liabilities for guaranteeing loans, often foreign currency loans, were not reported.
- Appropriate disclosures regarding loan loss provisions were not made.

Because of the problems associated with worldwide accounting diversity, attempts to reduce the accounting differences across countries have been ongoing for over three decades. This process is known as *harmonization*. The ultimate goal of harmonization is to have one set of international accounting standards that are followed by all companies around the world. Harmonization is the major topic of Chapter 3.

ACCOUNTING CLUSTERS

Given the discussion regarding factors influencing accounting practice worldwide, it should not be surprising to learn that there are clusters of countries that share common accounting orientation and practices. One classification scheme identifies three major accounting models: the Fair Presentation/Full Disclosure Model, the Legal Compliance Model, and the Inflation-Adjusted Model.[15] The Fair Presentation/Full Disclosure Model (also known as the Anglo-Saxon or Anglo-American model) is used to describe the approach used in the United Kingdom and United States, where accounting is oriented toward the decision needs of large

[13] M. Zubaidur Rahman, "The Role of Accounting in the East Asian Financial Crisis: Lessons Learned?" *Transnational Corporations* 7, no. 3 (December 1998), pp. 1–52.

[14] Ibid., p. 7.

[15] Helen Gernon and Gary Meek, *Accounting: An International Perspective,* 5th ed. (Burr Ridge, IL: Irwin/McGraw-Hill, 2001), pp. 10–11.

EXHIBIT 2.5
Nobes's Judgmental
Classification of
Accounting Systems

Source: Christopher W.
Nobes, "A Judgemental
International Classification
of Financial Reporting
Practices," *Journal of Business
Finance and Accounting,*
Spring 1983, p. 7.

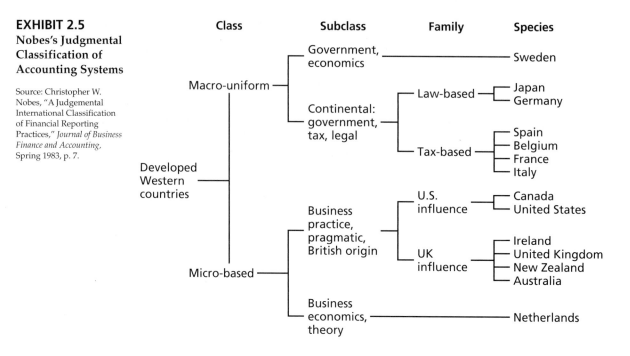

numbers of investors and creditors. This model is used in most English-speaking countries and other countries heavily influenced by the United Kingdom or the United States. Most of these countries follow a common law legal system. The Legal Compliance Model originated in the code law countries of continental Europe; it is also known as the Continental European model. It is used by most of Europe, Japan, and other code law countries. Companies in this group usually are tied quite closely to banks that serve as the primary suppliers of financing. Because these are code law countries, accounting is legalistic and is designed to provide information for taxation or government-planning purposes. The Inflation-Adjusted Model is found primarily in South America. This model resembles the Continental European model in its legalistic, tax, and government-planning orientation. This model distinguishes itself, however, through the extensive use of adjustments for inflation.

A Judgmental Classification of Financial Reporting Systems

Concentrating on the Anglo-Saxon and Continental European Model countries, Nobes developed a more refined classification scheme that attempts to show how the financial reporting systems in 14 developed countries relate to one another.[16] Exhibit 2.5 presents an adaptation of Nobes's classification.

The terms *micro-based* and *macro-uniform* describe the Anglo-Saxon and Continental European Models, respectively. Each of these classes is divided into two subclasses that are further divided into families. Within the micro-based class of accounting system, there is a subclass heavily influenced by business economics and accounting theory. The Netherlands is the only country in this subclass. One manifestation of the influence of theory is that Dutch companies may use current replacement cost accounting to value assets in their primary financial statements.

---

[16] Christopher W. Nobes, "A Judgemental International Classification of Financial Reporting Practices," *Journal of Business Finance and Accounting,* Spring 1983.

The other micro-based subclass, of British origin, is more pragmatic and is oriented toward business practice, relying less on economic theory in the development of accounting rules. The British-origin subclass is further split into two families, one dominated by the United Kingdom and one dominated by the United States. Nobes does not indicate how these two families differ.

On the macro-uniform side of the classification, a "government, economics" subclass has only one country, Sweden. Swedish accounting distinguishes itself from the other macro-uniform countries in being closely aligned with national economic policies. For example, income smoothing is allowed to promote economic stability and social accounting has developed to meet macroeconomic concerns. The "continental: government, tax, legal" subclass primarily has Continental European countries. This subclass is further divided into two families. Led by Germany, the law-based family includes Japan. The tax-based family consists of several Romance-language countries. The major difference between these families is that the accounting law is the primary determinant of accounting practice in Germany, whereas the tax law dominates in the Southern European countries.

The importance of this hierarchical model is that it shows the comparative distances between countries and could be used as a blueprint for determining where financial statement comparability is likely to be greater. For example, comparisons of financial statements between the United States and Canada (which are in the same family) are likely to be more valid than comparisons between the United States and the United Kingdom (which are not in the same family). However, the United States and the United Kingdom (which are in the same subclass) are more comparable than are the United States and the Netherlands (which are in different subclasses). Finally, comparisons between the United States and the Netherlands (which are in the same class) might be more meaningful than comparisons between the United States and any of the macro-uniform countries.

An Empirical Test of the Judgmental Classification

The judgmental classification in Exhibit 2.5 was empirically tested in 1990.[17] Data gathered on 100 financial reporting practices in 50 countries (including the 14 countries in Exhibit 2.3) were analyzed using the statistical procedure of hierarchical cluster analysis. The significant clusters arising from the statistical analysis are in Exhibit 2.6. Clusters are analogous to the families in Nobes's classification.

The results reported in Exhibit 2.6 clearly indicate the existence of two significantly different classes of accounting systems being used across these countries and are generally consistent with the classes, subclasses, and families of Nobes's classification. The major deviations from Nobes's classification are that the Netherlands is located in the UK-influence cluster (Cluster 1) rather than in a subclass by itself; Japanese accounting (Cluster 9) is not as similar to German accounting (Cluster 8) as hypothesized; and Belgium (located in Cluster 6) is not in the group with France, Spain, and Italy (Cluster 5). Indeed, there appears to be more diversity among the macro countries (as evidenced by the greater number of clusters) than among the countries comprising the micro class.

The large size of the UK-influence cluster (Cluster 1) shows the influence of British colonialism on accounting development. In contrast, Cluster 2, which includes the United States, is quite small. The emergence of Cluster 4, which

[17] Timothy S. Doupnik and Stephen B. Salter, "An Empirical Test of a Judgemental International Classification of Financial Reporting Practices," *Journal of International Business Studies,* First Quarter 1993, pp. 41–60.

EXHIBIT 2.6
**Results of
Hierarchical Cluster
Analysis on 100
Financial Reporting
Practices in 1990**

Source: Timothy S. Doupnik
and Stephen B. Salter, "An
Empirical Test of a
Judgemental International
Classification of Financial
Reporting Practices," *Journal
of International Business
Studies*, First Quarter 1993,
p. 53.

Micro Class		Macro Class		
Cluster 1	**Cluster 2**	**Cluster 3**	**Cluster 5**	**Cluster 7**
Australia	Bermuda	Costa Rica	Colombia	Finland
Botswana	Canada		Denmark	Sweden
Hong Kong	Israel	**Cluster 4**	France	
Ireland	United States	Argentina	Italy	**Cluster 8**
Jamaica		Brazil	Norway	Germany
Luxembourg		Chile	Portugal	
Malaysia		Mexico	Spain	**Cluster 9**
Namibia				Japan
Netherlands			**Cluster 6**	
Netherlands Antilles			Belgium	
Nigeria			Egypt	
New Zealand			Liberia	
Philippines			Panama	
Papua New Guinea			Saudi Arabia	
South Africa			Thailand	
Singapore			United Arab	
Sri Lanka			Emirates	
Taiwan				
Trinidad and Tobago				
United Kingdom				
Zambia				
Zimbabwe				

includes several Latin American countries, is evidence of the importance of inflation as a factor affecting accounting practice.

The two classes of accounting reflected in Exhibit 2.6 differ significantly on 66
of the 100 financial reporting practices examined. Differences exist for 41 of the
56 disclosure practices studied. In all but one case, the micro class of countries
provided a higher level of disclosure than the macro class of countries. There were
also significant differences for 25 of the 44 practices examined affecting income
measurement. Of particular importance is the item asking whether accounting
practice adhered to tax requirements. The mean level of agreement with this statement among macro countries was 72 percent, whereas it was only 45 percent
among micro countries. To summarize, companies in the micro-based countries
provide more extensive disclosure than do companies in the macro-uniform
countries, and companies in the macro countries are more heavily influenced by
taxation than are companies in the micro countries. These results are consistent
with the relative importance of equity finance and the relatively weak link between accounting and taxation in the micro countries.

THE INFLUENCE OF CULTURE ON FINANCIAL REPORTING

In addition to economic and institutional determinants, national culture has long
been considered a factor that affects the accounting system of a country.[18]

***

[18] One of the first to argue that accounting is determined by culture was W. J. Violet in "The Development of International Accounting Standards: An Anthropological Perspective," *International Journal of
Accounting,* 1983, pp. 1–12.

Hofstede's Cultural Dimensions

Using responses to an attitude survey of IBM employees worldwide, Hofstede identified four cultural dimensions that can be used to describe general similarities and differences in cultures around the world: (1) individualism, (2) power distance, (3) uncertainty avoidance, and (4) masculinity.[19] More recently, a fifth dimension, long-term orientation, was identified. *Individualism* refers to a preference for a loosely knit social fabric rather than a tightly knit social fabric (collectivism). *Power distance* refers to the extent to which hierarchy and unequal power distribution in institutions and organizations are accepted. *Uncertainty avoidance* refers to the degree to which individuals feel uncomfortable with uncertainty and ambiguity. *Masculinity* refers to an emphasis on traditional masculine values of performance and achievement rather than feminine values of relationships, caring, and nurturing. *Long-term orientation* stands for the "fostering of virtues oriented towards future rewards, in particular perseverance and thrift."[20]

Gray's Accounting Values

From a review of accounting literature and practice, Gray identified four widely recognized accounting values that can be used to define a country's accounting subculture: professionalism, uniformity, conservatism, and secrecy.[21] Gray describes these accounting values as follows:[22]

Professionalism versus Statutory Control—a preference for the exercise of individual professional judgment and the maintenance of professional self-regulation as opposed to compliance with prescriptive legal requirements and statutory control.

Uniformity versus Flexibility—a preference for the enforcement of uniform accounting practices between companies and for the consistent use of such practices over time as opposed to flexibility in accordance with the perceived circumstances of individual companies.

Conservatism versus Optimism—a preference for a cautious approach to measurement so as to cope with the uncertainty of future events as opposed to a more optimistic, laissez-faire, risk-taking approach.

Secrecy versus Transparency—a preference for confidentiality and the restriction of disclosure of information about the business only to those who are closely involved with its management and financing as opposed to a more transparent, open, and publicly accountable approach.

Gray argues that national culture values affect accounting values, as shown in Exhibit 2.7. The accounting values of conservatism and secrecy have the greatest relevance for the information content of a set of financial statements. The relationship between culture and each of these two accounting values is explained as follows:

Conservatism can be linked perhaps most closely with the uncertainty-avoidance dimension and the short-term versus long-term orientations. A preference for more

---

[19] G. Hofstede, *Culture's Consequences: International Differences in Work-Related Values* (London: Sage, 1980).

[20] G. Hofstede, *Culture's Consequences: Comparing Values, Behaviours, Institutions, and Organizations across Nations,* 2nd ed. (Thousand Oaks, CA: Sage, 2001), p. 359.

[21] S. J. Gray, "Towards a Theory of Cultural Influence on the Development of Accounting Systems Internationally," *Abacus,* March 1988, pp. 1–15.

[22] Ibid., p. 8.

EXHIBIT 2.7
Relationships between Accounting Values and Cultural Dimensions

Source: Lee H. Radebaugh and Sidney J. Gray, *International Accounting and Multinational Enterprises,* 5th ed. (New York: Wiley, 2001), p. 49.

Cultural Dimension	Accounting Values			
	Professionalism	Uniformity	Conservatism	Secrecy
Power distance	Neg.	Pos.	n/a	Pos.
Uncertainty avoidance	Neg.	Pos.	Pos.	Pos.
Individualism	Pos.	Neg.	Neg.	Neg.
Masculinity	Pos.	n/a	Neg.	Neg.
Long-term orientation	Neg.	n/a	Pos.	Pos.

Pos. = Positive relationship hypothesized between cultural dimension and accounting value.

Neg. = Negative relationship hypothesized between cultural dimension and accounting value.

n/a = No relationship hypothesized.

conservative measures of profits and assets is consistent with strong uncertainty avoidance following from a concern with security and a perceived need to adopt a cautious approach to cope with uncertainty of future events. A less conservative approach to measurement is also consistent with a short-term orientation where quick results are expected and hence a more optimistic approach is adopted relative to conserving resources and investing for long-term trends. There also seems to be a link, if less strong, between high levels of individualism and masculinity, on the one hand, and weak uncertainty avoidance on the other, to the extent that an emphasis on individual achievement and performance is likely to foster a less conservative approach to measurement.[23]

A preference for secrecy is consistent with strong uncertainty avoidance following from a need to restrict information disclosures so as to avoid conflict and competition and to preserve security. . . . [H]igh power-distance societies are likely to be characterized by the restriction of information to preserve power inequalities. Secrecy is also consistent with a preference for collectivism, as opposed to individualism, in that its concern is for the interests of those closely involved with the firm rather than external parties. A long-term orientation also suggests a preference for secrecy that is consistent with the need to conserve resources within the firm and ensure that funds are available for investment relative to the demands of shareholders and employees for higher payments. A significant but possibly less important link with masculinity also seems likely to the extent that in societies where there is more emphasis on achievement and material success there will be a greater tendency to publicize such achievements and material success.[24]

Gray extended Hofstede's model of cultural patterns to develop a framework that identifies the mechanism through which culture influences the development of corporate reporting systems on a national level. According to this framework (shown in Exhibit 2.8), the particular way in which a country's accounting system develops is influenced by accountants' accounting values and by the country's institutional framework, both of which are influenced by cultural values. Thus, culture is viewed as affecting accounting systems indirectly in two ways: through its influence on accounting values and through its institutional consequences.

Using measures of each of the cultural values for a group of 40 countries, Hofstede classified countries into 10 different cultural areas. The Anglo cultural area, for example, is characterized by high individualism, low uncertainty

[23] Lee H. Radebaugh and Sidney J. Gray, *International Accounting and Multinational Enterprises,* 5th ed. (New York: Wiley, 2001), p. 47.

[24] Ibid., p. 48.

EXHIBIT 2.8 Framework for the Development of Accounting Systems

Source: Adapted from S. J. Gray, "Towards a Theory of Cultural Influence on the Development of Accounting Systems Internationally," *Abacus,* March 1988, p. 7.

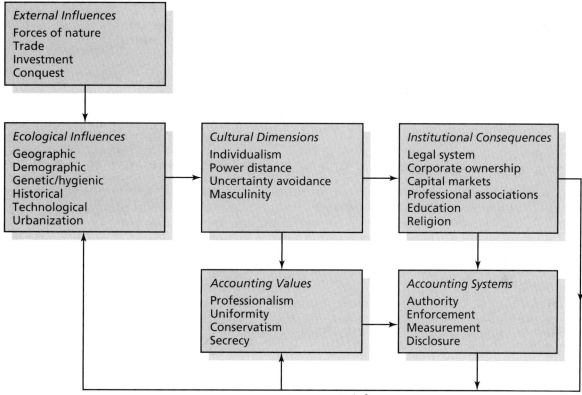

avoidance, low power distance, and moderate masculinity. Given this pattern of cultural values, Gray hypothesized that Anglo countries (which include Australia, Canada, New Zealand, the United States, and the United Kingdom) would rank relatively low on the accounting values of conservatism and secrecy (or high on optimism and high on transparency). Exhibiting the opposite pattern of cultural values, the countries of the less developed Latin cultural area (which includes countries like Colombia and Mexico) are expected to rank relatively high in conservatism and secrecy. Gray's expectation with respect to measurement and disclosure for the 10 different cultural areas is shown in Exhibit 2.9. Perhaps the most striking feature of the diagram is that all cultural areas are located in only two of the four quadrants, indicating the strong positive correlation expected to exist between conservatism and secrecy.

A number of studies have empirically examined the relationship between Hofstede's cultural values and national accounting systems.[25] Although the results of this research are mixed, most studies find a relationship between

[25] For a comprehensive review of this literature, see T. S. Doupnik and G. T. Tsakumis, "A Review of Empirical Tests of Gray's Framework and Suggestions for Future Research," *Journal of Accounting Literature*, 2004, pp. 1–48.

EXHIBIT 2.9
Measurement and Disclosure Expectations by Cultural Area

Source: S. J. Gray, "Towards a Theory of Cultural Influence on the Development of Accounting Systems Internationally," *Abacus,* March 1988, p. 13.

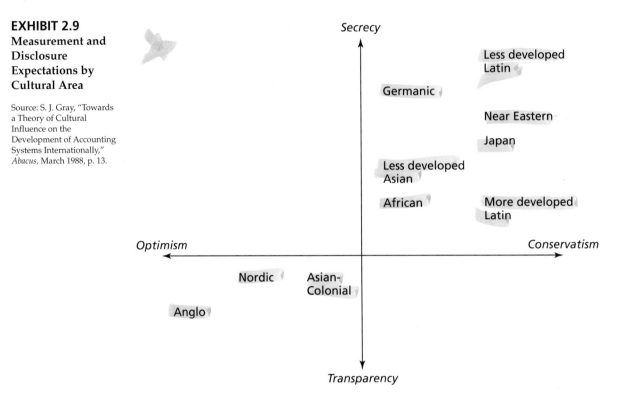

cultural values and disclosure consistent with Gray's hypothesis. However, these studies are unable to determine whether culture influences disclosure through its effect on accounting values or through its effect on institutional consequences. Research results on the relationship between culture and conservatism are less conclusive.

Religion and Accounting

Religion plays an important role in defining national culture in many parts of the world and can have a significant effect on business practice. Under Islam, for example, the Koran provides guidance with respect to issues such as making charitable contributions and charging interest on loans. In some Islamic countries, banking companies operate under Shariah, the Islamic law of human conduct derived from the Koran. Because traditional accounting rules do not cover many of the transactions carried out by Islamic financial institutions (IFIs), the Accounting and Auditing Organization for Islamic Financial Institutions (AAOIFI), a standard-setting body based in Bahrain, has been active in developing and promoting Islamic accounting standards.

Based on the AAOIFI's work, the Malaysian Accounting Standards Board (MASB) developed MASB i-1, *Presentation of Financial Statements of Islamic Financial Institutions,* in 2001. MASB i-1 states:

> The general purpose of financial statements is to provide information about the financial position, performance and cash flows of IFIs, which are useful to a wide range of users in making economic decisions. It also portrays aspects of the

management's stewardship of the resources entrusted to it. All these information, along with other information in the notes to financial statements, allows users in assessing the degree of compliance of the IFIs with the prescribed Shariah requirements (para. 10).

In developing MASB i-1, the MASB consulted with the Malaysian Central Bank's National Shariah Council on issues relating to Shariah. In April 2004, the MASB announced that it would introduce four new Islamic accounting standards related to *ijarah* (leasing), *zakat* (income tax), *takaful* (insurance), and *mudarabah* (deferred payments).

A SIMPLIFIED MODEL OF THE REASONS FOR INTERNATIONAL DIFFERENCES IN FINANCIAL REPORTING

Sifting through the many reasons that have been hypothesized to affect international differences in financial reporting, Nobes develops a model with two explanatory factors: culture and the nature of the financing system.[26] Nobes argues that the major reason for international differences in financial reporting is different purposes for that reporting. A country's financing system is seen as the most relevant factor in determining the purpose of financial reporting. Specifically, whether or not a country has a strong equity financing system with large numbers of outside shareholders will determine the nature of financial reporting in a country.

Nobes divides financial reporting systems into two classes, labeled A and B. Class A accounting systems are found in countries with strong equity–outside shareholder financing. In Class A accounting systems, measurement practices are less conservative, disclosure is extensive, and accounting practice differs from tax rules. Class A corresponds to what may be called Anglo-Saxon accounting. Class B accounting systems are found in countries with weak equity–outside shareholder financing systems. Measurement is more conservative, disclosure is not as extensive, and accounting practice more closely follows tax rules. Class B corresponds to Continental European accounting.

Nobes posits that culture, including institutional structures, determines the nature of a country's financing system. Although not explicitly defined, Nobes's notion of culture appears to go beyond the rather narrow definition used in Gray's framework, which relies on Hofstede's cultural dimensions. Nobes assumes (without explaining how) that some cultures lead to strong equity-outsider financing systems and other cultures lead to weak equity-outsider financing systems. His simplified model of reasons for international accounting differences is as follows:

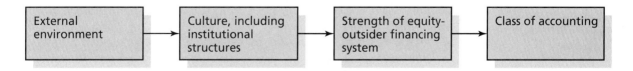

External environment → Culture, including institutional structures → Strength of equity-outsider financing system → Class of accounting

[26] Christopher W. Nobes, "Towards a General Model of the Reasons for International Differences in Financial Reporting," *Abacus* 34, no. 2 (1998), p. 166.

Most countries in the developed world have a self-sufficient culture. For these countries, Nobes applies his model as follows:

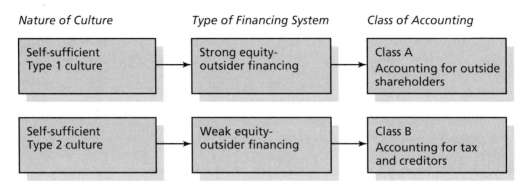

Nature of Culture	Type of Financing System	Class of Accounting
Self-sufficient Type 1 culture	→ Strong equity-outsider financing	→ Class A Accounting for outside shareholders
Self-sufficient Type 2 culture	→ Weak equity-outsider financing	→ Class B Accounting for tax and creditors

Many countries in the developing world are culturally dominated by another country often as a result of European colonialism. Nobes argues that culturally dominated countries use the accounting system of their dominating country regardless of the nature of the equity financing system. Thus, countries with a Type 1 culture as well as countries historically dominated by a Type 1 country use Class A accounting systems.

Examples of Countries with Class A Accounting

The United Kingdom is a culturally self-sufficient Type 1 country with a strong equity-outsider system. It has an outside shareholder–oriented Class A accounting system. New Zealand is culturally dominated by the United Kingdom. It also has a strong equity-outsider financing system, probably because of the influence of British culture. New Zealand also has a Class A accounting system. According to Nobes's model, this can be the result of New Zealand being culturally dominated by the United Kingdom (a Type 1 culture country), having a strong equity-outsider financing system, or both. The African nation of Malawi has a weak equity-outsider financing system, but as a former British colony (culturally dominated by the United Kingdom) it has adopted a Class A accounting system even though it has a weak equity-outsider financing system.

Nobes further suggests that as the financing system in a country evolves from weak equity to strong equity, the accounting system will also evolve in the direction of Class A accounting. He cites China as an example. Finally, Nobes argues that companies with strong equity-outsider financing will attempt to use Class A accounting even if they are located in a Class B accounting system country. He cites the German firms Deutsche Bank and Bayer and the Swiss company Nestlé as examples.

Recent Changes in Europe

Because of the desire for companies to be competitive in attracting international equity investment, several European countries (with Class B accounting systems) developed a two-tiered financial reporting system in the late 1990s. Austria, France, Germany, Italy, and Switzerland gave stock-exchange-listed companies the option to use International Financial Reporting Standards (IFRSs), a Class A accounting system, in preparing their consolidated financial statements.[27] The parent company

---

[27] International Financial Reporting Standards are issued by the International Accounting Standards Board and are discussed in more detail in Chapters 3 and 4.

statements, which serve as the basis for taxation, continued to be prepared using local accounting rules. Large numbers of German and Swiss companies (including Deutsche Bank, Bayer, and Nestlé), in particular, availed themselves of this opportunity to use IFRSs.

This desire for companies to be competitive in the international capital market led the European Commission in 2005 to require all publicly traded companies within the European Union to use IFRSs in preparing consolidated financial statements. Thus, it is no longer appropriate to think in terms of all German (or all French, all Italian, etc.) companies following the traditional Continental European model of accounting.

FURTHER EVIDENCE OF ACCOUNTING DIVERSITY

In the remainder of this chapter we provide additional evidence of some of the differences in accounting that exist across countries. We categorize accounting differences in the following manner and provide examples of each of these types of difference:

1. Differences in the financial statements included in an annual report.
2. Differences in the format used to present individual financial statements.
3. Differences in the level of detail provided in the financial statements.
4. Terminology differences.
5. Disclosures differences.
6. Recognition and measurement differences.

We illustrate these differences by considering a typical set of U.S. financial statements as a point of reference.

Financial Statements

U.S. companies are required to include a balance sheet, income statement, and statement of cash flows in a set of financial statements. In addition, schedules explaining the change in retained earnings and in accumulated other comprehensive income must be presented. Many U.S. companies provide this information in a separate statement of stockholders' equity.

Virtually all companies worldwide provide a balance sheet and an income statement in a set of financial statements. Although it has become more common over time, a statement of cash flows is not required in some countries. For example, firms in Mexico and Brazil are required to prepare a statement of changes in financial position rather than a statement of cash flows. In addition to a balance sheet, income statement, and statement of cash flows, the Austrian firm Bau Holding Strabag AG includes a statement of changes in noncurrent assets as one of its primary financial statements. This statement provides detail on the change during the year in the historical cost of noncurrent intangible, tangible, and financial assets. A statement of changes in noncurrent assets often also is found in financial statements prepared by German companies.

Format of Financial Statements

U.S. companies list assets and liabilities on the balance sheet in order of liquidity, from most liquid (cash) to least liquid (often intangible assets). The same is true in Canada and Japan. Companies in many countries (including most of Europe) list assets and liabilities in reverse order of liquidity. An example was presented in

EXHIBIT 2.10

EURO DISNEY SCA
Balance Sheet

Consolidated Balance Sheets

(€ in millions)	Notes	September 2004	As-Reported September 2003	September 2002
FIXED ASSETS				
Intangible assets		52.4	57.6	61.7
Tangible assets	3	2,343.9	928.0	1,004.3
Financial assets	4	115.3	1,332.2	1,323.5
		2,511.6	2,317.8	2,389.5
CURRENT ASSETS				
Inventories	5	41.5	41.8	38.7
Accounts receivable				
• Trade	6	72.7	76.9	100.6
• Other	7	59.8	45.9	70.7
Short-term investments	8	120.8	34.9	14.2
Cash		10.6	11.2	8.2
		405.4	210.7	232.4
DEFERRED CHARGES	9	59.6	55.1	86.7
Total assets		**2,876.6**	**2,583.6**	**2,708.6**
SHAREHOLDERS' EQUITY				
Share capital	10	10.8	802.5	804.9
Share premium	10	1,235.6	291.4	289.0
Retained earnings (Accumulated deficit)	10	(1,306.3)	(9.5)	150.9
		(59.9)	1,084.4	1,244.8
MINORITY INTERESTS	11	339.6	—	—
QUASI-EQUITY	12	—	152.8	152.8
PROVISIONS FOR RISKS AND CHARGES	13	98.2	120.1	35.5
BORROWINGS	14	2,052.8	867.5	821.3
CURRENT LIABILITIES				
Payable to related companies	15	73.3	56.9	82.5
Accounts payable and accrued liabilities	16	284.3	214.3	277.0
		357.6	271.2	359.5
DEFERRED REVENUES	17	88.3	87.6	94.7
Total shareholders' equity and liabilities		**2,876.6**	**2,583.6**	**2,708.6**

*See *Notes to Consolidated Financial Statements*

Exhibit 2.1 for a British company. Another example is presented for the French company Euro Disney SCA in Exhibit 2.10. Not only are assets presented in reverse order of liquidity, but their classification is different from that in U.S. statements as well. In addition to the familiar categories of fixed assets and current assets, a third class of assets consists of deferred charges. For Euro Disney, this category of assets primarily reflects prepaid expenses, both current and long-term. Deferred revenues are also not classified as current or long-term.

In the income statement format commonly used by U.S. companies, sales revenue and cost of goods sold are generally reported as separate line items, the difference being gross profit. Cost of goods sold includes manufacturing costs

EXHIBIT 2.11

THE HOME DEPOT, INC.
Income Statement

CONSOLIDATED STATEMENTS OF EARNINGS

amounts in millions, except per share data	Fiscal Year Ended[1]		
	February 1, 2004	February 2, 2003	February 3, 2002
NET SALES	$64,816	$58,247	$53,553
Cost of Merchandise Sold	44,236	40,139	37,406
GROSS PROFIT	20,580	18,108	16,147
Operating Expenses			
Selling and Store Operating	12,502	11,180	10,163
Pre-Opening	86	96	117
General and Administrative	1,146	1,002	935
Total Operating Expenses	13,734	12,278	11,215
OPERATING INCOME	6,846	5,830	4,932
Interest Income (Expense):			
Interest and Investment Income	59	79	53
Interest Expense	(62)	(37)	(28)
Interest, net	(3)	42	25
EARNINGS BEFORE PROVISION FOR INCOME TAXES	6,843	5,872	4,957
Provision for Income Taxes	2,539	2,208	1,913
NET EARNINGS	$ 4,304	$ 3,664	$ 3,044
Weighted Average Common Shares	2,283	2,336	2,335
BASIC EARNINGS PER SHARE	$ 1.88	$ 1.57	$ 1.30
Diluted Weighted Average Common Shares	2,289	2,344	2,353
DILUTED EARNINGS PER SHARE	$ 1.88	$ 1.56	$ 1.29

[1]*Fiscal years ended February 1, 2004 and February 2, 2003 include 52 weeks. Fiscal year ended February 3, 2002 includes 53 weeks.*

(materials, labor, and overhead) related to those items sold during the year. In addition to cost of goods sold, selling expense, administrative expense, research and development costs, and other operating expenses are subtracted to calculate operating income. Each of these line items includes costs related to materials (including supplies), labor, and overhead. The Home Depot income statement presented in Exhibit 2.11 illustrates the format typically used by U.S.-based companies.

In contrast to the operational format income statement commonly found in the United States, many European companies present their income statement using a type of expenditure format. An example is presented in Exhibit 2.12 for Südzucker AG, a German sugar manufacturer. Rather than presenting cost of goods sold as a single line item, Südzucker presents separate line items for cost of materials, personnel expenses, and depreciation (excluding goodwill). The line item *Personnel expenses* aggregates the total amount of personnel cost incurred by the company. In contrast, Home Depot allocates these expenses to the various categories of operating expense (manufacturing, selling, administrative, general). Similarly, the line item *Depreciation (excluding goodwill)* includes depreciation on manufacturing assets, as well as assets used in administration, marketing, and other departments. The second line in Südzucker's income statement, *Change in work in process and finished goods inventories and internal costs capitalized,* adjusts for the manufacturing

EXHIBIT 2.12

SÜDZUCKER AG
Income Statement

Statement of income

1 March 2003 to 29 February 2004 (€ million)

	Note	01.03.2003– 29.02.2004	01.03.2002– 28.02.2003
Sales	V.2.1	**4,575.0**	**4,383.8**
Change in work in process and finished goods			
inventories and internal costs capitalized	V.2.2	39.8	24.9
Other operating income	V.2.3	93.4	129.9
Cost of materials	V.2.4	(2,824.2)	(2,702.0)
Personnel expenses	V.2.5	(564.6)	(526.0)
Depreciation (excluding goodwill)	V.2.6	(198.1)	(189.2)
Other operating expenses	V.2.7	(642.3)	(601.1)
Operating profit		**479.0**	**520.3**
Restructuring costs and other exceptional items	V.2.8	(32.6)	(33.0)
Amortisation of goodwill	V.2.9	0.0	(72.5)
Income from ordinary operating activities		**446.4**	**414.8**
Financial expense, net	V.2.10	(52.8)	(41.1)
Earnings before income taxes		**393.6**	**373.7**
Taxes on income	V.2.11	(86.3)	(58.3)
Net earnings for the year		**307.3**	**315.4**
of which attributable to Südzucker AG shareholders . . .		254.6	259.4
of which attributable to minority interests		52.7	56.0
Earnings per share (€/share)		**1.48**	**1.52**

costs included in *Cost of materials, Personnel expenses, Depreciation (excluding good-will),* and *Other operating expenses* that are not part of cost of goods sold in the current year. As a result of this adjustment, the amount related to the cost of goods sold subtracted in calculating operating income is the same as if cost of goods sold had been reported as a separate line item. Although much different in appearance, the format Südzucker uses to report operating profit does not affect the amount reported. The amount is the same regardless of whether the company uses the type of expenditure format or the cost of goods sold format.

The format of the income statement prepared by Fiat SpA is very different from what can be found in most other countries (see Exhibit 2.13). Fiat presents the following components of income: *Difference between the value and costs of production, Total financial income and expenses, Total adjustments to financial assets,* and *Total extraordinary income and expenses.* The sum of these four measures is *Income (Loss) before Taxes.* Fiat does not report earnings per share on its income statement, as is required of U.S. and UK companies. This is consistent with the creditor, rather than investor, orientation of the Italian accounting system.

Most companies present their income statement using a vertical format in which expenses are subtracted from revenues to calculate income. However, some companies use a horizontal format to prepare their income statement. Exhibit 2.14 provides an example of a horizontal format income statement for Sol Melia SA, a Spanish hotel chain. The left-hand side of the statement reports expenses and the

EXHIBIT 2.13

FIAT GROUP
Income Statement

Consolidated Statement of Operations

(in millions of euros)		2003	2002	2001
VALUE OF PRODUCTION	(note 15)			
Revenues from sales and services		48,346	55,427	57,575
Change in work in progress, semifinished and finished products inventories		700	(816)	7
Change in contract work in progress		(1,075)	222	431
Additions to internally produced fixed assets		688	1,107	1,069
Other income and revenues:				
revenue grants	52		47	79
other	1,637		2,105	2,166
Total Other income and revenues		1,689	2,152	2,245
TOTAL VALUE OF PRODUCTION		50,348	58,092	61,327
COSTS OF PRODUCTION	(note 16)			
Raw materials, supplies and merchandise . . .		28,392	30,289	31,255
Services		8,505	9,890	9,835
Leases and rentals		367	468	487
Personnel:				
salaries and wages	4,707		5,457	5,862
social security contributions	1,249		1,365	1,551
employee severance indemnities	244		256	315
employee pensions and similar obligations . .	185		100	122
other costs	303		376	319
Total Personnel costs		6,688	7,554	8,169
Amortization, depreciation and writedowns:				
amortization of intangible fixed assets	519		595	593
depreciation of property, plant and equipment	1,750		2,019	2,287
writedown of fixed assets	35		3	8
writedown of receivables among current assets and liquid funds	278		366	538
Total Amortization, depreciation and writedowns		2,582	2,983	3,426
Change in raw materials, supplies and merchandise inventories		81	38	(110)
Provisions for risks		1,163	1,138	1,038
Other provisions		17	30	6
Other operating costs		1,028	1,304	1,309
Expenses of financial services companies		668	1,115	904
Insurance claims and other insurance costs . .		1,367	4,045	4,690
TOTAL COSTS OF PRODUCTION		50,858	58,854	61,009
DIFFERENCE BETWEEN THE VALUE AND COSTS OF PRODUCTION		(510)	(762)	318

Continued

EXHIBIT 2.13
(*Continued*)

FIAT GROUP
Income Statement

Consolidated Statement of Operations

(in millions of euros)	**2003**	2002	2001
TOTAL FINANCIAL INCOME AND EXPENSES*	**(963)**	(671)	(680)
TOTAL ADJUSTMENTS TO FINANCIAL ASSETS*	**(172)**	(881)	(494)
TOTAL EXTRAORDINARY INCOME AND EXPENSES*	**347**	(2,503)	359
LOSS BEFORE TAXES	**(1,298)**	(4,817)	(497)
Income taxes .... (note 20)	**650**	(554)	294
LOSS BEFORE MINORITY INTEREST	**(1,948)**	(4,263)	(791)
Minority interest	**48**	315	346
NET LOSS	**(1,900)**	(3,948)	(445)

*Author's note: Detail included on Fiat's income statement is not provided

right-hand side reports income. Various measures of profit—including *Operating Profit, Financial Profit, Profit from Ordinary Activities, Extraordinary Profit,* and *Consolidated Profit before Taxation*—are reported on the left-hand side of the statement. To verify the amount reported as operating profit, one must subtract the sum of lines 1 through 5 under *Expenses* (€876,599) from the sum of lines 1 and 2 under *Income* (€987,845). For readers unfamiliar with this format, making sense out of Sol Melia's income statement might require significant effort.

Level of Detail

Considerable differences exist in the level of detail provided in the individual financial statements. U.S. companies tend to provide relatively few line items on the face of the financial statements and then supplement these with additional detail in the notes. New Zealand–based building materials manufacturer Fletcher Building Limited provides even less detail on its income statement and little additional information in the notes (see Exhibit 2.15). Fletcher's notes to the financial statements provide some information regarding the expenses subtracted in determining operating earnings, but the company does not disclose the amount of cost of goods sold.

The level of detail provided by U.S. and New Zealand–based companies can be contrasted with the extremely detailed financial statements provided by many Italian companies. Fiat's income statement (see again Exhibit 2.14) is a case in point. For example, Fiat disaggregates personnel costs into five separate components. Exhibit 2.16 presents the noncurrent asset section of Fiat's consolidated balance sheet. The entire balance sheet comprises five pages of the annual report. Even though the company provides considerable detail on the face of the balance sheet, it includes additional information in the notes to provide further detail. For example, Note 3, Financial fixed assets, provides extensive information on acquisitions and disposals of subsidiaries and other equity investments carried out during the year.

Terminology

The examination of AstraZeneca PLC's balance sheet earlier in this chapter revealed a number of differences in the terminology used by AstraZeneca and a

EXHIBIT 2.14

SOL MELIA SA
Income Statement

Consolidated Profit and Loss Account
In thousands of Euros

A. EXPENSES	31/12/2003
1. Supplies and other external expenses	119,526
2. Personnel expenses	256,146
a) Salaries, wages and related expenses	66,059
b) Social Security cost	111,094
3. Deprecation and amortization	7,823
4. Changes in trade provisions	315,951
5. Other operating expense	
I. OPERATING PROFIT	**111,246**
6. Financial expenses	61,329
8. Foreign currency losses	38,217
II. FINANCIAL PROFIT	—
9. Amortization of consolidation goodwill	2,956
III. PROFIT FROM ORDINARY ACTIVITIES	**51,094**
10. Losses arising from sale of fixed assets	2,646
11. Changes in fixed asset provisions	3,382
12. Extraordinary expenses and losses	9,441
13. Expenses and losses from prior years	7,007
IV. EXTRAORDINARY PROFIT	**12,134**
V. CONSOLIDATED PROFIT BEFORE TAXATION	**63,228**
10. Corporate income tax	14,138
VI. CONSOLIDATED RESULT FOR THE YEAR (PROFIT)	**49,089**
11. Result attributed to minority shareholders	10,950
VII. RESULT FOR THE YEAR ATTRIBUTED TO PARENT COMPANY (PROFIT)	**38,139**

Consolidated Profit and Loss Account
In thousands of Euros

B. INCOME	31/12//2003
1. Net turnover	944,167
2. Other operating income	43,678
I. OPERATING LOSSES	—
3. Income from share capital investments	1,115
4. Other financial income	2,925
5. Foreign currency gains	38,387
II. FINANCIAL LOSSES	**57,118**
6. Particip. in profits from companies consolidated by equity method	(79)
III. LOSSES FROM ORDINARY ACTIVITIES	—
7. Gains on disposals of fixed assets	23,800
9. Capital grants transferred to results for the year	236
10. Extraordinary income or profits	6,847
11. Income or profit from previous years	3,727
IV. EXTRAORDINARY LOSSES	—
V. CONSOLIDATED LOSSES BEFORE TAXATION	—
VI. CONSOLIDATED RESULT FOR THE YEAR (LOSSES)	—
VII. RESULT FOR THE YEAR ATTRIBUTED TO PARENT COMPANY (LOSSES)	—

Author's note: Comparative information for 2001 and 2002 presented by the company is not provided.

EXHIBIT 2.15

FLETCHER BUILDING LIMITED
Income Statement

STATEMENT OF FINANCIAL PERFORMANCE FOR THE YEAR ENDED 30 JUNE 2004

	NOTE	FLETCHER BUILDING GROUP		FLETCHER BUILDING LIMITED	
		YEAR ENDED JUNE 2004 NZ$M	PRO FORMA YEAR ENDED JUNE 2003 NZ$M	YEAR ENDED JUNE 2004 NZ$M	YEAR ENDED JUNE 2003 NZ$M
Operating revenue	3,4	**3,958**	3,221	135	57
Operating expenses		**(3,498)**	(2,890)		
Operating earnings	4,5	**460**	331	135	57
Funding costs	6	**(75)**	(59)	(54)	(42)
Earnings before taxation		**385**	272	81	15
Taxation expense	7	**(124)**	(85)	11	13
Earnings after taxation		**261**	187	92	28
Minority interest		**(21)**	(19)		
Net earnings		**240**	168	92	28
Net earnings per share (cents)	9				
Basic		**55.7**	43.4		
Diluted		**50.9**	39.9		
Weighted average number of shares outstanding (millions of shares)	9				
Basic		**431**	387		
Diluted		**515**	469		
Dividends declared per share (cents)		**25.00**	19.00		

---

typical U.S. company. To facilitate non-British readers' understanding of its financial statements, AstraZeneca (along with other British companies) provides a glossary in the notes to the financial statements that "translates" terms used by the company in its annual report to its U.S. equivalent. Exhibit 2.17 presents the glossary included in AstraZeneca's 2003 annual report.

Exhibit 2.17 indicates some very fundamental differences in British and U.S. accounting terminology, including *interest receivable (interest income)*, *profit and loss account (income statement)*, and *turnover (sales/revenues)*. Many non-English-language companies translate their annual reports into English for the convenience of English speakers. These companies typically choose between the British and the American formats and terminology in preparing convenience translations. Occasionally terms unfamiliar to both British and U.S. accounting are found in English-language reports to reflect business and accounting practices unique to a specific country. For example, Euro Disney reported the line item *Quasi-Equity* in its balance sheet presented in Exhibit 2.10. Bonds issued by the company that are redeemable in common shares are treated either as shareholders' equity or as quasi-equity depending on whether certain rights have been waived.

Disclosure

Numerous differences exist across countries in the amount and types of information disclosed in a set of financial statements. Many of the disclosures provided by companies are required by law or other regulations. In addition, many companies around the world provide additional, voluntary disclosures

EXHIBIT 2.16

FIAT GROUP
Noncurrent Asset Section of Consolidated Balance Sheet

Consolidated Balance Sheet

ASSETS

(in millions of euros)		*December 31, 2003*		*December 31, 2002*
AMOUNTS DUE FROM STOCKHOLDERS FOR SHARES SUBSCRIBED BUT NOT CALLED		—		1
FIXED ASSETS				
Intangible fixed assets (note 1)				
Start-up and expansion costs	**144**		77	
Research, development and advertising expenses	**22**		18	
Industrial patents and intellectual property rights	**406**		416	
Concessions, licenses, trademarks and similar rights	**347**		467	
Goodwill	**151**		229	
Intangible assets in progress and advances	**246**		263	
Other intangible assets	**157**		359	
Differences on consolidation	**2,251**		3,371	
Total		**3,724**		5,200
Property, plant and equipment (note 2)				
Land and buildings	**2,736**		3,801	
Plant and machinery	**3,393**		3,721	
Industrial and commercial equipment	**1,504**		1,511	
Other assets	**1,314**		2,095	
Construction in progress and advances	**728**		978	
Total		**9,675**		12,106
Financial fixed assets (note 3)				
Investments in:				
unconsolidated subsidiaries	**435**		558	
associated companies	**3,202**		2,772	
other companies	**257**		682	
Total Investments		**3,894**		3,962
Receivables from:				
others:				
due within one year	**4**		19	
due beyond one year	**25**		28	
Total receivables from others	**29**		47	
Total receivables		**29**		47
Other securities		**56**		2,445
Treasury stock		**—**		231
Finance lease contracts receivable		**1,797**		2,947
Investments where the investment risk is borne by policyholders and those related to pension plan management		**—**		6,930
Total		**5,776**		16,562
TOTAL FIXED ASSETS		**19,175**		33,868

EXHIBIT 2.17

Source: AstraZeneca Annual
Report and Form 20-F
Information 2003, p. 134.

ASTRAZENECA PLC
Glossary

Terms Used in the Annual Report and Form 20-F Information	US Equivalent or Brief Description
Accruals	Accrued expenses
Allotted	Issued
Bank borrowings	Payable to banks
Called-up share capital	Issued share capital
Capital allowances	Tax term equivalent to US tax depreciation allowances
Creditors	Liabilities/payables
Current instalments of loans	Long term debt due within one year
Debtors	Receivables and prepaid expenses
Earnings	Net income
Finance lease	Capital lease
Fixed asset investments	Non-current investments
Freehold	Ownership with absolute rights in perpetuity
Interest receivable	Interest income
Interest payable	Interest expense
Loans	Long term debt
Prepayments	Prepaid expenses
Profit	Income
Profit and loss account	Income statement/consolidated statement of income
Reserves	Retained earnings
Short term investments	Redeemable securities and short term deposits
Share premium account	Premiums paid in excess of par value of Ordinary Shares
Statement of total recognised gains and losses	Statement of comprehensive income
Stocks	Inventories
Tangible fixed assets	Property, plant and equipment
Turnover	Sales/revenues

often to better compete in obtaining finance in the international capital markets. The disclosures required to be made by publicly traded companies in the United States generally are considered to be the most extensive in the world. Saudagaran and Biddle developed a ranking of the level of disclosure required by stock exchanges in eight major countries (see Exhibit 2.18). Consistent with Gray's expectations with respect to secrecy (presented in Exhibit 2.9), the Anglo countries rank 1, 2, and 3 in the amount of disclosure provided, whereas the Germanic countries rank 7 and 8.

One must be careful in generalizing these disclosure rankings to all companies within a country. For example, the Swiss banking firm UBS Group provides extensive notes (91 pages) to its consolidated financial statements that are similar in scope and content to what is found in the annual reports of Anglo companies. The same can be said for other Swiss multinational corporations as well as for many multinationals in other non-Anglo countries. As part of the two-tiered reporting system that has developed in Europe, publicly traded companies in the European Union (EU) as well as large non-EU companies (such as UBS Group) use IFRSs, which generally require more extensive disclosures than local accounting rules.

EXHIBIT 2.18
Stock Market Disclosure Levels

Source: S. M. Saudagaran and G. C. Biddle, "Foreign Listing Location: A Study of MNCS and Stock Exchanges in Eight Countries," *Journal of International Business Studies,* Second Quarter 1995, p. 331.

Country	Overall Disclosure Level	Rank
United States	7.28	1
Canada	6.41	2
United Kingdom	6.02	3
Netherlands	4.75	4
France	4.17	5
Japan	3.83	6
Germany	3.81	7
Switzerland	3.17	8

There are an infinite number of differences that can exist in the disclosures provided by companies. To illustrate the wide diversity, we provide several examples of disclosures uncommon in the United States and most other countries. The Swedish company Electrolux, introduced earlier in this chapter, includes a note in its financial statements titled *Employees, Salaries, Remunerations and Employer Contributions* (see Exhibit 2.19). This note reports the number of employees, their gender, and their total remuneration by geographical area. By splitting total remuneration into the amount paid to boards and senior managers and the amount paid to other employees, the statement allows interested readers to see that it is the latter group that receives the vast majority of compensation.

The Brazilian mining company Companhia Vale do Rio Doce (CVRD) includes a statement of value added and a social balance sheet in the notes to its financial statements (see Exhibits 2.20 and 2.21). CVRD explains that it includes these notes to provide better information to the market. The format of the statement of value added is based on a recommendation made by the Commissão de Valores Mobiliarios (CVM), the Brazilian securities commission. The social balance sheet is based on a model developed by the Brazilian Institute for Social and Economic Analysis (IBASE).

The statement of value added provides insight into the groups that benefit most from CVRD's existence. Stockholders and the government received the largest distributions of value added by the company in 2003. The social balance sheet indicates among other things the costs in addition to gross payroll the company incurs related to its labor force. These include costs related to food, health, education, and profit sharing. In 2003, these costs amounted to 88 percent of gross payroll, with the largest amount going to compulsory social charges.

Imperial Chemical Industries PLC (ICI) includes a line item in its balance sheet titled *Provision for Liabilities and Charges.* Provisions are long-term accrued liabilities that by their nature involve a substantial amount of estimation. In note 21 to the financial statements, ICI provides considerable detail about the various items for which provisions have been established and the change in each of these items during the year (see Exhibit 2.22). This information can be used to assess the quality of estimates made by the company with respect to expected future liabilities. For example, note 21 indicates that for the year 2003, ICI had a beginning restructuring provision of £64 million. During 2003, £54 million of the estimated liability related to restructuring was paid or became payable, and a downward adjustment of £3 million was made partly due to a strengthening of the British pound during the year (exchange and other movements). Note 21 also discloses that only £2 million of £40 million ICI expects in environmental cleanup costs was paid in 2003.

EXHIBIT 2.19

AB ELECTROLUX
Note 28: Employees, Salaries, Remunerations and Employer Contributions

Amounts in SEKm, unless otherwise stated

Average number of employees, by geographical area

	Group		
	2003	**2002**	**2001**
Europe	39,514	42,601	46,899
North America	21,169	20,117	21,294
Rest of the world	16,457	19,253	18,946
Total	77,140	81,971	87,139

In 2003, average number of employees was 77,140 (81,971), of whom 51,240 (54,755) were men and 25,900 (27,215) were women. A detailed specification of average number of employees by country has been submitted to the Swedish Patent and Registration Office and is available on request from AB Electrolux, Investor Relations and Financial Information. See also Electrolux website www.electrolux.com/ir.

Salaries, other remuneration and employer contributions

	2003		2002		2001	
	Salaries and remuneration	**Employer contributions**	**Salaries and remuneration**	**Employer contributions**	**Salaries and remuneration**	**Employer contributions**
Parent Company	1,081	647	993	559	1,046	462
(of which pension costs)		(194)[1]		(196)[1]		(149)[1]
Subsidiaries	16,073	4,958	18,415	5,764	19,284	6,021
(of which pension costs)		(489)		(423)		(354)
Group total	17,154	5,605	19,408	6,323	20,330	6,483
(of which pension costs)		(683)		(619)		(503)

[1]Of which SEK 1m (19) and (22) respectively refers to pension costs for the President and his predecessors.

Salaries and remuneration for board members, senior managers and other employees, by geographical area

	2003		2002		2001	
	Boards and senior managers	**Other employees**	**Boards and senior managers**	**Other employees**	**Boards and senior managers**	**Other employees**
Sweden						
Parent Company	45	1,036	32	961	30	1,016
Other	30	903	24	887	18	908
Total Sweden	**75**	**1,939**	**39**	**1,865**	**30**	**1,942**
EU excluding Sweden	119	7,445	142	8,456	135	8,786
Rest of Europe	45	931	51	973	44	999
North America	48	5,196	39	6,047	55	6,451
Latin America	19	271	18	328	24	449
Asia	24	232	31	371	32	426
Africa	—	30	—	23	2	33
Oceania	11	769	8	1,017	5	917
Total outside Sweden	**266**	**14,874**	**289**	**17,215**	**297**	**18,061**
Group total	**341**	**16,813**	**345**	**19,063**	**345**	**19,985**

Board members and senior managers in the Group were 395 men and 58 women, of whom 15 men and 8 women in the Parent Company.

EXHIBIT 2.19   (*Continued*)

Employee absence due to illness

%	Second half of 2003	
	Employees in the Parent Company	All employees in Sweden
Total absence due to illness		
as a percentage of total normal working hours	8.0	6.6
of which 60 days or more	57.9	54.5
Absence due to illness, by category		
Women	10.9	9.8
Men	6.5	5.4
29 years or younger	5.5	4.6
30–49 years	8.7	7.2
50 years or older	9.1	7.7

According to the new regulations in the Swedish Annual Accounts Act, effective as of July 1, 2000, absence due to illness for employees in the Parent Company and the Group's employees in Sweden is reported in the table. The Parent Company comprises the Group's head office, as well as a number of units and plants, and employs approximately half of the Group's employees in Sweden.

EXHIBIT 2.20

COMPANHIA VALE DO RIO DOCE SA
Statement of Value Added

7 STATEMENT OF VALUE ADDED (ADDITIONAL INFORMATION)

Years ended December 31

	In millions of reais							
	Parent Company				Consolidated			
	2003	%	2002	%	2003	%	2002	%
Generation of Value Added								
Sales revenue	**10,367**	**100**	**8,570**	**100**	**20,219**	**100**	**15,267**	**100**
Less: Acquisition of products	(1,192)	(12)	(1,039)	(12)	(2,214)	(11)	(1,401)	(9)
Outsourced services	(1,279)	(12)	(854)	(10)	(2,702)	(13)	(1,832)	(12)
Materials	(880)	(9)	(641)	(7)	(1,752)	(9)	(1,216)	(8)
Fuel oil and gas	(636)	(6)	(393)	(5)	(1,401)	(7)	(850)	(6)
Research and development commercial								
and administrative	(397)	(4)	(372)	(4)	(939)	(5)	(849)	(6)
Other operating expenses	(232)	(2)	(293)	(3)	(1,163)	(6)	(499)	(3)
Gross Value Added	5,751	55	**4.978**	59	10,048	49	8,620	56
Depreciation and depletion	(593)	(6)	(650)	(8)	(1,102)	(5)	(1,016)	(7)
Amortization of goodwill	(166)	(2)	(98)	(1)	(166)	(1)	(101)	(1)
Net Value Added	**4,992**	**47**	**4,328**	**(51)**	**8,780**	**43**	**7,503**	**48**
Received from third parties								
Financial revenue	53	1	597	7	196	1	360	2
Result of equity investments	1,122	11	1,564	18	(540)	(3)	(473)	(3)
Discontinued operations	—	—	—	—	174	1	—	—
Total Value Added to be Distributed	**6,167**	**59**	**6,489**	**76**	**8,610**	**42**	**7,390**	**47**
Distribution of Value Added								
Employees	770	12	699	11	1,213	15	1,153	16
Government	1,301	21	101	2	2,185	26	554	7
Creditors (interest and exchange								
rate differences, net)	(413)	(7)	3,646	56	351	4	3,761	51
Stockholders	2,254	37	1,029	16	2,254	26	1,029	14
Minority participation	—	—	—	—	253	3	(121)	(2)
Retained earnings	2,255	37	1,014	15	2,255	26	1,014	14
Total Distribution of Value Added	**6,167**	**100**	**6,489**	**100**	**8,610**	**100**	**7,390**	**100**

EXHIBIT 2.21

COMPANHIA VALE DO RIO DOCE SA
Social Balance Sheet

---

8 SOCIAL BALANCE SHEET (ADDITIONAL INFORMATION)
Years ended December 31

In millions of reais

Consolidated (unaudited)

Basis for computation	2003	2002
Gross revenues	20,219	15,267
Operating profit	6,371	5,131
Gross payroll	970	740

| | | % of | | | | % of | |
| | | Gross | Operating | | | Gross | Operating |
Labor indicators	Amount	payroll	profit	Amount		payroll	profit
Food	76	8	1	37		5	1
Compulsory social charges	351	36	6	277		37	5
Private pension plan	82	8	1	66		9	1
Health	62	6	1	44		6	1
Education	42	4	1	34		5	1
Profit sharing	146	15	2	117		16	2
Other benefits	96	11	1	74		10	1
Total—Labor indicators	**855**	**88**	**13**	**649**		**88**	**12**

| | | % of | | | | % of | |
| | | Gross | Operating | | | Gross | Operating |
Social indicators	Amount	payroll	profit	Amount		payroll	profit
Taxes	**2,079**	**33**	**10**	**1,159**		**23**	**8**
Social investments	**60**	**1**	**—**	**52**		**1**	**—**
Social projects and actions ..	42	1	—	41		1	—
Indigeneous communities ..	18	—	—	11		—	—
Environmental expenditures ...	**154**	**2**	**1**	**109**		**2**	**1**
Operational	134	2	1	97		2	1
On outside programs or projects	20	—	—	12		—	—
Total—Social indicators	**2,293**	**36**	**11**	**1,320**		**26**	**9**

Headcount	2003	2002
No. of employees at end of year	30,063	29,349
No. of new hires during year ..	6,567	5,089

Authors' note: Parent Company information provided by the company is not presented.

Recognition and Measurement

Perhaps the most important international differences that exist in financial reporting are those related to the recognition and measurement of assets, liabilities,
revenues, and expenses. *Recognition* refers to the decision of whether an item
should be included on a financial statement. *Measurement* refers to the determination of the amount to be included. For example, national accounting standards establish whether goodwill should be recognized as an asset on the balance sheet. If

EXHIBIT 2.22

IMPERIAL CHEMICAL INDUSTRIES PLC
Note 21: Provisions for Liabilities and Charges

	Deferred taxation £m	Pensions (note 36) £m	Post retirement healthcare (note 36) £m	Environ-mental provisions* £m	Disposal and legacy provisions (note 22) £m	Restructuring provisions (note 22) £m	Other provisions† £m	Total £m
Group								
At beginning of 2003	140	148	205	40	458	64	66	**1,121**
Profit and loss account ...	(52)	28	14	(2)	(6)	141	92	**215**
Increase due to effluxion of time	—	—	—	—	10	—	—	**10**
Net amounts paid or becoming payable	—	(38)	(15)	(2)	(105)	(54)	(9)	**(223)**
Movements due to acqui-sitions and disposals	—	(1)	—	—	—	—	—	**(1)**
Exchange and other movements	(9)	(3)	(16)	(1)	(9)	(3)	11	**(30)**
At end of 2003	**79**	**134**	**188**	**35**	**348**	**148**	**160†**	**1,092**

Under US GAAP, provisions for liabilities and charges would be shown under other creditors (note 19).
*Other than arising on disposal.
†Includes £70m relating to provisions for the write-down of shares under forward contrats to hedge employee share options.
Authors' note: Parent Company information provided by the company is not presented.

so, then guidance must be provided with respect to both the initial measurement of goodwill and measurement at subsequent balance sheet dates. Goodwill is a good example of an item for which accounting diversity exists across countries. Exhibit 2.23 summarizes practices related to goodwill in several economically significant countries.

Numerous other areas exist in which accounting treatment differs internationally. The remainder of this chapter provides three examples related to the valuation of fixed assets, research and development costs, and lease capitalization. A cross-section of economically significant countries and regions demonstrates the range of possible treatments that have developed throughout the world. These countries and regions are Japan and Korea in Asia; Canada, Mexico, and Brazil in the Americas; and the countries that comprise the European Union. Accounting practice in the United States serves as a point of reference.

Reported Value of Assets

The following are the possible methods of reporting assets on the balance sheet subsequent to acquisition:

1. Historical cost (HC).
2. Historical cost adjusted for changes in the general purchasing power (GPP) of the currency.
3. Current replacement cost (CRC).
4. Net realizable value (NRV), the net amount that could be received from selling the asset today.

EXHIBIT 2.23
Accounting for
Goodwill
Internationally

United States

U.S. rules require goodwill to be recognized as an asset on the balance sheet. It is initially measured as the excess of acquisition price over the fair market value of net assets. At subsequent balance sheet dates, goodwill is written down to a lower value only if deemed to be impaired.

Canada

Rules for accounting for goodwill are the same as in the United States.

Mexico

Goodwill is recognized as an asset and amortized over a reasonable period not exceeding 20 years.

Brazil

Brazilian firms initially measure goodwill as the excess of acquisition price over the *book value* of net assets. The cost of goodwill thus measured is divided into that portion attributable to unrecorded intangible assets such as customer lists, and that portion attributable to future profitability. The two components of goodwill are accounted for and amortized separately over appropriate time periods.

Japan

Initial measurement of goodwill is similar to the United States. However, the amount of goodwill may be charged directly to income if the amount is not considered significant. If capitalized, goodwill is amortized over a period of up to five years unless a longer period of time can be justified.

Korea

Goodwill is reported on the balance sheet as an intangible asset and amortized to income over a five-year period. To the extent that the excess of purchase price over fair market value of acquired net assets does not represent goodwill, it should be recorded as an expense immediately.

European Union

Beginning in 2005, publicly traded companies in the European Union follow International Financial Reporting Standards (IFRSs) in preparing consolidated financial statements. IFRSs also require goodwill to be recognized as an asset on the balance sheet and then tested annually for impairment.

In most cases, GPP, CRC, and NRV accounting results in assets being written up to an amount larger than historical cost. The counterpart generally is treated as an increase in stockholders' equity, often included in a Revaluation Reserve account. The larger asset value results in a larger depreciation expense and smaller net income.

U.S. GAAP requires fixed assets to be carried on the balance sheet at historical cost less accumulated depreciation. If an asset is impaired, that is, its carrying value exceeds the amount of cash expected to result from use of the asset, it must be written down to the amount of cash expected to be generated by the asset over its remaining useful life. Upward revaluation of fixed assets is not acceptable. HC accounting is also required in Japan. Although the specific rules vary, write-down to a smaller value is required if a permanent impairment of value has occurred.

In contrast, under IFRSs, publicly traded companies in the European Union are free to choose between two different methods for valuing their assets. Fixed assets may be carried on the balance sheet at historical cost or at revalued amounts. The basis of revaluation is the *fair value* of the asset at the date of revaluation, which in many cases will be determined through appraisals. If a company chooses to report assets at revalued amounts, it has an obligation to keep the valuations up to date, which might require annual adjustments.

In Mexico, fixed assets are reported initially at historical cost and then are restated to current values at subsequent balance sheet dates. For public companies, current value is defined as CRC. Nonpublic companies may use either CRC or GPP accounting to revalue fixed assets. Until the early 1990s, publicly traded companies in Brazil were required to use GPP in preparing financial statements. In addition to fixed assets, inventories and investments also were adjusted upward for inflation on each balance sheet date, and receivables were discounted to their present value. These procedures no longer are required in Brazil but still may be followed at the option of the company.

Korean companies generally use HC accounting. However, revaluation to market value is allowed if the wholesale price index has risen 25 percent or more since the date of an asset's acquisition or previous revaluation. Such adjustments are optional but can be made only on the first day of the business year. A revaluation is recorded through an increase in a capital reserve in stockholders' equity, and a 3 percent tax is imposed on the revaluation amount. Prior to 1990, Canadian companies were allowed to write assets up to an appraised value above cost. The procedure was rarely used and has been eliminated.

Research and Development Costs

The major issue related to the accounting for research and development costs is whether these costs should be expensed immediately or capitalized as an asset and then amortized to expense over their useful life.

In Mexico, all research and development costs are expensed as incurred. The United States follows a similar rule, except that computer software development costs are capitalized once technical feasibility has been established.

Publicly traded companies in the European Union are required to expense all research costs immediately, but development costs must be capitalized when certain specified criteria are met. Similarly, Canadian companies must capitalize development costs when certain criteria are met.

Japanese accounting allows not only development but also research costs to be capitalized if the research is directed toward new goods or techniques, development of markets, or exploitation of resources. Korean businesses capitalize their research and development costs when they are incurred in relation to a specific product or technology, when costs can be separately identified, and when the recovery of costs is reasonably expected. Brazil also allows research and development costs to be capitalized under certain conditions.

Lease Capitalization

There are two methods used internationally in accounting for long-term leases. Under the capitalized lease method, the asset being leased is recognized on the books of the lessee with an offsetting long-term lease obligation. The lessee depreciates the asset held under capital lease and allocates lease payments between interest expense and reduction of the long-term obligation. The alternative is the operating lease method. Under operating lease accounting, the lessee accounts for lease payments as rent expense; no asset or liability is recognized.

There is a split opinion internationally regarding the capitalization of leases. The European Union, the United States, Canada, Mexico, and Korea require capitalization when specified criteria are met. In contrast, all leases are accounted for as operating leases in Japan and Brazil.

Summary

1. Considerable diversity exists across countries with respect to the form and content of individual financial statements, the rules used to measure assets and liabilities and recognize and measure revenues and expenses, and the magnitude and nature of the disclosures provided in a set of financial statements.

2. Many environmental factors are thought to contribute to the differences in financial reporting that exist across countries. Some of the more commonly mentioned factors include legal system, the influence of taxation on financial reporting, corporate financing system, inflation, political and economic ties between countries, and national culture.

3. The diversity that exists in financial reporting creates problems for multinational corporations in preparing consolidated financial statements on the basis of a single set of accounting rules. Accounting diversity also can result in increased cost for companies in tapping into foreign capital markets. The comparison of financial statements across companies located in different countries is hampered by accounting diversity. Low-quality financial reporting contributed to the financial crisis in East Asia in the 1990s.

4. Several authors have classified countries according to similarities and differences in financial reporting. Two dominant models of accounting used in the developed world are the British-American model and the Continental European model.

5. Concentrating on the British-American and Continental model countries, Nobes developed a classification scheme that attempts to show how the financial reporting systems in 14 developed countries relate to one another. Nobes breaks down the two major classes of accounting system first into subclasses and then into families. This classification scheme shows how different families of accounting are related.

6. Culture has long been considered a determinant of accounting. Using the cultural dimensions identified by Hofstede, Gray developed a framework for the relationship between culture and accounting systems. Cultural values affect a country's accounting system in two ways: (1) through their influence on the accounting values of conservatism, secrecy, uniformity, and professionalism shared by a country's accountants and (2) through their influence on institutional factors such as the capital market and legal system.

7. In a more recent model of the reasons for international differences in financial reporting, Nobes suggests that the dominant factor is the extent to which corporate financing is obtained through the sale of equity securities to outsider shareholders. For whatever reason, some cultures lead to a strong equity-outsider financing system and other cultures lead to a weaker equity-outsider financing system. In countries with strong equity-outsider financing, measurement practices are less conservative, disclosure is extensive, and accounting practice differs from tax rules. This is consistent with what may be called Anglo-Saxon accounting. In accounting systems found in countries with weak equity–outside shareholder financing systems, measurement is more conservative, disclosure is not as extensive, and accounting practice follows tax rules. This is consistent with the Continental European accounting model.

8. Differences in financial reporting exist with regard to the financial statements provided by companies; the format, level of detail, and terminology used in presenting financial statements; the nature and amount of disclosure provided; and the principles used to recognize and measure assets, liabilities, revenues, and expenses.

Appendix to Chapter 2

The Case of Daimler-Benz

Daimler-Benz (now DaimlerChrysler) was the first German company to list on the New York Stock Exchange (NYSE), doing so in 1993. This was a major event for the NYSE and the Securities and Exchange Commission (SEC) because German companies had previously refused to make the adjustments necessary to reconcile their German law–based financial statements to U.S. generally accepted accounting principles (GAAP). After some compromise on the part of the SEC and because of Daimler's strong desire to enter the U.S. capital market (and be the first German company to do it), Daimler agreed to comply with SEC regulations.

Subsequent to its NYSE listing, Daimler-Benz filed an annual report on Form 20-F with the SEC.[1] In its 20-F filing, Daimler prepared financial statements in English, in both German deutschemarks (DM) and U.S. dollars, and, until 1996, according to German accounting principles. In the notes to the 1995 financial statements, Daimler provided a "Reconciliation to U.S. GAAP" in which adjustments were made to net income and stockholders' equity prepared in accordance with German accounting law to reconcile to U.S. GAAP. The net effect of these adjustments over the period 1993–1995 is shown in Exhibit A2.1.

The fact that in 1993 Daimler-Benz reported a profit under German GAAP but a loss under U.S. GAAP created quite a stir in the international financial community. Because German companies are notorious for intentionally understating income through the creation of hidden reserves, one would have expected German GAAP income to be smaller than U.S. GAAP income (as was true in 1994). In 1993, however, Daimler incurred a net loss for the year (as can be seen from the negative amount of U.S. GAAP income). To avoid reporting this loss, the company

EXHIBIT A2.1

DAIMLER-BENZ
Excerpt from Form 20-F: Reconciliation to U.S. GAAP 1995

(all amounts in DM)

	1993	1994	1995
Net income as reported in the consolidated income statement under German GAAP	615	895	(5,734)
Net income in accordance with U.S. GAAP	(1,839)	1,052	(5,729)
Stockholders' equity as reported in the consolidated balance sheet under German GAAP	18,145	20,251	13,842
Stockholders' equity in accordance with U.S. GAAP	26,281	29,435	22,860

[1]U.S. companies file their annual report with the SEC on Form 10-K; foreign companies file theirs on Form 20-F.

"released" hidden reserves that had been created in earlier years, thus reporting a profit of DM 615 million under German GAAP. The difference in German GAAP and U.S. GAAP income in 1993 of some DM 2.5 billion shows just how unreliable German GAAP income can be in reflecting the actual performance of a company. In fact, the German Financial Analysts Federation (DVFA) developed a method for adjusting German GAAP earnings to a more reliable amount (known as DVFA earnings).

In 1996, Daimler-Benz decided to abandon German GAAP and implement a U.S. GAAP accounting system worldwide. The 1996 annual report was prepared using U.S. GAAP and received a clean opinion on this basis from KPMG. The rationale for this decision was outlined in the 1996 annual report and is reproduced in Exhibit A2.2. The company indicates that U.S. GAAP figures not only allow external analysts to better evaluate the company but also serve as a better basis for the internal controlling of the company. This clearly points out the differences in orientation between a typical macro-uniform accounting system that is geared toward minimizing taxes and protecting creditors, and a micro-based accounting system that has the objective of providing information that is useful for making decisions, not only by external parties but by management as well.

EXHIBIT A2.2

DAIMLER-BENZ
Excerpts from Annual Report 1996

Excerpts from *Value-Based Management, U.S. GAAP, and New Controlling Instruments* (pages 44–45)

1996 Financial Statements Prepared Entirely in Accordance with U.S. GAAP for the First Time

Since our listing on the New York Stock Exchange we have increasingly aligned our external reporting in accordance with the information requirements of the international financial world . . . With our 1996 annual report, we are the first German company to present an entire year's financial statements in accordance with U.S. GAAP while at the same time complying with the German Law to Facilitate Equity Borrowing. The report thus also conforms with EU guidelines and European accounting principles.

Improved External Disclosure

Instead of providing various figures concerning the economic performance of the Company that are derived using the HGB and U.S. GAAP but that in some instances differ significantly from each other because of the distinct accounting philosophies, we supply a complete set of figures in conformance with U.S. GAAP for our shareholders, the financial analysts, and the interested public. In so doing, we fulfill accounting standards of the highest reputation worldwide, and we believe our approach more clearly and accurately reflects the economic performance, financial situation, and net worth of the Company than any other accounting system available at this time. This is not least due to the fact that U.S. accounting principles focus on investor information rather than creditor protection, which is the dominant concern under German accounting principles. Discretionary valuation is greatly limited, and the allocation of income and expenses to the individual accounting period is based on strict economic considerations.

Advantages for All Shareholders

Using U.S. accounting principles makes it significantly easier to internationally active financial analysts or experienced institutional investors to accurately assess the financial situation and development of the Company. Moreover, it improves disclosure at Daimler-Benz as well as comparability on an international scale. This helps promote the worldwide acceptance of our stock.

Internal Controlling on the Basis of Balance Sheet Values in Accordance with U.S. GAAP

The U.S. GAAP not only made Daimler-Benz more transparent from an external perspective. Because the earnings figures as derived with American accounting principles accurately reflect the economic

**EXHIBIT A2.2
(Continued)**

performance of the Company, we are now able to use figures from our external reporting for the internal controlling of the Company and its individual business units rather than relying on the internal operating profit used in the past. We thus make use of the same figures both internally and externally to measure the economic performance of the Company and the business units.

Excerpt from *Letter to the Stockholders and Friends of Our Company* (page 4)

1996 marks the first time we have prepared our accounts in accordance with U.S. accounting principles which gives our investors worldwide the transparency they require. This means that our success as well as our shortcomings will be reported with new clarity. The terms operating profit, return on capital employed, and cash flow have become part of the language of the entire company and part of our corporate philosophy.

Questions

1. What are the two most common methods used internationally for the order in which assets are listed on the balance sheet? Which of these two methods is most common in North America? In Europe?

2. What are the two major types of legal systems used in the world? How does the type of legal system affect accounting?

3. How does the relationship between financial reporting and taxation affect the manner in which income is measured for financial reporting purposes?

4. Who are the major providers of capital (financing) for business enterprises? What influence does the relative importance of equity financing in a country have on financial statement disclosure?

5. What are the major problems caused by worldwide accounting diversity for a multinational corporation?

6. What are the major problems caused by worldwide accounting diversity for international portfolio investment?

7. What are the hypothesized relationships between the cultural value of uncertainty avoidance and the accounting values of conservatism and secrecy?

8. How are the Anglo and less developed Latin cultural areas expected to differ with respect to the accounting values of conservatism and secrecy?

9. According to Nobes, what are the two most important factors influencing differences in accounting systems across countries?

10. What are the different ways in which financial statements differ across countries?

11. How are the various costs that comprise cost of goods sold reflected in a "type of expenditure" format income statement?

12. What do the following terms found on a British balance sheet represent: *fixed assets, stocks, debtors, share premium capital,* and *profit and loss account?*

13. What information is provided in a statement of value added?

14. What are the alternative methods used internationally to account for goodwill?

15. What are the alternative methods used internationally to present fixed assets on the balances sheet subsequent to acquisition?

16. What are the alternative approaches used internationally to account for research and development costs?

Exercises and Problems

1. Refer to the income statements presented in Exhibits 2.11, 2.12, 2.13, 2.14, and 2.15 for The Home Depot Inc., Südzucker AG, Fiat Group, Sol Melia SA, and Fletcher Building Limited.

   Required:
   a. Calculate gross profit margin (gross profit/sales), operating profit margin (operating profit/sales) and net profit margin (net earnings/sales) for each of these companies. If a particular ratio cannot be calculated, explain why not.
   b. Is it valid to compare the profit margins calculated in Part (a) across these companies in assessing relative profitability? Why or why not?

2. Refer to Exhibit 2.16, which presents the noncurrent asset section of the consolidated balance sheet for Fiat Group.

   Required:
   Identify any items listed in the noncurrent asset section on Fiat's balance sheet that you find unfamiliar or that you believe should not be reported as a noncurrent asset.

3. Access the financial statements from the most recent annual report of a foreign company and a domestic company with which you are familiar to complete this assignment.

   Required:
   a. Determine the accounting principles (GAAP) the foreign and domestic companies use to prepare financial statements.
   b. Determine whether the foreign and domestic companies provide a set of financial statements that includes the same components (e.g., consolidated balance sheet, consolidated income statement, consolidated cash flows statement).
   c. List five format differences in the companies' income statements.
   d. List five format differences in the companies' balance sheets.
   e. Note any terminology differences that exist between the two companies' income statements and balance sheets.
   f. Assess whether the scope and content of the information provided in the notes to the financial statements is similar between the two companies.
   g. Compare the overall presentation of the financial statements and notes to the financial statements between the two companies.

4. Access the financial statements from the most recent annual report of two foreign companies located in the same country to complete this assignment.

   Required:
   a. Determine the accounting principles (GAAP) the two foreign companies use to prepare financial statements.
   b. Determine whether the two foreign companies provide a set of financial statements that includes the same components (e.g., consolidated balance sheet, consolidated income statement, consolidated cash flows statement).
   c. List any format differences in the companies' income statements.
   d. List any format differences in the companies' balance sheets.
   e. Note any terminology differences that exist between the two companies' income statements and balance sheets.
   f. Assess whether the scope and content of the information provided in the notes to the financial statements is similar between the two companies.

g. Compare the overall presentation of the financial statements and notes to the financial statements between the two companies.

5. Cultural dimension index scores developed by Hofstede for six countries are reported in the following table:

Country	Power Distance Index	Power Distance Rank[a]	Uncertainty Avoidance Index	Uncertainty Avoidance Rank[a]	Individualism Index	Individualism Rank[a]	Masculinity Index	Masculinity Rank[a]	Long-Term Orientation Index	Long-Term Orientation Rank[b]
Belgium	65	20	94	5–6	75	8	54	22	38	18
Brazil	69	14	76	21–22	38	26–27	49	27	65	6
Korea (South)	60	27–28	85	16–17	18	43	39	41	75	5
Netherlands	38	40	53	35	80	4–5	14	51	44	11–12
Sweden	31	47–48	29	49–50	71	10–11	5	53	33	20
Thailand	64	21–23	64	30	20	39–41	34	44	56	8

[a]1 = highest rank; 53 = lowest rank.
[b]1 = highest rank; 34 = lowest rank.

Required:
Using Gray's hypothesis relating culture to the accounting value of secrecy, rate these six countries as relatively high or relatively low with respect to the level of disclosure you would expect to find in financial statements. Explain.

6. Refer to Nobes's judgmental classification of accounting systems in Exhibit 2.5 and consider the following countries: Austria, Brazil, Finland, Ivory Coast, Russia, South Africa.

Required:
Identify the family of accounting in which you would expect to find each of these countries. Explain your classification of these countries.

7. Five factors are often mentioned as affecting a country's accounting practices: (1) legal system, (2) taxation, (3) providers of financing, (4) inflation, and (5) political and economic ties.

Required:
Consider your home country. Identify which of these factors has had the strongest influence on accounting in your country. Provide specific examples to support your position.

8. As noted in the chapter, diversity in accounting practice across countries generates problems for a number of different groups.

Required:
Answer the following questions and provide explanations for your answers.
a. Which is the greatest problem arising from worldwide accounting diversity?
b. Which group is most affected by worldwide accounting diversity?
c. Which group can most easily deal with the problems associated with accounting diversity?

9. Various attempts have been made to reduce the accounting diversity that exists internationally. This process is known as harmonization and is discussed in more detail in Chapter 3. The ultimate form of harmonization would be a world in which all countries followed a similar set of financial reporting rules and practices.

Required:

Consider each of the following factors that contribute to existing accounting diversity as described in this chapter:

- Legal system
- Taxation
- Providers of financing
- Inflation
- Political and economic ties
- Culture

Which factor or factors do you believe represent the greatest impediment to harmonization? Which factor or factors do you believe create the smallest impediment to harmonization? Explain your reasoning.

Case 2-1

The Impact of Culture on Conservatism

PART I

The framework created by Professor Sidney Gray in 1988 to explain the development of a country's accounting system is presented in the chapter in Exhibit 2.8. Gray predicts that culture has an impact on a country's accounting system through its influence on accounting values. Focusing on that part of a country's accounting system comprised of financial reporting rules and practices, the model can be visualized as follows:

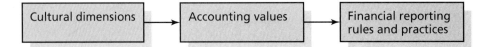

In short, cultural values shared by members of a society influence the accounting values shared by members of the accounting subculture. The shared values of the accounting subculture in turn affect the financial reporting rules and practices found within a country.

With respect to the accounting value of conservatism, Gray hypothesizes that the higher a country ranks on the cultural dimensions of uncertainty avoidance and long-term orientation, and the lower it ranks in terms of individualism and masculinity, then the more likely it is to rank highly in terms of conservatism. Conservatism is a preference for a cautious approach to measurement. Conservatism is manifested in a country's accounting system through a tendency to defer recognition of assets and items that increase net income and a tendency to accelerate the recognition of liabilities and items that decrease net income. One example of conservatism in practice would be a rule that requires an unrealized contingent liability to be recognized when it is probable that an outflow of future resources will arise but does not allow the recognition of an unrealized contingent asset under any circumstances.

Required:

Discuss the implications for the global harmonization of financial reporting standards raised by Gray's model.

PART II

Although Gray's model relates cultural values to the accounting value of conservatism as it is embodied in a country's financial reporting rules, it can be argued that the model is equally applicable to the manner in which a country's accountants apply those rules:

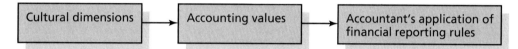

Cultural dimensions → Accounting values → Accountant's application of financial reporting rules

Required:

Discuss the implications this argument has for the comparability of financial statements across countries, even in an environment of international accounting harmonization. Identify areas in which differences in cultural dimensions across countries could lead to difference in the application of financial reporting rules.

PART III

Cancan Enterprises Inc. is a Canadian-based company with subsidiaries located in Brazil, Korea, and Sweden. (Hofstede's cultural dimension index scores for these countries are presented in Exercise 5.) Cancan Enterprises must apply Canadian GAAP worldwide in preparing consolidated financial statements. Cancan has developed a corporate accounting manual that prescribes the accounting policies based on Canadian GAAP that are to be applied by all the company's operations. Each year Cancan's internal auditors have the responsibility of ensuring that the company's accounting policies have been applied consistently company-wide.

Required:

Discuss the implications that the model presented in Part II of this case has for the internal auditors of Cancan Enterprises in carrying out their responsibilities.

Case 2-2

SKD Limited

SKD Limited is a biotechnology company that prepares financial statements using internally developed accounting rules (referred to as SKD GAAP). To be able to compare SKD's financial statements with those of companies in their home country, financial analysts in Country A and Country B prepared a reconciliation of SKD's current year net income and stockholders' equity. Adjustments were based on the actual accounting policies and practices followed by biotechnology companies in Country A and Country B. The following table shows the adjustments to income and stockholders' equity made by each country analyst:

	Country A	Country B
Income under SKD GAAP	1,050	1,050
Adjustments:		
Goodwill amortization	300	(100)
Capitalized interest	50	50
Depreciation related to capitalized interest	(20)	(20)
Depreciation related to revalued fixed assets	—	(8)
Income under local GAAP	1,380	972
Stockholders' equity under SKD GAAP	15,000	15,000
Adjustments:		
Goodwill	900	(300)
Capitalized interest	30	30
Revaluation of fixed assets	—	56
Stockholders' equity under local GAAP	15,930	14,786

Description of Accounting Differences

Goodwill. SKD capitalizes goodwill and amortizes it over a 20-year period. Goodwill is also treated as an asset in Country A and Country B. However, goodwill is not amortized in Country A, but instead is subjected to an annual impairment test. Goodwill is amortized over a 5-year period in Country B.

Interest. SKD expenses all interest immediately. In both Country A and Country B, interest related to self-constructed assets must be capitalized as a part of the cost of the asset.

Fixed assets. SKD carries assets on the balance sheet at their historical cost, less accumulated depreciation. The same treatment is required in Country A. In Country B, companies in the biotechnology industry generally carry assets on the balance sheet at revalued amounts. Depreciation is based on the revalued amount of fixed assets.

Required:

1. With respect to the adjustments related to goodwill, answer the following:
   a. Why does the adjustment for goodwill amortization increase net income under Country A GAAP but decrease net income under Country B GAAP?
   b. Why does the goodwill adjustment increase stockholders' equity in Country A but decrease stockholders' equity in Country B?
   c. Why are the adjustments to stockholders' equity larger than the adjustments to income?

2. With respect to the adjustments made by the analyst in Country A related to interest, answer the following:
   a. Why are there two separate adjustments to income related to interest?
   b. Why does the adjustment to income for capitalized interest increase income, whereas the adjustment for depreciation related to capitalized interest decreases income?
   c. Why is the positive adjustment to stockholders' equity for capitalized interest smaller than the positive adjustment to income for capitalized interest?

3. With respect to the adjustments made by the analyst in Country B related to fixed assets, answer the following:
   a. Why does the adjustment for depreciation related to revalued fixed assets decrease income, whereas the adjustment for revaluation of fixed assets increases stockholders' equity?

References

Afterman, Allan B. *International Accounting, Financial Reporting, and Analysis.* New York: Warren, Gorham & Lamont, 1995, pp. C1-17, C1-22.

Brooks, Jermyn Paul, and Dietz Mertin. *Neues Deutsches Bilanzrecht.* Düsseldorf: IDW-Verlag, 1986.

Cochrane, James L.; James E. Shapiro; and Jean E. Tobin. "Foreign Equities and U.S. Investors: Breaking Down the Barriers Separating Supply and Demand." NYSE Working Paper, 95-04, 1995.

Collins, Stephen H. "The Move to Globalization," *Journal of Accountancy*, March 1989.

Doupnik, Timothy S., and Stephen B. Salter. "An Empirical Test of a Judgemental International Classification of Financial Reporting Practices." *Journal of International Business Studies*, First Quarter 1993, pp. 41–60.

Doupnik, Timothy S., and George T. Tsakumis. "A Review of Empirical Tests of Gray's Framework and Suggestions for Future Research." *Journal of Accounting Literature*, 2004, pp. 1–48.

Gernon, H., and Gary Meek. *Accounting: An International Perspective*, 5th ed. Burr Ridge, IL: Irwin/McGraw-Hill, 2001.

Gray, S. J. "Towards a Theory of Cultural Influence on the Development of Accounting Systems Internationally." *Abacus*, March 1988, pp. 1–15.

Hofstede, G. *Culture's Consequences: International Differences in Work-Related Values.* London: Sage, 1980.

————. *Culture's Consequences: Comparing Values, Behaviors, Institutions, and Organizations across Nations*, 2nd ed. Thousand Oaks, CA: Sage, 2001.

Malaysian Accounting Standards Board. MASB i-1, "*Presentation of Financial Statements of Islamic Financial Institutions*, 2001.

Meek, Gary K., and Sharokh M. Saudagaran. "A Survey of Research on Financial Reporting in a Transnational Context." *Journal of Accounting Literature*, 1990, pp. 145–82.

Nobes, Christopher W. "A Judgemental International Classification of Financial Reporting Practices." *Journal of Business Finance and Accounting*, Spring 1983.

————. "Towards a General Model of the Reasons for International Differences in Financial Reporting." *Abacus* 34, no. 2 (1998), p. 166.

Periar, V.; R. Paterson; and A. Wilson. *UK/US GAAP Comparison*, 2nd ed. London: Kogan Page, 1992.

Radebaugh, Lee H., and Sidney J. Gray. *International Accounting and Multinational Enterprises*, 5th ed. New York: Wiley, 2002.

Rahman, Zubaidur M. "The Role of Accounting in the East Asian Financial Crisis: Lessons Learned?" *Transnational Corporations* 7, no. 3 (December 1998), pp. 1–52.

U.S. Department of Commerce. "U.S. International Transactions." *Survey of Current Business*, January 2005, pp. 45–76.

U.S. Securities and Exchange Commission. *Survey of Financial Statement Reconciliations by Foreign Registrants.* Washington, DC: SEC, 1993.

Violet, William J. 1983. "The Development of International Accounting Standards: An Anthropological Perspective." *International Journal of Accounting*, 1983, pp. 1–12.

Chapter **Three**

International Harmonization of Financial Reporting

Learning Objectives

After reading this chapter, you should be able to

- Explain the meaning of harmonization.
- Identify the arguments for and against international harmonization of accounting standards.
- Discuss major harmonization efforts at regional and global levels with particular emphasis on the International Accounting Standards Board (IASB).
- Explain the principles-based approach used by the IASB in accounting standards setting.
- Discuss the IASB's *Framework* and Standards related to the adoption of International Financial Reporting Standards (IFRSs) and the presentation of financial statements.
- Examine the support for, and the use of, IFRSs across countries.
- Describe the IASB/FASB convergence project.

INTRODUCTION

In Chapter 2, we discussed worldwide diversity in accounting practices and some of the problems caused by such diversity. Sir Bryan Carsberg, former secretary-general of the International Accounting Standards Committee (IASC), explained how accounting diversity affects international capital markets:

> Imagine the case of an international business, with operations in many different countries. It is likely to be required to prepare accounts for its operations in each country, in compliance with the rules of that country. It will then have to convert those accounts to conform to the rules of the country in which the holding company is resident, for the preparation of group accounts. If the company has listings on stock exchanges outside its home country, these exchanges or their regulators may require the accounts to be filed under some other basis. The extra cost could be enormous. Heavy costs also fall on investors in trying to compare the results of companies based in different countries and they may just be unable to make such

comparisons. . . . But the biggest cost may be in limiting the effectiveness of the international capital markets. Cross border investment is likely to be inhibited.[1]

The accounting profession and standard setters have been under pressure from multinational companies, stock exchanges, securities regulators, and international lending institutions, such as the World Bank, to reduce diversity and harmonize accounting standards and practices internationally. This chapter focuses on the major harmonization efforts worldwide, emphasizing the activities of the International Accounting Standards Board (IASB), which took the place of the IASC in 2001. We explain the meaning of harmonization, identify the arguments for and against harmonization, and discuss the use of International Financial Reporting Standards (IFRSs), including national efforts to converge with those standards.

WHAT IS HARMONIZATION?

The word *harmonization* appears to mean different things to different people. Some view harmonization as the same as standardization. However, whereas standardization implies the elimination of alternatives in accounting for economic transactions and other events, harmonization refers to the reduction of alternatives while retaining a high degree of flexibility in accounting practices. Harmonization allows different countries to have different standards as long as the standards do not conflict. For example, within the European Union harmonization program, if appropriate disclosures were made, companies were permitted to use different measurement methods: For valuing assets, German companies could use historical cost, while Dutch companies can use replacement costs without violating the harmonization requirements.

Harmonization is a process that takes place over time. Accounting harmonization can be considered in two ways, namely, harmonization of accounting regulations or standards (also known as formal or de jure harmonization), and harmonization of accounting practices (also known as material or de facto harmonization). Harmonization of accounting practices is the ultimate goal of international harmonization efforts. Harmonization of standards may not necessarily lead to harmonization of accounting practices adopted by companies. For example, a recent study in China found that despite the Chinese government's efforts through legislation to ensure harmonization between Chinese GAAP and IASC GAAP, there was no evidence that such efforts eliminated or significantly reduced the differences that exist between earnings calculated under Chinese and IASC GAAP.[2] Other factors such as differences in the quality of audits, enforcement mechanisms, culture, legal requirements, and socioeconomic and political systems may lead to noncomparable accounting numbers despite similar accounting standards. An empirical study conducted in 1996 to assess the impact of the IASC's harmonization efforts, focusing on the accounting practices of major companies based in France, Germany, Japan, the United Kingdom, and the United States, concluded that the impact had been quite modest. The study considered

---

[1] Excerpt from Sir Bryan Carsberg, "Global Issues and Implementing Core International Accounting Standards: Where Lies IASC's Final Goal?" Remarks made at the 50th Anniversary Dinner, Japanese Institute of CPAs, Tokyo, October 23, 1998.

[2] S. Chen, Z. Sun, and Y. Wang, "Evidence from China on Whether Harmonized Accounting Standards Harmonize Accounting Practices," *Accounting Horizons* 16, no. 3 (2002), pp. 183–97.

26 major accounting measurement issues and found that in 14 cases harmonization had increased, but in 12 cases harmonization had decreased.[3]

ARGUMENTS FOR AND AGAINST HARMONIZATION

Arguments for Harmonization

Proponents of accounting harmonization argue that comparability of financial statements worldwide is necessary for the globalization of capital markets. Financial statement comparability would make it easier for investors to evaluate potential investments in foreign securities and thereby take advantage of the risk reduction possible through international diversification. It would also simplify the evaluation by multinational companies of possible foreign takeover targets. Harmonization would reduce financial reporting costs for companies that seek to list their shares on foreign stock exchanges. Cross-listing of securities would allow companies to gain access to less expensive capital in other countries and would make it easier for foreign investors to acquire the company's stock. National differences in corporate reporting cause loss of investor confidence, which affects the availability and cost of capital. Investors often build in a premium to the required return on their investment if there is any uncertainty or lack of comparability about the figures—such premiums can be as large as 40 percent.[4]

One set of universally accepted accounting standards would reduce the cost of preparing worldwide consolidated financial statements and simplify their auditing. Multinational companies would find it easier to transfer accounting staff to other countries. This would be true for the international auditing firms as well.

Another argument is that harmonization would help raise the quality level of accounting practices internationally, thereby increasing the credibility of financial information. In relation to this argument, some point out that as a result of harmonization, developing countries would be able to adopt a ready-made set of high-quality standards with minimum cost and effort.

Arguments against Harmonization

The greatest obstacles to harmonization are the magnitude of the differences that exist between countries and the fact that the political cost of eliminating those differences would be enormous. As stated by Dennis Beresford, former chairman of the Financial Accounting Standards Board (FASB), "high on almost everybody's list of obstacles is nationalism. Whether out of deep-seated tradition, indifference born of economic power, or resistance to intrusion of foreign influence, some say that national entities will not bow to any international body."[5] Arriving at principles that satisfy all of the parties involved throughout the world seems an almost impossible task.

Not only is harmonization difficult to achieve, but the need for such standards is not universally accepted. As stated by Seagram's chief financial officer, Richard

---

[3] Emmanuel N. Emenyonu and Sidney J. Gray, "International Accounting Harmonization and the Major Developed Stock Market Countries: An Empirical Study," *International Journal of Accounting* 31, no. 3 (1996), pp. 269–79.

[4] David Illigworth, President of the Institute of Chartered Accountants in England and Wales, in a speech at the China Economic Summit 2004 of the 7th China Beijing International High-Tech Expo, May 21, 2004.

[5] Dennis R. Beresford, "Accounting for International Operations," *CPA Journal*, October 1988, pp. 79–80.

Goeltz: "Full harmonization of international accounting standards is probably neither practical nor truly valuable. . . . It is not clear whether significant benefits would be derived in fact. A well-developed global capital market exists already. It has evolved without uniform accounting standards."[6] Opponents of harmonization argue that it is unnecessary to force all companies worldwide to follow a common set of rules. They also point out that this would lead to a situation of standards overload as a result of requiring some enterprises to comply with a set of standards not relevant to them. The international capital market will force those companies that can benefit from accessing the market to provide the required accounting information without harmonization.

Yet another argument against harmonization is that because of different environmental influences, differences in accounting across countries might be appropriate and necessary. For example, countries that are at different stages of economic development or that rely on different sources of financing perhaps should have differently oriented accounting systems. Professor Frederick Choi refers to this as the dilemma of global harmonization: "The thesis of environmentally stimulated and justified differences in accounting runs directly counter to efforts at the worldwide harmonization of accounting. Hence, the dilemma."[7]

Regardless of the arguments against harmonization, substantial efforts to reduce differences in accounting practice have been ongoing for several decades. The question is no longer *whether* to strive for harmonization, but *to what extent* accounting practices can be harmonized and *how fast*.

MAJOR HARMONIZATION EFFORTS

Several international organizations are involved in harmonization efforts either regionally (such as the Association of South East Asian Nations) or worldwide (such as the United Nations). The two most important players in this effort have been the European Union (regionally) and the International Accounting Standards Board (globally). The International Organization of Securities Commissions and the International Federation of Accountants also have contributed to the harmonization efforts at the global level.

International Organization of Securities Commissions

Established in 1974, the International Organization of Securities Commissions (IOSCO) was initially limited to providing a *framework* in which securities regulatory agencies in the Americas could exchange information and providing advice and assistance to those agencies supervising emerging markets. In 1986, IOSCO opened its membership to regulatory agencies in other parts of the world, thus giving it the potential to become a truly international organization. Today, IOSCO is the leading organization for securities regulators around the world, with about 135 ordinary, associate, and affiliate members (including the U.S. Securities and Exchange Commission) from about 100 countries.

IOSCO aims, among other things, to ensure a better regulation of the markets on both the domestic and international levels. It provides assistance to ensure the

---

[6] Richard Karl Goeltz, "International Accounting Harmonization: The Impossible (and Unnecessary?) Dream," *Accounting Horizons,* March 1991, pp. 85–86.

[7] F. D. S. Choi, "A Cluster Approach to Harmonization," *Management Accounting,* August 1981, p. 29.

integrity of the markets by a rigorous application of the standards and by effective enforcement.

As one of its objectives, IOSCO works to facilitate cross-border securities offerings and listings by multinational issuers. It has consistently advocated the adoption of a set of high-quality accounting standards for cross-border listings. For example, a 1989 IOSCO report entitled "International Equity Offers" noted that cross-border offerings would be greatly facilitated by the development of internationally accepted accounting standards.[8] To this end, IOSCO supported the efforts of the International Accounting Standards Committee (IASC) in developing international accounting standards that foreign issuers could use in lieu of local accounting standards when entering capital markets outside of their home country. As one observer notes: "This could mean, for example, that if a French company had a simultaneous stock offering in the United States, Canada, and Japan, financial statements prepared in accordance with international standards could be used in all three nations."[9]

International Federation of Accountants

Formed in 1977, the International Federation of Accountants (IFAC) aims to develop international standards of auditing, ethics, education, and training. In pursuing these goals, IFAC has contributed to the harmonization process in many ways. For example, one of its objectives is to enhance the standards and development of the profession by issuing technical and professional guidance and by promoting the adoption of IFAC and IASB (formerly IASC) pronouncements.

In June 1999, IFAC launched the International Forum on Accountancy Development (IFAD) in response to a criticism from the World Bank (following the Asian financial crisis) that the accounting profession was not doing enough to enhance the accounting capacity and capabilities in developing and emerging nations. IFAD's membership includes the international financial institutions (such as the World Bank, International Monetary Fund, and Asian Development Bank); other key international organizations (such as IOSCO, IASB, SEC); and the large accountancy firms.[10] The primary aim of this forum is to promote transparent financial reporting, duly audited to high standards by a strong accounting and auditing profession.

In May 2000, IFAC and the large international accounting firms established the Forum of Firms, also aimed at raising standards of financial reporting and auditing globally in order to protect the interests of cross-border investors and promote international flows of capital. The forum works alongside IFAD in achieving common objectives.

At its July 2003 meeting, held in Quebec, IFAC approved a compliance program designed to provide clear benchmarks to current and potential member organizations in ensuring high-quality performance by accountants worldwide. For example, this program requires member bodies to implement, with appropriate investigation and disciplinary regulations, both IFAC standards and international financial reporting standards. IFAC's International Auditing and Assurance Standards Board (IAASB) has also issued new guidance clarifying when financial statements are in full compliance with international financial reporting standards.

---

[8] This report is available from IOSCO's Web site, www.iosco.org.

[9] Stephen H. Collins, "The SEC on Full and Fair Disclosure," *Journal of Accountancy,* January 1989, p. 84.

[10] Details at www.ifad.org.

European Union

The European Union (EU) was founded in March 1957 with the signing of the Treaty of Rome by six European nations: Belgium, France, Germany, Italy, Luxembourg, and the Netherlands.[11] Between 1973 and 1995, nine other countries joined the common market (Denmark, Ireland, and the United Kingdom in 1973; Greece in 1981; Portugal and Spain in 1986; and Austria, Finland, and Sweden in January 1995), creating a 15-nation trading bloc. Another 10 new members (namely, Latvia, Estonia, Lithuania, Poland, Hungary, Czech Republic, Slovakia, Slovenia, and the Mediterranean islands of Cyprus and Malta) joined the EU in May 2004. Until this most recent expansion, all EU countries possessed similar traits in many respects. They all were wealthy industrial nations with similar political goals, comparable standards of living, high volumes of trade within the union, and good transportation links. The 2004 additions to EU membership are likely to change the dynamics of the group, especially considering that 8 of the 10 new entrants were members of the former Soviet bloc.

The European Commission is responsible for administering the EU. From the beginning, the EU's aim has been to create a unified business environment. Accordingly, the harmonization of company laws and taxation, the promotion of full freedom in the movement of goods and labor between member countries, and the creation of a community capital market have been high on its agenda. In July 2002, most EU members adopted a single currency, the euro, as envisaged in the Treaty of Maastricht signed in 1991.[12]

The EU attempted to harmonize financial reporting practices within the community by issuing directives that member nations had to incorporate into their laws. EU directives possess the force of law.[13] They are binding on EU members with respect to the results to be achieved, but the manner in which the desired results are achieved is left to the discretion of the individual countries.

Two directives aimed at harmonizing accounting: The Fourth Directive (issued in 1978) dealt with valuation rules, disclosure requirements, and the format of financial statements, and the Seventh Directive (issued in 1983) dealt with consolidated financial statements. The latter required companies to prepare consolidated financial statements and outlined the procedures for their preparation. It had a significant impact on European accounting, as consolidations were previously uncommon in Continental Europe.

The Fourth Directive included comprehensive accounting rules covering the content of annual financial statements, their methods of presentation, and measurement and disclosure of information for both public and private companies. It established the "true and fair view" principle, which required financial statements to provide a true and fair view of a company's assets and liabilities, and of its financial position and profit and loss for the benefit of shareholders and third parties.

The Fourth Directive provided considerable flexibility. Dozens of provisions beginning with the expression "Member states may require or permit companies to . . .," which allowed countries to choose from among acceptable alternatives. For example, under Dutch and British law, companies could write assets up to

---

[11] The original European Economic Community (EEC) became the European Union (EU) on January 1, 1994.

[12] Several EU members—namely, Denmark, Sweden, and the United Kingdom—have not adopted the euro as their national currency.

[13] The EU has issued numerous directives covering a broad range of business issues, including directives related to accounting, auditing, taxation, e-commerce, and the prevention of money laundering.

higher market values, whereas in Germany this was strictly forbidden. Both approaches were acceptable under the Fourth Directive. By allowing different options for a variety of accounting issues, the EU directives opened the door for noncomparability in financial statements. As an illustration of the effects of differing principles within the EU, the profits of one case study company were measured using the accounting principles of various member states. The results, presented in the following table, reveal the lack of comparability:[14]

Most Likely Profit—Case Study Company	
Country	**ECUs (millions)**
Spain	131
Germany	133
Belgium	135
Netherlands	140
France	149
Italy	174
United Kingdom	192

Profit measurement across EU countries differed in part because the directives failed to cover several important topics, including lease accounting, foreign currency translation, accounting changes, contingencies, income taxes, and long-term construction contracts.

Notwithstanding the flexibility afforded by the directives, their implementation into local law caused extensive change in accounting practice in several EU member countries. The following are some of the changes in German accounting practice brought about by the integration of the EU's Fourth and Seventh Directives into German law in 1985:

1. Required inclusion of notes to the financial statements.
2. Preparation of consolidated financial statements on a worldwide basis (i.e., foreign subsidiaries no longer could be excluded from consolidation).
3. Elimination of unrealized intercompany losses on consolidation.
4. Use of the equity method for investments in associated companies.
5. Disclosure of comparative figures in the balance sheet and income statement.
6. Disclosure of liabilities with a maturity of less than one year.
7. Accrual of deferred tax liabilities and pension obligations.[15]

Most of these "innovations" had been common practice in the United States for several decades.

Although the EU directives did not lead to complete comparability across member nations, they helped reduce differences in financial statements. In addition, the EU directives have served as a basic framework of accounting that has been adopted by other countries in search of an accounting model. With the economic reforms in Eastern Europe since 1989, several countries in that region found it necessary to abandon the Soviet-style accounting system previously used in favor

---

[14] Anthony Carey, "Harmonization: Europe Moves Forward," *Accountancy,* March 1990.

[15] Timothy S. Doupnik, "Recent Innovations in German Accounting Practice Through the Integration of EC Directives," *Advances in International Accounting* 5 (1992), pp. 75–103.

of a Western, market-oriented system. For example, in the early 1990s, Hungary, Poland, and the Czech and Slovak Republics all passed new accounting laws primarily based on the EU directives in anticipation of securing EU membership. This is further evidence of the influence that economic ties among countries can have on accounting practice.

In 1990, the European Commission indicated that there would be no further EU directives related to accounting. Instead, the commission indicated in 1995 that it would associate the EU with efforts undertaken by the IASC toward a broader international harmonization of accounting standards. In June 2000, the European Commission issued the following communication to the European Parliament:

- Before the end of 2000, the Commission will present a formal proposal requiring all listed EU companies to prepare their consolidated accounts in accordance with one single set of accounting standards, namely International Accounting Standards (IAS).
- This requirement will go into effect, at the latest, from 2005 onwards.
- Member states will be allowed to extend the application of IAS to unlisted companies and to individual accounts.[16]

Thus, beginning in January 2005, stock-exchange-listed companies in the EU are required to prepare consolidated financial statements using International Financial Reporting Standards.

THE INTERNATIONAL ACCOUNTING STANDARDS BOARD

The International Accounting Standards Board (IASB) was created in 2001 to replace its predecessor, the International Accounting Standards Committee (IASC), which had been established in 1973 by an agreement of the leading professional accounting bodies in 10 countries (Australia, Canada, France, Germany, Ireland, Japan, Mexico, the Netherlands, the United Kingdom, and the United States) with the broad objective of formulating "international accounting standards." Prior to its dissolution, the IASC consisted of 156 professional accountancy bodies in 114 countries, representing over 2 million accountants in public practice, education, government service, industry, and commerce. The IASC was funded by contributions from member bodies, multinational companies, financial institutions, accounting firms, and the sale of IASC publications.

Early Harmonization Efforts

The IASC's harmonization efforts from 1973 to 2001 evolved in several different phases. In the initial phase, covering the first 15 years, the IASC's main activity was the issuance of 26 generic International Accounting Standards (IASs), many of which allowed multiple options. The IASC's approach to standard setting during this phase can be described as a lowest-common-denominator approach, as the standards reflected an effort to accommodate existing accounting practices in various countries. For example, International Accounting Standard (IAS) 11, *Construction Contracts*, as originally written in 1979, allowed companies to choose between the percentage of completion method and the completed contract method in accounting for long-term construction contracts, effectively sanctioning the two major methods used internationally. A study conducted by the IASB in 1988 found

---

[16] Commission of the European Communities, "EU Financial Reporting Strategy: The Way Forward," Communication from the Commission to the Council and the European Parliament, June 13, 2000.

that all or most of the companies listed on the stock exchanges of the countries included in Nobes's classification presented in Chapter 2 of this book (except for Germany and Italy) were in compliance with the International Accounting Standards.[17] Given the lowest-common-denominator approach adopted by the IASC, it was obvious that IASC standards existing in 1988 introduced little if any comparability of financial statements across countries.

The Comparability Project

Two significant activities took place from 1989 to 1993, which can be described as the IASC's second phase. The first was the 1989 publication of the *Framework for the Preparation and Presentation of Financial Statements* (hereafter referred to as the *Framework*), which set out the objectives of financial statements, the qualitative characteristics of financial information, definitions of the elements of financial statements, and the criteria for recognition of financial statement elements. The second activity was the Comparability of Financial Statements Project, the purpose of which was "to eliminate most of the choices of accounting treatment currently permitted under International Accounting Standards."[18] As a result of the Comparability Project, 10 revised International Accounting Standards were approved in 1993 and became effective in 1995. As an example of the changes brought about by the comparability project, IAS 11 was revised to require the use of the percentage of completion method when certain criteria are met, thereby removing the option to avoid the use of this method altogether.

The IOSCO Agreement

The final phase in the work of the IASC began with the IOSCO agreement in 1993 and ended with the creation of the IASB in 2001. The main activity during this phase was the development of a core set of international standards that could be endorsed by IOSCO for cross-listing purposes. This period also was marked by the proposal to restructure the IASC and the proposal's final approval. The formation of the IASB in 2001—with a change in focus from harmonization to global standard setting—marked the beginning of a new era in international financial reporting.

IOSCO became a member of the IASC's Consultative Group in 1987 and supported the IASC's Comparability Project. In 1993, IOSCO and the IASC agreed on a list of 30 core standards that the IASC needed to develop that could be used by companies involved in cross-border security offerings and listings. In 1995, the IASC and IOSCO agreed on a work program for the IASC to develop the set of core international standards, and IOSCO agreed to evaluate the standards for possible endorsement for cross-border purposes upon their completion.

To meet deadlines established in the work program, the IASC accelerated its pace of standards development, issuing or revising 16 standards in 1997–1998. With the publication of IAS 39, *Financial Instruments: Recognition and Measurement*, in December 1998, the IASC completed its work program to develop the set of 30 core standards. In May 2000, IOSCO's Technical Committee recommended that securities regulators permit foreign issuers to use the core IASC standards to gain access to a country's capital market as an alternative to using local standards. The Technical Committee consisted of securities regulators representing the 14 largest and most developed capital markets, including Australia, France, Germany, Japan,

[17] International Accounting Standards Committee, *Survey of the Use and Application of International Accounting Standards 1988* (London: IASC, 1988).

[18] International Accounting Standards Committee, *International Accounting Standards 1990* (London: IASC, 1990), p. 13.

the United Kingdom, and the United States. IOSCO's endorsement of IASC standards was an important step in the harmonization process. The Technical Committee has initiated a project on regulatory interpretations of International Financial Reporting Standards (IFRSs) to address communications among IOSCO members with the goal of promoting the consistent application and enforcement of IFRSs. This project is expected to generate a central database of regulatory decisions and a process for facilitating communications and cooperation among regulators and other enforcers relating to IFRSs.[19]

U.S. Reaction to International Accounting Standards

Of the 14 countries represented on IOSCO's Technical Committee, only Canada and the United States do not allow foreign companies to use International Accounting Standards (IASs) without reconciliation to local GAAP for listing purposes.[20] In 1996, the U.S. Securities and Exchange Commission (SEC) announced three criteria IASs would have to meet to be acceptable for cross-listing purposes. Namely, IASs would have to

- Constitute a comprehensive, generally accepted basis of accounting.
- Be of high quality, resulting in comparability and transparency, and providing for full disclosure.
- Be rigorously interpreted and applied.

Partly in response to the third criterion, the IASC created a Standing Interpretations Committee (SIC) to provide guidance on accounting issues where there is likely to be divergent or unacceptable treatment in the absence of specific guidance in an International Accounting Standard.

The SEC began its assessment of the IASC's core set of standards in 1999 and issued a concept release in 2000 soliciting comments on whether it should modify its requirement that all financial statements be reconciled to U.S. GAAP. In September 2004, at the IASB meeting with world standard setters, the chief accountant of the U.S. SEC stated that the SEC was considering the steps that needed to be taken to eliminate the reconciliation from IFRSs to U.S. GAAP, and that one such step was to review the quality and consistency of the application of IFRSs.

The FASB conducted a comparison of IASC standards and U.S. GAAP in 1996, identifying 218 items covered by both sets of standards.[21] The following table lists the degree of similarity across these items:

	Number	Percent
Similar approach and guidance	56	26%
Similar approach but different guidance	79	36
Different approach	56	26
Alternative approaches permitted	27	12
	218	100%

---

[19] IOSCO, *Final Communique of the XXIXth Annual Conference of the International Organization of Securities Commissions,* Amman, May 17–20, 2004.

[20] The SEC allows foreign companies listed on U.S. stock exchanges to file annual reports based on IASs but only if a reconciliation from IASs to U.S. GAAP for income and stockholders' equity is included in the notes to the financial statements. Many foreign companies find this reconciliation to be very costly and view this requirement as a significant barrier to entering the U.S. capital market.

[21] Financial Accounting Standards Board, *The IASC-U.S. Comparison Project: A Report on the Similarities and Differences between IASC Standards and U.S. GAAP,* ed. Carrie Bloomer (Norwalk, CT: FASB, 1996).

Although it was widely assumed that U.S. GAAP and IASs were generally consistent, the FASB's comparison showed that differences existed for 74 percent of the accounting items covered by both sets of standards.

Restructuring of the IASC/Creation of the IASB

The IASC as a global standard setter faced problems of legitimacy with regard to constituent support, independence, and technical expertise. For example, some interested parties perceived the fact that IASC board members worked at international standard setting only part-time and were not necessarily selected because of their technical expertise as an indication of the lack of commitment on the part of the IASC to develop the highest quality standards possible. Responding to these concerns, the IASC appointed a Strategy Working Party in 1996, which issued a discussion document in December 1998 entitled "Shaping IASC for the Future." This document proposed a vastly different structure and process for the development of international accounting standards.

The final recommendations of the IASC Strategy Working Party were approved at its Venice meeting in November 1999. These recommendations, designed to deal with the issue of legitimacy, attempted to balance calls for a structure based on geographic representativeness and those based on technical competence and independence. Accordingly, it was decided that representativeness would be provided by the geographic distribution of the trustees, who would be essential to ensuring the effectiveness and independence of the board, but that board members would be selected based on their expertise.

On April 1, 2001, the newly created International Accounting Standards Board (IASB) took over from the IASC as the creator of international accounting standards. The process of restructuring the IASC into the IASB took over five years and is summarized in Exhibit 3.1.

The Structure of the IASB

The standard-setting work of the IASB is funded and monitored by the IASC Foundation, whose constitution lists the following objectives:

(a) to develop, in the public interest, a single set of high quality, understandable and enforceable global accounting standards that require high quality, transparent and comparable information in financial statements and other financial reporting to help participants in the world's capital markets and other users make economic decisions;

(b) to promote the use and rigorous application of these standards; and

(c) to bring about convergence of national accounting standards and International Accounting Standards to high quality solutions.[22]

In addition to the IASB itself, the other main components of the new international standing-setting structure include the IASC Foundation and its trustees, the International Financial Reporting Interpretation Committee (IFRIC), and the Standards Advisory Council (SAC). The IASB follows a due process procedure and adopts a principles-based approach in developing international standards. These are briefly discussed in the following paragraphs.

---

[22] The new constitution is available at www.iasb.org/about/constitution/asp.

EXHIBIT 3.1
The Process of
Restructuring the
IASC into the IASB

Date	Activity
September 1996	IASC board approves formation of a Strategy Working Party (SWP) to consider what IASC's strategy and structure should be when it completes the Core Standards work program.
December 1998	SWP publishes a discussion paper, "Shaping IASC for the Future," and invites comments.
April to October 1999	SWP holds various meetings to discuss the comments on their initial proposal and to develop final recommendations.
December 1999	SWP issues final report, *Recommendations on Shaping IASC for the Future.* IASC board passes a resolution supporting the report and appoints a nominating committee for the initial trustees.
January 2000	Nominating committee elects SEC chairman Arthur Levitt as its chair and invites nominations from public.
March 2000	IASC board approves a new constitution reflecting the SWP proposals.
May 2000	Nominating committee announces initial trustees.
May 2000	IASC member bodies approve the restructuring and the new IASC constitution.
June 2000	Trustees appoint Sir David Tweedie as the first chairman of new IASC board.
July 1, 2000	New IASC constitution takes effect.
Starting in July 2000	Trustees invite nominations for membership on the new IASC board, narrow the list to approximately 45 finalists, and conduct interviews in London, New York, and Tokyo.
January 2001	Trustees invite nominations for membership on the new advisory council.
January 2001	Members of the IASB announced.
March 2001	IASC trustees activate Part B of IASC's constitution and establish a nonprofit Delaware corporation, named the International Accounting Standards Committee Foundation, to oversee the International Accounting Standards Board.
April 2001	On April 1, 2001, the new IASB takes over from the IASC the responsibility for setting International Accounting Standards.

The Board

The IASB is composed of 14 members: 12 full-time and 2 part-time. Seven of the full-time IASB members must have a formal liaison responsibility with one or more national standard setters. A minimum of five IASB members must have a background as practicing auditors, three must have a background as preparers of financial statements, three must be users of financial statements, and at least one must come from academia. The most important criterion for selection as a board member is technical competence. The IASC Foundation's constitution provides that the trustees shall "select members of the IASB so that it will comprise a group of people representing, within that group, the best available combination of technical skills and background experience of relevant international business and market conditions in order to contribute to the development of high quality, global accounting standards."[23]

[23] IASC Foundation constitution, para. 20.

All full-time members are required to sever their employment relationships with former employers and are not allowed to hold any position that gives rise to perceived economic incentives that might call their independence into question. The initial board members came from nine countries: one member each from Australia, Canada, France, Germany, Japan, South Africa, and Switzerland; four from the United Kingdom; and three from the United States. Sir David Tweedie, former chairman of the United Kingdom's Accounting Standards Board, became the first chairman of the IASB. Clearly, there is a very strong Anglo-American influence on the board.

The IASB announced in April 2001 that its accounting standards would be designated International Financial Reporting Standards (IFRSs). Also in April 2001, the IASB announced that it would adopt all of the International Accounting Standards issued by the IASC. IAS 1, *Presentation of Financial Statements,* was revised by the IASB in 2003 and defines IFRSs as Standards and Interpretations adopted by the IASB. They consist of:

- IASB International Financial Reporting Standards.
- IASC International Accounting Standards.
- Interpretations originated by the International Financial Reporting Interpretations Committee (IFRIC; formerly the SIC).

Under the new structure, the IASB has sole responsibility for establishing IFRSs.

The IASB, like its predecessor, is headquartered in London. The IASB published a new preface to the International Financial Reporting Standards in May 2002 that sets out the board's objectives; its procedures for due process reflecting the IASB's new structure; and the scope, authority, and timing of application of IFRSs.

IASC Foundation Trustees

The governance of the IASC Foundation rests with the trustees. The initial 19 trustees are from Europe (7), North America (6), Asia Pacific (4), Africa (1), and South America (1). They come from diverse functional backgrounds.

The trustees are not involved in technical matters relating to accounting standards. Their responsibilities include appointing the members of the board, IFRIC, and the SAC; establishing operating procedures for the board, IFRIC and the SAC; approving the IASB's annual budget and basis for funding; reviewing broad strategic issues affecting accounting standards; and generally promoting the IASB's efforts. The trustees act by simple majority vote, except for amendments to the constitution, which require a 75 percent majority.

The International Financial Reporting Interpretations Committee

In December 2001, the SIC was reconstituted as the International Financial Reporting Interpretations Committee (IFRIC). IFRIC has 12 members appointed by the trustees for terms of three years. IFRIC members are not salaried, but their expenses are reimbursed. This committee's main responsibilities are to interpret the application of IFRSs and to provide guidance on financial reporting issues not specifically addressed in an IAS or IFRS in the context of the IASB's *Framework.* It publishes draft interpretations for public comment and reports final interpretations to the board for approval. By allowing IFRIC to develop interpretations on financial reporting issues not specifically addressed in an IAS or IFRS, the new IASB constitution has broadened IFRIC's mandate beyond that of the former SIC.

Of 31 interpretations published by the original SIC, most have been superseded by either a new IFRS or a revised IAS issued by the IASB. For example, the revision of IAS 33, *Earnings per Share,* that occurred in 2003 incorporates SIC-24, *Earnings per Share—Financial Instruments and Other Contracts That May Be Settled in Shares,* thus superseding that interpretation.

The Standards Advisory Council

The Standards Advisory Council (SAC) has 49 members and provides a forum for interested organizations and individuals to participate in the standard-setting process. Members are appointed for a renewable term of three years and have diverse geographical and functional backgrounds. The chair of the IASB is also the chair of the SAC.

The SAC meetings, normally three times each year, are open to the public. The SAC has the responsibility to provide advice to the board and the trustees. In particular, it is expected to advise the board on priorities in its work and inform the board of the implications of proposed standards for users and preparers of financial statements.

Due Process

The process followed in developing an IFRS generally includes five steps. First, IASB staff members work to identify and review all the issues related to a topic and study other national accounting standards and practices. Second, a steering committee or advisory group may be formed to give advice on major projects. Third, a draft statement of principles or similar discussion document will be developed and published on major projects. Fourth, following receipt of comments on the initial discussion document, if any, the IASB will develop and publish an exposure draft (ED). Finally, following receipt of comments on the ED, the IASB will approve and issue a final standard. Approval of a standard requires a positive vote from 8 of the 14 members of the IASB.

Each draft statement of principles, discussion paper, and exposure draft of a proposed standard is issued for public comment. The usual comment period is 90 days. Draft interpretations are exposed for a 60-day comment period.

Review of the IASC Foundation's Constitution

The IASC Foundation's constitution states that the trustees should undertake:

> [A] review of the entire structure of the IASC Foundation and its effectiveness, such review to include consideration of changing the geographical distribution of Trustees in response to changing global economic conditions, and publishing the proposals of that review for public comment, the review commencing three years after the coming into force of this Constitution, with the objective of implementing any agreed changes five years after the coming into force of this Constitution (6 February 2006, five years after the date of the incorporation of the IASC Foundation [Section 18 (b)]).

Consistent with Section 18 of the constitution, the IASC Foundation's Constitution Committee initiated in May 2004 a broad review of the constitution and identified 10 issues for consideration. These issues are based on the concerns expressed by important constituencies through various processes of consultation. They are as follows:

1. Whether the objectives of the IASC Foundation should expressly refer to the challenges facing small and medium-sized entities (SMEs). (*Concern:* The

language of the constitution does not adequately address the position of SMEs and emerging economies.)

2. Number of trustees and their geographical and professional distribution. (*Concern:* Certain regions are overrepresented, while the Asia-Oceania region as well as emerging economies are underrepresented.)

3. The oversight role of the trustees. (*Concern:* Trustees should demonstrate more clearly how they are fulfilling the oversight function.)

4. Funding of the IASC Foundation. (*Concern:* The funding structure of the IASC Foundation needs to be examined.)

5. The composition of the IASB. (*Concern:* The geographic backgrounds of the IASB members need to be examined.)

6. The appropriateness of the IASB's existing formal liaison relationships. (*Concern:* More guidance is needed in the constitution regarding the role that liaison relationships play.)

7. Consultation arrangements of the IASB. (*Concern:* Consultative arrangements need to be improved.)

8. Voting procedures of the IASB. (*Concern:* For approval of a standard, the current "simple majority" approach should be replaced with a "super majority" approach.)

9. Resources and effectiveness of the International Financial Reporting Interpretations Committee (IFRIC). (*Concern:* given the likely increase in demand for IFRIC interpretations, the current arrangements are inadequate.)

10. The composition, role, and effectiveness of the SAC. (*Concern:* steps should be taken to make better use of the SAC.)

A PRINCIPLES-BASED APPROACH TO INTERNATIONAL FINANCIAL REPORTING STANDARDS

In developing accounting standards, the IASB uses a principles-based approach rather than a rules-based approach. Principles-based standards focus on establishing general principles derived from the IASB *Framework*, providing recognition, measurement, and reporting requirements for the transactions covered by the standard. By following this approach, IFRSs tend to limit guidance for applying the general principles to typical transactions and encourage professional judgment in applying the general principles to transactions specific to an entity or industry.

Sir David Tweedie, IASB chairman, explained the principles-based approach taken by the IASB as follows:

> The IASB concluded that a body of detailed guidance (sometimes referred to as *bright lines*) encourages a rule-based mentality of "where does it say I can't do this?" We take the view that this is counter-productive and helps those who are intent on finding ways around standards more than it helps those seeking to apply standards in a way that gives useful information. Put simply, adding the detailed guidance may obscure, rather than highlight, the underlying principles. The emphasis tends to be on compliance with the letter of the rule rather than on the spirit of the accounting standard.
>
> We prefer an approach that requires the company and its auditors to take a step back and consider with the underlying principles. This is not a soft option. Our approach requires both companies and their auditors to exercise professional judgement in the public interest. Our approach requires a strong commitment from

preparers to financial statements that provide a faithful representation of all transactions and strong commitment from auditors to resist client pressures. It will not work without those commitments. There will be more individual transactions and situations that are not explicitly addressed. We hope that a clear statement of the underlying principles will allow companies and auditors to deal with those situations without resorting to detailed rules.[24]

It is interesting that support for a principles-based approach has come from many quarters, including current and former U.S. regulators. It has been pointed out that as part of the commitment to convergence, the FASB and the SEC should change their behavior and become more like the rest of the world. For example, a former SEC chairman, expressing preference for the IASB's principles-based standards, referred to the IASB's approach as a "Ten Commandments" approach in contrast to FASB's "cookbook" approach.[25] The SEC chairman, in a speech made in Puerto Rico in February 2002, also expressed preference for a principles-based set of accounting standards.[26] In addition, in an editorial in the June 27, 2002, edition of *Financial Times* titled "The World after WorldCom," the U.S. regulators were urged to move to principles-based standards.

> It is time for US accounting standards to move away from prescriptive rulemaking towards the alternative used in many other countries, which focuses on "substance over form." US regulators have been suspicious of principles-based standards drafted by the International Accounting Standards Board, arguing that the US approach is superior. As the list of US accounting scandals mounts, it is hard to maintain such a position.

There is also other outside pressure on the U.S. regulators to recognize IFRSs. For example, on May 13, 2004, the director general of the Internal Market Directorate of the European Commission, in his testimony before the U.S. House Committee on Financial Services, expressed a hope that the U.S. SEC would recognize IFRSs as part of a program of mutual U.S.–EU recognition of each other's financial market regulations and elaborated the merits of such a recognition in detail.[27]

The U.S. Public Company Accounting Reform and Investor Protection Act of 2002 (the Sarbanes-Oxley Act) required the SEC to study the "adoption by the United States financial reporting system of a principles-based accounting system" and submit a report to specified committees of the Senate and House of Representatives.

INTERNATIONAL FINANCIAL REPORTING STANDARDS

As of March 2005, 41 International Accounting Standards (IASs) and 6 International Financial Reporting Standards (IFRSs) had been issued (see Exhibit 3.2). A conceptual *framework* similar in scope and nature to that developed by the U.S. FASB also has been created. Several IASs have been revised one or more times since original issuance. For example, IAS 21, *The Effects of Changes in Foreign Exchange Rates,* was originally issued in 1983 and then revised as part of the comparability project in 1993. This standard was again updated in 2003 as part of the

---

[24] Excerpt from a speech delivered before the Committee on Banking, Housing and Urban Affairs of the United States Senate, Washington, DC, February 14, 2002.

[25] http://banking.senate.gov/02_02hrg/021202/index.htm.

[26] www.sec.gov/news/speech/spch539.htm.

[27] Full text of the testimony is available at www.iasplus.com/index.htm.

EXHIBIT 3.2   International Financial Reporting Standards (IFRSs) as of March 2005

Title	Issued (Revised)	Effective Date
Framework for the Preparation and Presentation of Financial Statements[a]	1989	
IAS 1 *Presentation of Financial Statements*[a]	1975 (1997, 2003)	Jan. 1, 2005
IAS 2 *Inventories*[b]	1975 (1993, 2003)	Jan. 1, 2005
IAS 7 *Cash Flow Statements*[b]	1977 (1992)	Jan. 1, 1994
IAS 8 *Accounting Policies, Changes in Accounting Estimates and Errors*[b]	1978 (1993, 2003)	Jan. 1, 2005
IAS 10 *Events After the Balance Sheet Date*[b]	1978 (1999, 2003)	Jan. 1, 2005
IAS 11 *Construction Contracts*	1979 (1993)	Jan. 1, 1995
IAS 12 *Accounting for Taxes on Income*[b]	1979 (1997, 2000)	Jan. 1, 1998 (2001)
IAS 14 *Segment Reporting*[d]	1981 (1997)	July 1, 1998
IAS 16 *Property, Plant and Equipment*[b]	1982 (1993, 1998, 2003)	Jan. 1, 2005
IAS 17 *Leases*[b]	1982 (1997, 2003)	Jan. 1, 2005
IAS 18 *Revenue*[b]	1982 (1993)	Jan. 1, 1995
IAS 19 *Employee Benefits*[b]	1983 (1997, 2000)	Jan. 1, 2001 (31 May 2002)
IAS 20 *Accounting for Government Grants and Disclosure of Government Assistance*	1983	Jan. 1, 1984
IAS 21 *The Effects of Changes in Foreign Exchange Rates*[c]	1983 (1993, 2003)	Jan. 1, 2005
IAS 23 *Borrowing Costs*[b]	1984 (1993)	Jan. 1, 1995
IAS 24 *Related Party Disclosures*[b]	1984 (2003)	Jan. 1, 2005
IAS 26 *Accounting and Reporting by Retirement Benefit Plans*	1987	Jan. 1, 1988
IAS 27 *Consolidated Financial Statements and Accounting for Investments in Subsidiaries*[d]	1989 (2003)	Jan. 1, 2005
IAS 28 *Accounting for Investments in Associates*[d]	1989 (1998, 2003)	Jan. 1, 2005

Standard	Title	Issued	Effective
IAS 29	Financial Reporting in Hyperinflationary Economies[d]	1989	Jan. 1, 1990
IAS 30	Disclosures in the Financial Statements of Banks and Similar Financial Institutions	1990	Jan. 1, 1991
IAS 31	Financial Reporting of Interests in Joint Ventures[d]	1990 (1998, 2003)	Jan. 1, 2005
IAS 32	Financial Instruments: Disclosure and Presentation[b]	1995 (2003)	Jan. 1, 2005
IAS 33	Earnings per Share[b]	1997 (2003)	Jan. 1, 2005
IAS 34	Interim Financial Reporting[b]	1998	Jan. 1, 1999
IAS 36	Impairment of Assets[b]	1998 (2004)	April 1, 2004
IAS 37	Provisions, Contingent Liabilities and Contingent Assets[b]	1998	July 1, 1999
IAS 38	Intangible Assets[b]	1998 (2004)	April 1, 2004
IAS 39	Financial Instruments: Recognition and Measurement[b]	1998 (2000, 2003, 2004)	Jan. 1, 2005
IAS 40	Investment Property[b]	2000 (2003, 2004)	Jan. 1, 2005
IAS 41	Agriculture	2001	Jan. 1, 2003
IFRS 1	First-time Adoption of International Financial Reporting Standards[a]	2003	Jan. 1, 2004
IFRS 2	Share-based Payment[b]	2004	Jan. 1, 2005
IFRS 3	Business Combinations[d]	2004	March 31, 2004
IFRS 4	Insurance Contracts	2004	Jan. 1, 2005
IFRS 5	Non-current Assets Held for Sale and Discontinued Operations[b]	2004	Jan. 1, 2005
IFRS 6	Exploration for and Evaluation of Mineral Resources	2004	Jan. 1, 2006

Standards covered in this book:
[a]Denotes standards covered in Chapter 3.
[b]Denotes standards covered in Chapter 4.
[c]Denotes standards covered in Chapters 6 and 7.
[d]Denotes standards covered in Chapter 8.

improvements project undertaken by the IASB that resulted in revisions to 13 IASs. Other IASs have been withdrawn or replaced by later standards. Of 41 IASs issued by the IASC, only 31 were still in force as of March 2005. The first IFRS was issued by the IASB in 2003, providing guidance on the important question of how a company goes about restating its financial statements when it adopt IFRSs for the first time.

In the next three sections of this chapter, we discuss the following components of the IASB's body of authoritative literature:

- The *Framework for the Preparation and Presentation of Financial Statements*.
- IAS 1, *Presentation of Financial Statements*.
- IFRS 1, *First Time Adoption of IFRS*.

We provide detail on selected IFRSs dealing with accounting recognition and measurement and financial disclosure issues in Chapter 4.

THE IASB *FRAMEWORK*

The *Framework for the Preparation and Presentation of Financial Statements* was first approved by the IASC board in 1989 and was reaffirmed by the newly formed IASB in 2001. The objective of the *Framework* is to establish the concepts underlying the preparation and presentation of IFRS-based financial statements. It deals with the following:

1. Objective of financial statements and underlying assumptions.
2. Qualitative characteristics that affect the usefulness of financial statements.
3. Definition, recognition, and measurement of the financial statements elements.
4. Concepts of capital and capital maintenance.

Among other things, the purpose of the *Framework* is to assist the IASB in developing future standards and revising existing standards. It also is intended to assist preparers of financial statements in applying IFRSs and in dealing with topics that have not yet been addressed in IFRSs. The *Framework* identifies investors, creditors, employees, suppliers, customers, government agencies, and the general public as potential users of financial statements but concludes that financial statements that are designed to meet the needs of investors will also meet most of the information needs of other users. This is an important conclusion because it sets the tone for the nature of individual IFRSs, that is, that their application will result in a set of financial statements that is useful for making investment decisions.

Objective of Financial Statements and Underlying Assumptions

The *Framework* establishes that the primary objective of IFRS-based financial statements is to *provide information useful for decision making*. Financial statements also show the results of management's stewardship of enterprise resources, but that is not their primary objective. To meet the objective of decision usefulness, financial statements must be prepared on an *accrual basis*. The other underlying assumption is that the enterprise for which financial statements are being prepared is a *going concern*.

Qualitative Characteristics of Financial Statements

The four characteristics that make financial statement information useful are *understandability, relevance, reliability,* and *comparability*. Information is relevant if it can be used to make predictions of the future or if it can be used to confirm expectations from the past. The *Framework* indicates that the relevance of information is affected by its nature and its materiality. An item of information is material if its misstatement or omission could influence the decision of a user of financial statements.

Information is reliable when it is neutral (i.e., free of bias) and represents faithfully what it purports to. The *Framework* specifically states that reflecting items in the financial statements based on their economic substance rather than their legal form is necessary for faithful representation. The *Framework* also states that while the exercise of prudence (conservatism) in measuring accounting elements is necessary, it does not allow the creation of hidden reserves or excessive provisions to deliberately understate income, as this would be biased and therefore would not have the quality of reliability.

Elements of Financial Statements: Definition, Recognition, and Measurement

Assets are defined as resources controlled by the enterprise from which future economic benefits are expected to flow to the enterprise. Note that a resource need not be owned to be an asset of an enterprise. This allows, for example, for leased resources to be treated as assets. An *asset should be recognized only when it is probable that future economic benefits will flow to the enterprise and the asset has a cost or value that can be measured reliably*. The *Framework* acknowledges that several different measurement bases may be used to measure assets including historical cost, current cost, realizable value, and present value.

Liabilities are present obligations arising from past events that are expected to be settled through an outflow of resources. Obligations need not be contractual to be treated as a liability. Similar to assets, *liabilities should be recognized when it is probable that an outflow of resources will be required to settle them and the amount can be measured reliably*. Also as with assets, several different bases exist for measuring liabilities including the amount of proceeds received in exchange for the obligation, the amount that would be required to settle the obligation currently, undiscounted settlement value in the normal course of business, and the present value of future cash outflows expected to settle the liabilities.

The *Framework* identifies income and expenses as the two elements that constitute profit. *Income,* which encompasses both revenues and gains, is defined as increases in equity, other than from transactions with owners. *Expenses,* including losses, are decreases in equity, other than through distributions to owners. *Equity* is defined as assets minus liabilities. Income should be recognized when the increase in an asset or decrease in a liability can be measured reliably. The *Framework* does not provide more specific guidance with respect to income recognition. (This topic is covered in IAS 18, *Revenue.*) Expenses are recognized when the related decrease in assets or increase in liabilities can be measured reliably. The *Framework* acknowledges the use of the matching principle in recognizing liabilities but specifically precludes use of the matching principle to recognize expenses and a related liability when it does not meet the definition of a liability. For example, it is inappropriate to recognize an expense if a present obligation arising from a past event does not exist.

Concepts of Capital Maintenance

The *Framework* describes different concepts of capital maintenance (financial capital maintenance vs. physical capital maintenance) and acknowledges that each leads to a different basis for measuring assets (historical cost vs. current cost). The *Framework* does not prescribe one measurement basis (and related model of accounting) over another, but indicates that it (the *Framework*) is applicable to a range of accounting models.

The IASB *Framework* is similar in content and direction to the FASB's *Conceptual Framework* embodied in *Statements of Financial Accounting Concepts 1, 2, 5,* and 6. However, the IASB *Framework* is considerably less detailed.

IAS 1, *PRESENTATION OF FINANCIAL STATEMENTS*

IAS 1, *Presentation of Financial Statements,* is a single standard providing guidelines for the preparation and presentation of financial statements. It provides guidance in the following areas:

- *Purpose of financial statements.* To provide information for decision making.
- *Components of financial statements.* A set of financial statements must include a balance sheet, income statement, statement of cash flows, statement of changes in equity, and notes, comprising a summary of significant accounting polices and other explanatory notes.
- *Overriding principle of fair presentation.* IAS 1 states that financial statements "shall present fairly the financial position, financial performance and cash flows of an entity. Fair presentation requires the faithful representation of the effects of transactions, other events and conditions in accordance with the definitions and recognition criteria for assets, liabilities, income and expenses set out in the *Framework.*"[28] Compliance with IFRSs generally ensures fair presentation. In the *extremely rare* circumstance when management concludes that compliance with the requirement of a standard or interpretation would be so misleading that it would conflict with the objective of financial statements set out in the *Framework,* IAS 1 *requires* departing from that requirement with extensive disclosures made in the notes. If the local regulatory framework will not allow departing from a requirement, disclosures must be made to reduce the misleading aspects of compliance with that requirement.
- *Accounting policies.* Management should select and apply accounting policies to be in compliance with all IASB standards and all applicable interpretations. If guidance is lacking on a specific issue, management should refer to (a) the requirements and guidance in other IASB standards dealing with similar issues; (b) the definitions, recognition, and measurement criteria for assets, liabilities, income, and expenses set out in the IASB *Framework;* and (c) pronouncements of other standard-setting bodies and accepted industry practices to the extent, but only to the extent, that these are consistent with (a) and (b). IAS 1 does *not* indicate that this is a hierarchy. It is important to note that individual country GAAP may be used to fill in the blanks but only if consistent with other IASB standards and the IASB *Framework.*
- *Basic principles and assumptions.* IAS 1 reiterates the accrual basis and going concern assumptions and the consistency and comparative information principles found in the *Framework.* IAS 1 adds to the guidance provided in the *Framework* by indicating that immaterial items should be aggregated. It also stipulates

---

[28] IAS 1, paragraph 13.

that assets and liabilities, and income and expenses should not be offset and reported at a net amount unless specifically permitted by a standard or interpretation.

- *Structure and content of financial statements.* IAS 1 also provides guidance with respect to: (a) current/noncurrent distinction, (b) items to be presented on the face of financial statements, and (c) items to be disclosed in the notes.

IAS 1 requires companies to classify assets and liabilities as current and noncurrent on the balance sheet, except when a presentation based on liquidity provides information that is reliable and more relevant. IAS 1 also provides guidance with respect to the items, at a minimum, that should be reported on the face of the income statement or balance sheet. Exhibit 3.3 presents an illustrative income statement, and Exhibit 3.4 presents an illustrative balance sheet demonstrating minimum compliance with IAS 1. The line items comprising operating profit must be reflected using either a nature of expense format (common in Continental Europe) or a function of expense format (commonly found in Anglo countries). Both formats are presented in Exhibit 3.3. IAS 1 specifically precludes designating items as extraordinary on the income statement or in the notes.

In Exhibit 3.4, assets are presented on one side of the balance sheet and liabilities and equity are presented on the other side. Other formats are equally acceptable so long as the current/noncurrent distinction is clear. For example, British balance sheets commonly present noncurrent assets, net current assets (working capital), and noncurrent liabilities on one side of the balance sheet and equity on the other side. In addition, assets and liabilities may be presented in order of liquidity, as is common in North America.

EXHIBIT 3.3
Illustrative IFRS
Income Statement

Source: IAS 1, paragraphs 81, 82, 91, 92.

MODEL COMPANY
Consolidated Income Statement
For the year ended December 31, Year 1
(in thousands of currency units)

Nature of Expenses Format	Function of Expenses Format
Revenue	**Revenue**
Other income	Cost of sales
Changes in inventories of finished goods and work in progress	**Gross profit**
	Other income
Raw materials and consumables used	Distribution costs
Employee benefits expense	Administrative expenses
Depreciation and amortization expense	Other operating expenses
Other operating expenses	**Operating profit (or loss)**
Operating profit (or loss)	Finance costs
Finance costs	Equity method income (loss)
Equity method income (loss)	**Profit (or loss) before tax**
Profit (or loss) before tax	Income tax expense
Income tax expense	**Profit (loss)**
Profit (loss)	Attributable to:
Attributable to:	Parent company shareholders
Parent company shareholders	Minority interest
Minority interest	

Note: IAS 33, *Earnings per Share*, requires that basic and dilute earnings per share also be reported on the face of the income statement. Additional required disclosures must be made either on the face of the income statement or in the notes.

EXHIBIT 3.4
Illustrative IFRS
Balance Sheet

Source: IAS 1, paragraph 68.

MODEL COMPANY
Consolidated Balance Sheet
At December 31, Year 1
(in thousands of currency units)

Assets	Equity and Liabilities
Noncurrent assets	**Equity**
Property, plant and equipment	Issued capital
Investment property	Reserves
Intangible assets	Retained earnings
Investments in associates	Minority interest
Other non-current investments	**Total equity**
Current assets	**Noncurrent Liabilities**
Inventories	Long-term borrowings
Trade and other receivables	Deferred taxes
Other current assets	Provisions
Cash and cash equivalents	**Current liabilities**
Total assets	Trade and other payables
	Short-term borrowings
	Current taxes payable
	Total liabilities
	Total equity and liabilities

Note: Additional required disclosures must be made either on the face of the balance sheet or in the notes.

Compliance with International Financial Reporting Standards

Prior to the creation of the IASB, several studies investigated the extent of compliance by those firms that claimed to follow International Accounting Standards.[29] These studies found various levels of noncompliance with IASs.[30] Former IASC secretary-general David Cairns referred to the use of IASs with exceptions as "IAS lite."[31] In response to the use of IAS lite, IAS 1 was revised in 1997 to preclude a firm from claiming to be in compliance with IFRSs unless it complies with all requirements (including disclosure requirements) of each standard and each applicable interpretation. A number of firms that previously disclosed in their annual report their use of IFRSs "with exceptions" discontinued this disclosure subsequent to this revision to IAS 1.

[29] See, for example, Donna L. Street, Sidney J. Gray, and Stephanie M. Bryant, "Acceptance and Observance of International Accounting Standards: An Empirical Study of Companies Claiming to Comply with IASs," *International Journal of Accounting* 34, no. 1 (1999), pp. 11–48, and David Cairns, *Financial Times International Accounting Standards Survey* (London: FT Finance, 1999).

[30] Apparently concerned with the lack of full compliance with IFRS, one of the SEC's major requirements to allow foreign registrants to use IFRS without reconciliation to U.S. GAAP is the existence of "an infrastructure that ensures that the standards are rigorously interpreted and applied." SEC Concept Release: International Accounting Standards (2000).

[31] Ernst & Young, "Mind the GAAP: The Rise and Fall of IAS Lite," *Eye on IAS Newsletter,* June 2002, pp. 2–8. As reported in this newsletter, Cairns identifies three types of IAS lite: (1) disclosed IAS lite, where companies disclose exceptions from full IAS compliance; (2) implied IAS lite, where companies refer to the use of rather than compliance with IAS; and (3) undisclosed IAS lite, where companies claim to comply with IAS but fail to comply fully with it.

In its accounting policies note to its 1998 financial statements, the French firm Thomson-CSF stated:

> In a February 1998 recommendation, the C.O.B. [the French Securities Regulator] observed that for operating periods starting as from July 1, 1998, a company could no longer state that it complied with the International Accounting Standards Committee (I.A.S.C.) reference system, if it did not apply all I.A.S.C. standards currently in force. Consequently, as from the 1998 operating period, the consolidated financial statements of Thomson-CSF, prepared in accordance with accounting principles applicable in France, as also the provisions of the 7th European Directive, no longer refer to the I.A.S.C. standards. (p. 82)

Prior to 1998, Thomson-CSF claimed to follow IASs when it apparently did not. From the excerpt above, it appears that Thomson-CSF elected not to fully comply with IASs and in 1998 no longer claimed to do so as required by the French Securities Regulator. Because the IASB itself does not have the power to enforce it, IAS 1 must be enforced by national securities regulators and auditors.

IFRS 1, *FIRST-TIME ADOPTION OF INTERNATIONAL FINANCIAL REPORTING STANDARDS*

IFRS 1, *First-time Adoption of International Financial Reporting Standards*, issued in June 2003, was the first IFRS developed by the IASB. IFRS 1 sets out the requirements for adopting IFRSs and preparing a set of IFRS financial statements for the first time. As companies make the transition from their previous GAAP to IFRSs, guidance on this issue is very important.

In general, IFRS 1 requires an entity adopting IFRSs to comply with each IFRS effective at the reporting date of its first IFRS financial statements. For example, if an entity is preparing IFRS financial statements for the year ended December 31, 2005, it must comply with all IFRSs in force at that date. Moreover, if the entity provides comparative financial statements for the year 2004 in its 2005 IFRS financial statements, the comparative statements also must be prepared in accordance with IFRSs in force at December 31, 2005. In effect, the entity's date of transition to IFRSs is January 1, 2004. IFRS 1 requires the entity to prepare an "opening IFRS balance sheet" as of that date, which becomes the starting point for accounting under IFRSs.

In preparing its opening IFRS balance sheet, IFRS 1 requires an entity to do the following:

1. Recognize all assets and liabilities whose recognition is required by IFRSs.
2. Derecognize items previously recognized as assets or liabilities if IFRSs do not permit such recognition.
3. Reclassify items that it recognized under previous GAAP as one type of asset, liability, or component of equity, but are a different type of asset, liability, or component of equity under IFRSs.
4. Apply IFRSs in measuring all recognized assets and liabilities.

To understand the significance of these requirements, consider their implementation with respect to intangible assets. In preparing its opening IFRS balance sheet, an entity would need to (1) exclude previously recognized intangible assets that do not meet the recognition criteria in IAS 38, *Intangible Assets*, at the date of transition to IFRSs, and (2) include intangible assets that do meet the recognition criteria in IAS 38 at that date, even if they previously had been accounted for as an expense. For example, an entity adopting IFRSs must determine whether previously expensed development costs would have qualified for recognition as an intangible asset under IAS 38 at the date of transition to IFRSs. If so, then an asset should be recognized in the opening IFRS balance sheet even if the related costs had been expensed previously. Furthermore, if amortization methods and useful lives for intangible assets recognized under previous GAAP differ from those that would be acceptable under IFRSs, then the accumulated amortization in the opening IFRS balance sheet must be adjusted retrospectively to comply with IFRSs.

In specific areas where the cost of complying with an IFRS would likely exceed the benefits to users, IFRS 1 provides exemptions from complying with IFRSs. Exemptions are allowed with respect to specific aspects of accounting in the following areas: business combinations, asset revaluations, employee benefits, cumulative translation differences, and financial instruments.

USE OF INTERNATIONAL FINANCIAL REPORTING STANDARDS

As Exhibit 3.2 shows, IFRSs constitute a comprehensive system of financial reporting addressing accounting concerns ranging from accounting for income taxes to the recognition and measurement of financial instruments to the preparation of consolidated financial statements. Because the IASB is a private body, it does not have the ability to enforce its standards. Instead, the IASB develops IFRSs for the public good, making them available to any country or company that might choose to adopt them.

There are a number of different ways in which a country might adopt IFRSs, including requiring (or permitting) IFRSs to be used by the following:

1. *All* companies. In effect, IFRSs replace national GAAP.
2. Parent companies preparing *consolidated* financial statements. National GAAP is used in parent company-only financial statements.
3. *Stock-exchange-listed* companies preparing consolidated financial statements. Nonlisted companies use national GAAP.
4. *Foreign* companies listing on domestic stock exchanges. Domestic companies use national GAAP.
5. Domestic companies that list on *foreign stock exchanges*. Other domestic companies use national GAAP.

The endorsement of IFRSs for cross-listing purposes by IOSCO and the EU's decision to require domestic listed companies to use IFRSs for consolidated accounts beginning in 2005 have provided a major boost to the efforts of the IASB. The results of a survey of the use of IFRSs by domestic listed companies in preparing their consolidated financial statements is presented in Exhibit 3.5. Of the 130 countries included in the survey, more than 90 require or permit the use of IFRSs by domestic listed companies.

Many developing countries have adopted IFRSs with little or no amendment as their national standards. For some of them, it may have been a less expensive option than developing their own standards. The need to attract foreign investment also may have been an influencing factor. Countries changing from centrally planned to market-based economies also have found IFRSs attractive, as they offer a ready-made set of standards to facilitate the development of a market system.

EXHIBIT 3.5
Use of IFRSs in
Preparing
Consolidated
Financial
Statements

Source: Deloitte IAS PLUS
"Use of IFRS for Reporting
by Domestic Listed
Companies, by Country,"
www.iasplus.com.

IFRSs Required for All Domestic Listed Companies

Armenia	Finland*	Kuwait	Oman
Australia	France*	Kyrgyzstan	Panama
Austria*	Germany*	Lebanon	Papua New Guinea
Bahamas	Georgia	Latvia*	Peru
Barbados	Greece*	Liechtenstein	Poland*
Bangladesh	Guatemala	Lithuania*	Portugal*
Belgium*	Guyana	Luxembourg*	Slovenia*
Bosnia & Herzegovina	Haiti	Macedonia	Slovak Republic*
Bulgaria	Honduras	Malawi	Spain*
Costa Rica	Hungary*	Malta*	Sweden*
Croatia	Iceland	Mauritius	Tajikistan
Cyprus*	Ireland*	Nepal	Tanzania
Czech Republic*	Italy*	Netherlands*	Trinidad & Tobago
Dominican Republic	Jamaica	Netherlands Antilles	Ukraine
Denmark*	Jordan	Nicaragua	United Kingdom*
Ecuador	Kenya	Norway	Yugoslavia
Egypt			
Estonia*			

IFRSs Permitted for Domestic Listed Companies

Aruba	Dominica	Lesotho	Switzerland
Bermuda	El Salvador	Myanmar	Turkey
Bolivia	Gibraltar	Namibia	Uganda
Botswana	Hong Kong	South Africa	Zambia
Brunei	Laos	Swaziland	Zimbabwe
Cayman Islands			

IFRSs Required for Some Domestic Listed Companies

Bahrain	Romania	Russian Federation	United Arab
China			Emirates

IFRSs Not Permitted for Domestic Listed Companies

Argentina	Ghana	Moldova	Taiwan
Benin	India	New Zealand	Thailand
Brazil	Indonesia	Niger	Togo
Burkina Faso	Israel	Pakistan	Tunisia
Cambodia	Japan	Philippines	United States
Canada	Korea (S)	Saudi Arabia	Uruguay
Chile	Mali	Singapore	Uzbekistan
Côte d'Ivoire	Malaysia	Sri Lanka	Venezuela
Colombia	Mexico	Syria	Vietnam
Fiji			

*EU member.

Although many countries do not allow domestic listed companies to use IASB standards, some of these countries nevertheless allow *foreign* companies listed on domestic stock exchanges to use IFRSs in accordance with IOSCO's recommendation. Japan, for example, allows foreign companies listing on the Tokyo stock exchange to file financial statements prepared in accordance with IFRSs without any reconciliation to Japanese GAAP.

The region of the world that thus far has been least receptive to the use of IFRSs is the Western Hemisphere. The largest economies in this region—Argentina, Brazil, Canada, Chile, Mexico, and the United States—do not permit domestic or foreign listed companies to use IFRSs.

GAAP CONVERGENCE

Convergence with IFRSs

In 2002, the six largest public accounting firms worldwide conducted a survey of national efforts in 54 countries to promote and achieve convergence with IFRSs.[32] Almost all of the countries surveyed intend to converge with IFRSs, indicating that the IASB is the appropriate body to develop a global accounting language. Countries with a plan to achieve convergence included members of the European Union; the six countries of the Western Hemisphere with the largest economies (Argentina, Brazil, Canada, Chile, Mexico, and the United States); and China, India, Malaysia, New Zealand, South Korea, and Thailand. The survey identified three different convergence strategies:

1. Replacing national GAAP with IFRSs (supplemented for issues not addressed by IFRSs).
2. Adopting IFRSs as national GAAP on a standard-by-standard basis.
3. Eliminating differences between national GAAP and IFRSs when possible and practicable.

The European Union has adopted the first strategy with respect to the preparation of consolidated financial statements by listed companies. Nonlisted companies will continue to apply national GAAP. Two EU countries (Denmark and Estonia) have also adopted the third strategy with respect to nonlisted companies, by adopting a plan to converge national GAAP with IFRSs. This strategy could eventually result in no substantive differences between IFRSs and a country's national GAAP. In January 2003, the European Parliament approved amendments to the EU's Fourth and Seventh Directives, removing all inconsistencies between the directives and IFRSs.

The following were the major concerns expressed by survey respondents in achieving IFRS convergence:

- The complicated nature of particular standards, especially those related to financial instruments and fair value accounting (51 percent of countries).
- The tax-driven nature of the national accounting regime (47 percent).
- Disagreement with certain significant IFRSs, especially those related to financial instruments and fair value accounting (39 percent).
- Insufficient guidance on first-time application of IFRSs (35 percent).
- Limited capital markets, and therefore little benefit to be derived from using IFRSs (30 percent).
- Satisfaction with national accounting standards among investors/users (21 percent).
- IFRS language translation difficulties (18 percent).

[32] BDO, Deloitte Touche Tohmatsu, Ernst & Young, Grant Thornton, KPMG, and PricewaterhouseCoopers, *GAAP Convergence 2002: A Survey of National Efforts to Promote and Achieve Convergence with International Financial Reporting Standards,* available at www.ifad.net.

In October 2004, the EU decided to adopt a version of IAS 39 amended by the European Commission. This was not well received internationally, including in the United Kingdom. The concerns included that this could have adverse consequences for the cost of capital of European companies if the adopted standard prevents European companies from complying with the complete standard as issued by the IASB, as it will damage the credibility of European financial reporting. Further, it was pointed out that the adopted standard includes seriously weakened hedge accounting requirements and may give rise to artificial volatility in reported profits and difficulties in application as a result of limiting the fair value option.

In December 2004, the United Kingdom's Accounting Standards Board (ASB) issued five standards aligning the text of UK accounting standards with that of IFRSs as part the ASB's strategy for convergence with IFRSs.[33] In January 2005, the IASB and the Accounting Standards Board of Japan (ASBJ) announced their agreement to launch a joint project to reduce differences between IFRS and Japanese accounting standards.

The official language of the IASB is English, and IFRSs are developed in this language. The IASB has attempted to address the translation issue by permitting national accountancy bodies to translate IFRSs into more than 30 languages, including Chinese, French, German, Japanese, Portuguese, and Spanish. In addition to the problem that IFRSs have not yet been translated into very many languages, research has shown that translation can be problematic, as some terms in English have no direct equivalent in other languages.[34]

The switch to IFRSs will involve significant changes to the accounting policies of listed companies. The UK Institute of Chartered Accountants in England and Wales urged companies to provide investors and analysts with clear explanations of their preparations for adopting IFRSs and changes to accounting policies ahead of publication of the 2005 accounts, as this is important in securing investor confidence.

The Norwalk Agreement

In September 2002, at a meeting in Norwalk, Connecticut, the FASB and IASB pledged to use their best efforts to (1) make their existing financial reporting standards fully compatible as soon as is practicable and (2) to coordinate their work program to ensure that once achieved, compatibility is maintained. This has become known as the "Norwalk Agreement." Note that this agreement does not mean that the FASB will always try to move in the direction of IASB Standards to remove existing differences, but that the opposite also will occur. Significantly, the two standard setters have agreed to work together on future issues to try to develop common solutions. In March 2003, the IASB decided to use identical style and wording in the standards issued by the FASB and IASB on joint projects.

---

[33] They were: FRS 22 (IAS 33), *Earnings per Share;* FRS 23 (IAS 21), *The Effects of Changes in Foreign Exchange Rates;* FRS 24 (IAS 29), *Financial Reporting in Hyper Inflationary Economies;* FRS 25 (IAS 32), *Financial Instruments: Disclosure and Presentation;* and FRS 26 (IAS 39), *Financial Instruments—Measurement.*

[34] Timothy S. Doupnik and M. Richter, "Interpretation of Uncertainty Expressions: A Cross-national Study," *Accounting, Organizations and Society* 28, no. 1 (2003), pp. 15–35. These researchers find, for example, that German speakers do not view the English word *remote* (used in the context of the probability that a loss will occur) and its German translation *Wahrscheinlichkeit äußerst gering* as being equivalent.

The following are key FASB initiatives to further convergence between IFRSs and U.S. GAAP:

1. *Joint projects.* Joint projects involve sharing staff resources and working on a similar time schedule. Revenue recognition and business combinations are two major topics covered by joint projects.

2. *Short-term convergence project.* The two boards agreed to undertake a short-term project to remove a variety of differences that exist between IFRSs and U.S. GAAP. The scope of the short-term convergence project is limited to those differences between in which convergence is likely to be achieved in the short-term. Convergence is expected to occur by selecting either existing U.S. GAAP or IFRS requirements as the high-quality solution.

3. *Liaison IASB member.* A full-time IASB member is in residence at the FASB offices. This facilitates information exchange and cooperation between the FASB and the IASB.

4. *Monitoring of IASB projects.* The FASB monitors IASB projects according to the FASB's level of interest in the topic being addressed.

5. *The convergence research project.* The FASB staff embarked on a project to identify all of the substantive differences between U.S. GAAP and IFRSs and catalog differences according to the FASB's strategy for resolving them.

6. *Consideration of convergence potential in board agenda decisions.* All topics considered for addition to the FASB's agenda are assessed for the potential cooperation with the IASB.

The FASB expected that through these initiatives significant progress could be made toward convergence with IFRSs in the short to medium term. Toward the end of 2004 the FASB issued three standards designed to eliminate some differences between the U.S. and IASB standards: SFAS 123 (revised 2004), *Share-based Payments,* issued in December 2004; SFAS 151, *Inventory Costs* (an amendment of ARB 43, Chapter 4), issued in November 2004; and SFAS 153, *Exchange of Non-monetary Assets* (an amendment of APB Opinion 29), issued in December 2004. SFAS 123 requires that compensation cost relating to share-based payment transactions be recognized in financial statements. The cost is to be measured on the basis of the fair value of the equity or liability instrument issued. This standard eliminates the use of the intrinsic value method, which was allowed under Opinion 25, and it is expected to result in convergence with IFRS 2. ARB 43 states that under some circumstances, items such as idle facility expenses, excessive spoilage, double freight, and re-handling costs may be so abnormal as to require treatment as current period charges. SFAS 151 eliminates the term abnormal. The term was not defined in ARB 43. The language used in SFAS 151 is similar to that in IAS 2. SFAS 153 eliminates certain narrow differences between Opinion 29 and IAS 16. Opinion 29 provided an exception to the basic measurement principle (fair value) for exchanges of similar productive assets (commercially substantive assets). SFAS 153 eliminates that exception and brings the U.S. standard closer to IAS 16.[35]

---

[35] For a link to differences between IFRS and U.S. GAAP, refer to http://accountingeducation.com/news/news5639.html.

THE IASB AS A GLOBAL STANDARD SETTER

The IASB has earned a great deal of goodwill from many interested parties. Its new approach clearly reflects a change of role from a harmonizer to a global standard setter. According to its chairman, the IASB's strategy is to identify the best in standards around the world and build a body of accounting standards that constitute the highest common denominator of financial reporting. The IASB has adopted a principles-based approach to standard setting and has obtained the support of U.S. regulators (even though U.S. standard setters historically have taken a rules-based approach). However, the IASB's structure is similar to that of the U.S. standard setter, recognizing that the FASB has the best institutional structure for developing accounting standards.

The IASB also has taken initiatives to facilitate and enhance its role as a global standard setter. The issuance of IFRS 1 in 2004 is one such initiative. With the increasing trend in many countries, including Australia and the EU member nations, to adopt IFRSs, a large number of companies (over 7,000 listed companies in Europe alone) recently began using IFRSs in preparing their financial statements. The IASB's decision to hold a series of public roundtable forums to provide opportunities for those who have commented on an exposure draft to discuss their views on the proposals with members of the IASB is another important initiative.

As noted earlier, 7 of the 14 board members have direct liaison responsibility with national standard setters.[36] As a result, unlike its predecessor, the IASB is now formally linked to national standard setters, and the liaison board members are able to coordinate agendas and ensure that the IASB and national bodies are working toward convergence, based on Anglo-Saxon accounting. (Some of the defining features of Anglo-Saxon accounting are described in the appendix to this chapter.)

In the quest to achieve convergence with national accounting standards, the IASB must remain alert to the potential for it to be influenced by interested parties. Commenting on the IASB's strategy to engineer convergence through a process of formal liaison with leading national standard setters, Professor Steven Zeff warns about the political pressures that may be triggered by any board initiative to prescribe specific accounting treatments, eliminate alternative treatments, impose additional disclosure requirements, or tighten interpretations.[37] Most accounting issues are politically sensitive, because the need for standards often arises where there is controversy and because accounting can have economic consequences that affect the wealth of different groups. As a result, different groups interested in a particular accounting issue can be expected to lobby for the standard most beneficial to them, or to prevent the establishment of a proposed standard they believe would be less favorable than the status quo.

The issue of accounting standards convergence versus financial statement comparability also should not be overlooked. Convergence of standards does not necessarily produce comparable financial statements. Cultural and other factors could lead to different interpretations of standards and different levels of compliance across countries, leading to the production of financial statements that might not be comparable.

---

[36] The IASB initially had official liaison with national standard setters from Australia, Canada, France, Germany, Japan, New Zealand, the United Kingdom, and the United States.

[37] S. Zeff, "Political Lobbying on Proposed Standards: A Challenge to the IASB," *Accounting Horizons* 16, no. 1 (2002), pp. 43–54.

Summary

1. Harmonization is the process of reducing differences in financial reporting practices across countries. The major goal of harmonization is comparability of financial statements.

2. Harmonization of accounting standards might not necessarily result in harmonization of financial reporting practices, which is necessary for financial statement comparability.

3. Proponents of international accounting harmonization argue that cross-country comparability of financial statements is required for the globalization of capital markets. Opponents argue that globalization is occurring without harmonization and that it might be appropriate for countries with different environments to have different standards.

4. Several organizations are involved in the harmonization efforts at global and regional levels, including IOSCO, IFAC, the EU, and the IASB.

5. To achieve a common capital market, the European Union (EU) has attempted to harmonize accounting through the issuance of the Fourth and the Seventh Directives. Although the EU directives have reduced differences in accounting in Europe, complete comparability has not been achieved. Rather than developing additional directives, the European Commission decided to require the use of International Accounting Standards (IASs) beginning in 2005.

6. The International Accounting Standards Committee (IASC) was formed in 1973 to develop international accounting standards universally acceptable in all countries. In 2001, the IASC was replaced by the International Accounting Standards Board (IASB).

7. The IASB has 14 members (12 full-time and 2 part-time), 7 of whom have a formal liaison relationship with a national standard setter. The IASB adheres to an open process in developing standards, which are principles-based (rather than rules-based). With the establishment of the IASB, there has been a shift in emphasis from harmonization to global standard setting.

8. As of March 2005, International Financial Reporting Standards (IFRSs) consisted of 31 IASs, 5 IFRSs, and a number of interpretations. As a private organization, the IASB does not have the ability to require the use of its standards.

9. The International Organization of Securities Commissions (IOSCO) recommends that securities regulators permit foreign issuers to use IFRSs for cross-listing. Most major stock exchanges are in compliance with this recommendation. In addition, a large and growing number of countries either require or allow domestic listed companies to use IFRSs in preparing consolidated financial statements. The EU's adoption of IFRSs in 2005 was a major boost to the IASB's legitimacy as a global accounting standard setter.

10. The United States is one of the few economically important countries that does not allow domestic or foreign companies to use IFRSs in stock exchange listings. The SEC requires foreign registrants that use IFRSs (or foreign GAAP) in preparing their financial statements to reconcile their net income and stockholders' equity on a U.S. GAAP basis.

11. The IASB's *Framework for the Preparation and Presentation of Financial Statements* establishes usefulness for decision making as the primary objective of financial statements prepared under IFRSs. Understandability, relevance, reliability, and comparability are the primary qualitative characteristics that make financial statements useful. The *Framework* also provides workable definitions of the accounting elements.

12. IAS 1 is a single standard providing guidelines for the presentation of financial statements. The standard stipulates that a set of IFRS-based financial statements must include a balance sheet, an income statement, a statement of cash flows, a statement of changes in equity, and accounting polices and explanatory notes. IAS 1 establishes the overriding principle of fair presentation and permits an override of a requirement of an IASB standard in the extremely rare situation where management concludes that compliance with a requirement of a standard would be misleading.

13. IFRS 1 provides guidance to companies that are adopting IFRSs for the first time. IFRS 1 requires an entity to comply with each IFRS effective at the reporting date of its first IFRS financial statements. However, IFRS 1 provides exemptions to this rule where the cost of complying with this requirement would likely exceed the benefit to users.

14. In 2002, the FASB and IASB signed the Norwalk Agreement, in which they agreed to work toward convergence of their two sets of financial reporting standards.

Appendix to Chapter 3

What Is This Thing Called Anglo-Saxon Accounting?

The term *Anglo-Saxon* or *Anglo-American* is used for a group of countries that includes the United States, the United Kingdom, Canada, Australia, and New Zealand. This group often figures in international accounting textbooks and articles, particularly with regard to international classification of accounting systems and international harmonization of accounting standards. The efforts of the IASB (and its predecessor, the IASC) are usually associated with Anglo-Saxon accounting. Some even criticize the IASB for attempting to promote Anglo-Saxon accounting throughout the world. However, many non-Anglo countries are already using IFRSs. Given this, it is important to examine some of the important features of Anglo-Saxon accounting, which is the basis for IFRSs.

In a broad sense, the term *Anglo-Saxon accounting* refers to the accounting systems prevalent in the English-speaking countries mentioned in the preceding paragraph. Although the accounting systems in these countries are not identical, they share some fundamental features that distinguish them from other systems of accounting:

- A focus on how businesses operate at the firm level (micro orientation), with an emphasis on the importance of professional judgment (recognition of professional rules and professional self-regulation).

- An investor orientation, with the provision of information for efficient operation of the capital market as the primary aim (recognition of the importance of being transparent).

- Less emphasis on prudence and measurement of taxable income or distributable income, and willingness to go beyond superficial legal form (substance over form).[1]

[1]Christopher W. Nobes, "On the Myth of 'Anglo-Saxon' Financial Accounting: A Comment," *International Journal of Accounting* 38 (2003), pp. 95–104.

There are other recognizable commonalities that are related to the above features. For example, because of the investor orientation and emphasis on transparency in accounting reports, the principle of true and fair view or fair presentation is predominant in Anglo-Saxon financial reporting. Auditors are required to report on whether, in their opinion, the financial statements have been prepared in such a way that they adhere to this principle. In the United Kingdom, the concept of *true and fair view* has not been clearly defined in legislation. The courts have placed considerable reliance on expert witnesses in developing a meaning for this concept. The UK government's view has been that this is a highly technical matter and therefore should be dealt with by the profession. This leaves open the possibility for different interpretations. There is no single true and fair view. There are also some differences in how the concept of true and fair view is applied. For example, in the United Kingdom, it is an overriding requirement. In other words, complying with the legal requirements does not necessarily lead to a true and fair view, in which case additional information should be provided. However, in Canada and Australia, a true-and-fair-view override does not apply. Further, the U.S. equivalent to true and fair view, *present fairly,* is defined in terms of conformity with U.S. GAAP. In other words, if the financial statements have been prepared in accordance with the U.S. GAAP, then it is assumed that the information is presented fairly. In general, it is recognized that the application of the qualitative characteristics and appropriate accounting standards would normally result in financial statements that convey a true and fair view of such information, or that present it fairly.[2]

The qualitative characteristics such as understandability, relevance, reliability, and objectivity or representational faithfulness are found in the conceptual frameworks developed by all Anglo-Saxon countries and by the IASB. The use of a conceptual framework to provide guidance for developing accounting standards is another common feature among these countries. The IASB's conceptual framework is largely based on that of the U.S. FASB. This has been one of the reasons for the view that the IASB has been heavily influenced by Anglo-Saxon accounting. Another recognizable common feature among Anglo-Saxon countries is that they all have common law traditions rather than code law traditions. This means they all use common law legal systems, which tend to be flexible in terms of legislation and rely heavily on private sector and market mechanisms for regulation. Related to this, all these countries have private-sector standard-setting bodies recognizing the profession's capacity to self-regulate.[3]

Some differences can be observed among Anglo-Saxon countries with regard to the recognizable common features described in the preceding paragraph. For example, the conceptual frameworks are not always used as the basis for developing accounting standards. As a case in point, SFAS 87, *Employers' Accounting for Pensions*, in the United States specifically states that it does not follow the FASB's conceptual framework. Further, a common law legal system does not necessarily lead to flexible standards. U.S. accounting standards are increasingly becoming more detailed and rigidly prescriptive as compared to accounting standards developed in the United Kingdom. With regard to private-sector standard setting, traditionally the U.S. standard-setting system is significantly more public-sector-oriented than the UK system, because the U.S. Securities and Exchange Commission (SEC) has the ultimate responsibility for authorizing accounting standards. On the basis

---

[2]IASC, *Framework for the Preparation and Presentation of Financial Statements* (London: IASC, 1989).
[3]Nobes (2003), Op cit.

of these differences, some commentators have argued that Anglo-Saxon accounting is a myth.[4] However, such differences do not necessarily indicate that these countries cannot usefully be seen as members of the same group.[5]

[4]David Alexander and Simon Archer, "On the Myth of 'Anglo-Saxon' Accounting," *International Journal of Accounting* 35, no. 4 (2000), pp. 539–57.
[5]Nobes (2003), Op cit.

Questions

1. How does harmonization differ from standardization?
2. What are the potential benefits that a multinational corporation could derive from the international harmonization of accounting?
3. Were the EU directives effective in generating comparability of financial statements across companies located in member nations? Why or why not?
4. What were the three phases in the life of the IASC?
5. Why was IOSCO's endorsement of IASs so important to the IASC's efforts?
6. How does the structure of the IASB help to establish its legitimacy as a global standard setter?
7. What is a principles-based approach to accounting standard setting? Who uses such an approach?
8. Are there any major accounting issues that have not yet been covered by IFRSs?
9. Do you see a major change of emphasis in the harmonization process since the establishment of the IASB? Explain.
10. What are the different ways in which IFRSs might be used within a country?
11. Would the worldwide adoption of IFRSs result in worldwide comparability of financial statements? Why or why not?
12. In what way is the IASB's *Framework* intended to assist firms in preparing IFRS-based financial statements?
13. As expressed in IAS 1, what is the overriding principle that should be followed in preparing IFRS-based financial statements?
14. Under what conditions should a firm claim to prepare financial statements in accordance with IFRSs?
15. How are IFRSs currently used in the United States? What are the different ways in which IFRSs might be used in the United States in the future?

Exercises and Problems

1. "The IASB has been repeatedly accused of devising accounting standards that pay insufficient attention to the concerns and practices of companies. . . . Some European banks and insurers complain about poor due process by the IASB, and Frits Bolkestein, European commissioner responsible for accounting matters, endorsed their concerns earlier this month" (*Financial Times*, March 24, 2004, p. 20).

Required:
Elaborate on the concerns raised in the preceding quote, and discuss the measures that have been taken by the IASB to alleviate those concerns.

2. Since 2005, publicly traded companies in the European Union have been required to use IFRSs in preparing their consolidated financial statements.

   Required:
   a. Explain the EU's objective in requiring the use of IFRSs.
   b. Identify and describe two issues that might hamper the EU from achieving the objective underlying the use of IFRSs.

3. Assume that you have been invited to advise the newly established accounting oversight body in one of the former eastern European countries that became a member of the EU in May 2004. The accounting oversight body is charged with the task of identifying the main issues to be addressed in implementing the use of IFRSs.

   Required:
   Prepare a report outlining the key points you would include in your advice to this accounting oversight body.

4. Refer to Exhibit 3.5 in this chapter and note the countries that do not permit domestic listed companies to use IFRSs.

   Required:
   Identify three countries from this group that are likely to have different reasons for not permitting the use of IFRSs by domestic listed companies. Describe those reasons.

5. On May 19, 2004, the IASB published a single volume of its official pronouncements that will be applicable from January 1, 2005.

   Required:
   Access the IASB Web site (www.iasb.org), search for these pronouncements, and prepare a list of them.

6. The professional accounting bodies in many countries have taken, or are taking, steps to adopt IFRSs.

   Required:
   Go to the Web site of a professional accounting body of your choice and outline the steps it has taken so far to facilitate adoption of IFRSs.

7. The appendix to this chapter describes what is commonly referred to as Anglo-Saxon accounting.

   Required:
   Explain why Anglo-Saxon accounting might be of interest to Chinese accounting regulators.

8. In its 2003 annual report, Honda Motor Company Ltd. states:

   > Honda's manufacturing operations are principally conducted in 25 separate factories, 5 of which are located in Japan. Principal overseas manufacturing factories are located in the United States of America, Canada, The United Kingdom, France, Italy, Spain, India, Pakistan, the Philippines, Thailand, Vietnam, Brazil, and Mexico. . . . The company and its domestic subsidiaries maintain their books of account in conformity with financial accounting standards of Japan, and its foreign subsidiaries generally maintain their books of account in conformity with those of the countries of their domicile.

> The consolidated financial statements presented herein have been prepared in a manner and reflect the adjustments which are necessary to conform them with accounting principles generally accepted in the United States of America. (p. 59)

Required:
Discuss the possible reasons for Honda to prepare its consolidated financial statements in conformity with U.S. GAAP.

9. A list of foreign companies with shares traded on the New York Stock Exchange (NYSE) can be found on the NYSE's Web site (www.nyse.com).

Required:
a. Refer to Exhibit 3.5. Identify a developing country in Asia, Africa, and Latin America listed in Exhibit 3.5, and determine how many companies from each of these countries is listed on the NYSE. If the country you select first from a region does not have any NYSE-listed companies, identify another country included in Exhibit 3.5 from that region that does.
b. Describe the manner in which IFRSs are used in each of the countries you have selected.

10. The *Financial Times*, on Tuesday, April 13, 2004, made the following comment in its editorial "Parmalat: Perennial Lessons of European Scandal: **Urgent need for better enforcement and investor scepticism:**"

> After the accounting scandals in the US, there was an unseemly amount of crowing in Europe. As it happens, Parmalat is a much older scandal than Enron or WorldCom. It just took longer to come out at the Italian dairy company. . . . Convergence of standards—in accounting, for instance—will help spread best practice. So will high level meetings between regulators, such as take place within the International Organisation of Securities Commission. But we are nowhere near having a world super-regulator. . . . In Italy regulation has been weak because of fragmentation and lack of clout and resources. Attempts to tackle this and to ensure regulators' independence from political interference should be urgently pursued." (p. 12)

Required:
Discuss the lessons referred to above concerning the objectives of the current efforts at setting global standards for accounting and financial reporting.

11. The chapter describes different phases in the harmonization efforts of the IASC and IASB.

Required:
Identify one such phase and prepare a brief report describing its importance in the overall scheme of international harmonization of accounting standards. You should consult relevant literature in preparing this report.

12. Geneva Technology Company (GTC), a Swiss-based company founded in 1999, is considering the use of IFRSs in preparing its annual report for the year ended December 31, 2007. You are the manager of GTC's fixed assets accounting department.

Required:
Identify the steps that you will need to take in your department to comply with the requirements of IFRS 1.

Case 3-1

Jardine Matheson Group (Part 1)

With its broad portfolio of market-leading businesses, the Jardine Matheson Group is an Asian-based conglomerate with extensive experience in the region. Its business interests include Jardine Pacific, Jardine Motors Group, Hongkong Land, Dairy Farm, Mandarin Oriental, Cycle & Carriage and Jardine Lloyd Thompson. These companies are leaders in the fields of engineering and construction, transport services, motor trading, property, retailing, restaurants, hotels and insurance broking.

The Group's strategy is to build its operations into market leaders across Asia Pacific, each with the support of Jardine Matheson's extensive knowledge of the region and its long-standing relationships. Through a balance of cash producing activities and investment in new businesses, the Group aims to produce sustained growth in shareholder value.

Incorporated in Bermuda, Jardine Matheson has its primary share listing in London, with secondary listings in Singapore and Bermuda. Jardine Matheson Limited operates from Hong Kong and provides management services to Group companies, making available senior management and providing financial, legal, human resources and treasury support services throughout the Group.[1]

Jardine Matheson uses International Financial Reporting Standards in preparing its financial statements and has done so for a number of years.

Required:

Access Jardine Matheson's most recent annual report on the company's Web site (www.jardine-matheson.com). Review the company's consolidated financial statements to evaluate whether the financial statements presented comply with the presentation requirements in IAS 1, *Presentation of Financial Statements*. Document your evaluation.

[1] www.jardine-matheson.com/profile/intro.html

Case 3-2

Comments on the IASB's ED 4, *Disposal of Non-current Assets and Presentation of Discontinued Operations*

In July 2003, the IASB released Exposure Draft (ED) 4, *Disposal of Non-current Assets and Presentation of Discontinued Operations,* for public comment. This proposed IFRS was the first resulting from the IASB's short-term convergence project with the FASB in the United States, part of the so-called Norwalk Agreement. It was intended to achieve consistency between IFRSs and the FASB's SFAS 144, *Accounting for the Impairment or Disposal of Long-Lived Assets.*

The main features of the proposal are that it

1. Establishes "held for sale" as a separate classification for noncurrent assets.
2. Creates the concept of a "disposal group."

3. Requires an asset held for sale (or included in a disposal group) to be carried at the lower of carrying value and fair value less costs to sell.
4. Requires discontinuance of depreciation on assets held for sale.
5. Requires assets held for sale to be reported separately on the balance sheet.

Appendix B to ED 4 provides criteria for determining when a noncurrent asset should be classified as held for sale. In addition, ED 4 would withdraw IAS 35, *Discontinuing Operations*, replacing it with the following:

1. The definition of a discontinued operation would be changed from a separate major line of business or geographical area to any unit whose operations and cash flows can be clearly distinguished operationally and for financial reporting purposes.
2. An operation would be classified as discontinued on the date the entity has actually disposed of it or when the operation meets the criteria to be classified as held for sale.
3. The results of discontinued operations would be reported separately on the face of the income statement.

The IASB received 86 letters from 25 different countries commenting on the proposals embodied in ED 4. Companies, professional associations, international accounting firms, national institutes of accountants, national standard setting bodies, and private citizens wrote letters. As part of its public process, the IASB makes the full text of comment letters available on its Web site. In the "Invitation to Comment" section of ED 4, the IASB asked for feedback to nine specific questions. Many of the comment letters provide question-by-question responses to those questions, in most cases simply expressing agreement with the approach proposed in ED 4. Other comment letters focused on specific issues where the commenter disagreed with the ED's proposals.

Required:

1. Access the comment letters related to ED 4 on the IASB's Web site (www.iasb.org) under "Current Issues," "Comment Letters." Read the letters written by BP PLC (UK) and Bundesverband deutscher Banken (BdB) (Germany).
2. Prepare a brief report summarizing the issues raised by the authors of these letters with respect to the proposed IFRS. In your report, discuss the level of specificity in the comments made by the authors of these letters.
3. Discuss the implications raised by the authors' comments with respect to the "Norwalk Agreement" leading to comparability of U.S. GAAP and IFRS-based financial statements.
4. Discuss the implications raised by the authors' comments with respect to the impact the "Norwalk Agreement" might have on the IASB's status as global standard setter.

Note: IFRS 5, *Non-current Assets Held for Sale and Discontinued Operations*, was issued in March 2004 as the first IFRS to arise from the IASB's joint project with the FASB. It substantially incorporates the proposal requirements included in ED 4.

Case 3-3

The European Perspective on International Financial Reporting Standards

Excerpts from three articles from the financial press related to the European Union's adoption of International Financial Reporting Standards are presented below.

Required:

Read each article and identify the key concerns related to the work of the IASB and adoption of IFRSs in Europe.

> **Convergence of Accounting Rules Proving to Be "All Pain and No Gain": The outgoing head of the accountants' institute tells Andrew Parker of his worries surrounding the international harmonisation of standards**

Accountants could be hamstrung by highly prescriptive reporting rules because of the drive towards an international standard, Britain's most senior accountant has warned.

Peter Wyman, outgoing president of the Institute of Chartered Accountants in England and Wales, criticised efforts to achieve convergence between US and international accounting standards. He also attacked the work of the International Accounting Standards Board, which writes the global financial reporting rules. Mr Wyman urged the IASB to reconsider its efforts to achieve convergence with US accounting standards because he claimed the body's recent standards were too complex and did not give auditors sufficient leeway to exercise professional judgment.

He singled out the IASB's controversial financial reporting rules on derivatives, known as IAS 39, which are largely based on US accounting rules. The deepening row over these rules is threatening to undermine the European Union's plans for EU-listed companies to use international accounting standards from 2005.

US business scandals gave fresh momentum towards the longstanding goal of convergence between US and international accounting standards. The Securities and Exchange Commission, the chief US financial regulator, signalled last October that it could drop the requirement for non-US companies to issue accounts under US accounting standards as well as international financial reporting rules in 2005.

But Mr Wyman claimed the SEC was now unlikely to drop its requirement for reconciliation between international and US financial reporting rules. He said: "I do not believe that in anything like the foreseeable future we are going to achieve recognition by the SEC of international standards without reconciliation. The IASB should concentrate on producing the very best standards, and look to convergence with US generally accepted accounting principles as a secondary focus. . . . I do think we should urge the IASB to row back on convergence as a primary goal."

Mr Wyman claimed the IASB had bent too far towards the US in its recent work. "I am very unhappy with the style of standards," he said. "They are getting more and more rules-based. They are longer, and less judgment is involved. . . . It is all pain and no gain."

Mr Wyman has warned that the quality of UK financial reporting could deteriorate because EU companies are due to use international accounting standards from 2005. "The worrying thing is if it is more than one step backwards. We are quite close to it."[1]

---

[1] *Financial Times,* Wednesday London Edition 2, May 28, 2003, p. 6.

Accounting: IAS Endorsed by EU Member States

The European Union's 15 Member States officially endorsed the existing set of International Accounting Standards (IAS) on July 16, after getting the go-ahead from Finance Ministers the day before. However, through their representatives sitting in the Accounting Regulatory Committee, they postponed a decision on two contested standards, IAS 32 on disclosure and presentation and IAS 39 on recognition and measurement, which cover fair value reporting. France has been leading the call for these two IAS to be dropped altogether, judging them causes of "nefarious consequences" for financial stability, in the words of French President Jacques Chirac (see European Report 2793). Adoption of the standards into EU law will go ahead in September and they will be published in the *Official Journal of the European Communities* in all eleven official EU languages.

But the London-based International Accounting Standards Board says that it has no intention of suppressing the two standards. IAS Board Chairman Sir David Tweedie said that such a move would destroy the credibility of the IAS, and undermine their convergence with US GAAP standards. Redrafting work is continuing on IAS 32 and 39 to take into account the concerns of non-EU countries. But the Member States will have to arrive at a decision at some point soon, if they are to stick to the January 2005 deadline for adoption. A spokesman for the Department of Trade and Industry which represents the UK at the Committee said, "We are prepared to support the Commissions' proposals on the basis that we expect IAS 32 and 39 to be considered for adoption as soon as the IASB has finalised them."[2]

The IASB Must Be Watched Closely

Purchase-pooling, mandatory expensing of stock options, and consolidating variable interest entities. These are three of the recent high-stakes battles we have had with the U.S.-based Financial Accounting Standards Board (FASB). Two were successfully resolved, while the third, on mandatory expensing, is ongoing.

But what if we were constantly fighting a two-front war? The broad mandate and increasing reach of European accounting standards setters could mean trouble for VCs at home and abroad.

Created in 2000, the International Accounting Standards Board (IASB) has the stated goal of developing "a single set of high-quality, understandable and enforceable global accounting standards." The European Union (EU) has agreed that rules of the IASB are binding for all European companies starting in 2005, but the European Commission will retain the power to overturn an international standard. This is not unlike the situation in the United States, in which the FASB writes the GAAP rules and the SEC approves them and enforces them. In addition to determining how businesses operate is Europe, the IASB is significant because of its ongoing project with FASB to achieve convergence or harmonization between IAS and GAAP standards.

Clearly, a set of global accounting standards could be beneficial as our industry increasingly looks for opportunities abroad and could, in the long-term, aid in capital formation for countries whose capital markets are not as efficient as our own. But we share the concerns of those in Europe, here in the States, and in other industrialized countries that the IASB's initial projects cast suspicion upon whether high-quality, consensus-based accounting standards are achievable.

The IASB has not shied away from controversy. Thus, it is under tremendous pressure from many businesses for its proposals and from politicians in the EU for its process in producing those proposals.

[2] *European Report,* July 19, 2003.

Among its first projects were the mandatory expensing of stock options and fair-value accounting for derivatives. As we have discussed previously in this column (see June VCJ), the IASB's proposal on expensing stock options, ED 2, fails to address the significant problems with valuation, among other problems. IAS 32 and IAS 39 are draft standards that would require that all investment assets of financial institutions, such as banks and insurance companies, to be measured at fair or market value rather than historic cost, which the industries fear would lead to artificial volatility in quarterly earnings reports.

In Brussels on July 15, EU finance ministers stepped up political pressure on the IASB, demanding that European viewpoints—especially when it comes to calculating the value of derivatives in company audits—carry greater influence in decision-making. The EU finance ministers endorsed all IASB standards except the two involving derivatives.

On July 9, commenting on the flaws in the IASB's processes with particular regard to the handling of IAS 32 and 39, Mr. Bolkenstein, a Member of the European Commission wrote: "There is growing unease concerning the standard setting process itself. The perception seems to be that there is a lack of willingness on the part of the IASB to move away from theoretical concepts to accept solutions that are based upon solid, practical experience. I am convinced that in the future the IAS-endorsement process will become more and more difficult unless ways and means are found to ensure that the standard setting procedures become more open and thorough allowing all parties concerned to fully participate in the process at all stages."

French President Jacques Chirac also had harsh words for the IASB's process, writing the following: "Several other standards could also have negative effects on companies and the European economy [referring to the expensing of stock options]. More in general, I believe it urgent and necessary, given my experience, to quickly start thinking thoroughly about the institutional *framework* which is put in place to adopt accounting standards which would be of application for our companies."

Although these comments were made in reference to the IASB's work on derivatives, we believe the same criticisms can be leveled against its proposal on stock options. Thus, while we will continue to oppose mandatory expensing, we recognize that it is essential for our industry's long-term success to constructively engage all the parties to develop a well-functioning, collaborative process at the IASB that actually results in a set of consensus-built, high-quality, understandable accounting rules.[3]

---

[3] Mark Heesen, President of the National Venture Capital Association, writing in *Venture Capital Journal*, October 1, 2003.

References

Alexander, David, and Simon Archer. "On the Myth of 'Anglo-Saxon' Accounting." *International Journal of Accounting* 35, no. 4 (2000), pp. 539–57.

BDO, Deloitte Touche Tohmatsu, Ernst & Young, Grant Thornton, KPMG, PricewaterhouseCoopers. *GAAP Convergence 2002: A Survey of National Efforts to Promote and Achieve Convergence with International Financial Reporting Standards.* Available at www.ifad.net

Beresford, Dennis R. "Accounting for International Operations." *CPA Journal*, October 1988, pp. 79–80.

Cairns, David. "Compliance Must Be Enforced." *Accountancy International*, September 1998, pp. 64–65.

———. *Financial Times International Accounting Standards Survey.* London: FT Finance, 1999.

Carey, Anthony. "Harmonization: Europe Moves Forward." *Accountancy*, March 1990.

Carsberg, Sir Bryan. "Global Issues and Implementing Core International Accounting Standards: Where Lies IASC's Final Goal?" Remarks made at the 50th Anniversary Dinner, Japanese Institute of CPAs, Tokyo, October 23, 1998.

Chen, S.; Z. Sun; and Y. Wang. "Evidence from China on Whether Harmonized Accounting Standards Harmonize Accounting Practices." *Accounting Horizons* 16, no. 3 (2002), pp. 183–97.

Choi, F. D. S. "A Cluster Approach to Harmonization." *Management Accounting*, August 1981, pp. 27–31.

Collins, Stephen H. "The SEC on Full and Fair Disclosure." *Journal of Accountancy*, January 1989, p. 84.

Commission of the European Communities. "EU Financial Reporting Strategy: The Way Forward." Communication from the Commission to the Council and the European Parliament, June 13, 2000.

Doupnik, Timothy S. "Recent Innovations in German Accounting Practice Through the Integration of EC Directives," *Advances in International Accounting* 5 (1992), pp. 75–103.

———, and M. Richter. "Interpretation of Uncertainty Expressions: A Cross-national Study." *Accounting, Organizations and Society* 28, no. 1 (2003), pp. 15–35.

Emenyonu, Emmanuel N., and Sidney J. Gray. "International Accounting Harmonization and the Major Developed Stock Market Countries: An Empirical Study." *International Journal of Accounting* 31, no. 3 (1996), pp. 269–79.

Ernst & Young. "Mind the GAAP: The Rise and Fall of IAS Lite." *Eye on IAS Newsletter*, June 2002, pp. 2–8.

Financial Accounting Standards Board. *The IASC-U.S. Comparison Project: A Report on the Similarities and Differences between IASC Standards and U.S. GAAP*, ed. Carrie Bloomer. Norwalk, CT: FASB, 1996.

Financial Accounting Standards Board. *The IASC-U.S. Comparison Project*, 2nd ed. Norwalk, CT: FASB, 1999.

Goeltz, Richard Karl. 1991. "International Accounting Harmonization: The Impossible (and Unnecessary?) Dream." *Accounting Horizons*, March 1991, pp. 85–86.

International Accounting Standards Committee. *Survey of the Use and Application of International Accounting Standards 1988.* London: IASC, 1988.

IOSCO. *Final Communique of the XXIXth Annual Conference of the International Organization of Securities Commissions.* Amman, May 17–20, 2004.

Nobes, Christopher W. "On the Myth of 'Anglo-Saxon' Financial Accounting: A Comment." *International Journal of Accounting* 38 (2003), pp. 95–104.

Street, Donna L.; Sidney J. Gray; and Stephanie M. Bryant. "Acceptance and Observance of International Accounting Standards: An Empirical Study of Companies Claiming to Comply with IASs," *International Journal of Accounting* 34, no. 1 (1999), pp. 11–48.

"The World After WorldCom," *Financial Times,* June 27, 2002.

Zeff, S. "Political Lobbying on Proposed Standards: A Challenge to the IASB." *Accounting Horizons* 16, no. 1 (2002), pp. 43–54.

Chapter **Four**

International Financial Reporting Standards

Learning Objectives

After reading this chapter, you should be able to

- Describe the requirements of International Financial Reporting Standards (IFRSs) on the recognition and measurement of assets.
- Explain the differences between IFRSs and U.S. generally accepted accounting principles (GAAP) on recognition and measurement issues.
- Describe the requirements of IFRSs related to the disclosure of financial information.
- Explain the difference between IFRSs and U.S. GAAP on disclosure issues.
- Use numerical examples to highlight the differences between IFRSs and U.S. GAAP.

INTRODUCTION

As noted in Chapter 3, International Financial Reporting Standards (IFRSs) have been adopted as generally accepted accounting principles (GAAP) for listed companies in a number of countries around the world and are accepted for cross-listing purposes by most major stock exchanges.[1] Increasingly, accountants are being called on to prepare and audit, and users are finding it necessary to read and analyze, IFRS-based financial statements. This chapter describes and demonstrates the requirements of selected IASB standards, particularly those relating to the recognition and measurement of assets, through numerical examples. IFRSs that deal exclusively with disclosure issues also are briefly summarized. The appendix to this chapter includes IFRSs related to the measurement and recognition of liabilities, revenues, financial instruments, and other issues.

The International Accounting Standards Committee (IASC) issued a total of 41 International Accounting Standards (IASs) during the period 1973–2001. Ten of these standards have been superseded or withdrawn. Most of the 31 remaining standards have been revised one or more times.[2] Since 2001, the IASB has issued

---

[1] The term *International Financial Reporting Standards (IFRSs)* describes the body of authoritative pronouncements issued or adopted by the IASB. IFRSs consist of International Accounting Standards issued by the IASC (and adopted by the IASB), International Financial Reporting Standards issued by the IASB, and interpretations developed by IFRIC or the former SIC.

[2] In December 2003, 13 IASs were revised as part of the IASB's *Improvements to International Accounting Standards* (London: IASB, 2003); and IAS 36, *Impairment of Assets*, and IAS 38, *Intangible Assets,* were revised in March 2004 in conjunction with the issuance of IFRS 3, *Business Combinations*.

six International Financial Reporting Standards (IFRSs). Exhibit 3.2 in Chapter 3 provides a list of IASs and IFRSs issued by the IASB as of March 2005.

In September 2002, the IASB and the U.S. Financial Accounting Standards Board (FASB) agreed to work together to reduce differences between IFRSs and U.S. GAAP. The goal of this so-called Norwalk Agreement is to make the two sets of existing standards compatible as soon as possible and to coordinate future projects to ensure that, once achieved, compatibility is maintained. In this chapter, in describing the guidance provided by IFRSs, we make comparisons with U.S. GAAP to indicate the differences and similarities between the two sets of standards.[3] In this way we can begin to appreciate the impact a choice between the two sets of standards has on financial statements.

TYPES OF DIFFERENCES BETWEEN IFRSs AND U.S. GAAP

The FASB has identified numerous differences between IFRSs and U.S. GAAP.[4] The types of differences that exist can be classified as follows:

- *Definition differences.* Differences in definitions exist even though concepts are similar. Definition differences can lead to recognition or measurement differences.
- *Recognition differences.* Differences in recognition criteria and/or guidance are related to (1) whether an item is recognized or not, (2) how it is recognized, and/or (3) when it is recognized (timing difference).
- *Measurement differences.* Differences in approach for determining the *amount* recognized result from either (1) a difference in the method required or (2) a difference in the detailed guidance for applying a similar method.
- *Alternatives.* One set of standards allows a choice between two or more alternative methods; the other set of standards requires one specific method to be used.
- *Lack of requirements or guidance.* IFRSs may not cover an issue addressed by U.S. GAAP, and vice versa.
- *Presentation differences.* Differences exist in the presentation of items in the financial statements.
- *Disclosure differences.* Differences in information presented in the notes to financial statements are related to (1) whether a disclosure is required or not, and (2) the manner in which disclosures are required to be made.

In many cases, IFRSs are more flexible than U.S. GAAP. Several IASs allow firms to choose between a "benchmark treatment" and an "allowed alternative treatment" in accounting for a particular item. Also, IFRSs generally have less bright-line guidance than U.S. GAAP; therefore, more judgment is required in applying IFRSs. IFRSs are said to constitute a principles-based accounting system (broad principles with limited detailed rules), whereas U.S. GAAP is a rules-based system.[5] However, in some cases, IFRSs are more detailed than U.S. GAAP.

---

[3] It is worth noting that both IFRSs and U.S. GAAP are moving targets, constantly changing. This chapter describes IFRSs and makes comparisons with U.S. GAAP as of March 2005.

[4] Financial Accounting Standards Board, *The IASC-U.S. Comparison Project*, 2nd ed. (Norwalk, CT: FASB, 1999).

[5] In response to several accounting scandals, including those at Enron and Worldcom, the Sarbanes-Oxley Act passed by the U.S. Congress in 2002 requires the FASB to investigate the desirability of U.S. GAAP shifting to a principles-based approach.

RECOGNITION AND MEASUREMENT STANDARDS

IAS 2, *Inventories*

IAS 2, *Inventories*, is an example of an International Accounting Standard that provides more extensive guidance than U.S. GAAP, especially with regard to inventories of service providers and disclosures related to inventories. The cost of inventory includes all costs of purchase, costs of conversion, and an allocation of production overhead (variable and fixed). IAS 2 specifically allows capitalization of interest for those inventories that "require a substantial period of time to bring them to a saleable condition."

IAS 2 does not allow as much choice with regard to cost flow assumption as does U.S. GAAP. First in, first out (FIFO) and weighted-average cost are acceptable treatments under IAS 2, but last in, first out (LIFO) is not. The standard cost method and retail method also are acceptable provided that they approximate cost as defined in IAS 2.

Lower of Cost or Net Realizable Value

IAS 2 requires inventory to be reported on the balance sheet at the lower of cost or net realizable value. *Net realizable value* is defined as "estimated selling price in the ordinary course of business less the estimated costs of completion and the estimated costs necessary to make the sale." This rule may be applied item by item or to pools of items. Write-downs to net realizable value must be reversed when the selling price increases.

U.S. GAAP requires inventory to be reported at the lower of cost or replacement cost with a ceiling (net realizable value) and a floor (net realizable value less normal profit margin). The two sets of standards will provide similar results only when replacement cost is greater than net realizable value. Under U.S. GAAP, write-downs to market may not be reversed if replacement costs should subsequently increase.

Example: Application of Lower of Cost or Net Realizable Value Rule

Assume that Distributor Company Inc. has the following inventory item on hand at December 31, Year 1:

Historical cost	$1,000.00
Replacement cost	800.00
Estimated selling price	880.00
Estimated costs to complete and sell	50.00
Net realizable value	830.00
Normal profit margin—15%	124.50
Net realizable value less normal profit margin	$ 705.50

IFRSs Net realizable value is $830, which is lower than historical cost. Inventory must be written down by $170 ($1,000 − $830).

The journal entry at December 31, Year 1, is:

Inventory loss	$170	
Inventory		$170
To record the write-down on inventory due to decline in net realizable value.		

U.S. GAAP Market is replacement cost of $800 (falls between $705.50 and $830), which is lower than historical cost. Inventory must be written down by $200 ($1,000 − $800).

The journal entry at December 31, Year 1, is:

Inventory loss	$200	
Inventory		$200
To record the write-down on inventory due to decline in market value.		

Assume that at the end of the first quarter in Year 2, replacement cost has increased to $900, the estimated selling price has increased to $980, and the estimated cost to complete and sell remains at $50. The item now has a net realizable value of $930.

IFRSs The net realizable value is $930, which is $100 greater than carrying value (and $70 less than historical cost). $100 of the write-down that was made at December 31, Year 1, is reversed through the following journal entry:

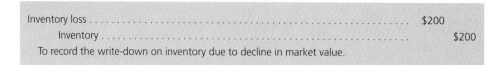

Inventory	$100	
Recovery of inventory loss (increase in income)		$100
To record a recovery of inventory loss taken in the previous period.		

U.S. GAAP The new cost for the item is $800, which is less than the current replacement cost of $900. No adjustments are necessary.

In effect, under IFRSs, the historical cost of $1,000 is used in applying the lower of cost or net realizable value rule over the entire period the inventory is held. In contrast, under U.S. GAAP, the inventory write-down at the end of Year 1 establishes a new cost used in subsequent periods in applying the lower of cost or market rule.

Over the period of time that inventory is held by a firm, the two sets of standards result in the same amount of expenses (cost of goods sold plus any inventory loss). However, the amount of expense recognized in any given accounting period can differ between the two rules as can the amount at which inventory is measured on the balance sheet.

IAS 16, *Property, Plant, and Equipment*

IAS 16, *Property, Plant, and Equipment,* provides guidance for the following aspects of accounting for fixed assets:

1. Recognition of initial costs of property, plant, and equipment.
2. Recognition of subsequent costs.
3. Measurement at initial recognition.
4. Measurement after initial recognition.
5. Depreciation.
6. Derecognition (retirements and disposals).

Impairment of assets, including property, plant, and equipment, is covered by IAS 36, *Impairment of Assets.* Accounting for impairments is discussed later in this chapter.

Recognition

Relying on the definition of an asset provided in the IASB's *Framework for the Preparation and Presentation of Financial Standards*, both initial costs and subsequent costs related to property, plant, and equipment should be recognized as an asset when (1) it is probable that future economic benefits will flow to the enterprise and (2) the cost can be measured reliably. Replacement of part of an asset should be capitalized if (1) and (2) are met, and the carrying amount of the replaced part should be derecognized (removed from the accounts).

Depreciation and Derecognition

Depreciation is based on estimated useful lives, taking residual value into account. The depreciation method should reflect the pattern in which the asset's future economic benefits are expected to be consumed. The carrying value of an item of property, plant, and equipment should be derecognized when it is retired or otherwise disposed of. Gains and loss on retirement and disposal of fixed assets should be recognized in income.

Measurement at Initial Recognition

Property, plant, and equipment should be initially measured at cost, which includes (1) purchase price, including import duties and taxes; (2) all costs directly attributable in bringing the asset to the location and condition necessary for it to perform as intended; and (3) an estimate of the costs of dismantling and removing the asset and restoring the site on which it is located.

An item of property, plant, and equipment acquired in exchange for a nonmonetary asset or combination of monetary and nonmonetary assets should be initially measured at fair value unless the exchange transaction lacks commercial substance. *Fair value* is defined as the "amount for which an asset could be exchanged between knowledgeable, willing parties in an arm's length transaction."[6] If the fair value of an asset acquired in a nonmonetary exchange cannot be determined, its cost is measured as the carrying value of the asset given up.

Measurement Subsequent to Initial Recognition

A substantive area of difference between IFRSs and U.S. GAAP relates to the measurement of property, plant, and equipment subsequent to initial recognition. IAS 16 allows two treatments for reporting fixed assets on balance sheets subsequent to their acquisition: the cost model (the benchmark treatment) and the revaluation model (the allowed alternative treatment).

Under the cost model, an item of property, plant, and equipment is carried on the balance sheet at cost less accumulated depreciation and any accumulated impairment losses. This is consistent with U.S. GAAP.

Under the revaluation model, an item of property, plant, and equipment is carried at a revalued amount, measured as fair value at the date of revaluation, less any subsequent accumulated depreciation and any accumulated impairment losses. If an enterprise chooses to follow this measurement model, revaluations must be made often enough that the carrying amount of assets does not differ materially from the assets' fair value. When revaluations are made, an entire class of property, plant, and equipment must be revalued. Revaluation increases are credited directly to equity as a revaluation surplus; revaluation decreases are recorded

---

[6] IAS 16, paragraph 6.

as an expense. The revaluation surplus may be transferred to retained earnings on disposal of the asset. Revalued assets may be presented either (1) at a gross amount less a separately reported accumulated depreciation (both revalued) or (2) at a net amount. Allowing firms the option to revalue fixed assets is one of the most substantial differences between IFRSs and U.S. GAAP. Guidelines for applying this option are presented in more detail in the following paragraphs.

Determination of Fair Value   The basis of revaluation is the *fair value* of the asset at the date of revaluation. The definition in IAS 16 indicates that fair value is the amount at which an asset could be exchanged between knowledgeable, willing parties in an arm's-length transaction. The fair value of land and buildings is usually determined through appraisals conducted by professionally qualified valuers. The fair value of plant and equipment is also usually determined through appraisal. In the case of a specialized asset that is not normally sold, fair value may need to be estimated using, for example, a depreciated replacement cost approach.

Frequency of Revaluation   IAS 16 requires that revalued amounts should not differ materially from fair values at the balance sheet date. The effect of this rule is that, once an enterprise has opted for the fair value model, it has an obligation to keep the valuations up to date. Although the IASB avoids mandating annual revaluations, these will be necessary in some circumstances in order to comply with the standard. In other cases, annual changes in fair value will be insignificant and revaluation may be necessary only every several years.

Selection of Assets to Be Revalued   IAS 16 requires that all assets of the same class be revalued at the same time. Selectivity *within* a class is not permitted, but selection *of* a class is. Following are examples of classes of assets described in the standard:

- Land
- Land and buildings
- Machinery
- Ships
- Aircraft
- Motor vehicles
- Furniture and fixtures
- Office equipment

Detailed disclosures are required for each class of property, plant, and equipment (whether revalued or not). Thus, if a company divides its assets into many classes to minimize the effect of the rule about revaluing a whole class of assets, it will incur the burden of being required to make additional disclosures for each of those classes.

Accumulated Depreciation   Two alternative treatments are described in IAS 16 for the treatment of accumulated depreciation when an item of property, plant, and equipment is revalued:

1. Restate the accumulated depreciation proportionately with the change in the gross carrying amount of the asset, so that the carrying amount of the asset after revaluation equals its revalued amount. The Standard comments that this method is often used where an asset is revalued by means of an index and is the appropriate method for those companies using current cost accounting.

2. Eliminate the accumulated depreciation against the gross carrying amount of the asset and restate the net amount to the revalued amount of the asset.

Example: Treatment of Accumulated Depreciation upon Revaluation

Assume that Kiely Company Inc. has buildings that cost $1,000,000, have accumulated depreciation of $600,000, and a carrying amount of $400,000 on December 31, Year 1. On that date, Kiely Company determines that the market value for these buildings is $750,000. Kiely Company wishes to carry buildings on the December 31, Year 1, balance sheet at a revalued amount. Under treatment 1, Kiely Company would restate both the buildings account and accumulated depreciation on buildings such that the ratio of net carrying amount to gross carrying amount is 40 percent ($400,000/$1,000,000) and the net carrying amount is $750,000. To accomplish this, the following journal entry would be made at December 31, Year 1:

Buildings	$875,000	
Accumulated depreciation—buildings		$525,000
Revaluation surplus		350,000
To revalue buildings and related accumulated depreciation		

	Original Cost		**Revaluation**		**Total**	**%**
Gross carrying amount	$1,000,000	+	$875,000	=	$1,875,000	100%
Accumulated depreciation	600,000	+	525,000	=	1,125,000	60
Net carrying amount	$ 400,000	+	350,000	=	$ 750,000	40%

Under treatment 2, accumulated depreciation of $600,000 is first eliminated against the buildings account and then the buildings account is increased by $350,000 to result in a net carrying amount of $750,000. The necessary journal entries are as follows:

Accumulated depreciation—buildings	$600,000	
Buildings		$600,000
To eliminate accumulated depreciation on buildings to be revalued.		
Buildings	$350,000	
Revaluation surplus		$350,000
To revalue buildings.		

As a result of making these two entries, the buildings account has a net carrying amount of $750,000 ($1,000,000 − 600,000 + 350,000). Under both treatments, both assets and equity are increased by a net amount of $350,000.

Treatment of Revaluation Surpluses and Deficits   On the first revaluation after initial recording, the treatment of increases and decreases in carrying amount as a result of revaluation is very straightforward:

- Increases are credited directly to a revaluation surplus in equity.
- Decreases are charged to the income statement as an expense.

At subsequent revaluations, the following rules apply:

- To the extent that there is a previous revaluation surplus with respect to an asset, a decrease first should be charged against it and any excess of deficit over that previous surplus should be expensed.
- To the extent that a previous revaluation resulted in a charge to expense, a subsequent upward revaluation first should be recognized as income to the extent of the previous expense and any excess should be credited to equity.

Example: Treatment of Revaluation Surplus

Assume that Kiely Company Inc. has elected to measure property, plant, and equipment at revalued amounts. Costs and fair values for Kiely Company's three classes of property, plant, and equipment at December 31, Year 1 and Year 2, are as follows:

	Land	Buildings	Machinery
Cost	$100,000	$500,000	$200,000
Fair value at 12/31/Y1	120,000	450,000	210,000
Fair value at 12/31/Y2	150,000	460,000	185,000

The following journal entries are made at December 31, Year 1, to adjust the carrying amount of the three classes of property, plant, and equipment to fair value:

Land	$20,000	
Revaluation surplus—land		$20,000
Loss on revaluation—buildings (expense)	$50,000	
Buildings		$50,000
Machinery	$10,000	
Revaluation surplus—machinery		$10,000

At December 31, Year 2, the following journal entries are made:

Land	$30,000	
Revaluation surplus—land		$30,000
Buildings	$10,000	
Recovery of loss on revaluation—buildings (income)		$10,000
Revaluation surplus—machinery	$10,000	
Loss on revaluation—machinery (expense)	15,000	
Machinery		$25,000

IAS 16 indicates that the revaluation surplus in equity may be transferred to retained earnings when the surplus is realized. The surplus may be considered to be realized either through use of the asset or upon its sale or disposal. Accordingly,

- The revaluation surplus in equity may be transferred to retained earnings as a lump sum at the time the asset is sold or scrapped, or
- Each period, an amount equal to the difference between depreciation on the revalued amount and depreciation on the historical cost of the asset may be transferred to retained earnings.

A third possibility apparently allowed by IAS 16 would be to do nothing with the revaluation surplus. However, this would result in revaluation surpluses being reported in equity related to assets no longer owned by the firm.

With shares traded on the New York Stock Exchange, China Eastern Airlines Corporation (CEA) is required to reconcile IFRS-based income and shareholders' equity to a U.S. GAAP basis. Exhibit 4.1 presents CEA's reconciliation to U.S. GAAP, along with the note describing significant differences between IFRSs and U.S. GAAP with respect to revaluation of property, plant, and equipment. In 2003, CEA's reversal of the depreciation taken on revalued property, plant, and equipment caused U.S. GAAP income to be $7.72 million larger than IFRS income. This amount represents 6.7 percent of IFRS income.

IAS 40, *Investment Property*

IAS 40, *Investment Property,* prescribes the accounting treatment for investment property, that is, land and/or buildings held to earn rentals, capital appreciation, or both. The principles related to accounting for plant, property, and equipment generally apply to investment property, including the option to use either a cost model or a fair value model in measuring investment property subsequent to original acquisition. The fair value model for investment property differs from the revaluation method for property, plant, and equipment in that changes in fair value are recognized as gains or loss in current income and not as a revaluation surplus.

IAS 38, *Intangible Assets*

IAS 38, *Intangible Assets,* provides accounting rules for purchased intangible assets, intangible assets acquired in a business combination, and internally generated intangible assets. (Goodwill is covered by IFRS 3, *Business Combinations.*)

IAS 38 defines an intangible asset as an *identifiable,* nonmonetary asset without physical substance held for use in the production of goods or services, for rental to others, or for administrative purposes. As an asset, it is a resource *controlled* by the enterprise as a result of past events from which *future economic benefits are expected* to arise. If a potential intangible asset does not meet this definition (i.e., it is identifiable, controlled, and future benefits are probable) or cannot be measured reliably, it should be expensed immediately, unless it is obtained in a business combination, in which case it should be included in goodwill.

Purchased Intangibles

Purchased intangibles are initially measured at cost, and their useful life is assessed as finite or indefinite. The cost of intangible assets with a finite useful life is amortized on a systematic basis over the useful life. The residual value is assumed to be zero unless (1) a third party has agreed to purchase the asset at the end of its useful life or (2) there is an active market for the asset from which a residual value can be estimated.

EXHIBIT 4.1

CHINA EASTERN AIRLINES CORPORATION LIMITED
Form 20-F
2003
Revaluation of Property, Plant, and Equipment

Notes to the Consolidated Financial Statements

Excerpt from Note 40. Significant Differences between IFRS and U.S. GAAP

Differences between IFRS and U.S. GAAP which have significant effects on the consolidated profits/(loss) attributable to shareholders and consolidated owners' equity of the Group are summarized as follows:

Consolidated profit/(loss) attributable to shareholders

(Amounts in thousands except per share data)

	Note	2001 RMB	2002 RMB	2003 RMB	2003 US$ (note 2a)
				Year Ended December 31	
As stated under IFRS		541,713	83,369	(949,816)	(114,758)
U.S. GAAP adjustments:					
Reversal of difference in depreciation charges arising from revaluation of fixed assets	(a)	94,140	20,370	63,895	7,720
Reversal of revaluation deficit of fixed assets	(a)	—	171,753	—	—
Gain/(loss) on disposal of aircraft and related assets	(b)	5,791	(26,046)	(10,083)	(1,218)
Others	(c)	(11,295)	23,767	6,860	829
Deferred tax effect on U.S. GAAP adjustments	(d)	(155,877)	(28,477)	(9,101)	(1,100)
As stated under U.S. GAAP		474,472	247,736	(892,245)	(108,527)
Basic and fully diluted earnings/(loss) per share under U.S. GAAP		RMB0.097	RMB0.051	(RMB0.185)	(US$0.022)
Basic and fully diluted earnings/(loss) per American Depository Share ("ADS") under U.S. GAAP		RMB9.75	RMB5.09	(RMB18.46)	(US$2.23)

Consolidated owners' equity

(Amounts in thousands)

	Note	2002 RMB	2003 RMB	2003 US$ (note 2a)
			December 31	
As stated under IFRS		7,379,103	6,382,151	771,099
U.S. GAAP adjustments:				
Reversal of net revaluation surplus of fixed assets	(a)	(908,873)	(908,873)	(109,811)
Reversal of difference in depreciation charges and accumulated depreciation and loss on disposals arising from the revaluation of fixed assets	(a),(b)	637,423	691,235	83,516
Others	(c)	29,111	35,971	4,346
Deferred tax effect on U.S. GAAP adjustments	(d)	20,844	9,225	1,115
As stated under U.S. GAAP		7,157,608	6,209,709	750,264

Notes:

(a) Revaluation of fixed assets

Under IFRS, fixed assets of the Group are initially recorded at cost and are subsequently restated at revalued amounts less accumulated depreciation. Fixed assets of the Group were revalued as of June 30, 1996, as part of the restructuring of the Group for the purpose of listing. In addition, as of December 31, 2002, a revaluation of the Group's aircraft and engines was carried out and difference between the valuation and carrying amount was recognized. Under U.S. GAAP, the revaluation surplus or deficit and the related difference in depreciation are reversed since fixed assets are required to be stated at cost.

An intangible asset is deemed to have an indefinite life when there is no fore-seeable limit to the period over which it is expected to generate cash flows for the entity. If the useful life of an intangible asset is indefinite, no amortization should be taken until the life is determined to be definite.

The distinction made in IAS 38 between intangibles with a finite life and those with an indefinite life and corresponding accounting treatment is consistent with U.S. GAAP. A departure from U.S. GAAP is that IAS 38 allows intangible assets to be carried on the balance sheet at cost less accumulated amortization (*benchmark*) or fair value (*allowed alternative*). However, the fair value method is applicable only for intangibles with an active secondary market—which is rare.

Intangibles Acquired in a Business Combination

Under both IAS 38 and U.S. GAAP, intangibles such as patents, trademarks, and customer lists acquired in a business combination should be recognized as assets apart from goodwill at their fair value. The acquiring company should recognize these intangibles as assets even if they were not recognized as assets by the ac-quiree, so long as their fair value can be measured reliably. If fair value cannot be measured reliably, the intangible is not recognized as a separate asset but is in-cluded in goodwill.

A special situation arises with respect to development costs that have been incurred by the acquiree prior to the business combination. Under U.S. GAAP, in-process research and development costs acquired in a business combination must be written off immediately. In accordance with IAS 38, in-process develop-ment costs that meet certain criteria (described in more detail in the following subsections) must be capitalized as an intangible asset unless their fair value cannot be measured reliably, in which case they are included in goodwill. In either case, the development costs are capitalized under IFRSs but expensed under U.S. GAAP.

Internally Generated Intangibles

A major difference between IFRSs and U.S. GAAP lies in the treatment of inter-nally generated intangibles. To determine whether an internally generated intan-gible should be recognized as an asset, IAS 38 requires the expenditures giving rise to the potential intangible to be classified as either research or development expenditures. If the two cannot be distinguished, all expenditures should be classi-fied as research expenditures. Research expenditures must be expensed as incurred. Development expenditures, in contrast, must be recognized as an intangible asset when an enterprise can demonstrate all of the following:

1. The technical feasibility of completing the intangible asset so that it will be available for use or sale.
2. Its intention to complete the intangible asset and use or sell it.
3. Its ability to use or sell the intangible asset.
4. How the intangible asset will generate probable future economic benefits. Among other things, the enterprise should demonstrate the existence of a mar-ket for the output of the intangible asset or the existence of the intangible asset itself or, if it is to be used internally, the usefulness of the intangible asset.
5. The availability of adequate technical, financial, and other resources to complete the development and to use or sell the intangible asset.
6. Its ability to reliably measure the expenditure attributable to the intangible asset during its development.

Items that might qualify as assets under IAS 38 include the following:

- Computer software costs
- Patents, copyrights
- Motion picture films
- Mortgage servicing rights
- Fishing licenses
- Franchises
- Customer or supplier relationships
- Customer loyalty
- Market share
- Marketing rights
- Import quotas

IAS 38 specifically excludes the following from being recognized as internally generated intangible assets:

- Brands
- Mastheads
- Publishing titles
- Customer lists
- Advertising costs
- Training costs
- Business relocation costs

The recognition of development costs in general as an asset is a major difference from U.S. GAAP, which allows such recognition only with respect to computer software development costs. Internally generated goodwill may not be capitalized under IFRSs or U.S. GAAP.

Considerable management judgment is required in determining whether development costs should be capitalized. Managers must determine the point at which research ends and development begins. IAS 38 provides the following examples of activities generally included in research:

- Activities aimed at obtaining new knowledge.
- The search for application of research findings or other knowledge.
- The search for alternatives for materials, devices, products, processes, systems, or services.
- The formulation, design, evaluation, and selection of possible alternatives for new or improved materials, devices, products, processes, systems, or services.

Development activities typically include the following:

- The design, construction, and testing of preproduction prototypes and models.
- The design of tools, jigs, molds, and dies involving new technology.
- The design, construction, and operation of a pilot plant that is not of a scale economically feasible for commercial production.
- The design, construction, and testing of a chosen alternative for new or improved materials, devices, products, processes, systems, or services.

IAS 38 also provides a list of activities that are neither research nor development, including the following:

- Engineering follow-through in an early phase of commercial production.
- Quality control during commercial production, including routine testing of products.
- Troubleshooting in connection with breakdowns during commercial production.
- Routine efforts to refine, enrich, or otherwise improve upon the qualities of an existing product.
- Adaptation of an existing capability to a particular requirement or customer's need as part of a continuing commercial activity.
- Seasonal or other periodic design changes to existing products.
- Routine design of tools, jigs, molds, and dies.
- Activities, including design and construction engineering, related to the construction, relocation, rearrangement, or start-up of facilities or equipment other than facilities or equipment used solely for a particular research and development project.

Once the research and development phases of a project have been determined, management must assess whether all six criteria (listed earlier) for development cost capitalization have been met. Judgments of future circumstances often will be necessary and may be highly subjective. The ultimate decision can depend on the degree of optimism or pessimism of the persons making the judgment.

Development costs consist of (1) all costs directly attributable to development activities and (2) those costs that can be reasonably allocated to such activities, including:

- Personnel costs.
- Materials and services costs.
- Depreciation of plant, property, and equipment.
- Amortization of patents and licenses.
- Overhead costs, other than general administrative costs.

In other words, development costs are similar to costs incurred in producing inventory. Because the costs of some, but not all, development projects will be deferred as assets, it is necessary to accumulate costs for each development project as if it were a separate work in progress.

Borrowing costs could be included in research and development costs if the allowed alternative treatment (capitalization) in IAS 23, *Borrowing Costs*, is adopted. Under that treatment, borrowing costs should be included as part of the cost of development activities to the extent that the costs of those activities constitute a "qualifying asset." IAS 23 is discussed in more detail later in this chapter.

Deferred (capitalized) development costs are accounted for using the same rules as any other intangible. They must be amortized over a period not to exceed 20 years, using a method that best reflects the pattern in which the asset's economic benefits are consumed. Declining-balance, units-of-production, and straight-line methods are among the acceptable methods. Amortization begins when the intangible asset is available for sale or use.

Example: Accounting for Deferred Development Costs

Assume that Szabo Company Inc. incurred costs to develop a specific product for a customer in Year 1, amounting to $300,000. Of that amount, $250,000 was incurred up to the point at which the technical feasibility of the product could be demonstrated. In Year 2, Szabo Company incurred an additional $300,000 in costs in the development of the product. The product was available for sale on January 2, Year 3, with the first shipment to the customer occurring in mid-February, Year 3. Sales of the product are expected to continue for four years, at which time it is expected that a replacement product will need to be developed. The total number of units expected to be produced over the product's four-year economic life is 2,000,000. The number of units produced in Year 3 is 800,000. Residual value is zero.

In Year 1, $250,000 of development costs is expensed and $50,000 is recognized as an asset. The journal entry is as follows:

Development expense	$250,000	
Deferred development costs (intangible asset)	50,000	
Cash, payables, etc		$300,000
To record development expense and deferred development costs.		

In Year 2, $300,000 of development costs is recognized as an asset:

Deferred development costs (asset)	$300,000	
Cash, payables, etc.		$300,000
To record deferred development costs.		

Amortization of deferred development costs begins on January 2, Year 3, when the product becomes available for sale. Szabo Company determines that the units-of-production method best reflects the pattern in which the asset's economic benefits are consumed. Amortization expense for Year 3 is calculated as follows:

Carrying amount of deferred development cost		$350,000
Units produced in Year 3	800,000	
Total number of units to be produced over economic life	2,000,000	
% of total units produced in Year 3		40%
Amortization expense in Year 3		$140,000

The journal entry to record amortization of deferred development costs at December 31, Year 3, is as follows:

Amortization expense	$140,000	
Deferred development costs (asset)		$140,000
To record annual amortization expense.		

If Szabo Company were unable to estimate with reasonable certainty the number of units to be produced, it would be appropriate to amortize the deferred development costs on a straight-line basis over the four-year expected life. In that case, the journal entry to record amortization in Year 3 is as follows:

Amortization expense	$87,500	
Deferred development costs (asset)		$87,500
To record annual amortization expense.		

Impairment of Development Costs

IAS 36, *Impairment of Assets,* must be applied to determine whether deferred development costs have been impaired and recognition of an impairment loss is appropriate. We discuss IAS 36 in the next section of this chapter.

Finnish cellular telephone manufacturer Nokia Corporation is a European multinational that has used IFRSs for several years. Exhibit 4.2 presents the reconciliation of net income from IFRSs to U.S. GAAP provided by Nokia in its Form 20-F filed with the U.S. Securities and Exchange Commission (SEC), and the note describing the U.S. GAAP adjustment related to development costs. Adjusting for the capitalization of development costs under IFRSs that would not be allowed under U.S. GAAP resulted in U.S. GAAP net income being €66 million less than IFRS income in 2002. However, in 2003 and 2004, U.S. GAAP net income was €322 million and €42 million greater than IFRS income, respectively. The larger income under U.S. GAAP in these years most likely is attributable to the amount of amortization expense related to deferred development costs under IFRSs exceeding the development costs expensed immediately under U.S. GAAP.

IAS 36, *Impairment of Assets*

IAS 36, *Impairment of Assets,* requires impairment testing and recognition of impairment losses for property, plant, and equipment; intangible assets; goodwill; and investments in subsidiaries, associates, and joint ventures. It does not apply to inventory, construction in progress, deferred tax assets, employee benefit assets, or financial assets such as accounts and notes receivable. U.S. GAAP also requires impairment testing of assets. However, several important differences exist between the two sets of standards.

Definition of Impairment

Under IAS 36, an asset is impaired when its carrying amount (book value) exceeds its recoverable amount.

- *Recoverable amount* is the greater of *net selling price* and *value in use.*
- *Net selling price* is the price of an asset in an active market less disposal costs.
- *Value in use* is determined as the present value of future net cash flows expected to arise from continued use of the asset over its remaining useful life and upon disposal. In calculating value in use, projections of future cash flows should be based on approved budgets and should cover a maximum of five years (unless a longer period can be justified). The discount rate used to determine present value should reflect current market assessments of the time value of money and the risks specific to the asset under review.

EXHIBIT 4.2

NOKIA
Form 20-F
2004
Development Costs

Notes to the Consolidated Financial Statements

Excerpt from Note 37. Differences between International Financial Reporting Standards and U.S. Generally Accepted Accounting Principles

The Group's consolidated financial statements are prepared in accordance with International Financial Reporting Standards, which differ in certain respects from accounting principles generally accepted in the United States (U.S. GAAP). The principal differences between IFRS and U.S. GAAP are presented below together with explanations of certain adjustments that affect consolidated net income and total shareholders' equity as of and for the years ended December 31:

	2004 EURm	2003 EURm	2002 EURm
Reconciliation of net income:			
Net income reported under IFRS	3,207	3,592	3,381
U.S GAAP adjustments:			
Pension expense	—	(12)	(5)
Development costs	42	322	(66)
Provision for social security cost on stock options	(8)	(21)	(90)
Stock compensation expense	(21)	(9)	(35)
Cash flow hedges	89	9	6
Net investment in foreign companies	—	—	48
Amortization of identifiable intangible assets acquired	(11)	(22)	(22)
Impairment of identifiable intangible assets acquired	(47)	—	—
Amortization of goodwill	106	162	206
Impairment of goodwill	—	151	104
Deferred tax effect of U.S. GAAP adjustments	(14)	(75)	76
Net income under U.S. GAAP	3,343	4,097	3,603

Development costs

Development costs have been capitalized under IFRS after the product involved has reached a certain degree of technical feasibility. Capitalization ceases and depreciation begins when the product becomes available to customers. The depreciation period of these capitalized assets is between two and five years.

Under U.S. GAAP, software development costs would similarly be capitalized after the product has reached a certain degree of technical feasibility. However, certain non-software related development costs capitalized under IFRS would not be capitalizable under U.S. GAAP and therefore would have been expensed under U.S. GAAP.

Under U.S. GAAP, impairment exists when an asset's carrying amount exceeds the future cash flows (undiscounted) expected to arise from its continued use and disposal. Net selling price is not involved in the test, and future cash flows are not discounted to their present value. When value in use is the recoverable amount under IAS 36, an impairment is more likely to arise under IFRSs (discounted cash flows) than under U.S. GAAP (undiscounted cash flows).

Measurement of Impairment Loss

The measurement of impairment loss under IAS 36 is straightforward. It is the amount by which carrying value exceeds recoverable amount and it is recognized in income. In the case of property, plant, and equipment carried at a revalued amount, the impairment loss is first taken against revaluation surplus and then to income.

The comparison of carrying value and undiscounted future cash flows under U.S. GAAP is done to determine whether an asset is impaired. The impairment loss is then measured as the amount by which carrying value exceeds *fair value*. Fair value may be determined by reference to quoted market prices in active markets, estimates based on the values of similar assets, or estimates based on the results of valuation techniques. It is unlikely that fair value (U.S. GAAP) and recoverable amount (IFRSs) for an asset will be the same, resulting in differences in the amount of impairment loss recognized between the two sets of standards.

Example: Determination and Measurement of Impairment Loss

At December 31, Year 1, Toca Company has specialized equipment with the following characteristics:

Carrying value	$50,000
Selling price	40,000
Costs of disposal	1,000
Expected future cash flows	55,000
Present value of expected future cash flows	46,000

IFRSs In applying IAS 36, the asset's recoverable amount would be determined as follows:

Net selling price	$40,000 − 1,000 = $39,000	
Value in use	$46,000	
Recoverable amount (greater of the two)		$46,000

The determination and measurement of impairment loss would be:

Carrying value	$50,000
Recoverable amount	46,000
Impairment loss	$ 4,000

The following journal entry would be made to reflect the impairment of this asset:

Impairment loss	$4,000	
Equipment		$4,000
To recognize an impairment loss on equipment.		

U.S. GAAP Under U.S. GAAP, an impairment test would be carried out as follows:

Carrying value	$50,000
Expected future cash flows (undiscounted)	55,000

Because expected future cash flows exceed the asset's carrying value, no impairment is deemed to exist. The asset would be reported on the December 31, Year 1, balance sheet at $50,000.

Reversal of Impairment Losses

At each balance sheet date, a review should be undertaken to determine if impairment losses have reversed. (Indicators of impairment reversal are provided in IAS 36.) If subsequent to recognizing an impairment loss, the recoverable amount of an asset is determined to exceed its new carrying amount, the impairment loss should be reversed. However, the loss should be reversed only if there are changes in the estimates used to determine the original impairment loss or there is a change in the basis for determining the recoverable amount (from value in use to net selling price or vice versa). The carrying value of the asset is increased but not to exceed what it would have been if no impairment loss had been recognized. The reversal of an impairment loss should be recognized in income immediately. U.S. GAAP does not allow the reversal of a previously recognized impairment loss.

The shares of Lihir Gold Limited, a mining company based in Papua New Guinea, are traded on the NASDAQ national market in the United States. Lihir Gold uses IFRSs in preparing its financial statements. The reconciliation of net income to U.S. GAAP and procedures followed by Lihir Gold in complying with IAS 36's impairment rules are summarized in Exhibit 4.3. The company explains that impairment losses were recorded in 1999 and 2000 under IAS 36, but only the loss in 2000 would have been recognized under U.S. GAAP. In 2002 and 2003, previous impairment losses were determined to have been overstated and a reversal was recognized under IAS 36. The reversal of impairment loss would not have been acceptable under U.S. GAAP. As a result, IFRS income was reduced by $31.1 million in 2003 ($37.9 million in 2002) to reconcile to U.S. GAAP.

Impairment of Goodwill

The recoverable amount of goodwill must be determined annually regardless of whether impairment indicators are present. The recoverable amount is determined for the cash-generating unit (e.g., an acquired business) to which the goodwill belongs by first applying a bottom-up test. In this test, goodwill is allocated to the individual cash-generating unit under review, if possible, and impairment of that cash-generating unit is then determined by comparing (1) the carrying amount plus allocated goodwill and (2) the recoverable amount.

If goodwill cannot be allocated on a reasonable and consistent basis to the cash-generating unit under review, then both a bottom-up test and a top-down test should be applied. Under the top-down test, goodwill is allocated to the smallest group of cash-generating units to which it can be allocated on a reasonable and consistent basis, and impairment of the group of cash-generating units is then determined by comparing (1) the carrying amount of the group plus allocated goodwill and (2) the recoverable amount. U.S. GAAP requires only a bottom-up test and only for that goodwill associated with those assets that are being reviewed for impairment.

Example: Application of the Bottom-Up and Top-Down Tests for Goodwill

In Year 1, Lebron Company acquired another company that operates a chain of three restaurants, paying $300,000 for goodwill. By the end of Year 4, it is clear that the restaurants are not generating the profit and cash flows expected at the date of purchase. Therefore, Lebron Company is required to test for impairment.

Each restaurant is a cash-generating unit, but Lebron cannot allocate the goodwill on a reasonable and consistent basis to individual restaurants. Both a bottom-up test and a top-down test must be applied.

EXHIBIT 4.3

LIHIR GOLD LIMITED
Form 20-F
2003
Impairment of Assets

Notes to the Financial Statements

Excerpt from Note 30: Reconciliation to US GAAP

The basis of preparation of these financial statements is set out in Note 1. These accounting policies vary in certain important respects from the accounting principles generally accepted in the United States ("US GAAP"). The material differences affecting the profit and loss account and shareholders' equity between generally accepted accounting principles followed by the Company and those generally accepted in the US are summarised below.

	As Restated		
	2003 US$'000	2002 US$'000	2001 US$'000
Net income/(loss) in accordance with IAS GAAP	34,778	53,247	59,176
Adjusted as follows:			
Rehabilitation, restoration and environmental provision (i)	—	(374)	(420)
Mine properties—capitalized interest (ii)	—	—	—
Depreciation of mine properties (iii)	353	—	—
Impairment charge/(reversal) under IAS GAAP (v)	(31,061)	(37,893)	—
Deferred tax benefit under IAS GAAP (vi)	—	16,426	(16,426)
Deferred mining costs under IAS GAAP (vii)	(7,163)	(3,675)	—
Deferred mining costs under US GAAP (vii)	3,067	10,894	—
Net income/(loss) under US GAAP before cumulative effect of change in accounting policy	(26)	38,625	42,330
Cumulative effect of change in accounting policy (i)	400	—	—
Net income/(loss) under US GAAP after cumulative effect of change in accounting policy	374	38,625	42,330

v) Impairment: Under IAS 36, the impairment test for determining the recoverable amount of non-current assets is the higher of net selling price and value in use. At 31 December 1999 and again at 31 December 2000, the Company determined that an impairment charge was necessary as the discounted cash flows were less than the carrying value of the asset. Under US GAAP, the mine property assets were evaluated for impairment on an undiscounted basis and, because the sum of expected (undiscounted) future cash flows exceeded the asset's carrying amount, no impairment loss was recognised in 1999. During 2000 the undiscounted value of expected future cash flows were less than the asset's carrying values, which resulted in an impairment provision calculated on the same basis as for IFRS. In 2003, having revised critical assumptions, including life of mine, remaining reserves, a long term gold price assumption of $US340 (2002: $US305) and a pre-tax real discount rate of 7% (2002: 7%), the directors resolved to partially reverse previously recognised impairments, to the value of $US31.1 million (2002: $US37.9 million). US GAAP does not allow the reversal of impairment provisions previously recognised.

Bottom-Up Test   A bottom-up test is applied to each restaurant by estimating the recoverable amount of the assets of each restaurant and comparing with the carrying value of those assets. An impairment loss is recognized for the amount by which a restaurant's carrying value exceeds its recoverable amount. The loss is allocated to the impaired restaurant's assets on a pro rata basis according to the relative carrying value of the assets. The bottom-up test checks for impairment of the assets of the individual restaurants but provides no information about the impairment of the goodwill that was purchased in the acquisition of the chain of restaurants. Assume the following carrying values and recoverable amounts for the three restaurants acquired:

Cash-Generating Unit (restaurant location)	Carrying Value	Recoverable Amount	Impairment Loss
Anaheim	$1,000,000	$ 970,000	$30,000
Buena Park	1,000,000	1,050,000	0
Cerritos	1,000,000	1,020,000	0

An impairment loss of $30,000 is recognized, and the assets of the Anaheim restaurant are written down by the same amount. The carrying value of Anaheim's net assets is now $970,000.

Top-Down Test Lebron determines that the smallest cash-generating unit to which goodwill can be allocated is the entire chain of restaurants. Therefore, Lebron estimates the recoverable amount of the chain of restaurants and compares this with the carrying value of the assets of all the restaurants plus goodwill. Goodwill is considered to be impaired to the extent that the carrying value of the assets plus goodwill exceeds the restaurant chain's recoverable amount.

Cash-Generating Unit (restaurant location)	Carrying Value
Anaheim	$ 970,000
Buena Park	1,000,000
Cerritos	1,000,000
Subtotal	2,970,000
Goodwill	300,000
Total	$3,270,000

Lebron estimates the recoverable amount of the chain of restaurants to be $3,000,000. Lebron compares this amount with the total carrying value of $3,270,000 to determine that goodwill is impaired. A loss on the impairment of goodwill of $270,000 must be recognized.

IAS 23, *Borrowing Costs*

IAS 23, *Borrowing Costs*, provides two methods of accounting for borrowing costs:

1. *Benchmark treatment:* Expense all borrowing costs in the period incurred.
2. *Allowed alternative treatment*: Capitalize borrowing costs to the extent they are attributable to the acquisition, construction, or production of a qualifying asset; other borrowing costs are expensed in the period incurred.

Adoption of the benchmark treatment would not be acceptable under U.S. GAAP. The allowed alternative is similar to U.S. GAAP, but some definitional and implementation differences exist. The IASB requires those enterprises adopting a capitalization policy to apply that treatment consistently to all qualifying assets; picking and choosing between assets is not allowed.

IAS 23 defines *borrowing costs* as interest and other costs incurred by an enterprise in connection with the borrowing of funds. This definition is broader in scope than the definition of *interest cost* under U.S. GAAP. Borrowing costs in accordance with IAS 23 specifically include foreign exchange gains and losses on foreign currency borrowings to the extent they are regarded as an adjustment to interest costs.

An asset that qualifies for borrowing cost capitalization is one that necessarily takes a substantial period to get ready for its intended use or sale. Both IAS 23 and U.S. GAAP exclude inventories that are routinely manufactured or produced in large quantities on a repetitive basis over a short period. However, IAS 23 specifically includes inventories that require a substantial period to bring them to a marketable condition.

The amount to be capitalized is the amount of interest cost that could have been avoided if the expenditure on the qualifying asset had not been made. This is determined by multiplying the weighted-average accumulated expenditures by an appropriate interest rate. The appropriate interest rate is determined similarly under both IAS 23 and U.S. GAAP, being a weighted-average interest rate on borrowings outstanding. If a specific new borrowing can be associated with a qualifying asset, the actual interest rate is used to the extent the weighted-average accumulated expenditures are less than the amount of the specific borrowing.

The capitalization of borrowing costs begins when expenditures for the asset are incurred and ceases when substantially all the activities necessary to prepare the asset for sale or use are completed. Similar rules exist under U.S. GAAP.

IAS 17, *Leases*

IAS 17, *Leases,* distinguishes between finance (capitalized) leases and operating leases. IAS 17 provides guidance for classifying leases as finance or operating, and then describes the accounting procedures that should be used by lessees and lessors in accounting for each type of lease. IAS 17 also provides rules for sale-leaseback transactions. IAS 17 and U.S. GAAP are conceptually similar, but IAS 17 provides less specific guidance than U.S. GAAP.

Lease Classification

As a case in point, IAS 17 indicates that a lease should be classified and accounted for as a finance lease when it transfers substantially all the risks and rewards of ownership to the lessee. The standard then provides five situations that would normally lead to a lease being capitalized:

1. The lease transfers ownership of the asset to the lessee by the end of the lease term.
2. The lessee has the option to purchase the asset at a price less than fair market value.
3. The lease term is for the major part of the leased asset's economic life.
4. The present value of minimum lease payments at the inception of the lease is equal to substantially all the fair value of the leased asset.
5. The leased asset is of a specialized nature such that only the lessee can use it.

In contrast, U.S. GAAP stipulates that if any one of four very specific criteria is met, a lease must be capitalized. These criteria are similar to 1–4 above; in fact, the first two are exactly the same as (1) and (2). In the U.S. GAAP version of criterion (3), *major part* is specifically defined as 75 percent, and in criterion (4), *substantially all* is defined as 90 percent. Depending on the manner in which a financial statement preparer defines these terms, application of IAS 17 and U.S. GAAP might or might not lead to similar classification of leases.

Finance Leases

IAS 17 requires leases classified as finance leases to be recognized by the lessee as assets and liabilities at an amount equal to the fair value of the leased property or, if lower, at the present value of the future minimum lease payments. Lease payments are apportioned between interest expense and a reduction in the lease obligation using an effective interest method to amortize the lease obligation, and the leased asset is depreciated in a manner consistent with assets owned by the lessee.

The lessor should treat the same lease as a finance sale. The leased asset is replaced by the "net investment" in the lease, which is equal to the present value of future minimum lease payments (including any unguaranteed residual value). Any profit on the "sale" is recognized at the inception of the lease, and interest is recognized over the life of the lease using an effective interest method. Under U.S. GAAP, the net investment in the lease is determined simply as the lessor's cost or carrying amount for the leased asset.

Operating Leases

Any lease not classified as a finance lease is an operating lease. With an operating lease, lease payments are recognized by the lessee as an expense and by the lessor as income. The asset remains on the books of the lessor and is accounted for similarly to any other asset owned by the lessor.

Sale-Leaseback Transaction

A sale-leaseback transaction involves the sale of an asset by the initial owner of the asset and the leasing of the same asset back to the initial owner. If the lease is classified as a finance lease, IAS 17 requires the initial owner to defer any gain on the sale and amortize it to income over the lease term. U.S. GAAP rules are generally similar. If the fair value of property at time of sale-leaseback is less than undepreciated cost, IAS 17 allows recognition of a loss only if the loss is due to an impairment in the value of the asset sold. U.S. GAAP requires immediate recognition of the loss regardless of its source.

If the lease in a sale-leaseback transaction is classified as an operating lease, U.S. GAAP again requires the seller to amortize any gain over the lease term. IAS 17, in contrast, requires immediate recognition of the gain in income.

The difference in accounting treatment for gains on sale-leaseback transactions between IAS 17 and U.S. GAAP is described by Swisscom AG in Exhibit 4.4. In its reconciliation to U.S. GAAP, Swisscom made an adjustment for this accounting difference that resulted in an increase in income, as stated under U.S. GAAP, of 24 million Swiss francs.

Other Differences

Other differences between IAS 17 and U.S. GAAP with respect to finance leases include the following:

- The lessee's discount rate for determining present value of the future payments and interest expense. The implicit rate in the lease is generally used under IAS 17; the lessee's incremental borrowing rate is generally used under U.S. GAAP.
- Initial direct costs of the lessee in connection with negotiating the lease. These costs are capitalized as part of the cost of the asset under IAS 17; U.S. GAAP is silent with respect to this issue, but common practice is to defer and amortize the costs over the lease term.

EXHIBIT 4.4

SWISSCOM AG
Form 20-F
2003
Sale and Leaseback Transactions

Notes to Consolidated Financial Statements

Excerpt from Note 42. Differences between International Financial Reporting Standards and U.S. Generally Accepted Accounting Principles

The consolidated financial statements of Swisscom have been prepared in accordance with International Financial Reporting Standards (IFRS), which differ in certain respects from generally accepted accounting principles in the United States (U.S. GAAP). Application of U.S. GAAP would have affected the balance sheet as of December 31, 2001, 2002 and 2003 and net income for each of the years in the three-year period ended December 31, 2003 to the extent described below. A description of the material differences between IFRS and U.S. GAAP as they relate to Swisscom are discussed in further detail below

Reconciliation of net income from IFRS to U.S. GAAP

The following schedule illustrates the significant adjustments to reconcile net income in accordance with IFRS to the amounts determined in accordance with U.S. GAAP for each of the three years ended December 31.

CHF in millions	2001	2002	2003
Net income according to IFRS	**4,964**	**824**	**1,569**
U.S. GAAP adjustments:			
a) Capitalization of interest cost	(31)	(1)	(1)
b) Retirement benefits	32	(17)	(12)
c) Stock based compensation	(8)	9	6
d) Termination benefits	50	(20)	11
e) Write-down of long-lived assets	(30)	—	—
f) Capitalization of software	(124)	—	—
g) Impairment of investments	24	00	00
h) Cross-border tax leases	14	(13)	15
i) Debitel purchase accounting	(142)	(82)	(86)
j) Application of SAB 101	18	9	31
k) Site restoration	18	14	(13)
l) Telephone poles	10	4	—
m) Goodwill amortization	—	304	213
m) Goodwill impairment	1,130	(283)	280
n) Dilution gains	(72)	—	—
o) Derivative accounting	21	(21)	—
p) Sale and leaseback transaction	(286)	30	24
q) Income taxes	114	29	21
Net income before cumulative effect of accounting change according to U.S. GAAP	**5,702**	**786**	**2,058**
k) l) m) Cumulative effect of accounting change, net of tax	—	(1,649)	38
Net income (loss) according to U.S. GAAP	**5,702**	**(863)**	**2,096**

In March 2001 Swisscom entered into two master agreements for the sale of real estate. The first relates to the sale of 30 commercial and office properties for CHF 1,272 million to a consortium led by Credit Suisse Asset Management. The second concerns the sale of 166 commercial and office properties for CHF 1,313 million to PSP Real Estate AG and WTF Holding (Switzerland) Ltd. At the same time Swisscom entered into agreements to lease back part of the sold property space. The gain on the sale of the properties after transaction costs of CHF 105 million and including the reversal of environmental provisions (see Note 28), was CHF 807 million under IFRS.

Continued

EXHIBIT 4.4 (*Continued*)

A number of the leaseback agreements are accounted for as finance leases under IFRS and the gain on the sale of these properties of CHF 239 million is deferred and released to income over the individual lease terms. See Note 28. The accounting is similar under U.S. GAAP. The remaining gain of CHF 568 million represents the gain on the sale of buildings which were either sold outright or which under IFRS qualify as operating leases. Under IFRS, the gain on a leaseback accounted for as an operating lease is recognized immediately. Under U.S. GAAP, the gain is deferred and amortized over the lease term. If the lease back was minor, the gain was immediately recognized. In addition, certain of the agreements did not qualify as sale and leaseback accounting because of continuing involvement. These transactions are accounted for under the finance method and the sales proceeds would be reported as a financing obligation and the properties would remain on the balance sheet and would be depreciated as in the past. The lease payments would be split into an interest part and an amortization of the obligation.

Other Recognition and Measurement Standards

The appendix to this chapter summarizes several IFRSs pertaining to the recognition and measurement of liabilities, revenue, and financial instruments. IAS 21, *Foreign Currency Translation*, which provides guidance for dealing with foreign currency transactions and the translation of foreign currency financial statements, is covered in detail in Chapters 6 and 7. IFRSs related to business combinations (IFRS 3), consolidated financial statements (IAS 27), investments in associates (IAS 28), investments in joint ventures (IAS 31), and financial reporting in hyperinflationary economies (IAS 29) are covered in Chapter 8, Additional Financial Reporting Issues.

DISCLOSURE AND PRESENTATION STANDARDS

Several IFRSs deal primarily with disclosure and presentation issues. This section summarizes those standards. While briefly introduced here, IAS 14, *Segment Reporting*, is discussed in greater detail in Chapter 8.

IAS 7, *Cash Flow Statements*
- IAS 1 requires presentation of a cash flow statement in a set of IFRS-based financial statements. IAS 7 requires cash flows to be classified into operating, investing, and financial activities. Operating cash flows may be presented using either the direct or indirect methods. Investing and financing activities that do not give rise to cash flows should be disclosed separately. There are no substantive differences between IAS 7 and U.S. GAAP, although classification of some items might differ between the two sets of standards. For example, IAS 7 allows dividends paid to be classified as either an operating or a financing cash flow, whereas U.S. GAAP classifies dividends paid as a financing activity. Interest received and paid may be classified as an operating, investing, or financing activity under IAS 7, but must be classified as an operating activity under U.S. GAAP.

IAS 8, *Accounting Policies, Changes in Accounting Estimates, and Errors*
- IAS 8 provides guidance on selecting and changing accounting policies, and prescribes the accounting treatment and disclosures related to changes in accounting polices. It also prescribes accounting for changes in accounting estimates and corrections of errors.
- Changes in accounting estimates are handled prospectively.

- Material prior-period errors should be corrected retrospectively through the restatement of comparative amounts for the prior period(s) in which the error(s) occurred.

- A change in accounting policy is allowed only if required by an IASB standard or interpretation, or if the change results in reliable and more relevant information being provided in the financial statements. A change in accounting policy required by an IASB standard or interpretation should be accounted for in accordance with the transitional provisions in that standard or interpretation, if provided. Otherwise, changes in accounting policies should be handled retrospectively, by adjusting comparative amounts as if the new accounting policy had always been applied.

- The amount of a correction of a prior-period error and the cumulative effect of a change in accounting policy may not be included in income; comparative information for prior periods is presented as if the error had never occurred and the new accounting method had always been applied.

IAS 10, *Events After the Balance Sheet Date*

- Financial statements should be adjusted for certain events (adjusting events) that occur after the balance sheet date. Adjusting events are those that provide evidence of conditions that existed, but were unknown, at the balance sheet date. U.S. GAAP requirements are very similar.

IAS 14, *Segment Reporting*

- Disclosures are required for both business segments and geographical segments, one of which is identified as the primary reporting format and the other as secondary. Disclosures required for the primary segments include segment revenues, profit, assets, liabilities, capital expenditures, depreciation expense, and noncash expenses. Segment revenues, assets, and capital expenditures should be disclosed for the secondary type of segment. U.S. GAAP requires operating segments to be determined using a management approach that might result in a different segmentation from what is required by IAS 14. Whereas IAS 14 allows geographical segments to be an individual country or groups of countries, U.S. GAAP requires disclosures to be made by individual countries.[7]

IAS 24, *Related Party Disclosures*

- Transactions between related parties must be disclosed in the notes to financial statements. Parties are related if one party has the ability to control or exert significant influence over the other party. Related parties can include parent companies, subsidiaries, equity method associates, individual owners, and key management personnel. Similar rules exist in U.S. GAAP.

IAS 33, *Earnings per Share*

- Basic and diluted earnings per share must be reported on the face of the income statement. IAS 33 provides guidance for calculating earnings per share. U.S. GAAP provides more detailed guidance with respect to the calculation of diluted earnings per share. Application of this guidance would appear to be consistent with IAS 33.

---

[7] In January 2005, as part of its short-term convergence project with the FASB, the IASB announced its decision to adopt the management approach of FASB Statement 131, *Disclosures about Segments of an Enterprise and Related Information*. A revision of IAS 14 had not been completed at the time this book went to press.

IAS 34, *Interim Financial Reporting*

- IAS 34 does not mandate which companies should prepare interim statements, how frequently, or how soon after the end of an interim period. The standard defines the minimum content to be included in interim statements and identifies the accounting principles that should be applied. With certain exceptions, IAS 34 requires interim periods to be treated as discrete reporting periods. This differs from the position in U.S. GAAP, which treats interim periods as an integral part of the full year.

IFRS 5, *Non-current Assets Held for Sale and Discontinued Operations*

- Noncurrent assets held for sale must be reported separately on the balance sheet at the lower of (1) carrying value or (2) fair value less costs to sell. Assets held for sale are not depreciated. Similar rules exist in U.S. GAAP.

- A discontinued operation is a component of an entity that represents a major line of business or geographical area of operations, or is a subsidiary acquired exclusively with a view to resell, that either has been disposed of or has been classified as held for sale. The after-tax profit or loss and after-tax gain or loss on disposal (or from measurement to fair value less costs to sell) must be reported as a single amount on the face of the income statement. Detail of the revenues, expenses, gain or loss on disposal, and income taxes comprising this single amount must be disclosed in the notes or on the face of the income statement. If presented on the face of the income statement, it must be presented in a section identified as discontinued operations. The definition of the type of operation that can be classified as discontinued is somewhat narrower than under U.S. GAAP. In addition, U.S. GAAP requires both pretax and after-tax profit or loss to be reported on the income statement. Otherwise the two sets of standards are substantially similar.

Summary

1. Differences exist between IFRSs and U.S. GAAP with respect to recognition, measurement, presentation, disclosure, and choice among alternatives. In 2002, the IASB and FASB agreed to work together to converge their two sets of standards as soon as possible.

2. In many cases, IFRSs are more flexible than U.S. GAAP. Several IFRSs allow firms to choose between a benchmark treatment and an allowed alternative in accounting for a particular item. Also, IFRSs generally have less bright-line guidance than U.S. GAAP; therefore, more judgment is required in applying individual IFRSs. However, in some cases, IFRSs are more detailed than U.S. GAAP.

3. A small number of foreign firms required to file Form 20-F with the U.S. Securities and Exchange Commission use IFRSs as their primary set of accounting principles. The reconciliation of IFRS income and shareholders' equity to a U.S. GAAP basis included in Form 20-F provides considerable insight into the differences that exist in practice between IFRSs and U.S. GAAP.

4. Some of the more important recognition and measurement differences between IFRSs and U.S. GAAP relate to the following issues: inventory valuation; revaluation of property, plant, and equipment; capitalization of development costs; measurement of impairment losses; and expensing of all borrowing costs.

5. IAS 2 requires inventory to be reported on the balance sheet at the lower of cost and net realizable value. Write-downs to realizable value must be reversed

when the selling price increases. IAS 2 no longer allows the use of last in, first out (LIFO) in determining the cost of inventory.

6. IAS 16 allows property, plant, and equipment to be carried at cost less accumulated depreciation and impairment losses or at a revalued amount less any subsequent accumulated depreciation and impairment losses. Specific guidance is provided for those firms that choose the revaluation option.

7. IAS 38 requires development costs to be capitalized as an intangible asset when six specific criteria are met. Development costs can include personnel costs; materials and services; depreciation of property, plant, and equipment; amortization of patents and licenses; and overhead costs, other than general administrative costs. Deferred development costs are amortized over their useful life, not to exceed 20 years.

8. IAS 36 requires impairment testing of property, plant, and equipment; intangibles, including goodwill; and long-term investments. An asset is impaired when its carrying value exceeds its recoverable amount, which is the greater of net selling price and value in use. An impairment loss is the amount by which carrying value exceeds recoverable amount. If subsequent to recognizing an impairment loss, the recoverable amount of an asset exceeds its new carrying value, the impairment loss must be reversed.

9. IAS 23 provides two methods of accounting for borrowing costs: (1) Expense all borrowing costs in the period incurred, or (2) capitalize borrowing costs to the extent they are attributable to the acquisition of a qualifying asset, while expensing other borrowing costs immediately.

Appendix to Chapter **4**

Other Recognition and Measurement Standards

This appendix summarizes selected International Financial Reporting Standards (IFRSs) related to the recognition and measurement of liabilities (IAS 37, IAS 19, IFRS 2, and IAS 12); revenues (IAS 18); and financial instruments (IAS 32 and IAS 39).

IAS 37, *Provisions, Contingent Liabilities and Contingent Assets*

IAS 37, *Provisions, Contingent Liabilities and Contingent Assets,* attempts to provide a consistent framework and approach for accounting for liabilities (and assets) for which the timing, amount, or existence is uncertain. IAS 37 also contains specific rules related to onerous contracts and restructuring costs. By way of examples in appendixes, guidance is also provided with regard to issues such as environmental costs and nuclear decommissioning costs.

Contingent Liabilities and Provisions

IAS 37 distinguishes between a contingent liability, which is not recognized on the balance sheet, and a provision, which is. *A provision* is defined as a "liability of uncertain timing or amount." A provision should be recognized when

1. The entity has a *present* obligation as a result of a past event.
2. It is *probable* (more likely than not) that an outflow of resources embodying economic events will be required to settle the obligation.
3. A reliable estimate of the obligation can be made.

Contingent liabilities are defined as

- *Possible* obligations that arise from past events and whose existence will be confirmed by the occurrence or nonoccurrence of a future event, or
- A *present* obligation that is *not recognized* because (1) it is *not* probable that an outflow of resources will be required to settle the obligation or (2) the amount of the obligation *cannot* be measured with sufficient reliability.

Contingent liabilities are disclosed unless the possibility of an outflow of resources embodying the economic future benefits is *remote.*

The rules for recognition of a provision and disclosure of a contingent liability are generally similar to the U.S. GAAP rules related to contingent liabilities. Under U.S. GAAP, a contingent liability is neither recognized nor disclosed if the likelihood of an outflow of resources is remote; it is disclosed if such an outflow is possible but not probable; and it is recognized on the balance sheet when an outflow of resources is probable. The main difference is that U.S. GAAP requires accrual when it is probable that a loss has occurred, with no guidance as to how the word *probable* should be interpreted. In defining a provision, IAS 37 specifically defines *probable* as "more likely than not."

IAS 37 requires the recognition of a provision for the present obligation related to an "onerous contract," that is, a contract in which the unavoidable costs of meeting the obligation of the contract exceed the economic benefits expected to be received from it. However, recognition of a provision for expected future operating losses is not allowed.

IAS 37 provides guidance for measuring a provision as the best estimate of the expenditure required to settle the present obligation at the balance sheet date. The *best estimate* is the expected value when a range of estimates exist; the midpoint within a range if all estimates are equally likely. Provisions must be discounted to present value. Subsequent reduction of provisions can be made only for the expenditures for which the provision was established, and provisions should be reversed to the extent they are no longer required for particular expenditures. Under U.S. GAAP, contingent liabilities should be recognized as the low end of the range of possible amounts when a range of estimates exist; in some cases, the amount is not discounted to present value.

With respect to disclosure of contingent liabilities, IAS 37 allows an enterprise "in extremely rare cases" to omit disclosures that "can be expected to prejudice seriously the position of the enterprise in a dispute with other parties." No such exemption exists under U.S. GAAP.

Contingent Assets

A contingent asset is a probable asset that arises from past events and whose existence will be confirmed only by the occurrence or nonoccurrence of a future event. Contingent assets should not be recognized, but should be disclosed when the inflow of economic benefits is *probable.* If the realization of income from a contingency is determined to be *virtually certain*, then the related benefit is considered to meet the definition of an asset and recognition is appropriate. IAS 37 allows earlier recognition of a contingent asset (and related gain) than does U.S. GAAP, which generally requires the asset to be realized before it can be recognized.

Summary of IAS 37, *Recognition and Disclosure Guidelines*		
Contingent Element	**Likelihood of Realization**	**Accounting Treatment**
Contingent liability	Probable (more likely than not)	
	— Reliably measurable	Recognize provision
	— Not reliably measurable	Disclosure
	Not probable	Disclosure
	Remote	No disclosure
Contingent asset	Virtually certain	Recognize asset
	Probable	Disclosure
	Not probable	No disclosure

Appendix C to IAS 37 provides many illustrations of the application of the standard's recognition principles. Example 6 illustrates just how restrictive the concept of "present obligation" is intended to be in determining whether a provision should be recognized. In the example, there is a legislative requirement to install smoke filters by a particular date. The firm does not comply by the deadline. At the balance sheet date subsequent to the missed deadline, there is no present obligation related to the cost of installing smoke filters because no obligating event (i.e., installation) has occurred. Therefore, no provision would be recognized. However, if it is more likely than not (probable) that a penalty will be paid for missing the deadline, the best estimate of that penalty should be recognized as a provision because an obligating event (i.e., noncompliance) has occurred.

Restructuring

A difference exists between IAS 37 and U.S. GAAP with respect to when a provision should be recognized related to a restructuring plan. IAS 37 indicates that the provision should be recognized only when (1) a detailed formal plan exists, and (2) the plan's main features have been announced to those affected by it or implementation of the plan has begun.

U.S. GAAP does not allow recognition of a restructuring provision until a liability has been incurred. The existence of a restructuring plan and its announcement does not necessarily create a liability. Thus, the recognition of a restructuring provision may occur at a later date under U.S. GAAP.

IAS 19, *Employee Benefits*

IAS 19, *Employee Benefits,* is a comprehensive standard covering the following types of employee benefits:

1. Short-term employee benefits (such as compensated absences and bonuses).
2. Postemployment benefits (pensions, medical benefits, and other postemployment benefits).
3. Other long-term employee benefits.
4. Termination benefits (such as severance pay and early retirement benefits).

Pension Plans

Both IAS 19 and U.S. GAAP distinguish between defined contribution and defined benefit pension plans. The definition of a defined contribution plan differs between the two sets of standards and could lead to differences in classification (and therefore accounting) of pension plans. In addition to a potential difference in classification of pension plans, IAS 19 and U.S. GAAP differ on a number of issues with respect to the accounting for defined benefit plans. Each of these issues is discussed in the following paragraphs.

Past Service Cost

Past service cost arises when an employer improves the benefits to be paid employees in conjunction with a defined benefit plan. IAS 19 provides the following rules related to past service cost:

- Past service cost related to retirees and vested active employees is expensed immediately.
- Past service cost related to nonvested employees is recognized on a straight-line basis over the remaining vesting period.

In comparison, U.S. GAAP requires that the past service cost related to retirees be amortized over their remaining expected life, and the past service cost to active employees be amortized over their remaining service period.

Example: Recognition of Past Service Cost

Assume that on January 1, Year 7, Eagle Company Inc. amends its defined benefit pension plan to increase the amount of benefits to be paid. The benefits vest after five years of service. At the date of the plan amendment, the increase in the present value of the defined benefit obligation attributable to vested and nonvested employees is as follows:

Employees with more than five years of service at 1/1/Y7	$10,000
Employees with less than five years of service at 1/1/Y7	8,000
Total present value of additional benefits	$18,000

On average, the nonvested employees have two years of service at 1/1/Y7.

IFRSs Eagle Company recognizes the past service cost attributable to vested employees in Year 7 and the past service cost attributable to nonvested employees is amortized on a straight-line basis over Years 7, 8, and 9 (average three years until vesting). The total amount of past service cost recognized as a component of pension expense in Year 7 is computed as follows:

Past service cost (vested employees)	$10,000
Past service cost (nonvested employees) $8,000/3 years	2,667
Total	$12,667

The unrecognized past service cost of $5,333 is subtracted from the present value of the defined benefit obligation in determining the amount of asset or liability to be recognized on the balance sheet.

U.S. GAAP Under U.S. GAAP, because all of the employees affected by the plan amendment are active employees, the past service cost of $18,000 would be amortized to expense over the remaining service life of those employees. Assuming an average remaining service life of 12 years, $1,500 of past service cost would be recognized as a component of pension expense in Year 7.

Minimum Liability

U.S. GAAP requires recognition of at least the unfunded accumulated pension benefit obligation as a minimum liability on the balance sheet. There is no minimum liability recognition requirement in IAS 19.

Anticipation of Changes in Future Benefits

IAS 19 permits anticipation of future changes in the law in measuring the employer's pension benefit obligation. This is especially relevant in those situations where the level of pension benefits provided by the employer is linked to the level of retirement benefit that will be provided by national and local governments. U.S. GAAP does *not* permit anticipation of future changes in the law.

Amortization of Actuarial Gains and Losses

Both IAS 19 and U.S. GAAP allow a similar "corridor" approach to smooth the impact that actuarial gains and losses have on net income. IAS 19 also permits any systematic method of amortization that results in faster recognition of gains and losses (including immediate recognition) provided the same basis is applied to gains and losses and is applied consistently period to period. If a company chooses to recognize actuarial gains and losses in the period in which they occur, it may do so by including them either in net income or in a separate component of shareholders' equity. Bypassing income to accumulate actuarial gains and losses in equity is not acceptable under U.S. GAAP.

Curtailments and Settlements

A pension plan curtailment arises when there is a material reduction in the number of employees covered by a plan (such as when a plant is closed as part of a restructuring) or when the future service by current employees will no longer qualify for pension benefits or will qualify only for reduced benefits. A pension plan settlement involves lump-sum cash payments to employees in exchange for their rights to received defined pension benefits. Gains and losses usually arise in conjunction with plan curtailments and settlements. IAS 19 treats these gains and losses similarly; both are recognized in income in the period in which the entity is demonstrably committed and a curtailment or settlement has been announced. U.S. GAAP treats gains and losses on plan curtailments and settlements differently, with losses generally recognized earlier than gains. A curtailment gain cannot be recognized until the related employees terminate or the plan has been adopted.

Balance Sheet Recognition and Limitation

The amount recognized on the balance sheet related to a defined benefit plan can be either an asset or a liability and is equal to the present value of the defined benefit obligation plus (minus) unrecognized actuarial gains (losses) minus any unrecognized past service cost (related to nonvested benefits) minus the fair value of plan assets.

However, if the resulting amount is negative (net pension asset), the amount of asset to be reported on the balance sheet is limited to the sum of any unrecognized actuarial losses and past service cost, and the present values of any refunds available from the plan and any available reduction in future employer contributions to the plan.

Under U.S. GAAP, there is no limitation of the amount of pension asset to be recognized.

Example: Application of the Limitation on the Recognition of the Net Asset

Assume that the defined benefit plan of Fortsen Company Inc. has the following characteristics at December 31, Year 9:

Present value of defined benefit obligation	$10,000
Fair value of plan assets	(10,800)
Subtotal	(800)
Unrecognized actuarial losses	(50)
Unrecognized past service cost	(30)
Negative amount (possible asset)	$ (880)
Present value of available future refunds and reduction in future contributions	$ 525

The limit as to the amount of asset that may be recognized is computed as follows:

Unrecognized actuarial losses	$ 50
Unrecognized past service cost	30
Present value of available future refunds and reduction in future contributions	525
Limit	$605

Fortsen Company recognizes a prepaid pension cost (pension asset) of $605 on its 12/31/Y9 balance sheet and must disclose the fact that the limit reduced the carrying amount of the asset by $275. Under U.S. GAAP, Fortsen Company would recognize a pension asset in the amount of $880.

Exhibit A4.1 presents the note in Bayer AG's reconciliation from IFRSs to U.S. GAAP related to the accounting for pension plans. Differences between IAS 19 and U.S. GAAP resulted in adjustments related to the asset limitation included in IAS 19, the additional minimum liability of U.S. GAAP, the amortization of a transition obligation, and the accounting for curtailment in certain plans.

Medical Benefits

IAS 19 does not provide separate guidance for other postemployment benefits such as medical benefits. The procedures described above for pension plans is equally applicable for other forms of postemployment benefits provided to employees, such as medical benefits and life insurance contracts.

U.S. GAAP provides considerably more guidance than IAS 19 with regard to the assumptions to be used and the measurement of the employer's obligation for postemployment medical benefits. As allowed by the IASB's *Framework*, companies using IFRSs could refer to the guidance provided in U.S. GAAP (or other national standards) to identify an appropriate method for determining the amount of expense to recognize related to postemployment benefits other than pensions.

Termination Benefits

IAS 19 requires termination benefits to be recognized when an enterprise is *demonstrably committed* to either (1) terminating the employment of an employee or group of employees, or (2) providing termination benefits as a result of an offer made by the enterprise to encourage voluntary termination. A demonstrable commitment arises when a detailed formal plan exists from which the enterprise cannot withdraw.

EXHIBIT A4.1

BAYER AG
Form 20-F
2004
Pension Expense

Notes to the Consolidated Financial Statements of the Bayer Group

Excerpt from Note [44] U.S. GAAP Information

c. Pension Provisions

Under IFRS, pension costs and similar obligations are accounted for in accordance with IAS 19, "Employee Benefits". For purposes of U.S. GAAP, pension costs for defined benefit plans are accounted for in accordance with SFAS No. 87 "Employers' Accounting for Pensions". Using an accommodation of the United States Securities and Exchange Commission ("SEC") for foreign private issuers, the Group adopted SFAS No. 87 on January 1, 1994, for its non-U.S. plans, which was also the date of adoption for IAS 19 for those plans. It was not feasible to apply SFAS No. 87 on the effective date specified in the standard. IAS 19 as applied by the Group from 1994 was substantially similar to the methodology required under SFAS No. 87. The adjustment between IFRS and U.S. GAAP comprises required SFAS 87 amortization of the unrecognized transition obligation over the remaining average service lives of employees from 1994 of €238 million, the recognition of an asset limitation under IAS 19, which is not allowed under SFAS No. 87, and the recognition of an additional minimum liability under SFAS No. 87, which is not required under IAS 19. As of December 31, 2003 the unrecognized transition obligation from 1994 was fully amortized.

Following is a reconciliation of the balance sheet and income statement amounts recognized for IFRS and U.S. GAAP for both pension and post-retirement benefit plans:

	2002	2003	2004
	(€ million)		
Pension benefits:			
Liability recognized for IFRS	(3,741)	(3,812)	(3,827)
Asset limitation under IAS 19	1,187	1,193	1,196
Additional minimum liability under SFAS No. 87	(480)	(637)	(1,024)
Difference in unrecognized transition obligation	23	—	—
Difference in pension curtailment	—	—	(44)
Liability recognized for U.S. GAAP	(3,011)	(3,256)	(3,699)
Net periodic benefit cost recognized for IFRS	521	747	581
Amortization of transition obligation	24	23	—
Difference pension curtailment	—	—	48
Net periodic benefit recognized for U.S. GAAP	545	770	629

U.S. GAAP distinguishes between three different types of termination benefits and provides different timing recognition criteria for each:

1. Special termination benefits should be recognized when an employee accepts the offer.
2. Contractual termination benefits should be recognized when it is probable that employees will be entitled to benefits.
3. Termination benefits offered in conjunction with a restructuring should be recognized when the plan is approved by management.

A difference also exists with respect to the amount of termination benefit to recognize.

IAS 19 indicates that measurement should be based on the number of employees *expected to accept* the offer, discounted to present value if benefits fall due more than 12 months after the balance sheet date. Under U.S. GAAP, measurement is based on the number of employees that *actually accept* the offer and discounting is not required.

IFRS 2, *Share-based Payment*

IFRS 2, *Share-based Payment*, sets out measurement principles and specific requirements for three types of share-based payment transactions:

1. Equity-settled share-based payment transactions, in which the entity receives goods or services as consideration for equity instruments of the entity (including stock options granted to employees).
2. Cash-settled share-based payment transactions, in which the entity acquires goods or services by incurring liabilities to the supplier of those goods or services for amounts that are based on the price (or value) of the entity's shares or other equity instruments of the entity (e.g., share appreciation rights).
3. Transactions in which the entity receives or acquires goods or services and the terms of the arrangement provide either the entity or the supplier of those goods or services with a choice of whether the entity settles the transaction in cash or by issuing equity instruments.

IFRS 2 requires an entity to recognize all share-based payment transactions in its financial statements; there are no exceptions.

Stock Options Granted to Employees

IFRS 2 requires the fair value method to be used in accounting for stock options granted to employees. Under this method, total compensation expense is computed as the fair value of the options expected to vest on the date the options are granted. Total compensation expense is recognized (allocated) over the service period for which the employee is being compensated. The fair value of the options should be based on market prices, if available. In the absence of market prices, fair value is estimated, using a valuation technique (e.g., a Black-Scholes model).

The IASB and the FASB worked closely in developing new standards related to accounting for share-based payments. Concurrent with the IASB's issuance of IFRS 2, the FASB published an exposure draft in March 2004, and subsequently issued a final standard on this topic in December 2004. Although minor differences exist between the two standards, IFRS 2 and U.S. GAAP are substantially similar.

IAS 12, *Income Taxes*

IAS 12, *Income Taxes,* and U.S. GAAP take a similar approach to accounting for income taxes. Both standards adopt an asset-and-liability approach that recognizes deferred tax assets and liabilities for temporary differences and for operating loss and tax credit carryforwards. However, differences do exist. The accounting for income taxes is a very complex topic, and only some of the major differences are discussed here.

Tax Laws and Rates

IAS 12 requires that current and deferred taxes be measured on the basis of tax laws and rates that have been enacted or substantively enacted by the balance sheet date, but it provides no guidance for determining when a law has been substantively enacted. U.S. GAAP requires measurement of income taxes using actually enacted tax laws and rates. IAS 12 provides no guidance on which tax rate to use in jurisdictions where different tax rates exist for distributed and undistributed income, such as Germany and Greece, or how to deal with alternative tax systems, such as the alternative minimum tax in the United States. Each of these issues is covered by U.S. GAAP.

Recognition of Deferred Tax Asset

IAS 12 requires recognition of a deferred tax asset if future realization of a tax benefit is probable, where *probable* is undefined. Under U.S. GAAP, a deferred tax asset must be recognized if its realization is more likely than not. If the word *probable* can be considered to imply a probability of occurrence that is greater than the phrase *more likely than not,* then IAS 12 provides a more stringent threshold for the recognition of a deferred tax asset.[1]

Exceptions in Recognizing Deferred Taxes

Both IAS 12 and U.S. GAAP contain exceptions to the general rule that deferred taxes are recognized for temporary differences. In some cases, IAS 12 requires recognition of a difference that U.S. GAAP prohibits; in other cases, U.S. GAAP requires recognition of a difference not allowed by IAS 12.

Application of IFRSs

Application of IFRSs can create temporary differences unknown under U.S. GAAP. For example, the revaluation of property, plant, and equipment for financial statement purposes (in accordance with IAS 16's allowed alternative treatment) with no equivalent adjustment for tax purposes will result in a temporary difference that cannot exist under U.S. GAAP. Other differences between IFRSs and U.S. GAAP can create different amounts of temporary differences. For example, because of different definitions of impairment, differences in the amount of an impairment loss can exist under the two sets of standards. With no equivalent tax adjustment, the amount of temporary difference related to the impairment loss will be different in a set of IFRS-based financial statements form the amount recognized under U.S. GAAP.

IAS 18, *Revenue*

IAS 18, *Revenue,* is a single standard that covers most revenues, in particular revenues from the sale of goods; the rendering of services; and interest, royalties, and dividends. There is no similar single standard in U.S. GAAP. U.S. rules related to revenue recognition are found in various authoritative pronouncements; making a direct comparison between IAS 18 and U.S. GAAP difficult.

General Measurement Principle

IAS 18 requires revenue to be measured at the fair value of the consideration received or receivable.

Identification of the Transaction Generating Revenue

If a transaction consists of distinct elements, each element should be accounted for separately. For example, if a sale of computer software is accompanied by an

---

[1]Research shows that, on average, accountants associate a probability of about 75–80 percent with the term *probable.* See, for example, J. L. Reimers, "Additional Evidence on the Need for Disclosure Reform," *Accounting Horizons,* March 1992, pp. 36–41.

agreement to provide maintenance (postcontract support) for a period of time, the proceeds received by the seller should be allocated between the amount applicable to the software (recognized at the time of sale) and the amount identifiable with the postcontract support (recognized over the period of support). Conversely, there may be situations where it is necessary to treat two or more separate transactions as one economic transaction to properly reflect their true economic substance.

Sale of Goods

Five criteria must be met in order for revenue from the sale of goods to be recognized:

- The significant risks and rewards of ownership of the goods has been transferred to the buyer.
- Neither continuing managerial involvement normally associated with ownership nor effective control of the goods sold is retained.
- The amount of revenue can be measured reliably.
- It is probable that the economic benefits associated with the sale will flow to the seller.
- The costs incurred or to be incurred with respect to the sale of goods can be measured reliably.

Evaluating whether significant risks and rewards of ownership have been transferred to the buyer can sometimes be difficult and require the exercise of judgment. IAS 18 provides a list of examples in which significant risks and rewards might be retained by the seller. These include the following:

- The seller assumes an obligation for unsatisfactory performance not covered by normal warranty provisions.
- Receipt of revenue by the seller is contingent on the buyer's generating revenue through its sale of the goods.
- Goods sold are subject to installation, installation is a significant part of the contract, and installation has not yet been completed.
- The sales contract gives the buyer the right to rescind the purchase, and the probability of return is uncertain.

Similarly, in determining whether the seller has relinquished managerial involvement or control over the goods sold, a careful evaluation is required for some types of sales.

Rendering of Services

When the outcome of a service transaction can be estimated reliably and it is probable that economic benefits of the transaction will flow to the enterprise, revenue should be recognized in proportion to some measure of the extent of services rendered (that is, on a percentage-of-completion basis). The outcome of a transaction can be estimated reliably when (1) the amount of revenue, (2) the costs incurred and the costs to be incurred, (3) and the stage of completion can all be measured reliably. Guidelines provided in IAS 11, *Construction Contracts,* related to the application of the percentage-of-completion method are generally applicable to the recognition of revenue for service transactions.

When the outcome of a transaction cannot be estimated reliably, revenue should be recognized only to the extent that expenses incurred are probable of recovery. If such underlying expenses are not probable of recovery, the expense should be recognized, but not the revenue.

Interest, Royalties, and Dividends

If it is *probable* that the economic benefits of interest, royalties, and dividends will flow to the enterprise and the amounts can be measured *reliably*, revenue should be recognized on the following bases:

- Interest income is recognized on an effective yield basis.
- Royalties are recognized on an accrual basis in accordance with the terms of the relevant agreement.
- Dividends are recognized when the shareholders' right to receive payment is established.

Exchanges of Goods or Services

If the exchanged goods are similar in nature and in value, no gain or loss is recognized. If the exchanged goods or services are dissimilar in nature, revenue is recognized at the fair value of the goods or services received, adjusted for the amount of any cash paid or received. When the fair value of the goods or services received cannot be measured reliably, revenue should be measured as the fair value of the goods or services given up, adjusted for the amount of any cash paid or received.

Appendix

The appendix to IAS 18 provides examples illustrating the application of the standard to most major types of revenues. Most of the examples are self-explanatory. The examples accompany IAS 18 but technically are not part of the standard.

IAS 32 and IAS 39, *Financial Instruments*

IAS 32, *Financial Instruments: Disclosure and Presentation,* and IAS 39, *Financial Instruments: Recognition and Measurement,* were developed on the basis of U.S. GAAP. Both sets of standards

- Require financial assets and liabilities to be measured and reported at fair value.
- Allow the use of hedge accounting when certain criteria are met. (Hedge accounting is discussed in Chapter 6 of this book.)

However, numerous differences exist between IAS 32 and IAS 39 and U.S. GAAP. For example, IAS 32 requires a convertible debt instrument to be split into its liability and equity components and classified accordingly, whereas U.S. GAAP treats convertible debt as a liability. The discussion of other differences, especially with respect to derivative financial instruments, is beyond the scope of this book.

It should be noted that the adoption of IAS 39 met with considerable resistance in the European Union. The European Commission ultimately decided in 2004 to endorse IAS 39, but with exceptions. The commission modified the version of IAS 39 to be applied by publicly traded companies in the EU with respect to certain provisions on the use of a full fair value option and on hedge accounting. According to the European Commission, these "carve-outs" are temporary, in effect only until the IASB modifies IAS 39 in line with European requests.[2]

[2]Ernst & Young, "The Evolution of *IAS 39* in Europe," *Eye on IFRS Newsletter,* November 2004, pp. 1–4.

Questions

1. What are two issues related to the recognition and measurement of assets for which IFRSs provide both a benchmark treatment and an allowed alternative treatment?

2. How does application of the lower of cost or market rule for inventories differ between IAS 2 and U.S. GAAP?

3. What is the alternative treatment allowed by IAS 16 for measuring property, plant, and equipment at dates subsequent to original acquisition?

4. How is an impairment loss on property, plant, and equipment determined and measured under IAS 36? How does this differ from U.S. GAAP?

5. What is the IAS 23 benchmark treatment with respect to borrowing costs? How does this treatment differ from U.S. GAAP?

6. How do the criteria for determining whether a lease qualifies as a finance (capitalized) lease differ between IAS 17 and U.S. GAAP?

7. How do the criteria for the recognition of contingencies differ between IAS 37 and U.S. GAAP?

8. What are the rules under IAS 19 for dealing with the past service cost that arises when an employer improves the benefits to be paid employees in conjunction with a defined benefit plan? How do these rules differ from U.S. GAAP?

Exercises and Problems

1. To determine the amount at which inventory should be reported on the December 31, Year 1, balance sheet, Monroe Company compiles the following information for its inventory of Product Z on hand at that date:

Historical cost	$20,000
Replacement cost	$14,000
Estimated selling price	$17,000
Estimated costs to complete and sell	$2,000
Normal profit margin as % of selling price	20%

The entire inventory of Product Z that was on hand at December 31, Year 1, was completed in Year 2 at a cost of $1,800 and sold at a price of $17,150.

Required:

a. Use the information provided in this chapter related to the accounting for inventories to determine the impact on Year 1 and Year 2 income related to Product Z (1) under IFRSs and (2) under U.S. GAAP.

b. Summarize the difference in income, total assets, and total stockholders' equity using the two different sets of accounting rules over the two-year period.

2. In Year 1, in a project to develop Product X, Lincoln Company incurred research and development costs totaling $10 million. Lincoln is able to clearly distinguish the research phase from the development phase of the project. Research-phase costs are $6 million, and development-phase costs are $4 million. All of the IAS 38 criteria have been met for recognition of the development costs as an asset. Product X was brought to market in Year 2 and is expected to be marketable for five years. Total sales of Product X are estimated at over $100 million.

Required:

a. Use the information provided in this chapter related to the accounting for internally generated intangible assets to determine the impact on Year 1 and

Year 2 income related to research and development costs (1) under IFRSs and (2) under U.S. GAAP.

b. Summarize the difference in income, total assets, and total stockholders' equity related to Product X over its five-year life under the two different sets of accounting rules.

3. Jefferson Company acquired equipment on January 2, Year 1, at a cost of $10 million. The asset has a five-year life, no residual value, and is depreciated on a straight-line basis. On January 2, Year 3, Jefferson Company determines the fair value of the asset (net of any accumulated depreciation) to be $12 million.

Required:

a. Determine the impact the equipment has on Jefferson Company's income in Years 1–5 (1) using IFRSs, assuming that IAS 16's allowed alternative treatment for measurement subsequent to initial recognition is followed, and (2) using U.S. GAAP.

b. Summarize the difference in income, total assets, and total stockholders' equity using the two different sets of accounting rules over the period Year 1–Year 5.

4. Madison Company acquired a depreciable asset at the beginning of Year 1 at a cost of $12 million. At December 31, Year 1, Madison gathered the following information related to this asset:

Carrying amount (net of accumulated depreciation)	$10 million
Fair value of the asset (net selling price)	$7.5 million
Sum of future cash flows from use of the asset	$10 million
Present value of future cash flows from use of the asset	$8 million
Remaining useful life of the asset	5 years

Required:

a. Use the information provided in this chapter related to the impairment of assets to determine the impact on Year 2 and Year 3 income from the depreciation and possible impairment of this equipment (1) under IFRSs and (2) under U.S. GAAP.

b. Summarize the difference in income, total assets, and total stockholders' equity for the period Year 1–Year 6 under the two different sets of accounting rules.

Note: If the asset is determined to be impaired, there would be no adjustment to Year 1 depreciation expense of $2 million.

5. Garfield Company begins construction of a building for its own use on January 2, Year 1. Construction is complete and Garfield moves in to the building on December 30, Year 1. The total cost of construction, which is incurred evenly throughout Year 1, is $10 million. (Weighted-average accumulated expenditures during Year 1 were $5 million.) Garfield obtains a loan of $8 million at an interest rate of 10 percent on January 2, Year 1. Garfield Company has no other borrowings. The building is estimated to have a useful life of 20 years and a residual value of $2 million.

Required:

a. Use the information provided in this chapter related to borrowing costs to determine the impact on Year 1 and Year 2 income (1) under IFRSs, assuming IAS 23's benchmark treatment is followed, and (2) under U.S. GAAP.

b. Summarize the difference in income, total assets, and total stockholders' equity over the 20-year life of the building under the two different sets of accounting rules.

6. Iptat International Ltd. provided the following reconciliation from IFRSs to U.S. GAAP in its most recent annual report (amounts in thousands of CHF):

	Net Income	Shareholders' Equity
As stated under IFRSs	541,713	7,638,794
U.S. GAAP adjustments		
(a) Reversal of additional depreciation charges arising from revaluation of fixed assets	85,720	643,099
(b) Reversal of revaluation surplus of fixed assets. . . .	—	(977,240)
As stated under U.S. GAAP	627,433	7,305,653

would have increased on IFRS · *cumulative*

Required:
a. Explain why U.S. GAAP adjustment (a) results in an addition to net income. Explain why U.S. GAAP adjustment (a) results in an addition to shareholders' equity that is greater than the addition to net income. What is the shareholders' equity account affected by adjustment (a)? *Retained Earnings*
b. Explain why U.S. GAAP adjustment (b) results in a subtraction from shareholders' equity but does not affect net income. What is the shareholders' equity account affected by adjustment (b)? *lowered asset and lowered equity — both BS therefore income not affected*

7. Xanxi Petrochemical Company provided the following reconciliation from IFRSs to U.S. GAAP in its most recent annual report (amounts in thousands of RMB):

	Net Income	Shareholders' Equity
As stated under IFRSs	938,655	4,057,772
U.S. GAAP adjustments		
(a) Reversal of amortization charge on goodwill	5,655	16,965
(b) Gain on sale and leaseback of building	(40,733)	(66,967)
As stated under U.S. GAAP	903,577	4,007,770

Required:
a. Explain why U.S. GAAP adjustment (a) results in an addition to net income. Explain why U.S. GAAP adjustment (a) results in an addition to shareholders' equity that is greater than the addition to net income. What is the shareholders' equity account affected by adjustment (a)?
b. Explain why U.S. GAAP adjustment (b) reduces net income. Explain why U.S. GAAP adjustment (b) reduces shareholders' equity by a larger amount than it reduces net income. What is the shareholders' equity account affected by adjustment (b)?

8. On October 1, Year 1, Clinton Company purchased all of the outstanding shares of Gore Company by paying $250,000 in cash. Gore has several assets with market values that differ from their book values. In addition, Gore has internally generated intangibles that remain unrecorded on its books. In deriving a purchase price, Clinton made assessments of the fair value of Gore's net assets as follows:

	Book Value	Fair Value
Cash	$30,000	$30,000
Equipment	40,000	50,000
Computer software	20,000	40,000
Brands	0	50,000
Liabilities	(40,000)	(40,000)

In addition, in-process research and development costs incurred by Gore up to the date of acquisition were $100,000. Sixty percent of in-process research and development costs were related to research. One-half of the costs related to development were incurred prior to the technical feasibility of completing and the ability to sell the product could be demonstrated.

Required:

Determine the amount of goodwill to be reported in accordance with IAS 22 by Clinton Company as a result of its purchase of Gore Company.

9. Buch Corporation purchased Machine Z at the beginning of Year 1 at a cost of $100,000. The machine is used in the production of Product X. The machine is expected to have a useful life of 10 years and no residual value. The straight-line method of depreciation is used. Adverse economic conditions develop in Year 3 that result in a significant decline in demand for Product X. At December 31, Year 3, the company develops the following estimates related to Machine Z:

Expected future cash flows	$75,000
Present value of expected future cash flows	55,000
Selling price	70,000
Costs of disposal	7,000

At the end of Year 5, Buch's management determines that there has been a substantial improvement in economic conditions resulting in a strengthening of demand for Product Z. The following estimates related to Machine Z are developed at December 31, Year 5:

Expected future cash flows	$70,000
Present value of expected future cash flows	53,000
Selling price	50,000
Costs of disposal	7,000

Required:

Apply IAS 36 to determine:

a. The carrying value for Machine Z to be reported on the balance sheet at the end of Years 1–5.

b. The amounts to be reported in the income statement related to Machine Z for Years 1–5.

10. On January 1, Year 1, Holzer Company hired a general contractor to begin construction of a new office building. Holzer negotiated a $900,000, five-year, 10 percent loan on January 1, Year 1, to finance construction. Payments made to the general contractor for the building during Year 1 amount to $1,000,000. Payments were made evenly throughout the year. Construction is completed at the end of Year 1 and Holzer moves in and begins using the building on January 1, Year 2. The building is estimated to have a 40-year life and no residual value. On December 31, Year 3, Holzer Company determines that the market value for the building is $970,000. On December 31, Year 5, the company estimates the market value for the building to be $950,000.

Required:

Using the benchmark and allowed alternative treatments provided in (1) IAS 16 with respect to the measurement of property, plant, and equipment subsequent to initial recognition and (2) IAS 23 with respect to borrowing costs attributable to the construction of qualifying assets, there are four different combinations that could be used to determine the carrying value of the building over its useful life. For each of the four possible combinations determine:

a. The carrying value of the building that would be reported on the balance sheet at the end of Years 1–5.

b. The amounts to be reported in the income statement related to this building for Years 1–5.

In each case, assume that the building's value in use exceeds its carrying value at the end of each year and therefore impairment is not an issue.

11. Access the most recent Form 20-F filed with the U.S. Securities and Exchange Commission by one of the following foreign companies:

> Bayer
> China Southern Airlines
> Nokia
> Novartis
> Swisscom

Find the reconciliation from IFRSs to U.S. GAAP. Select three line items included in the reconciliation to fulfill the requirements of this exercise.

Required:

For each of the three line items:

a. Describe, in your own words, the difference between the rules in IFRSs and the rules in U.S. GAAP that caused a reconciliation adjustment to be made.

b. Explain the sign of the adjustments (positive or negative) related to net income and stockholders' equity. If possible, also explain the magnitude of the adjustments related to net income and stockholders' equity and/or the relative magnitude of the adjustment to net income and the adjustment to stockholders' equity.

Case 4-1

Jardine Matheson Group (Part 2)

With a broad portfolio of market-leading businesses, the Jardine Matheson Group is an Asian-based conglomerate with extensive experience in the region. Its business interests include Jardine Pacific, Jardine Motors Group, Hongkong Land, Dairy Farm, Mandarin Oriental, Jardine Cycle & Carriage and Jardine Lloyd Thompson. These companies are leaders in the fields of engineering and construction, transport services, motor trading, property, retailing, restaurants, hotels and insurance broking.

The Group's strategy is to build its operations into market leaders across Asia Pacific, each with the support of Jardine Matheson's extensive knowledge of the region and its long-standing relationships. Through a balance of cash producing activities and investment in new businesses, the Group aims to produce sustained growth in shareholder value.

Incorporated in Bermuda, Jardine Matheson has its primary share listing in London, with secondary listings in Singapore and Bermuda. Jardine Matheson Limited operates from Hong Kong and provides management services to Group companies, making available senior management and providing financial, legal, human resources and treasury support services throughout the Group.[1]

Jardine Matheson uses International Financial Reporting Standards in preparing its financial statements and has done so for a number of years.

Required:

Access Jardine Matheson's most recent annual report on the company's Web site (www.jardine-matheson.com). Review the company's list of principal accounting policies to evaluate whether the accounting policies followed are in accordance with IFRSs. Document your evaluation. In those areas in which IFRSs allow choice among accounting alternatives, identify the alternative selected by Jardine Matheson.

[1] www.jardine-matheson.com/profile/intro.html, accessed March 2005.

References   Financial Accounting Standards Board. *The IASC-U.S. Comparison Project,* 2nd ed. Norwalk, CT: FASB, 1999.

Ernst & Young. "The Evolution of IAS 39 in Europe," *Eye on IFRS Newsletter,* November 2004, pp. 1–4.

Reimers, J. L. "Additional Evidence on the Need for Disclosure Reform." *Accounting Horizons,* March 1992, pp. 36–41.

Chapter **Five**

Comparative Accounting

Learning Objectives

After reading this chapter, you should be able to

- Describe some aspects of the environment in which accounting operates in five countries, China, Germany, Japan, Mexico, and the United Kingdom.
- Explain the nature of the accounting profession in the selected countries.
- Discuss the mechanisms in place for regulating accounting and financial reporting in the selected countries.
- Examine some of the accounting principles and practices used by companies in these countries.
- Identify the areas where national accounting practices in these countries differ from International Financial Reporting Standards (IFRSs).

INTRODUCTION

This chapter describes the accounting environments in five countries: China, Germany, Japan, Mexico, and the United Kingdom. We selected these countries because they are economically important and they represent a cross section of the different accounting systems used around the world. Further, their accounting systems reflect their unique historical and cultural backgrounds. Exhibit 5.1 provides comparative demographic and economic data for these countries. Germany, Japan, and the United Kingdom are among the wealthiest nations in the world, whereas China and Mexico are developing economies. China, with a population of over 1.2 billion, has been one of the fastest-growing economies in recent years. As a result of recent economic reforms, Chinese accounting is experiencing a period of rapid evolution. Germany is one of the economic powerhouses in Europe, and its accounting system is one of the most important examples of the Continental European approach to accounting. Japan became a major economic power within a short period after World War II, focusing on high-tech industries. Its unique system of business interrelationships has had a profound impact on accounting. Mexico is representative of Latin American countries. As a member of the North American Free Trade Agreement (NAFTA), Mexico has been under external pressure to change its accounting system. The United Kingdom represents the Anglo-Saxon model of accounting. Recently, accounting in the United Kingdom has been strongly affected by the country's membership in the European Union.

EXHIBIT 5.1 Country Profiles

	China	Germany	Japan	Mexico	United Kingdom
Area	9.6 million sq. km. (3.7 million sq. miles)	357,000 sq. km. (138,000 sq. miles)	378,000 sq. km. (146,000 sq. miles)	1.96 million sq. km. (756,000 sq. miles)	243,000 sq. km. (94,000 sq. miles)
Population	1,248 million	83 million (2001) (Approx. 80% in former W. Germany)	127 million (2001)	97 million (2000)	60 million (2001)
Population Growth	0.9% (1999)	0.1% (1999)	0.3% (1999)	1.9% (2000)	0.2% (2001)
Life Expectancy	Male: 69.1 years Female: 73.5 years	Male: 75 years Female: 81.1 years	Male: 77.8 years Female: 85 years	Male: 70.4 years Female: 76.4 years	Male: 75.7 years Female: 80.7 years
Capital City	Beijing (Population: 7.4 million)	Berlin (Population: 3.5 million)	Tokyo (Population: 11.9 million)	Mexico City (Population: 16.7 million)	London (Population: 7.3 million)
Currency	Renminbi yuan of 10 jiao or 100 fen	Euro (€) of 100 cents	Yen (¥)	Peso of 100 centavos	Pound sterling (£) of 100 pence
GNP (US$ million) Per capita	1,064,537 (2000) 780 (1999)	2,057,633 (2000) 25,620 (1999)	4,337,268 (2000) 32,030 (1999)	498,018 (2000) 4,440 (1999)	1,463,474 (2000) 23,590 (1999)
GDP (US$ million) Per capita	959,001 (1998) 798 (1999)	2,150,480 (1998) 25,749 (1999)	3,782,834 (1998) 34,276 (1999)	414,350 (1998) 5,036 (1999)	1,403,668 (2000) 24,323 (1999)
Annual Average Growth of GDP	8.0% (2000)	3.1% (2000)	0.5% (2000)	6.9% (2000)	3.1% (2000)
Inflation Rate	1.4% (2001)	1.9% (2000)	0.1% (2001)	9.5% (2000)	2.7% (2001)
Unemployment	3.1% (1999)	7.8% (2001)	4.7% (2001)	1.7% (1999)	5.2% (2000)

Source: *2003 Whitaker's Almanack*, 135th ed. (London: A&C Black, 2003).

The discussion related to each country's accounting system is organized into four parts: (1) background, (2) accounting profession, (3) accounting regulation, and (4) accounting principles and practices. We discuss the countries in alphabetical order.

PEOPLE'S REPUBLIC OF CHINA (PRC)

Background

The ultimate legislative authority in China rests with the National People's Congress, the highest organ of state power. It is elected for a term of five years and has the power to amend the constitution; make laws; select the president, vice president, and other leading officials of the state; approve the national economic plan, the state budget, and the final state accounts; and decide on questions of war and peace. The State Council is the highest organ of the state administration. It is composed of the premier, the vice premiers, the state councillors, heads of ministries and commissions, the auditor general, and the secretary-general.

With the formation of the People's Republic of China (PRC) in 1949, the government adopted a policy of establishing a single public ownership economy with centralized management of businesses and control of all economic resources. By 1956, all private companies had been transformed into state or collective ownership. However, these state-owned enterprises (SOEs) eventually proved to be economic failures. For example, during 1995–1997, more than half of them were in the red, and the losses in 1995 alone were close to 100 billion renminbi (US$12 billion).[1] Restructuring the loss-making SOEs was a major part of the subsequent economic reforms, which aimed at transforming the centrally planned economy into a socialist market economy, that is, a market economy based on socialist principles. Under the reform agenda, private enterprises, cooperatives, and joint ventures coexist and compete with state-run entities. The radical economic changes implemented over the last decade have made China one of the fastest-growing and largest economies, with annual economic growth rates among the highest in the world. In terms of gross domestic product (GDP), China ranks fourth behind the United States, the European Union (combined), and Japan.

To carry out its reform program, China needed capital and advanced technology. This led to an open-door policy of attracting foreign direct investment (FDI), which emphasized the importance of developing a capital market. With nearly 500,000 FDI enterprises, China is now the world's number one recipient of foreign direct investment.

Chinese companies were encouraged to raise funds on international capital markets as well as on the domestic one by issuing shares and bonds. The government took steps to develop its domestic capital market. The history of the capital market in China is short, and the market itself is relatively small. Shanghai's municipal government approved the first securities regulation in China in 1984. Share dealings did not become popular until the beginning of the next decade, when the Shanghai Stock Exchange (SHSE) was reactivated in December 1990 and a second stock exchange, the Shenzhen Stock Exchange (SZSE), was established in April 1991.[2] The

---

[1] C. J. Lee, "Financial Restructuring of State Owned Enterprises in China: the Case of Shanghai Sunve Pharmaceutical Corporation," *Accounting, Organizations and Society* 26 (2001), p. 673.

[2] I. Haw, D. Qi, and W. Wu, "The Nature of Information in Accruals and Cash Flows in an Emerging Capital Market: The Case of China," *International Journal of Accounting* 36 (2001), pp. 391–406.

capital market in China is controlled by the government. In July 1992, the Chinese Security Regulatory Commission (CSRC) was set up as China's equivalent of the U.S. Securities and Exchange Commission to monitor and regulate the stock market. This provided an encouragement for investors to engage in capital market activities. The number of companies listed on the two stock exchanges increased from 50 in 1992 to 1,200 in 2003, with a market capitalization approaching US$500 billion. About 100 Chinese companies also trade on exchanges outside of China, including 20 companies trading on the New York Stock Exchange.

Long-term investment in China's highly speculative stock market is still an exception to the rule. The turnover rates of China's two stock exchanges in 2000, for example, were more than 450 percent per annum.[3] Stock holdings typically range from days to a few months. Investors basically strive for short-term stock price gains, which are not necessarily based on fundamental company data. The validity and reliability of financial disclosure are therefore of limited importance to investors.

Companies in China issue four categories of shares:

1. "A" shares, which can be owned only by Chinese citizens, and are traded on the two stock exchanges.
2. "B" shares (introduced in 1992), which can be owned by foreigners.
3. "C" shares, which are nontradable and held mainly by the government and other SOEs.
4. "H" shares, which can be owned only by foreigners and are traded in Hong Kong.

The market capitalization of A shares on the two stock exchanges accounts for more than 90 percent of the total market capitalization. B shares are for foreign individuals, institutional investors, and Chinese nationals able to trade in foreign currency. At the end of 1999, only about 5 percent of B shareholders were institutional investors.[4] As of late 2001, only 112 out of China's 1,160 listed firms issued B shares; approximately 50 were listed in Hong Kong, and another 20 were listed in New York.[5] Companies listed on the local capital market have a distinctive capital structure in which a large portion is made up of C shares, which cannot be traded publicly.

Accounting Profession

Accounting has a long history and a close association with the development of Chinese culture. Its roots can be found in the teachings of the philosopher and educator Confucius, which highlight the imperative to keep history and view accounting records as part of that history. The word *accounting* is noted as far back as the Hsiu Dynasty, around 2200 BC, when the stewardship function of accounting was emphasized. Later, in the Xia Dynasty (2000–1500 BC), the concept of measuring wealth and accomplishment was mentioned. More recently, the master–apprentice system was used to train accountants up until the 1900s. Also, in the early 1900s, university study in accounting became an accepted way to understand and advance the principles and practice of accounting. Since 1949, Chinese scholars returning home after completing their accounting studies abroad, mainly

[3] China Securities Regulatory Commission, *China Securities and Futures Statistical Yearbook* (Beijing: CSRC, 2002), p. 27.

[4] China Securities Regulatory Commission, *China Securities and Futures Statistical Yearbook* (Beijing: CSRC, 2000).

[5] CSRC, *Yearbook,* 2002.

in the Soviet Union, pioneered the development of a body of new knowledge in China, which resulted in existing practices.[6]

However, until the 1980s, those who carried out accounting work were not held in high regard in Chinese society compared with their Western counterparts. This was partly due to the traditional Chinese culture of "respecting the peasants and despising the merchants."[7] Consequently, accounting education has never been well developed in China and was particularly disrupted during the Cultural Revolution (beginning in the mid-1960s). Graham explains some aspects of the accounting environment in China as follows:

> Accounting became focused on reporting compliance with State economic plans, using a specified structure of accounts and following a sources and uses of funds concept. But it is commonly agreed the period of the Cultural Revolution (1966–1976) marks a dark period for the profession, as accounting was overly simplified with the objective of making accounting accessible and understandable to the "masses," University professors were ousted and occasionally brutalized, and accounting theory all but abandoned. . . . The consequence of this simplification on top of an already crude Soviet-based system was the loss of a generation or so of true accounting thought, and the absence of any need to reflect the nature of modern transactions or business concepts in the accounting system.[8]

The economic reform and the open-door policy introduced in the 1980s brought about a large number of Sino–foreign joint ventures in China. This resulted in the reemergence of a private auditing profession, supported by the Accounting Law issued in 1985 and the CPA Regulations in 1986. The CPA Regulations, promulgated by the State Council, prescribed the scope of practice for certified public accountants (CPAs) and some working and ethical rules. These developments led to the formation of the Chinese Institute of Certified Public Accountants (CICPA) in 1988, the first professional accounting body in China since the establishment of the PRC in 1949.

Unlike in the United States, accounting and auditing in China took different paths in their development processes. For many years, auditing firms mainly audited domestic companies, whereas accounting firms focused on companies using foreign investments. Accounting firms were sponsored by the Ministry of Finance (MoF), and auditing firms were under the State Administration of Audit (SAA), a department within the State Council responsible for government audits. In 1991, the SAA, in competition with the CICPA, issued its "Tentative Rules on Certified Public Auditors" to regulate auditors employed in audit firms. In 1992, the Chinese Association of Certified Practicing Auditors (CACPA) was formed under the auspices of the SAA.[9]

The competition between accountants and auditors with their own rules issued by different government departments was confusing, particularly to international accounting firms. Consequently, steps were taken to merge the CICPA and CACPA. In 1993, the CPA Regulations were upgraded to become the CPA Law.[10]

---

[6] L. E. Graham and C. Li, "Cultural and Economic Influences on Current Accounting Standards in the People's Republic of China," *International Journal of Accounting* 32, no. 3 (1997), pp. 247–78.

[7] Y. Chen, P. Jubb, and A. Tran, "Problems of Accounting Reform in the People's Republic of China," *International Journal of Accounting* 32, no. 2 (1997), pp. 139–53.

[8] L. E. Graham, "Setting a Research Agenda for Auditing Issues in the People's Republic of China," *International Journal of Accounting* 31, no. 1 (1996), p. 22.

[9] J. Z. Xiao, Y. Zhang, and Z. Xie, "The Making of Independent Auditing Standards in China," *Accounting Horizons* 14, no. 1 (2000), pp. 69–89.

[10] In China, laws have a higher legal status than regulations, as laws are stipulated by the National Peoples' Congress, whereas regulations are promulgated by the State Council (ibid.).

As a result, the MoF was given the authority to regulate both the accounting and the auditing firms. The CICPA became a member of the IASC (and IFAC) in 1997. The merger between the CICPA and the CACPA was completed in 1998.

By way of comparison, there are some clear differences between the evolution of the accounting profession in China and in other countries such as the United Kingdom. For example, in the United Kingdom, auditors enjoyed a good legislative and judicial environment during the early stages of development, whereas a market-oriented legal and judicial infrastructure is still emerging in China. Further, UK auditors were able to establish and maintain high quality because they had the support of their professional accounting bodies, which emphasized professional education, training, and examinations. By contrast, these support mechanisms are still lacking in China.[11] Finally, unlike in the United Kingdom, accounting and auditing firms in China have been treated separately. This is evident from the coexistence of the CICPA and the CACPA, with their admission requirements governed by the respective sponsoring agencies (i.e., the MoF and the SAA). By the end of 1997, there were 62,460 practicing CPAs and 6,900 accounting and auditing firms in China.[12]

The economic reform program, with its open-door policy, has stimulated the growth of accounting and related activities in China in many ways. Prior to reforms, the accounting system was no more than a way to provide information to the government. The economic reforms rapidly changed, among other things, the ownership structure of organizations.[13] The joint stock company was recognized by the state as the desired organizational structure to reform the SOEs. This created new demands for financial information from investors and other interested parties. The establishment of the two stock exchanges aiming to develop capital market activities led to major changes in China's accounting system. For example, companies that issue B shares are now required to restate their earnings according to International Financial Reporting Standards, and to provide two annual reports—one prepared by an international auditing firm, and one certified by a local accounting firm.

Many aspects of the reform program rely on accounting and auditing services to assist the market to work in an orderly manner. Various government regulations on the implementation of economic reform measures require the involvement of independent auditors. The laws on Sino–foreign joint ventures require the audit of annual statements and income tax returns and the verification of capital contributions by registered Chinese CPAs. These additional demands for accounting services created new opportunities for international accounting firms to enter the Chinese market.

By providing services to foreign investors, the international accounting firms have assisted in the implementation of the open-door policy. They also have assisted in the development of the Chinese capital market by, for example, undertaking financial audits of Chinese companies that offer shares to overseas investors and that wish to obtain a foreign stock exchange listing. In addition, the international firms have been involved in training Chinese auditors and setting auditing standards. More than 200 of the world's top 500 companies have invested in China. All of the leading international accounting firms, following their clients, have moved into China by opening representative offices.

---

[11] Xiao, Zhang, and Xie, "The Making. . . ."

[12] Y. Tang, "Bumpy Road Leading to Internationalization: A Review of Accounting Development in China," *Accounting Horizons* 14, no. 1 (2000), pp. 93–102.

[13] Z. Xiao and A. Pan, "Developing Accounting Standards on the Basis of a Conceptual Framework by the Chinese Government," *International Journal of Accounting* 32, no. 3 (1997), pp. 279–99.

Accounting Regulation

In recent years, accounting regulation in China has been influenced mainly by China's desire to harmonize domestic accounting practices (the various uniform accounting systems used in different industries produced inconsistent practices across industries), harmonize Chinese accounting with IFRSs, and meet the requirements of economic reforms.

The movement toward private ownership has required a revision of China's accounting and disclosure standards. Several major Chinese financial scandals in the early 1990s highlighted the problems associated with the accounting system, which was modeled on the system that existed in the former Soviet Union. One of the most notorious was the Great Wall fund-raising scandal, which implicated the Zhongchen accounting firm.

> In this case, the Great Wall Electrical Engineering Science and Technology Co. illegally raised one billion Yuan in a few months between 1992 and 1993 by issuing very high coupon securities to over 100,000 private investors in 17 large cities in China. The money raised was partly embezzled and partly used to establish over 20 subsidiaries and more than 100 branches all over the country. A branch of the Zhongchen accounting firm played a key role in the fraud: its three CPAs provided an unfounded certificate confirming 0.3 billion Yuan capital after just one day's work with only 25 pages of working papers. . . . Five CPAs from the accounting firm were disqualified and the whole firm was dismantled. The president of the client company received the death penalty, a deputy minister was jailed for bribery, and the president of the People's Bank of China was terminated.[14]

The MoF establishes accounting standards and regulations, while the CSRC issues disclosure requirements for listed companies. The MoF began setting accounting standards in 1988, the same year in which the CICPA was established. The MoF adopted a policy of following international accounting practice in setting Chinese standards. To this end, in 1992, it developed the *Basic Standard of Accounting for Business Enterprises* (similar to a conceptual framework). In 1993, it appointed an international accounting firm (with technical assistance funds from the World Bank) as consultants to the MoF's standard-setting program and established two advisory committees, one consisting of international accounting experts and the other consisting of Chinese accounting experts.[15] The promulgation of a conceptual framework by the MoF in 1992 was a landmark event in the recent accounting reforms in China. It was a clear signal that Anglo-American accounting principles were to replace the rigid Soviet accounting model practiced in China since 1949.

The CPA Law requires auditors to audit Chinese enterprises' financial statements; verify the enterprises' capital contribution; engage in the audit work of the enterprises' merger, demerger, and liquidation; and provide professional services specified by the law and regulations.[16] Accountants who intentionally provide false certificates may be sentenced to up to five years of fixed-term imprisonment or criminal detention and a fine. The law requires a CPA to refuse to issue any relevant report where (1) the client suggests, overtly or covertly, that a false or misleading report or statement be issued; (2) the client intentionally fails to provide

[14] Xiao, Zhang, and Xie, "The Making. . . ."

[15] Y. Tang, "Bumpy Road. . . ."

[16] K. Z. Lin, and K. H. Chan, "Auditing Standards in China: A Comparative Analysis with Relevant International Standards and Guidelines," *International Journal of Accounting* 35, no. 4 (2000), pp. 559–77.

relevant accounting material and documents; and (3) the report to be issued by a certified public accountant cannot correctly represent all material information due to the client's unreasonable behavior.

The China Accounting Standards Committee (CASC)—comprising government experts, academics, and members of accounting firms—was established within the MoF in 1998. China has not adopted IFRSs, but it has stated that it will develop its own standards based on IFRSs. However, different types of companies are required to comply with different sets of standards; for example, companies with B shares must follow IFRSs, companies with A shares must follow Chinese GAAP, and companies with H shares must follow either Hong Kong GAAP or IFRSs.

In June 2002, the CICPA issued new guidelines on professional ethics as a supplement to the *General Standard on Professional Ethics*. The guidelines stress the importance of a CPA's independence and also contain extensive discussion on change in a professional appointment, service fees charged to clients, practice promotion, and confidentiality.[17]

The CSRC requires companies listed on the two stock exchanges to post their annual reports on the exchanges' respective Web sites.[18] The CSRC and the two stock exchanges have also adopted new corporate governance rules that require listed companies to disclose detailed related-party transaction information relating to intangible assets.[19]

In November 2003 (effective January 2004), the CSRC and the MoF issued a joint document requiring companies to rotate their auditors every five years and to take a two-year break before auditing the same client again. China is following the international trend toward tighter regulation of auditing practices, which has gained momentum following the collapse of Arthur Andersen in the aftermath of the Enron scandal. The CSRC seems to follow the recommendations of the Sarbanes-Oxley Act in the United States.

The pressure is on for China to harmonize its accounting standards and practices with international standards. As a result, international harmonization has been recognized as a priority for the development of the profession. China's desire to join the World Trade Organization (WTO) was a major incentive for the push toward international harmonization. WTO membership, granted in 2002, was conditional upon, among other things, the adoption of internationally acceptable accounting and financial reporting practices, and the opening up of the accounting and auditing markets.

Accounting Principles and Practices

China is an economy in transition, and its market-based systems are still at an early stage of development. Traditionally in China, there has been a close link between taxation and accounting, and the calculation of taxable income has been a major purpose of accounting. Further, under China's communist ideological influences, accounting conservatism has long been criticized as a tool used to manipulate accounting numbers and maximize the profits of capitalists in exploiting workers. Accounting conservatism is the principle that stipulates that, in a situation where there are acceptable accounting alternatives, the one that produces lower current amounts for net income and net assets ought to be chosen. This accounting

---

[17] For more details, see IAS PLUS, July 2002, at www.iasplus.com

[18] Shanghai Stock Exchange Web site (www.sse.com.cn) and the Shenzhen Stock Exchange Web site (www.cninfo.com.cn).

[19] See IAS PLUS, January 2001, at www.iasplus.com

convention has virtually been prohibited in China since 1949.[20] A lack of conservatism in Chinese accounting standards and practices continues to be a major difference between Chinese GAAP and IFRSs.

The financial statements published by Chinese companies typically include a balance sheet, an income statement, a cash flow statement, notes to financial statements, and other supporting schedules. One of the major problems associated with accounting practices adopted by enterprises in China is the lack of coherent interpretation of the relevant requirements. Regulations are subject to different interpretations and applications on the part of government agencies in different locations. As a result, the formal harmonization of accounting and auditing standards that has occurred within China has not brought about a harmonization of accounting practices. China, being a transitional economy, is only beginning to develop the infrastructure required to support credible financial reporting. As China intensifies its integration into the global economy and fulfills its obligations agreed on in the WTO accession treaty, for example, to open up its market to foreign auditors,[21] market forces in the accounting and auditing sector undoubtedly will become more active, which should strengthen the effectiveness of private safeguard mechanisms.

The conceptual framework, first issued in 1992, has since been superseded by 16 Chinese Accounting Standards (see Exhibit 5.2) and other regulations, such as the Accounting System for Business Enterprises (ASBE) issued in 2001. The ASBE aims, among other things, to enhance comparability of financial information, separate accounting and taxation treatments, and ensure harmonization with internationally accepted accounting practices.

The ASBE defines fundamental principles (going concern, accounting period, substance over form, consistency, timeliness, understandability, accrual basis, matching, impairment recognition, prudence, materiality, and measurement currency vs. presentation currency) and financial statement elements (assets, liabilities, owners' equity, revenues, expenses, and profits), which are similar to those found in IFRSs. It also specifies the contents of financial reports (which financial statements are to be presented annually, semiannually, quarterly, and monthly); minimum notes to the financial statements; and how soon after the end of the accounting period reports should be published.

The ASBE also includes

1. Classifications within the asset, liability, and equity elements, as well as recognition and measurement principles for a wide variety of assets and liabilities.
2. Revenue recognition principles for goods, services, royalties, and interest.
3. Expense recognition principles for bad debts, cost of goods sold, depreciation, major overheads, and impairment of assets.
4. Accounting principles for nonmonetary transactions, assets contributed by investors, accounting for income taxes, foreign currency transactions, changes in accounting policies, changes in estimates, corrections of errors, post–balance sheet events, contingencies, and related-party transactions.
5. Principles for consolidated financial statements and accounting for investments in joint ventures.

---

[20] Lin and Chan, "Auditing Standards in China."

[21] Foreign firms that have obtained CPA licenses are permitted to affiliate with Chinese firms and enter into contractual agreements to provide accounting, auditing and bookkeeping services. (World Trade Organization, *Report of the Working Party on the Accession to China, Addendum, Schedule of Specific Commitment on Services,* October 1, 2001, available at www.wto.org/english/thewto_e/completeacc_e.htm.)

EXHIBIT 5.2
Chinese
Accounting
Standards as at
January 1, 2002

	Accounting Standard	Effective Date	Applicability
1	*Disclosure of Related Party Relationships and Transactions*	January 1, 1997	Listed enterprises
2	*Cash Flow Statements* (minor revision in 2001)	January 1, 2001	All enterprises
3	*Events Occuring After the Balance Sheet Date*	January 1, 1998	Listed enterprises
4	*Debt Restructuring* (revised significantly in 2001)	January 1, 2002	All enterprises
5	*Revenue*	January 1, 1999	Listed enterprises
6	*Investments* (minor revision in 2001)	January 1, 2001	Joint stock limited enterprises (prior to January 1, 2001, listed enterprises only)
7	*Construction Contracts*	January 1, 1999	Listed enterprises
8	*Changes in Accounting Policies and Estimates and Corrections of Accounting Errors* (minor revision in 2001)	January 1, 2001	All enterprises (prior to January 1, 2001 listed enterprises only)
9	*Non-monetary Transactions* (revised significantly in 2001)	January 1, 2001	All enterprises
10	*Contingencies*	July 1, 2000	All enterprises
11	*Intangible Assets*	January 1, 2001	Joint stock limited enterprises
12	*Borrowing Costs*	January 1, 2001	All enterprises
13	*Leases*	January 1, 2001	All enterprises
14	*Interim Financial Reporting*	January 1, 2002	Listed enterprises
15	*Inventories*	January 1, 2002	Joint stock limited enterprises
16	*Fixed Assets*	January 1, 2002	Joint stock limited enterprises

In addition, it requires that expenses be classified as operating, administrative, or financing expenses and that profit be classified between operating profit, investment income, subsidy income, and several other nonoperating income categories. Finally, its requirement to include management discussion of financial condition is similar to requirements in the United States.

Nearly half a million enterprises in China, including all listed companies, now follow one unified ASBE. The MoF required all 170,000 SOEs to adopt the ASBE in 2005. The ASBE and Chinese Accounting Standards together form the structure of financial reporting in modern China.

Chinese accounting practices differ in some respects from those required under IFRSs. In some areas covered by IFRSs, there are no specific rules in China. In other areas, transactions are treated differently under the two sets of rules. For example, there are no specific rules in the areas of business combinations, including provisions in the context of acquisitions (IAS 22); impairment of assets, particularly as (except for investments) diminutions in value are not allowed (IAS 36); the definitions of operating and finance leases (IAS 17); employee benefits obligations (IAS 19); and accounting for an issuer's financial instruments (IAS 32). Further, there are no specific rules requiring disclosures of discontinuing operations (IAS 35), segment liabilities (IAS 14), or diluted earnings per share (IAS 33). The methods of treating certain transactions are different from those required under IFRSs. In

EXHIBIT 5.3 Differences between Chinese GAAP and IFRSs

Issue	IFRSs	Chinese GAAP
Profit or loss on disposal of fixed assets	IAS 16: Included in operating profit or loss.	Presented as a nonoperating gain or loss.
Requirement to provide segment information	IAS 14: Listed companies only.	Listed companies and other enterprises applying the system.
Measurement of property, plant, and equipment	IAS 16: May use either fair value or historical cost.	Generally required to use historical cost.
Borrowing costs related to self-use assets that take a substantial time to complete	IAS 23: May either capitalize as part of the asset's cost or charge to expenses.	Must capitalize as part of the asset's cost.
Impairment of assets that do not generate cash flows individually	IAS 36: An asset is impaired when its book value exceeds its recoverable amount, which is the greater of net realizable value and the net present value of future net cash flows expected to arise from continued use of the asset.	Specific guidance is not provided.
Research and development costs	IAS 38: Expense all research costs. Capitalize development costs if certain criteria are met.	Expense all research and development costs (except patent registration and legal costs, which are capitalized).
Preoperating expenses	IAS 38: Charged to expenses when incurred.	Deferred until the entity begins operations, then charged to expenses.
Land use rights	IAS 38: Accounted for as an operating lease. Cost of land use rights is treated as prepaid lease payments.	Accounted for as a purchased intangible asset until the construction or development commences, then accounted for as fixed assets under construction or property development costs until the construction or development is complete; on completion, total costs are transferred to property held for use.
Amortization of intangible assets	IAS 38: Amortize over the estimated useful life, which is presumed to be 20 years or less.	Amortized over the shorter of the estimated useful life and the contractual or legal life; if no contractual or legal life, amortize over the estimated useful life, but not more than 10 years.
Revaluation of intangible assets	IAS 38: Permitted only if the intangible asset trades in an active market.	Prohibited.

China, proposed dividends are accrued before being approved (IAS 10); preoperating expenses are deferred and amortized (IAS 38); a wider definition of extraordinary items is used (IAS 8); and in segment reporting, the line of business basis is always treated as primary (IAS 14). Each of these practices is inconsistent with IFRSs. Exhibit 5.3 presents some of the differences between IFRSs and Chinese GAAP.

Several Chinese companies provide financial statements prepared in accordance with both Chinese (PRC) GAAP and IFRSs. Exhibit 5.4 provides an excerpt from Sinopec Shanghai Petrochemical Company Ltd.'s 2003 annual report, in which the company (1) describes major differences between PRC GAAP and IFRSs and (2) quantifies the effects of these differences on net income and stockholders' equity.

EXHIBIT 5.4

SINOPEC SHANGHAI PETROCHEMICAL COMPANY LTD.
Excerpt from Annual Report
2003

Differences between Financial Statements Prepared under PRC Accounting Rules and Regulations and IFRSs

The Company also prepares a set of financial statements which complies with PRC Accounting Rules and Regulations. A reconciliation of the Group's net profit and shareholders' equity prepared under PRC Accounting Rules and Regulations and IFRS is presented below.

Other than the differences in classification of certain financial statements assertions and the accounting treatment of the items described below, there are no material differences between the Group's financial statements prepared in accordance with PRC Accounting Rules and Regulations and IFRS. The major differences are:

(i) Capitalisation of general borrowing costs

Under IFRS, to the extent that funds are borrowed generally and used for the purpose of obtaining a qualifying asset, the borrowing costs should be capitalised as part of the cost of that asset. Under PRC Accounting Rules and Regulations, only borrowing costs on funds that are specially borrowed for construction are eligible for capitalisation as fixed assets.

(ii) Valuation surplus

Under PRC Accounting Rules and Regulations, the excess of fair value over the carrying value of assets given up in part exchange for investments should be credited to capital reserve fund. Under IFRS, it is inappropriate to recognise such excess as a gain as its realisation is uncertain.

(iii) Government grants

Under PRC Accounting Rules and Regulations, government grants should be credited to capital reserve. Under IFRS, such grants for the purchase of equipment used for technology improvements are offset against the cost of asset to which the grants related. Upon transfer to property, plant and equipment, the grant is recognised as income over the useful life of the property, plant and equipment by way of a reduced depreciation charge.

(iv) Revaluation of land use rights

Under IFRS, land use rights are carried at historical cost less accumulated amortisation under IFRS. Under PRC Accounting Rules and Regulations, land use rights are carried at revalued amount less accumulated amortisation.

(v) Pre-operating expenditure

Under IFRS, expenditure on start-up activities should be recognised as expenses when it is incurred. Under PRC Accounting Rules and Regulations, all expenses incurred during the start-up period are aggregated in long-term deferred expenses and then fully charged to the income statement in the month of commencement of operations.

Effects on the Group's net profit and shareholders' equity of significant differences between PRC Accounting Rules and Regulations and IFRS are summarised below:

		Years ended 31 December	
	Note	**2003** *RMB'000*	**2002** *RMB'000*
Net profit under PRC			
Accounting Rules and Regulations		1,385,556	908,965
Adjustments:			
Capitalisation of borrowing costs, net of depreciation effect	(i)	6,187	5,833
Reduced depreciation on government grants	(iii)	26,760	15,411
Amortisation of revaluation of land use rights	(iv)	3,498	3,498
Write off of pre-operating expenditure	(v)	(18,858)	(15,942)
Tax effects of the above adjustments		(1,453)	(1,400)
Profit attributable to shareholders under IFRS*		1,401,690	916,365

Continued

EXHIBIT 5.4 *(Continued)*

| | Note | As at 31 December | |
		2003 RMB'000	2002 RMB'000
Shareholders' equity under PRC Accounting Rules and Regulations		15,507,016	14,481,460
Adjustments:			
Capitalisation of borrowing costs	(i)	64,308	58,121
Valuation surplus	(ii)	(44,887)	(44,887)
Government grants	(iii)	(344,199)	(370,959)
Revaluation of land use right	(iv)	(136,359)	(139,857)
Write off of pre-operating expenditure	(v)	(34,800)	(15,942)
Tax effects of the above adjustments		10,807	12,260
Shareholders' equity under IFRS*		15,021,886	13,980,196

*The above figures are extracted from the financial statements prepared in accordance with IFRS, which have been audited by KPMG.

GERMANY

Background

After the Second World War, Germany was divided into American, French, British, and Soviet zones of occupation. In 1949, the Federal Republic of Germany was created out of the western zones, and the communist-led German Democratic Republic was established in the Soviet zone. After reunification in October 1990, Germany became a federal republic composed of 16 *Länder* (states): 10 from the former West, 5 from the former East, and Berlin, the capital city. The constitution provides for a president, elected by a federal convention for a five-year term; the *Bundestag* (Lower House) of 667 members elected by direct universal suffrage for a four-year term of office; and the *Bundesrat* (Upper House), composed of 69 members appointed by the governments of the *Länder* in proportion to their populations, without a fixed term of office.

Unlike in the United States, traditionally the primary source of finance for German companies is bank loans, rather than equity raised through the capital market. In Germany, as in Japan, banks not only provide loans to companies but also control major proportions of their equity capital, either directly or as trustees for their customers. This determines to a large extent the purpose for financial reporting by companies. Since reunification, German accounting has been greatly affected by the increasing internationalization of the German economy and the growing integration of the world's capital markets. In recent years, an increasing number of German companies, such as DaimlerChrysler and Deutsche Telekom, have been raising capital on international markets, particularly the New York Stock Exchange.

The most common legal forms of business enterprise are the *Aktiengesellschaft* (AG), which is a publicly traded stock corporation, and the *Gesellschaft mit beschränkter Haftung* (GMBH), which is a limited liability company that is not publicly traded.

Historically, Germany has had a considerable influence on the accounting systems in many countries, especially Japan, Austria, Switzerland, and some Nordic countries such as Denmark and Sweden. These countries adapted the ideas and concepts developed in Germany to suit their conditions. This is reflected in the intellectual basis of accounting and auditing education and in the source of the various laws in those countries. For example, the Commercial Code in Japan was modeled on the German Commercial Code.

Accounting Profession

Auditing dominates the financial reporting related professional activities in Germany. The title for certified auditors, *Wirtschaftsprüfer* (WP) (economic or enterprise examiner), was created by the Companies Act of 1931. *The Institut der Wirtschaftsprüfer* (Institute of Auditors) is a private association of public auditors and public audit firms. It comprises approximately 10,800 public auditors and over 900 public audit firms, and represents about 85 percent of the profession. It provides for the education and continuing professional development. Stock corporations and other large companies must be audited by WPs. Stringent requirements to become a WP are found in the *Wirtschaftsprüferordnung* (Auditors Law). These generally include obtaining a university degree in business administration, economics, law, engineering, or agriculture; passing examinations covering accounting, auditing, business adminsitration, law, taxation, and general economics; and four years of practical experience, including two years in auditing. The German auditing profession is much smaller than its counterpart in the United States (about 11,000 WPs vs. over 250,000 CPAs).

The auditing profession is headed by the *Wirtschaftsprüferkammer* (WPK) (Chamber of Auditors), an independent organization responsible for the supervision of its members and for the representation of the profession to other parties. It is a state-supervised organization. All public accountants are mandatory members of the WPK. A second important organization is the Institute of Auditors, whose main task is to publish statements on accounting and auditing questions, which usually serve as generally accepted accounting and auditing standards.

There also is a second-tier body of certified accountants, *vereidigte Buchprüfer* (VB). The requirements to become a VB are less onerous than to become a WP. VBs are allowed to perform only voluntary audits and audits of medium-sized limited liability companies (GMBHs). A third type of professional accountant in Germany are the *Steuerberater* (tax advisers), who focus on offering tax services to their clients.

Accounting Regulation

Financial reporting in Germany is dominated by commercial law, tax law, and pronouncements issued by the profession. The German Commercial Code contains most of the country's financial reporting principles, which include the general accounting and auditing rules applicable to all companies, together with a special section relating to stock corporations and limited liability companies. It also specifies sanctions for noncompliance, such as punitive measures, penalties, and fines to be imposed by the courts. Unlike in the United States, partnership accounting is regulated in Germany. The German Stock Exchange listing requirements have much less influence on financial reporting compared to those in the United States.

A stock corporation (AG) is required to prepare statutory nonconsolidated annual financial statements comprising a balance sheet, income statement, and the notes to the financial statements, along with a management report. These financial statements should (1) be prepared in accordance with the German principles of proper accounting applicable to all commercial business and (2) provide a true and fair view of the net assets, financial position, and results of operations of the corporation. In addition, parent companies are required to prepare statutory consolidated annual financial statements and a group management report. A parent company may be exempted from this requirement if, for example, it is itself a subsidiary of another parent company. Further, the executive board of a stock corporation is required to file at the Commercial Registrar the nonconsolidated (and consolidated, if applicable) financial statements, the management report, the auditor's report and the proposed, and resolved appropriation of retained earnings and net income (including any dividend proposal or resolution). These documents are also published in the official federal gazette, the *Bundesanzeiger*.

In Germany, the predominance of the principle of prudence (conservatism) is clearly established in the law. Accordingly, profits must be recognized only when they have been realized, but losses should be recorded as soon as they appear possible. During the worldwide economic crisis of the late 1920s and early 1930s (the Great Depression), the existing accounting practices failed to protect adequately the creditors of German companies in cases of insolvency. As a consequence, the principle of prudence was incorporated in the 1937 Stock Corporation Law, which also specifically required that the compulsory audits of public corporations be performed by WPs.

In the mid-1960s, there were signs of a change in financial reporting in Germany from a creditor orientation towards a shareholder orientation. The Companies Act of 1965 can be regarded as the initiator of this change, and for the first time it required greater financial disclosures from companies, including preparation of consolidated statements and disclosure of the valuation bases used. For two decades, the Companies Act provided the primary source of accounting regulation for listed companies, supplemented by provisions in the Commercial Code and income tax law.

More recently, German accounting regulation has been heavily influenced by the EU directives. The Accounting Act of 1985 implemented the EU's Fourth, Seventh, and Eighth Directives, and transformed them into German Commercial Law. The act specifies different financial reporting requirements according to company size. Since then the Financial Statement Directives Law, which amended the Commercial Code, has been the legal basis for financial reporting in Germany.

Until 1998 the Federal Ministry of Justice coordinated the accounting rule development process, and the accounting profession played only a relatively minor role in that process. In May 1998, German law was amended to allow a private-sector body to develop accounting standards. Accordingly, the German Accounting Standards Committee (GASC) was created in May 1998. It was charged with the responsibility of developing accounting standards for consolidated financial reporting, representing German interests in international fora, and advising the Ministry of Justice on the development of accounting legislation. The GASC is a private standard-setting body that is supported and funded by 137 German companies and individual members, and managed by an executive board of up to 14 members.

The GASC has two standing committees, the German Accounting Standards Board (GASB) and the Accounting Interpretations Committee (AIC). The GASB is solely responsible for the preparation and adoption of its pronouncements, which may consist of accounting standards, comments on accounting issues addressed to national and international bodies, working papers, and other comments and publications considered appropriate by the GASB. The main objective of the AIC is to promote international convergence of interpretations of core accounting issues in close cooperation with the IASB's International Financial Reporting Interpretations Committee (IFRIC). The GASB develops its accounting standards through a due process of public consultation, which includes the following steps:

1. Publication of exposure drafts of standards with a call for comments to be submitted within 45 days.
2. Publication of comments received (unless the party submitting the comments requests otherwise), along with an analysis and discussion of material objections and proposed amendments.
3. Publication of a revised exposure draft with a call for comments to be submitted within 30 days (in those cases where the GASB determines the comments received warrant material amendments of the original exposure draft).
4. Public discussion on the draft standard, which must be announced at least 14 days in advance; minutes of the public discussion must be published within 30 days.
5. Adoption of standards at meetings open to the public.
6. Publication of adopted standards including, where applicable dissenting votes, with a brief basis for conclusion.

The GASB was given the task of adapting German accounting principles to international norms by 2004. The establishment of this committee also provided a vehicle for the German accounting profession to participate formally in the activities of international bodies such as the IASB. The GASB, modeled on the FASB, is staffed by independent experts—three from industry, two auditors, one financial analyst, and one academic.

Germany has created a new legal code for financial accounting. Accordingly, in May 2004, representatives of 15 professional and industry associations established, under the auspices of the Federal Ministry of Justice, an independent private-sector enforcement body, the Financial Reporting Enforcement Panel (FREP). The objective of this panel is to serve as the sponsoring organization for an independent body enforcing financial reporting requirements as provided for in the draft *Bilanzkontrollgesetz* (Financial Reporting Enforcement Law). The panel's charge solely is to discover infringements of financial reporting requirements by listed companies. It does not have any authority to impose sanctions.

Accounting Principles and Practices

The German financial reporting requirements are mainly based on the Commercial Code. The historical cost basis for valuing tangible assets is strictly adhered to. In addition, the approved standards of the GASB must be followed in preparing the consolidated accounts of listed companies. Accordingly, starting from 2005, listed companies are required to use IFRSs in their consolidated financial statements, so long as these comply with EU directives.

Given the traditional role of bank credit in corporate finance the principle of creditor protection plays an important role in German accounting practices. Accordingly, the primary function of financial accounting is the conservative determination of distributable income, which represents that part of the actual income of the company that can be paid out to shareholders without impairing the position of the creditors or the long-term prospects of the firm. Consequently, the information needs of investors and presenting a *true and fair view* in the financial statements have not been the primary focus in financial reporting.

German accounting is heavily influenced by tax law. The relationship between financial accounting and taxation in Germany is explained by the "authoritative principle," which basically states that the financial statements are the basis for taxation. There also is a "reverse authoritative principle," which requires an expense to be included in accounting income to be tax deductible. These principles have the effect of minimizing differences between tax and accounting income, thereby reducing the need to account for deferred income taxes.

The reason for the link between financial reporting and taxation in Germany is historical. The duty of bookkeeping and annual accounting was codified in the German Commercial Code in 1862. Corporate income taxation was introduced 12 years later, in 1874. The easiest course of action was to link corporate income taxation to existing financial statements. In contrast, when income tax was introduced in the United Kingdom in 1799 and reformed substantially in 1803, there was no set of accounting rules to refer to. The first accounting rules appeared only in 1844. This explains the different traditions followed in Germany and the United Kingdom with regard to the link between taxation and financial reporting.[22]

For the average company, financial accounting is influenced to a great extent by the desire to minimize taxes. For example, in years with high profits, firms will attempt to report a more moderate level of income to reduce taxes by adopting the most conservative options available under the rules. (This is less the case for companies that compete for funds in international capital markets.) In some cases, what is acceptable for tax purposes is not acceptable under German accounting rules. To meet the requirement that tax deductions must be reported in financial statements, German accounting law allows companies to report "special tax items" on the balance sheet, located between accrued liabilities and stockholders' equity. For example, assume tax law allows a special depreciation rate of 75 percent in the year in which an asset with a 20-year life that costs 100 euros is acquired. Depreciation of 75 euros (a debit) would be taken in calculating both taxable and accounting income, but accumulated depreciation (a credit) would be reflected on the balance sheet in the amount of only 5 euros (5 percent annual depreciation). The difference of 70 euros is reported as a special tax item on the equity side (a credit) of the balance sheet.

The conservative measurement of income in Germany is also influenced by a desire to mitigate labor unions' demands for higher wages and to report stable income over time for dividend purposes.[23] Income stability (or smoothing) is accomplished by estimating liabilities such as provisions for warranties, pensions, and "uncertain future liabilities" at relatively high amounts, with a corresponding increase in expenses. The extra amounts accrued as liabilities on the balance sheet are known as hidden or silent reserves. In later, less profitable years, adjustments can be made to these liabilities to release the hidden reserves with a corresponding amount of revenue recognized in income. German accounting rules allow firms to smooth their profits over time in this fashion.[24] The process of using accounting options available within the accounting law to generate the desired amount of reported profit is referred to as *Bilanzpolitik* (financial statement policy).

The EU's Fourth Directive requires companies to apply the true and fair view principle in preparing financial statements. Some suggest that the German

[22] E. L. E. Eberhartinger, "The Impact of Tax Rules on Financial Reporting in Germany, France, and the UK," *International Journal of Accounting* 34, no. 1 (1999), pp. 93–119.

[23] Timothy S. Doupnik, "Recent Innovations in German Accounting Practice Through the Integration of EC Directives," *Advances in International Accounting,* 1992, p. 80.

[24] M. Glaum and U. Mandler, "Global Accounting Harmonization from a German Perspective: Bridging the GAAP," *Journal of International Financial Management and Accounting* 7, no. 3 (1996), pp. 215–42.

understanding of true and fair view differs from how the concept is understood in Anglo-Saxon countries. Alexander and Archer state:

> According to the thinking of the Germans, and to a certain extent of most other member states, the true and fair view is not an operational concept; accounting measurement rules are simply conventions that are agreed on by due democratic process, and if they allow hidden reserves, then such reserves are fair.[25]

The German Accounting Act of 1985 increased the required note disclosures. It appears that extensive note disclosures are seen as a way of achieving the true and fair view without changing the tax-based, income-smoothing approach to financial reporting.

Globalization has had a dramatic effect on German financial reporting in recent years. Since 1998, parent companies whose shares or other issued securities are publicly traded have been allowed to prepare their consolidated financial statements in accordance with IFRSs or other internationally accepted accounting standards, such as U.S. GAAP. In 2001, of the 100 blue-chip companies making up the DAX/MDAX stock market index, 39 were using IFRSs and 22 used U.S. GAAP.[26] Since January 1, 2005, all German listed companies have been required to use IFRSs in preparing their consolidated financial statements. German GAAP continues to be used by nonpublicly traded companies and by publicly traded companies in preparing their parent company, that is, nonconsolidated financial statements, which serve as the basis for taxation.

German accounting practices differ in some respects from IFRSs, partly because German accounting law contains no specific rules in some areas. For example, the law provides no guidance with respect to the translation of foreign currency financial statements of foreign subsidiaries (IAS 21), or annual impairment reviews when a useful life in excess of 20 years is used for intangible assets (IAS 38). Further, there are no specific rules requiring disclosures of a primary statement of changes in equity (IAS 1); fair values of financial assets and liabilities (IAS 32); related-party transactions other than those with equity participants (IAS 24); and earnings per share (IAS 33). There are also inconsistencies between German rules and IFRSs in some areas; for example, goodwill arising on consolidation can be deducted immediately against equity (IFRS 3); foreign currency payables and receivables are generally translated at the worse of transaction and closing rates so as to avoid the recognition of gains on unsettled balances (IAS 21); leases are normally classified according to tax rules and are therefore seldom recognized as finance leases (IAS 17); and inventories can be valued at replacement cost (IAS 2). Exhibit 5.5 summarizes some of the differences between IFRSs and German GAAP.

Another area where German GAAP differs from IFRSs is in the management report, which is, according to the German tradition, an important part of a company's financial statements. The IFRSs do not include specific requirements regarding the management report. However, even companies that publish their financial statements according to IFRSs[27] still have to provide a management report

---

[25] David Alexander and Simon Archer, eds., *European Accounting Guide,* 5th ed. (New York: Aspen, 2004), p. 1.15.

[26] Ibid., p. 7.09.

[27] In early February 2005, it was reported that more than half of German companies, which are in the FTSEurofirst 300 index, adopt IFRSs. Due to globalization pressures, German companies are now competing in a worldwide capital market where the quality of the information provided to investors has to match up to that of international competitors.

EXHIBIT 5.5 Differences between German GAAP and IFRSs

Issue	IFRSs	German GAAP
Business combinations	IFRS 3: Must use purchase method; pooling of interests prohibited.	Certain business combinations may be accounted for as pooling of interests even though an acquirer can be identified.
Goodwill on consolidation	IFRS 3: Not amortized, but tested for impairment annually (effective March 31, 2004).	Goodwill arising on consolidation can be deducted immediately against equity.
Internally generated intangible assets	IAS 38: Internally generated goodwill can be recognized as an asset under certain conditions.	Internally generated intangible assets, which are expected to provide ongoing service to the enterprise must not be recognized.
Foreign currency translation	IAS 21: Foreign currency monetary items should be reported using the closing rate.	Foreign currency monetary balances are generally translated at the worse of transaction and closing rates so as to avoid the recognition of gains on unsettled balances.
Leases	IAS 17: Distinguishes between finance leases and operating leases, and provides guidance for classifying them.	Leases are normally classified according to tax rules; therefore, leases are seldom recognized as finance leases.
Inventory valuation	IAS 2: Requires inventories to be stated at the lower of cost and net realizable value.	Inventories can be stated at the lowest of cost, net realizable value, or replacement cost.
Construction contracts	IAS 11: The stage of completion of the contract activity at the balance sheet date should be used to recognize contract revenue.	In general the completed contract method is used for the recognition of revenue on construction contracts and services.
Exclusion of subsidiaries from consolidation	IAS 27: Subsidiaries whose activities are dissimilar to those of its parent must be consolidated.	Certain subsidiaries with dissimilar activities should be excluded from consolidation.
Start-up costs	IAS 38: Start-up costs must be charged to expenses when incurred.	Start-up costs may be capitalized and amortized over four years.

providing information on a company's future situation, for example, regarding research and development or exposure to financial or operating risks.[28]

In June 2004, 17 German companies were listed on the New York Stock Exchange (NYSE). Prior to the adoption of IFRSs in the European Union in 2005, BASF AG was one of the few NYSE-listed German companies that prepared its consolidated financial statements on the basis of German GAAP; the others used either IFRSs (e.g., Bayer and Schering), or U.S. GAAP (e.g., DaimlerChrysler and Siemens). We can gain some insight into the differences that exist between German GAAP and U.S. GAAP by investigating the reconciliation to U.S. GAAP prepared by BASF in its Form 20-F annual report filed with the U.S. Securities and Exchange Commission. Exhibit 5.6 presents excerpts from this reconciliation for the year ended December 31,

[28] In February 2005, the Federal Ministry of Justice published German Accounting Standard 15, *Management Reporting,* and subsequently the GASB reported that it adopted GAS 15.

EXHIBIT 5.6

BASF GROUP
Form 20-F
2003
Excerpt from Notes to the Consolidated Financial Statements

4. Reconciliation to U.S. GAAP

BASF Aktiengesellschaft
Form 20-F
Notes to the Consolidated Financial Statements

3. Reconciliation to U.S. GAAP

The Consolidated Financial Statements comply with IFRS as far as permissible under German GAAP. The differences between German and U.S. GAAP relate to valuation methods that are required under U.S. GAAP but which are not permissible under German GAAP.

The following is a summary of the significant adjustments to net income and stockholders' equity that would be required if U.S. GAAP had been fully applied rather than German GAAP.

	Note	Year Ended December 31,			
		2004	2004	2003	2002
				(As Restated, Note 3(1))	
			(Million € and Million $, Except Per Share Amounts)		
Reconciliation of Net Income to U.S. GAAP					
Net income as reported in the Consolidated Financial Statements of income under German GAAP		$2,549.2	€1,883.0	€910.2	€1,504.4
Adjustments required to conform with U.S. GAAP:					
Capitalization of interest	(a)	(6.1)	(4.5)	(7.3)	(6.4)
Capitalization of software developed for internal use	(b)	(72.4)	(53.5)	(2.8)	30.5
Accounting for pensions	(c)	55.5	41.0	69.0	71.2
Accounting for provisions	(d)	(11.0)	(8.1)	157.6	12.4
Accounting for derivatives at fair value and valuation of long-term foreign currency items at year end rates	(e)	263.3	194.5	(24.8)	(143.9)
Valuation of securities at market values	(f)	9.2	6.8	(6.2)	.
Valuation adjustments relating to companies accounted for under the equity method	(g)	(218.8)	(161.6)	62.4	12.9
Inventory valuation	(h)	(4.6)	(3.4)	(26.3)	(1.1)
Reversal of goodwill amortization and write-offs due to permanent impairment	(i)	201.3	148.7	167.3	211.0
Other adjustments	(j)	40.3	29.8	1.0	(12.9)
Deferred taxes and recognition of tax effects for dividend payments	(k)	(284.8)	(210.4)	8.9	48.5
Minority interests	(l)	0.7	0.5	10.7	(10.4)
Net income in accordance with U.S. GAAP		**2,521.8**	**1,862.8**	**1,319.7**	**1,716.2**

Earnings per share

The calculation of earnings per common share is based on the weighted-average number of common shares outstanding during the applicable period. The calculation of diluted earnings per common share reflects the effect of all dilutive potential common shares that were outstanding during the respective period. Shares awarded under the BASF employee participation program "plus" have been included in the computation of diluted earnings per share. Due to a resolution by the Board of Executive Directors and the Supervisory Board in 2002, settlements of stock options from the BASF stock option program (BOP) for senior management are made in cash, therefore such stock options have no dilutive effect.

Continued

EXHIBIT 5.6 (*Continued*)

The earnings per share from continuing operations based on income from ordinary activities after taxes were not impacted by any dilutive effect in 2004, 2003 and 2002, because the impact of potential common shares was anti-dilutive in each year.

	Year Ended December 31,			
	2004	**2004**	**2003**	**2002**
	(Million € and Million $, Except per Share Amounts)			
Net income in accordance with U.S. GAAP	$2,521.9	€1,862.8	€1,319.7	€1,716.2
Number of shares (1,000)				
Weighted average undiluted number of shares	548,714	548,714	561,887	579,118
Dilutive effect	—	—	—	—
Weighted average diluted number of shares	548,714	548,714	561,887	579,118
Basic earnings per share in accordance with U.S. GAAP	**4.59**	**3.39**	**2.35**[1]	**2.96**[1]
Dilutive effect	—	—	—	—
Diluted earnings per share in accordance with U.S. GAAP	4.59	3.39	2.35[1]	2.96[1]

	Note	Year Ended December 31,		
		2004	**2004**	**2003**
				(As Restated, Note 3(1))
		(Million € and Million $)		
Reconciliation of Stockholders' Equity to U.S. GAAP				
Stockholders' equity as reported in the Consolidated Balance Sheets under German GAAP		$21,342.7	€15,765.0	€15,878.4
Minority interests		(449.2)	(331.8)	(388.1)
Stockholders' equity excluding minority interests		20,893.5	15,433.2	15,490.3
Adjustments required to conform with U.S. GAAP:				
Capitalization of interest	(a)	639.9	472.7	493.9
Capitalization of software developed for internal use	(b)	173.7	128.3	184.1
Accounting for pensions	(c)	1,251.3	924.3	982.5
Accounting for provisions	(d)	330.9	244.4	206.8
Accounting for derivatives at fair value and valuation of long-term foreign currency items at year end rates	(e)	4.3	3.2	(138.8)
Valuation of securities at market values	(f)	259.3	191.5	89.1
Valuation adjustments relating to companies accounted for under the equity method	(g)	52.8	39.0	182.0
Inventory valuation	(h)	25.6	18.9	167.6
Reversal of goodwill amortization and write-offs due to permanent impairment	(i)	635.6	469.5	337.1
Other adjustments	(j)	79.3	58.6	43.4
Deferred taxes and recognition of tax effects of dividend payments	(k)	(1,097.7)	(810.8)	(698.7)
Minority interests	(l)	(18.5)	(13.7)	(15.3)
Stockholders' equity in accordance with U.S. GAAP		**23,230.0**	**17,159.1**	**17,324.0**

[1]As reported in (h), BASF changed its method of inventory costing from the last-in first-out (LIFO) method to the average cost method. The new method was adopted to provide a better measure of the current value of inventory and because the LIFO method is not allowed under IFRS. The balances of U.S. GAAP shareholders' equity for 2003 and 2002 have been adjusted for the effect of retroactively not applying the LIFO method. The change in inventory costing increased shareholders' equity as of January 1, 2002 by €120.9 million. The following table presents the effect of the change on previously reported net income for 2003 and 2002.

The following table presents the effect of the change in the inventory costing method:

	As Previously Reported	Change in Inventory Costing Method	Restated
	(Million €, Except per Share Data)		
2003			
Net income	1,337.7	(18.0)	1,319.7
Basic earnings per share	2.38	(0.03)	2.35
Diluted earnings per share	2.38	(0.03)	2.35
Stockholders' equity as of December 31	17,221.8	102.2	17,324.0
2002			
Net income	1,716.9	(0.7)	1,716.2
Basic earnings per share	2.96	—	2.96
Diluted earnings per share	2.96	—	2.96
Stockholders' equity as of December 31	17,919.8	120.2	18,040.0

(a) Capitalization of interest

For U.S. GAAP purposes, the Company capitalizes interest on borrowings during the active construction period of major capital projects. Capitalized interest is added to the cost of the underlying assets and is amortized over the useful lives of the assets. The capitalization of interest relating to capital projects is not permissible under German GAAP. In calculating capitalized interest, the Company has made assumptions with respect to the capitalization rate and the average amount of accumulated expenditures. The Company's subsidiaries generally use the entity-specific weighted-average borrowing rate as the capitalization rate.

(b) Capitalization of software developed for internal use

Certain costs incurred for computer software developed or obtained for the Company's internal use are to be capitalized and amortized over the expected useful life of the software. Such costs have been expensed in these financial statements because the capitalization of self-developed intangible assets is not permissible under German GAAP.

(c) Accounting for pensions

Pension benefits under Company pension schemes are partly funded in a legally independent fund "BASF Pensionskasse VVaG" ("BASF Pensionskasse"). Pension liabilities and plan assets of BASF Pensionskasse are not included in BASF Group's balance sheet. However, contributions to the BASF Pensionskasse are included in expenses for pensions and assistance.

BASF guarantees the commitments of the BASF Pensionskasse. For U.S. GAAP purposes, BASF Pensionskasse would be classified as a defined benefit plan and therefore included in the calculation of net periodic benefit cost as well as the projected benefit obligation and plan assets. The valuation of the pension obligations under the projected unit credit method and of the fund assets of BASF Pensionskasse at market values would result in a prepaid pension asset in accordance with U.S. GAAP that is not recorded in the Consolidated Financial Statements under German GAAP.

Net periodic benefit cost in accordance with U.S. GAAP would be lower than showing the Company's contribution to the BASF Pensionskasse as expense.

Information about the funded status of the BASF Pensionskasse is provided in the following table:

	2004	2003
	(Million €)	
Plan assets as of December 31, ...	4,034.1	3,781.2
Projected benefit obligation as of December 31, ...	3,871.9	3,569.3
Funded status	162.2	211.9
Unrecognized actuarial losses	667.0	575.0
Prepaid pension asset	829.2	786.9

Continued

EXHIBIT 5.6 *(Continued)*

The accumulated pension benefit obligation (ABO) in 2004 is €3,725.2 million and in 2003 is €3,429.8 million.

The valuation of certain pension plans of foreign subsidiaries, in accordance with SFAS 87 also resulted in prepaid pension assets. After consideration of unrecognized actuarial gains and losses, €95.1 million in 2004, and €195.6 million in 2003 were included in the reconciliation to U.S. GAAP. In addition, the change in treatment of pension liabilities explained in Note 2, and the associated charge of accumulated actuarial gains and losses to shareholders' equity is eliminated for U.S. GAAP as the SFAS 87 accounting treatment is to be continued. In the case of an additional minimum liability, equity according to U.S. GAAP is reduced.

(d) Accounting for provisions

The reconciliation item contains the following deviations:

Provisions for part-time programs for employees nearing retirement age:

In these financial statements agreed upon top-up payments within the pre-retirement part-time programs are immediately accrued in their full amount, and discounted at a rate of 3.0% (see note 22). A provision is also recorded for the expected costs for agreements that are anticipated to be concluded during the term of the collective bargaining agreements, taking into consideration the ceilings on the number of employee participants provided in such collective bargaining agreements. In accordance with U.S. GAAP, provisions may only be recorded for employees who have accepted an offer, and the supplemental payments are accrued over the employee's remaining service period. This results in a (decrease)/increase in income under U.S. GAAP of €(22.3) million in 2004, €124.4 million in 2003, and €6.0 million in 2002. Stockholders' equity increased by €154.7 million in 2004 and €140.0 million in 2003.

Provisions for omitted maintenance procedures:

German GAAP requires companies to accrue provisions as of the end of the year for expected costs of omitted maintenance procedures expected to take place in the first three months of the following year. Such costs would be expensed as incurred under U.S. GAAP. The amounts included in the reconciliation of net income related to maintenance provisions were €(8.3) million in 2004, €(1.7) million in 2003, and €6.4 million in 2002. The amounts in the reconciliation of stockholders' equity were €23.7 million in 2004, and €32.0 million in 2003.

Provisions for restructuring measures:

SFAS 146, "Accounting for Costs Associated with Exit and Disposal Activities," requires expected costs associated with the exit or disposal of business activities to be accrued only when a liability against a third party exists. This includes severance payments for employees, the cancellation of contracts, the shutdown of production facilities, and the relocation of employees.

Since the accruals for restructuring measures under German GAAP are recorded based upon management decisions, the application of SFAS 146 (decreased)/increased net income in accordance with U.S. GAAP by €(20.9) million in 2004 (€23.5 million in 2003), and stockholders' equity by €1.6 million (€23.3 million in 2003).

Provisions for environmental measures:

In the current financial statement, obligations for recultivation obligations due to oil and gas extraction are accrued. SFAS 143, "Accounting for Asset Retirement Obligations," addresses financial accounting and reporting for obligations and costs associated with the retirement of tangible long-lived assets. The expected obligations and costs associated with the demolition of plants and removal of potential damage to the environment have to be accrued as of the start of the production as additional cost for the related plants and are depreciated over the useful life. This also includes the change of these potential liabilities due to adjustments to the conditions as of the balance sheet date.

In addition, provisions accrued in 2004 for adaptation obligations in connection with the operation of production plants are not to be taken into consideration according to SOP 96-1, and have therefore been eliminated. Income was thereby increased by €13.9 million in 2004 and €3.8 million in 2003. Equity increased by €25.8 million in 2004 and €11.4 million in 2003.

Discounting of provisions and liabilities:

Provisions and liabilities are to be shown at nominal value according to German GAAP. According to U.S. GAAP, the values may be discounted if the aggregate amount of the liability and the timing of payments are reliably determinable. This results in an income effect in 2004 of €38.6 million, which leads to an equity increase in the same amount.

(e) Accounting for derivatives at fair value and valuation of long-term foreign currency items

As required by SFAS 133, as amended, derivative contracts are to be accounted for at fair values. Where hedge accounting is not applicable, changes in the fair values of derivative contracts are to be included in net income, together with foreign exchange gains and losses of the underlying transactions.

Under German GAAP, long-term receivables and liabilities denominated in a foreign currency are converted into euros at the exchange rates of the date when the transactions took place or the lower exchange rates at the end of the year for receivables and the higher exchange rates for liabilities. U.S. GAAP requires conversion at the exchange rate at the end of the year.

Under German GAAP, unrealized gains on swaps and other forward contracts are deferred until settlement or termination while unrealized expected losses from firm commitments are recognized as of each period end. Under U.S. GAAP, these contracts are marked to market.

Under German GAAP, hedge accounting is achieved by a combined valuation of underlying hedged transactions and derivatives. Under U.S. GAAP such accounting is not permitted. SFAS 133 requires that the hedged transaction and the derivative be accounted for separately, and extensive documentation regarding the hedge relationship be provided.

(f) Valuation of securities

Under U.S. GAAP, available-for-sale securities are recorded at market values on the balance sheet date. If the effect comes from unrealized profits or temporary decreases in value, the change in valuation is immediately recognized in a separate component of stockholders' equity. Realized profits and losses are credited or charged to income, as are other than temporary impairments of value. The major part of securities and other investments are considered to be available-for-sale. Under German GAAP, such securities and other investments are valued at the lower of acquisition cost or market value at the balance sheet date.

(g) Valuation adjustments relating to companies accounted for under the equity method

For purposes of the reconciliation to U.S. GAAP, the earnings of companies accounted for using the equity method have been determined using valuation principles prescribed by U.S. GAAP. The write-down of the interests in Basell N.V., the Netherlands, and Svalöf Weibull, Sweden, affected net income under German GAAP in 2004. This also applies to the catch-up of scheduled amortization of goodwill of these companies under U.S. GAAP that was eliminated according to SFAS 142 (Goodwill and Other Intangible Assets) in the previous years.

(h) Inventory valuation

In connection with the conversion to IFRS as of January 1, 2005, the current inventory valuation methods are being changed. This specifically affects the LIFO method, which is not allowed under IFRS. This change requires prior years' amounts to be restated, according to APB 20.27. In the current year there were differences resulting from the deductions required by German GAAP.

(i) Reversal of goodwill amortization and write-offs due to permanent impairment

Goodwill is amortized over its useful life in accordance with German GAAP, however, the U.S. GAAP standard SFAS 142, "Goodwill and Other Intangible Assets," requires write-offs only based on annual impairment tests. The recoverability of goodwill is reviewed at the reporting-unit level by comparing the fair value of the reporting unit determined using discounted future cash flows, to the carrying value. There were no material impairment write-downs required in 2004 or 2003. The regular goodwill amortization included in these financial statements is reversed and added back to net income.

(j) Other adjustments

This item primarily includes the adjustment of provisions for stock compensation.

Following a resolution by the Board of Executive Directors in 2002, stock options are to be settled in cash. Under U.S. GAAP, such obligations are to be accounted for as stock appreciation rights based on the intrinsic value of the options on the balance sheet date. However, options granted in prior years, for which cash settlement was not foreseen, are to be accounted for in accordance with SFAS 123 as equity instruments based upon the fair value on the grant date.

In the present Financial Statements, all obligations resulting from stock options are accounted for based upon the fair value on the balance sheet date. A provision is accrued over the vesting period of the options. The different accounting methods led to an increase in net income in accordance with U.S. GAAP of €16.1 million in 2004, and €17.2 million in 2003, and a decrease of €10.7 million in 2002.

In the present Financial Statements, obligations resulting from stock options are shown as provisions. In accordance with U.S. GAAP, options for which cash settlement was not originally foreseen are recorded as additions to stockholders' equity.

Overall, the accounting for stock options resulted in a decrease in stockholders' equity of €9.4 million in 2004, and €14.6 million in 2003.

Continued

EXHIBIT 5.6 (*Continued*)

(k) Deferred taxes

The adjustments required to conform with U.S. GAAP would result in taxable temporary differences between the valuation of assets and liabilities in the Consolidated Financial Statements and the carrying amount for tax purposes. Resulting adjustments for deferred taxes primarily relate to the following:

	Note	Stockholders' Equity			Net Income	
		2004	2003	2004	2003	2002
		(Million €)				
Capitalization of interest	(a)	(158.4)	(171.5)	8.9	11.0	7.3
Capitalization of software developed for internal use	(b)	(47.7)	(69.7)	21.0	1.0	(10.4)
Accounting for pensions	(c)	(351.1)	(360.6)	(14.3)	(27.7)	(22.2)
Accounting for provisions	(d)	(82.2)	(78.8)	13.9	(59.1)	(5.8)
Accounting for derivatives at fair value and valuation of long-term foreign currency items at year end rates	(e)	13.4	48.9	(58.9)	6.3	35.3
Valuation of securities at market values	(f)	(3.8)	0.1	(4.0)	(17.2)	62.2
Valuation adjustments relating to companies accounted for under the equity method	(g)	—	—	—	—	45.7
Inventory valuation	(h)	(7.2)	(65.4)	1.3	8.3	0.4
Reversal of goodwill amortization and write-offs due to permanent impairment	(i)	(122.0)	(97.0)	(31.2)	(45.9)	(60.7)
Other adjustments	(j)	55.7	95.3	(39.6)	8.0	(5.5)
Tax effects of dividend payments	(k)	(107.5)	—	(107.5)	124.2	2.2
		(810.8)	**(698.7)**	**(210.4)**	**8.9**	**48.5**

The change of the deferred taxes for foreign currency translation adjustments is recognized in other comprehensive income.

In 2004, following a change to the German Corporate Income Tax Act (Section 8b), deferred taxes were, for the first time, accrued for tax effects of future dividend payments from BASF Group companies, according to the financial plan.

In 2003, capitalized tax credits related to the distribution of retained earnings previously taxed at higher rates had to be written off in the German GAAP financial statements due to a legal change. In accordance with U.S. GAAP, such tax credits are recognized as a reduction of income tax expenses in the period in which the tax credits are recognized for tax purposes. The resulting burden on income therefore had to be eliminated in 2003 for U.S. GAAP purposes.

(l) Minority interests

The share of minority shareholders in the aforementioned reconciliation items to U.S. GAAP of net income and stockholders' equity are reported separately.

Consolidation of majority-owned subsidiaries: U.S. GAAP requires the consolidation of all controlled subsidiaries. Under German GAAP, the Company does not consolidate certain subsidiaries if their individual or their combined effect on financial position, results of operations and cash flows is not material. The effect of non-consolidated subsidiaries for 2004, 2003 and 2002, on total assets, total liabilities, stockholders' equity, net sales and net income was less than 2%.

Additionally, under German GAAP, the Company accounts on a prospective basis for previous unconsolidated subsidiaries that are added to the scope of consolidation. U.S. GAAP requires consolidation for all periods that a subsidiary is controlled. The effects of adding previously unconsolidated companies to the scope of consolidation on net sales, net income, assets and liabilities was immaterial.

Proportional consolidation: The Company accounts for its investments in 12 jointly operated companies (2003: 12, 2002: 11) using the proportional consolidation method, as permitted under German GAAP. Under U.S. GAAP, all investments in jointly operated companies must be accounted for using the equity method. The differences in accounting treatment between proportional consolidation and the equity method of accounting have no impact on reported stockholders' equity or net income. Rather, they relate solely to matters of classification and display. The United States Securities and Exchange Commission (SEC) permits the omission of such differences in classification and display in the reconciliation to U.S. GAAP appearing above.

Balance Sheet presentation: The classification of the balance sheet is as required by German GAAP. Noncurrent portions of receivables and prepaid expenses are disclosed in Notes 15 and 17. Current portions of provisions and liabilities are disclosed in Notes 22 and 23.

New U.S. GAAP accounting standards not yet adopted

The standards adopted in 2004—SFAS 151 "Inventory Costs," SFAS 152 "Accounting for Real Estate Time-Sharing Transactions," SFAS 153 "Exchange of Nonmonetary Assets," and EITF 03-1 "The Meaning of Other Than Temporary Impairment and its Application to Certain Investments"—were examined to determine their effect on the BASF Group financial statements. According to SFAS 151, certain abnormal costs for the production of inventories are to be charged against income in the period they occur, rather than being capitalized as production costs. SFAS 152 covers the accounting treatment of timesharing of property and property rights. SFAS 153 states that the exchange of nonmonetary assets are generally to be valued at fair value. EITF 03-1 provides guidance regarding the impairment of certain investments and the related disclosures. In September 2004, the Emerging Issues Task Force issued EITF Issue 4-10 "Determining Whether to Aggregate Operating Segments That Do Not Meet the Quantitative Thresholds" ("EITF 4-10"), which addresses the criteria for aggregating operating segments. We have reviewed our segment reporting and have determined that our aggregation of segments is consistent with the guidance in EITF Issue No. 4-10. These new standards have no effect on the financial statements of the BASF Group.

Reporting of comprehensive income

Comprehensive income in accordance with SFAS 130, "Reporting Comprehensive Income," includes the impact of expenses and earnings that are not included in net income under U.S. GAAP.

	Year Ended December 31,		
	2004	**2003**	**2002**
	(Million €)		
Comprehensive income			
Net income in accordance with U.S. GAAP (before other comprehensive income)	1,862.8	1,319.7	1,716.2
Change of foreign currency translation adjustments			
/*/ Gross	(291.3)	(729.3)	(908.6)
/*/ Deferred taxes	17.2	38.0	24.3
Changes in unrealized holding gains on securities			
/*/ Gross	95.6	(5.2)	(262.8)
/*/ Deferred taxes	0.3	17.2	71.8
Changes in unrealized losses from cash flow hedges			
/*/ Gross	(54.0)	0.5	(4.6)
/*/ Deferred taxes	18.7	(0.2)	1.6
Additional minimum liability for pensions			
/*/ Gross	(514.7)	(18.5)	(17.8)
/*/ Deferred taxes	197.0	—	5.4
Other comprehensive income (loss), net of tax	(531.2)	(697.5)	(1,090.7)
Comprehensive income, net of tax	**1,331.6**	**622.2**	**625.5**

Continued

EXHIBIT 5.6   *(Continued)*

	Year Ended December 31,	
	2004	2003
	(Million €)	
Statement of stockholders' equity		
Stockholders' equity in accordance with U.S. GAAP before accumulated other comprehensive income	18,694.7	18,328.4
Accumulated other comprehensive income:		
Translation adjustments		
/*/ Gross	(1,369.0)	(1,077.7)
/*/ Deferred taxes	69.2	52.0
Unrealized holding gains on securities		
/*/ Gross	196.2	100.6
/*/ Deferred taxes	(45.4)	(45.7)
Unrealized losses from cash flow hedges		
/*/ Gross	(58.1)	(4.1)
/*/ Deferred taxes	20.1	1.4
Additional minimum liability for pensions		
/*/ Gross	(551.0)	(36.3)
/*/ Deferred taxes	202.4	5.4
Accumulated other comprehensive income	(1,535.6)	(1,004.4)
Total stockholders' equity in accordance with U.S. GAAP including comprehensive income	**17,159.1**	**17,324.0**

Reconciliation of stockholders' equity under U.S. GAAP

	Year Ended December 31,	
	2004	2003
	(Million €)	
Stockholders' equity in accordance with U.S. GAAP on January 1	17,324.0	18,040.0
Comprehensive income, net of tax	1,331.6	622.2
Share buyback and cancellation, including own shares intended to be cancelled	(725.7)	(499.8)
Dividend paid (excluding minority interests)	(774.1)	(788.7)
BASF stock option program	(9.4)	(14.6)
Change in scope of consolidation and other changes	12.7	(35.1)
Total stockholders' equity in accordance with U.S. GAAP on December 31	**17,159.1**	**17,324.0**

2003. Note that BASF has adopted accounting policies consistent with U.S. GAAP to the extent that these practices are permissible under German GAAP. Nonetheless, BASF's accountants have determined that there are 11 accounting issues in which U.S. GAAP and German GAAP are incompatible and for which an adjustment must be made. The largest adjustments relate to the accounting for goodwill and the accrual of provisions. The adjustment related to provisions reverses accruals of liabilities (and expenses) that were made under German GAAP in 2003 that would not have met the definition of a liability under U.S. GAAP in that period.

JAPAN

Background

Legislative authority in Japan rests with the *Kokkai*, the bicameral diet, which consists of a 480-member House of Representatives and a 247-member House of Councillors. Members of the House of Representatives serve a four-year term. The House of Councillors elects half of its members every three years for a six-year term.

In 1868, groups of feudal lords, known as samurai, and aristocrats overthrew the military government and installed an imperial government under the Meiji Empire. This ended Japan's self-isolation policy and led to rapid economic change. Prior to World War II, the Japanese economy was dominated by *zaibatsu* (family financial combines). They derived their power from both economic strength and political affiliations. Each of these conglomerates usually included a major bank as the source of finance for the group. During the postwar occupation of Japan by the allied forces, *zaibatsu* were dissolved by the Anti-Monopoly Law of 1947. However, when the allied forces left Japan in 1952, the old conglomerates started to reappear under a different name, *keiretsu*. Douthett and Jung describe the disappearance of *zaibatsu* and the reappearance of *keiretsu* as follows:

> An interesting aspect of Japanese ownership structure is the industrial groupings known as the *keiretsu*. The *keiretsu* is a successor of pre-war *zaibatsu*, which originated as family-controlled concerns such as Yasuda banking complex, Mitsubishi shipping conglomerate, and Mitsui trading company, and existed as early as the 1870s. After the *zaibatsu* were dissolved by the Anti-Monopoly Law (1947) during the occupation of Japan by the allied forces following World War II, the pre-existing inter-firm relations gradually re-emerged as *keiretsu* through coordination by the previous *zaibatsu* banks and other large commercial banks.
>
> After the occupation forces left Japan in April 1952, Ministry of International Trade and Industry (MITI) began to permit formation of cartels among the small businesses as an exception to the anti-Monopoly Law. . . . As a result, the old *zaibatsu* names were restored and MITI encouraged the formation of *keiretsu*. Banks continued to be the major nexus of inter-locking shareholding ties in these "financial *keiretsu*." The main banking groups of Mitsubishi, Sumitomo, Mitsui and Fuyo as well as the newer groups of Sanwa and Dai-ichi Kangyo Group (DKB) were the initial six financial *keiretsu*. These financial *keiretsu* are referred to as horizontal *keiretsu* since the member firms have common ties with a main bank, including shared stockholdings as well as normal banking relations. In contrast, a vertical *keiretsu* normally involves a very large trading company with many small, subservient companies such as Toyota Motor Corporation.[29]

A unique aspect of Japanese business is cross-corporate ownership. About 70 percent of the equity shares of listed firms in Japan are cross-owned by corporate

[29] E. B. Douthett and K. Jung, "Japanese Corporate Groupings (*Keiretsu*) and the Informativeness of Earnings," *Journal of International Financial Management and Accounting* 12, no. 2 (2001), pp. 135–36.

shareholders such as financial institutions and other companies. *Keiretsu* control about a half of the top 200 firms in Japan through cross-corporate shareholdings, which amount to more than 25 percent of all the assets in Japan.[30] The manner in which business is organized in Japan reflects its cultural value of collectivism.

The ways in which businesses are financed influences financial reporting and attitudes of interested parties toward accounting information. The main sources of finance for Japanese business are through bank credit and cross-corporate ownership. Unlike in the United States, outside equity financing is relatively minor. In addition to providing credit, banks also have control over major portions of corporate equity capital. As "insiders," banks have access to their clients' financial information, so there is less pressure for public disclosure. This helps to explain the relatively low level of information disclosure in the annual reports of Japanese companies. The heavy reliance on bank credit and the long-term nature of cross-corporate equity ownership also lead to a weaker emphasis on short-term earnings in Japanese companies compared to those in the United States. Corporate earnings are regarded as the source of funds that can be distributed, at the discretion of the shareholders, and not as a measure of corporate performance.

In the 1990s, however, as their ability to raise capital from domestic sources contracted significantly, Japanese companies were compelled to look beyond the national borders to raise capital. This was due to the major recessionary pressures experienced by the Japanese economy during this period involving large-scale capital losses among Japanese banks and other financial companies, as well as the collapse of Japanese asset prices, including stock prices.[31] As the need to attract foreign investment grew, Japanese businesses and regulators found it necessary to respond to the demands of the international capital markets.

Accounting Profession

The Certified Public Accountants Law of 1948 established the Japanese Institute of Certified Public Accountants (JICPA). This can be considered the beginning of the modern accounting profession in Japan. The JICPA has been heavily involved in the international harmonization process, being one of the nine founding members of the IASC. Compared to the AICPA in the United States, the influence of the JICPA on financial reporting in Japan has been minor. Its traditional role has been basically to implement the decisions made by the Ministry of Finance (MoF). It has issued recommendations on minor accounting issues, guidelines, and interpretations of accounting and auditing standards.[32]

Members of the accountancy profession in Japan practice with the title of CPA under the CPA Law of 1948. The CPA law deals with issues such as examinations, qualifications, registration, duties, and responsibilities of CPAs; audit corporations; the CPA board; JICPA; and disciplinary procedures. Because of the cultural value of collectivism, an independent auditor in Japan does not fit the role of someone to be trusted or relied on and the auditor has difficulty being accepted by clients. Japanese corporations do not typically trust outsiders, and that includes

---

[30] L. Jiang and J. Kim, "Cross-Corporate Ownership, Information Asymmetry and the Usefulness of Accounting Performance Measures in Japan," *International Journal of Accounting* 35, no. 1 (2000), p. 96.

[31] W. R. Singleton and S. Globerman, "The Nature of Financial Disclosure in Japan," *International Journal of Accounting* 37 (2002), pp. 95–111.

[32] Tax experts have their own separate profession, and it is much larger in terms of membership.

(Japanese) auditors.[33] The relatively low status of the accounting profession within Japanese society is reflected in the fact that very few CPAs hold top positions in industry and commerce. Instead, such positions are often held by people with engineering and science backgrounds. Although the population of Japan is about one-third the size of the U.S. population, Japan has about 15,000 CPAs, compared to about 250,000 in the United States.

The relatively small number of CPAs in Japan is caused partially by the rigorous requirements one must meet to become an accountant. The preliminary requirement includes a series of general examinations, but university graduates are exempt from this requirement. A candidate then must pass intermediate exams covering topics such as economics, bookkeeping, financial and cost accounting, the Commercial Code, and auditing theory. The pass rates for this exam are relatively low, but a candidate who does pass is considered to be a junior CPA. A three-year apprenticeship then is required, which includes one year in training and two years of practical experience. Upon completion of the apprenticeship, the CPA candidate must take a final technical exam and submit a written thesis. The final exam also has a very low pass rate. The JICPA recently reformed the certification process. Under this reform, the three levels of examinations have been reduced to one, the three-year internship has been reduced to two years, and the notion of junior CPA has been eliminated.

Accounting Regulation

Accounting and financial reporting in Japan are regulated primarily through a triangle of laws: the Commercial Code, the Securities and Exchange Law (SEL), and the Corporate Income Tax Law. The Commercial Code of Japan is administered by the Ministry of Justice. It was enacted in 1890, as mentioned earlier, borrowing heavily from the German Commercial Code. This law requires *kabushiki kaisha* (joint stock corporations) to prepare an annual report for submission to the general meeting of shareholders. The annual report must include a balance sheet, an income statement, and a statement of proposed appropriation of earnings. These must be accompanied by a number of supplementary schedules, including schedules detailing the acquisition and disposal of fixed assets, transactions with directors and shareholders, and details of changes to share capital and reserves. Recent amendments to the code also require certain "large corporations" (as defined by the code) to include a *consolidated* balance sheet and income statement in annual reports for the business years ending in or after 2004. Prior to this, there was no legal requirement for consolidated financial statements in Japan.

Japan has six stock exchanges, the most important being the Tokyo Stock Exchange. From the early 1990s, while the total number of listings in the Japanese exchanges has increased rapidly, the number of foreign companies listed on Japanese stock exchanges has gradually fallen. From 1991 to 2003, the total number of companies listed on the Tokyo stock exchange increased from 1,532 to 2,194; during the same period the number of foreign listings fell from 127 to 32.

Stock exchanges in Japan are government regulated rather than self-regulated. The SEL for listed companies was enacted in 1948 and is administered by the MoF. In 1951 the SEL required that financial statements of stock-exchange-listed companies should be audited by CPAs. This requirement also was added to the Commercial Code in 1974. However, there were difficulties in implementing the SEL,

---

[33] J. Aono, "The Auditing Environment in Japan," in *International Auditing Environment,* ed. I. Shiobara (Tokyo: Zeimukeiri-Kyokai, 2001), pp. 199–211.

particularly during its first two decades. CPA firms at the time were relatively small, often with fewer than 10 assistants, and therefore did not have the capacity to undertake audits of major corporations such as Mitsubishi, Toyota, and Sumitomo. Understandably, these small CPA firms were not able to ensure compliance with the SEL and independence was an issue. As a result, the 1966 revision to the CPA Law allowed many smaller audit companies to merge to form *kansa hajin,* large corporations that operate like partnerships in terms of their liability and auditing activities and often are affiliated with large international accounting firms. Modeled on the U.S. SEC regulations, the financial reporting requirements under SEL are more demanding compared to those of the Commercial Code. In addition to SEL requirements, the stock exchanges have their own listing requirements.

Some Japanese companies, including well-known companies such as Honda Motor Company, Sony Corporation, and Pioneer Corporation, have listed on foreign stock exchanges, in particular the New York Stock Exchange. Foreign companies that list their shares on the U.S. stock market must register with the U.S. Securities and Exchange Commission (SEC). Japanese companies are the fourth largest group of foreign SEC registrants. Interestingly, although the U.S. SEC allows foreign registrants to file financial statements based on foreign GAAP with a reconciliation of income and stockholders' equity only to U.S. GAAP, most Japanese companies with U.S. stock listings use U.S. GAAP in preparing the consolidated financial statements included in their SEC filings.

Unlike in the United States, and as in Germany, financial reporting in Japan is strongly influenced by tax law. The corporate income tax law in Japan provides methods for calculating taxable income and requires revenues and expenses to be recognized in the books of account in accordance with the tax law. The tax law is considered to be less vague than the Commercial Code and the SEL, so it is often referred to for more detailed regulations. Depreciation, allowance for bad debts, and profit from installment sales are examples of accounting issues that are generally reported in financial statements in conformity with the tax law.

In addition to the three laws just discussed, all listed companies are required to comply with Business Accounting Principles issued by the MoF. Business Accounting Principles consist of a set of seven general guidelines that form the equivalent of a conceptual framework in Japan:

1. *True and fair view.* Financial statements should provide a true and fair view of a company's financial situation.
2. *Orderly bookkeeping.* A company must use an orderly system in accounting for its activities.
3. *Distinction between capital and earnings.* A company should clearly distinguish earnings from capital, earnings being the amount that can be distributed to stockholders as a dividend.
4. *Clear presentation.* Financial statements must be presented in a manner that is straightforward and logical.
5. *Continuity.* A company should follow the same accounting principles from year to year, unless a specific and understandable reason to change arises.
6. *Conservatism.* A company should use cautious judgment in applying accounting principles.
7. *Consistency.* A company should prepare only one set of financial statements to be used by various users of financial statements.

In the 1990s, the Business Accounting Principles increasingly came under criticism, mainly from international investors, for lacking a requirement of transparency in corporate reporting.

The Business Accounting Principles are developed by the Business Accounting Deliberation Council (BADC), an advisory body to the MoF. Members of the BADC have a wide variety of backgrounds. They include accountants who work in industry, public accounting, government, and higher education. The BADC has been the primary standard-setting body in Japan.

Japan's economy experienced unprecedented growth from the mid-1950s to the 1980s. In the late 1980s, however, exports and stock prices began to fall, and economic growth ground to a halt. In November 1996, the Japanese government announced its strategy for financial reforms, and the prime minister commissioned the BADC to reform the financial reporting system. This triggered a series of major changes to the regulation of financial reporting in Japan. These changes have been referred to as the Big Bang.[34] One of the major objectives of the Big Bang is to ensure that Japanese accounting standards fall into line with international standards. As a result of the Big Bang, companies in Japan are now required to

- Publish consolidated accounts, including those for all associates over which they have influence.
- Disclose the market value of pension liabilities and whether they have shortfalls.
- Report tradable financial securities, such as derivatives and equities, at market values, not historical cost.[35]

Another outcome of the Big Bang was the creation, in 2001, of the Financial Accounting Standards Foundation (FASF) and a new private-sector standard-setting body modeled on the FASB, the Accounting Standards Board of Japan (ASBJ). The FASF oversees the ASBJ. The ASBJ was established by a joint committee of the Financial Services Agency, the JICPA, and the *Keidanren* (Federation of Economic Organizations). Similar to the manner in which the FASB obtains its authority to establish U.S. GAAP from the U.S. SEC, the FASF and ASBJ derive standard-setting authority from the BADC. The BADC reserves the right, however, to override any ASBJ pronouncement that is considered to be inconsistent with the "true and fair view" principle. The FASF was established partly to facilitate harmonization with international accounting standards. The JICPA takes part in setting accounting standards by sending board members to the FASF and the ASBJ. Additionally, many CPAs participate in various technical committees at the ASBJ as technical staff.

In May 2002, the FASF confirmed that accounting standards issued by the ASBJ are considered to set forth standards for financial accounting and, together with other pronouncements such as Financial Accounting Standards Implementation Guidance and Report of Practical Issues, constitute a coherent set of standards that must be complied with or otherwise referred to by members of the founding organizations and other concerned parties.[36]

In terms of accounting regulation, Japanese tradition differs in several aspects from the approach taken in Anglo-American countries. The government has the

---

[34] T. Ravlic, "Japan Looks to Higher Standards," *Australian CPA* 69, no. 10 (1999), pp. 48–49.

[35] N. Yamori and T. Baba, "Japanese Management Views on Overseas Exchange Listings: Survey Results," *Journal of International Financial Management and Accounting* 12, no. 3 (2001), pp. 312–14.

[36] FASF, "Concerning Treatment (Compliance) of Accounting Standards and other Pronouncements Issued by the Accounting Standards Board of Japan," May 2002. For details, go to www.jicpa.or.jp/n_eng/e200201.html.

strongest influence on accounting through the Commercial Code, the Securities Law, and the Tax Law and Regulations. Further, until recently the Japanese accounting profession, represented by the JICPA, had only a relatively minor influence on determining standards for accounting and financial reporting. Finally, stock exchanges are government regulated rather than self-regulated.

International influences have played a major role in shaping accounting regulation in Japan. The Commercial Code reflects a German influence on the Japanese company legislation, including financial reporting requirements. The Securities and Exchange Law clearly reflects the influence of U.S. securities and exchange regulations. Indications are that the forces of globalization are having a significant impact on accounting and financial reporting in Japan and will continue to do so in the future.[37]

Accounting Principles and Practices

As mentioned earlier, Japanese disclosure requirements are based on the Commercial Code, the SEL, and ASBJ accounting standards. Accounting periods ending on March 31 are the most common in Japan. Corporate net income tends to be used as a measure of funds available for distribution to shareholders, and not as a measure of corporate performance. Financial reporting practices in Japan reflect some of the inherent cultural values in Japanese society, such as group consciousness. Prior to the U.S. occupation of Japan following World War II, there was no outside auditing profession. Many Japanese corporations viewed the introduction of the CPA law in 1949 as unnecessary, and the audit as a necessary inconvenience.[38]

In general, companies are not under pressure from their main providers of finance to disclose information publicly, and Japanese companies are reluctant to provide information voluntarily. Research has found that Japanese financial analysts are concerned that Japanese firms do not define segments meaningfully and consistently and are arbitrary in the allocation of common costs,[39] and that there is a general reluctance on the part of Japanese firms to disclose segment and other information, particularly to nonshareholders.[40]

Efforts are being made to bring Japanese accounting principles and practices closer to international standards. In January 2005, the IASB and the ASBJ announced that they had agreed to launch a joint project to reduce differences between IFRSs and Japanese accounting standards. Specific elements of the agreement include the following:

- Identification and assessment of differences in their existing standards on the basis of their respective conceptual frameworks or basic philosophies with the aim of reducing those differences where economic substance or market environments such as legal systems are equivalent.

---

[37] For information on developments in Japanese accounting activity, go to www.jicpa.or.jp/n_eng/e-jicpa.html.

[38] Aono, "The Auditing Environment. . . ."

[39] V. Mande and R. Ortman, "Are Recent Segment Disclosures of Japanese Firms Useful? Views of Japanese Financial Analysts," *International Journal of Accounting* 37 (2002), pp. 27–46.

[40] C. Ozu and S. Gray, "The Development of Segment Reporting in Japan: Achieving International Harmonization Through a Process of National Consensus," *Advances in International Accounting* 14 (2001), pp. 1–13; and J. L. McKinnon and G. L. Harrison, "Cultural Influence on Corporate and Governmental Involvement in Accounting Policy Determination in Japan," *Journal of Accounting and Public Policy*, Autumn (1985), pp. 201–23.

- Addressing the differences in their respective conceptual frameworks.
- Considering their respective due process requirements in arriving at agreement.
- Undertaking a study by the ASBJ to get an overall picture of major differences between Japanese accounting standards and IFRSs with a view to identifying topics to be discussed.

Under this project, five topics will be considered by both boards for the first phase:

- Measurement of inventories (IAS 2).
- Segment reporting (IAS 14).
- Related-party disclosures (IAS 24).
- Unification of accounting policies applied to foreign subsidiaries (IAS 27).
- Investment property (IAS 40).

The differences between Japanese accounting standards and IFRSs can be identified in many areas. There are no specific Japanese rules in some areas covered by IFRSs, such as classification of business combinations as acquisitions or poolings of interest (IAS 22), impairment of assets (IAS 36), and accounting for employee benefits other than severance indemnities (IAS 19). Further, there are no specific rules requiring disclosures of a primary statement of changes in equity (IAS 1), discontinuing operations (IAS 35), and segment liabilities (IAS 14). In some other areas, there are inconsistencies between Japanese GAAP and IFRSs. For example, under Japanese GAAP, leases, except those that transfer ownership to the lessee, are treated as operating leases (IAS 17); inventories generally can be valued at cost rather than at the lower of cost or net realizable value (IAS 2); proposed dividends can be accrued in consolidated financial statements (IAS 10); and extraordinary items are defined more broadly (IAS 8). Exhibit 5.7 shows some of differences between IFRSs and Japanese GAAP.

Nineteen Japanese companies were listed on the New York Stock Exchange in June 2004. Each of these companies uses U.S. GAAP to prepare the financial statements included in the Form 20-F annual report filed with the U.S. Securities and Exchange Commission, so there are no reconciliations from Japanese GAAP to U.S. GAAP that we can look at to learn about the effect differences in the two sets of accounting standards have on financial statements. However, in its 2003 Form 20-F, Nidec Corporation (a Japanese motor manufacturer) provided the following information related to differences between Japanese and U.S. GAAP:

> There are differences between Japanese GAAP and U.S. GAAP. They primarily relate to the statement of cash flows, disclosure of segment information, the scope of consolidation, accounting for derivatives, deferred income taxes, accounting for investments in certain equity securities, accounting for lease transactions, accrued compensated absences, accounting for employee retirement and severance benefits, accounting for the impairment of long-lived assets, earnings per share and comprehensive income. Also, under Japanese GAAP, a restatement of prior years' financial statements reflecting the effect of a change in accounting policies is not required.
>
> Our results of operations for the year ended March 31, 2003, as reported in our U.S. GAAP and Japanese GAAP consolidated financial statements differ substantially mainly because of the difference in the scope of consolidation. For that year, we consolidated 18 more entities in our Japanese GAAP consolidated financial statements than in our U.S. GAAP consolidated financial statements. We were required to consolidate these additional entities in our Japanese GAAP consolidated financial statements because, with respect to each of those entities: (i) we were

EXHIBIT 5.7 Differences between Japanese GAAP and IFRSs

Issue	IFRSs	Japanese GAAP
Accounting policies for overseas subsidiaries	IAS 27: Consolidated financial statements should be prepared using uniform accounting policies for like transactions and other events in similar circumstances. If it is not practicable to use uniform accounting policies, that fact should be disclosed together with the proportions of the items in the consolidated financial statements to which the different accounting policies have been applied.	It is acceptable that overseas subsidiaries apply different accounting policies if they are appropriate under the requirements of the country of those subsidiaries.
Revaluation of land	IAS 16: Revaluations should be made with sufficient regularity such that the carrying amount does not differ materially from that which would be determined using fair value at the balance sheet date.	Land can be revalued, but the revaluation does not need to be kept up to date.
Preoperating costs	IAS 38: Start-up costs should be recognized as an expense when incurred.	Preoperating costs can be capitalized.
Inventory valuation	IAS 2: Inventories should be measured at the lower of cost or net realizable value.	Inventories can be valued at cost rather than at the lower of cost and net realizable value.
Construction contracts	IAS 11: The stage of completion of the contract activity at the balance sheet date should be used to recognize contract revenue.	The completed contract method can be used for the recognition of revenue on construction contracts.
Provisions	IAS 37: Provisions can be made only if an enterprise has a present obligation as result of a past transaction.	Provisions can be made on the on the basis of decisions by directors before an obligation arises.
Segment reporting	IAS 14: Disclosure requirements for segments are provided in terms of primary and secondary reporting formats.	Segment reporting does not use the primary/secondary basis.
Financial statements of hyperinflationary subsidiaries	IAS 21: The financial statements of a foreign entity that reports in the currency of a hyperinflationary economy should be restated before they are translated into the reporting currency of the reporting entity.	There are no requirements concerning the translation of the financial statements of hyperinflationary subsidiaries.

regarded as possessing a majority of the entity's voting shares because of the existence of a sufficient number of shareholders of the company that did not exercise their voting rights at the shareholders' general meetings; or (ii) our current or former executives or employees comprised a majority of the board of directors of the entity. These 18 entities had combined net sales of ¥86 billion in the year ended March 31, 2003. (p. 4)

Nidec Corporation also provided two sets of consolidated financial statements for the year ended March 31, 2003, on its corporate Web site—one set prepared under Japanese GAAP and the second set prepared under U.S. GAAP. The company's consolidated balance sheets and income statements prepared under the two different sets of accounting rules are presented in Exhibit 5.8. A comparison of

EXHIBIT 5.8

NIDEC CORPORATION
Consolidated Balance Sheets and Income Statements
Prepared in Accordance with Japanese GAAP and U.S. GAAP
2004

<u>Japanese GAAP</u>

4. CONSOLIDATED FINANCIAL STATEMENTS

1) Consolidated Balance Sheets

Assets

	Japanese Yen (Millions)				
	March 31, 2004		March 31, 2003		Increase (decrease)
	Amount	%	Amount	%	
Current assets:					
Cash and bank deposits	¥ 74,487		¥ 49,491		¥ 24,996
Note & accounts receivable	117,896		80,144		37,752
Marketable securities	217		266		(49)
Inventories	42,262		24,298		17,964
Deferred income taxes	2,778		4,144		(1,366)
Other current assets	8,906		10,176		(1,270)
Allowances for doubtful accounts	(624)		(550)		(74)
Total current assets	245,925	56.7	167,972	55.0	77,953
Fixed assets:					
Property, plant and equipment	138,610	32.0	112,484	36.9	26,126
Buildings and structures	38,131		35,372		2,759
Machinery and vehicles	41,806		34,419		7,387
Tools, furniture and fixtures	14,564		11,541		3,023
Land	36,726		28,691		8,035
Construction in progress	7,383		2,459		4,924
Intangible assets	24,866	5.7	9,174	3.0	15,692
Goodwill	24,071		8,402		15,669
Other intangible assets.	794		771		23
Investments and other assets	24,303	5.6	15,673	5.1	8,630
Investment securities	15,472		7,342		8,130
Deferred income taxes	4,016		4,608		(592)
Other investments	5,560		4,374		1,186
Allowances for doubtful accounts	(745)		(651)		(94)
Total fixed assets	187,779	43.3	137,332	45.0	50,447
Deferred charges	0	0.0	13	0.0	(13)
Total assets	¥433,706	100.0	¥305,318	100.0	¥128,388

Continued

EXHIBIT 5.8 (*Continued*)

Liabilities and Shareholders' Equity

	Japanese Yen (Millions)				
	March 31 2004		March 31 2003		Increase (decrease)
	Amount	%	Amount	%	
Current liabilities:					
Notes and accounts payable	¥ 83,961		¥ 53,113		¥ 30,848
Short-term borrowings	86,944		65,496		21,448
Current portion of long-term debt	1,650		3,349		(1,699)
Current portion of convertible bonds	—		5,027		(5,027)
Income taxes payable	3,790		3,045		745
Deferred income taxes	48		0		48
Accrued bonus to employees	4,670		3,325		1,345
Other current liabilities	23,489		19,129		4,360
Total current liabilities	204,554	47.2	152,485	49.9	52,069
Non-current liabilities:					
Corporate bonds	30,000		—		30,000
Convertible bonds	9,274		9,279		(5)
Long-term debt	3,008		5,187		(2,179)
Deferred income taxes	2,730		1,192		1,538
Accrued severance benefit costs	25,701		9,081		16,620
Accrued retirement benefit to directors	1,921		1,255		666
Other non-current liabilities	2,524		811		1,713
Total non-current liabilities	75,161	17.3	26,807	8.8	48,354
Total liabilities	279,716	64.5	179,293	58.7	100,423
Minority interests	49,308	11.4	35,882	11.8	13,426
Shareholders' equity:					
Common stock	28,994	6.7	26,485	8.7	2,509
Additional paid-in capital	32,378	7.4	26,360	8.6	6,018
Retained earnings	53,639	12.4	44,282	14.5	9,357
Land revaluation reserve	(701)	(0.2)	(701)	(0.2)	—
Net unrealized loss on securities	1,966	0.4	(561)	(0.2)	2,527
Foreign currency translation Adjustment	(11,473)	(2.6)	(5,656)	(1.9)	(5,817)
Treasury stock	(123)	(0.0)	(65)	(0.0)	(58)
Total shareholders' equity	104,681	24.1	90,142	29.5	14,539
Total liabilities and shareholders' equity	¥433,706	100.0	¥305,318	100.0	¥128,388

2) Consolidated Statements of Income

	Japanese Yen (Millions)					
	March 31, 2004		March 31, 2003		Increase/ decrease	2004/ 2003 %
	Amount	%	Amount	%		
Net sales	¥329,003	100.0	¥298,641	100.0	¥30,362	110.2
Cost of sales	256,879	78.1	238,851	80.0	18,028	107.5
Gross profit	72,123	21.9	59,789	20.0	12,334	120.6
Selling, general, and administrative expenses	41,044	12.5	36,928	12.3	4,116	111.1
Amortization of goodwill	3,531		3,320		211	
Operating income	31,078	9.4	22,861	7.7	8,217	135.9
Other income	1,851	0.6	2,060	0.7	(209)	89.9
Interest income	243		324		(81)	75.0
Dividend income	219		229		(10)	95.6
Other	1,388		1,506		(118)	92.2
Other expenses	9,253	2.8	7,105	2.4	2,148	130.2
Interest expenses	728		897		(169)	81.2
Equity in loss of affiliates	1,946		110		1,836	1,769.1
Loss on write off of inventories	1,478		1,453		25	101.7
Foreign exchange loss, net	3,339		3,538		(199)	94.4
Other	1,760		1,105		655	159.3
Recurring profit	23,676	7.2	17,816	6.0	5,860	132.9
Extraordinary gains	2,440	0.7	211	0.1	2,229	1,156.4
Gain on sale of fixed assets	205		102		103	201.0
Gain on sale of marketable securities	472		—		472	—
Gain on sale of investments in affiliates	2		34		(32)	5.9
Equity in earnings (losses) of affiliates	191		32		159	596.9
Gain on reversal of allowances for doubtful accounts	93		32		61	290.6
Gain on reversal of allowances for retirement	459		—		459	—
Gain on return of substitutional portion of govt. welfare pension prog................	972		—		972	—
Other	44		9		35	488.9
Extraordinary losses	3,308	1.0	5,315	1.8	(2,007)	62.2
Loss on disposal of property, plant & equipment ...	1,344		1,266		78	106.2
Loss on write-down of investment securities	6		1,255		(1,249)	0.5
Recognition of Unrecognized net Transition obligation	1,207		1,462		(255)	82.6
Relocation of HQ and laboratory	316		—		316	—
Lump sum license fee	—		975		(975)	—
Other	433		354		79	122.3
Income before income taxes and minority Interests ...	22,809	6.9	12,712	4.3	10,097	179.4
Income taxes	6,994	2.1	5,035	1.7	1,959	138.9
Income taxes (deferred)	604	0.2	(1,114)	(0.4)	1,718	(54.2)
Minority interests in subsidiaries	3,761	1.1	2,305	0.8	1,456	163.2
Net income	¥ 11,448	3.5	¥ 6,485	2.2	¥ 4,963	176.5

Continued

EXHIBIT 5.8 (*Continued*)

U.S. GAAP

NIDEC CORPORATION
Form 20-F
2004
Consolidated Balance Sheets

Assets:

	Yen (Millions)		U.S. Dollars (Thousands)
	March 31, 2003	March 31, 2004	March 31, 2004
	Amount	Amount	
Current assets:			
Cash and cash equivalents	¥ 33,039	¥ 73,392	$ 694,408
Trade notes and accounts receivable, net of allowance for doubtful accounts of ¥465 million in 2003 and ¥623 million ($5,895 thousand) in 2004:			
Notes	8,708	17,431	164,926
Accounts	50,780	96,509	913,133
Inventories	17,036	45,245	428,092
Prepaid expenses and other current assets	11,750	13,838	130,929
Total current assets	121,313	246,415	2,331,488
Marketable securities and other securities investments	5,324	19,892	188,211
Investments in and advances to affiliates	29,051	2,259	21,374
	34,375	22,151	209,585
Property, plant and equipment:			
Land	18,490	30,532	288,883
Buildings	47,220	73,860	698,836
Machinery and equipment	83,624	163,401	1,546,040
Construction in progress	2,425	7,411	70,120
	151,759	275,204	2,603,879
Less—Accumulated depreciation	(61,050)	(142,792)	(1,351,046)
	90,709	132,412	1,252,833
Goodwill	3,658	28,078	265,664
Other non-current assets	7,877	14,830	140,316
Total assets	¥257,932	¥443,886	$4,199,886

The accompanying notes are an integral part of these financial statements.

Liabilities and Shareholders' Equity

	Yen (Millions)		U.S. Dollars (Thousands)
	March 31, 2003	March 31, 2004	March 31, 2004
	Amount	Amount	
Current liabilities:			
Short-term borrowings	¥ 64,597	¥ 86,636	$ 819,718
Current portion of long-term debt	8,951	2,653	25,102
Trade notes and accounts payable	49,276	93,418	883,887
Other current liabilities	10,351	24,087	227,902
Total current liabilities	133,175	206,794	1,956,609
Long-term liabilities:			
Long-term debt	16,388	45,025	426,010
Accrued pension and severance costs	10,357	29,836	282,297
Other long-term liabilities	347	3,054	28,896
Total long-term liabilities	27,092	77,915	737,203
Minority interest in consolidated subsidiaries	9,108	49,131	464,859
Commitments and contingencies (Note 24)			
Shareholders' equity:			
Common stock authorized: 240,000,000 shares in 2003 and 2004; issued and outstanding: 63,574,729 shares in 2003 and 65,017,898 shares in 2004	26,485	28,995	274,340
Additional paid-in capital	25,817	31,822	301,088
Retained earnings	43,708	57,887	547,706
Accumulated other comprehensive loss	(7,387)	(8,535)	(80,755)
Foreign currency translation adjustments	(5,690)	(11,475)	(108,572)
Unrealized gains on securities	225	2,972	28,120
Minimum pension liability adjustment	(1,922)	(32)	(303)
Treasury stock, at cost: 8,648 shares in 2003 and 14,360 shares in 2004	(66)	(123)	(1,164)
Total shareholders' equity	88,557	110,046	1,041,215
Total liabilities and shareholders' equity	¥257,932	¥443,886	$4,199,886

The accompanying notes are an integral part of these financial statements.

Continued

EXHIBIT 5.8 *(Continued)*

Consolidated Statements of Income

	Yen (Millions)			U.S. Dollars (Thousands)
	For the year ended March 31			For the year ended March 31, 2004
	2002	**2003**	**2004**	
	Amount	Amount	Amount	
Net sales	¥193,332	¥231,836	¥277,497	$2,625,575
Operating expenses:				
Cost of products sold	159,442	187,306	218,189	2,064,424
Selling, general and administrative expenses..............	17,691	21,302	28,542	270,054
Research and development expenses	5,727	6,824	8,751	82,799
	182,860	215,432	255,482	2,417,277
Operating income	10,472	16,404	22,015	208,298
Other income (expense):				
Interest and dividend income	572	364	362	3,425
Interest expense	(1,167)	(890)	(862)	(8,156)
Foreign exchange gain (loss), net........	2,107	(3,511)	(3,149)	(29,795)
Gain (loss) from derivative instruments, net	8	23	(5)	(47)
(Loss) gain on marketable securities, net	(1,400)	(1,583)	816	7,720
Gain from issuance of securities by affiliated companies	—	39	—	—
Gain (loss) from sales of investments in affiliated companies	11	(4)	45	426
Other, net	874	69	417	3,946
	1,005	(5,493)	(2,376)	(22,481)
Income before provision for income taxes	11,477	10,911	19,639	185,817
Provision for income taxes	(2,162)	(1,053)	(5,424)	(51,320)
Income before minority interest and equity in earnings of affiliated companies	9,315	9,858	14,215	134,497
Minority interest in income (loss) of consolidated subsidiaries	318	644	648	6,131
Equity in net (income)/losses of affiliated companies	2,417	(1,466)	(2,522)	(23,862)
Net income	¥ 6,580	¥ 10,680	¥ 16,089	$ 152,228

	Yen			U.S. Dollars
Per share data:				
Net income — basic	¥103.53	¥168.01	¥251.14	$2.38
— diluted	¥ 98.85	¥159.82	¥241.53	$2.29
Cash dividends	¥ 27.50	¥ 20.00	¥ 30.00	$0.28

The accompanying notes are an integral part of these financial statements.

these two sets of statements reveals differences in format, levels of aggregation, and the amounts reported. For the year ended March 31, 2003, Nidec reported net sales of ¥298,641 million under Japanese GAAP and ¥231,838 million under U.S. GAAP, a difference of ¥67 billion. This is different from the amount (¥86 billion) attributable to differences in the scope of consolidation. Apparently other differences exist in the recognition of revenues under the two sets of accounting principles.

MEXICO

Background

Mexico became an independent nation in 1821 after being held for three centuries as a Spanish colony. The legislative authority in Mexico rests with the president and the Congress. The chief executive of the government is the president, who is elected for a six-year term and may not be reelected. The Mexican Congress consists of a Senate, with 128 members, elected for six years, and a Chamber of Deputies, with 500 members, elected for three years.

Until about two decades ago, a substantial proportion of the Mexican business sector was government controlled, and a large number of business enterprises were government owned. From the mid-1970s until the late 1980s Mexico faced persistent balance-of-payments problems resulting from the government's efforts to defend the overvalued peso while incurring massive external debt. These and other economic problems were attributed largely to government acquisition and control of private enterprises. In recent years, there has been a major effort to privatize state-owned enterprises as part of a new economic program designed to accelerate long-term economic growth. Many of the restrictions on investment by foreigners have been removed, opening the door to external capital. This process has been further encouraged by Mexico's joining the United States and Canada under the North American Free Trade Agreement (NAFTA) in 1993. Among other things, NAFTA aims to reduce most barriers to trade in goods, liberalize the cross-border flow of services and capital, and open up new areas of opportunity in each country to conduct business in the other two countries.

In December 1994, Mexico devalued the peso and plunged into a financial crisis (known as the Tequila crisis) as billions in short-term, dollar-denominated bonds held largely by foreigners came due. Unable to pay, Mexico accepted a $40 billion bailout from the U.S. Treasury and the International Monetary Fund. The bailout was accompanied by some tough conditions. For example, Mexico's Central Bank and Finance Secretariat had to shed light on all of their financial transactions and start communicating better with investors and creditors. Within seven months, Mexico managed to raise money on international financial markets once again. Currently, Mexico has a largely free-market economy.

Mexico has one stock exchange, the Bolsa Mexicana de Valores, located in Mexico City. Historically, the Mexican business sector has been predominantly family-owned. The influx of foreign capital and the return of Mexican capital previously invested abroad in the late 1980s and early 1990s have stimulated the growth of the Mexican stock market. The stock exchange is a private institution jointly owned by 32 brokerage houses. Prior approval of the National Banking and Securities Commission (NBSC) is required for listing on the stock exchange. Mexican companies can issue three categories of shares, Series A, Series B, and Series N. Series A shares can be held only by Mexican nationals, and these shares account for at least 51 percent of voting rights; Series B shares are open to foreigners and may account for only up to 49 percent of ownership; and Series N shares, called neutral shares and created under the Foreign Investment Law in January 1994, involve a trust mechanism designed for foreign investors. They have no voting rights and limited corporate rights.

Accounting Profession

The first professional organization of public accountants in Mexico, the *Asociacion de Contadores Publicos,* was established in 1917.[41] This organization was replaced by the Mexican Institute of Public Accountants (MIPA) in 1964. MIPA was officially recognized in 1977 as a federation of state and local associations of registered public accountants in Mexico. An independent, nongovernmental professional association, it is governed by three bodies, the General Conference of Members, the Governance Group, and the National Executive Committee (NEC). The first two bodies mainly perform sponsoring and oversight functions, whereas the NEC's major responsibilities relate to overseeing the day-to-day activities of MIPA. MIPA's primary responsibility is to establish and communicate, in the public interest, the accounting principles to be followed in preparing financial information for external users and to promote their acceptance and observance throughout the nation.[42] MIPA was one of the nine founding members of the IASC.

Public accounting services in Mexico mainly consist of bookkeeping, tax, and audit services. As stipulated in the law regulating the practice of professions, a "professional diploma" is required to practice as a public accountant in Mexico. The professional diploma is a certificate issued by the state or other authorized body to a person who has completed the requisite studies and demonstrated the necessary skills. To become certified, Mexican accountants usually must complete four or more years of post–high school education. On completion of formal education, the candidate is tested verbally and must prepare a thesis before obtaining the title of *contador publico* (CP) (public accountant).

Accounting Regulation

Regulation of accounting and financial reporting in Mexico is through legislation, stock exchange listing requirements, and bulletins issued by MIPA. Mexican law requires all companies incorporated in Mexico to appoint one or more statutory auditors. Annual financial statements of listed companies must be audited by a Mexican CPA and be published in a nationally circulated medium. The statutory audit report must include, at a minimum, the auditor's opinion as to whether the accounting and reporting policies followed by the company are appropriate and adequate in the circumstances and have been consistently applied, and whether the information presented by management gives a true and adequate picture of the company's financial position and operating results.

The NBSC, an equivalent of the U.S. Securities and Exchange Commission, is the most important federal agency that oversees information disclosure by publicly

[41] For an excellent discussion of the early development of Mexican Accounting, see S. A. Zeff, *Forging Accounting Principles in Five Countries: A History and Analysis of Trends* (Champaign, IL: Stipes, 1972), pp. 91–109.

[42] Certain regulated enterprises, such as government-owned banks, may follow special accounting rules and thus depart from GAAP.

owned companies in Mexico. It is a semi-independent entity within the Ministry of Finance that administers Mexico's securities law and regulates the operation of securities markets. The current Mexican Securities Law was enacted in 1975, with some amendments introduced in 1993, mainly to accommodate the foreign investment requirements under NAFTA.

MIPA is responsible for issuing standards of accounting and auditing in Mexico. In fact, it is both the standard-setting and enforcement body in Mexico. It follows a due process in developing standards, which includes issuance of exposure drafts of proposed standards for public comment. MIPA also has developed a code of ethics, which, among other things, prohibits media advertising for public accountants. Two special commissions within MIPA are responsible for the actual development of standards. The Auditing Standards and Procedures Commission develops auditing standards, and the Accounting Principles Commission (APC) develops accounting standards. APC members are volunteers, appointed by MIPA's NEC. About half of the APC members are public accountants working as independent auditors; another 25 percent are public accountants working in other areas; and the balance consists of representatives of user, preparer, private sector, and public sector groups.

MIPA issues four kinds of pronouncements, known as bulletins. Series A bulletins deal with the basic accounting principles that define the framewok of accounting principles. For example, Bulletin A-8 requires companies to apply International Financial Reporting Standards for issues that are not covered by Mexican generally accepted accounting principles. MIPA has translated and published IFRSs into Spanish. Series B bulletins deal with the accounting principles that are pervasive to all financial statements. For example, Bulletin B-1 states the objectives of financial statements, B-2 deals with revenue recognition, and so on. Bulletin B-10 deals with the recognition of the effects of inflation in the financial statements. Series C bulletins provide guidance with respect to specific balance sheet and income statement accounts, such as cash and short-term investments (Bulletin C-1), inventories (Bulletin C-4), liabilities (Bulletin C-9), and contingencies and commitments (Bulletin C-12). Series D bulletins deal with specific topics that are key to detemining the net income of an enterprise, such as accounting for income taxes (Bulletin D-4) and leasing (Bulletin D-5).

Compliance with tax regulations requires a report prepared in accordance with generally accepted Mexican accounting principles and audited in accordance with Mexican generally accepted auditing standards.

Accounting Principles and Practices

Mexico has a conceptual framework for financial reporting, which is basically included in three bulletins: A-1, *Structure of the Basic Theory of Financial Accounting*; A-11, *Definition of Basic Concepts Integrating Financial Statements*; and B-1, *Objectives of Financial Statements*. The generally accepted accounting principles in Mexico consist of the following, in order of importance:

1. MIPA bulletins.
2. MIPA circulars or interpretations. These are opinions relating to specific topics on which there may or may not be a specific standard. Compliance with these is not mandatory, but highly recommended.
3. International Financial Reporting Standards.

4. Accounting principles of other countries that would be applicable in the circumstances. In practice, U.S. GAAP are the main source applied.

In recent years Mexican accounting principles have been heavily influenced by U.S. accounting practice because of Mexico's membership in NAFTA. The U.S. influence is through the presence of subsidiaries of U.S. companies and the prominence of local representatives of the Big Four international accounting firms. As a result, although there are differences in accounting between the two countries, Mexican and U.S. accounting standards are generally consistent. In those areas where Mexican accounting principles do not exist, such as earnings per share or line-of-business disclosures, it is common for companies to use the corresponding U.S. standard.

In addition to the basic balance sheet and income statement, a statement of changes in financial position also is prepared. This latter statement is very similar to the U.S. statement of cash flows in appearance but reflects sources and uses of funds, rather than cash. Notes to the financial statements and a report from the statutory auditor are attached to the financial statements. Mexican parent companies are required to prepare consolidated financial statements. In doing so, Mexican companies use both the purchase method and the pooling of interests method. Goodwill is amortized over a period not exceeding 20 years.

One of the unique features of Mexican accounting practice, and the greatest difference from U.S. accounting, is the treatment of the effects of inflation in financial statements by using general purchasing power accounting. Mexico has a history of high rates of inflation, often exceeding 20 percent per year. Bulletin B-10, *Recognition of the Effects of Inflation in Financial Information,* became compulsory for all Mexican companies in 1984. The bulletin has been amended and refined several times. This is an example of how accounting practices reflect specific needs of the local environment, in this case, the economic environment.

Bulletin B-10 requires all nonmonetary assets and liabilities to be restated for changes in the purchasing power of the peso using the National Consumer Price Index (NCPI) published by the Central Bank. Prior to the Fifth Amendment to B-10 in 1996, estimated replacement costs were acceptable for restating inventory and fixed assets, but now this is only permissible for inventory. Equity accounts also must be restated using the NCPI to reflect paid-in capital at constant purchasing power. The third important element of the Mexican inflation accounting system is the recognition in income of the gain or loss from the net monetary asset or liability position. All comparative financial statements from prior years also should be restated to constant pesos as of the date of the most recent balance sheet. Both large and small enterprises follow the same set of accounting standards.

Bulletin B-10 also introduced a novel concept called the integral result of financing, which is reported as a separate line item on the income statement. This is calculated by adding the nominal interest expense, the gain or loss due to price-level changes on the company's net monetary position, and the gains and losses due to exchange rate fluctuations on the company's monetary assets and liabilities denominated in foreign currencies.

Mexican accounting rules require research and development costs to be expensed as incurred, and leases to be classified into financial and operating categories. Mexican GAAP differs from IFRSs in the following areas: The definition of an associate is based on a threshold of an investment of 10 percent of voting shares (IAS 28); preoperating and setup costs can be capitalized (IAS 38); a

EXHIBIT 5.9 Differences between Mexican GAAP and IFRSs

Issue	IFRSs	Mexican GAAP
Definition of an associate	IAS 28: An associate is an enterprise in which the investor has significant influence and which is neither a subsidiary nor a joint venture of the investor.	The definition of an associate is based on a threshold of an investment of 10 percent of voting shares.
Preoperating and setup costs	IAS 38: Charge to expenses when incurred.	Preoperating and setup costs can be capitalized.
Calculation of impairment of fixed assets	IAS 36: Impairment is calculated when the book value of an asset exceeds its recoverable amount, which is the greater of net realizable value and the net present value of future net cash flows expected to arise from continued use of the asset.	For the calculation of impairment, assets for sale are valued at net selling price and assets for continued use are valued at value in use.
Statement of cash flows	IAS 7: A statement of cash flows is required.	A statement of changes in financial position is required instead of a statement of cash flows.
Inflation accounting	IAS 29: Required for hyperinflationary countries.	Restatement for inflation is mandatory, irrespective of the inflation rate.
Inflation accounting method	IAS 29: Adjust the subsidiary financial statements for general effects of inflation, with the gain or loss on net monetary position in net income.	Companies can follow either the general price-level method or that method combined with the current cost method for restatement for inflation, and if the current cost method is followed, the results of holding nonmonetary assets (difference between indexed cost and current cost) is recorded in equity.
Negative goodwill	IFRS 3: Recognized in profit and loss immediately.	Negative goodwill is shown as a deferred credit and amortized over a period of up to five years.

statement of changes in financial position is required instead of a statement of cash flows (IAS 7); and restatement of inflation is mandatory, irrespective of the inflation rate (IAS 29). Exhibit 5.9 summarizes some of the differences between IFRSs and Mexican GAAP.

CEMEX SA de CV is one of more than 20 Mexican companies listed on the New York Stock Exchange. Note 23 to the consolidated financial statements included in the company's 2003 Form 20-F reconciles Mexican GAAP income and stockholders' equity to U.S. GAAP (see Exhibit 5.10). The largest adjustments in 2003 to reconcile net income to U.S. GAAP pertain to goodwill (adjustment 1); derivative financial instruments (adjustments 7, 12, and 13); and inflation accounting (adjustment 11). The adjustment related to goodwill is highly material, amounting to 28 percent of Mexican GAAP net income.

EXHIBIT 5.10

CEMEX SA DE CV AND SUBSIDIARIES
Form 20-F
2003
(millions of constant Mexican Pesos as of December 31, 2003)
Excerpt from Notes to the Consolidated Financial Statements

---

23. DIFFERENCES BETWEEN MEXICAN AND UNITED STATES ACCOUNTING PRINCIPLES—Some examples

The consolidated financial statements are prepared in accordance with accounting principles generally accepted in Mexico (Mexican GAAP) which differ in certain significant respects from those applicable in the United States (U.S. GAAP).

The Mexican GAAP consolidated financial statements include the effects of inflation as provided for under Bulletin B-10 and Bulletin B-15, whereas financial statements prepared under U.S. GAAP are presented on a historical cost basis. The reconciliation to U.S. GAAP includes (i) a reconciling item for the reversal of the effect of applying Bulletin B-15 for restatement to constant pesos for the years ended December 31, 2001 and 2002, and (ii) a reconciling item to reflect the difference in the carrying value of machinery and equipment of foreign origin and related depreciation between the methodology set forth by Bulletin B-10 (integrated document) and the amounts that would be determined by using the historical cost/constant currency method. As described below, these provisions of inflation accounting under Mexican GAAP do not meet the requirements of Rule 3-20 of Regulation S-X of the Securities and Exchange Commission. The reconciliation does not include the reversal of other Mexican GAAP inflation accounting adjustments as these adjustments represent a comprehensive measure of the effects of price level changes in the inflationary Mexican economy and, as such, is considered a more meaningful presentation than historical cost-based financial reporting for both Mexican and U.S. accounting purposes. The other principal differences between Mexican GAAP and U.S. GAAP for the years ended December 31, 2001, 2002 and 2003, and their effect on consolidated net income and earnings per share, are presented below:

	Years ended December 31		
	2001	2002	2003
Net income under Mexican GAAP	Ps 13,126.6	5,966.9	7,067.4
Inflation adjustment (*)	(1,181.2)	(357.5)	—
Net income reported under Mexican GAAP after inflation adjustment	11,845.4	5,609.4	7,067.4
Approximate additional U.S. GAAP adjustments:			
1. Amortization of goodwill (see 23(a))	(549.4)	1,729.4	1,946.4
2. Deferred income taxes (see 23(b))	(285.9)	2,316.8	(61.8)
3. Deferred employees' statutory profit sharing (see 23(b))	(190.8)	(194.4)	89.3
4. Other employee benefits (see 23(c))	(9.7)	(31.8)	86.4
5. Capitalized interest (see 23(d))	15.1	(40.0)	(45.7)
6. Minority interest (see 23(e)):			
a) Financial transactions	303.6	(167.0)	(175.0)
b) Effect of U.S. GAAP adjustments	135.3	33.6	(24.4)
7. Hedge accounting (see 23(l))	633.3	(2,555.3)	(826.7)
8. Depreciation (see 23(f))	(18.1)	13.1	48.8
9. Accruals for contingencies (see 23(g))	(9.6)	7.6	(108.9)
10. Equity in net income of affiliated companies (see 23(h))	0.6	11.9	(9.7)
11. Inflation adustment of fixed assets (see 23(i))	(481.3)	(377.2)	(262.0)
12. Temporary equity from forward contracts (see 23(j))	(461.6)	(538.0)	740.5
13. Derivative instruments and equity forward contracts in CEMEX stock (see 23(1) and 23(m))	32.3	—	415.0
14. Other U.S. GAAP adjustments (see 23(k))	(410.6)	(494.3)	(257.1)
15. Monetary effect of U.S. GAAP adjustments	495.0	542.4	291.9
Approximate U.S. GAAP adjustments before cumulative effect of accounting change	(801.8)	256.8	1,847.0
Approximate net income under U.S. GAAP before cumulative effect of accounting change	11,043.6	5,866.2	8,914.4
Cumulative effect of accounting change (see 23(k) and 23(m))	—	—	(640.7)
Approximate net income under U.S. GAAP after cumulative effect of change	Ps 11,043.6	5,866.2	8,273.7
Basic EPS under U.S. GAAP before cumulative effect of accounting change..	Ps 2.60	1.31	1. 89
Diluted EPS under U.S. GAAP before cumulative effect of accounting change	2.53	1.31	1.84
Basic EPS under U.S. GAAP after cumulative effect of accounting change	Ps 2.60	1.31	1.75
Diluted EPS under U.S. GAAP after cumulative effect of accounting change	2.53	1.31	1.71

At December 31, 2002 and 2003, the other principal differences between Mexican GAAP and U.S. GAAP, and their effect on consolidated stockholders' equity, with an explanation of the adjustments, are presented below:

	At December 31,	
	2002	**2003**
Total stockholders' equity reported under Mexican GAAP	Ps 79,721.3	76,051.5
Inflation adjustment (*)	(4,776.6)	—
Total stockholders' equity reported under Mexican GAAP after inflation adjustment	74,944.7	76,051.5
Approximate additional U.S. GAAP adjustments:		
1. Goodwill (see 23 (a))	(1,938.1)	1,261.8
2. Deferred income taxes (see 23(b))	(888.6)	768.2
3. Deferred employees' statutory profit sharing (see 23(b))	(3,314.2)	(3,008.1)
4. Other employee benefits (see 23(c))	(328.3)	(175.8)
5. Capitalized interest (see 23(d))	(480.5)	(523.5)
6. Minority interest—effect of financing transactions (see 23(e))	(976.7)	(741.8)
7. Minority interest—U.S. GAAP presentation (see 23(e))	(13,115.5)	(5,419.1)
8. Depreciation (see 23(f))	(208.1)	(55.1)
9. Accruals for contingencies (see 23(g))	120.9	31.4
10. Investment in net assets of affiliated companies (see 23(h))	(218.2)	(249.9)
11. Inflation adjustment for machinery and equipment (see 23(i))	6,354.9	3,770.6
12. Temporary equity from forward contracts (see 23(j))	(5,878.5)	—
13. Derivative instruments and equity forward contracts in CEMEX's stock (see 23(l) and (m))	—	397.0
14. Other U.S. GAAP adjustments (see 23(k))	(377.4)	(458.5)
Approximate U.S. GAAP adjustments before cumulative effect of accounting change	(21,248.3)	(4,402.8)
Approximate stockholders' equity under U.S. GAAP before cumulative effect of accounting change	53,696.4	71,648.7
Cumulative effect of accounting change (see 23(k) and (m))	—	(527.5)
Approximate stockholders' equity under U.S. GAAP after cumulative effect of accounting change	Ps 53,696.4	71,121.2

(*) Adjustment that reverses the restatement of prior periods into constant pesos as of December 31, 2003, using the CEMEX weighted average inflation factor (see note 2B), and restates such prior periods into constant pesos as of December 31, 2003 using the Mexican-only inflation factor, in order to comply with current requirements of Regulation S-X. The Mexican and U.S. GAAP prior periods amounts, included throughout note 23, were restated using the Mexican inflation index, with the exception of those amounts of prior periods that are also disclosed in notes 1 to 22, which were not restated in note 23 using the Mexican inflation in order to have more straightforward cross-references between note 23 and the Mexican GAAP notes.

Net income and stockholders' equity reconciliations to U.S. GAAP for the year ended december 31, 2003 have been prepared on a basis that is substantially consistent with the accounting principles applied in our Annual Report on Form 20-F for the year ended December 31, 2002, excpet for the adoption of SFAS 143 *Accounting for Asset Retirement Obligations* ("SFAS 143") and SFAS 150 *Accounting for Certain Financial Instruments with Characteristics of both Liabilities and Equity* ("SFAS 150"), as of and for the year ended December 31, 2003 (see note 23(k) and 23(m). The term "SFAS" as used herein refers to Statement of Financial Accounting Standards.

(a) *Goodwill*

Goodwill represents the diffrence between the purchase price and the estimated fair value of the acquired entityat the acqusition date. CEMEX's goodwill recognized under Mexican GAAP gas been adjusted for U.S. GAAP purposes for (i) the effects on goodwill for the U.S. GAAP adjustments as of the dates the subsidiaries were acquired; (ii) until December 31, 2001, for the difference

Continued

EXHIBIT 5.10 (*Continued*)

between amortization of goodwill as determined under sinking fund method over 20 to 40 years for Mexican GAAP purposes (see note 2(l)) and the straight-line method over 40 years for U.S. GAAP purposes. Beginning January 1, 2002, SFAS 142, *Goodwill and Other Intangible Assets,* eliminates the amortization of goodwill under U.S. GAAP (see note 23(s)) and (iii) the difference between goodwill amounts carried in the reporting unit's functional currency, restated by the inflation factor of the reporting unit's country and then translated into Mexican pesos at the exchange rates prevailing at the reporting date, under U.S. GAAP, against goodwill amounts carried in the currencies of the reporting units' holding companies, translated into pesos and then restated using the Mexican inflation index under Mexican GAAP.

In the condensed income statement under U.S. GAAP for the year ended December 31, 2001, presented in note 23(0), amortization of goodwill is reflected as an operating expense versus other expense under Mexican GAAP.

For purpposes of reconciliation to U.S. GAAP, CEMEX adopted in 2002, SFAS 142 and SFAS 144, *Accounting for the Impairment or Disposal of Long-Lived Assets* (see note 23(s)). As a result of this adoption, effective January 1, 2002, amortization ceased for goodwilll under U.S. GAAP; therefore, beginning in 2002, goodwill amortization recorded under Mexican GAAP is adjusted for purposes of the reconciliation of net income and stockholders' equity to U.S. GAAP.

CEMEX assesses goodwill for impairment unless events occur that require more frequent reviews. Discounted cash flow analyses are used to assess goodwill impairment (see note 23(s)). If an assessment indicates impairment, the impaired asset is written down to its fair market value based on the best information available. Estimated fair market value is generally measured using estimated discounted future cash flows. Considerable management judgment is necessary to estimate discounted future cash flows. Assumptions used for these cash flows are consistent with internal forecasts.

(d) *Capitalized Interest*

Under Mexican GAAP, CEMEX capitalizes interest on property, machinery and equipment under construction, which is comprehensively measured in order to include the following effects from the debt incurred to finance the construction project: (i) the interest cost, plus (ii) any foreign currency fluctuations, and less (iii) the related monetary position result. Under U.S. GAAP, only interest is considered an additional cost of constructed assets to be capitalized and depreciated over the lives of the related assets. The U.S. GAAP reconciliation removes the foreign currency gain or loss and the monetary position result capitalized for Mexican GAAP derived from borrowing denominated in foreign currency.

(f) *Depreciation*

A subsidiary of CEMEX in Colombia records depreciation expense utilizing the sinking fund method. This methodology for depreciation was in place before CEMEX acquired the subsidiary in 1997. For Mexican GAAP purposes, CEMEX has maintained this accounting practice due to tax consequences in Colombia arising from a change in methodology and the immateriality of the effects in CEMEX's consolidated results. For U.S. GAAP purposes, depreciation is calculated on a straight-line basis over the estimated useful lives of the assets. As a result, for the years ended December 31, 2001, 2002 and 2003, expense of Ps44.5 and income of Ps13.1 and Ps48.8, respectively, have been reflected in the reconciliation of net income to U.S. GAAP.

Additionally, as a result of the application of APB 16 in the acquisition of Solid (formerly Rizal), one of CEMEX's subsidiaries in the Philippines, for U.S. GAAP purposes, CEMEX reduced the value of its fixed assets by Ps215.7 in 2001, net of depreciation, corresponding to the appraisal value, determined at the acquisition date, related to the minority owners. The change in the appraised fixed assets amount resulted in a decrease in depreciation expense under U.S. GAAP of Ps26.4 for the year ended December 31, 2001. As mentioned in note 8A, during July 2002, CEMEX acquired the remaining 30% economic interest in Solid from the minority shareholders. As a result, in 2002, the adjustment made to the appraised fixed assets amount was reversed against minority interest, given that the reversed amount is part of the proportional net assets' fair value assigned to the 30% economic interest acquired. There is no further effect on earnings under U.S. GAAP.

(i) *Inflation Adjustment of Machinery and Equipment*

For purposes of the reconciliation to U.S. GAAP, fixed assets of foreign origin are restated by applying the inflation rate of the country that holds the assets, regardless of the assets' origin countries, instead of using the Mexican GAAP methodology, under which fixed assets of foreign origin are restated by applying a factor that considers the inflation of the asset's origin country, not the inflation of the country that holds the asset, and the fluctuation of the functional currency (currency of the country that holds the asset) against the currency of the asset's origin country. Depreciation expense is based upon the revised amounts.

(p) *Supplemental Cash Flow Information Under U.S. GAAP*

Under Mexican GAAP, statement of changes in financial position identify the sources and uses of resources based on the differences between beginning and ending financial statements in constant pesos. Monetary position results and unrealized foreign exchange results are treated as cash items in the determination of resources provided by operatons. Under U.S. GAAP (SFAS 95), statement of cash flows present only cash items and exclude non-cash items. SFAS 95 does not provide any guidance with respect to inflation-adjusted financial statements. The differences between Mexican GAAP and U.S. GAAP in the amounts reported is primarily due to (i) the elimination of inflationary effects of monetary assets and liabilities from financing and investing activities against the corresponding monetary position result in oerating activities, (ii) the elimination of foreign exchange results from financing and investing activities against the corresponding inrealized foreign exchange result included in operating activities and (iii) the recognition in operating, financing and investing activities of the U.S. GAAP adjustments.

The following table summarizes the cash flow items as required under SFAS 95 provided by (used in) operating, financing and investing activities for the years ended December 31, 2001, 2002 and 2003, giving effect to the U.S. GAAP adjustments, excluding the effects of inflation required by Bulletin B-10 and Bulletin B-15. The following information is presented in millions of pesos on a historical peso basis and is not presented in pesos of constant purchasing power:

	Years ended December 31		
	2001	**2002**	**2003**
Net cash provided by operating activities	Ps 18,786.5	9,526.4	9,771.8
Net cash provided by (used in) financing activities	(9,250.1)	(1,323.7)	(4,874.0)
Net cash used in investing activities	(8,433.3)	(8,380.4)	(5,419.4)

Net cash flow from operating activities reflects cash payments for interest and income taxes as follows:

	Years ended December 31		
	2001	**2002**	**2003**
Interest paid.	Ps 3,594.9	3,467.1	4,897.4
Income taxes paid	559.2	1,350.3	576.2

Non-cash activities are comprised of the following:

1. Acquisition of fixed assets through capital leases amounting to Ps23.2 in 2001. CEMEX did not acquire assets through capital leases during 2002 and 2003.
2. Liabilities assumed through the acquisition of businesses (see note 8A) were Ps275.6 in 2001, Ps1,873.7 in 2002 and Ps137.8 in 2003.

(q) *Restatement to Constant Pesos of Prior Years*

The following table presents summarized financial information under Mexican GAAP of the consolidated income statements for the years ended December 31, 2001 and 2002, and balance sheet information as of December 31, 2002, in constant Mexican pesos as of December 31, 2003, using the Mexican inflation index:

	Years ended December 31,	
	2001	**2002**
Sales	Ps 69,630.1	70,545.9
Gross profit	30,464.3	31,133.3
Majority interest net income	11,845.5	5,609.4

	At December 31, 2002
Current assets.	Ps 21,053.2
Non-current assets	150,747.7
Current liabilities	31,849.9
Non-current liabilities	65,006.3
Majority interest stockholders' equity	61,933.5
Minority interest stockholders' equity	

UNITED KINGDOM

Background

The United Kingdom consists of four constituent regions: England, Wales, Scotland, and Northern Ireland. The legislative authority lies with Parliament, which includes the House of Commons and the House of Lords. The House of Commons has 659 directly elected members, whose term of office is a maximum of five years. The House of Lords is appointed and consists of 92 hereditary peers, over 500 life peers, certain senior judges, and 26 bishops of the Church of England.

The limited liability company is the main form of business organization in the United Kingdom, and the capital market provides the main source of funding for business. Consequently, facilitating the efficient working of the capital market is the primary purpose of accounting. There are approximately 15,000 private limited companies (PLCs), of which about 2,500 are listed on the London Stock Exchange.[43] The United Kingdom has by far the greatest number of companies listed on a regulated market in the European Union. Listed companies and other large companies file a full set of audited annual financial statements with the Registrar of Companies. The annual report of a UK-listed company typically includes, in addition to financial statements, a chairperson's statement, an operating and financial review, the report of the directors, the report of the remuneration committee, a statement on corporate governance, and shareholding information.

Accounting Profession

Accounting in the United Kingdom grew as an independent discipline, responding to business needs, and has had a significant influence on the development of accounting profession in many countries including the United States and member countries of the British Commonwealth such as Canada, Australia, and New Zealand. The establishment of the first professional accounting body, the Society of Accountants in Edinburgh, in 1853 can be regarded as the beginning of the modern accounting profession.[44] There are six professional bodies in the United Kingdom. In order of membership size, these are the Institute of Chartered Accountants in England and Wales (ICAEW), the Association of Chartered Certified Accountants (ACCA), the Chartered Institute of Management Accountants (CIMA), the Institute of Chartered Accountants in Scotland (ICAS), the Chartered Institute of Public Finance and Accountancy (CIPFA), and the Institute of Chartered Accountants in Ireland (ICAI). The ICAEW alone has more than 126,000 members. It is the largest professional accounting body in Europe. The activities of the six bodies are coordinated through the Consultative Committee of Accountancy Bodies (CCAB), established in May 1974. Members of CIMA and CIPFA are not allowed to sign audit opinions.

Professional accounting bodies in the United Kingdom do not require aspiring members to have an undergraduate degree in accounting. However, those who possess an undergraduate degree in accounting would qualify for exemptions from the full examination structure. The three Institutes of Chartered Accountants have been the main training bodies for the members of the big accounting firms in

---

[43] David Alexander and Simon Archer, eds., *European Accounting Guide*, 4th ed. (New York: Aspen, 2003), p. 14.04.

[44] For details about early developments of the accounting profession in United Kingdom, see Zeff, *Forging Accounting Principles*, and L. Goldburgh, "The Development of Accounting," in *Accounting Concepts Readings*, ed. C. T. Gibson, G. G. Meredith, and R. Peterson (Melbourne: Cassell, 1971), pp. 18–22.

the respective regions of the United Kingdom. The membership of ACCA mainly consists of small practitioners and individuals from the corporate sector, while the main foci of CIMA and CIPFA are on management accounting and accounting in government organizations, respectively. All six professional accounting bodies set comprehensive exams for admission to their bodies. The examinations test knowledge at the basic, intermediate, and advanced levels. Those aspiring to be members of the three Institutes of Chartered Accountants are required to enter into training contracts with approved organizations (traditionally accounting firms but now extended to large companies) while completing their examinations.

The ICAEW in September 2000 introduced a new examination structure consisting of a professional stage and an advanced stage. The professional stage, which students can take prior to entering a training contract, consists of six subjects and two modules in law whose assessment is devolved to tuition providers. Students can gain exemptions from individual subjects at this stage if they have completed relevant diplomas, degrees, or examinations of other professional bodies. The advanced stage consists of a Test of Advanced Technical Competence (TATC) and an Advanced Case Study. The advanced stage adopts "a multidisciplinary approach, breaking down the old subject by subject 'tunnel vision,' integrating tax, audit, financial reporting and business topics, including business strategy, knowledge management and communication, digital economy, financial strategy, mergers and acquisition, change management, and business recovery."[45]

In December 2004, it was reported that there was a major consolidation initiative within the UK accountancy profession to merge three chartered bodies (CIMA, CIPFA, and ICAEW) and form a new combined institute. This would create an organization with 200,000 members and become the authoritative voice across the accountancy profession in the United Kingdom.

Traditionally, the UK accounting profession has favored a principles-based approach, rather than a rules-based approach, to standard setting. Peter Wyman, president of the ICAEW, explained the importance of this approach as follows:

> To remain a profession, accountancy must be about the exercise of professional integrity and judgment. If we are driven down the road of simply ticking boxes to show that rules have been complied with, we will end up with a clerical activity that is carried out without thought, and possibly without regard to the special context of the business at hand.
>
> Not only will this fail to attract people with intellect, but will also, inevitably from time to time, produce the wrong answers. No standard setter, no lawmaker is able to predict every likely situation. It is for this reason that we have constantly called for principles rather than rules in our standards. However, such an approach can only operate successfully if the principles are being applied by people with integrity and with the suitable skill, insight and application to do so effectively.[46]

Accounting Regulation

Regulation of accounting and financial reporting in the United Kingdom primarily is through legislation (Companies Act), professional pronouncements, and stock exchange listing requirements. The idea that determination of acceptable accounting principles and standards should be left in the hands of the profession

---

[45] www.icaew.co.uk/students/newaca/document.asp.

[46] Peter Wyman, "The Enron Aftermath—Where Next?" speech delivered October 10, 2002, at a conference held in Brussels (available at www.icaew.co.uk).

has been part of the UK tradition. Unlike their counterparts in the United States, traditionally, UK legislators have never felt the need to have a powerful securities commission to regulate accounting and financial reporting with detailed rules. Recent developments, however, suggest a change to this attitude.

The United Kingdom joined the European Union in 1973. Since then, EU directives have had a strong impact on UK accounting regulation. EU directives are transformed into UK legislation through the Companies Act. The EU Fourth Directive was integrated into British law in 1981 through amendments to the Companies Act of 1948. These amendments were prescriptive to a degree previously unknown in the United Kingdom. Traditionally, the Companies Act would normally set out the general principles leaving the specific requirements to be developed through other channels, particularly the accounting profession. However, the 1981 amendments to the Companies Act state exactly how certain matters are to be disclosed, with no latitude, for example, in matters of format. Similarly, the Companies Act of 1989 introduced the EU Seventh and Eighth Directives.[47]

As a result of the EU Eighth Directive, in order to qualify to practice as an auditor in the United Kingdom, a candidate is required to be registered in a statutory register maintained by one of the professional bodies. The 1989 Companies Act also requires companies to state whether the financial statements have been prepared in accordance with applicable accounting standards and, if not, give reasons for the departure. This is also an important change, because, prior to the 1989 Companies Act, UK accounting standards were not referred to in company legislation.

In 2000, the British government, in partnership with the professional accountancy bodies, established the Accountancy Foundation, to be responsible for the nonstatutory independent regulation of the six professional chartered accountancy bodies comprising the CCAB. The purpose of establishing the Accountancy Foundation was to ensure that self-regulation would be conducted in the public interest.

In response to accounting scandals in the United States, such as those related to Enron and WorldCom, several steps have been taken to improve regulation of financial reporting in the United Kingdom. The Department of Trade and Industry initiated a review of the Accountancy Foundation in October 2002 by publishing a consultation document on how the UK accountancy and auditing professions are regulated. It highlighted a number of issues:

- Whether the professional organizations should continue to set their own ethical standards and monitor the work and conduct of audit firms, or whether there should be stronger independent oversight or intervention.
- Whether the Accountancy Foundation should focus on the company auditor rather than on the regulation of accountants in general.
- Whether the structure and funding of the Accountancy Foundation should be reviewed.

The second main element of the UK regulatory system is professional pronouncements. The establishment of the Accounting Standards Steering Committee

---

[47] In January 2003, the European Parliament approved amendments to the EU Fourth and Seventh Directives that removed all inconsistencies between the directives and IFRSs. In December 2004, the EU adopted a directive on minimum transparency requirements for listed companies, completing a package of measures to establish a common financial disclosure regime across the EU for issuers of listed securities. The text of the directive is at www.europa.eu.int/comm/internal_market/securities/transparency/index_en.htm.

in 1970 by the ICAEW was the beginning of the development of formal accounting standards in the United Kingdom. The committee was later redesignated as the Accounting Standards Committee (ASC), which was reconstituted as a joint committee of the six professional bodies in 1976. The ASC standard-setting mechanism came under heavy criticism in the 1980s for a lack of effective means of monitoring compliance and the low quality of its standards known as Statements of Standard Accounting Practice (SSAP). In response, the Dearing Report recommended significant changes to the UK standard-setting process, which included the creation of the following:[48]

1. The Accounting Standards Board (ASB), with the authority to issue standards in its own right.
2. The Financial Reporting Council (FRC), given the responsibility of overall policy control over the standard setting process.
3. The Financial Reporting Review Panel (FRRP), to oversee compliance.

The creation of the ASB in August 1990 marked the beginning of a new era in accounting standards setting in the United Kingdom. It reduced the direct influence of the accounting profession on standard setting, because the ASB, like the U.S. FASB, is institutionally separated from the accounting institutes. The role of the FRC, also created in 1991, is to secure funding for the ASB and FRRP, which function under its purview. The FRC also acts as a high-level policy body that provides guidance to the ASB on priorities and work programs, advises the board in broad terms on issues of public concern, and encourages compliance.

In January 2003, the Secretary of State for Trade and Industry announced a package of reforms to raise standards of corporate governance, strengthen the accountancy and audit professions, and provide for an independent system of regulation for those professions. Accordingly, the FRC assumed the functions of the Accountancy Foundation, and the FRC and its operating boards would have the following three specific roles:

• Set accounting and auditing standards.
• Proactively enforce and monitor those standards.
• Oversee the self-regulatory professional bodies.

With the assumption of these responsibilities, the FRC became the single independent regulator of accounting and auditing in the United Kingdom. The FRC retains its current responsibilities for the work of the ASB and the FRRP. In addition, three other boards fall under the FRC's umbrella to meet its additional responsibilities. One of these boards is the newly established Professional Oversight Board for Accountancy (POBA). The others are two existing boards from the Accountancy Foundation: the Auditing Practices Board (APB) and the Accountancy Investigation and Discipline Board (AIDB). The FRC is funded equally by government, business, and the accountancy profession, thereby guaranteeing its independence because no single interest group dominates.

The ASB, adopting a principles-based approach, develops its standards on the basis of a conceptual framework known as the *Statement of Principles for Financial Reporting*. The ASB makes, amends, and withdraws accounting standards, assisted by four committees: (1) the Urgent Issues Task Force, (2) the Financial Sector and

---

[48] Consultative Committee on Accountancy Bodies, *The Making of Accounting Standards: Report of the Review Committee (Dearing Committee)* (London: ICAEW, 1988).

Other Special Industries Committee, (3) the Public Sector and Not-for-Profit Committee, and (4) the Committee on Accounting for Smaller Entities. The standards issued by the ASB are called Financial Reporting Standards (FRSs).

The ASB is one of several national standard setters that have a formal liaison relationship with the IASB. The ASB is committed to align UK accounting standards with IFRSs wherever practicable, by a phased replacement of existing UK standards with new UK standards based on IFRSs.[49] Accordingly, in December 2004, the ASB issued six standards to align the text of UK accounting standards with that of IFRSs:

- FRS 22 (IAS 33), *Earnings per Share.*
- FRS 23 (IAS 21), *The Effects of Changes in Foreign Exchange Rates.*
- FRS 24 (IAS 29), *Financial Reporting in Hyperinflationary Economies.*
- FRS 25 (IAS 32), *Financial Instruments: Disclosure and Presentation.*
- FRS 26 (IAS 39), *Financial Instruments: Measurement.*
- Amendment to FRS 2, *Accounting for Susidiary Undertakings: Legal Changes.*

FRS 26 implements in full the measurement and hedge accounting provisions of IAS 39.[50] It introduces for the first time requirements for the measurement of financial instruments. The amendments to FRS 2 include removal of the requirement for exclusion from consolidation of subsidiaries with dissimilar operations to the parent undertaking.[51]

The main purpose of the FRRP, which was established in 1991, is to review companies' financial statements to ensure fair presentation of information. The FRRP adopts a proactive role for the enforcement of accounting standards in which the Financial Services Authority (FSA), the UK finance watchdog, plays an active part.[52] The FRRP can ask directors to explain apparent departures from the accounting requirements. If the panel is not satisfied by the directors' explanations, it persuades them to adopt a more appropriate accounting treatment. Failing this, the panel can exercise its powers to secure the necessary revision of the original accounts through a court order.

Under the Companies Act of 2004, which came into effect in October 2004,[53] the authority of the FRRP would be extended to cover financial information, other

[49] In July 2003, the Department of Trade and Industry announced that all UK companies will be able to use IFRSs as an alternative to UK standards from 2005. (Department of Trade and Industry Press Release, "UK Extends Use of International Accounting Standards," July 17, 2003.)

[50] It was announced in December 2004 that the IASB had issued limited amendments to IAS 39, allowing, but not requiring, entities to adopt an approach to transition that is easier to implement than that in the previous version of IAS 39.

[51] A report published by the ICAEW at the end of October 2004 stated that the threat of aggressive earnings management to UK corporate reporting was likely to increase with the introduction of IFRSs. The report included the results of interviews with audit partners, finance directors, audit committee chairs, investment analysts and senior financial journalists. They identified two key motivating factors giving rise to this threat—the need to meet or exceed market expectations and the gearing of directors and management income to results.

[52] The FSA is an independent body that regulates the financial services industry in the United Kingdom. It aims to maintain confidence in the UK financial system, promote public understanding of the financial system, secure the right degree of protection for consumers, and help to reduce financial crime. For details see, www.fsa.gov.uk.

[53] The Companies (Audit, Investigations and Community Enterprise) Act of 2004 forms part of the government's stategy to help restore investor confidence in companies and financial markets following major corporate failures. The act amends relevant provisions of the Companies Acts of 1985 and 1989.

than annual accounts, published by entities that have securities listed on a UK market and where mandatory accounting requirements may apply.

Auditing standards in the United Kingdom are issued by the Auditing Practices Board (APB). They include Statements of Auditing Standards (SASs), Auditing Guidelines, and Statements of Investment Circular Reporting Standards (SIRs). The APB is funded by the CCAB, and its membership consists of practicing auditors and others from business, academia, law, and the public sector.

The third element of the UK regulatory system is stock exchange listing requirements. The London Stock Exchange (LSE) requires publication of a semi-annual interim report and disclosure of information about corporate governance and directors' remuneration. Unlike in Germany or Japan, taxation rules are not a major influence on financial reporting in the United Kingdom.

Accounting Principles and Practices

Accounting principles in the United Kingdom emphasize investor needs and the importance of transparency. UK financial statements typically include a profit and loss account, a balance sheet, a cash flow statement, a statement of total gains and losses, a statement of accounting policies, notes to financial statements, and the auditor's report. The United Kingdom has a differential financial reporting system in which small and medium-size companies are exempt from many reporting requirements.

The 1985 Companies Act requires corporate financial statements to provide a true and fair view of the firm's financial position and results of operations for the financial year. Auditors are given the corresponding duty to render an opinion on whether a true and fair view is provided. The term *true and fair view* is not specifically defined in law, but it is overriding and may require more than just compliance with accounting standards. The Companies Act specifically stipulates that if compliance with the act "would not be sufficient to give a true and fair view, the necessary additional information shall be given in the accounts or in a note to them" [Section 226 (2)].

Since January 1, 2005, UK-listed companies must use European Union–adopted IFRSs to prepare their group financial statements.[54] They are permitted, but not required, to use IFRSs for their individual accounts. Other companies and limited liability partnerships are permitted, but not required, to use IFRSs both for their consolidated and individual accounts. UK standards will therefore still be available for all financial statements other than the consolidated accounts of listed groups.

Financial statements generally are prepared on the basis of historical cost, but companies are allowed to revalue tangible assets. In general, UK accounting standards are very similar to IFRSs, as the international standards have been heavily influenced by British accounting. However, specific differences do exist between IFRSs and UK GAAP. In some areas, there is a difference in requirements under the two sets of standards. For example, segment reporting in the United Kingdom does not follow the primary–secondary reporting format approach found in IAS 14. In other areas, UK rules are more flexible. For example, whereas IFRS 3 requires that goodwill should not be amortized systematically, but instead should be subject to an annual impairment test, UK GAAP allows amortization at the

---

[54] The EU made certain amendments to IAS-39 prior to its adoption. However, the ASB has adopted the unamended version of IAS 39 in the United Kingdom.

EXHIBIT 5.11 Differences between UK GAAP and IFRSs

Issue	IFRSs	UK GAAP
Goodwill	IFRS 3: Prohibits amortization. Must be tested for impairment annually.	Goodwill can be amortized at the firm's choice.
Proposed dividends	IAS 10: Should not be recognized as a liability at the balance sheet date.	Accrued as a liability.
Related party disclosures	IAS 24: Requires transactions to be disclosed by type of related party. Does not require names to be disclosed.	Names of transacting related parties should be disclosed.
Segment reporting	IAS 14: More disclosure for primary segments than for secondary segments.	Segment reporting does not use the primary/secondary basis. Reports net assets rather than assets and liabilities separately.
Cash flow statements	IAS 7: Cash flows include both cash and cash equivalents.	Cash flow statements reconcile to a narrowly defined "cash" rather than to "cash and cash equivalents."
Translation of profit and loss account of a foreign subsidiary	IAS 21: The average rate of exchange for the period should be used.	Allows the closing rate to be used.
Reporting on a hyperinflationary subsidiary	IAS 21: The financial statements of a foreign entity that reports in the currency of a hyperinflationary economy should be restated before they are translated into the reporting currency of the reporting entity.	The financial statements of a hyperinflationary subsidiary can be remeasured using a stable currency as the measurement currency.
Revaluation gains/losses on investment properties	IAS 40: Allows the choice of either fair value or depreciated cost as an accounting policy for measuring investment property. Where fair value is used, gains and losses from changes in fair value are recognized in the income statement.	Fair value should be used, but gains on revaluation are taken though the statement of total recognized gains and losses not through profit and loss (except for permanent deficits below cost, or their reversals).
Intangible assets	IAS 38: Requires capitalization of development expenditure in R&D. Requires Web site costs, when capitalized, to be treated as intangible asset.	Permits capitalization of development expenditure in R&D.

firm's discretion. Exhibit 5.11 provides a summary of several differences that exist between UK GAAP and IFRSs.

The United Kingdom has the second greatest number of foreign companies listed on the New York Stock Exchange (Canada has the most). Exhibit 5.12 presents the reconciliation to U.S. GAAP included in Vodafone Group's 2003 Form 20-F. As is true for BASF (Germany) and CEMEX (Mexico) presented earlier in this chapter, the single largest adjustment made to reconcile to U.S. GAAP net income pertains to goodwill. The goodwill adjustment is followed closely in size by an adjustment required because of the very different rules in the United States and the United Kingdom pertaining to the accounting for income taxes.

EXHIBIT 5.12

VODAFONE GROUP PLC
Form 20-F
2003
Excerpt from Notes to the Consolidated Financial Statements

---

36. US GAAP Information

Reconciliations to US GAAP

The following is a summary of the effects of the differences between US GAAP and UK GAAP. The translation of pounds sterling amounts into US dollars is provided solely for convenience based on the Noon Buying Rate on 31 March 2004 of $1.8400: £1.

Net loss for the years ended 31 March

	Reference	2004 $m	2004 £m	2003 £m	2002 £m
Revenue from continuing operations in accordance with UK GAAP(1)		60,244	32,741	28,547	21,767
Items (decreasing)/increasing Revenues:					
Non-consolidated entities	(a)	(9,703)	(5,276)	(4,371)	(4,162)
Connection revenues	(b)	346	188	(1,760)	(1,044)
Revenues from continuing operations in accordance with US GAAP(1)		50,882	27,653	22,416	16,561
Net loss reported in accordance with UK GAAP		(16,588)	(9,015)	(9,819)	(16,155)
Items (increasing)/decreasing net loss:					
Investments accounted for under the equity method	(a)	2,491	1,354	289	(537)
Connection revenues and costs	(b)	53	29	16	(15)
Goodwill and other intangible assets	(c)	(11,997)	(6,520)	(5,487)	(5,120)
Licence fee amortisation	(d)	(140)	(76)	(6)	—
Exceptional items	(e)	(646)	(351)	270	(85)
Capitalised interest.	(f)	747	406	408	387
Income taxes	(g)	11,377	6,183	5,320	4,873
Other	(i)	(251)	(137)	(46)	(53)
Net loss before change in accounting principle in accordance with US GAAP		(14,954)	(8,127)	(9,055)	(16,705)
Effect of change in accounting principle(2)		—	—	—	17
Net loss after change in accounting principle, in accordance with US GAAP		(14,954)	(8,127)	(9,055)	(16,688)
US GAAP basic and diluted loss per share:	(k)				
—from continuing operations(1)		(20.90)c	(11.36)p	(13.40)p	(24.20)p
—net loss.		(21.95)c	(11.93)p	(13.29)p	(24.56)p

Shareholders' equity at 31 March

	Reference	2004 $m	2004 £m	2003 £m
Equity shareholders' funds in accordance with UK GAAP(2)		205,940	111,924	128,630
Items increasing/(decreasing) equity shareholders' funds:				
Investments accounted for under the equity method	(a)	10,241	5,566	4,630
Connection revenues and costs	(b)	(101)	(55)	(84)
Goodwill and other intangible assets..	(c)	83,389	45,320	51,144
Licence fee amortisation.	(d)	(201)	(109)	(43)
Exceptional items	(e)	—	—	270
Capitalised interest	(f)	(2,972)	1,615	1,073
Income taxes.	(g)	(73,736)	(40,074)	(45,446)
Proposed dividends	(h)	1,340	723	612
Other	(i)	209	114	(350)
Shareholders' equity in accordance with US GAAP		230,053	125,029	140,436

Continued

EXHIBIT 5.12   *(Continued)*

Total assets at 31 March

	Reference	2004 $m	2004 £m	2003 £m
Total assets in accordance with UK GAAP(2)		270,718	147,129	163,239
Items (decreasing)/increasing total assets:				
Investments accounted for under the equity method	(a)	3,733	2,029	1,849
Connection costs	(b)	6,775	3,682	4,179
Goodwill and other intangible assets	(c)	83,389	45,320	51,144
Licence fee amortisation	(d)	(201)	(109)	(43)
Exceptional items.	(e)	—	—	270
Capitalised interest	(f)	2,972	1,615	1,073
Income taxes	(g)	—	—	45
Other	(i)	1,076	585	(344)
Total assets in accordance with US GAAP.		368,462	200,251	221,412

Notes:

The reconciliations of net loss for the years ended 31 March 2003 and 2002 and shareholders' equity and total assets as at 31 March 2003 include reclassifications to provide comparability with the presentation as at 31 March 2004 and for the year then ended. The Group now shows amounts previously reported as "other" related to licence fee amortisation as a separate line item in the reconciliation. In addition, the Group now reflects only the Group's interest in each adjustment. These reclassifications had no impact on the Group's previously reported net loss or shareholders' equity under US GAAP.

(1) The results of operations of Japan Telecom are reported as discontinued operations under US GAAP and are included in the segment "Other operations—Asia Pacific". The pre-tax loss, including the loss on sale, was £515 million for the year ended 31 March 2004 (2003: income of £133 million; 2002: loss of £428 million).

(2) Change in accounting principle for 2002 relates to the Group's transitional adjustment in respect of the adoption of Statement of Financial Accounting Standards ("SFAS") No. 133, "Accounting for Derivative Instruments and Hedging Activities", on 1 April 2001.

The Group's retrospective adoption of UITF 38 "Accounting for ESOP Trusts" resulted in the UK GAAP equity shareholders' funds and total assets for prior years being restated (see note 37). The reconciliations of shareholders' equity and total assets have been restated to reflect this change in UK GAAP reporting which had no effect on previously reported US GAAP net income, shareholders' equity or total assets.

Summary of differences between UK GAAP and US GAAP

The Consolidated Financial Statements are prepared in accordance with UK GAAP, which differ in certain material respects from US GAAP. The differences that are material to the Group relate to the following items.

(a) Non-consolidated entities and investments accounted for under the equity method

Under UK GAAP, the results and assets of Vodafone Italy have been consolidated in the Group's financial statements from 12 April 2000. Under US GAAP, as a result of significant participating rights held by minority shareholders, the Group's interest in Vodafone Italy has been accounted for as an associated undertaking under the equity method of accounting. Under UK GAAP, Vodafone Spain has been consolidated in the Group's financial statements from 29 December 2000. Under US GAAP, the Group's interests in Vodafone Spain, have been accounted for as an associated undertaking under the equity method of accounting up to 29 June 2001 and consolidated thereafter, following the completion of the acquisition of a further 17.8% shareholding.

Under UK GAAP, charges for interest and taxation for associated undertakings are aggregated within the Group interest and taxation amounts shown on the face of the consolidated profit and loss account. The Group's share of the turnover of associated undertakings is also permitted to be disclosed on the face of the consolidated profit and loss account. US GAAP does not permit the Group's share of turnover of associated undertakings to be disclosed on the face of the consolidated income statement.

Equity accounting for Vodafone Italy and Vodafone Spain under US GAAP results in the Group operating loss, Group net interest payable, Group taxation payable and equity minority interests being less than/(more than) the equivalent UK GAAP amount by £1,325 million, £(55) million, £583 million and £459 million (2003: £1,955 million, £(45) million, £478 million and £264 million; 2002: £2,060 million, £(9) million, £402 million and £249 million), respectively. Equity accounting for Vodafone Italy and Vodafone Spain results in the Group's share of the operating loss, interest payable and taxation payable of associated undertakings being greater/(lower) under US GAAP than UK GAAP by £1,907 million, £(42) million and £448 million (2003: £2,305 million, £(34) million and £367 million; 2002: £2,402 million, £(7) million and £307 million), respectively. The Group's investment in the entity consolidated under UK GAAP but equity accounted under US GAAP at 31 March 2004 was £24,028 million (2003: £21,512 million).

(b) Connection revenues and costs

The Group's UK GAAP accounting policy on revenue recognition was amended during the year in relation to the deferral of certain equipment, connection, upgrade and tariff migration fees following the issuance of Application Note G to FRS 5 "Reporting the Substance of Transactions". Following the prospective adoption of EITF 00-21, "Accounting for Revenue Arrangements with Multiple Deliverables" on 1 October 2003 under US GAAP the Group's UK and US GAAP accounting policies have been substantially aligned.

For transactions prior to 1 October 2003, connection revenues under US GAAP are recognised over the period that a customer is expected to remain connected to a network. Connection costs directly attributable to the income deferred are recognised over the same period. Where connection costs exceed connection revenues, the excess costs were charged in the profit and loss account immediately upon connection. The balances of deferred revenue and deferred charges as of 30 September 2003 will continue to be recognised over the period that a customer is expected to remain connected to a network.

(c) Goodwill and other intangible assets

Under UK GAAP, the policy followed prior to the introduction of FRS 10, "Goodwill and Intangible Assets", which is effective for accounting periods ended on or after 23 December 1998 and was adopted on a prospective basis, was to write off goodwill against shareholders' equity in the year of acquisition. FRS 10 requires goodwill to be capitalised and amortised over its estimated useful economic life. Under US GAAP, following the introduction of SFAS No. 142, "Goodwill and Other Intangible Assets", which was effective for accounting periods starting after 15 December 2001 and, transitionally, for acquisitions completed after 30 June 2001, goodwill and intangible assets with indefinite lives are capitalised and not amortised, but tested for impairment, at least annually, in accordance with SFAS No. 142. Intangible assets with finite lives continue to be capitalised and amortised over their useful economic lives.

The Group believes that the nature of the licences and the related goodwill acquired in business combinations is substantially indistinguishable. In acquisitions where the primary asset is a licence, the Group, therefore, allocates the surplus of the purchase price over the fair value attributed to the share of net assets acquired to licences. In a number of the Group's previous acquisitions, the primary assets acquired were licences to provide mobile telecommunications services. As a result of the adoption of SFAS 142 and these considerations, on 1 April 2002, £33,664 million of goodwill was reclassified as licences. In accordance with the provision of SFAS No. 109, "Accounting for Income Taxes", a related deferred tax liability and a corresponding increase to licence value of £19,077 million has also been recognised related to the resulting difference in the tax basis versus the book basis of the licences.

Under UK GAAP and US GAAP the purchase price of a transaction accounted for as an acquisition is based on the fair value of the consideration. In the case of share consideration, under UK GAAP the fair value of such consideration is based on the share price at completion of the acquisition or the date when the transaction becomes unconditional. Under US GAAP the fair value of the share consideration is based on the average share price over a reasonable period of time before and after the proposed acquisition is agreed to and announced. This has resulted in a difference in the fair value of the consideration for certain acquisitions and consequently in the amount of goodwill capitalised under UK GAAP and US GAAP.

Under UK GAAP, costs incurred in reorganising acquired businesses are charged to the profit and loss account as post-acquisition expenses. Under US GAAP, certain of such costs are considered in the allocation of purchase consideration.

(d) Licence fee amortisation

Under UK GAAP, the Group has adopted a policy of amortising licence fees in proportion to the capacity of the network during the start up period and then on a straight line basis. Under US GAAP, licence fees are amortised on a straight line basis from the date that operations commence to the date the licence expires.

(e) Exceptional items

In the year ended 31 March 2003, the Group recorded an impairment charge under UK GAAP of £405 million in relation to the fixed assets of Japan Telecom. Under US GAAP, the Group evaluated the recoverability of these fixed assets in accordance with the requirements of SFAS No. 144, "Accounting for the Impairment or Disposal of Long-Lived Assets", and determined that the carrying amount of these assets was recoverable. As a result, the UK GAAP impairment charge of £405 million (£270 million net of minority interests) was not recognised under US GAAP during the year ended 31 March 2003. On disposal of Japan Telecom in the year ended 31 March 2004, an incremental loss on sale of £476 million (£351 million net of minority interests) was recognised under US GAAP resulting in a total loss on sale of £555 million (£399 million net of minority interests).

The reconciling item arising in the year ended 31 March 2002 represented the loss on sale of a business, which was sold fifteen months after the date of acquisition. Under UK GAAP, the fair value of an acquired business can be amended up until the end of the financial year after acquisition. Under US GAAP, the fair value can only be adjusted for one year following acquisition.

In addition, the exceptional non-operating items recorded under UK GAAP, disclosed in note 6, are reclassified as operating items under US GAAP and reduce operating profit accordingly.

Continued

EXHIBIT 5.12   (*Continued*)

(f) Capitalised interest

Under UK GAAP, the Group's policy is not to capitalise interest costs on borrowings in respect of the acquisition of tangible and intangible fixed assets. Under US GAAP, the interest cost on borrowings used to finance the construction of network assets is capitalised during the period of construction until the date that the asset is placed in service. Interest costs on borrowings to finance the acquisition of licences are also capitalised until the date that the related network service is launched. Capitalised interest costs are amortised over the estimated useful lives of the related assets.

(g) Income taxes

Under UK GAAP, deferred tax is provided in full on timing differences that result in an obligation at the balance sheet date to pay more tax, or a right to pay less tax, at a future date, at rates expected to apply when they crystallise based on current tax rates and law. Under US GAAP, deferred tax assets and liabilities are provided in full on all temporary differences and a valuation adjustment is established in respect of those deferred tax assets where it is more likely than not that some portion will not be realised. The most significant component of the income tax adjustment is due to the temporary difference between the assigned values and tax values of intangible assets acquired in a business combination, which results in the recognition of a deferred tax liability under US GAAP. Under UK GAAP, no deferred tax liability is recognised.

Under UK GAAP, the tax benefit received on the exercise of share options by employees, being the tax on the difference between the market value on the date of exercise and the exercise price, is shown as a component of the tax charge for the period. Under US GAAP, the tax benefit for deductions not exceeding the US GAAP accounting charge is recognised in earnings. Any incremental tax benefit from tax deductions in excess of the US GAAP accounting charge is shown as a component of paid-in capital on issue of shares.

In addition, deferred tax assets are recognised for future deductions and utilisation of tax carry-forwards, subject to a valuation allowance. The valuation allowance established against deferred tax assets as at 31 March 2004 was £11,150 million (2003: £11,446 million), the movement in the year being £296 million. The valuation allowance is mainly in respect of tax losses amounting to £11,018 million (2003: £11,226 million) not recognised.

(h) Proposed dividends

Under UK GAAP, final dividends are included in the financial statements when recommended by the Board to the shareholders in respect of the results for a financial year. Under US GAAP, dividends are included in the financial statements when declared by the Board.

(i) Other

Pension costs—Under both UK GAAP and US GAAP pension costs provide for future pension liabilities. There are differences, however, in the prescribed methods of valuation, which give rise to GAAP adjustments to the pension cost and the pension prepayment/liability. In addition, in certain circumstances an additional minimum liability must also be recognised with changes therein reported net of tax in other comprehensive income.

Capitalisation of computer software costs—Under UK GAAP, costs that are directly attributable to the development of computer software for continuing use in the business, whether purchased from external sources or developed internally, are capitalised. Under US GAAP, data conversion costs and costs incurred during the research stage of software projects are not capitalised.

Marketable securities—Under US GAAP, SFAS No. 115, "Accounting for Certain Investments in Debt and Equity Securities", the Group classifies its marketable equity securities with readily determinable fair values as available for sale and are stated at fair value with the unrealised loss or gain, net of deferred taxes, reported in comprehensive income. Under UK GAAP such investments are generally carried at cost and reviewed for other than temporary impairment.

Minority interests—Where losses in a subsidiary undertaking attributable to the minority interest result in its interest being one in net liabilities, UK GAAP requires a parent company make provision only to the extent it has a commercial or legal obligation to provide funding that may not be recoverable in respect of the accumulated losses attributable to the minority interest. US GAAP requires all losses allocable to minority interests in excess of their interest in the equity of the respective subsidiary to be charged to the majority shareholder.

Stock based compensation—Under UK GAAP, options granted over the Company's ordinary shares are accounted for using the intrinsic value method, with the difference between the fair value of shares at grant date and the exercise price charged to the profit and loss over the period until the shares first vest. Grants under the Company's SAYE schemes are exempt from this accounting methodology.

Under US GAAP, the Group accounts for option plans in accordance with the requirements of Accounting Principles Board ("APB") 25, "Accounting for Stock Issued to Employees" and applies the disclosure provisions of SFAS No. 148, "Accounting for Stock-Based Compensation—Transition and Disclosure". Under APB 25, such plans are accounted for as variable and the cost is calculated by reference to the market price of the shares at the measurement date and amortised over the period until the shares first vest. Where the measurement period has not yet been completed, the cost is calculated by reference to the market price of the relevant shares at the end of each accounting period.

Derivative instruments—All the Group's transactions in derivative financial instruments are undertaken for risk management purposes only and are used to hedge its exposure to interest rate and foreign currency risk. In accordance with UK GAAP, to the extent that such instruments are matched against an underlying asset or liability, they are accounted for as hedging transactions and recorded at appropriate historical amounts, with fair value information disclosed in the notes to the consolidated financial statements. Under US GAAP, in accordance with SFAS No. 133, the Group's derivative financial instruments, together with any separately identified embedded derivatives, are reported as assets or liabilities on the Group's balance sheet at fair value. In a hedge of fair values, changes in the fair value of the derivative are recorded in earnings with a corresponding change in the fair value of the hedged item also being recorded in earnings. For hedges of future cash flows, the changes in fair value of the derivative are recorded in other comprehensive income and reclassified to earnings when the hedged item affects earnings. Under US GAAP, all changes in fair value of derivatives not designated in hedging relationships are accounted for in the consolidated profit and loss account. The Group does not pursue hedge accounting treatment for:

—interest rate futures, which are typically used to switch floating interest rates to fixed interest rates; or

—derivatives entered into for funding and liquidity purposes, including forwards; or

—individual contracts where the underlying value of the transactions amounts to less than £10 million.

Upon first adopting SFAS No. 133, on 1 April 2002, a cumulative transition adjustment was made which increased US GAAP net income and other comprehensive income by £17 million and £nil, respectively.

Summary

1. China:
   a. In China, accounting and auditing have taken different paths in their development.
   b. There is strong government involvement in the activities of the stock market.
   c. The accounting profession in China has a lower social recognition compared to its counterparts in Anglo-Saxon countries.
   d. The recent economic reforms in China have had a major impact on that country's accounting standards and practices.
   e. China became a member of the IASC in 1997, and has expressed commitment to develop accounting standards based on IFRSs.

2. Japan:
   a. The Japanese economy is dominated by large conglomerates known as *keiretsu*.
   b. A unique feature of Japanese companies is cross-corporate ownership, mutual holding of equity interests among companies.
   c. In Japan, financial reporting has a creditor orientation, and is strongly influenced by tax law.
   d. Traditionally, accounting regulation in Japan is heavily influenced by government, and the accounting profession has played only a minor role, compared to its counterpart in the United States.
   e. Recent developments indicate a willingness to bring Japanese accounting practices more in line with international best practice.

3. Germany:
   a. Traditionally, the primary source of finance for German companies has been bank credit, and as a result, financial reporting has a creditor orientation rather than an equity shareholder orientation.
   b. Company, commercial, and tax laws and regulations are the main sources of accounting requirements (or "principles of orderly bookkeeping").
   c. Financial reporting is strongly influenced by EU directives.

d. The German stock exchange has much less influence on financial reporting compared to those in the United Kingdom or United States.

e. Traditionally, the influence of the accounting profession on developing accounting standards has been minor compared to that of its counterpart in the United Kingdom or United States.

f. Recent developments indicate a willingness to align German accounting standard setting process more closely with international best practice.

4. Mexico:

a. In recent years, the economy has been transforming from a centrally controlled economy to a market economy.

b. The Mexican stock exchange is a privately owned institution.

c. Mexico has a conceptual framework for financial reporting.

d. A unique feature of Mexican accounting is the treatment of the effects of inflation in financial statements.

e. The changes to Mexican accounting standards in recent years highlight, among other things, the potential conflict between the pressures for international harmonization and the need to consider the local circumstances in a given country.

5. United Kingdom:

a. The main purpose of accounting in the United Kingdom is to facilitate the effective functioning of the capital market.

b. The primary sources of accounting standards are the Companies Act, professional pronouncements, and stock exchange listing requirements.

c. Unlike in Germany or Japan, taxation rules do not have a major influence on financial reporting in the United Kingdom.

d. The UK Accounting Standards Board uses a statement of principles as a conceptual framework for developing financial reporting standards.

e. A principles-based approach is taken in setting standards for accounting and financial reporting.

f. Traditionally, there has been no government agency similar to the U.S. SEC in the United Kingdom. However, recent changes to the regulatory structure have strengthened enforcement.

Questions

1. How might the liberalization of accounting and auditing services in China result in an improved level of investor protection?

2. How have economic reforms affected the demand for accounting services in China?

3. In what way has the development of accounting and auditing in China differed from other countries?

4. What are the main pressures for accounting regulation in modern China?

5. How have cultural factors influenced accounting practices in Japan?

6. What was the accounting Big Bang in Japan?

7. Why is the principle of prudence clearly established in the German law?

8. Why does tax law have a strong influence on German accounting?

9. What are the main external factors that have influenced financial reporting in Germany in recent years?

10. What is the role of the National Banking and Securities Commission in the area of financial reporting by Mexican companies?

11. What is the significance of Bulletin A-8 of the Mexican Institute of Public Accountants?

12. What are the main external factors that have influenced financial reporting in Mexico in recent years?

13. What is an important contribution that Mexican accounting has made to international accounting?

14. What has been the impact of EU membership on accounting regulation in the United Kingdom?

15. What is the role of the UK Financial Reporting Council?

16. What are the main features of the approach taken in the United Kingdom in setting accounting standards?

Exercises and Problems

1. This chapter describes accounting regulation in five countries: China, Germany, Japan, Mexico, and the United Kingdom.

   Required:
   Compare the mechanisms in place to regulate accounting and financial reporting in your own country with those of any of the five countries mentioned above, and explain the possible reasons for any noticeable differences.

2. The number of professional accountants in a country indicates the status of the accounting profession in that country.

   Required:
   Determine the number of accountants per 100,000 of population in the United Kingdom and Japan. Explain why the numbers are so different. The membership details of professional accounting bodies in different countries are available at www.iasplus.com/links.htm#proforg.

3. Chapter 1 identified and described six major reasons for accounting diversity: legal system, taxation, providers of financing, inflation, political and economic ties, and culture.

   Required:
   a. Which factor or factors appear to have exerted the greatest influence on the development of accounting in each of the five countries covered in this chapter?
   b. Identify the distinguishing features of the accounting system in each of these countries.

4. Refer to the IASB Web site (www.iasb.org.uk).

   Required:
   a. Determine the manner in which IFRSs are used in each of the five countries included in this chapter.
   b. Determine which of these countries has a resident who is a member of the IASB.

5. Refer to Exhibits 5.3, 5.5, 5.7, 5.9, and 5.11.

   Required:
   Identify
   a. An issue in respect of which the practices of several countries discussed in this chapter are at variance with IFRSs.
   b. The most important financial accounting practice for each of the five countries, which is at variance with IFRSs. Also explain the reason(s) for your selection.

6. Visit the New York Stock Exchange Web site (www.nyse.com).

   Required:
   Determine the number of companies listed on the NYSE from each of the five countries covered in this chapter.

7. This chapter describes the mechanisms in place to regulate accounting and financial reporting in five countries.

   Required:
   Compare and contrast these mechanisms in the United Kingdom and China.

8. This chapter describes the major changes that have been introduced recently in Germany and Japan in the area of accounting regulation.

   Required:
   Describe any similarities between those changes in Germany and Japan.

9. The financial reporting issues facing Mexico are different in some respects from those of other countries covered in this chapter.

   Required:
   Provide two main reasons to support the above statement.

10. Refer to Exhibits 5.3, 5.7, and 5.9.

    Required:
    Explain the main areas you would focus on in comparing financial statements prepared by companies in China, Japan, and Mexico with those prepared by companies using IFRSs.

Case 5-1

Toyota Signs an Engine Joint Venture in China

Toyota, Japan's largest automaker, announced a new $152 million joint venture in China to build engines for upscale sedans, expanding the company's presence in a market where it has lagged behind its global competitors. The venture with First Automotive Works (FAW), China's largest carmaker, aims at annual production of 130,000 3.0-litre V6 gasoline engines. Initial production is scheduled to start in 2005, when annual output will be about 40,000 engines.

The 50-50 JV, to be called FAW Toyota Changchun Engine, will be based in Changchun in Jilin Province, one of China's major auto centers. The engine will be used in the Toyota Crown, which in China will be positioned in the sub-luxury segment of the market. The model will be built at the Toyota's JV factory with FAW in Tianjin, near Beijing, where the Vios sedan has been manufactured since 2002. Toyota, which is well behind Volkswagen and General Motors in China's car market, have committed more than $2 bn to a series of ventures with different Chinese partners over the last 18 months.[1]

Required:

Discuss some of the accounting issues that Toyota is likely to encounter in preparing its financial statements concerning its 50-50 joint venture with FAW.

[1]Richard, McGregor, "Toyota and Volvo Sign Engine JVs in China," *Financial Times*, March 29, 2004.

Case 5-2
China Petroleum and Chemical Corporation

China Petroleum and Chemical Corporation (CPCC) is one of a growing number of Chinese companies that has cross-listed its stock on foreign stock exchanges. To provide information that might be useful for a wide audience of readers outside of China, CPCC provides a reconciliation of income and stockholders' equity from Chinese GAAP to IFRSs. Further, to provide information specifically for its North American shareholders, the company also provides a reconciliation of net income and stockholders' equity from IFRSs to U.S. GAAP. The following is the section of CPCC's 2003 annual report providing this information.

Differences Between Financial Statements Prepared under the Chinese GAAP and IFRSs

The major differences are:

i. **Depreciation of oil and gas properties**

Under the PRC accounting rules and regulations, oil and gas properties are depreciated on a straight-line basis. Under IFRS, oil and gas properties are depreciated on the unit of production method.

ii. **Disposal of oil and gas properties**

Under the PRC accounting rules and regulations, gains and losses arising from the retirement or disposal of an individual item of oil and gas properties are recognized as income or expense in the income statement and are measured as the difference between the estimated net disposal proceeds and the carrying amount of the asset.

Under IFRS, gains and losses on the retirement or disposal of an individual item of proved oil and gas properties are not recognized unless the retirement or disposal encompasses an entire property. The costs of the asset abandoned or retired are charged to accumulated depreciation with the proceeds received on disposals credited to the carrying amounts of oil and gas properties.

iii. **Capitalisation of general borrowing costs**

Under the PRC accounting rules and regulations, only borrowing costs on funds that are specially borrowed for construction are capitalized as part of the cost of fixed assets. Under IFRS, to the extent that funds are borrowed generally and used for the purpose of obtaining a qualifying asset, the borrowing costs should be capitalized as part of the cost of that asset.

iv. Acquisition of Sinopec National Star, Sinopec Maoming, Xi'an Petrochemical and Tahe Petrochemical

Under the PRC accounting rules and regulations, the acquisition of Sinopec National Star, Sinopec Maoming, Xi'an Petrochemical and Tahe Petrochemical (the "Acquisitions") are accounted for by the acquisition method. Under the acquisition method, the income of an acquiring enterprise includes the operations of the acquired enterprise subsequent to the acquisition. The difference between the cost of acquiring Sinopec National Star and the fair value of the net assets acquired is capitalized as an exploration and production right, which is amortised over 27 years.

Under IFRS, as the Group, Sinopec National Star, Sinopec Maoming, Xi'an Petrochmical and Tahe Petrochemical are under the common control of Sinopec Group Company, the Acquisitions are considered "combination of entities under common control" which are accounted in a manner similar to a pooling-of-interests ("as in pooling of interests accounting"). Accordingly, the assets and liabilities of Sinopec National Star, Sinopec Maoming, Xi'an Petrochemicals and Tahe Petrochemicals acquired have been accounted for at historical cost and the financial statements of the Group for periods prior to the Acquisitions have been restated to include the financial statements and results of operations of Sinopec National Star, Sinopec Maoming, Xi'an Petrochemicals and Tahe Petrochemical on a combined basis. The consideration paid by the Group are treated as an equity transaction.

v. Gains from issuance of shares by a subsidiary

Under the PRC accounting rules and regulations, the increase in the company's share of net assets of a subsidiary after the sale of additional shares by the subsidiary is credited to capital reserve. Under IFRS, such increase is recognised as income.

vi. Gain from debt restructuring

Under the PRC accounting rules and regulations, gain from debt restructuring resulting from the difference between the carrying amount of liabilities extinguished or assumed by other parties and the amount paid is credited to capital reserve. Under IFRS, the gain resulting from such difference is recognised as income.

vii. Revaluation of land use rights

Under the PRC accounting rules and regulations, land use rights are carried at revalued amounts. Under IFRS, land use rights are carried at historical cost less amortisation. Accordingly, the surplus on the revaluation of land use rights, credited to revaluation reserve, was eliminated.

viii. Unrecognised losses of subsidiaries

Under the PRC accounting rules and regulations, the results of subsidiaries are included in the Group's consolidated income statement to the extent that the subsidiaries' accumulated losses do not result in their carrying amount being reduced to zero, without the effect of minority interests. Further, losses are debited to a separate reserve in the shareholders' funds.

Under IFRS, the results of subsidiaries are included in the Group's consolidated income statement from the date that control effectively commences until the date that control effectively ceases.

ix. Pre-operating expenditures

Under the PRC accounting rules and regulations, expenditures incurred during the start-up period are aggregated in long-term deferred expenses and charged to the income statement when operations commence. Under IFRS, expenditures on start-up activities are recognized as an expense when they are incurred.

x. Impairment losses on long-lived assets

Under the PRC accounting rules and regulations and IFRS, impairment charges are recognized when the carrying value of long-lived assets exceeds the higher of their net selling price and the value in use which incorporates discounting the asset's estimated future cash flows. Due to the difference in the depreciation method of oil and gas properties discussed in (i) above, the provision for impairment losses and reversal of impairment loss under the PRC Accounting Rules and Regulations are different from the amounts recorded under IFRS.

xi. Government grants

Under the PRC accounting rules and regulations, government grants should be credited to capital reserve. Under IFRS, government grants relating to the purchase of equipment used for technology improvements are initially recorded as long term liabilities and are offset against the cost of assets to which the grants related when construction commences. Upon transfer to property, plant and equipment, the grants are recognized as an income over the useful life of the property, plant and equipment by way of reduced depreciation charge.

Effects of major differences between the PRC Accounting Rules and Regulations and IFRS on net profit are analysed as follows:

	Note	2003 RMB millions
Net profit under PRC GAAP		19,011
Adjustments:		
Depreciation of oil and gas properties	(i)	1,784
Disposal of oil and gas properties	(ii)	1,260
Capitalisation of general borrowing costs	(iii)	389
Acquisition of Sinopec Maoming, Xi'an Petrochemical and Tahe Petrochemical	(iv)	326
Acquisition of Sinopec National Star	(iv)	117
Gain from issuance of shares by subsidiary	(v)	136
Gain from debt restructuring	(vi)	82
Revaluation of land use rights	(vii)	18
Unrecognised losses of subsidiaries	(viii)	(182)
Pre-operating expenditures	(ix)	(169)
Effects of the above adjustments on taxation		(1,179)
*Net profit under IFRS**		*21,593*

Effects of major differences between the PRC Accounting Rules and Regulations and IFRS on shareholders' funds are analysed as follows:

	Note	2003 RMB millions
Shareholders' funds under the PRC GAAP		162,946
Adjustments:		
Depreciation of oil and gas properties	(i)	10,885
Disposal of oil and gas properties	(ii)	1,260
Capitalisation of general borrowing costs	(iii)	1,125
Acquisition of Sinopec Maoming, Xi'an Petrochemical and Tahe Petrochemical	(iv)	—
Acquisition of Sinopec National Star	(iv)	(2,812)
Revaluation of land use rights	(vii)	(870)
Effect on minority interests on unrecognised losses of subsidiaries	(viii)	61
Pre-operating expenditures	(ix)	(169)
Impairment losses on long-lived assets	(x)	(113)
Government grants	(xi)	(326)
Effect of the above adjustment on taxation		(4,088)
*Shareholders' funds under IFRS**		*167,899*

*The above figure is extracted from the financial statements prepared in accordance with IFRS which have been audited by KPMG.

SUPPLEMENTAL INFORMATION FOR NORTH AMERICAN SHAREHOLDERS

The Group's accounting policies conform with IFRS which differ in certain significant respects from accounting principles generally accepted in the United States of America ("US GAAP"). Information relating to the nature and effect of such differences are set out below. The US GAAP reconciliation presented below is included as supplemental information, is not required as part of the basic financial statements and does not include differences related to classification, display or disclosures.

a. **Foreign exchange gains and losses**

In accordance with IFRS, foreign exchange differences on funds borrowed for construction are capitalized as property, plant and equipment to the extent that they are regarded as an adjustment to interest costs during the construction period. Under US GAAP, all foreign exchange gains and losses on foreign currency debts are included in current earnings.

b. **Capitalisation of property, plant and equipment**

In the years prior to those presented herein, certain adjustments arose between IFRS and US GAAP with regard to the capitalization of interest and pre-production results under IFRS that were reversed and expensed under US GAAP. For the years presented herein, there were no adjustments related to the capitalization of interest and pre-production results. Accordingly, the US GAAP adjustments represent the amortisation effect of such originating adjustments described above.

c. **Revaluation of property, plant and equipment**

As required by the relevant PRC regulations with respect to the Reorganisation, the property, plant and equipment of the Group were revalued at 30 September 1999. In addition, the property, plant and equipment of Sinopec National Star, Sinopec Maoming and Refining Assets were revalued at 31 December 2000, 30 June 2003 and 31 October 2003 respectively in connection with the Acquisitions. Under IFRS, such revaluations result in an increase in shareholders' funds with respect to the increase in carrying amount of certain property, plant and equipment below their cost bases.

Under US GAAP, property, plant and equipment, including land use rights, are stated at their historical cost less accumulated depreciation. However, as a result of the tax deductibility of the net revaluation surplus, a deferred tax asset related to the reversal of the revaluation surplus is created under US GAAP with a corresponding increase in shareholders' funds.

Under IFRS, effective 1 January 2002, land use rights, which were previously carried at revalued amount, are carried at cost under IFRS. The effect of this change resulted in a decrease to revaluation reserve net of minority interests of RMB 840 million as of 1 January 2002. This revaluation reserve was previously included as part of the revaluation reserve of property, plant and equipment. This change under IFRS eliminated the US GAAP difference relating to the revaluation of land use rights. However, as a result of the tax deductibility of the revalued land use rights, the reversal of the revaluation reserve resulted in a deferred tax asset.

In addition, under IFRS, on disposal of a revalued asset, the related revaluation surplus is transferred from the revaluation reserve to retained earnings. Under US GAAP, the gain and loss on disposal of an asset is determined with reference to the asset's historical carrying amount and included in current earnings.

d. **Exchange of assets**

During 2002, the Company and Sinopec Group Company entered into an asset swap transaction. Under IFRS, the cost of property, plant and equipment acquired in an exchange for a similar item of property, plant and equipment is measured at fair value. Under US GAAP, as the exchange of assets was between entities under common control, the assets received from Sinopec Group Company are measured at historical cost. The difference between the historical cost of the net assets transferred and the net assets received is accounted fro as an equity transaction.

e. **Impairment of long-lived assets**

Under IFRS, impairment charges are recognized when a long-lived asset's carrying amount exceeds the higher of an asset's net selling price and value in use, which incorporates discounting the asset's estimated future cash flows.

Under US GAAP, determination of the recoverability of a long-lived asset is based on an estimate of undiscounted future cash flows resulting from the use of the asset and its eventual disposition. If the sum of the expected future cash flows is less than the carrying amount of the asset, an impairment loss is recognized. Measurement of an impairment loss for a long-lived asset is based on the fair value of the asset.

In addition, under IFRS, a subsequent increase in the recoverable amount of an asset is reversed to the consolidated income statement to the extent that an impairment loss on the same asset was previously recognized as an expense when the circumstances and events that led to the write-down or write-off cease to exist. The reversal is reduced by the amount that would have been recognized as depreciation had the write-off not occurred.

Under US GAAP, an impairment loss establishes a new cost basis for the impaired asset and the new cost basis should not be adjusted subsequently other than for further impairment losses.

The US GAAP adjustment represents the effect of reversing the recovery of previous impairment charge recorded under IFRS.

f. Capitalised interest on investment in associates

Under IFRS, investment accounted for by the equity method is not considered a qualifying asset for which interest is capitalized. Under US GAAP, an investment accounted for by the equity method while the investee has activities in progress necessary to commence its planned principal operations, provided that the investee's activities include the use of funds to acquire qualifying assets for its operations, is a qualifying asset for which interest is capitalized.

g. Goodwill amortisation

Under IFRS, goodwill and negative goodwill are amortised on a systematic basis over their useful lives.

Under US GAAP, with reference to Statement of Financial Accounting Standard No.142, "Goodwill and Other Intangible Assets" ("SFAS No. 142"), goodwill is no longer amortised beginning 1 January 2002, the date that SFAS No. 142 was adopted. Instead, goodwill is reviewed for impairment upon adoption of SFAS No. 142 and annually thereafter. In connection with SFAS No. 142's transitional goodwill impairment evaluation, the Group determined that no goodwill impairment existed as of the date of adoption. In addition, under US GAAP, negative goodwill of RMB 11 million, net of minority interests that existed at the date of adoption of SFAS No. 142 was written off as a cumulative effect of a change in accounting principle.

h. Companies included in consolidation

Under IFRS, the Group consolidates less than majority owned entities in which the Group has the power, directly or indirectly, to govern the financial and operating policies of an entity do as to obtain benefits from its activities, and proportionately consolidates jointly controlled entities in which the Group has joint control with other venturers. However, US GAAP requires that any entity of which the Group owns 20% to 50% of total outstanding voting stock not be consolidated nor proportionately consolidated, but rather be accounted for under the equity method. Accordingly, certain of the Group's subsidiaries of which the Group owns between 40.72% to 50% of the outstanding voting stock, and the Group's jointly controlled entities are not consolidated nor proportionately consolidated under US GAAP and instead accounted for under the equity method. This exclusion does not affect the profit attributable to shareholders or shareholders' funds reconciliation between IFRS and US GAAP.

Presented below is summarized financial information of such subsidiaries and jointly controlled entities.

	Year ended 31 December 2003 RMB millions
Revenue	21,735
Profit before taxation	1,329
Net Profit	1,090

	At 31 December 2003 RMB millions
Current assets	4,986
Total assets	27,607
Current liabilities	5,902
Total liabilities	9,238
Total equity	18,369

i. Related party transactions

Under IFRS, transactions of state-controlled enterprises with other state-controlled enterprises are not required to be disclosed as related party transactions. Furthermore, government departments and agencies are deemed not to be related parties to the extent that such dealings are in the normal course of business. Therefore, related party transactions as disclosed in Note 33 in the financial statements prepared under IFRS only refers to transactions with enterprises over which Sinopec Group Company is able to exercise significant influence.

Under US GAAP, there are no similar exemptions. Although the majority of the Group's activities are with PRC government authorities and affiliates and other PRC state-owned enterprises, the Group believes that it has provided meaningful disclosures of related party transactions in Note 33 to the financial statements prepared under IFRS.

The effect on profit attributable to shareholders of significant differences between IFRS and US GAAP is as follows:

	Reference in Note above	Year ended 12-31-2003	
		US$ millions	RMB millions
Profit attributable to shareholders under IFRS		2,60911	21,593
US GAAP adjustments			
Foreign exchange gains and losses	(a)	9	76
Capitalisation of property, plant and equipment ...	(b)	1	12
Reversal of deficit on revaluation of property, plant and equipment	(c)	10	86
Depreciation on revalued property, plant	(c)	483	3,998
Disposal of property, plant and equipment	(c)	159	1,316
Exchange of assets	(d)	3	23
Reversal of impairment of long-lived assets, Net of depreciation effect	(e)	6	47
Capitalised interest on investments in associates ...	(f)	17	141
Goodwill amortisation for the year	(g)	—	—
Cumulative effect of adopting SFAS No.142	(g)	—	—
Deferred tax effect of US GAAP adjustments		(207)	(1,715)
Profit attributable to shareholders under US GAAP		**3,090**	**25,577**
Basic and diluted earnings per share under US GAAP		**US$0.04**	**RMB0.30**
Basic and diluted earning per ADS under US GAAP*		**US$3.56**	**RMB29.50**

*Basic and diluted earnings per ADS is calculated on the basis that one ADS is equivalent to 100 shares.

The effect on shareholders' funds of significant differences between IFRS and US GAAP is as follows:

	Reference in note above	At December 2003	
		US$ millions	RMB millions
Shareholders' funds under IFRS		20,286	167,899
US GAAP adjustments:			
Foreign exchange gains and losses	(a)	(43)	(352)
Capitalisation of property, plant and equipment ...	(b)	(1)	(12)
Revaluation of property, plant and equipment	(c)	(1,564)	(12,943)
Deferred tax adjustments on revaluation	(c)	484	4,004
Exchange of assets	(d)	(67)	(555)
Reversal of impairment of long-lived assets	(e)	(68)	(561)
Capitalised interest on investments in associates ...	(f)	39	321
Goodwill	(g)	2	17
Deferred tax effect of US GAAP adjustments		48	398
Shareholders' funds under US GAAP		***19,116***	***158,216***

Note: United States dollar equivalents

For the convenience of readers, amounts in Renminbi have been translated into United States dollars at the rate of US$1.00 = RMB 8.2767 being the noon buying rate in New York City on 31 December 2003 for cable transfers in Renminbi as certified for customs purposes by the Federal Reserve Bank of New York. No representation is made that the Renminbi amounts could have been, or could be, converted into United States dollars at that rate.

Source: China Petroleum and Chemical Corporation 2003 annual report, pp. 158–63.

Required:

1. Critically comment on the results reported by CPCC under PRC GAAP, IFRSs, and U.S. GAAP.
2. Identify the main areas of difference for CPCC between:
   a. PRC GAAP and IFRSs.
   b. IFRSs and U.S. GAAP.
3. Should UK readers of these financial statements find the information useful?
4. Should U.S. readers of these financial statements find the information useful?
5. Would you recommend that other companies adopt the multiple standards approach taken by CPCC? Explain.

References

Alexander, David, and Simon Archer, eds. *European Accounting Guide*, 5th ed. New York: Aspen, 2004, p. 1.15.

Aono, J. "The Auditing Environment in Japan." In *International Auditing Environment*, ed. I. Shiobara. Tokyo: Zeimukeiri-Kyokai, pp. 199–211.

Chen, S.; Z. Sun; and Y. Wang. "Evidence from China on Whether Harmonized Accounting Standards Harmonize Accounting Practices." *Accounting Horizons* 16, no. 3 (2002), pp. 183–97.

Chen, Y.; P. Jubb; and A. Tran. "Problems of Accounting Reform in the People's Republic of China." *International Journal of Accounting* 32, no. 2 (1997), pp. 139–53.

China Securities Regulatory Commission. *China Securities and Futures Statistical Yearbook*. Beijing: CSRC, 2000 and 2002.

Consultative Committee on Accountancy Bodies. *The Making of Accounting Standards: Report of the Review Committee (Dearing Committee)*. London: ICAEW, 1988.

Doupnik, Timothy S. "Recent Innovations in German Accounting Practice Through the Integration of EC Directives." *Advances in International Accounting*, 1992, p. 80.

Douthett, E. B. Jr., and K. Jung. "Japanese Corporate Groupings (*Keiretsu*) and the Informativeness of Earnings." *Journal of International Financial Management and Accounting* 12, no. 2 (2001), pp. 133–59.

Eberhartinger, E. L. E. "The Impact of Tax Rules on Financial Reporting in Germany, France, and the UK." *International Journal of Accounting* 34, no. 1 (1999), pp. 93–119.

FASF. "Concerning Treatment (Compliance) of Accounting Standards and other Pronouncements Issued by the Accounting Standards Board of Japan," May 2002. For details, go to www.jicpa.or.jp/n_eng/e200201.html.

Glaum, M., and U. Mandler. "Global Accounting Harmonization from a German Perspective: Bridging the GAAP." *Journal of International Financial Management and Accounting* 7, no. 3 (1996), pp. 215–42.

Goldburgh, L. "The Development of Accounting." In *Accounting Concepts Readings*, ed. C. T. Gibson, G. G. Meredith, and R. Peterson. Melbourne: Cassell, 1971.

Graham, L. E. "Setting a Research Agenda for Auditing Issues in the People's Republic of China." *International Journal of Accounting* 31, no. 1 (1996), pp. 19–37.

Graham, L. E., and C. Li. "Cultural and Economic Influences on Current Accounting Standards in the People's Republic of China." *International Journal of Accounting* 32, no. 3 (1997), pp. 247–78.

Haw, I.; D. Qi; and W. Wu. "The Nature of Information in Accruals and Cash Flows in an Emerging Capital Market: The Case of China." *International Journal of Accounting* 36 (2001), pp. 391–406.

IASC. *Insight*. London: IASC, March 1999.

Jiang, L., and J. Kim. "Cross-Corporate Ownership, Information Asymmetry and the Usefulness of Accounting Performance Measures in Japan," *International Journal of Accounting* 35, no. 1 (2000), pp. 85–98.

Lee, C. J. "Financial Restructuring of State Owned Enterprises in China: The Case of Shanghai Sunve Pharmaceutical Corporation." *Accounting, Organizations and Society* (2001), pp. 673–89.

Lin, J., and F. Chen. "Applicability of the Conservatism Accounting Convention in China: Empirical Evidence." *International Journal of Accounting* 34, no. 4 (1999), pp. 517–37.

Lin, K. Z., and K. H. Chan. "Auditing Standards in China: A Comparative Analysis with Relevant International Standards and Guidelines." *International Journal of Accounting* 35, no. 4 (2000), pp. 559–77.

Mande, V., and R. Ortman. "Are Recent Segment Disclosures of Japanese Firms Useful? Views of Japanese Financial Analysts." *International Journal of Accounting* 37 (2002), pp. 27–46.

McKinnon, J. L., and G. L. Harrison. "Cultural Influence on Corporate and Governmental Involvement in Accounting Policy Determination in Japan." *Journal of Accounting and Public Policy*, Autumn 1985, pp. 201–23.

Ozu, C., and S. Gray. "The Development of Segment Reporting in Japan: Achieving International Harmonization Through a Process of National Consensus." *Advances in International Accounting* 14 (2001), pp. 1–13.

Ravlic, T. "Japan Looks to Higher Standards." *Australian CPA* 69, no. 10 (1999), pp. 48–49.

Singleton, W. R., and S. Globerman. "The Nature of Financial Disclosure in Japan." *International Journal of Accounting* 37 (2002), pp. 95–111.

Tang, Y. "Bumpy Road Leading to Internationalization: A Review of Accounting Development in China." *Accounting Horizons* 14, no. 1 (2000), pp. 93–102.

World Trade Organization. *Report of the Working Party on the Accession to China, Addendum, Schedule of Specific Commitment on Services*, October 1, 2001, available at www.wto.org/english/thewto_e/completeacc_e.htm.

Wyman, P. "The Enron Aftermath—Where Next?" speech delivered October 10, 2002, at a conference held in Brussels (available at www.icaew.co.uk/index/cfm?AUB=TB2I_37723).

Xiao, J. Z.; Y. Zhang; and Z. Xie. "The Making of Independent Auditing Standards in China." *Accounting Horizons* 14, no. 1 (2000), pp. 69–89.

Xiao, Z., and A. Pan. "Developing Accounting Standards on the Basis of a Conceptual Framework by the Chinese Government." *International Journal of Accounting* 32, no. 3 (1997), pp. 279–99.

Yamori, N., and T. Baba. "Japanese Management Views on Overseas Exchange Listings: Survey Results." *Journal of International Financial Management and Accounting* 12, no. 3 (2001), pp. 286–316.

Zeff, S. A. *Forging Accounting Principles in Five Countries: A History and Analysis of Trends*. Champaign, IL: Stipes, 1972.

Chapter **Six**

Foreign Currency Transactions and Hedging Foreign Exchange Risk

Learning Objectives

After reading this chapter, you should be able to

- Provide an overview of the foreign exchange market.
- Explain how fluctuations in exchange rates give rise to foreign exchange risk.
- Demonstrate the accounting for foreign currency transactions.
- Describe how foreign currency forward contracts and foreign currency options can be used to hedge foreign exchange risk.
- Describe the concepts of cash flow hedges, fair value hedges, and hedge accounting.
- Demonstrate the accounting for forward contracts and options used as cash flow hedges and fair value hedges to hedge foreign currency assets and liabilities, foreign currency firm commitments, and forecasted foreign currency transactions.

INTRODUCTION

International trade (imports and exports) constitutes a significant portion of the world economy. According to the World Trade Organization, over $7 trillion worth of merchandise was exported (and imported) in 2003.[1] Recent growth in trade has been phenomenal. From 1990 to 2001, global exports increased by 75 percent while global gross domestic product increased by only 27 percent.

The number of companies involved in trade also has grown substantially. From 1987 to 1999, the number of U.S. companies making export sales rose by 233 percent to a total of 231,420 companies.[2] Raytheon Company is a U.S.-based electronics and defense systems company with more than $3.5 billion of annual export

---

[1] World Trade Organization, *International Trade Statistics 2004,* Table I.5: Leading Exporters and Importers in World Merchandise Trade, 2004 (www.wto.org).

[2] U.S. Department of Commerce, International Trade Administration, "Small and Medium-Sized Enterprises Play an Important Role," *Export America,* September 2001, pp. 26–29.

sales. In 2004, 18 percent of Raytheon's sales were outside of the United States.[3] Even small businesses are significantly involved in exporting. Companies with fewer than 500 workers comprise 97 percent of U.S. exporters.

Collections from export sales or payments for imports are not always made in a company's domestic currency; they may be made in a foreign currency depending on the negotiated terms of the transaction. As the exchange rate for the foreign currency fluctuates, so does the domestic currency value of these export sales and import purchases. Companies often find it necessary to engage in some form of hedging activity to reduce losses arising from fluctuating exchange rates. For example, at the end of 2004, Raytheon reported having "foreign currency forward contracts with commercial banks to fix the dollar value of specific commitments and payments to international vendors and the value of foreign currency denominated receipts."[4] At December 31, 2004, the company had outstanding foreign currency contracts to buy foreign currency totaling $831 million and to sell foreign currency in the amount of $495 million. At year-end 2003, Italian automaker Fiat SpA reported having contracts to hedge foreign exchange risks amounting to 4.8 billion euros (approximately $3.8 billion at the time).

This chapter covers accounting issues related to foreign currency transactions and foreign currency hedging activities. To provide background for subsequent discussion of the accounting issues, we begin with a description of foreign exchange markets. We then discuss the accounting for import and export transactions, followed by coverage of various types of hedging techniques. The discussion concentrates on forward contracts and options because these are the most popular types of hedging instruments. Understanding how to account for these items is important for any company engaged in international transactions.

FOREIGN EXCHANGE MARKETS

Each country uses its own currency as the unit of value for the purchase and sale of goods and services. The currency used in the United States is the U.S. dollar, the currency used in Japan is the Japanese yen, and so on. If a U.S. citizen travels to Japan and wishes to purchase local goods, Japanese merchants require payment to be made in Japanese yen. To make the purchase, a U.S. citizen has to purchase yen using U.S. dollars. The price at which the foreign currency can be acquired is known as the *foreign exchange rate*. A variety of factors determine the exchange rate between two currencies; unfortunately for those engaged in international business, the exchange rate fluctuates.[5] In some cases, a change in the exchange rate is quite large and unexpected.

Exchange Rate Mechanisms

Exchange rates have not always fluctuated. During the period 1945–1973, countries fixed the par value of their currency in terms of the U.S. dollar and the value of the U.S. dollar was fixed in terms of gold. Countries agreed to maintain the value of their currency within 1 percent of the par value. If the exchange rate for a

---

[3] Raytheon Company, 2004 Form 10-K, p. 14.

[4] Ibid., p. 51.

[5] Several theories attempt to explain exchange rate fluctuations but with little success, at least in the short run. A discussion of exchange rate determination can be found in any international finance textbook. An understanding of the causes of exchange rate changes is not necessary for an understanding of the concepts underlying the accounting for changes in exchange rates.

particular currency began to move outside of this 1 percent range, the country's central bank was required to intervene by buying or selling its currency in the foreign exchange market. Due to the law of supply and demand, the purchase of currency by a central bank would cause the price of the currency to stop falling and the sale of currency would cause the price to stop rising.

The integrity of the system hinged on the ability of the U.S. dollar to maintain its value in terms of gold and the ability of foreign countries to convert their U.S.-dollar holdings into gold at the fixed rate of $35 per ounce. As the United States began to incur balance-of-payment deficits in the 1960s, a glut of U.S. dollars arose worldwide and foreign countries began converting their U.S. dollars into gold. This resulted in a decline in the U.S. government's gold reserve from a high of $24.6 billion in 1949 to a low of $10.2 billion in 1971. In the latter year, the United States suspended the convertibility of the U.S. dollar into gold, signaling the beginning of the end for the fixed exchange rate system. In March 1973, most currencies were allowed to float in value.

Today, several different currency arrangements exist. The following are some of the more important ones and the countries they affect:

1. *Independent float.* The value of the currency is allowed to fluctuate freely according to market forces with little or no intervention from the central bank (Brazil, Canada, Japan, Mexico, Switzerland, United States).
2. *Pegged to another currency.* The value of the currency is fixed (pegged) in terms of a particular foreign currency, and the central bank intervenes as necessary to maintain the fixed value. For example, 25 countries peg their currency to the U.S. dollar (including the Bahamas and Syria).
3. *European Monetary System (euro).* In 1998, the countries comprising the European Monetary System adopted a common currency called the euro and established the European Central Bank.[6] Until 2002, local currencies such as the German mark and French franc continued to exist but were fixed in value in terms of the euro. On January 1, 2002, local currencies disappeared and the euro became the currency in 12 European countries. The value of the euro floats against other currencies such as the U.S. dollar.

Foreign Exchange Rates

Exchange rates between the U.S. dollar and most foreign currencies are published daily in *The Wall Street Journal* and other major U.S. newspapers. Current and past exchange rates are readily obtainable from a variety of Web sites, such as OANDA.com and X-rates.com. U.S.-dollar exchange rates for several foreign currencies for Wednesday, March 16, 2005, as reported in *The Wall Street Journal,* are presented in Exhibit 6.1. These exchange rates were quoted in New York at 4:00 p.m. Eastern time. The U.S.-dollar price for one Mexican peso on Wednesday, March 16, at 4:00 p.m. in New York was $0.0891. The U.S.-dollar price for a peso at 3:00 p.m. or 5:00 p.m. Eastern time was probably something different, as exchange rates fluctuate constantly. These exchange rates are for trades between banks in amounts of $1 million or more; that is, these are interbank or wholesale prices. Prices charged when selling foreign currency to retail customers such as companies engaged in international business are higher, and prices offered to buy foreign

---

[6] Most members of the European Union (EU) are euro-zone countries. The major exception is the United Kingdom, which decided not to participate. Switzerland is another important European country not part of the euro zone because it is not a member of the EU.

EXHIBIT 6.1
Foreign Exchange
Rates on
Wednesday,
March 16, 2005

Source: *The Wall Street
Journal*, March 17, 2005,
p. C12.

Country	US$ Equivalent		Currency per US$	
	Wednesday, March 16	Tuesday, March 15	Wednesday, March 16	Tuesday, March 15
China (renminbi)	0.1208	0.1208	8.2764	8.2764
Mexico (peso)	0.0891	0.0890	11.2221	11.2385
Switzerland (franc)	0.8676	0.8587	1.1526	1.1646
One month forward.....	0.8691	0.8602	1.1506	1.1625
Three months forward ..	0.8727	0.8636	1.1459	1.1579
Six months forward	0.8785	0.8696	1.1383	1.1500
Taiwan (dollar)	0.03224	0.03239	31.0170	30.8740
United Kingdom (pound) ..	1.9268	1.9121	0.5190	0.5230
One month forward	1.9236	1.9088	0.5199	0.5239
Three months forward ..	1.9176	1.9031	0.5215	0.5255
Six months forward	1.9105	1.8958	0.5234	0.5275
Euro	1.3420	1.3313	0.7452	0.7511

currency from retail customers are lower. The difference between the buying and selling rates is the spread through which the banks earn a profit on foreign exchange trades.

The Wall Street Journal presents comparative exchange rates for the two most recent days so that readers can quickly see the change that has occurred from one day to the next. Two types of exchange rate quotes are presented for each day. The columns labeled "US$ Equivalent" indicate the number of U.S. dollars needed to purchase one unit of foreign currency. These are known as direct quotes. The direct quote for the UK pound on March 16 was $1.9268; in other words, one British pound could be purchased for $1.9268. The columns labeled "Currency per US$" indicate the number of foreign currency units that can be purchased with one U.S. dollar. These are called indirect quotes. Indirect quotes are simply the inverse of direct quotes. If one British pound costs $1.9268, then $1.00 can purchase only 0.5190 pounds. To avoid confusion, we use direct quotes exclusively in this chapter.

In most cases, there was a change in the exchange rate from Tuesday, March 15, 2005, to Wednesday, March 16, 2005. Some currencies, such as the euro, increased in price, or *appreciated*, against the U.S. dollar (from $1.3313 to $1.3420). Other currencies, such as the Taiwanese dollar, decreased in price, or *depreciated*, against the U.S. dollar (from $0.03239 to $0.03224). However, for currencies such as the Chinese renminbi, whose value is pegged to the dollar, there was no change in the exchange rate from March 15 to March 16.

Spot and Forward Rates

Foreign currency trades can be executed on a *spot* or *forward* basis. The *spot rate* is the price at which a foreign currency can be purchased or sold today. In contrast, the *forward rate* is the price today at which foreign currency can be purchased or sold sometime in the future. Because many international business transactions take some time to be completed, the ability to lock in a price today at which foreign currency can be purchased or sold at some future date has definite advantages.

Most of the quotes published in *The Wall Street Journal* are spot rates. In addition, the journal publishes forward rates quoted by New York banks for the major currencies (Canadian dollar, Japanese yen, Swiss franc, and British pound) on a daily basis. This is only a partial listing of possible forward contracts. A firm and its bank can tailor forward contracts in other currencies and for other time periods to meet the needs of the firm. There is no up-front cost to enter into a forward contract.

The forward rate can exceed the spot rate on a given date, in which case the foreign currency is said to be selling at a *premium* in the forward market, or the forward rate can be less than the spot rate, in which case it is selling at a *discount*. Currencies sell at a premium or a discount because of differences in interest rates between two countries. When the interest rate in the foreign country exceeds the interest rate domestically, the foreign currency sells at a discount in the forward market. Conversely, if the foreign interest rate is less than the domestic rate, the foreign currency sells at a premium.[7] Forward rates are said to be unbiased predictors of the future spot rate.

The spot rate for Swiss francs on March 16, 2005, indicates that 1 franc could have been purchased on that date for $0.8676. On the same day, the one-month forward rate was $0.8691. The Swiss franc was selling at a premium in the one-month forward market. By entering into a forward contract on March 16, it was possible to guarantee that Swiss francs could be purchased one month later at a price of $0.8691 per franc, regardless of what the spot rate turned out to be on that date. Entering into the forward contract to purchase francs would have been beneficial if the spot rate in one month turned out to be greater than $0.8691. However, such a forward contract would have been detrimental if the future spot rate turned out to be less than $0.8691. In either case, the forward contract must be honored and Swiss francs must be purchased at $0.8691.

On the same day that the Swiss franc was selling at a premium in the forward market, the British pound was selling at a discount. On March 16, 2005, when the British pound spot rate was $1.9268, a U.S. importer of British goods could have locked in a rate of only $1.9105 to purchase British pounds in six months. This action would eliminate the risk to the importer that the British pound might actually appreciate against the U.S. dollar over the next six months, which would increase the U.S.-dollar cost of the British imports.

Option Contracts

To provide companies more flexibility than exists with a forward contract, a market for *foreign currency options* has developed. A foreign currency option gives the holder of the option *the right but not the obligation* to trade foreign currency in the future. A *put option* is for the sale of foreign currency by the holder of the option; a *call option* is for the purchase of foreign currency by the holder of the option. The *strike price* is the exchange rate at which the option will be executed if the holder of the option decides to exercise the option. The strike price is similar to a forward rate. There are generally several strike prices to choose from at any particular time. Foreign currency options may be purchased either on the Philadelphia Stock Exchange or directly from a bank in the so-called over-the-counter market.

Unlike forward contracts, where banks earn their profit through the spread between buying and selling rates, options must actually be purchased by paying an *option premium*. The option premium is a function of two components: intrinsic value and time value. The *intrinsic value* of an option is equal to the gain that could be realized by exercising the option immediately. For example, if the spot rate for a foreign currency is $1.00, a call option (to purchase foreign currency) with a

---

[7] This relationship is based on the theory of interest rate parity, which indicates that the difference in national interest rates should be equal to but opposite in sign to the forward rate discount or premium. This topic is covered in detail in international finance textbooks.

strike price of $0.97 has an intrinsic value of $0.03, whereas a put option with a strike price of $1.00 or less has an intrinsic value of zero. An option with a positive intrinsic value is said to be "in the money."

The *time value* of an option relates to the fact that the spot rate can change over time and cause the option to become in the money. Even though a 90-day call option with a strike price of $1.00 has zero intrinsic value when the spot rate is $1.00, it will still have a positive time value if there is a chance that the spot rate could increase over the next 90 days and bring the option into the money.

The value of a foreign currency option can be determined by applying an adaptation of the Black-Scholes option pricing formula. This formula is discussed in detail in international finance books. In very general terms, the value of an option is a function of the difference between the current spot rate and strike price, the difference between domestic and foreign interest rates, the length of time to expiration, and the potential volatility of changes in the spot rate. In this book, we will give the premium originally paid for a foreign currency option and its subsequent fair value up to the date of expiration derived from applying the pricing formula.

FOREIGN CURRENCY TRANSACTIONS

Export sales and import purchases are international transactions. When two parties from different countries enter into a transaction, they must decide which of the two countries' currencies to use to settle the transaction. For example, if a U.S. computer manufacturer sells to a customer in Japan, the parties must decide whether the transaction will be denominated (i.e., whether payment will be made) in U.S. dollars or Japanese yen. In some cases, a third country's currency might be used to denominate the transaction.

Assume that a U.S. exporter (Eximco) sells goods to a Spanish customer with payment to be made in euros. In this situation, Eximco has entered into a foreign currency transaction. It must restate the euro amount that actually will be received into U.S. dollars to account for this transaction. This is because Eximco keeps its books and prepares financial statements in U.S. dollars. Although the Spanish importer has entered into an international transaction, it does not have a foreign currency transaction (payment will be made in its home currency) and no restatement is necessary.

Assume that, as is customary in its industry, Eximco does not require immediate payment and allows its Spanish customer three months to pay for its purchases. By doing this, Eximco runs the risk that from the date the sale is made until the date of payment, the euro might decrease in value (depreciate) against the U.S. dollar and the actual number of U.S. dollars generated from the sale will be less than expected. In this situation Eximco is said to have an *exposure to foreign exchange risk*. Specifically, Eximco has a *transaction exposure*.

Transaction exposure can be summarized as follows:

- *Export sale.* A transaction exposure exists when the exporter allows the buyer to pay in a foreign currency and also allows the buyer to pay sometime after the sale has been made. The exporter is exposed to the risk that the foreign currency might decrease in value between the date of sale and the date of payment, thereby decreasing the amount of domestic currency (U.S. dollars for Eximco) into which the foreign currency can be converted.

- *Import purchase.* A transaction exposure exists when the importer is required to pay in foreign currency and is allowed to pay sometime after the purchase has been made. The importer is exposed to the risk that the foreign currency might increase in price (appreciate) between the date of purchase and the date of payment, thereby increasing the amount of domestic currency that has to be paid for the imported goods.

Accounting Issue

The major issue in accounting for foreign currency transactions is how to deal with the change in the domestic currency value of the sales revenue and account receivable resulting from the export when the foreign currency changes in value. The corollary issue is how to deal with the change in the domestic currency value of the foreign currency account payable and goods being acquired in an import purchase.

Assume that Eximco sells goods to a Spanish customer at a price of 1 million euros (€) when the spot exchange rate is $1.00 per euro. If payment were received at the date of sale, Eximco could have converted €1,000,000 into $1,000,000 and this amount clearly would be the amount at which the sales revenue would be recognized. Instead, Eximco allows the Spanish customer three months to pay for its purchase. At the end of three months, the euro has depreciated to $0.98 and Eximco is able to convert the €1,000,000 received on that date into only $980,000. How should Eximco account for this $20,000 decrease in value?

Accounting Alternatives

Conceptually, the two methods of accounting for changes in the value of a foreign currency transaction are the one-transaction perspective and the two-transaction perspective. The *one-transaction perspective* assumes that an export sale is not complete until the foreign currency receivable has been collected and converted into U.S. dollars. Any change in the U.S.-dollar value of the foreign currency will be accounted for as an adjustment to Accounts Receivable and to Sales. Under this perspective, Eximco would ultimately report Sales at $980,000 and an increase in the Cash account of the same amount. This approach can be criticized because it hides the fact that the company could have received $1,000,000 if the Spanish customer had been required to pay at the date of sale. The company incurs a $20,000 loss because of the depreciation in the euro, but that loss is buried in an adjustment to Sales. This approach is not acceptable under International Financial Reporting Standards (IFRSs) or U.S. GAAP.

Instead, both International Accounting Standard (IAS) 21, *The Effects of Changes in Foreign Exchange Rates,* and Statement of Financial Accounting Standards (SFAS) 52[8] require companies to use a *two-transaction perspective* in accounting for foreign currency transactions. This perspective treats the export sale and the subsequent collection of cash as two separate transactions. Because management has made two decisions—(1) to make the export sale, and (2) to extend credit in foreign currency to the customer—the income effect from each of these decisions should be reported separately.

Under the two-transaction perspective, Eximco records the U.S. dollar value of the sale at the date the sale occurs. At that point the sale has been completed; there are no subsequent adjustments to the Sales account. Any difference between the number of U.S. dollars that could have been received at the date of sale and the number of U.S. dollars actually received at the date of payment due to fluctuations in the exchange rate is a result of the decision to extend foreign currency credit to the customer. This difference is treated as a Foreign Exchange Gain or Loss that is reported separately

---

[8] FASB, Statement of Financial Accounting Standards 52, *Foreign Currency Translation* (Stamford, CT: FASB, December 1981).

from Sales in the income statement. Using the two-transaction perspective to account for its export sale to Spain, Eximco would make the following journal entries:

Date of Sale:	Accounts Receivable (€)	1,000,000	
	Sales		1,000,000
	To record the sale and euro receivable at the spot rate of $1.00.		
Date of Payment:	Foreign Exchange Loss	20,000	
	Accounts Receivable (€)		20,000
	To adjust the U.S.-dollar value of the euro receivable to the new spot rate of $0.98 and record a foreign exchange loss resulting from the depreciation in the euro.		
	Cash	980,000	
	Accounts Receivable (€)		980,000
	To record the receipt of €1,000,000 and conversion into U.S. dollars at the spot rate of $0.98.		

Sales are reported in income at the amount that would have been received if the customer had not been given three months to pay the €1,000,000, that is, $1,000,000. A separate Foreign Exchange Loss of $20,000 is reported in income to indicate that because of the decision to extend foreign currency credit to the Spanish customer and because the euro decreased in value, fewer U.S. dollars are actually received.[9]

Note that Eximco keeps its Account Receivable (€) account separate from its U.S.-dollar receivables. Companies engaged in international trade need to keep separate payable and receivable accounts in each of the currencies in which they have transactions. Each foreign currency receivable and payable should have a separate account number in the company's chart of accounts.

We can summarize the relationship between fluctuations in exchange rates and foreign exchange gains and losses as follows:

		Foreign Currency (FC)	
Transaction	Type of Exposure	Appreciates	Depreciates
Export sale	Asset	Gain	Loss
Import purchase	Liability	Loss	Gain

A foreign currency receivable arising from an export sale creates an *asset exposure* to foreign exchange risk. If the foreign currency appreciates, the foreign currency asset increases in terms of domestic currency and a foreign exchange gain arises; depreciation of the foreign currency causes a foreign exchange loss. A foreign currency payable arising from an import purchase creates a *liability exposure* to foreign exchange risk. If the foreign currency appreciates, the foreign currency liability increases in domestic currency value and a foreign exchange loss results; depreciation of the currency results in a foreign exchange gain.

Balance Sheet Date before Date of Payment

The question arises as to what accounting should be done if a balance sheet date falls between the date of sale and the date of payment. For example, assume that

[9] Note that the foreign exchange loss results because the customer is allowed to pay in euros and is given 30 days to pay. If the transaction were denominated in U.S. dollars, no loss would result. There would also be no loss if the euros had been received at the date the sale was made.

Eximco shipped goods to its Spanish customer on December 10, Year 1, with payment to be received on March 1, Year 2. Assume that at December 10 the spot rate for euros is $1.00, but by December 31 the euro has appreciated to $1.05. Is any adjustment needed at December 31, Year 1, when the books are closed to account for the fact that the foreign currency receivable has changed in U.S. dollar value since December 10?

The general consensus worldwide is that a foreign currency receivable or foreign currency payable should be revalued at the balance sheet date to account for the change in exchange rates. Under the two-transaction perspective, this means that a foreign exchange gain or loss arises at the balance sheet date. The next question then is what should be done with these foreign exchange gains and losses that have not yet been realized in cash. Should they be included in net income?

The two approaches to accounting for unrealized foreign exchange gains and losses are the deferral approach and the accrual approach. Under the *deferral approach,* unrealized foreign exchange gains and losses are deferred on the balance sheet until cash is actually paid or received. When cash is paid or received, a *realized* foreign exchange gain or loss would be included in income. This approach is not acceptable under either IFRSs or U.S. GAAP.

IAS 21 (as well as SFAS 52) requires companies to use the *accrual approach* to account for unrealized foreign exchange gains and losses. Under this approach, a firm reports unrealized foreign exchange gains and losses in net income in the period in which the exchange rate changes. SFAS 52 justifies this approach by saying: "This is consistent with accrual accounting; it results in reporting the effect of a rate change that will have cash flow effects when the event causing the effect takes place."[10] Thus, any change in the exchange rate from the date of sale to the balance sheet date would result in a foreign exchange gain or loss to be reported in income in that period. Any change in the exchange rate from the balance sheet date to the date of payment would result in a second foreign exchange gain or loss that would be reported in the second accounting period. The journal entries Eximco would make under the accrual approach would be as follows:

12/1/Y1	Accounts Receivable (€)	1,000,000	
	Sales		1,000,000
	To record the sale and euro receivable at the spot rate of $1.00.		
12/31/Y1	Accounts Receivable (€)	50,000	
	Foreign Exchange Gain		50,000
	To adjust the value of the euro receivable to the new spot rate of $1.05 and record a foreign exchange gain resulting from the appreciation in the euro since December 10.		
3/1/Y2	Foreign Exchange Loss	70,000	
	Accounts Receivable (€)		70,000
	To adjust the value of the euro receivable to the new spot rate of $0.98 and record a foreign exchange loss resulting from the depreciation in the euro since December 31.		
	Cash	980,000	
	Accounts Receivable (€)		980,000
	To record the receipt of €1,000,000 and conversion at the spot rate of $0.98.		

[10] SFAS 52, paragraph 124.

The net impact on income in Year 1 includes Sales of $980,000 and a Foreign Exchange Gain of $50,000; in Year 2, a Foreign Exchange Loss of $70,000 is recorded. This results in a net increase in Retained Earnings of $980,000 that is balanced by an equal increase in Cash.[11]

One criticism of the accrual approach is that it leads to a *violation of conservatism* when an unrealized foreign exchange gain arises at the balance sheet date. In fact, this is one of only two situations in U.S. GAAP (the other relates to trading marketable securities reported at market value) where it is acceptable to recognize an unrealized gain in income. Historically, several European Union (EU) countries (such as Germany and Austria) more strictly adhered to the concept of conservatism. In those countries, if at the balance sheet date the exchange rate had changed such that an unrealized gain arises, the change in exchange rate was ignored and the foreign currency account receivable or payable continued to be carried on the balance sheet at the exchange rate that existed at the date of the transaction. In contrast, if the exchange rate had changed to cause a foreign exchange loss, the account receivable would have been revalued and an unrealized loss would have been recorded and reported in income. This is a classic application of conservatism. With the introduction of the requirement to use IFRSs, this practice is no longer used by EU-based companies in preparing consolidated financial statements.

All foreign currency assets and liabilities carried on a company's books must be restated at the balance sheet date. In addition to foreign currency payables and receivables arising from import and export transactions, companies also might have dividends receivable from foreign subsidiaries, loans payable to foreign lenders, lease payments receivable from foreign customers, and so on that are denominated in a foreign currency and therefore must be restated at the balance sheet date. Each of these foreign-currency-denominated assets and liabilities is exposed to foreign exchange risk; therefore, fluctuations in the exchange rate will result in foreign exchange gains and losses.

Many U.S. companies report foreign exchange gains and losses on the income statement in a line item often titled "Other Income (Expense)." Other incidental gains and losses such as gains and losses on sales of assets would be included in this line item as well. SFAS 52 requires companies to disclose the magnitude of foreign exchange gains and losses if material. For example, in the Notes to Financial Statements in its 2004 annual report, Merck & Company Inc. indicated that the income statement item "Other (Income) Expense, Net" included exchange gains of $18.4 million, $28.4 million, and $7.8 million in 2004, 2003, and 2002, respectively.[12]

HEDGING FOREIGN EXCHANGE RISK

In the preceding example, Eximco has an asset exposure in euros when it sells goods to the Spanish customer and it allows the customer three months to pay for its purchase. If the euro depreciates over the next three months, Eximco incurs a

---

[11] Note that the journal entries recorded at March 1, Year 2, could have been combined into the following single entry:

3/1/Y2	Foreign Exchange Loss	70,000	
	Cash	980,000	
	Accounts Receivable (€)		1,050,000

[12] Merck & Company, Inc., annual report 2004, Note 16 Other (Income) Expense, Net, p. 54.

foreign exchange loss. For many companies, the uncertainty of not knowing exactly how much domestic currency will be received on this export sale is of great concern. To avoid this uncertainty, companies often use foreign currency derivatives to hedge against the effect of unfavorable changes in the value of foreign currencies.[13] The two most common derivatives used to hedge foreign exchange risk are foreign currency forward contracts and foreign currency options. Through a forward contract, Eximco can lock in the price at which it will sell the euros it receives in three months. An option establishes a price at which Eximco will be able, but is not required, to sell the euros it receives in three months. If Eximco enters into a forward contract or purchases an option on the date the sale is made, the derivative is being used as a *hedge of a recognized foreign-currency-denominated asset* (the euro account receivable).

Companies engaged in foreign currency activities often enter into hedging arrangements as soon as a noncancelable sales order is received or a noncancelable purchase order is placed. A noncancelable order that specifies the foreign currency price and date of delivery is a known as a *foreign currency firm commitment*. Assume that, on April 1, Eximco accepts an order to sell parts to a customer in Thailand at a price of 20 million Thai baht. The parts will be delivered and payment will be received on May 15. On April 1, before the sale has been made, Eximco enters into a forward contract to sell 20 million Thai baht on May 15. In this case, Eximco is using a foreign currency derivative as a *hedge of an unrecognized foreign currency firm commitment*.

Some companies have foreign currency transactions that occur on a regular basis and can be reliably forecast. For example, Eximco regularly purchases components from a supplier in Singapore making payment in Singapore dollars. Even if Eximco has no contract to make future purchases, it has an exposure to foreign currency risk if it plans to continue making purchases from the Singapore supplier. Assume that, on October 1, Eximco forecasts that it will make a purchase from the Singapore supplier in one month. To hedge against a possible increase in the price of the Singapore dollar, Eximco acquires a call option on October 1 to purchase Singapore dollars in one month. The foreign currency option represents a *hedge of a forecast foreign-currency-denominated transaction*.

ACCOUNTING FOR DERIVATIVES

In the development of a core set of standards for global use, the International Organization of Securities Commissions (IOSCO) required the International Accounting Standards Board (IASB) to include a standard on the recognition and measurement of financial instruments, off-balance-sheet items, and hedging activities. In 1988, the IASB embarked on a joint project with the Canadian Institute of Chartered Accountants to develop a comprehensive standard in this area. Due to the critical response to an early Exposure Draft, the project was subsequently divided into two parts and IAS 32, *Financial Instruments: Disclosure and Presentation,* was issued in 1995. Work continued on the recognition and measurement dimensions of the project with a discussion paper published in 1997. Comments on the discussion paper raised numerous issues that caused the IASB to conclude that developing a final standard in the near term was not possible. Therefore, to

[13] A derivative is a financial instrument whose value changes in response to the change in a specified interest rate, security price, commodity price, index of prices or rates, or other variable. The value of a foreign currency derivative changes in response to changes in foreign exchange rates.

provide users of IASs with some guidance in this area, an interim statement, IAS 39, *Financial Statements: Recognition and Measurement,* was issued in 1999. The IASB continues to work on an integrated standard on financial instruments. IAS 39 provides the following general principles with respect to the accounting for derivatives:

1. All derivatives should be reported on the balance sheet at fair value (off-balance-sheet treatment is not acceptable).
2. "Hedge accounting" is acceptable for those derivatives used for hedging purposes provided the hedging relationship is clearly defined, measurable, and actually effective.

Hedge accounting is described in more detail later in this chapter.

Although derivatives are widely used throughout the world to hedge foreign exchange risk, there are very few national accounting standards that provide specific guidance on the accounting for derivatives in general and foreign currency derivatives in particular. The major exception is U.S. GAAP. SFAS 133, *Accounting for Derivative Instruments and Hedging Activities,* which went into effect in 2001, governs the accounting for all derivatives, including those used to hedge foreign exchange risk. In response to concerns expressed by many companies, SFAS 138, *Accounting for Certain Derivative Instruments and Certain Hedging Activities,* amends SFAS 133 with respect to the accounting for hedges of recognized foreign currency denominated assets and liabilities.

SFAS 133 (as amended by SFAS 138) provides guidance for hedges of the following sources of foreign exchange risk:

1. Recognized foreign-currency-denominated assets and liabilities.
2. Unrecognized foreign currency firm commitments.
3. Forecast foreign-currency-denominated transactions.
4. Net investments in foreign operations.

Different accounting applies to each of these different types of foreign currency hedge. Because U.S. GAAP provides the most comprehensive rules with respect to the accounting for hedges of foreign exchange risk and application of these rules is consistent with IAS 39, we focus on U.S. rules in this area.[14] This chapter demonstrates the accounting for the first three types of hedge. Hedges of net investments in foreign operations are covered in Chapter 7.

Fundamental Requirement of Derivatives Accounting

Consistent with IAS 39, the fundamental requirement of SFAS 133 (and SFAS 138) is that all derivatives must be carried on the balance sheet at their fair value. Derivatives are reported on the balance sheet as assets when they have a positive fair value and as liabilities when they have a negative fair value. The first issue in accounting for derivatives is the determination of fair value.

The fair value of derivatives can change over time, causing adjustments to be made to the carrying values of the assets and liabilities. The second issue in accounting for derivatives is the treatment of the gains and losses that arise from these adjustments.

---

[14] The basic concepts and procedures applied in accounting for foreign currency hedges are essentially similar under both IAS 39 and SFAS 133.

Determining the Fair Value of Derivatives

The *fair value of a foreign currency forward contract* is determined by reference to changes in the forward rate over the life of the contract, discounted to the present value. Three pieces of information are needed to determine the fair value of a forward contract at any time:

1. The forward rate when the forward contract was entered into.
2. The current forward rate for a contract that matures on the same date as the forward contract entered into.
3. A discount rate—typically, the company's incremental borrowing rate.

Assume that Interco enters into a forward contract on November 1 to sell 1 million South African rand on May 1 at a forward rate of $0.15 per rand, or a total of $150,000. There is no cost to Interco to enter into the forward contract, and the forward contract has no value on November 1. On December 31, when Interco closes its books to prepare financial statements, the forward rate to sell South African rand on May 1 has changed to $0.147. On that date a forward contract for the delivery of 1 million South African rand could be negotiated that would result in a cash inflow on May 1 of only $147,000. This represents a favorable change in the value of Interco's forward contract of $3,000 ($150,000 − $147,000). The fair value of the forward contract on December 31 is $3,000, discounted to its present value. Assuming that the company's incremental borrowing rate is 12 percent per annum, the fair value of the forward contract must be discounted at the rate of 1 percent per month for four months (from the current date of December 31 to the settlement date of May 1). The fair value of the forward contract at December 31 is $2,883 ($3,000 × 0.96098).[15]

The manner in which the *fair value of a foreign currency option* is determined depends on whether the option is traded on an exchange or has been acquired in the over-the-counter market. The fair value of an exchange-traded foreign currency option is its current market price quoted on the exchange. For over-the-counter options, fair value can be determined by obtaining a price quote from an option dealer (such as a bank). If dealer price quotes are unavailable, the company can estimate the value of an option using the modified Black-Scholes option pricing model (briefly mentioned earlier in this chapter). Regardless of who does the calculation, principles similar to those in the Black-Scholes pricing model will be used in determining the fair value of the option.

Accounting for Changes in the Fair Value of Derivatives

Under U.S. GAAP, changes in the fair value of derivatives must be included in comprehensive income. The Financial Accounting Standards Board (FASB) introduced the reporting of comprehensive income in 1997.[16] *Comprehensive income* is defined as all changes in equity from nonowner sources and consists of two components: net income and other comprehensive income. *Other comprehensive income* consists of income items that previous FASB statements required to be deferred in stockholders' equity such as gains and losses on available-for-sale marketable securities. Other comprehensive income is accumulated and reported as a separate line in the stockholders' equity section of the balance sheet. The account title

---

[15] The present value factor for four months at 1 percent per month is calculated as $1/1.01^4$, or 0.96098.

[16] FASB Statement 130, *Reporting Comprehensive Income*, issued in June 1997.

Accumulated Other Comprehensive Income is used in this chapter to describe this stockholders' equity line item.

In accordance with SFAS 133 (as amended by SFAS 138), gains and losses arising from changes in the fair value of derivatives are recognized initially either (1) on the income statement as a part of net income or (2) on the balance sheet as a component of other comprehensive income. Recognition treatment partly depends on whether the derivative is used for hedging purposes or for speculation.[17] For speculative derivatives, the change in the fair value of the derivative (the gain or loss) is recognized immediately in net income. The accounting for changes in the fair value of derivatives used for hedging depends on the nature of the foreign exchange risk being hedged, and whether the derivative qualifies for hedge accounting.

HEDGE ACCOUNTING

Companies enter into hedging relationships to minimize the adverse effect that changes in exchange rates have on cash flows and net income. As such, companies would like to account for hedges in such a way that the gain or loss from the hedge is recognized in net income in the same period as the loss or gain on the risk being hedged. This approach is known as *hedge accounting.* SFAS 133 and SFAS 138 allow hedge accounting for foreign currency derivatives only if three conditions are satisfied:

1. The derivative is used to hedge either a fair value exposure or cash flow exposure to foreign exchange risk.
2. The derivative is highly effective in offsetting changes in the fair value or cash flows related to the hedged item.
3. The derivative is properly documented as a hedge.

Each of these conditions is discussed in turn.

Nature of the Hedged Risk

A *fair value exposure* exists if changes in exchange rates can affect the fair value of an asset or liability reported on the balance sheet. To qualify for hedge accounting the fair value risk must have the potential to affect net income if it is not hedged. For example, there is a fair value risk associated with a foreign currency account receivable. If the foreign currency depreciates, the receivable must be written down with an offsetting loss recognized in net income. The FASB has determined that a fair value exposure also exists for foreign currency firm commitments.

A *cash flow exposure* exists if changes in exchange rates can affect the amount of cash flow to be realized from a transaction with changes in cash flow reflected in net income. A cash flow exposure exists for (1) recognized foreign currency assets and liabilities, (2) foreign currency firm commitments, and (3) forecast foreign currency transactions.

---

[17] Companies can acquire derivative financial instruments as investments for speculative purposes. For example, assume the three-month forward rate for Swiss francs is $0.60, and a speculator believes the Swiss franc spot rate in three months will be $0.57. In that case, the speculator would enter into a three-month forward contract to sell Swiss francs. At the future date, the speculator purchases francs at the spot rate of $0.57 and sells them at the contracted forward rate of $0.60, reaping a gain of $0.03 per franc. Of course, such an investment might just as easily generate a loss if the spot rate does not move in the expected direction.

Derivatives for which companies wish to use hedge accounting must be designated as either a *fair value hedge* or a *cash flow hedge.* For hedges of recognized foreign currency assets and liabilities and hedges of foreign currency firm commitments, companies must choose between the two types of designation. Hedges of forecasted foreign currency transactions can qualify only as cash flow hedges. Accounting procedures differ for the two types of hedge. In general, gains and losses on fair value hedges are recognized immediately in net income, whereas gains and losses on cash flow hedges are included in other comprehensive income.[18]

Hedge Effectiveness

For hedge accounting to be used initially, the hedge must be expected to be highly effective in generating gains and losses that offset losses and gains on the item being hedged. The hedge actually must be effective in generating offsetting gains and losses for hedge accounting to continue to be applied.

At inception, a foreign currency derivative can be considered an effective hedge if the critical terms of the hedging instrument match those of the hedged item. Critical terms include the currency type, currency amount, and settlement date. For example, a forward contract to purchase 1 million Japanese yen in 30 days would be an effective hedge of a liability of 1 million Japanese yen that is payable in 30 days. Assessing hedge effectiveness on an ongoing basis can be accomplished using a cumulative dollar offset method.

Hedge Documentation

For hedge accounting to be applied, SFAS 133 requires formal documentation of the hedging relationship at the inception of the hedge, that is, on the date a foreign currency forward contract is entered into or a foreign currency option is acquired. The hedging company must prepare a document that identifies the hedged item, the hedging instrument, the nature of the risk being hedged, how the hedging instrument's effectiveness will be assessed, and the risk management objective and strategy for undertaking the hedge.

HEDGING COMBINATIONS

The specific entries required to account for a foreign currency hedging relationship are determined by a combination of the following factors:

1. The type of item being hedged:
   a. Foreign-currency-denominated asset/liability,
   b. Foreign currency firm commitment, or
   c. Forecast foreign currency transaction.
2. The nature of the item being hedged:
   a. Existing (or future) asset, or
   b. Existing (or future) liability.

---

[18] Many companies choose not to designate derivatives used to hedge recognized foreign currency assets and liabilities as hedges per se. In that case, the derivative is accounted for in exactly the same manner as if it had been designated as a fair value hedge; gains and losses are recognized immediately. As a result, designating a hedge of a recognized foreign currency asset/liability as a fair value hedge is of no importance.

3. The type of hedging instrument being used:
   a. Forward contract, or
   b. Option.
4. The nature of the hedged risk:
   a. Fair value exposure, or
   b. Cash flow exposure.

To measure the fair value of a firm commitment, a choice must be made between using

1. Changes in the spot rate, or
2. Changes in the forward rate.

We do not have enough space in this chapter to demonstrate the accounting for over 20 different combinations of hedging relationships. However, it is important to see the differences in accounting for (1) foreign-currency-denominated assets/ liabilities, (2) firm commitments, and (3) forecast transactions. We show this by focusing on the accounting that would be done by an exporter who has an existing or future foreign currency asset. We also demonstrate the use of both forward contracts and options for different types of items being hedged, and we selectively demonstrate the accounting for fair value and cash flow hedges. The appendix to this chapter demonstrates the accounting for hedges entered into by an importer who has existing and future foreign currency liabilities.

HEDGES OF FOREIGN-CURRENCY-DENOMINATED ASSETS AND LIABILITIES

Hedges of foreign-currency-denominated assets and liabilities, such as accounts receivable and accounts payable, can qualify as either *cash flow hedges* or *fair value hedges.* To qualify as a cash flow hedge, the hedging instrument must completely offset the variability in the cash flows associated with the foreign currency receivable or payable. If the hedging instrument does not qualify as a cash flow hedge, or if the company elects not to designate the hedging instrument as a cash flow hedge, the hedge is designated as a fair value hedge. The following lists summarize the basic accounting for the two types of hedges.

Cash Flow Hedge
At each balance sheet date:

1. The hedged asset or liability is adjusted to fair value according to changes in the spot exchange rate, and a foreign exchange gain or loss is recognized in net income.
2. The derivative hedging instrument is adjusted to fair value (resulting in an asset or liability reported on the balance sheet), with the counterpart recognized as a change in accumulated other comprehensive income (AOCI).
3. An amount equal to the foreign exchange gain or loss on the hedged asset or liability is then transferred from AOCI to net income; the net effect is to offset any gain or loss on the hedged asset or liability.
4. An additional amount is removed from AOCI and recognized in net income to reflect (*a*) the current period's amortization of the original discount or premium on the forward contract (if a forward contract is the hedging instrument) or

(*b*) the change in the *time value* of the option (if an option is the hedging instrument).

Fair Value Hedge

At each balance sheet date:

1. The hedged asset or liability is adjusted to fair value according to changes in the spot exchange rate, and a foreign exchange gain or loss is recognized in net income.
2. The derivative hedging instrument is adjusted to fair value (resulting in an asset or liability reported on the balance sheet), with the counterpart recognized as a gain or loss in net income.

FORWARD CONTRACT USED TO HEDGE A RECOGNIZED FOREIGN-CURRENCY-DENOMINATED ASSET

We now return to the Eximco example in which the company has a foreign currency account receivable to demonstrate the accounting for a recognized foreign-currency-denominated asset. In the preceding example, Eximco has an asset exposure in euros when it sells goods to the Spanish customer and allows the customer three months to pay for its purchase. To hedge its exposure to a decline in the U.S. dollar value of the euro, Eximco decides to enter into a forward contract.

Assume that on December 1, Year 1, the three-month forward rate for euros is $0.985 and Eximco signs a contract with First National Bank to deliver €1,000,000 in three months in exchange for $985,000. No cash changes hands on December 1. Given that the spot rate on December 1 is $1.00, the euro is selling at a discount in the three-month forward market (the forward rate is less than the spot rate). Because the euro is selling at a discount of $0.015 per euro, Eximco receives $15,000 less than if payment had been received at the date the goods are delivered ($985,000 vs. $1,000,000). This $15,000 reduction in cash flow can be seen as an expense; it is the cost of extending foreign currency credit to the foreign customer.[19] Conceptually, this expense is similar to the transaction loss that arises on the export sale. It exists only because the transaction is denominated in a foreign currency. The major difference is that Eximco knows the exact amount of the discount expense at the date of sale, whereas, if the receivable is left unhedged, Eximco does not know the size of the transaction loss until three months pass. In fact, it is possible that the unhedged receivable could result in a transaction gain rather than a transaction loss.

Given that the future spot rate turns out to be only $0.98, selling euros at a forward rate of $0.985 is obviously better than leaving the euro receivable unhedged—Eximco will receive $5,000 more as a result of the hedge. This can be viewed as a gain resulting from the use of the forward contract. Unlike the discount expense, the exact size of this gain is not known until three months pass. (In fact, it is possible that use of the forward contract could result in an additional loss. This would occur if the spot rate on March 1, Year 2 is higher than the forward rate of $0.985.)

---

[19] This should not be confused with the cost associated with normal credit risk; that is, the risk that the customer will not pay for its purchase. That is a separate issue unrelated to the currency in which the transaction is denominated.

EXHIBIT 6.2 Hedge of a Foreign Currency Account Receivable with a Forward Contract

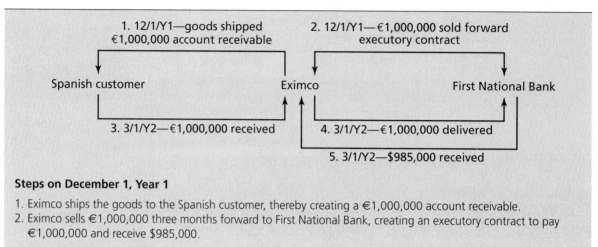

Steps on December 1, Year 1

1. Eximco ships the goods to the Spanish customer, thereby creating a €1,000,000 account receivable.
2. Eximco sells €1,000,000 three months forward to First National Bank, creating an executory contract to pay €1,000,000 and receive $985,000.

Steps on March 1, Year 2

3. The Spanish customer sends €1,000,000 to Eximco to settle the account receivable; Eximco now has €1,000,000 in foreign currency.
4. Eximco delivers €1,000,000 to First National Bank.
5. First National Bank pays Eximco $985,000.

Eximco must account for its foreign currency transaction and the related forward contract simultaneously but separately. The process can be better understood by referring to the steps involving the three parties—Eximco, the Spanish customer, and First National Bank—shown in Exhibit 6.2.

Because the settlement date, currency type, and currency amount of the forward contract match the corresponding terms of the account receivable, the hedge is expected to be highly effective. If Eximco properly designates the forward contract as a hedge of its euro account receivable position, hedge accounting may be applied. Because it completely offsets the variability in the cash flows related to the accounting receivable, the forward contract may be designated as a cash flow hedge. Alternatively, Eximco may elect to account for this forward contract as a fair value hedge.

In either case, Eximco determines the fair value of the forward contract by referring to the change in the forward rate for a contract maturing on March 1, Year 2. The relevant exchange rates, U.S.-dollar value of the euro receivable, and fair value of the forward contract are determined as follows:

		Account Receivable (€)			Forward Contract	
Date	Spot Rate	U.S.-Dollar Value	Change in U.S.-Dollar Value	Forward Rate to 3/1/Y2	Fair Value	Change in Fair Value
12/1/Y1	$1.00	$1,000,000	—	$0.985	$0	—
12/31/Y1	$1.05	$1,050,000	+$50,000	$0.996	$(10,783)*	−$10,783
3/1/Y2	$0.98	$980,000	−$70,000	$0.980	$5,000†	+$15,783

*$985,000 − $996,000 = $(11,000) × 0.9803 = $(10,783), where 0.9803 is the present value factor for two months at an annual interest rate of 12% (1% per month) calculated as $1/1.01^2$.

†$985,000 − $980,000 = $5,000.

Eximco pays nothing to enter into the forward contract at December 1, Year 1, and the forward contract has a fair value of zero on that date. At December 31, Year 1, the forward rate for a contract to deliver euros on March 1, Year 2 is $0.996. A forward contract could be entered into on December 31, Year 1, to sell €1,000,000 for $996,000 on March 1, Year 2. Because Eximco is committed to sell €1,000,000 for $985,000, the nominal value of the forward contract is negative $11,000. The fair value of the forward contract is the present value of this amount. Assuming that Eximco has an incremental borrowing rate of 12 percent per year (1 percent per month), and discounting for two months (from 12/31/Y1 to 3/1/Y2), the fair value of the forward contract at December 31, Year 1, is negative $10,783 (a liability). On March 1, Year 2, the forward rate to sell euros on that date is the spot rate—$0.98. At that rate, €1,000,000 could be sold for $980,000. Because Eximco has a contract to sell euros for $985,000, the fair value of the forward contract on March 1, Year 2, is $5,000. This represents an increase in fair value from December 31, Year 1, of $15,783. The original discount on the forward contract is determined by the difference in the euro spot rate and three-month forward rate on December 1, Year 1: ($0.985 − $1.00) × €1,000,000 = $15,000.

Forward Contract Designated as Cash Flow Hedge

Assume that Eximco designates the forward contract as a *cash flow hedge* of a foreign-currency-denominated asset. In this case, the original forward discount or premium is allocated to net income over the life of the forward contract using an effective interest method. The company would prepare the following journal entries to account for the foreign currency transaction and the related forward contract:

Year 1 Journal Entries—Forward Contract Designated as a Cash Flow Hedge

12/1/Y1	Accounts Receivable (€)	$1,000,000	
	Sales		$1,000,000
	To record the sale and €1,000,000 account receivable at the spot rate of $1.00 (Step 1 in Exhibit 6.2).		

There is no formal entry for the forward contract as it is an executory contract (no cash changes hands) and has a fair value of zero (Step 2 in Exhibit 6.2).

A memorandum would be prepared designating the forward contract as a hedge of the risk of changes in the cash flow to be received on the foreign currency account receivable resulting from changes in the U.S. dollar–euro exchange rate.

12/31/Y1	Accounts Receivable (€)	$50,000	
	Foreign Exchange Gain		$50,000
	To adjust the value of the euro receivable to the new spot rate of $1.05 and record a foreign exchange gain resulting from the appreciation of the euro since December 1.		
	Loss on Forward Contract	$50,000	
	Accumulated Other Comprehensive Income (AOCI) ...		$50,000
	To record a loss on forward contract to offset the foreign exchange gain on account receivable with a corresponding debit to AOCI.		

Accumulated Other Comprehensive Income (AOCI)	$10,783	
Forward Contract[20]		$10,783
To record the forward contract as a liability at its fair value of $10,783 with a corresponding debit to AOCI.		
Discount Expense	$4,975	
Accumulated Other Comprehensive Income (AOCI) ...		$4,975
To allocate the forward contract discount to net income over the life of the contract using the effective interest method with a corresponding credit to AOCI.		

The implicit interest rate associated with the forward contract is calculated by considering the fact that the forward contract will generate cash flow of $985,000 from a foreign currency asset with an initial value of $1,000,000. Because the discount of $15,000 accrues over a three-month period, the effective interest rate is calculated as $1 - \sqrt[3]{\$985,000/\$1,000,000} = 0.005051$. The amount of discount to be allocated to net income for the month of December Year 1 is $985,000 \times 0.5051\% = \$4,975$.

The impact on Year 1 net income is as follows:

Sales		$1,000,000
Foreign Exchange Gain	$50,000	
Loss on Forward Contract	(50,000)	
Net gain (loss)		0
Discount Expense		(4,975)
Impact on net income		$ 995,025

The effect on the December 31, Year 1, balance sheet is as follows:

Assets		Liabilities and Stockholders' Equity	
Accounts receivable (€)	$1,050,000	Forward contract	$ 10,783
		Retained earnings	995,025
		AOCI	44,192
			$1,050,000

Year 2 Journal Entries—Forward Contract Designated as Cash Flow Hedge

3/1/Y2	Foreign Exchange Loss	$70,000	
	Accounts Receivable (€)		$70,000
	To adjust the value of the euro receivable to the new spot rate of $0.98 and record a foreign exchange loss resulting from the depreciation of the euro since December 31.		

[20] "Forward Contract" is a generic account title. In practice, the balance sheet line item in which forward contract assets and liabilities are recognized will differ across companies. ChevronTexaco Corporation, for example, indicates that the fair values of forward contracts "are reported on the Consolidated Balance Sheet as "Accounts and notes receivable" or "Accounts payable," with gains and losses reported in "Other income" (2004 Form 10-K, Note 8: Financial and Derivative Instruments).

Accumulated Other Comprehensive Income (AOCI)	$70,000	
Gain on Forward Contract		$70,000
To record a gain on forward contract to offset the foreign exchange loss on account receivable with a corresponding debit to AOCI.		
Forward Contract	$15,783	
Accumulated Other Comprehensive Income (AOCI)		$15,783
To adjust the carrying value of the forward contract to its current fair value of $5,000 with a corresponding credit to AOCI.		
Discount Expense	$10,025	
Accumulated Other Comprehensive Income (AOCI)		$10,025
To allocate the remaining forward contract discount to net income ($15,000 − $4,975 = $10,025) with a corresponding credit to AOCI.		

As a result of these entries, the balance in AOCI is zero: $44,192 − $70,000 + $15,783 + $10,025 = $0.

Foreign Currency (€)	$980,000	
Accounts Receivable (€)		$980,000
To record receipt of €1,000,000 from the Spanish customer as an asset (Foreign Currency) at the spot rate of $0.98 (Step 3 in Exhibit 6.2).		
Cash	$985,000	
Foreign Currency (€)		$980,000
Forward Contract		5,000
To record settlement of the forward contract, that is, record receipt of $985,000 in exchange for delivery of €1,000,000, and remove the forward contract from the accounts (Steps 4 and 5 in Exhibit 6.2).		

The impact on Year 2 net income is:

Foreign Exchange Loss	$(70,000)	
Gain on Forward Contract	70,000	
Net gain (loss)		0
Discount Expense		(10,025)
Impact on net income		$(10,025)

The net effect on the balance sheet over the two years is an increase in cash of $985,000 with a corresponding increase in retained earnings of $985,000 ($995,025 − $10,025). The cumulative Discount Expense of $15,000 reflects the cost of extending credit to the Spanish customer.

The net benefit from having entered into the forward contract is $5,000. Eximco has a cash inflow of $985,000 rather than only the $980,000 that would have been received without a forward contract. This "gain" is reflected in net income as the difference between the net Gain on Forward Contract and the cumulative Discount Expense ($20,000 − $15,000 = $5,000) recognized over the two periods.

Effective Interest versus Straight-Line Methods

Use of the effective interest method results in allocation of the forward contract discount of $4,975 at the end of the first month and $10,025 at the end of the next two months. Straight-line allocation on a monthly basis of the $15,000 discount would result in a reasonable approximation of these amounts:

12/31/Y1	$15,000 \times \dfrac{1}{3} = \$5,000$
3/1/Y2	$15,000 \times \dfrac{2}{3} = \$10,000$

Determining the effective interest rate is complex and no conceptual insights are gained by its use. For the remainder of this chapter, we use straight-line allocation of forward contract discounts and premiums, as is allowed by the FASB's Derivatives Implementation Group. The important thing to keep in mind in this example is that, with a cash flow hedge, an expense equal to the original forward contract discount is recognized in net income over the life of the contract.

What if the forward rate on December 1, Year 1, had been $1.06 (i.e., the euro was selling at a premium in the forward market)? In that case, Eximco would receive $6,000 more through the forward sale of euros ($1,006,000) than if the euros had been received and converted into dollars at the date of sale ($1,000,000). The forward contract premium would be allocated as an increase in net income at the rate of $2,000 per month; $2,000 at 12/31/Y1 and $4,000 at 3/1/Y2.

Forward Contract Designated as Fair Value Hedge

Assume that Eximco decides not to designate the forward contract as a cash flow hedge, but instead elects to treat it as a fair value hedge. In that case, the gain or loss on the forward contract is taken directly to net income and there is no separate amortization of the original discount on the forward contract.

Year 1 Journal Entries—Forward Contract Designated as a Fair Value Hedge

12/1/Y1	Accounts Receivable (€)	$1,000,000	
	Sales		$1,000,000
	To record the sale and €1,000,000 account receivable at the spot rate of $1.00 (Step 1 in Exhibit 6.2).		

There is no formal entry for the forward contract (Step 2 in Exhibit 6.2). A memorandum would be prepared designating the forward contract as a hedge of the risk of changes in the fair value of the foreign currency account receivable resulting from changes in the U.S. dollar–euro exchange rate.

12/31/Y1	Accounts Receivable (€)	$50,000	
	Foreign Exchange Gain		$50,000
	To adjust the value of the euro receivable to the new spot rate of $1.05 and record a foreign exchange gain resulting from the appreciation of the euro since December 1.		
	Loss on Forward Contract	$10,783	
	Forward Contract		$10,783
	To record the forward contract as a liability at its fair value of $10,783 and record a forward contract loss for the change in the fair value of the forward contract since December 1.		

The impact on Year 1 net income is:

Sales		$1,000,000
Foreign Exchange Gain	$50,000	
Loss on Forward Contract	(10,783)	
Net gain (loss)		39,217
Impact on net income		$1,039,217

The effect on the December 31, Year 1, balance sheet is:

Assets		Liabilities and Stockholders' Equity	
Accounts receivable (€)	$1,050,000	Forward contract	$ 10,783
		Retained earnings	1,039,217
			$1,050,000

Year 2 Journal Entries—Forward Contract Designated as a Fair Value Hedge

3/1/Y2	Foreign Exchange Loss	$70,000	
	Accounts Receivable (€)		$70,000
	To adjust the value of the euro receivable to the new spot rate of $0.98 and record a foreign exchange loss resulting from the depreciation of the euro since December 31.		
	Forward Contract	$15,783	
	Gain on Forward Contract		$15,783
	To adjust the carrying value of the forward contract to its current fair value of $5,000 and record a forward contract gain for the change in the fair value since December 31.		
	Foreign Currency (€)	$980,000	
	Accounts Receivable (€)		$980,000
	To record receipt of €1,000,000 from the Spanish customer as an asset at the spot rate of $0.98 (Step 3 in Exhibit 6.2).		
	Cash	$985,000	
	Foreign Currency (€)		$980,000
	Forward Contract		5,000
	To record settlement of the forward contract, that is, record receipt of $985,000 in exchange for delivery of €1,000,000 and remove the forward contract from the accounts (Steps 4 and 5 in Exhibit 6.2).		

The impact on Year 2 net income is as follows:

Foreign Exchange Loss	$(70,000)
Gain on Forward Contract	15,783
Impact on net income	$(54,217)

The net effect on the balance sheet for the two years is an increase in cash of $985,000 with a corresponding increase in retained earnings of $985,000 ($1,039,217 − $54,217).

EXHIBIT 6.3

COCA-COLA COMPANY
Annual Report
2004

Notes to the Consolidated Financial Statements

Excerpt from Note 10: Hedging Transactions and Derivative Financial Instruments

Foreign Currency Management

The purpose of our foreign currency hedging activities is to reduce the risk that our eventual U.S. dollar net cash inflows resulting from sales outside the United States will be adversely affected by changes in exchange rates.

We enter into forward exchange contracts and purchase currency options (principally euro and Japanese yen) and collars to hedge certain portions of forecasted cash flows denominated in foreign currencies. The effective portion of the changes in fair value for these contracts, which have been designated as cash flow hedges, are reported in AOCI and reclassified into earnings in the same financial statement line item and in the same period or periods during which the hedged transaction affects earnings. Any ineffective portion (which was not significant in 2004, 2003 or 2002) of the change in fair value of these instruments is immediately recognized in earnings. These contracts had maturities up to one year on December 31, 2004.

Additionally, the Company enters into forward exchange contracts that are not designated as hedging instruments under SFAS No. 133. These instruments are used to offset the earnings impact relating to the variability in exchange rates on certain monetary assets and liabilities denominated in nonfunctional currencies. Changes in the fair value of these instruments are immediately recognized in earnings in the line item other income (loss)—net of our consolidated statements of income to offset the effect of remeasurement of the monetary assets and liabilities.

Author's note: Emphasis added.

Under fair value hedge accounting, the original forward contract discount is not amortized systematically over the life of the contract. Instead, it is recognized in income as the difference between the Foreign Exchange Gain (Loss) on the account receivable and the Gain (Loss) on the Forward Contract, that is, $39,217 in Year 1 and $(54,217) in Year 2. The net impact on net income over the two years is $(15,000), which reflects the cost of extending credit to the Spanish customer. The net Gain on Forward Contract of $5,000 ($10,783 loss in Year 1 and $15,783 gain in Year 2) reflects the net benefit—that is increase in cash inflow—from Eximco's decision to hedge the euro receivable.

The accounting for a fair value hedge of a foreign currency denominated asset or liability is the same as if the forward contract were not designated as a hedging instrument; changes in the fair value of the forward contract are immediately recognized in net income. Exhibit 6.3 provides an excerpt from the Coca-Cola Company annual report describing the accounting for forward contracts used as hedges of foreign-currency-denominated assets and liabilities that demonstrates this point. Coca-Cola uses the term *remeasurement* to refer to the process of adjusting the value of foreign currency "monetary assets and liabilities," that is, receivables and payables.

FOREIGN CURRENCY OPTION USED TO HEDGE A RECOGNIZED FOREIGN-CURRENCY-DENOMINATED ASSET

As an alternative to a forward contract, Eximco could hedge its exposure to foreign exchange risk arising from the euro account receivable by purchasing a foreign currency put option. A put option would give Eximco the right but not the obligation to sell €1,000,000 on March 1, Year 2, at a predetermined strike price. Assume that on December 1, Year 1, Eximco purchases an over-the-counter option from its bank with a strike price of $1.00 when the spot rate is $1.00 and pays a premium of $0.009 per euro.[21] Thus, the purchase price for the option is $9,000 (€1,000,000 × $0.009).

Because the strike price and spot rate are the same, there is no intrinsic value associated with this option. The premium is based solely on time value; that is, it is possible that the euro will depreciate and the spot rate on March 1, Year 2, will be less than $1.00, in which case the option will be in the money. If the spot rate for euros on March 1, Year 2, is less than the strike price of $1.00, Eximco will exercise its option and sell its €1,000,000 at the strike price of $1.00. If the spot rate for euros in three months is greater than the strike price of $1.00, Eximco will not exercise its option and instead will sell euros at the higher spot rate. By purchasing this option, Eximco is guaranteed a minimum cash flow from the export sale of $991,000 ($1,000,000 from exercising the option less the $9,000 cost of the option). There is no limit to the maximum number of U.S. dollars that could be received.

As is true for other derivative financial instruments, SFAS 133 requires foreign currency options to be reported on the balance sheet at fair value. The fair value of a foreign currency option at the balance sheet date is determined by reference to the premium quoted by banks on that date for an option with a similar expiration date. Banks (and other sellers of options) determine the current premium by incorporating relevant variables at the balance sheet date into the modified Black-Scholes option pricing model. Changes in value for the euro account receivable and the foreign currency option are summarized as follows:

Date	Spot Rate	Account Receivable (€) U.S. Dollar Value	Change in U.S. Dollar Value	Option Premium for 3/1/Y2	Foreign Currency Option Fair Value	Change in Fair Value
12/1/Y1	$1.00	$1,000,000	—	$0.009	$9,000	—
12/31/Y1	$1.05	$1,050,000	+$50,000	$0.006	$6,000	−$3,000
3/1/Y2	$0.98	$980,000	−$70,000	$0.020	$20,000	+$14,000

The fair value of the foreign currency option can be decomposed into its intrinsic value and time value components as follows:

Date	Fair Value	Intrinsic Value	Time Value	Change in Time Value
12/1/Y1	$9,000	$0	$9,000	—
12/31/Y1	$6,000	$0	$6,000	−$3,000
3/1/Y2	$20,000	$20,000	$0	−$6,000

Because the option strike price is less than or equal to the spot rate at both December 1 and December 31, the option has no intrinsic value at those dates. The entire fair value is attributable to time value only. On March 1, the date of expiration, there is no time value remaining and the entire amount of fair value is attributable to intrinsic value.

---

[21] The price of the option (the premium) was determined by the seller of the option through the use of a variation of the Black-Scholes option pricing formula.

Option Designated as Cash Flow Hedge

Assume that Eximco designates the foreign currency option as a *cash flow hedge* of a foreign-currency-denominated asset. In this case, the change in the option's time value is recognized immediately in net income. The company prepares the following journal entries to account for the foreign currency transaction and the related foreign currency option:

Year 1 Journal Entries—Option Designated as a Cash Flow Hedge

12/1/Y1	Accounts Receivable (€)	$1,000,000	
	Sales		$1,000,000
	To record the sale and €1,000,000 account receivable at the spot rate of $1.00.		
	Foreign Currency Option	$9,000	
	Cash		$9,000
	To record the purchase of the foreign currency option as an asset at its fair value of $9,000.		
12/31/Y1	Accounts Receivable (€)	$50,000	
	Foreign Exchange Gain		$50,000
	To adjust the value of the euro receivable to the new spot rate of $1.05 and record a foreign exchange gain resulting from the appreciation of the euro since December 1.		
	Loss on Foreign Currency Option	$50,000	
	Accumulated Other Comprehensive Income (AOCI)		$50,000
	To record a loss on foreign currency option to offset the foreign exchange gain on the euro account receivable with a corresponding credit to AOCI.		
	Accumulated Other Comprehensive Income (AOCI)	$3,000	
	Foreign Currency Option		$3,000
	To adjust the fair value of the option from $9,000 to $6,000 with a corresponding debit to AOCI.		
	Option Expense	$3,000	
	Accumulated Other Comprehensive Income (AOCI)		$3,000
	To recognize the change in the time value of the option as a decrease in net income with a corresponding credit to AOCI.		

The impact on Year 1 net income is as follows:

Sales		$1,000,000
Foreign Exchange Gain	$50,000	
Loss on Foreign Currency Option	(50,000)	
Net gain (loss)		0
Option Expense		(3,000)
Impact on net income		$ 997,000

The effect on the December 31, Year 1, balance sheet is:

Assets		Liabilities and Stockholders' Equity	
Cash	$ (9,000)	Retained earnings	$ 997,000
Accounts receivable (€)	1,050,000	AOCI	50,000
Foreign currency option	6,000		$1,047,000
	$1,047,000		

At March 1, Year 2, the option has increased in fair value by $14,000—time value decreases by $6,000 and intrinsic value increases by $20,000. The accounting entries made in Year 2 are as follows:

Year 2 Journal Entries—Option Designated as a Cash Flow Hedge

3/1/Y2	Foreign Exchange Loss	$70,000	
	Accounts Receivable (€)		$70,000
	To adjust the value of the euro receivable to the new spot rate of $0.98 and record a foreign exchange loss resulting from the depreciation of the euro since December 31.		
	Accumulated Other Comprehensive Income (AOCI)	$70,000	
	Gain on Foreign Currency Option		$70,000
	To record a gain on foreign currency option to offset the foreign exchange gain on account receivable with a corresponding debit to AOCI.		
	Foreign Currency Option	$14,000	
	Accumulated Other Comprehensive Income (AOCI). .		$14,000
	To adjust the fair value of the option from $6,000 to $20,000 with a corresponding credit to AOCI.		
	Option Expense	$6,000	
	Accumulated Other Comprehensive Income (AOCI)		$6,000
	To recognize the change in the time value of the option as a decrease in net income with a corresponding credit to AOCI.		
	Foreign Currency (€)	$980,000	
	Accounts Receivable (€)		$980,000
	To record receipt of €1,000,000 from the Spanish customer as an asset at the spot rate of $0.98.		
	Cash	$1,000,000	
	Foreign Currency (€)		$980,000
	Foreign Currency Option		20,000
	To record exercise of the option, that is, record receipt of $1,000,000 in exchange for delivery of €1,000,000, and remove the foreign currency option from the accounts.		

The impact on Year 2 net income is as follows:

Foreign Exchange Loss	$(30,000)	
Gain on Foreign Currency Option	30,000	
Net gain (loss)		0
Option Expense.		(6,000)
Impact on net income		$(6,000)

Over the two accounting periods, Eximco would report Sales of $1,000,000 and a cumulative Option Expense of $9,000. The net effect on the balance sheet is an increase in cash of $991,000 ($1,000,000 − $9,000) with a corresponding increase in retained earnings of $991,000 ($997,000 − $6,000).

The net benefit from having acquired the option is $11,000. Eximco has a net cash inflow of $991,000 rather than only $980,000 if the option had not been purchased. This "gain" is reflected in net income as the net Gain on Foreign Currency Option less the cumulative Option Expense ($20,000 − $9,000 = $11,000) recognized over the two accounting periods.

Spot Rate Exceeds Strike Price

If the spot rate at March 1, Year 2, had been greater than the strike price of $1.00, Eximco would allow its option to expire unexercised. Instead it would sell its foreign currency (€) at the spot rate. The fair value of the foreign currency option on March 1, Year 2, would be zero. The journal entries for Year 1 to reflect this scenario would be the same as above. The option would be reported as an asset on the December 31, Year 1, balance sheet at $6,000 and the euro receivable would have a carrying value of $1,050,000. The entries on March 1, Year 2, assuming a spot rate on that date of $1.02 (rather than $0.98), would be as follows:

3/1/Y2	Foreign Exchange Loss	$30,000	
	Accounts Receivable (€)		$30,000
	To adjust the value of the euro receivable to the new spot rate of $1.02 and record a foreign exchange loss resulting from the depreciation of the euro since December 31.		
	Accumulated Other Comprehensive Income (AOCI)	$30,000	
	Gain on Foreign Currency Option		$30,000
	To record a gain on foreign currency option to offset the foreign exchange gain on account receivable with a corresponding debit to AOCI.		
	Loss on Foreign Currency Option	$6,000	
	Foreign Currency Option		$6,000
	To adjust the fair value of the option from $6,000 to $0 and record a loss on foreign currency option for the change in fair value since December 31.		
	Foreign Currency (€)	$1,020,000	
	Accounts Receivable (€)		$1,020,000
	To record receipt of €1,000,000 from the Spanish customer as an asset at the spot rate of $1.02.		
	Cash	$1,020,000	
	Foreign Currency (€)		$1,020,000
	To record the sale of €1,000,000 at the spot rate of $1.020.		

Option Designated as Fair Value Hedge

If Eximco had decided to designate the foreign currency option as a fair value hedge, the gain or loss on the option would have been taken directly to net income and there would have been no separate recognition of the change in the time value of the option. The net gain (loss) recognized in Year 1 and Year 2 would be different from the amounts recognized under the cash flow hedge, but over the two-year period, the same amount of net income would be recognized. The accounting method (fair value hedge or cash flow hedge) has no impact on cash flows or on the net amount of income recognized.

HEDGES OF UNRECOGNIZED FOREIGN CURRENCY FIRM COMMITMENTS

In the examples thus far, Eximco does not enter into a hedge of its export sale until the sale is actually made. Assume now that on December 1, Year 1, Eximco receives and accepts an order from a Spanish customer to deliver goods on March 1, Year 2, at a price of €1,000,000. Assume further that under the terms of the sales agreement Eximco will ship the goods to the Spanish customer on March 1, Year 2, and will receive immediate payment on delivery. In other words, Eximco will not allow the Spanish customer time to pay. Although Eximco will not make the sale until March 1, Year 2, it has a firm commitment to make the sale and receive €1,000,000 in three months. This creates a euro asset exposure to foreign exchange risk as of December 1, Year 1. On that date, Eximco wants to hedge against an adverse change in the value of the euro over the next three months. This is known as a hedge of a foreign currency firm commitment. Although SFAS 133 indicated that only fair value hedge accounting was appropriate for hedges of foreign currency firm commitments, the FASB's Derivatives Implementation Group subsequently concluded that cash flow hedge accounting also could be used. However, because the results of fair value hedge accounting are intuitively more appealing, we do not cover cash flow hedge accounting for firm commitments.

Under fair value hedge accounting, (1) the gain or loss on the hedging instrument is recognized currently in net income and (2) the gain or loss (i.e., the change in fair value) on the firm commitment attributable to the hedged risk is also recognized currently in net income. This accounting treatment requires (1) measurement of the fair value of the firm commitment, (2) recognizing the change in fair value in net income, and (3) reporting the firm commitment on the balance sheet as an asset or liability. This raises the conceptual question of how the fair value of the firm commitment should be measured. Two possibilities are (1) through reference to changes in the spot exchange rate or (2) through reference to changes in the forward rate. These two approaches are demonstrated in the examples that follow.

Forward Contract Used as Fair Value Hedge of a Firm Commitment

To hedge its firm commitment exposure to a decline in the U.S.-dollar value of the euro, Eximco decides to enter into a forward contract on December 1, Year 1. Assume that on December 1, Year 1, the three-month forward rate for euros is $0.985 and Eximco signs a contract with New Manhattan Bank to deliver €1,000,000 in three months in exchange for $985,000. No cash changes hands on December 1, Year 1. Eximco elects to measure the fair value of the firm commitment through changes in the forward rate. As the fair value of the forward contract is also measured using changes in the forward rate, the gains and losses on the firm commitment and forward contract exactly offset. The fair value of the forward contract and firm commitment are determined as follows:

Date	Forward Rate to 3/1/Y2	Forward Contract		Firm Commitment	
		Fair Value	Change in Fair Value	Fair Value	Change in Fair Value
12/1/Y1	$0.985	$0	—	$0	—
12/31/Y1	$0.996	$(10,783)*	−$10,783	$10,783*	+$10,783
3/1/Y2	$0.98 (spot)	$5,000†	+$15,783	$(5,000)†	−$15,783

*($985,000 − $996,000) = $(11,000) × 0.9803 = $(10,783); where 0.9803 is the present value factor for two months at an annual interest rate of 12% (1% per month) calculated as $1/1.01^2$.
†($985,000 − $980,000) = $5,000.

Eximco pays nothing to enter into the forward contract at December 1, Year 1. Both the forward contract and the firm commitment have a fair value of zero on that date. At December 31, Year 1, the forward rate for a contract to deliver euros on March 1, Year 2, is $0.996. A forward contract could be entered into on December 31, Year 1, to sell €1,000,000 for $996,000 on March 1, Year 2. Because Eximco is committed to sell €1,000,000 for $985,000, the value of the forward contract is negative $11,000; present value is negative $10,783 (a liability). The fair value of the firm commitment is also measured through reference to changes in the forward rate. As a result, the fair value of the firm commitment is equal in amount but of opposite sign to the fair value of the forward contract. At December 31, Year 1, the firm commitment is an asset of $10,783.

On March 1, Year 2, the forward rate to sell euros on that date is the spot rate—$0.98. At that rate, €1,000,000 could be sold for $980,000. Because Eximco has a contract to sell euros for $985,000, the fair value of the forward contract on March 1, Year 2, is $5,000 (an asset). The firm commitment has a value of negative $5,000 (a liability). The journal entries to account for the forward contract fair value hedge of a foreign currency firm commitment are as follows:

Year 1 Journal Entries—Forward Contract Fair Value Hedge of Firm Commitment

12/1/Y1	There is no entry to record either the sales agreement or the forward contract as both are executory contracts. A memorandum would be prepared designating the forward contract as a hedge of the risk of changes in the fair value of the firm commitment resulting from changes in the U.S. dollar–euro forward exchange rate.		
12/31/Y1	Loss on Forward Contract	$10,783	
	Forward Contract		$10,783
	To record the forward contract as a liability at its fair value of $(10,783) and record a forward contract loss for the change in the fair value of the forward contract since December 1.		
	Firm Commitment	$10,783	
	Gain on Firm Commitment		$10,783
	To record the firm commitment as an asset at its fair value of $10,783 and record a firm commitment gain for the change in the fair value of the firm commitment since December 1.		

Consistent with the objective of hedge accounting, the gain on the firm commitment offsets the loss on the forward contract and the impact on Year 1 net income is zero. The Forward Contract is reported as a liability and the Firm Commitment is reported as an asset on the 12/31/Y1 balance sheet. This achieves the FASB's objective of making sure that derivatives are recognized on the balance sheet and at the same time ensures that there is no impact on net income.

Year 2 Journal Entries—Forward Contract Fair Value Hedge of Firm Commitment

3/1/Y2	Forward Contract	$15,783	
	Gain on Forward Contract		$15,783
	To adjust the fair value of the forward contract from $(10,783) to $5,000 and record a forward contract gain for the change in fair value since December 31.		
	Loss on Firm Commitment	$15,783	
	Firm Commitment		$15,783
	To adjust the fair value of the firm commitment from $10,783 to $(5,000) and record a firm commitment loss for the change in fair value since December 31.		
	Foreign Currency (€)	$980,000	
	Sales		$980,000
	To record the sale and the receipt of €1,000,000 as an asset at the spot rate of $0.98.		
	Cash	$985,000	
	Foreign Currency (€)		$980,000
	Forward Contract		5,000
	To record settlement of the forward contract (receipt of $985,000 in exchange for delivery of €1,000,000), and remove the forward contract from the accounts.		
	Firm Commitment	$5,000	
	Adjustment to Net Income		$5,000
	To close the firm commitment as an adjustment to net income.		

Once again, the gain on forward contract and the loss on firm commitment offset. As a result of the last entry, the export sale increases Year 2 net income by $985,000 ($980,000 in Sales plus a $5,000 Adjustment to Net Income). This is exactly equal to the amount of cash received. In practice, companies might use a variety of account titles for the adjustment to net income that results from closing the firm commitment account.

The net Gain on Forward Contract of $5,000 ($10,783 loss in Year 1 plus $15,783 gain in Year 2) measures the net benefit to the company from hedging its firm commitment. Without the forward contract, Eximco would have sold the €1,000,000 received on March 1, Year 2, at the spot rate of $0.98, generating cash flow of $980,000. Through the forward contract, Eximco is able to sell the euros for $985,000, a net gain of $5,000.

Option Used as Fair Value Hedge of Firm Commitment

Now assume that to hedge its exposure to a decline in the U.S.-dollar value of the foreign currency firm commitment, Eximco purchases a put option to sell €1,000,000 on March 1, Year 2, at a strike price of $1.00. The premium for such an option on December 1, Year 1, is $0.009 per euro. With this option, Eximco is guaranteed a minimum cash flow from the export sale of $991,000 ($1,000,000 from option exercise less $9,000 cost of the option).

Eximco elects to measure the fair value of the firm commitment through reference to changes in the U.S. dollar–euro spot rate. In this case, the fair value of the firm commitment must be discounted to its present value. The fair value and changes in fair value for the firm commitment and foreign currency option are summarized as follows:

| | Option | Foreign Currency Option | | | Firm Commitment | |
| | Premium | | Change in | Spot | | Change in |
Date	for 3/1/Y2	Fair Value	Fair Value	Rate	Fair Value	Fair Value
12/1/Y1	$0.009	$9,000	—	$1.00	—	—
12/31/Y1	$0.006	$6,000	−$3,000	$1.05	$49,015*	+$49,015
3/1/Y2	$0.020	$20,000	+$14,000	$0.98	$(20,000)[†]	−$69,015

* $1,050,000 − $1,000,000 = $50,000 × 0.9803 = $49,015, where 0.9803 is the present value factor for two months at an annual interest rate of 12% (1% per month) calculated as $1/1.01^2$.
[†] $980,000 − $1,000,000 = $(20,000)$.

At December 1, Year 1, given the spot rate of $1.00, the firm commitment to receive €1,000,000 in three months would generate a cash flow of $1,000,000. At December 31, Year 1, the cash flow that could be generated from the firm commitment increases by $50,000 to $1,050,000. The fair value of the firm commitment at December 31, Year 1, is the present value of $50,000 discounted at 1 percent per month for two months. The fair value of the firm commitment on March 1, Year 2, is determined through reference to the change in the spot rate from December 1, Year 1, to March 1, Year 2. Because the spot rate declines by $0.02 over that period, the firm commitment to receive €1,000,000 has a fair value of negative $20,000 on March 1, Year 2. The journal entries to account for the foreign currency option and related foreign currency firm commitment are as follows:

Year 1 Journal Entries—Option Fair Value Hedge of Firm Commitment

12/1/Y1	Foreign Currency Option	$9,000	
	Cash		$9,000
	To record the purchase of the foreign currency option as an asset.		

There is no entry to record the sales agreement as it is an executory contract. A memorandum would be prepared designating the option as a hedge of the risk of changes in the fair value of the firm commitment resulting from changes in the spot exchange rate.

12/31/Y1	Firm Commitment	$49,015	
	Gain on Firm Commitment		$49,015
	To record the firm commitment as an asset at its fair value of $49,015 and record a firm commitment gain for the change in the fair value of the firm commitment since December 1.		
	Loss on Foreign Currency Option	$3,000	
	Foreign Currency Option		$3,000
	To adjust the fair value of the option from $9,000 to $6,000 and record the change in the value of the option as a loss.		

The impact on Year 1 net income is as follows:

Gain on firm commitment	$49,015
Loss on foreign currency option	(3,000)
Impact on net income	$46,015

The effect on the December 31, Year 1, balance sheet is as follows:

Assets		Liabilities and Stockholders' Equity	
Cash	$ (9,000)	Retained earnings	$46,015
Foreign currency option.	6,000		
Firm commitment	49,015		
	$46,015		

Year 2 Journal Entries—Option Fair Value Hedge of Firm Commitment

3/1/Y2	Loss on Firm Commitment	$69,105	
	Firm Commitment		$69,105
	To adjust the fair value of the firm commitment from $49,105 to $(20,000) and record a firm commitment loss for the change in fair value since December 31.		
	Foreign Currency Option	$14,000	
	Gain on Foreign Currency Option		$14,000
	To adjust the fair value of the foreign currency option from $6,000 to $20,000 and record a gain on foreign currency option for the change in fair value since December 31.		
	Foreign Currency (€)	$980,000	
	Sales		$980,000
	To record the sale and the receipt of €1,000,000 as an asset at the spot rate of $0.98.		
	Cash	$1,000,000	
	Foreign Currency (€)		$980,000
	Foreign Currency Option		20,000
	To record exercise of the foreign currency option (receipt of $1,000,000 in exchange for delivery of €1,000,000), and remove the foreign currency option from the accounts.		
	Firm Commitment	$20,000	
	Adjustment to Net Income		$20,000
	To close the firm commitment as an adjustment to net income.		

The impact on Year 2 net income is as follows:

Sales	$980,000
Loss on Firm Commitment	(69,015)
Gain on Foreign Currency Option	14,000
Adjustment to Net Income	20,000
Impact on net income	$944,985

The net increase in net income over the two accounting periods is $991,000 ($46,015 in Year 1 plus $944,985 in Year 2), which is exactly equal to the net cash flow realized on the export sale ($1,000,000 from exercising the option less $9,000 to purchase the option). The net gain on option of $11,000 (loss of $3,000 in Year 1 plus gain of $14,000 in Year 2) reflects the net benefit from having entered into the hedge. Without the option, Eximco would have sold the €1,000,000 received on March 1, Year 2, at the spot rate of $0.98 for $980,000.

HEDGE OF FORECASTED FOREIGN-CURRENCY-DENOMINATED TRANSACTION

SFAS 133 also allows the use of cash flow hedge accounting for foreign currency derivatives used to hedge the cash flow risk associated with a forecasted foreign currency transaction. For hedge accounting to apply, the forecasted transaction must be probable (likely to occur), the hedge must be highly effective in offsetting fluctuations in the cash flow associated with the foreign currency risk and the hedging relationship must be properly documented.

The accounting for a hedge of a forecasted transaction differs from the accounting for a hedge of a foreign currency firm commitment in two ways:

1. Unlike the accounting for a firm commitment, there is no recognition of the forecasted transaction or gains and losses on the forecasted transaction.
2. The hedging instrument (forward contract or option) is reported at fair value, but because there is no gain or loss on the forecasted transaction to offset against, changes in the fair value of the hedging instrument are not reported as gains and losses in net income. Instead they are reported in other comprehensive income. On the projected date of the forecasted transaction, the cumulative change in the fair value of the hedging instrument is transferred from other comprehensive income (balance sheet) to net income (income statement).

Option Designated as a Cash Flow Hedge of a Forecasted Transaction

To demonstrate the accounting for a hedge of a forecasted foreign currency transaction, assume that Eximco has a long-term relationship with its Spanish customer and can reliably forecast that the customer will require delivery of goods costing €1,000,000 in March of Year 2. Confident that it will receive €1,000,000 on March 1, Year 2, Eximco hedges its forecasted foreign currency transaction by purchasing a €1,000,000 put option on December 1, Year 1. The facts are essentially the same as for the option hedge of a firm commitment, except that Eximco does not receive a sales order from the Spanish customer until late February, Year 2.

The option, which expires on March 1, Year 2, has a strike price of $1.00 and a premium of $0.009 per euro. The fair value of the option at relevant dates is as follows:

| Date | Option Premium for 3/1/Y2 | Foreign Currency Option | | | | |
		Fair Value	Change in Fair Value	Intrinsic Value	Time Value	Change in Time Value
12/1/Y1	$0.009	$9,000	—	$0	$9,000	—
12/31/Y1	$0.006	$6,000	−$3,000	$0	$6,000	−$3,000
3/1/Y2	$0.020	$20,000	−$14,000	$20,000	$0	−$6,000

Year 1 Journal Entries—Option Hedge of a Forecasted Transaction

12/1/Y1	Foreign Currency Option	$9,000	
	Cash		$9,000
	To record the purchase of the foreign currency option as an asset.		

There is no entry to record the forecasted sale. A memorandum would be prepared designating the foreign currency option as a hedge of the risk of changes in the cash flows related to the forecasted sale.

12/31/Y1	Option Expense	$3,000	
	Foreign Currency Option		$3,000
	To adjust the carrying value of the option to its fair value and recognize the change in the time value of the option as an expense.		

The impact on Year 1 net income is as follows:

Option Expense	$(3,000)
Impact on net income	$(3,000)

A Foreign Currency Option of $6,000 is reported as an asset on the December 31, Year 1, balance sheet. Cash decreases by $9,000 and retained earnings decreases by $3,000.

Year 2 Journal Entries—Option Hedge of a Forecasted Transaction

3/1/Y2	Foreign Currency Option	$14,000	
	Option Expense	6,000	
	Accumulated Other Comprehensive Income (AOCI) ..		$20,000
	To adjust the carrying value of the option to its fair value and recognize the change in the time value of the option as an expense, with a corresponding credit to AOCI.		
	Foreign Currency (€)	$980,000	
	Sales		$980,000
	To record the sale and the receipt of €1,000,000 as an asset at the spot rate of $0.98.		
	Cash	$1,000,000	
	Foreign Currency (€)		$980,000
	Foreign Currency Option		20,000
	To record exercise of the foreign currency option (receipt of $1,000,000 in exchange for delivery of €1,000,000), and remove the foreign currency option from the accounts.		
	Accumulated Other Comprehensive Income (AOCI)	$20,000	
	Adjustment to Net Income		$20,000
	To close AOCI as an adjustment to net income.		

The impact on Year 2 net income is as follows:

Sales	$980,000
Option Expense	(6,000)
Adjustment to Net Income	20,000
Impact on net income	$994,000

Over the two-year period, net income increases by $991,000 ($994,000 in Year 2 minus $3,000 in Year 1), equal to the net cash inflow realized from the export sale.

USE OF HEDGING INSTRUMENTS

There probably are as many different corporate strategies regarding hedging foreign exchange risk as there are companies exposed to that risk. Some companies simply require hedges of all foreign currency transactions. Others require the use of a forward contract hedge when the forward rate results in a greater cash inflow or smaller cash outflow than with the spot rate. Still other companies have proportional hedging policies that require hedging on some predetermined percentage (e.g., 50 percent, 60 percent, or 70 percent) of transaction exposure.

It is quite common for companies to use foreign currency derivatives to hedge the exposure to foreign exchange risk arising from forecasted foreign currency transactions. Exhibit 6.4 presents information provided by two U.S.-based

EXHIBIT 6.4
Hedges of
Forecasted Foreign
Currency
Transactions

INTERNATIONAL BUSINESS MACHINES CORPORATION
Annual Report
2004

Excerpt from Note L. Derivatives and Hedging Transactions

Anticipated royalties and cost transactions

The company's operations generate significant nonfunctional currency, third-party vendor payments and intercompany payments for royalties, and goods and services among the company's non-U.S. subsidiaries and with the parent company. In anticipation of these foreign currency cash flows and in view of the volatility of the currency markets, the company selectively employs foreign exchange forward and option contracts to manage its currency risk. In general, these hedges have maturities of one year or less, but from time to time extend beyond one year commensurate with the underlying hedged anticipated cash flow. At December 31, 2004, the weighted-average remaining maturity of these derivative instruments was approximately one year.

THE BOEING COMPANY
Form 10-K
2004

Excerpt from Note 19—Derivative Financial Instruments

Cash flow hedges

Our cash flow hedges include certain interest rate swaps, cross currency swaps, foreign currency forward contracts, and commodity purchase contracts. Interest rate swap contracts under which we agree to pay fixed rates of interest are designated as cash flow hedges of variable-rate debt obligations. *We use foreign currency forward contracts to manage currency risk associated with certain forecasted transactions, specifically sales and purchase commitments made in foreign currencies. Our foreign currency forward contracts hedge forecasted transactions principally occurring up to five years in the future.* We use commodity derivatives, such as fixed-price purchase commitments, to hedge against potentially unfavorable price changes for items used in production. These include commitments to purchase electricity at fixed prices through December 2005. The changes in fair value of the percentage of the commodity derivatives that are not designated in a hedging relationship are recorded in earnings immediately. There were no significant changes in fair value reported in earnings for the years ended December 31, 2004, 2003 and 2002.

Author's note: Emphasis added.

EXHIBIT 6.5

ABBOT LABORATORIES
Form 10-K
2004

Notes to Consolidated Financial Statements

Note 4—Financial Instruments and Derivatives

Certain Abbott foreign subsidiaries enter into foreign currency forward exchange contracts to manage exposures to changes in foreign exchange rates for anticipated intercompany purchases by those subsidiaries whose functional currencies are not the U.S. dollar. These contracts, totaling $984 million, $602 million and $857 million at December 31, 2004, 2003 and 2002, respectively, are designated as cash flow hedges of the variability of the cash flows due to changes in foreign exchange rates. Abbott records the contracts at fair value, resulting in charges of $40.0 million and $28.8 million to Accumulated other comprehensive income (loss) in 2004 and 2002, respectively, and a $3.6 million credit to Accumulated other comprehensive income (loss) in 2003. No hedge ineffectiveness was recorded in income in 2004, 2003 or 2002. Accumulated gains and losses as of December 31, 2004 will be included in Cost of products sold at the time the products are sold, generally through the end of 2005.

Abbott enters into foreign currency forward exchange contracts to manage currency exposures for foreign currency denominated third-party trade payables and receivables, and for intercompany loans and trade accounts payable where the receivable or payable is denominated in a currency other than the functional currency of the entity. For intercompany loans, the contracts require Abbott to sell or buy foreign currencies, primarily European currencies and Japanese yen, in exchange for primarily U.S. dollars and other European currencies. For intercompany and trade payables and receivables, the currency exposures are primarily the U.S. dollar, European currencies and Japanese yen. These contracts are recorded at fair value, with the resulting gains or losses reflected in income as Net foreign exchange (gain) loss. At December 31, 2004, 2003 and 2002, Abbott held $3.3 billion, $3.0 billion and $1.9 billion, respectively, of such foreign currency forward exchange contracts.

---

companies with respect to hedging forecasted transactions. International Business Machines Corporation (IBM) uses a combination of options and forward contracts to hedge transactions that primarily are anticipated to take place within one year. In contrast, Boeing Company uses only forward contracts to hedge future transactions that may occur up to five years in the future.

The notes to financial statements of multinational companies also indicate the magnitude of foreign exchange risk and the importance of hedging contracts. Exhibit 6.5 presents information extracted from Abbott Laboratories' 2004 Form 10-K. At December 31, 2004, Abbott had $984 million in foreign currency forward contracts related to anticipated foreign currency transactions and $3.3 billion in forward contracts used to hedge foreign-currency-denominated payables and receivables. To better appreciate the significance of these amounts, consider that Abbott had assets of $28.8 billion, sales of $19.7 billion, and net earnings of $3.2 billion in 2004.

Dell Inc. uses foreign currency options and forward contracts "to hedge its exposure on forecasted transactions and firm commitments in most of the foreign countries in which it operates. The principal currencies hedged during fiscal 2005 were the Euro, British Pound, Japanese Yen, and Canadian Dollar."[22] The Coca-Cola Company reports using a combination of forward contracts, options, and collars in its foreign currency hedging strategy.[23]

The Euro

The introduction of the euro as a common currency throughout much of Europe greatly reduces the need for hedging in that region of the world. For example,

---

[22] Dell Inc., 2004 Form 10-K, p. 29.

[23] A foreign currency collar can be created by simultaneously purchasing a call option and selling a put option to fix a range of prices at which foreign currency can be purchased at a predetermined future date.

a Finnish company purchasing goods from a Spanish supplier no longer has an exposure to foreign exchange risk, because the two countries use a common currency. This also is true for Finnish subsidiaries of U.S. (or other non-euro-zone) parent companies. However, any transactions denominated in euros between the U.S. parent and its Finnish (or other euro-zone) subsidiary continue to be exposed to foreign exchange risk.

One advantage of the euro for U.S. (and other non-euro-zone) companies is that a euro account receivable from sales to a customer in, say, the Netherlands, will act as a *natural hedge* of a euro account payable on purchases from, say, a supplier in Italy. Assuming that similar amounts and time periods are involved, any foreign exchange loss (gain) arising from the euro payable will be offset by a foreign exchange gain (loss) on the euro receivable. There will be no need to hedge the euro account payable with a contractual hedging instrument.

FOREIGN CURRENCY BORROWING

In addition to the receivables and payables that arise from import and export activities, companies often must account for foreign currency borrowings, another type of foreign currency transaction. Companies borrow foreign currency from foreign lenders either to finance foreign operations or perhaps to take advantage of more favorable interest rates. Accounting for a foreign currency borrowing is complicated by the fact that both the principal and interest are denominated in foreign currency and both create an exposure to foreign exchange risk.

To demonstrate the accounting for foreign currency debt, assume that on July 1, Year 1, Mapleleaf International (a company based in Canada) borrowed 1 billion Japanese yen (¥) on a one-year note at a per annum interest rate of 5 percent. Interest is payable and the note comes due on July 1, Year 2. The following exchange rates apply:

Date	Canadian Dollars (C$) per Japanese Yen (¥) Spot Rate
July 1, Year 1	C$0.00921
December 31, Year 1	0.00932
July 1, Year 2	0.00937

On July 1, Year 1, Mapleleaf borrows ¥1,000,000,000 and converts it into C$9,210,000 in the spot market. Over the life of the note, Mapleleaf must record accrued interest expense at year-end and interest payments on the anniversary date of July 1. In addition, the Japanese yen note payable must be revalued at year-end, with foreign exchange gains and losses reported in income. The journal entries to account for this foreign currency borrowing are as follows:

July 1, Year 1	Dr. Cash	9,210,000	
	Cr. Note Payable (¥)		9,210,000
	To record the yen note payable at the spot rate of C$0.00921 and the conversion of ¥1,000,000,000 into Canadian dollars.		

December 31, Year 1	Dr. Interest Expense	233,000	
	Cr. Accrued Interest Payable (¥)		233,000
	To accrue interest for the period July 1– December 31, Year 2: ¥1,000,000,000 × 5% × $\frac{1}{2}$ year = ¥25,000,000 × C$0.00932 = C$233,000.		
	Dr. Foreign Exchange Loss	110,000	
	Cr. Note Payable (¥)		110,000
	To revalue the yen note payable at the spot rate of C$0.00932 and record a foreign exchange loss of C$110,000 (¥1,000,000,000 × [C$0.00932 − C$0.00921]).		
July 1, Year 2	Dr. Interest Expense	234,250	
	Accrued Interest Payable (¥)	233,000	
	Foreign Exchange Loss	1,250	
	Cr. Cash		468,500
	To record the interest payment of ¥50,000,000 acquired at the spot rate of C$0.00937 for C$468,500; interest expense for the period January 1–July 1, Year 2 (¥25,000,000 × C$0.00937); and a foreign exchange loss on the yen accrued interest payable (¥25,000,000 × [C$0.00937 − C$0.00932]).		
	Dr. Foreign Exchange Loss	50,000	
	Cr. Note Payable (¥)		50,000
	To revalue the yen note payable at the spot rate of C$0.00937 and record a foreign exchange loss of C$50,000 (¥1,000,000,000 × [C$0.00937 − C$0.00932]).		
	Dr. Note Payable (¥)	9,370,000	
	Cr. Cash		9,370,000
	To record repayment of the ¥1,000,000,000 note through purchase of yen at the spot rate of C$0.00937.		

Foreign Currency Loan

At times companies might lend foreign currency to related parties, creating the opposite situation as with a foreign currency borrowing. The accounting will involve keeping track of a note receivable and interest receivable, both of which are denominated in foreign currency. Fluctuations in the U.S.-dollar value of the principal and interest will generally give rise to foreign exchange gains and losses, which would be included in income. Under SFAS 52, an exception arises when the foreign currency loan is being made on a long-term basis to a foreign branch, subsidiary, or equity method affiliate. Foreign exchange gains and losses on "intercompany foreign currency transactions that are of a long-term investment nature (that is, settlement is not planned or anticipated in the foreseeable future)" are reported in other comprehensive income until the loan is repaid.[24] Only the foreign exchange gains and losses related to the interest receivable would be recorded currently in net income.

[24] SFAS 52, paragraph 20 (b).

Summary

1. There are a variety of exchange rate mechanisms in use around the world. A majority of national currencies are allowed to fluctuate in value against other currencies over time.

2. Exposure to foreign exchange risk exists when a payment to be made or received is denominated in terms of a foreign currency. Appreciation in a foreign currency will result in a foreign exchange gain on a foreign currency receivable and a foreign exchange loss on a foreign currency payable. Conversely, a decrease in the value of a foreign currency will result in a foreign exchange loss on a foreign currency receivable and a foreign exchange gain on a foreign currency payable.

3. Under both IAS 21 and SFAS 52, foreign exchange gains and losses on foreign currency balances are recorded in income in the period in which an exchange rate change occurs; this is a two-transaction perspective, accrual approach. Foreign currency balances must be revalued to their current domestic currency equivalent using current exchange rates whenever financial statements are prepared. This approach violates the conservatism principle when unrealized foreign exchange gains are recognized as income.

4. Exposure to foreign exchange risk can be eliminated through hedging. Hedging involves establishing a price today at which a foreign currency to be received in the future can be sold in the future or at which a foreign currency to be paid in the future can be purchased in the future.

5. The two most popular instruments for hedging foreign exchange risk are foreign currency forward contracts and foreign currency options. A forward contract is a binding agreement to exchange currencies at a predetermined rate. An option gives the buyer the right, but not the obligation, to exchange currencies at a predetermined rate.

6. Both IAS 39 and SFAS 133 (as amended by SFAS 138) require derivative financial instruments to be reported on the balance sheet at their fair value. Hedge accounting is appropriate if the derivative is (*a*) used to hedge an exposure to foreign exchange risk, (*b*) highly effective in offsetting changes in the fair value or cash flows related to the hedged item, and (*c*) properly documented as a hedge. Under hedge accounting, gains and losses on the hedging instrument are reported in net income in the same period as gains and loss on the item being hedged.

7. SFAS 133 (as amended by SFAS 138) provides guidance for hedges of (*a*) recognized foreign-currency-denominated assets and liabilities, (*b*) unrecognized foreign currency firm commitments, and (*c*) forecast foreign-currency-denominated transactions. Cash flow hedge accounting can be used for all three types of hedges; fair value hedge accounting can be used only for (*a*) and (*b*).

Appendix to Chapter 6

Illustration of the Accounting for Foreign Currency Transactions and Hedging Activities by an Importer

This appendix provides illustrations of the accounting for the following types of hedges used by an importing company:

1. Forward contract cash flow hedge of a recognized foreign currency liability.
2. Forward contract fair value hedge of a recognized foreign currency liability.

3. Option cash flow hedge of a recognized foreign currency liability.
4. Forward contract fair value hedge of a foreign currency firm commitment.
5. Option fair value hedge of a foreign currency firm commitment.
6. Option cash flow hedge of a forecasted foreign currency transaction.

BASIC FACTS

Telectro Company is a U.S. company that produces electronic switches for the telecommunications industry. Telectro regularly imports component parts from a supplier located in Guadalajara, Mexico, with payments made in Mexican pesos (Mex$). The following spot exchange rates, forward exchange rates, and call option premiums for Mexican pesos exist during the period August to October.

	US$ per Mexican Peso		
Date	Spot Rate	Forward Rate to October 31	Call Option Premium for October 31 (strike price $0.080)
August 1	$0.080	$0.085	$0.0052
September 30	0.086	0.088	0.0095
October 31	0.091	0.091	0.0110

1. Forward Contract Cash Flow Hedge of a Recognized Foreign Currency Liability

On August 1, Telectro imports parts from its Mexican supplier at a price of Mex$1,000,000. The parts are received on August 1, but are not paid for until October 31. In addition, on August 1, Telectro enters into a forward contract to purchase Mex$1,000,000 on October 31. The forward contract is appropriately designated as a *cash flow hedge* of the Mexican peso liability exposure. Telectro's incremental borrowing rate is 12 percent per annum (1 percent per month), and the company uses a straight-line method on a monthly basis for allocating forward discounts and premia.

Journal Entries and Impact on the September 30 and October 31 Trial Balances

8/1	Parts Inventory	$80,000	
	Accounts Payable (Mex$)		$80,000
	To record the purchase of parts and a Mexican peso account payable at the spot rate of $0.080.		

There is no formal entry for the forward contract. A memorandum would be prepared designating the forward contract as a hedge of the risk of changes in the cash flow to be paid on the foreign currency payable resulting from changes in the U.S. dollar–Mexican peso exchange rate.

9/30	Foreign Exchange Loss	$6,000	
	Accounts Payable (Mex$)		$6,000
	To adjust the value of the peso payable to the new spot rate of $0.086 and record a foreign exchange loss resulting from the appreciation of the peso since August 1.		
	Accumulated Other Comprehensive Income (AOCI)	$6,000	
	Gain on Forward Contract		$6,000
	To record a gain on forward contract to offset the foreign exchange loss on account payable with a corresponding debit to AOCI.		
	Forward Contract	$2,970	
	Accumulated Other Comprehensive Income (AOCI) . . .		$2,970
	To record the forward contract as an asset at its fair value of $2,970 with a corresponding credit to AOCI.		

The fair value of the forward contract is determined by reference to the change in the forward rate for a contract that settles on October 31: ($0.088 − $0.085) × Mex$1,000,000 = $3,000. The present value of $3,000 discounted for one month (from October 31 to September 30) at an interest rate of 12 percent per year (1 percent per month) is calculated as follows: $3,000 × 0.9901 = $2,970.

Premium Expense	$3,333	
Accumulated Other Comprehensive Income (AOCI)		$3,333
To allocate the forward contract premium to income over the life of the contract using a straight-line method on a monthly basis ($5,000 × $\frac{2}{3}$ = $3,333).		

The original premium on the forward contract is determined by the difference in the Mexican peso spot rate and three-month forward rate on August 1: ($0.085 − $0.080) × Mex$1,000,000 = $5,000.

Trial Balance—September 30	Debit	Credit
Parts Inventory	$80,000	
Accounts Payable (Mex$)		$86,000
Forward Contract (asset)	2,970	
AOCI		303
Foreign Exchange Loss	6,000	
Gain on Forward Contract		6,000
Premium Expense	3,333	
	$92,303	$92,303

10/31	Foreign Exchange Loss	$5,000	
	Accounts Payable (Mex$)		$5,000
	To adjust the value of the peso payable to the new spot rate of $0.091 and record a foreign exchange loss resulting from the appreciation of the peso since September 30.		
	Accumulated Other Comprehensive Income (AOCI)	$5,000	
	Gain on Forward Contract		$5,000
	To record a gain on forward contract to offset the foreign exchange loss on account payable with a corresponding debit to AOCI.		
	Forward Contract	$3,030	
	Accumulated Other Comprehensive Income (AOCI) . .		$3,030
	To adjust the carrying value of the forward contract to its current fair value of $6,000 with a corresponding credit to AOCI.		

The current fair value of the forward contract is determined by reference to the difference in the spot rate on October 31 and the original forward rate: ($0.091 − $0.085) × Mex$1,000,000 = $6,000. The forward contract adjustment on October 31 is calculated as the difference in the current fair value and the carrying value at September 30: $6,000 − $2,970 = $3,030.

Premium Expense	$1,667	
Accumulated Other Comprehensive Income (AOCI)		$1,667
To allocate the forward contract premium to income over the life of the contract using a straight-line method on a monthly basis ($5,000 × $\frac{1}{3}$ = $1,667).		
Foreign Currency (Mex$)	$91,000	
Cash		$85,000
Forward Contract		6,000
To record settlement of the forward contract; record payment of $85,000 in exchange for Mex$1,000,000, record the receipt of Mex$1,000,000 as an asset at the spot rate of $0.91, and remove the forward contract from the accounts.		
Accounts Payable (Mex$)	$91,000	
Foreign Currency (Mex$)		$91,000
To record remittance of Mex$1,000,000 to the Mexican supplier.		

Trial Balance—October 31	Debit	Credit
Cash		$85,000
Parts Inventory	$80,000	
Retained Earnings, 9/30	3,333	
Foreign Exchange Loss	5,000	
Gain on Forward Contract		5,000
Premium Expense	1,667	
	$90,000	$90,000

2. Forward Contract Fair Value Hedge of a Recognized Foreign Currency Liability

The facts are the same as in (1), with the exception that Telectro designates the forward contract as a *fair value hedge* of the Mexican peso liability exposure.

Journal Entries and Impact on the September 30 and October 31 Trial Balances

8/1	Parts Inventory	$80,000	
	Accounts Payable (Mex$)		$80,000
	To record the purchase of parts and a Mexican peso account payable at the spot rate of $0.080.		

There is no formal entry for the forward contract. A memorandum would be prepared designating the forward contract as a hedge of the risk of changes in the cash flow to be paid on the foreign currency payable resulting from changes in the U.S. dollar–Mexican peso exchange rate.

9/30	Foreign Exchange Loss	$6,000	
	Accounts Payable (Mex$)		$6,000
	To adjust the value of the peso payable to the new spot rate of $0.086 and record a foreign exchange loss resulting from the appreciation of the peso since August 1.		
	Forward Contract	$2,970	
	Gain on Forward Contract		$2,970
	To record the forward contract as an asset at its fair value of $2,970 and record a forward contract gain for the change in the fair value of the forward contract since August 1.		

Trial Balance—September 30	Debit	Credit
Parts Inventory	$80,000	
Accounts Payable (Mex$)		$86,000
Forward Contract (asset)	2,970	
Foreign Exchange Loss	6,000	
Gain on Forward Contract		2,970
	$88,970	$88,970

10/31	Foreign Exchange Loss	$5,000	
	Accounts Payable (Mex$)		$5,000
	To adjust the value of the peso payable to the new spot rate of $0.091 and record a foreign exchange loss resulting from the appreciation of the peso since September 30.		
	Forward Contract	$3,030	
	Gain on Forward Contract		$3,030
	To adjust the carrying value of the forward contract to its current fair value of $6,000 and record a forward contract gain for the change in fair value since September 30.		

Foreign Currency (Mex$)	$91,000	
Cash		$85,000
Forward Contract		6,000
To record settlement of the forward contract: record payment of $85,000 in exchange for Mex$1,000,000, record the receipt of Mex$1,000,000 as an asset at the spot rate of $0.91, and remove the forward contract from the accounts.		
Accounts Payable (Mex$)	$91,000	
Foreign Currency (Mex$)		$91,000
To record remittance of Mex$1,000,000 to the Mexican supplier.		

Trial Balance—October 31	Debit	Credit
Cash		$85,000
Parts Inventory	$80,000	
Retained Earnings, 9/30	3,030	
Foreign Exchange Loss	5,000	
Gain on Forward Contract		3,030
	$88,030	$88,030

3. Option Cash Flow Hedge of a Recognized Foreign Currency Liability

On August 1, Telectro imports parts from its Mexican supplier at a price of Mex$1,000,000. The parts are received on August 1 but are not paid for until October 31. In addition, on August 1, Telectro purchases a three-month call option on Mex$1,000,000 with a strike price of $0.080. The option is appropriately designated as a *cash flow hedge* of the Mexican peso liability exposure.

The following schedule summarizes the changes in the components of the fair value of the Mexican peso call option with a strike price of $0.080:

Date	Spot Rate	Option Premium	Fair Value	Change in Fair Value	Intrinsic Value	Time Value	Change in TimeValue
8/1	$0.080	$0.0052	$5,200	—	$0	$5,200[a]	—
9/30	$0.086	$0.0095	$9,500	+$4,300	$6,000[b]	$3,500[b]	−$1,700
10/31	$0.091	$0.0110	$11,000	+$1,500	$11,000	$0[c]	−$3,500

[a]Because the strike price and spot rate are the same, the option has no intrinsic value. Fair value is attributable solely to the time value of the option.
[b]With a spot rate of $0.086 and a strike price of $0.080, the option has an intrinsic value of $6,000. The remaining $3,500 of fair value is attributable to time value.
[c]The time value of the option at maturity is zero.

Journal Entries and Impact on the September 30 and October 31 Trial Balances

8/1	Parts Inventory	$80,000	
	Accounts Payable (Mex$)		$80,000
	To record the purchase of parts and a Mexican peso account payable at the spot rate of $0.080.		
	Foreign Currency Option	$5,200	
	Cash		$5,200
	To record the purchase of a foreign currency option as an asset.		

9/30	Foreign Exchange Loss	$6,000	
	Accounts Payable (Mex$)		$6,000
	To adjust the value of the peso payable to the new spot rate of $0.086 and record a foreign exchange loss resulting from the appreciation of the peso since August 1.		
	Accumulated Other Comprehensive Income (AOCI)	$6,000	
	Gain on Foreign Currency Option		$6,000
	To record a gain on forward currency option to offset the foreign exchange loss on account payable with a corresponding debit to AOCI.		
	Foreign Currency Option	$4,300	
	Accumulated Other Comprehensive Income (AOCI) . . .		$4,300
	To adjust the fair value of the option from $5,200 to $9,500 with a corresponding credit to AOCI.		
	Option Expense	$1,700	
	Accumulated Other Comprehensive Income (AOCI)		$1,700
	To recognize the change in the time value of the foreign currency option as an expense with a corresponding credit to AOCI.		

Trial Balance—September 30	Debit	Credit
Parts Inventory	$80,000	
Accounts Payable (Mex$)		$86,000
Foreign Currency Option (asset)	9,500	
Cash		5,200
Foreign Exchange Loss	6,000	
Gain on Foreign Currency Option		6,000
Option Expense	1,700	
	$97,200	$97,200

10/31	Foreign Exchange Loss	$5,000	
	Accounts Payable (Mex$)		$5,000
	To adjust the value of the peso payable to the new spot rate of $0.091 and record a foreign exchange loss resulting from the appreciation of the peso since September 30.		
	Accumulated Other Comprehensive Income (AOCI)	$5,000	
	Gain on Foreign Currency Option		$5,000
	To record a gain on foreign currency option to offset the foreign exchange loss on account payable with a corresponding debit to AOCI.		
	Foreign Currency Option	$1,500	
	Accumulated Other Comprehensive Income (AOCI)		$1,500
	To adjust the carrying value of the foreign currency option to its current fair value of $11,000 with a corresponding credit to AOCI.		

Option Expense	$3,500	
Accumulated Other Comprehensive Income (AOCI)		$3,500
To recognize the change in the time value of the foreign currency option as an expense with a corresponding credit to AOCI.		
Foreign Currency (Mex$)	$91,000	
Cash		$80,000
Foreign Currency Option		11,000
To record exercise of the foreign currency option: record payment of $80,000 in exchange for Mex$1,000,000, record the receipt of Mex$1,000,000 as an asset at the spot rate of $0.91, and remove the option from the accounts.		
Accounts Payable (Mex$)	$91,000	
Foreign Currency (Mex$)		$91,000
To record remittance of Mex$1,000,000 to the Mexican supplier.		

Trial Balance—October 31	Debit	Credit
Cash ($5,000 credit + $80,000 credit)		$85,200
Parts Inventory	$80,000	
Retained Earnings, 9/30	1,700	
Foreign Exchange Loss	5,000	
Gain on Foreign Currency Option		5,000
Option Expense	3,500	
	$90,200	$90,200

4. Forward Contract Fair Value Hedge of a Foreign Currency Firm Commitment

On August 1, Telectro orders parts from its Mexican supplier at a price of Mex$1,000,000. The parts are received and paid for on October 31. On August 1, Telectro enters into a forward contract to purchase Mex$1,000,000 on October 31. The forward contract is designated as a *fair value hedge* of the Mexican peso firm commitment. The fair value of the firm commitment is determined through reference to changes in the forward exchange rate.

Journal Entries and Impact on the September 30 and October 31 Trial Balances

8/1	There is no formal entry for the forward contract or the purchase order. A memorandum would be prepared designating the forward contract as a fair value hedge of the foreign currency firm commitment.		
9/30	Forward Contract	$2,970	
	Gain on Forward Contract		$2,970
	To record the forward contract as an asset at its fair value of $2,970 and record a forward contract gain for the change in the fair value of the forward contract since August 1.		

Loss on Firm Commitment		$2,970	
Firm Commitment			$2,970
To record the firm commitment as a liability at its fair value of $2,970 based on changes in the forward rate and record a firm commitment loss for the change in fair value since August 1.			

Trial Balance—September 30	Debit	Credit
Forward Contract (asset)	$2,970	
Firm Commitment (liability)		$2,970
Gain on Forward Contract		2,970
Loss on Firm Commitment	2,970	
	$5,940	$5,940

10/31	Forward Contract	$3,030	
	Gain on Forward Contract		$3,030
	To adjust the carrying value of the forward contract to its current fair value of $6,000 and record a forward contract gain for the change in fair value since September 30.		
	Loss on Firm Commitment	$3,030	
	Firm Commitment		$3,030
	To adjust the value of the firm commitment to $6,000 based on changes in the forward rate and record a firm commitment loss for the change in fair value since September 30.		
	Foreign Currency (pesos)	$91,000	
	Cash		$85,000
	Forward Contract		6,000
	To record settlement of the forward contract; record payment of $85,000 in exchange for Mex$1,000,000, record the receipt of 1 million pesos as an asset at the spot rate of $0.91, and remove the forward contract from the accounts.		
	Parts Inventory	$91,000	
	Foreign Currency (Mex$)		$91,000
	To record the purchase of parts through the payment of Mex$1,000,000 to the Mexican supplier.		
	Firm Commitment	$6,000	
	Adjustment to Net Income		$6,000
	To close the firm commitment account as an adjustment to net income.		

Note that the final entry to close the Firm Commitment as an Adjustment to Net Income will be made only in the period in which the Parts Inventory affects net income through Cost of Goods Sold. The Firm Commitment remains on the books as a liability until that time.

Trial Balance—October 31	Debit	Credit
Cash		$85,000
Parts Inventory (Cost of Goods Sold)	$91,000	
Gain on Forward Contract		3,030
Loss on Firm Commitment	3,030	
Adjustment to Net Income		6,000
	$94,030	$94,030

5. Option Fair Value Hedge of a Foreign Currency Firm Commitment

On August 1, Telectro orders parts from its Mexican supplier at a price of Mex$1,000,000. The parts are received and paid for on October 31. On August 1, Telectro purchases a three-month call option on Mex$1,000,000 with a strike price of $0.080. The option is appropriately designated as a *fair value hedge* of the Mexican peso firm commitment. The fair value of the firm commitment is determined through reference to changes in the spot exchange rate.

Journal Entries and Impact on the September 30 and October 31 Trial Balances

8/1	Foreign Currency Option	$5,200	
	Cash		$5,200
	To record the purchase of a foreign currency option as an asset.		
9/30	Foreign Currency Option	$4,300	
	Gain on Foreign Currency Option		$4,300
	To adjust the fair value of the option from $5,200 to $9,500 and record an option gain for the change in fair value since August 1.		
	Loss on Firm Commitment	$5,940	
	Firm Commitment		$5,940
	To record the firm commitment as a liability at its fair value of $5,940 based on changes in the spot rate and record a firm commitment loss for the change in fair value since August 1.		

The fair value of the firm commitment is determined through reference to changes in the spot rate from August 1 to September 30: ($0.080 − $0.086) × Mex$1,000,000 = $(6,000). This amount must be discounted for one month at 12 percent per annum (1 percent per month): $(6,000) × 0.9901 = $(5,940).

Trial Balance—September 30	Debit	Credit
Cash		$ 5,200
Foreign Currency Option (asset)	$9,500	
Firm Commitment (liability)		5,940
Gain on Foreign Currency Option		4,300
Loss on Firm Commitment	5,940	
	$15,440	$15,440

10/31	Foreign Currency Option	$1,500	
	Gain on Foreign Currency Option		$1,500
	To adjust the fair value of the option from $9,500 to $11,000 and record an option gain for the change in fair value since September 30.		
	Loss on Firm Commitment	$5,060	
	Firm Commitment		$5,060
	To adjust the fair value of the firm commitment from $5,940 to $11,000 and record a firm commitment loss for the change in fair value since September 30.		

The fair value of the firm commitment is determined through reference to changes in the spot rate from August 1 to October 31: ($0.080 − $0.091) × Mex$1,000,000 = $(11,000).

Foreign Currency (Mex$)	$91,000	
Cash		$80,000
Foreign Currency Option		11,000
To record exercise of the foreign currency option; record payment of $80,000 in exchange for Mex$1,000,000, record the receipt of Mex$1,000,000 as an asset at the spot rate of $0.91, and remove the option from the accounts.		
Parts Inventory	$91,000	
Foreign Currency (Mex$)		$91,000
To record the purchase of parts through the payment of Mex$1,000,000 to the Mexican supplier.		
Firm Commitment	$11,000	
Adjustment to Net Income		$11,000
To close the firm commitment account as an adjustment to net income.		

Note that the final entry to close the Firm Commitment as an Adjustment to Net Income will be made only in the period in which the Parts Inventory affects net income through Cost of Goods Sold. The Firm Commitment remains on the books as a liability until that point in time.

Trial Balance—October 31	Debit	Credit
Cash ($5,200 credit + $80,000 credit)		$85,200
Parts Inventory (Cost of Goods Sold)	$91,000	
Retained Earnings, 9/30	1,640	
Gain on Foreign Currency Option		1,500
Loss on Firm Commitment	5,060	
Adjustment to Net Income		11,000
	$97,700	$97,700

6. Option Cash Flow Hedge of a Forecasted Foreign Currency Transaction

Telectro anticipates that it will import component parts from its Mexican supplier in the near future. On August 1, Telectro purchases a three-month call option on Mex$1,000,000 with a strike price of $0.080. The option is appropriately designated as a *cash flow hedge* of a forecasted Mexican peso transaction. Parts costing Mex$1,000,000 are received and paid for on October 31.

Journal Entries and Impact on the September 30 and October 31 Trial Balances

8/1	Foreign Currency Option	$5,200	
	Cash		$5,200
	To record the purchase of a foreign currency option as an asset.		
9/30	Foreign Currency Option	$4,300	
	Accumulated Other Comprehensive Income (AOCI)		$4,300
	To adjust the fair value of the option from $5,200 to $9,500 with a corresponding adjustment to AOCI.		
	Option Expense	$1,700	
	Accumulated Other Comprehensive Income (AOCI)		$1,700
	To recognize the change in the time value of the foreign currency option as an expense with a corresponding credit to AOCI.		

Trial Balance—September 30	Debit	Credit
Cash		$ 5,200
Foreign Currency Option (asset)	$ 9,500	
Accumulated Other Comprehensive Income		6,000
Option Expense	1,700	
	$11,200	$11,200

10/31	Foreign Currency Option	$1,500	
	Accumulated Other Comprehensive Income (AOCI)		$1,500
	To adjust the fair value of the option from $9,500 to $11,000 with a corresponding adjustment to AOCI.		
	Option Expense	$3,500	
	Accumulated Other Comprehensive Income (AOCI)		$3,500
	To recognize the change in the time value of the foreign currency option as an expense with a corresponding credit to AOCI.		
	Foreign Currency (Mex$)	$91,000	
	Cash		$80,000
	Foreign Currency Option		11,000
	To record exercise of the foreign currency option; record payment of $80,000 in exchange for Mex$1,000,000, record the receipt of Mex$1,000,000 as an asset at the spot rate of $0.91, and remove the option from the accounts.		

	Debit	Credit
Parts Inventory	$91,000	
Foreign Currency (Mex$)		$91,000
To record the purchase of parts through the payment of Mex$1,000,000 to the Mexican supplier.		
Accumulated Other Comprehensive Income (AOCI)	$11,000	
Adjustment to Net Income		$11,000
To close AOCI as an adjustment to net income.		

Note that the final entry to close AOCI as an Adjustment to Net Income is made at the date that the forecasted transaction was expected to occur, regardless of when the Parts Inventory affects net income.

Trial Balance—October 31	Debit	Credit
Cash ($5,200 credit + $80,000 credit)		$85,200
Parts Inventory (Cost of Goods Sold)	$91,000	
Retained Earnings, 9/30	1,700	
Loss on Foreign Currency Option	3,500	
Adjustment to Net Income		11,000
	$96,200	$96,200

Questions

1. What is the concept underlying the two-transaction perspective to accounting for foreign currency transactions?

2. A company makes an export sale denominated in a foreign currency and allows the customer one month to pay. Under the two-transaction perspective, accrual approach, how does the company account for fluctuations in the exchange rate for the foreign currency?

3. What factors create a foreign exchange gain on a foreign currency transaction? What factors create a foreign exchange loss?

4. What does the word *hedging* mean? Why do companies hedge foreign exchange risk?

5. How does a foreign currency option differ from a foreign currency forward contract?

6. How does the timing of hedges of the following differ?
   a. Foreign currency denominated assets and liabilities.
   b. Foreign currency firm commitments.
   c. Forecasted foreign currency transactions.

7. Why might a company prefer a foreign currency option rather than a forward contract in hedging a foreign currency firm commitment? Why might a company prefer a forward contract over an option in hedging a foreign currency asset or liability?

8. How are foreign currency derivatives such as forward contracts and options reported on the balance sheet?

9. How is the fair value of a foreign currency forward contract determined? How is the fair value of an option determined?

10. What is hedge accounting?

11. Under what conditions can hedge accounting be used to account for a foreign currency option used to hedge a forecasted foreign currency transaction?

12. What are the differences in accounting for a forward contract used as (*a*) a cash flow hedge and (*b*) a fair value hedge of a foreign-currency-denominated asset or liability?

13. What are the differences in accounting for a forward contract used as a fair value hedge of (*a*) a foreign-currency-denominated asset or liability and (*b*) a foreign currency firm commitment?

14. What are the differences in accounting for a forward contract used as a cash flow hedge of (*a*) a foreign-currency-denominated asset or liability and (*b*) a forecasted foreign currency transaction?

15. How are changes in the fair value of an option accounted for in a cash flow hedge? In a fair value hedge?

16. In what way is the accounting for a foreign currency borrowing more complicated than the accounting for a foreign currency account payable?

Exercises and Problems

1. Which of the following combinations correctly describes the relationship between foreign currency transactions, exchange rate changes, and foreign exchange gains and losses?

Type of Transaction	Foreign Currency	Foreign Exchange Gain or Loss
a. Export sale	Appreciates	Loss
b. Import purchase	Appreciates	Gain
c. Import purchase	Depreciates	Gain
d. Export sale	Depreciates	Gain

2. Gracie Corporation had a Japanese yen receivable resulting from exports to Japan and a Brazilian real payable resulting from imports from Brazil. Gracie recorded foreign exchange gains related to both its yen receivable and real payable. Did the foreign currencies increase or decrease in dollar value from the date of the transaction to the settlement date?

	Yen	Real
a.	Increase	Increase
b.	Decrease	Decrease
c.	Decrease	Increase
d.	Increase	Decrease

3. On December 1, Year 1, Tackett Company (a U.S.-based company) entered into a three-month forward contract to purchase 1 million Mexican pesos on March 1, Year 2. The following U.S. dollar per peso exchange rates apply:

Date	Spot Rate	Forward Rate (to March 1, Year 2)
December 1, Year 1	$0.088	$0.084
December 31, Year 1	0.080	0.074
March 1, Year 2	0.076	

Tackett's incremental borrowing rate is 12 percent. The present value factor for two months at an annual interest rate of 12 percent (1 percent per month) is 0.9803.

Which of the following correctly describes the manner in which Tackett Company will report the forward contract on its December 31, Year 1, balance sheet?

a. As an asset in the amount of $3,921.20.

b. As an asset in the amount of $7,842.40.

c. As a liability in the amount of $13,724.20.

d. As a liability in the amount of $9,803.00.

Use the following information for Exercises 4 and 5: Reiter Corp. (a U.S.-based company) sold parts to an Israeli customer on December 1, Year 1, with payment of 100,000 Israeli shekels to be received on March 31, Year 2. The following exchange rates apply:

Date	Spot Rate	Forward Rate (to March 31, Year 2)
December 1, Year 1	$0.24	$0.23
December 31, Year 1	0.22	0.20
March 31, Year 2	0.25	

Reiter's incremental borrowing rate is 12 percent. The present value factor for three months at an annual interest rate of 12 percent (1 percent per month) is 0.9706.

4. Assuming no forward contract was entered into, how much foreign exchange gain or loss should Reiter report on its Year 1 income statement with regard to this transaction?

a. A $5,000 gain.

b. A $3,000 gain.

c. A $2,000 loss.

d. A $1,000 loss.

5. Assuming a forward contract to sell 100,000 Israeli shekels was entered into on December 1, Year 1, as a fair value hedge of a foreign currency receivable, what would be the net impact on net income in Year 1 resulting from a fluctuation in the value of the shekel?

a. No impact on net income.

b. A $58.80 decrease in net income.

c. A $2,000 decrease in income.

d. A $911.80 increase in income.

Use the following information for Exercises 6 through 8: On September 1, Year 1, Keefer Company received an order to sell a machine to a customer in Canada at a price of 100,000 Canadian dollars. The machine was shipped and payment was received on March 1, Year 2. On September 1, Year 1, Keefer Company purchased a put option giving it the right to sell 100,000 Canadian dollars on March 1, Year 2, at a price of $75,000. Keefer Company properly designates the option as a fair value hedge of the Canadian-dollar firm commitment. The option cost $1,700 and had a fair value of $2,800 on December 31, Year 1. The fair value of the firm commitment is measured through reference to changes in the spot rate. The following spot exchange rates apply:

Date	U.S. Dollar per Canadian Dollar
September 1, Year 1	$0.75
December 31, Year 1 . . .	0.73
March 1, Year 2	0.71

Keefer Company's incremental borrowing rate is 12 percent. The present value factor for two months at an annual interest rate of 12 percent (1 percent per month) is 0.9803.

6. What was the net impact on Keefer Company's Year 1 income as a result of this fair value hedge of a firm commitment?
   a. $0.
   b. An $860.60 decrease in income.
   c. A $1,100.00 increase in income.
   d. A $1,960.60 increase in income.

7. What was the net impact on Keefer Company's Year 2 income as a result of this fair value hedge of a firm commitment?
   a. $0.
   b. An $839.40 decrease in income.
   c. A $74,160.60 increase in income.
   d. A $76,200.00 increase in income.

8. What was the net increase or decrease in cash flow from having purchased the foreign currency option to hedge this exposure to foreign exchange risk?
   a. $0.
   b. A $1,000 increase in cash flow.
   c. A $1,700 decrease in cash flow.
   d. A $2,300 increase in cash flow.

   Use the following information for problems 9 and 10: On November 1, Year 1, Black Lion Company forecasts the purchase of raw materials from an Argentinian supplier on February 1, Year 2, at a price of 200,000 Argentinian pesos. On November 1, Year 1, Black Lion pays $1,200 for a three-month call option on 200,000 Argentinian pesos with a strike price of $0.35 per peso. The option is properly designated as a cash flow hedge of a forecasted foreign currency transaction. On December 31, Year 1, the option has a fair value of $900. The following spot exchange rates apply:

Date	U.S. Dollar per Argentinian Peso
November 1, Year 1 ...	$0.35
December 31, Year 1 ..	0.30
February 1, Year 2	0.36

9. What is the net impact on Black Lion Company's Year 1 net income as a result of this hedge of a forecasted foreign currency purchase?
   a. $0.
   b. A $200 increase in net income.
   c. A $300 decrease in net income.
   d. An $800 decrease in net income.

10. What is the net impact on Black Lion Company's Year 2 net income as a result of this hedge of a forecast foreign currency purchase? Assume that the raw materials are consumed and become a part of cost of goods sold in Year 2.
    a. A $70,000 decrease in net income.
    b. A $70,900 decease in net income.
    c. A $71,100 decrease in net income.
    d. A $72,900 decrease in net income.

11. Garden Grove Corporation made a sale to a foreign customer on September 15, Year 1, for 100,000 foreign currency units (FCU). Payment was received on October 15, Year 1. The following exchange rates apply:

Date	U.S. Dollar per FCU
September 15, Year 1 . . .	$0.40
September 30, Year 1 . . .	0.42
October 15, Year 1	0.37

Required:

Prepare all journal entries for Garden Grove Corporation in connection with this sale assuming that the company closes its books on September 30 to prepare interim financial statements.

12. On December 1, Year 1, El Primero Company purchases inventory from a foreign supplier for 40,000 coronas. Payment will be made in 90 days after El Primero has sold this merchandise. Sales are made rather quickly and El Primero pays this entire obligation on February 15, Year 2. The following exchange rates for 1 corona apply:

Date	U.S. Dollar per Corona
December 1, Year 1	$0.87
December 31, Year 1	0.82
February 15, Year 2	0.91

Required:

Prepare all journal entries for El Primero in connection with the purchase and payment.

13. On September 30, Year 1, the Lester Company negotiated a two-year loan of 1,000,000 markkas from a foreign bank at an interest rate of 2 percent per annum. Interest payments are made annually on September 30 and the principal will be repaid on September 30, Year 3. Lester Company prepares U.S.-dollar financial statements and has a December 31 year-end. Prepare all journal entries related to this foreign currency borrowing assuming the following exchange rates for 1 markka:

Date	U.S. Dollars per Markka
September 30, Year 1	$0.20
December 31, Year 1	0.21
September 30, Year 2	0.23
December 31, Year 2	0.24
September 30, Year 3	0.27

Required:

Prepare all journal entries for the Lester Company in connection with the foreign currency borrowing. What is the effective annual cost of borrowing in dollars in each of the three years Year 1, Year 2, and Year 3?

14. The Budvar Company sells parts to a foreign customer on December 1, Year 1, with payment of 20,000 crowns to be received on March 1, Year 2. Budvar enters into a forward contract on December 1, Year 1, to sell 20,000 crowns on March 1,

Year 2. Relevant exchange rates for the crown on various dates are as follows:

Date	Spot Rate	Forward Rate (to March 1, Year 2)
December 1, Year 1	$1.00	$1.04
December 31, Year 1	1.05	1.10
March 1, Year 2	1.12	

Budvar's incremental borrowing rate is 12 percent. The present value factor for two months at an annual interest rate of 12 percent (1 percent per month) is 0.9803. Budvar must close its books and prepare financial statements at December 31.

Required:
a. Assuming that Budvar designates the forward contract as a cash flow hedge of a foreign currency receivable, prepare journal entries for these transactions in U.S. dollars. What is the impact on Year 1 net income? What is the impact on Year 2 net income? What is the impact on net income over the two accounting periods?

b. Assuming that Budvar designates the forward contract as a fair value hedge of a foreign currency receivable, prepare journal entries for these transactions in U.S. dollars. What is the impact on Year 1 net income? What is the impact on Year 2 net income? What is the impact on net income over the two accounting periods?

15. The same facts apply as in Exercise 14 except that Budvar Company purchases parts from a foreign supplier on December 1, Year 1, with payment of 20,000 crowns to be made on March 1, Year 2. On December 1, Year 1, Budvar enters into a forward contract to purchase 20,000 crowns on March 1, Year 2. The parts purchased on December 1, Year 1, become a part of the cost of goods sold on March 15, Year 2.

Required:
a. Assuming that Budvar designates the forward contract as a cash flow hedge of a foreign currency payable, prepare journal entries for these transactions in U.S. dollars. What is the impact on Year 1 net income? What is the impact on Year 2 net income? What is the impact on net income over the two accounting periods?

b. Assuming that Budvar designates the forward contract as a fair value hedge of a foreign currency payable, prepare journal entries for these transactions in U.S. dollars. What is the impact on Year 1 net income? What is the impact on Year 2 net income? What is the impact on net income over the two accounting periods?

16. On November 1, Year 1, Alexandria Company sold merchandise to a foreign customer for 100,000 francs with payment to be received on April 30, Year 2. At the date of sale, Alexandria Company entered into a six-month forward contract to sell 100,000 francs. The forward contract is properly designated as a cash flow hedge of a foreign currency receivable. Relevant exchange rates for the franc are:

Date	Spot Rate	Forward Rate (to April 30, Year 2)
November 1, Year 1	$0.23	$0.22
December 31, Year 1	0.20	0.18
April 30, Year 2	0.19	

Alexandria Company's incremental borrowing rate is 12 percent. The present value factor for four month at an annual interest rate of 12 percent (1 percent per month) is 0.9610.

Required:

Prepare all journal entries, including December 31 adjusting entries, to record the sale and forward contract. What is the impact on net income in Year 1? What is the impact on net income in Year 2?

17. Artco Inc. engages in various transactions with companies in the country of Santrica. On November 30, Year 1, Artco sold artwork at a price of 400,000 ricas to a Santrican customer with payment to be received on January 31, Year 2. In addition, on November 30, Year 1, Artco purchased art supplies from a Santrican supplier at a price of 300,000 ricas; payment will be made on January 31, Year 2. The art supplies are consumed by the end of November, Year 1. To hedge its net exposure in ricas, Artco entered into a two-month forward contract on November 30, Year 1, wherein Artco will deliver 100,000 ricas to the foreign currency broker in exchange for U.S dollars at the agreed-on forward rate. Artco properly designates its forward contract as a fair value hedge of a foreign currency receivable. The following rates for the rica apply:

Date	Spot Rate	Forward Rate (to January 31, Year 2)
November 30, Year 1	$0.13	$0.12
December 31, Year 1	0.10	0.08
January 31, Year 2	0.09	

Artco Inc.'s incremental borrowing rate is 12 percent. The present value factor for one month at an annual interest rate of 12 percent (1 percent per month) is 0.9901.

Required:

Prepare all journal entries, including December 31 adjusting entries, to record these transactions and forward contract. What is the impact on net income in Year 1? What is the impact on net income in Year 2?

18. On October 1, Year 1, Butterworth Company entered into a forward contract to sell 100,000 rupees in four months (on January 31, Year 2). Relevant exchange rates for the rupee are as follows:

Date	Spot Rate	Forward Rate (to January 31, Year 2)
October 1, Year 1	$0.069	$0.065
December 31, Year 1	0.071	0.074
January 31, Year 2	0.072	

Butterworth Company's incremental borrowing rate is 12 percent. The present value factor for one month at an annual interest rate of 12 percent (1 percent per month) is 0.9901. Butterworth must close its books and prepare financial statements on December 31.

Required:

a. Prepare journal entries assuming the forward contract was entered into as a fair value hedge of a 100,000-rupee receivable arising from a sale made on October 1, Year 1. Include entries for both the sale and the forward contract.

b. Prepare journal entries assuming the forward contract was entered into as a fair value hedge of a firm commitment related to a 100,000-rupee sale that will be made on January 31, Year 2. Include entries for both the firm commitment and the forward contract. The fair value of the firm commitment is measured through reference to changes in the forward rate.

19. On August 1, Year 1, Huntington Corporation placed an order to purchase merchandise from a foreign supplier at a price of 100,000 dinars. The merchandise is received and paid for on October 31, Year 1, and is fully consumed by December 31, Year 1. On August 1, Huntington entered into a forward contract to purchase 100,000 dinars in three months at the agreed-on forward rate. The forward contract is properly designated as a fair value hedge of a foreign currency firm commitment. The fair value of the firm commitment is measured through reference to changes in the forward rate. Relevant exchange rates for the dinar are as follows:

Date	Spot Rate	Forward Rate (to October 31, Year 1)
August 1	$1.300	$1.310
September 30	1.305	1.325
October 31	1.320	

Huntington's incremental borrowing rate is 12 percent. The present value factor for one month at an annual interest rate of 12 percent (1 percent per month) is 0.9901. Huntington Corporation must close its books and prepare its third-quarter financial statements on September 30, Year 1.

Required:

Prepare journal entries for the forward contract and firm commitment. What is the impact on net income in Year 1? What is the net cash outflow on the purchase of merchandise from the foreign customer?

20. On June 1, Year 1, Tsanumis Corporation (a U.S.-based manufacturing firm) received an order to sell goods to a foreign customer at a price of 1 million euros. The goods will be shipped and payment will be received in three months on September 1, Year 1. On June 1, Tsanumis Corporation purchased an option to sell 1 million euros in three months at a strike price of $1.00. The option is properly designated as a fair value hedge of a foreign currency firm commitment. The fair value of the firm commitment is measured through reference to changes in the spot rate. Relevant exchange rates and option premia for the euro during Year 1 are as follows:

Date	Spot Rate	Call Option Premium for September 1, Year 1 (strike price $1.00)
June 1	$1.00	$0.010
June 30	0.99	0.015
September 1	0.97	

Tsanumis Corporation's incremental borrowing rate is 12 percent. The present value factor for two months at an annual interest rate of 12 percent (1 percent per month) is 0.9803. Tsanumis Corporation must close its books and prepare its second-quarter financial statements on June 30.

Required:

Prepare journal entries for the foreign currency option and firm commitment. What is the impact on Year 1 net income? What is the net cash inflow resulting from the sale of goods to the foreign customer?

21. The Zermatt Company ordered parts from a foreign supplier on November 20 at a price of 100,000 francs when the spot rate was $0.80 per peso. Delivery and payment were scheduled for December 20. On November 20, Zermatt acquired a call option on 100,000 francs at a strike price of $0.80, paying a premium of $0.008 per franc. The option is designated as fair value hedge of a foreign currency firm commitment. The fair value of the firm commitment is measured through reference to changes in the spot rate. The parts are delivered and paid for according to schedule. Zermatt does not close its books until December 31.

Required:

a. Assuming a spot rate of $0.83 per franc on December 20, prepare all journal entries to account for the option and firm commitment.

b. Assuming a spot rate of $0.78 per franc on December 20, prepare all journal entries to account for the option and firm commitment.

22. Given its experience, Garnier Corporation expects that it will sell goods to a foreign customer at a price of 1 million lire on March 15, Year 2. To hedge this forecasted transaction, a three-month put option to sell 1 million lire is acquired on December 15, Year 1. Garnier selects a strike price of $0.15 per lire, paying a premium of $0.005 per unit, when the spot rate is $0.15. The spot rate decreases to $.14 at December 31, Year 1, causing the fair value of the option to increase to $12,000. By March 15, Year 2, when the goods are delivered and payment is received from the customer, the spot rate has fallen to $0.13, resulting in a fair value for the option of $20,000.

Required:

Prepare all journal entries for the option hedge of a forecast transaction and for the export sale assuming that December 31 is Garnier Corporation's year-end. What is the overall impact on net income over the two accounting periods? What is the net cash inflow from this export sale?

Case 6-1

Zorba Company

Zorba Company, a U.S.-based importer of specialty olive oil, placed an order with a Greek supplier for 500 cases of olive oil at a price of 100 euros per case. The total purchase price is 50,000 euros. Relevant exchange rates are as follows:

Date	Spot Rate	Forward Rate (to January 31, Year 2)	Call Option Premium for January 31, Year 2 (strike price $1.00)
December 1, Year 1.....	$1.00	$1.08	$0.04
December 31, Year 1...	1.10	1.17	0.12
January 31, Year 2.......	1.15	1.15	0.15

Zorba Company has an incremental borrowing rate of 12 percent (1 percent per month) and closes the books and prepares financial statements on December 31.

Required:

1. Assume the olive oil was received on December 1, Year 1, and payment was made on January 31, Year 2. There was no attempt to hedge the exposure to foreign exchange risk. Prepare journal entries to account for this import purchase.

2. Assume the olive oil was received on December 1, Year 1, and payment was made on October January 31, Year 2. On December 1, Zorba Company entered into a two-month forward contract to purchase 50,000 euros. The forward contract is properly designated as a fair value hedge of a foreign currency payable. Prepare journal entries to account for the import purchase and foreign currency forward contract.

3. The olive oil was ordered on December 1, Year 1. It was received and paid for on January 31, Year 1. On December 1, Zorba Company entered into a two-month forward contract to purchase 50,000 euros. The forward contract is properly designated as a fair value hedge of a foreign currency firm commitment. The fair value of the firm commitment is measured through reference to changes in the forward rate. Prepare journal entries to account for the foreign currency forward contract, firm commitment, and import purchase.

4. The olive oil was received on December 1, Year 1, and payment was made on January 31, Year 2. On December 1, Zorba Company purchased a two-month call option for 50,000 euros. The option was properly designated as a cash flow hedge of a foreign currency payable. Prepare journal entries to account for the import purchase and foreign currency option.

5. The olive oil was ordered on December 1, Year 1. It was received and paid for on December 31, Year 2. On December 1, Zorba Company purchased a two-month call option for 50,000 euros. The option was properly designated as a fair value hedge of a foreign currency firm commitment. The fair value of the firm commitment is measured through reference to changes in the spot rate. Prepare journal entries to account for the foreign currency option, firm commitment, and import purchase.

Case 6-2

Portofino Company

Portofino Company made purchases on account from three foreign suppliers on December 15, 2003, with payment made on January 15, 2004. Information related to these purchases is as follows:

Supplier	Location	Invoice Price
Borboleta SA de CV	Guadalajara, Mexico	225,000 Mexican pesos
Beija Flor Ltda.	São Paulo, Brazil	60,000 Brazilian reals
Quetzala SA	Guatemala City, Guatemala	150,000 Guatemalan quetzals

Portofino Company's fiscal year ends December 31.

Required:

1. Use historical exchange rate information available on the Internet at www.oanda.com to find exchange rates between the U.S. dollar and each foreign currency for the period December 15, 2003, to January 15, 2004.

2. Determine the foreign exchange gains and losses that Portofino would have recognized in net income in 2003 and 2004, and the overall foreign exchange gain or loss for each transaction. Determine for which transaction it would have been most important for Portofino to hedge its foreign exchange risk.

3. Portofino could have acquired a one-month call option on December 15, 2003, to hedge the foreign exchange risk associated with each of the three import purchases. In each case, the option would have had an exercise price equal to the spot rate at December 15, 2003, and would have cost $100. Determine for which hedges, if any, Portofino would have recognized a net gain on the foreign currency option.

Case 6-3

Better Food Corporation

Better Food Corporation (BFC) regularly purchases nutritional supplements from a supplier in Japan with the invoice price denominated in Japanese yen. BFC has experienced several foreign exchange losses in the past year due to increases in the U.S.-dollar price of the Japanese currency. As a result, BFC's CEO, Harvey Carlisle, has asked you to investigate the possibility of using derivative financial instruments, specifically foreign currency forward contracts and foreign currency options, to hedge the company's exposure to foreign exchange risk.

Required:

Draft a memo to CEO Carlisle comparing the advantages and disadvantages of using forward contracts and options to hedge foreign exchange risk. Make a recommendation for which type of hedging instrument you believe the company should employ and provide your justification for this recommendation.

References

U.S. Department of Commerce. "Small and Medium-Sized Enterprises Play an Important Role," *Export America*, September 2001.

World Trade Organization. *International Trade Statistics 2004* (www.wto.org).

Chapter **Seven**

Translation of Foreign Currency Financial Statements

Learning Objectives

After reading this chapter, you should be able to

- Describe the conceptual issues involved in translating foreign currency financial statements.
- Explain balance sheet exposure and how it differs from transaction exposure.
- Describe the concepts underlying the current rate and temporal methods of translation.
- Apply the current rate and temporal methods of translation and compare the results of the two methods.
- Describe the requirements of applicable International Financial Reporting Standards (IFRSs) and U.S. generally accepted accounting principles (GAAP).
- Discuss hedging of balance sheet exposure.
- Highlight translation procedures used internationally.

INTRODUCTION

In today's global business environment, many companies have operations in foreign countries. In its 2004 10-K report, Ford Motor Company provided a list of subsidiaries located in some 18 different countries around the world. The German automaker Volkswagen AG reports having wholly owned subsidiaries in 20 countries other than Germany. Most operations located in foreign countries keep their accounting records and prepare financial statements in the local currency using local accounting principles. To prepare consolidated financial statements, parent companies must restate their foreign subsidiaries' financial statements in terms of the parent company's reporting generally accepted accounting principles (GAAP) and then translate the statements into the parent company's reporting currency. The diversity in national accounting standards and the problems associated with that diversity (such as the GAAP reconciliation for consolidation purposes) are discussed in Chapter 2.

This chapter focuses on the *translation* of foreign currency financial statements for the purpose of preparing consolidated financial statements. We begin by examining the conceptual issues related to translation and then describe the manner in which these issues have been addressed by the International Accounting Standards Board (IASB) and by the Financial Accounting Standards Board (FASB) in the United States. We then illustrate application of the two methods prescribed by those standard setters and compare the results from applying the two different methods. We also discuss hedging the net investment in foreign operations to avoid the adverse impact the translation of foreign currency financial statements can have on the consolidated accounts.

TWO CONCEPTUAL ISSUES

In translating foreign currency financial statements into the parent company's reporting currency, two questions must be addressed:

1. What is the appropriate exchange rate to be used in translating each financial statement item?
2. How should the translation adjustment that inherently arises from the translation process be reflected in the consolidated financial statements?

We introduce these issues and the basic concepts underlying the translation of financial statements through the following example.

Example

Parentco, a U.S.-based company, establishes a wholly owned subsidiary, Foreignco, in Foreign Country on January 1 by investing US$600 when the exchange rate between the U.S. dollar and the foreign currency (FC) is FC1 = US$1.00. The equity investment of US$600 is physically converted into FC600. In addition, Foreignco borrows FC400 from local banks on January 2. Foreignco purchases inventory that costs FC900 and maintains FC100 in cash. Foreignco's opening balance sheet appears as follows:

FOREIGNCO			
Opening Balance Sheet			
Cash	FC 100	Liabilities	FC 400
Inventory	900	Common stock	600
Total	FC1,000	Total	FC1,000

To prepare a consolidated balance sheet at the date of acquisition, all FC balances on Foreignco's balance sheet are translated at the exchange rate of US$1.00 per FC. There is no other exchange rate that possibly could be used on that date. A partial consolidation worksheet at the date of acquisition would appear as follows:

Consolidation Worksheet at Date of Acquisition for Parentco and Its Subsidiary Foreignco

	Parentco US$	Foreignco			Eliminations		Consolidated Balance Sheet US$
		FC	Exchange Rate	US$	Dr.	Cr.	
Investment	600	—				(1) 600*	0
Cash	(600)	100	$1.00	100			(500)
Inventory	xx	900	$1.00	900			900
Total	xxx	1,000		1,000			400
Liabilities	xx	400	$1.00	400			400
Common stock	xx	600	$1.00	600	(1) 600		0
Total	xxx	1,000		1,000			400

*The elimination entry eliminates Parentco's Investment in Subsidiary account against Foreignco's Common Stock account.

By translating each FC balance on Foreignco's balance sheet at the same exchange rate (US$1.00), Foreignco's US$ translated balance sheet reflects an equal amount of total assets and total liabilities and equity.

Three Months Later

During the period January 1 to March 31, Foreignco engages in no transactions. However, during that period the FC appreciates in value against the US$ such that the exchange rate at March 31 is US$1.20 per FC.

In preparing the March 31 interim consolidated financial statements, Parentco now must choose between the current exchange rate of US$1.20 and the past (historical) exchange rate of US$1.00 to translate Foreignco's balance sheet into U.S. dollars. Foreignco's stockholders' equity must be translated at the historical rate of US$1.00 so that Parentco's Investment account can be eliminated against the subsidiary's common stock in the consolidation worksheet. Two approaches exist for translating the subsidiary's assets and liabilities:

1. All assets and liabilities are translated at the *current exchange rate* (the spot exchange rate on the balance sheet date).
2. Some assets and liabilities are translated at the current exchange rate, and other assets and liabilities are translated at *historical exchange rates* (the exchange rates that existed when the assets and liabilities were acquired).

All Assets and Liabilities Are Translated at the Current Exchange Rate

If the first approach is adopted, in which all assets and liabilities are translated at the current exchange rate, the consolidation worksheet on March 31 would appear as follows:

Consolidation Worksheet Three Months after Date of Acquisition for Parentco and Its Subsidiary Foreignco

	Parentco US$	Foreignco FC	Foreignco Exchange Rate	Foreignco US$	Change in US$ Value Since January 1	Eliminations Dr.	Eliminations Cr.	Consolidated Balance Sheet US$
Investment	600	—					600	0
Cash.	(600)	100	**$1.20**	120	**+20**			(480)
Inventory	xx	900	**$1.20**	1,080	**+180**			1,080
Total	xxx	1,000		1,200	+200			600
Liabilities	xx	400	**$1.20**	480	**+80**			480
Common stock . . .	xx	600	$1.00	600	0	600		0
Subtotal	xxx	1,000		1,080	+80			480
Translation adjustment				*120*	**+120**			120
Total				1,200	+200			600

By translating all assets at the higher current exchange rate, assets are written up in terms of their U.S.-dollar value by US$200. Liabilities are also written up by US$80. To keep the U.S. dollar translated balance sheet in balance, a *positive* (credit) translation adjustment of US$120 must be recorded. As a result, total assets on the consolidated balance sheet are US$120 greater than on January 1, as are consolidated total liabilities and stockholders' equity.

Translating foreign currency balances at the current exchange rate is similar to revaluing foreign currency receivables and payables at the balance sheet date. The translation adjustment is analogous to the *net* foreign exchange gain or loss caused by a change in the exchange rate:

$20 gain on cash + $180 gain on inventory − $80 loss on liabilities = $120 net gain

The net foreign exchange gain (positive translation adjustment) is *unrealized*, that is, it does not result in a cash inflow of US$120 for Parentco. However, the gain can be *realized* by selling Foreignco at the book value of its net assets (FC600) and converting the proceeds into U.S. dollars at the current exchange rate (FC600 × $1.20 = US$720). In that case, Parentco would realize a gain from the sale of its investment in Foreignco that would be due solely to the appreciation in value of the foreign currency:

Proceeds from the sale	$720
Original investment	600
Realized gain	$120

The translation adjustment reflects the *change in the dollar value of the net investment* in Foreignco if the subsidiary were to be sold. In addition, a *positive* translation adjustment signals that the appreciation of the foreign currency will result in an increase in the U.S. dollar value of future foreign-currency dividends to be paid by Foreignco to its parent. For example, a dividend of FC10 distributed on March 31 can be converted into US$12, whereas the same amount of foreign-currency dividend would have been worth only US$10 at the beginning of the year.

Monetary Assets and Liabilities Are Translated at the Current Exchange Rates

Now assume that only monetary assets (cash and receivables) and monetary liabilities (most liabilities) are translated at the current exchange rate. The worksheet to translate Foreignco's financial statements into U.S. dollars on March 31 appears as follows:

Consolidation Worksheet Three Months after Date of Acquisition for Parentco and Its Subsidiary Foreignco							
	Parentco	Foreignco			Change in US$ Value Since	Eliminations		Consolidated Balance Sheet
	US$	FC	Exchange Rate	US$	January 1	Dr.	Cr.	US$
Investment	600	—					600	0
Cash	(600)	100	**$1.20**	120	+20			(480)
Inventory	XX	900	$1.00	900	0			900
Total	XXX	1,000		1,020	+20			420
Liabilities	XX	400	**$1.20**	480	+80			480
Common stock . .	XX	600	$1.00	600	0	600		0
Subtotal	XXX	1,000		1,080	+80			480
Translation adjustment				(60)	**−60**			(60)
Total				1,020	+20			420

Using this approach, cash is written up by US$20 and liabilities are written up by US$80. To keep the balance sheet in balance, a *negative* (debit) translation adjustment of US$60 must be recorded. As a result, both total assets and total liabilities and stockholders' equity on the consolidated balance sheet are US$20 greater than on January 1.

The translation adjustment is analogous to the *net* foreign exchange gain or loss caused by a change in the exchange rate:

$$\$20 \text{ gain on cash} - \$80 \text{ loss on liabilities} = \$60 \text{ net loss}$$

This net foreign exchange loss (negative translation adjustment) also is *unrealized*. However, the loss can be *realized* through the following process:

1. The subsidiary uses its cash (FC100) to pay its liabilities to the extent possible.
2. The parent sends enough U.S. dollars to the subsidiary to pay its remaining liabilities (FC300). At January 1, the parent would have sent US$300 to pay FC300 of liabilities (at the $1.00/FC1 exchange rate). At March 31, the parent must send US$360 to pay FC300 of liabilities (at the $1.20/FC1 exchange rate). A foreign exchange loss (negative translation adjustment) of US$60 (US$360 − US$300) arises on the net monetary liability position because the foreign currency has appreciated from January 1 to March 31.

Note that under this translation approach, the *negative* translation adjustment does not reflect the change in the U.S.-dollar value of the net investment in Foreignco. Moreover, the *negative* translation adjustment is not consistent with the change in the U.S.-dollar value of future foreign currency dividends. As the foreign currency appreciates, the U.S. dollar value of foreign currency dividends received from Foreignco increases.

Balance Sheet Exposure

As exchange rates change, assets and liabilities translated at the *current* exchange rate change in value from balance sheet to balance sheet in terms of the parent company's reporting currency (for example, U.S. dollar). These items are *exposed* to translation adjustment. Balance sheet items translated at *historical* exchange rates do not change in parent currency value from one balance sheet to the next. These items are *not* exposed to translation adjustment. Exposure to translation adjustment is referred to as balance sheet, translation, or accounting exposure. *Balance sheet exposure* can be contrasted with the *transaction exposure* discussed in Chapter 6 that arises when a company has foreign currency receivables and payables in the following way:

> Transaction exposure gives rise to foreign exchange gains and losses that are ultimately realized in cash; translation adjustments that arise from balance sheet exposure do not directly result in cash inflows or outflows.

Each item translated at the current exchange rate is exposed to translation adjustment. In effect, a separate translation adjustment exists for each of these exposed items. However, positive translation adjustments on assets when the foreign currency appreciates are offset by negative translation adjustments on liabilities. If total exposed assets are equal to total exposed liabilities throughout the year, the translation adjustments (although perhaps significant on an individual basis) net to a zero balance. The *net* translation adjustment needed to keep the consolidated balance sheet in balance is based solely on the net asset or net liability exposure.

A foreign operation will have a *net asset balance sheet exposure* when assets translated at the current exchange rate are greater in amount than liabilities translated at the current exchange rate. A *net liability balance sheet exposure* exists when liabilities translated at the current exchange rate are greater than assets translated at the current exchange rate. The relationship between exchange rate fluctuations, balance sheet exposure, and translation adjustments can be summarized as follows:

Balance Sheet Exposure	Foreign Currency (FC)	
	Appreciates	**Depreciates**
Net asset	Positive translation adjustment	Negative translation adjustment
Net liability	Negative translation adjustment	Positive translation adjustment

Exactly how the translation adjustment should be reported in the consolidated financial statements is a matter of some debate. The major question is whether the translation adjustments should be treated as a *translation gain or loss reported in income* or whether the translation adjustment should be treated as a *direct adjustment to owners' equity without affecting income*. This issue is considered in this chapter in more detail after first examining different methods of translation.

TRANSLATION METHODS

Four major methods of translating foreign currency financial statements have been used worldwide: (1) the current/noncurrent method, (2) the monetary/nonmonetary method, (3) the temporal method, and (4) the current rate (or closing rate) method.

Current/Noncurrent Method

The rules for the current/noncurrent method are as follows: current assets and current liabilities are translated at the current exchange rate; noncurrent assets, noncurrent liabilities, and stockholders' equity accounts are translated at historical exchange rates. There is no theoretical basis underlying this method. Although once the predominant method, the current/noncurrent method has been unacceptable in the United States since 1975, has never been allowed under International Financial Reporting Standards, and is seldom used in other countries.

Monetary/Nonmonetary Method

To remedy the lack of theoretical justification for the current/noncurrent method, Hepworth developed the monetary/nonmonetary method of translation in 1956.[1] Under this method, monetary assets and liabilities are translated at the current exchange rates; nonmonetary assets, nonmonetary liabilities, and stockholders' equity accounts are translated at historical exchange rates. Monetary assets are those assets whose value does not fluctuate over time—primarily cash and receivables. Nonmonetary assets are assets whose monetary value can fluctuate. They consist of marketable securities, inventory, prepaid expenses, investments, fixed assets, and intangible assets; that is, all assets other than cash and receivables. Monetary liabilities are those liabilities whose monetary value cannot fluctuate over time, which is true for most payables.

[1] Samuel R. Hepworth, *Reporting Foreign Operations* (Ann Arbor: University of Michigan, Bureau of Business Research, 1956).

Under the monetary/nonmonetary method, cash, receivables, and payables carried on the foreign operation's balance sheet are exposed to foreign exchange risk. There is a net asset exposure when cash plus receivables exceed payables, and a net liability exposure when payables exceed cash plus receivables.

Cash + Receivables > Payables → Net asset exposure

Cash + Receivables < Payables → Net liability exposure

The previous example in which Foreignco's monetary assets and monetary liabilities were translated at the current exchange rate demonstrates the monetary/nonmonetary method. In that example, Foreignco had a net liability exposure that, when coupled with an appreciation in the foreign currency, resulted in a negative translation adjustment.

One way to understand the concept of exposure underlying the monetary/nonmonetary method is to assume that the foreign operation's cash, receivables, and payables are actually foreign currency assets and liabilities of the parent company. For example, consider the Japanese subsidiary of a New Zealand parent company. The Japanese subsidiary's yen receivables that result from sales in Japan may be thought of as Japanese yen receivables of the New Zealand parent resulting from export sales to Japan. If the New Zealand parent had yen receivables on its balance sheet, an increase in the value of the yen would result in a foreign exchange gain. There also would be a foreign exchange gain on the Japanese yen held in cash by the parent. These foreign exchange gains would be offset by a foreign exchange loss on the parent's Japanese yen payables resulting from foreign purchases. Whether a net gain or a net loss exists depends on the relative size of yen cash and receivables versus yen payables. Under the monetary/nonmonetary method, the translation adjustment measures the net foreign exchange gain or loss on the foreign operation's cash, receivables, and payables as if those items were actually carried on the books of the parent.

Temporal Method

The basic objective underlying the temporal method of translation is to produce a set of parent currency translated financial statements as if the foreign subsidiary had actually used the parent currency in conducting its operations. For example, land carried on the books of a foreign subsidiary should be translated such that it is reported on the consolidated balance sheet at the amount of parent currency that would have been spent if the parent had sent parent currency to the subsidiary to purchase the land. Assume that a piece of land costs ¥12,000,000 and is acquired at a time when one yen costs NZ$0.016. A New Zealand parent would send NZ$192,000 to its Japanese subsidiary to acquire the land—this is the land's historical cost in parent currency terms.

Consistent with the temporal method's underlying objective, assets and liabilities reported on the foreign operation's balance sheet at historical cost are translated at historical exchange rates to yield an equivalent historical cost in parent currency terms. Conversely, assets and liabilities reported on the foreign operation's balance sheet at a current (or future) value are translated at the current exchange rate to yield an equivalent current value in parent currency terms. (As is true under any translation method, equity accounts are translated at historical exchange rates.) Application of these rules maintains the underlying valuation method (historical cost or current value) used by the foreign subsidiary in accounting for its assets and liabilities.

Cash, receivables, and most liabilities are carried at current or future values under the traditional historical cost model of accounting. These balance sheet accounts are translated at the current exchange rate under the temporal method. By coincidence, the temporal method and monetary/nonmonetary method produce similar results in this situation. The two methods diverge from one another only when nonmonetary assets are carried at current value. Many national accounting standards require inventory to be carried on the balance sheet at the lower of historical cost or current market value. Although a nonmonetary asset, the temporal method requires translation of inventory at the current exchange rate when it is written down to market value. In those jurisdictions in which marketable securities are carried at current market value, such as is required by International Financial Reporting Standards (IFRSs) and U.S. GAAP, marketable securities are also translated at the current exchange rate.

The temporal method generates either a net asset or a net liability balance sheet exposure depending on whether assets carried at current value are greater than or less than liabilities carried at current value. This can be generalized as follows:

Cash + Marketable securities + Receivables + Inventory (when carried at current value) > Liabilities → Net asset exposure

Cash + Marketable securities + Receivables + Inventory (when carried at current value) < Liabilities → Net liability exposure

Because liabilities (current plus long-term) usually are greater than assets translated at current rates, *a net liability exposure generally exists when the temporal method is used.*

Under the temporal method, income statement items are translated at exchange rates that exist when the revenue is generated or the expense is incurred. For most items, an assumption can be made that the revenue or expense is incurred evenly throughout the accounting period and an average-for-the-period exchange rate can be used for translation. Some expenses—such as cost of goods sold, depreciation of fixed assets, and amortization of intangibles—are related to assets carried at historical cost. Because these assets are translated at historical exchange rates, the expenses related to them must be translated at historical exchange rates as well.

The major difference between the translation adjustment resulting from the use of the temporal method and a foreign exchange gain or loss on a foreign currency transaction is that the translation adjustment is not necessarily realized through inflows or outflows of cash. The translation adjustment *could be realized* as a gain or loss only if (1) the foreign subsidiary collects all its receivables in yen cash and then uses its cash to pay off liabilities to the extent possible, and (2) *if there is a net asset exposure* the excess of cash over liabilities is remitted to the parent where it is converted into parent currency, or *if there is a net liability exposure* the parent sends parent currency to its foreign subsidiary which is converted into foreign currency to pay the remaining liabilities.

Current Rate Method

The fourth major method used in translating foreign currency financial statements is the current rate method. The fundamental concept underlying the current rate method is that a parent's entire investment in a foreign operation is exposed to foreign exchange risk and translation of the foreign operation's financial statements should reflect this risk. To measure the net investment's exposure to foreign exchange risk:

- All assets and liabilities of the foreign operation are translated using the *current exchange rate*.
- Equity accounts are translated at *historical exchange rates*.

The balance sheet exposure measured by the current rate method is equal to the foreign operation's net asset position (total assets minus total liabilities).

$$\text{Total assets} > \text{Total liabilities} \rightarrow \text{Net asset exposure}$$

A positive translation adjustment results when the foreign currency appreciates, and a negative translation adjustment results when the foreign currency depreciates (assuming that assets exceed liabilities). The translation adjustment arising when the current rate method is used also is unrealized. It can become a realized gain or loss if the foreign operation is sold (for its book value) and the foreign currency proceeds from the sale are converted into parent currency.

Under the current rate method, revenues and expenses are translated using the exchange rate in effect at the date of accounting recognition. In most cases an assumption can be made that the revenue or expense is incurred evenly throughout the year and an average-for-the-period exchange rate is used. However, when an income item, such as a gain or loss on the sale of an asset, occurs at a specific point in time, the exchange rate at that date should be used for translation. Alternatively, all income statement items may be translated at the current exchange rate.

The example above in which all of Foreignco's assets and liabilities were translated at the current exchange rate demonstrates the current rate method. Foreignco has a net asset exposure that, because of the appreciation in the foreign currency, resulted in a positive translation adjustment. The positive translation adjustment that arises under the current rate method becomes a realized foreign exchange gain if the foreign subsidiary is sold at its foreign currency book value and the foreign currency proceeds are converted into parent currency.

The current rate method and the temporal method are the two methods required to be used under IAS 21, *The Effects of Changes in Foreign Exchange Rates*, and Statement of Financial Accounting Standards (SFAS) 52, *Foreign Currency Translation*. A summary of the appropriate exchange rate for selected financial statement items under these two methods is presented in Exhibit 7.1.

Translation of Retained Earnings

Stockholders' equity items are translated at historical exchange rates under both the temporal and current rate methods. This creates somewhat of a problem in translating retained earnings, which is a composite of many previous transactions: revenues, expenses, gains, losses, and declared dividends occurring over the life of the company. At the end of the first year of operations, foreign currency (FC) retained earnings are translated as follows:

Net income in FC	[Translated per method used to translate income statement items]	= + Net income in PC
− Dividends in FC	× Historical exchange rate	
Ending R/E in FC	when declared	= − Dividends in PC
		Ending R/E in PC

EXHIBIT 7.1
Exchange Rates
Used under the
Current Rate
Method and the
Temporal Method
for Selected
Financial Statement
Items

	Balance Sheet	
	Exchange Rate Used under the Current Rate Method	**Exchange Rate Used under the Temporal Method**
Assets		
Cash and receivables	Current	Current
Marketable securities	Current	Current*
Inventory at market	Current	Current
Inventory at cost	Current	Historical
Prepaid expenses	Current	Historical
Property, plant, and equipment	Current	Historical
Intangible assets	Current	Historical
Liabilities		
Current liabilities	Current	Current
Deferred income	Current	Historical
Long-term debt	Current	Current
Stockholders' Equity		
Capital stock	Historical	Historical
Additional paid-in capital	Historical	Historical
Retained earnings	Historical	Historical
Dividends	Historical	Historical

	Income Statement	
	Exchange Rate Used under the Current Rate Method	**Exchange Rate Used under the Temporal Method**
Revenues	Average	Average
Most expenses	Average	Average
Cost of goods sold	Average	Historical
Depreciation of property, plant, and equipment	Average	Historical
Amortization of intangibles	Average	Historical

*Under IAS 39 and SFAS 105, marketable debt securities classified as hold-to-maturity are carried at cost and therefore are translated at the historical exchange rate under the temporal method.

The ending parent currency retained earnings in Year 1 becomes the beginning parent currency retained earnings for Year 2 and the translated retained earnings in Year 2 (and subsequent years) is then determined as follows:

Beginning R/E in FC (from last year's translation) =   Beginning R/E in PC
+ Net income in FC   [Translated per method
                        used to translate income
                        statement items]   = + Net income in PC

− Dividends in FC   × Historical exchange rate
Ending R/E in FC   when declared   = − Dividends in PC
                                                      Ending R/E in PC

The same approach is used for translating retained earnings under both the current rate and the temporal methods. The only difference is that translation of the current period's net income is done differently under the two methods.

Complicating Aspects of the Temporal Method

Under the temporal method, it is necessary to keep a record of the exchange rates that exist when inventory, prepaid expenses, fixed assets, and intangible assets are acquired because these assets, carried at historical cost, are translated at historical exchange rates. Keeping track of the historical rates for these assets is not necessary under the current rate method. Translating these assets at historical rates makes application of the temporal method more complicated than the current rate method.

Calculation of Cost of Goods Sold (COGS)

Under the *current rate method*, cost of goods sold (COGS) in foreign currency (FC) is simply translated into the parent currency (PC) using the average-for-the-period exchange rate (ER):

$$\text{COGS in FC} \times \text{Average ER} = \text{COGS in PC}$$

Under the *temporal method*, COGS must be decomposed into beginning inventory, purchases, and ending inventory and each component of COGS must then be translated at its appropriate historical rate. For example, if beginning inventory (FIFO basis) in Year 2 was acquired evenly throughout the fourth quarter of Year 1, then the average exchange rate in the fourth quarter of Year 1 will be used to translate beginning inventory. Likewise, the fourth-quarter (4thQ) Year 2 exchange rate will be used to translate Year 2 ending inventory. If purchases were made evenly throughout Year 2, then the average Year 2 exchange rate will be used to translate purchases:

Beginning inventory in FC	× Historical ER (e.g., 4thQ Year 1) =	Beginning inventory in PC
+ Purchases in FC	× Average ER, Year 2 =	+ Purchases in PC
− Ending inventory in FC	× Historical ER (e.g., 4thQ Year 2) =	− Ending Inventory in PC
COGS in FC		COGS in PC

There is no single exchange rate that can be used to directly translate COGS in FC into COGS in PC.

Application of the Lower of Cost and Market Rule

Under the *current rate method*, the ending inventory reported on the foreign currency balance sheet is translated at the current exchange rate regardless of whether it is carried at cost or at a lower market value. Application of the *temporal method* requires the foreign currency cost and foreign currency market value of the inventory to be translated into parent currency at appropriate exchange rates, and the *lower of the parent currency cost or parent currency market value* is reported on the consolidated balance sheet. As a result of this procedure, it is possible for inventory to be carried at cost on the foreign currency balance sheet and at market value on the parent currency consolidated balance sheet, and vice versa.

Fixed Assets, Depreciation, Accumulated Depreciation

Under the *temporal method*, fixed assets acquired at different times must be translated at different (historical) exchange rates. The same is true for depreciation of fixed assets and accumulated depreciation related to fixed assets.

For example, assume that a company purchases a piece of equipment on January 1, Year 1, for FC1,000 when the exchange rate is $1.00 per FC1. Another item of equipment is purchased on January 1, Year 2, for FC4,000 when the exchange rate is $1.20 per FC1. Both pieces of equipment have a five-year useful life. Under the temporal method, the amount at which equipment would be reported on the consolidated balance sheet on December 31, Year 2, when the exchange rate is $1.50 per FC1, would be:

$$
\begin{array}{ll}
\text{FC1,000} \times \$1.00 = \$1,000 \\
\underline{\text{FC4,000}} \times \$1.20 = \underline{\$4,800} \\
\text{FC5,000} \qquad\qquad \$5,800
\end{array}
$$

Depreciation expense for Year 2 under the temporal method would be calculated as follows:

$$
\begin{array}{ll}
\text{FC} \ \ 200 \times \$1.00 = \$ \ \ 200 \\
\underline{\text{FC} \ \ 800} \times \$1.20 = \underline{\$ \ \ 960} \\
\text{FC1,000} \qquad\qquad \$1,160
\end{array}
$$

Accumulated depreciation at December 31, Year 2, under the temporal method would be calculated as follows:

$$
\begin{array}{ll}
\text{FC} \ \ 400 \times \$1.00 = \$ \ \ 400 \\
\underline{\text{FC} \ \ 800} \times \$1.20 = \underline{\$ \ \ 960} \\
\text{FC1,200} \qquad\qquad \$1,360
\end{array}
$$

Similar procedures apply for intangible assets as well.

Under the *current rate method*, equipment would be reported on the December 31, Year 2, balance sheet at FC5,000 × $1.50 = $7,500. Depreciation expense would be translated at the average Year 2 exchange rate of $1.40: FC1,000 × $1.40 = $1,400, and accumulated depreciation would be FC1,200 × $1.50 = $1,800.

In this example, the foreign subsidiary has only two fixed assets that require translation. For subsidiaries that own hundreds and thousands of fixed assets, the temporal method, versus the current rate method, can require substantial additional work.

DISPOSITION OF TRANSLATION ADJUSTMENT

The first issue related to the translation of foreign currency financial statements is selection of the appropriate method. The second issue in financial statement translation relates to *where the resulting translation adjustment should be reported in the consolidated financial statements*. There are two prevailing schools of thought with regard to this issue:

1. *Translation gain or loss in net income.* Under this treatment, the translation adjustment is considered to be a gain or loss analogous to the gains and losses that arise from foreign currency transactions and should be reported in income in the period in which the fluctuation in exchange rate occurs.

The first of two conceptual problems with treating translation adjustments as gains/losses in net income is the gain or loss is unrealized; that is, there is no accompanying cash inflow or outflow. The second problem is the gain or loss may not be consistent with economic reality. For example, the depreciation of a foreign currency may have a *positive* impact on the foreign operation's export sales and income, but the particular translation method used gives rise to a translation *loss*.

2. *Cumulative translation adjustment in stockholders' equity (other comprehensive income)*. The alternative to reporting the translation adjustment as a gain or loss in net income is to include it in stockholders' equity as a component of other comprehensive income. In effect, this treatment defers the gain or loss in stockholders' equity until it is realized in some way. As a balance sheet account, other comprehensive income is not closed at the end of the accounting period and will fluctuate in amount over time.

The two major translation methods and the two possible treatments for the translation adjustment give rise to four possible combinations:

Combination	Translation Method	Disposition of Translation Adjustment
A	Temporal	Gain or loss in net income
B	Temporal	Deferred in stockholders' equity (other comprehensive income)
C	Current rate	Gain or loss in net income
D	Current rate	Deferred in stockholders' equity (other comprehensive income)

U.S. GAAP

Prior to 1975, there were no authoritative rules in the United States as to which translation method to use or where the translation adjustment should be reported in the consolidated financial statements. Different companies used different combinations, creating a lack of comparability across companies. In 1975, to eliminate this noncomparability, the FASB issued SFAS 8, *Accounting for the Translation of Foreign Currency Transactions and Foreign Currency Financial Statements*. SFAS 8 mandated use of the temporal method with translation gains/losses reported in income by all companies for all foreign operations (Combination A).

U.S. multinational companies were strongly opposed to SFAS 8. Specifically, they considered reporting translation gains and losses in income to be inappropriate given that the gains and losses are unrealized. Moreover, because currency fluctuations often reverse themselves in subsequent quarters, artificial volatility in quarterly earnings resulted.

After releasing two exposure drafts proposing new translation rules, the FASB finally issued SFAS 52, *Foreign Currency Translation*, in 1981. This resulted in a complete overhaul of U.S. GAAP with regard to foreign currency translation. SFAS 52 was approved by a narrow four-to-three vote of the FASB, indicating how contentious the issue of foreign currency translation has been.

SFAS 52

Implicit in the *temporal method* is the assumption that foreign subsidiaries of U.S. multinational corporations have very close ties to their parent company and would actually carry out their day-to-day operations and keep their books in the U.S. dollar if they could. To reflect the integrated nature of the foreign subsidiary with its U.S. parent, the translation process should create a set of U.S.-dollar translated financial statements as if the dollar had actually been used by the foreign subsidiary. This is the *U.S.-dollar perspective* to translation that was adopted in SFAS 8.

In SFAS 52, the FASB recognized that, whereas some foreign entities are closely integrated with their parent and do in fact conduct much of their business in U.S. dollars, other foreign entities are relatively self-contained and integrated with the local economy and primarily use a foreign currency in their daily operations. For the first type of entity, the FASB determined that the U.S.-dollar perspective still applies and therefore SFAS 8 rules are still relevant.

For the second relatively independent type of entity, a *local-currency perspective* to translation is applicable. For this type of entity, the FASB determined that a different translation methodology is appropriate; namely, the *current rate method* should be used for translation and translation adjustments should be reported as a separate component in other comprehensive income (Combination D in the preceding table).

Functional Currency

To determine whether a specific foreign operation is (1) integrated with its parent or (2) self-contained and integrated with the local economy, SFAS 52 created the concept of the functional currency. The *functional currency* is the primary currency of the foreign entity's operating environment. It can be either the parent's currency (US$) or a foreign currency (generally the local currency). SFAS 52's functional currency orientation results in the following rule:

Functional Currency	Translation Method	Translation Adjustment
U.S. dollar	Temporal method	Gain (loss) in income
Foreign currency	Current rate method	Separate component of stockholders' equity (accumulated other comprehensive income)

When a foreign operation is sold or otherwise disposed of, the cumulative translation adjustment related to it that has been deferred in a separate component of stockholders' equity is transferred to income as a realized gain or loss.

In addition to introducing the concept of the functional currency, SFAS 52 also introduced some new terminology. The *reporting currency* is the currency in which the entity prepares its financial statements. For U.S.-based corporations, this is the U.S. dollar. If a foreign operation's functional currency is the U.S. dollar, foreign currency balances must be *remeasured* into U.S. dollars using the temporal method with translation adjustments reported as remeasurement gains and losses in income. When a foreign currency is the functional currency, foreign currency balances are *translated* using the current rate method and a translation adjustment is reported on the balance sheet.

The functional currency is essentially a matter of fact. However, SFAS 52 states that for many cases "management's judgment will be required to determine the functional currency in which financial results and relationships are measured with the greatest degree of relevance and reliability" (paragraph 8). SFAS 52 provides a list of indicators to guide parent company management in its determination of a foreign entity's functional currency (see Exhibit 7.2). SFAS 52 provides no guidance

EXHIBIT 7.2
SFAS 52 Indicators
for Determining
the Functional
Currency

	Indication That the Functional Currency Is the:	
Indicator	**Foreign Currency (FC)**	**Parent's Currency**
Cash flow	Primarily in FC and does not affect parent's cash flows	Directly impacts parent's cash flows on a current basis
Sales price	Not affected on short-term basis by changes in exchange rates	Affected on short-term basis by changes in exchange rates
Sales market	Active local sales market	Sales market mostly in parent's country or sales denominated in parent's currency
Expenses	Primarily local costs	Primarily costs for components obtained from parent's country
Financing	Primarily denominated in FC, and FC cash flows are adequate to service obligations	Primarily obtained from parent or denominated in parent currency or FC cash flows not adequate to service obligations
Intercompany transaction	Low volume of intercompany transactions; no extensive interrelationships with parent's operations	High volume of intercompany transactions and extensive interrelationships with parent's operations

as to how these indicators are to be weighted in determining the functional currency. Leaving the decision about identifying the functional currency up to management allows some leeway in this process.

Different companies approach the selection of functional currency in different ways: "For us it was intuitively obvious" versus "It was quite a process. We took the six criteria and developed a matrix. We then considered the dollar amount and the related percentages in developing a point scheme. Each of the separate criteria was given equal weight (in the analytical methods applied)."[2]

Research has shown that the weighting schemes used by U.S. multinationals for determining the functional currency might be biased toward selection of the foreign currency as the functional currency.[3] This would be rational behavior for multinationals given that, when the foreign currency is the functional currency, the translation adjustment is reported on the balance sheet and does not affect net income.

Highly Inflationary Economies

For those foreign entities located in a *highly inflationary economy*, SFAS 52 mandates use of the *temporal method* with *translation gains/losses reported in income*. A country is defined as a highly inflationary economy if its cumulative three-year inflation exceeds 100 percent. With compounding, this equates to an average of approximately 26 percent per year for three years in a row. Countries that have met this definition at some time since SFAS 52 was implemented include Argentina, Brazil, Israel, Mexico, and Turkey. In any given year, a country may or may not be classified as highly inflationary depending on its most recent three-year experience with inflation.

[2] Jerry L. Arnold and William W. Holder, *Impact of Statement 52 on Decisions, Financial Reports and Attitudes* (Morristown, NJ: Financial Executives Research Foundation, 1986), p. 89.

[3] Timothy S. Doupnik and Thomas G. Evans, "Functional Currency as a Strategy to Smooth Income," *Advances in International Accounting,* 1988.

One reason for this rule is to avoid a "disappearing plant problem" that exists when the current rate method is used in a country with high inflation. Remember that under the current rate method, all assets (including fixed assets) are translated at the current exchange rate. To see the problem this creates in a highly inflationary economy, consider the following hypothetical example: The Brazilian subsidiary of a U.S. parent purchased land at the end of 1984 for 10,000,000 cruzeiros (CR$) when the exchange rate was $0.001 per CR$1. Under the *current rate method*, the land would be reported in the parent's consolidated balance sheet at $10,000.

	Historical Cost		Current Exchange Rate		Consolidated Balance Sheet
1984	CR$10,000,000	×	$0.001	=	$10,000

In 1985, Brazil experienced roughly 200 percent inflation. Accordingly, with the forces of purchasing power parity at work, the cruzeiro plummeted against the U.S. dollar to a value of $0.00025 at the end of 1985. Under the current rate method, land now would be reported in the parent's consolidated balance sheet at $2,500 and a negative translation adjustment of $7,500 would result.

	Historical Cost		Current Exchange Rate		Consolidated Balance Sheet
1985	CR$10,000,000	×	$0.00025	=	$2,500

Using the current rate method, land has lost 75 percent of its U.S.-dollar value in one year, and land is not even a depreciable asset!

High rates of inflation continued in Brazil, reaching the high point of roughly 1,800 percent in 1993. As a result of applying the current rate method, the land, which was originally reported on the 1984 consolidated balance sheet at $10,000, was carried on the 1993 balance sheet at less than $1.00.

In the exposure draft leading to SFAS 52, the FASB proposed requiring companies with operations in highly inflationary countries to first *restate* the historical costs for inflation and then *translate* using the current rate method. For example, with 200 percent inflation in 1985, the land would have been written up to CR$40,000,000 and then translated at the current exchange rate of $0.00025. This would have produced a translated amount of $10,000, the same as in 1984.

Companies objected to making inflation adjustments, however, because of a lack of reliable inflation indexes in many countries. The FASB backed off from requiring the restate/translate approach. Instead, SFAS 52 requires that the temporal method be used in highly inflationary countries. In our example, land would be translated at the historical rate of $0.001 at each balance sheet date and carried at $10,000, thus avoiding the disappearing plant problem.

INTERNATIONAL FINANCIAL REPORTING STANDARDS

IAS 21, *The Effects of Changes in Foreign Exchange Rates*, contains guidance for the translation of foreign currency financial statements. To determine the appropriate translation method, IAS 21 originally required foreign subsidiaries to be classified as either (1) foreign operations that are integral to the operations of the reporting enterprise or (2) foreign entities. As part of a comprehensive improvements project, IAS 21 was revised in 2003, adopting the functional currency approach developed years earlier by the FASB. The revised standard defines *functional currency* as the currency of the primary economic environment in which a subsidiary operates. It can be either the same as the currency in which the parent presents its financial statements or it can be a different, foreign currency. IAS 21 provides a list of factors that should be considered in determining the functional currency. While not identical, these factors are generally consistent with the guidance provided in SFAS 52 for determining the functional currency.

IAS 21 requires the financial statements of a foreign subsidiary that has a functional currency different from the reporting currency of the parent to be translated using the current rate method, with the resulting translation adjustment reported as a separate component of stockholders' equity. Upon disposal of a foreign subsidiary, the cumulative translation adjustment related to that particular foreign subsidiary is transferred to income in the same period in which the gain or loss on disposal is recognized. The financial statements of a foreign subsidiary whose functional currency is the same as the parent's reporting currency are translated using the temporal method, with the resulting translation adjustment reported currently as a gain or loss in income. The same combinations are required by SFAS 52.

For foreign subsidiaries whose functional currency is the currency of a hyperinflationary economy, IAS 21 requires the parent first to restate the foreign financial statements for inflation using rules in IAS 29, *Financial Reporting in Hyperinflationary Economies,* and then translate the statements into parent company currency using the current rate method. This approach is substantively different from the requirement of SFAS 52 that requires translation of financial statements of a foreign subsidiary operating in a highly inflationary economy using the temporal method. IAS 29 provides no specific definition for hyperinflation but suggests that a cumulative three-year inflation rate approaching or exceeding 100 percent is evidence that an economy is hyperinflationary. We describe the process of adjusting financial statements for inflation under IAS 29 in Chapter 8.

THE TRANSLATION PROCESS ILLUSTRATED

To provide a basis for demonstrating the translation procedures prescribed by IAS 21 and SFAS 52, assume that Multico (a U.S.-based company) forms a wholly owned subsidiary in Italy (Italco) on December 31, Year 0. On that date, Multico invests $1,000,000 in exchange for all of the subsidiary's capital stock. Given the exchange rate of €1.00 = $1.00, the initial capital investment is €1,000,000, of which €600,000 is immediately invested in inventory and the remainder is held in cash. Thus, Italco begins operations on January 1, Year 1, with stockholders' equity (net assets) of €1,000,000 and net monetary assets of €400,000. Italco's beginning balance sheet on January 1, Year 1, is shown in Exhibit 7.3.

During Year 1, Italco purchased property and equipment, acquired a patent, and made additional purchases of inventory, primarily on account. A five-year loan was negotiated to help finance the purchase of equipment. Sales were made, primarily on account, and expenses were incurred. Income after taxes of €825,000 was generated, with dividends of €325,000 declared on December 1, Year 1. Financial statements for Year 1 (in euros) appear in Exhibit 7.4.

To properly translate the euro financial statements into U.S. dollars, we must gather exchange rates between the euro and the U.S. dollar at various times.

EXHIBIT 7.3

ITALCO				
Beginning Balance Sheet				
January 1, Year 1				
Assets	**€**	**Liabilities and Equity**		**€**
Cash	400,000	Capital stock		1,000,000
Inventory	600,000			1,000,000
	1,000,000			

EXHIBIT 7.4
Italco's Financial
Statements, Year 1

Income Statement
Year 1

	€
Sales.....	8,000,000
Cost of goods sold	6,000,000
Gross profit......	2,000,000
Selling and administrative expenses	500,000
Depreciation expense	200,000
Amortization expense......................................	20,000
Interest expense	180,000
Income before income taxes	1,100,000
Income taxes	275,000
Net income........	825,000

Statement of Retained Earnings
Year 1

	€
Retained earnings, 1/1/Y1.....................................	0
Net income, Y1...	825,000
less: Dividends, 12/1/Y1	(325,000)
Retained earnings, 12/31/Y1..................................	500,000

Balance Sheet
December 31, Year 1

Assets	**€**	**Liabilities and Equity**	**€**
Cash	550,000	Accounts payable	330,000
Accounts receivable	600,000	Total current liabilities ...	330,000
Inventory*	800,000	Long-term debt	2,000,000
Total current assets	1,950,000	Total liabilities	2,330,000
Property and equipment ...	2,000,000	Capital stock	1,000,000
Less: Accumulated		Retained earnings	500,000
depreciation	(200,000)	Total	3,830,000
Patents, net	80,000		
Total assets	3,830,000		

*Inventory is carried at first-in, first-out (FIFO) cost; ending inventory was acquired evenly throughout the month of December.

Relevant exchange rates are as follows:

January 1, Year 1	$1.00
Rate when property and equipment were acquired and long-term debt was incurred, January 15, Year 1	0.98
Rate when patent was acquired, February 1, Year 1	0.97
Average Year 1	0.95
Rate when dividends were declared, December 1, Year 1	0.92
Average for the month of December	0.91
December 31, Year 1	0.90

As can be seen, the euro steadily declined in value against the U.S. dollar during the year.

TRANSLATION OF FINANCIAL STATEMENTS: CURRENT RATE METHOD

The first step in translating foreign currency financial statements is the determination of the functional currency. Assuming that the euro is the functional currency, the income statement and statement of retained earnings would be translated into U.S. dollars using the current rate method, as shown in Exhibit 7.5.

All revenues and expenses are translated at the exchange rate in effect at the date of accounting recognition. The weighted-average exchange rate for Year 1 is used because each revenue and expense in this illustration would have been recognized evenly throughout the year. However, when an income account, such as a gain or loss, occurs at a specific time, the exchange rate as of that date is applied.

EXHIBIT 7.5
Translation of Income Statement and Statement of Retained Earnings: Current Rate Method

Income Statement Year 1			
	€	**Translation Rate***	**US$**
Sales	8,000,000	$0.95 (A)	7,600,000
Cost of goods sold	6,000,000	0.95 (A)	5,700,000
Gross profit	2,000,000		1,900,000
Selling and administrative expenses . . .	500,000	0.95 (A)	475,000
Depreciation expense.	200,000	0.95 (A)	190,000
Amortization expense	20,000	0.95 (A)	19,000
Interest expense.	180,000	0.95 (A)	171,000
Income before income taxes	1,100,000		1,045,000
Income taxes	275,000	0.95 (A)	261,250
Net income	825,000		783,750

Statement of Retained Earnings Year 1			
	€	**Translation Rate***	**US$**
Retained earnings, 1/1/Y1 . . .	0		0
Net income, Year 1	825,000	From income statement	783,750
Less: Dividends, 12/1/Y1	(325,000)	0.92 (H)	(299,000)
Retained earnings, 12/31/Y1 .	500,000		484,750

*Indicates the exchange rate used and whether the rate is the current rate (C), the average rate (A), or a historical rate (H).

Depreciation and amortization expense are also translated at the average rate for the year. These expenses accrue evenly throughout the year even though the journal entry may have been delayed until year-end for convenience.

The translated amount of net income for Year 1 is transferred from the income statement to the statement of retained earnings. Dividends are translated at the exchange rate that exists on the date of declaration.

Translation of the Balance Sheet

Italco's translated balance sheet is shown in Exhibit 7.6. All assets and liabilities are translated at the current exchange rate. Capital stock is translated at the exchange rate that existed when the capital stock was originally issued. Retained earnings at December 31, Year 1, is brought down from the statement of retained earnings. Application of these procedures results in total assets of $3,447,000, and total liabilities and equities of $3,581,750. The balance sheet is brought back into balance by creating a negative translation adjustment of $134,750, which is treated as a decrease in stockholders' equity.

Note that the translation adjustment for Year 1 is a *negative* $134,750 (debit balance). The sign of the translation adjustment (positive or negative) is a function of two factors: (1) the nature of the balance sheet exposure (asset or liability) and (2) the direction of change in the exchange rate (appreciation or depreciation). In this illustration, Italco has a *net asset exposure* (total assets translated at the current exchange rate are greater than total liabilities translated at the current exchange rate), and the euro has *depreciated*, creating a *negative translation adjustment*.

The translation adjustment can be derived as a balancing figure that brings the balance sheet back into balance. The translation adjustment also can be calculated

EXHIBIT 7.6
Translation of Balance Sheet: Current Rate Method

Balance Sheet December 31, Year 1			
Assets	**€**	**Translation Rate***	**US$**
Cash	550,000	$0.90 (C)	495,000
Accounts receivable	600,000	0.90 (C)	540,000
Inventory	800,000	0.90 (C)	720,000
Total current assets	1,950,000		1,755,000
Property and equipment	2,000,000	0.90 (C)	1,800,000
Less: Accumulated depreciation	(200,000)	0.90 (C)	(180,000)
Patents, net	80,000	0.90 (C)	72,000
Total assets	3,830,000		3,447,000
Liabilities and Equity			
Accounts payable	330,000	$0.90 (C)	297,000
Total current liabilities	330,000		297,000
Long-term debt	2,000,000	0.90 (C)	1,800,000
Total liabilities	2,330,000		2,097,000
Capital stock	1,000,000	1.00 (H)	1,000,000
Retained earnings	500,000	from statement of retained earnings	484,750
Cumulative translation adjustment	—	to balance	(134,750)
Total equity	1,500,000		1,350,000
	3,830,000		3,447,000

by considering the impact of exchange rate changes on the beginning balance and subsequent changes in the net asset position. The following steps are applied:

1. The net asset balance of the subsidiary at the beginning of the year is translated at the exchange rate in effect on that date.
2. Individual increases and decreases in the net asset balance during the year are translated at the rates in effect when those increases and decreases occur. Only a few events actually change net assets (e.g., net income, dividends, stock issuance, and the acquisition of treasury stock). Transactions such as the acquisition of equipment or the payment of a liability have no effect on total net assets.
3. The translated beginning net asset balance (*a*) and the translated value of the individual changes (*b*) are then combined to arrive at the relative value of the net assets being held prior to the impact of any exchange rate fluctuations.
4. The ending net asset balance is then translated at the current exchange rate to determine the reported value after all exchange rate changes have occurred.
5. The translated value of the net assets prior to any rate changes (*c*) is compared with the ending translated value (*d*). The difference is the result of exchange rate changes during the period. If (*c*) is greater than (*d*), then a negative (debit) translation adjustment arises. If (*d*) is greater than (*c*), a positive (credit) translation adjustment results.

Computation of Translation Adjustment

According to the process just described, determination of the translation adjustment to be reported for Italco in this example is calculated as follows:

	€				US$
Net asset balance, 1/1/Y1	1,000,000	×	$1.00	=	1,000,000
Change in net assets:					
Net income, Year 1	825,000	×	0.95	=	783,750
Dividends, 12/1/Y1	(325,000)	×	0.92	=	(299,000)
Net asset balance, 12/31/Y1	1,500,000				1,484,750
Net asset balance, 12/31/Y1, at current					
exchange rate	1,500,000	×	0.90	=	1,350,000
Translation adjustment, Year 1(negative). . .					134,750

Since this subsidiary began operations at the beginning of the current year, $134,750 is the amount of cumulative translation adjustment reported on the consolidated balance sheet. The translation adjustment is reported as a separate component of equity only until the foreign operation is sold or liquidated. SFAS 52 stipulates that "in the period in which sale or liquidation occurs, the cumulative translation adjustment related to the particular entity must be removed from equity and reported as part of the gain or loss on the sale of the investment" (paragraph 14).

REMEASUREMENT OF FINANCIAL STATEMENTS: TEMPORAL METHOD

Now assume that a careful examination of the functional currency indicators leads Mulitco's management to conclude that Italco's functional currency is the U.S. dollar. In that case, the euro financial statements will be remeasured into U.S. dollars

EXHIBIT 7.7
Translation of
Balance Sheet:
Temporal Method

	Balance Sheet December 31, Year 1		
Assets	**€**	**Translation Rate***	**US$**
Cash	550,000	$0.90 (C)	495,000
Accounts receivable	600,000	0.90 (C)	540,000
Inventory	800,000	0.91 (H)	728,000
Total current assets	1,950,000		1,763,000
Property and equipment	2,000,000	0.98 (H)	1,960,000
Less: Accumulated depreciation . . .	(200,000)	0.98 (H)	(196,000)
Patents, net	80,000	0.97 (H)	77,600
Total assets	3,830,000		3,604,600
Liabilities and Equity			
Accounts payable	330,000	$0.90 (C)	297,000
Total current liabilities	330,000		297,000
Long-term debt	2,000,000	0.90 (C)	1,800,000
Total liabilities	2,330,000		2,097,000
Capital stock	1,000,000	1.00 (H)	1,000,000
Retained earnings	500,000	to balance	507,600
Total equity	1,500,000		1,507,600
	3,830,000		3,604,600

using the temporal method and the remeasurement gain or loss will be reported in income. To ensure that the remeasurement gain or loss is reported in income, it is easier to remeasure the balance sheet first (as shown in Exhibit 7.7).

According to the procedures outlined in Exhibit 7.1, under the temporal method, cash, receivables, and liabilities are remeasured into U.S. dollars using the current exchange rate of $0.90. Inventory, carried at first-in, first-out (FIFO) cost; property and equipment; patents; and the capital stock account are remeasured at historical rates. These procedures result in total assets of $3,604,600, and liabilities and capital stock of $3,097,000. In order for the balance sheet to balance, retained earnings must be $507,600. The accuracy of this amount is verified below.

Remeasurement of Income Statement

The remeasurement of Italco's income statement and statement of retained earnings is demonstrated in Exhibit 7.8. Revenues and expenses incurred evenly throughout the year (sales, selling and administrative expenses, interest expense, and income taxes) are remeasured at the average exchange rate. Expenses related to assets remeasured at historical exchange rates (depreciation expense and amortization expense) are themselves remeasured at relevant historical rates.

Cost of goods sold is remeasured at historical exchange rates using the following procedure. Beginning inventory was acquired on January 1 and is remeasured at the exchange rate from that date ($1.00). Purchases were made evenly throughout the year and are therefore remeasured at the average rate for the year ($0.95). Ending inventory (at FIFO cost) was purchased evenly throughout the month of December and the average exchange rate for that month ($0.91) is used to remeasure

EXHIBIT 7.8
Translation of
Income Statement
and Statement of
Retained Earnings
Temporal Method

Income Statement Year 1			
	€	Translation Rate*	US$
Sales	8,000,000	$0.95 (A)	7,600,000
Cost of goods sold	6,000,000	calculation (H)	5,762,000
Gross profit	2,000,000		1,838,000
Selling and administrative expenses. . . .	500,000	0.95 (A)	475,000
Depreciation expense	200,000	0.98 (H)	196,000
Amortization expense	20,000	0.97 (H)	19,400
Interest expense	180,000	0.95 (A)	171,000
Income before income taxes	1,100,000		976,600
Income taxes	(275,000)	0.95 (A)	(261,250)
Remeasurement gain	—	to balance	91,250
Net income	825,000		806,600

Statement of Retained Earnings Year 1			
	€	Translation Rate*	US$
Retained earnings, 1/1/Y1	0		0
Net income, Year 1	825,000	From income statement	806,600
Less: Dividends, 12/1/Y1	(325,000)	0.92 (H)	(299,000)
Retained earnings, 12/31/Y1	500,000		507,600

that component of cost of goods sold. These procedures result in cost of goods sold of $5,762,000, calculated as follows:

	€				US$
Beginning inventory	600,000	×	$1.00	=	600,000
Plus: Purchases.	6,200,000	×	$0.95	=	5,890,000
Less: Ending inventory	(800,000)	×	$0.91	=	(728,000)
Cost of goods sold.	6,000,000				5,762,000

The ending balance in retained earnings on the balance sheet and in the statement of retained earnings must reconcile with one another. Given that dividends are remeasured into a U.S.-dollar equivalent of $299,000 and the ending balance in retained earnings on the balance sheet is $507,600, net income must be $806,600.

In order for the amount of income reported in the statement of retained earnings and in the income statement to reconcile with one another, a remeasurement gain of $91,250 is required in the calculation of income. Without this remeasurement gain, the income statement, statement of retained earnings, and balance sheet will not be consistent with one another.

The remeasurement gain can be calculated by considering the impact of exchange rate changes on the subsidiary's balance sheet exposure. Under the temporal method, Italco's balance sheet exposure is defined by its net monetary asset or net monetary liability position. Italco began Year 1 with net monetary assets (cash) of €400,000. During the year, however, expenditures of cash and the incurrence of liabilities caused monetary liabilities (Accounts payable + Long-term debt = €2,330,000) to exceed monetary assets (Cash + Accounts receivable = €1,150,000). A net monetary liability position of €1,180,000 exists at December 31, Year 1. The remeasurement gain is computed by translating the beginning net monetary asset position and subsequent changes in monetary items at appropriate exchange rates and then comparing this with the U.S.-dollar value of net monetary liabilities at year-end based on the current exchange rate.

Computation of Remeasurement Gain

	€	Translation Rate	US$
Net monetary assets, 1/1/Y1	400,000	$1.00	400,000
Increase in monetary items:			
Sales, Year 1	8,000,000	0.95	7,600,000
Decrease in monetary items:			
Purchases of inventory, Year 1	(6,200,000)	0.95	(5,890,000)
Selling and administrative expenses, Year 1	(500,000)	0.95	(475,000)
Payment of interest, Year 1	(180,000)	0.95	(171,000)
Income taxes, Year 1	(275,000)	0.95	(261,250)
Purchase of property and equipment, 1/15/Y1	(2,000,000)	0.98	(1,960,000)
Acquisition of patent, 2/1/Y1	(100,000)	0.97	(97,000)
Dividends, 12/1/Y1	(325,000)	0.92	(299,000)
Net monetary liabilities, 12/31/Y	(1,180,000)		(1,153,250)
Net monetary liabilities, 12/31/Y1, at the current exchange rate	(1,180,000)	0.90	(1,062,000)
Remeasurement gain			(91,250)

If Italco had maintained its net monetary asset position (cash) of €400,000 for the entire year, a remeasurement loss of $40,000 would have resulted. (The euro amount held in cash was worth $400,000 [€400,000 × $1.00] at the beginning of the year and $360,000 [€400,0000 × $0.90] at year-end.) However, the net monetary asset position is not maintained. Indeed, a net monetary liability position arises. The *depreciation* of the foreign currency coupled with an increase in *net monetary liabilities* generates a *remeasurement gain* for the year.

COMPARISON OF THE RESULTS FROM APPLYING THE TWO DIFFERENT METHODS

The use of different translation methods can have a significant impact on Multico's consolidated financial statements. The chart below shows differences for Italco in several key items under the two different translation methods:

Item	Translation Method		
	Current Rate	Temporal	Difference
Net income	$783,750	$806,600	+2.9%
Total assets	$3,447,000	$3,604,600	+4.6%
Total equity	$1,350,000	$1,507,600	+11.7%
Return on equity	58.1%	53.5%	−9.4%

If the temporal method is applied, net income is 2.9 percent greater, total assets are 4.6 percent greater, and total equity is 11.7 percent greater than if the current rate method is applied. Because of the larger amount of equity under the temporal method, return on equity (net income/total equity) is only 53.5 percent as opposed to 58.1 percent using the current rate method.

It should be noted that the temporal method does not always result in larger net income (and a greater amount of equity) than the current rate method. For example, if Italco had maintained its net monetary asset position throughout the year, a remeasurement loss would have been computed under the temporal method, leading to lower income than under the current rate method. Moreover, if the euro had appreciated during Year 1, the current rate method would have resulted in higher net income.

The important point is that selection of translation method can have a significant impact on the amounts reported by a parent company in its consolidated financial statements. Different functional currencies selected by different companies in the same industry could have a significant impact on the comparability of financial statements within that industry.

In addition to differences in amounts reported in the consolidated financial statements, the results of the Italco illustration can be used to demonstrate several conceptual differences between the two translation methods.

Underlying Valuation Method

Using the temporal method, Italco's property and equipment was remeasured as follows:

| Property and equipment . . . . | €2,000,000 | × | $0.98 H | = | $1,960,000 |

By multiplying the historical cost in euros by the historical exchange rate, $1,960,000 represents the U.S.-dollar equivalent historical cost of this asset. It is the amount of U.S. dollars that the parent company would have had to pay to acquire assets having a cost of €2,000,000 when the exchange rate was $0.98 per euro.

Property and equipment was translated under the current rate method as follows:

| Property and equipment . . . . | €2,000,000 | × | $0.90 C | = | $1,800,000 |

The $1,800,000 amount is not readily interpretable. It does not represent the U.S.-dollar equivalent historical cost of the asset; that amount is $1,960,000. It also does not represent the U.S.-dollar equivalent current cost of the asset, because €2,000,000 is not the current cost of the asset in Italy. The $1,800,000 amount is simply the product of multiplying two numbers together!

Underlying Relationships

The following table reports the values for selected financial ratios calculated from the original foreign currency financial statements and from the U.S.-dollar translated statements using the two different translation methods.

		US$	
Ratio	€	Current Rate	Temporal
Current ratio (Current assets/Current liabilities)	5.91	5.91	5.94
Debt/equity ratio (Total liabilities/Total equities)	1.55	1.55	1.39
Gross profit ratio (Gross profit/Sales)	25.0%	25.0%	24.2%
Return on equity (Net income/Total equity)	55.0%	58.1%	53.5%

The temporal method distorts all of the ratios as measured in the foreign currency. The subsidiary appears to be more liquid, less highly leveraged, and less profitable than it does in euro terms.

The current rate method maintains the first three ratios, but return on equity is distorted. This distortion occurs because income was translated at the average-for-the-period exchange rate whereas total equity was translated at the current exchange rate. In fact, any ratio that combines balance sheet and income statement figures, such as turnover ratios, will be distorted because of the use of the average rate for income and the current rate for assets and liabilities.

Conceptually, when the current rate method is employed, income statement items can be translated either at exchange rates in effect when sales are made and expenses are incurred (approximated by the average rate) or at the current exchange rate at the balance sheet date. IAS 21 and SFAS 52 require the average exchange rate to be used. In this illustration, if revenues and expenses had been translated at the current exchange rate, net income would have been $742,500 (€825,000 × $0.90), and the return on equity would have been 55.0 percent ($742,500/ $1,350,000), exactly the amount reflected in the euro financial statements. In several countries in which the current rate method is used, companies are allowed to choose between the average exchange rate and the current exchange rate in translating income. This is true, for example, in France and the United Kingdom.

HEDGING BALANCE SHEET EXPOSURE

When a foreign operation is highly integrated with the operations of its parent or is located in a highly inflationary economy, remeasurement gains and losses will be reported in the consolidated income statement. Management of multinational companies might wish to avoid reporting remeasurement losses in income because of the perceived negative impact this has on the company's stock price or the adverse effect on incentive compensation. Likewise, when the foreign operation is independent of its parent, management might wish to avoid reporting negative translation adjustments in stockholders' equity because of the adverse impact on ratios such as the debt to equity ratio.

Translation adjustments and remeasurement gains/losses are a function of two factors: (1) changes in the exchange rate and (2) balance sheet exposure. While individual companies have no influence over exchange rates, there are several techniques that parent companies can use to hedge the balance sheet exposures of their foreign operations. Each of these techniques involves creating an equilibrium between foreign currency asset and foreign currency liability balances that are translated at current exchange rates.

Balance sheet exposure can be hedged through the use of a derivative financial instrument such as a forward contract or foreign currency option, or through the use of a nonderivative hedging instrument such as a foreign currency borrowing. To illustrate, assume that Italco's functional currency is the euro; this creates a *net asset balance sheet exposure*. Multico believes that the euro will lose value over the course of the next year, thereby generating a negative translation adjustment that will reduce consolidated stockholders' equity. Multico can hedge this balance sheet exposure by borrowing euros for a period of time, thus creating an offsetting euro liability exposure. As the euro depreciates, a foreign exchange gain will arise on the euro liability that offsets the negative translation adjustment arising from the translation of Italco's financial statements.

EXHIBIT 7.9

INTERNATIONAL BUSINESS MACHINES CORPORATION
Annual Report
2004

Excerpt from Note L. Derivatives and Hedging Transactions

Long-Term Investments in Foreign Subsidiaries (Net Investment)

A significant portion of the company's foreign currency denominated debt portfolio is designated as a hedge of net investment to reduce the volatility in stockholders' equity caused by changes in foreign currency exchange rates in the functional currency of major foreign subsidiaries with respect to the U.S. dollar. The company also uses currency swaps and foreign exchange forward contracts for this risk management purpose. The currency effects of these hedges (approximately $156 million in 2004 and approximately $200 million in 2003, net of tax) are reflected as a loss in the Accumulated gains and (losses) not affecting retained earnings section of the Consolidated Statement of Stockholders' Equity, thereby offsetting a portion of the translation of the applicable foreign subsidiaries' net assets.

As an alternative to the euro borrowing, Multico might have acquired a euro call option to hedge its balance sheet exposure. As the euro depreciates, the fair value of the call option should increase resulting in a gain. SFAS 133 provides that the gain or loss on a hedging instrument that is designated and effective as a *hedge of the net investment in a foreign operation* should be reported in the same manner as the translation adjustment being hedged. Thus, the foreign exchange gain on the euro borrowing or the gain on the foreign currency option would be included in other comprehensive income along with the negative translation adjustment arising from the translation of Italco's financial statements.[4] In the event that the gain on the hedging instrument is greater than the translation adjustment being hedged, the excess is taken to net income. Exhibit 7.9 contains disclosures made by International Business Machines Corporation (IBM) in its 2004 annual report with respect to hedging net investments in foreign operations.

The paradox of hedging a balance sheet exposure is that in the process of avoiding an unrealized translation adjustment, realized foreign exchange gains and losses can result. Consider Multico's foreign currency borrowing to hedge a euro exposure. At initiation of the loan, Multico will convert the borrowed euros into U.S. dollars at the spot exchange rate. When the liability matures, Multico will purchase euros at the spot rate prevailing at that date to repay the loan. The change in exchange rate over the life of the loan will generate a realized gain or loss. If the euro depreciates as expected, the result will be a realized foreign exchange gain that will offset the negative translation adjustment in other comprehensive income. Although the net effect on other comprehensive income is zero, there is a net increase in cash as a result of the hedge. If the euro unexpectedly appreciates, a realized foreign exchange loss will occur. This will be offset by a positive translation adjustment in other comprehensive income, but a net decrease in cash will arise. While a hedge of a net investment in a foreign operation eliminates the possibility of reporting a negative translation adjustment in other comprehensive income, the result can be realized gains and losses that affect cash flow.

Exhibit 7.10 presents an excerpt from the notes to the consolidated financial statements in Nokia Corporation's 2004 annual report filed on Form 20-F. Nokia prepares its financial statements in accordance with IFRSs, and the excerpt

---

[4] As an exception to the general rule that foreign currency gains and losses are taken directly to income, IAS 21 likewise stipulates that gains and losses on foreign currency borrowings used to hedge the net investment in a foreign operation should be reflected in equity.

EXHIBIT 7.10

NOKIA CORPORATION
Form 20-F
2004

Excerpt from Note 1. Accounting Principles

Foreign currency hedging of net investments

The Group also applies hedge accounting for its foreign currency hedging on net investments. Qualifying hedges are those properly documented hedges of the foreign exchange rate risk of foreign currency–denominated net investments that meet the requirements set out in IAS 39. The hedge must be effective both prospectively and retrospectively.

The Group claims hedge accounting in respect of forward foreign exchange contracts, foreign currency–denominated loans, and options, or option strategies, which have zero net premium or a net premium paid, and where the terms of the bought and sold options within a collar or zero premium structure are the same.

For qualifying foreign exchange forwards the change in fair value that reflects the change in spot exchange rates is deferred in shareholders' equity. The change in fair value that reflects the change in forward exchange rates less the change in spot exchange rates is recognized in the profit and loss account. For qualifying foreign exchange options the change in intrinsic value its deferred in shareholders' equity. Changes in the time value are at all times taken directly to the profit and loss account. If a foreign currency–denominated loan is used as a hedge, all foreign exchange gains and losses arising from the transaction are recognized in shareholders' equity.

Accumulated fair value changes from qualifying hedges are released from shareholders' equity into the profit and loss account only if the legal entity in the given country is sold or liquidated.

---

describes Nokia's compliance with IAS 39 with respect to hedging of net investments. Nokia uses forward contracts, options, and foreign currency borrowings to hedge its balance sheet exposures. Hedge accounting is applied when hedges are properly documented and effective. Changes in fair value of forward contracts attributable to changes in the spot rate, changes in the intrinsic value of options, and foreign exchange gains and losses on foreign currency borrowings are deferred in stockholders' equity until the subsidiary whose balance sheet exposure is being hedged is sold or liquidated. This also is consistent with the guidance provided under U.S. GAAP.

DISCLOSURES RELATED TO TRANSLATION

SFAS 52 (paragraph 31) requires an analysis of the change in the cumulative translation adjustment account to be presented in the financial statements or notes thereto. Many companies comply with this requirement by including a column titled "Accumulated Other Comprehensive Income (AOCI)" in their statement of stockholders' equity. Exhibit 7.11 demonstrates this method of disclosure as used by Hewlett-Packard (HP). In each year from 2002 to 2004, Hewlett-Packard has four items that affect AOCI, including a cumulative translation adjustment. The company does not disclose the balance in cumulative translation adjustment at the end of each year, just the change in the account for the year. A positive translation adjustment (credit balance) was added to AOCI each year—$7 million in 2002, $2 million in 2003, and $21 million in 2004. The relatively small amount of translation adjustment in each of these years is at least partially attributable to the fact that "HP uses forward contracts designated as net investment hedges to hedge net investments in certain foreign subsidiaries whose functional currency is the local

EXHIBIT 7.11

HEWLETT-PACKARD COMPANY
Form 10-K
2004

Consolidated Statements of Stockholders' Equity

In millions, except number of shares in thousands

	Common Stock		Additional Paid-in Capital	Retained Earnings	Accumulated Other Comprehensive Income (Loss)	Total
	Number of Shares	Par Value				
Balance October 31, 2001	1,938,828	$19	$200	$13,693	$41	$13,953
Net loss				(903)		(903)
Net unrealized loss on available-for-sale securities					(9)	(9)
Net unrealized loss on cash flow hedges					(61)	(61)
Minimum pension liability, net of taxes					(379)	(379)
Cumulative translation adjustment					7	7
Comprehensive loss						(1,345)
Issuance of common stock and options assumed in connection with business Acquisitions	1,114,673	11	24,706			24,717
Issuance of common stock in connection with employee stock plans and other	29,855		388			388
Repurchases of common stock	(39,623)		(655)	(16)		(671)
Tax benefit from employee stock plans			21			21
Dividends				(801)		(801)
Balance October 31, 2002	3,043,733	$30	$24,660	$11,973	($401)	$36,262
Net earnings				2,539		2,539
Net unrealized loss on available-for-sale securities					33	33
Net unrealized loss on cash flow hedges					(48)	(48)
Minimum pension liability, net of taxes					211	211
Cumulative translation adjustment					2	2
Comprehensive income						2,737
Issuance of common stock in connection with employee stock plans and other	38,808		451			451
Repurchases of common stock	(39,780)		(548)	(203)		(751)
Tax benefit from employee stock plans			24			24
Dividends				(977)		(977)
Balance October 31, 2003	3,042,761	$30	$24,587	$13,332	($203)	$37,746
Net earnings				3,497		3,497
Net unrealized loss on available-for-sale securities					(20)	(20)
Net unrealized loss on cash flow hedges					(28)	(28)
Minimum pension liability, net of taxes					(13)	(13)
Cumulative translation adjustment					21	21
Comprehensive income						3,457
Assumption of stock options in connection with business acquisitions			15			15
Issuance of common stock in connection						0
with employee stock plans and other	40,467		592			592
Repurchases of common stock	(172,468)	(1)	(3,100)	(208)		(3,309)
Tax benefit from employee stock plans			35			(937)
Dividends				(972)		
Balance October 31, 2004	2,910,760	$29	$22,129	$15,649	($243)	$37,564

EXHIBIT 7.12

THE GILLETTE COMPANY AND SUBSIDIARY COMPANIES
Annual Report
2003

Notes to Consolidated Financial Statements

Note 4. Accumulated Other Comprehensive Loss

An analysis of accumulated other comprehensive loss follows.

(millions)	Foreign Currency Translation	Pension Adjustment	Cash Flow Hedges	Accumulated Other Comprehensive Loss
Balance at December 31, 2000	$(1,280)	$ (34)	$ —	$(1,314)
Change in period	(48)	(53)	(13)	(114)
Income tax benefit (expense)	(45)	31	5	(9)
Balance at December 31, 2001	$(1,373)	$ (56)	$ (8)	$(1,437)
Change in period	196	(183)	5	18
Income tax benefit (expense)	(155)	53	(2)	(104)
Balance at December 31, 2002	$(1,332)	$(186)	$ (5)	$(1,523)
Change in period	409	(10)	12	411
Income tax benefit (expense)	25	3	(4)	24
Balance at December 31, 2002	$ (898)	$(193)	$ 3	$(1,088)

Net exchange gains or losses resulting from the translation of assets and liabilities of foreign subsidiaries, except those in highly inflationary economies, are accumulated in a separate section of stockholders' equity. Also included are the effects of exchange rate changes on intercompany balances of a long-term investment nature and transactions designated as hedges of net foreign investments. The gains of $434 million in accumulated foreign currency translation in 2003 were due primarily to the strength of the Euro, but also in part to the weakening of the U.S. dollar against other currencies, as well as the recognition of deferred taxes on the foreign currency translation adjustment for those non-U.S. subsidiaries that are included in the Company's U.S. tax return. Gains in 2002 of $41 million were primarily due to strengthening European currencies that were partially offset by weakening Latin American currencies. Losses in 2001 were $93 million, primarily from currency devaluation in Argentina and Brazil.

Included in Other charges (income)—net in the Consolidated Statement of Income are a net exchange gain of $14 million in 2003, a net exchange gain of $16 million in 2002, and a net exchange loss of $3 million in 2001 for the foreign currency effects of transactions (including translation of hyperinflationary entities) in those years.

---

currency. As of October 31, 2004, HP had a total notional amount of $750 million in forward contracts."[5]

Other companies provide separate disclosures related to the cumulative translation adjustment in the notes to financial statements. An example of this type of disclosure is found in Exhibit 7.12 for the Gillette Company.

Gillette reports an "Accumulated other comprehensive loss" as a separate line item in the stockholders' equity section of the balance sheet. The December 31, 2003, balance in this line item was negative $1,088 million. The balance in the "Foreign currency translation" component of this item was negative $898 million. According to the explanation provided in Exhibit 7.12, this amount includes a positive translation adjustment (including related tax benefit) of $434 million in 2003

---

[5] Hewlett-Packard Company, 2004 Form 10-K, Note 8: Financial Instruments, p. 115.

(Gillette refers to this as a "gain"), a net positive translation adjustment of $41 million in 2002, and a negative translation adjustment of $93 million in 2001. The sign of these translation adjustments indicates that, in aggregate, the foreign currencies in which Gillette has operations strengthened against the U.S. dollar in both 2002 and 2003, but decreased in value in 2001.

Gillette's "Foreign currency translation" component of "Accumulated other comprehensive loss" includes not only "net exchange gains or losses resulting from the translation of assets and liabilities of foreign subsidiaries" but also gains and losses on "intercompany balances of a long-term investment nature" (as mentioned in Chapter 6) and on "transactions designated as hedges of net foreign investments." Gillette includes gains and losses from foreign currency transactions and the remeasurement of foreign currency financial statements in an "Other charges (income)—net" line item on the income statement. These gains and losses were relatively small in the period 2001–2003.

Although there is no specific requirement to do so, many companies include a description of their translation procedures in their "summary of significant accounting policies" in the notes to the financial statements. The following excerpt from IBM's 2004 annual report illustrates this type of disclosure:

Translation of Non-U.S. Currency Amounts

Assets and liabilities of non-U.S. subsidiaries that operate in a local currency environment are translated to U.S. dollars at year-end exchange rates. Income and expense items are translated at weighted-average rates of exchange prevailing during the year. Translation adjustments are recorded in Accumulated gains and (losses) not affecting retained earnings within Stockholders' equity.

Inventories, Plant, rental machines and other property—net, and other nonmonetary assets and liabilities of non-U.S. subsidiaries and branches that operate in U.S. dollars, or whose economic environment is highly inflationary, are translated at approximate exchange rates prevailing when the company acquired the assets or liabilities. All other assets and liabilities are translated at year-end exchange rates. Cost of sales and depreciation are translated at historical exchange rates. All other income and expense items are translated at the weighted-average rates of exchange prevailing during the year. Gains and losses that result from translation are included in net income.[6]

TRANSLATION IN OTHER COUNTRIES

IAS 21 and SFAS 52 are generally consistent with respect to the translation of foreign currency financial statements. Both standards use the functional currency approach to determine the appropriate translation method and specifically indicate whether or not the translation adjustments should be reported in net income. Except for subsidiaries located in highly inflationary environments, there are no substantive differences in the foreign currency translation methods followed by companies in the United States and companies located in the European Union, Australia, and other countries using IFRSs. Some countries either have no rules with respect to translation or follow procedures that differ from the general

---

[6] IBM Corporation, 2004 annual report, Significant Accounting Policies, p. 53.

approach of IAS 21 and SFAS 52. Translation rules followed in selected countries are summarized in this section.

Canada: Translation rules in Canada are very similar to those in the United States. The major difference is that, when the temporal method is used, the translation adjustment related to long-term monetary items may be deferred and amortized to income over the life of the item.

Mexico: No regulations pertain to the translation of foreign currency financial statements. Many companies follow the U.S. rule, SFAS 52. Where the U.S. rule is not followed, practice varies considerably.

Brazil: Firms use the current rate method and recognize translation gains and losses in the income statement.

Japan: Japanese translation rules are much different from those in IAS 21 or SFAS 52. Assets carried at historical cost, noncurrent liabilities, and equity accounts must be translated at historical rates. Assets carried at current value and current liabilities are translated at current rates. Revenues and expenses are translated at average rates except for expenses related to assets carried at historical cost, which are translated at historical rates. Cumulative translation adjustments are reported as assets or liabilities in the consolidated balance sheet, depending on whether they have a debit or credit balance. Actual compliance with these rules, however, is limited.

Korea: Korean firms use the current rate method only to translate the financial statements of foreign subsidiaries. Average exchange rates are used to translate income.

Summary

1. The two major issues related to the translation of foreign currency financial statements are (*a*) which method should be used, and (*b*) where the resulting translation adjustment should be reported in the consolidated financial statements.

2. Translation methods differ on the basis of which accounts are translated at the current exchange rate and which are translated at historical rates. Accounts translated at the current exchange rate are exposed to translation adjustment. Different translation methods give rise to different concepts of balance sheet exposure and translation adjustments of differing sign and magnitude.

3. Under the current rate method, all assets and liabilities are translated at the current exchange rate, giving rise to a net asset balance sheet exposure. Appreciation in the foreign currency will result in a positive translation adjustment. Depreciation in the foreign currency will result in a negative translation adjustment. By translating assets carried at historical cost at the current exchange rate, the current rate method maintains relationships that exist among account balances in the foreign currency financial statements but distorts the underlying valuation method used by the foreign operation.

4. Under the temporal method, assets carried at current or future value (cash, marketable securities, receivables) and liabilities are translated (remeasured) at the current exchange rate. Assets carried at historical cost and stockholders' equity are translated (remeasured) at historical exchange rates. When liabilities are greater than the sum of cash, marketable securities, and receivables, a net liability balance sheet exposure exists. Appreciation in the foreign currency will result in a negative translation adjustment (remeasurement loss).

Depreciation in the foreign currency will result in a positive translation adjustment (remeasurement gain). By translating (remeasuring) assets carried at historical cost at historical exchange rates, the temporal method maintains the underlying valuation method used by the foreign operation but distorts relationships that exist among account balances in the foreign currency financial statements.

5. The appropriate combination of translation method and disposition of translation adjustment is determined under both IAS 21 and SFAS 52 by identifying the functional currency of a foreign operation. The financial statements of foreign operations whose functional currency is different from the parent's reporting currency are translated using the current rate method, with the translation adjustment included in stockholders' equity. The financial statements of foreign operations whose functional currency is the same as the parent's reporting currency are translated using the temporal method, with the resulting translation gain or loss reported currently in net income.

6. The only substantive difference in translation rules between IAS 21 and SFAS 52 relates to foreign operations that report in the currency of a hyperinflationary economy. IAS 21 requires the parent first to restate the foreign financial statements for inflation using rules in IAS 29 and then to translate the statements into parent-company currency using the current rate method. SFAS 52 requires the financial statements of foreign operations that report in the currency of a highly inflationary economy to be translated using the temporal method, as if the U.S. dollar were the functional currency. A country is considered highly inflationary if its cumulative three-year inflation rate exceeds 100 percent.

7. Some companies hedge their balance sheet exposures to avoid reporting remeasurement losses in income and/or negative translation adjustments in stockholder's equity. Foreign exchange gains and losses on foreign currency borrowings or foreign currency derivatives employed to hedge translation-based exposure (under the current rate method) are treated as part of the cumulative translation adjustment in stockholders' equity. Foreign exchange gains and losses on balance sheet hedges used to hedge remeasurement-based exposure (under the temporal method) are offset against remeasurement gain and losses on the income statement.

Questions

1. What are the two major conceptual issues that must be resolved in translating foreign currency financial statements?

2. What factors create a balance sheet (or translation) exposure to foreign exchange risk? How does balance sheet exposure compare with transaction exposure?

3. What is the concept underlying the current rate method of translation? What is the concept underlying the temporal method of translation? How does balance sheet exposure differ under these two methods?

4. What are the major procedural differences in applying the current rate and temporal methods of translation?

5. How does a parent company determine the appropriate method for translating the financial statements of a foreign subsidiary?

6. What are the major differences between IAS 21 and SFAS 52?

7. What does the term *functional currency* mean? How is the functional currency determined?

8. Which translation method does SFAS 52 require for operations in highly inflationary countries? What is the rationale for mandating use of this method?

9. Why might a company want to hedge its balance sheet exposure? What is the paradox associated with hedging balance sheet exposure?

10. How are gains and losses on foreign currency borrowings used to hedge the net investment in a foreign subsidiary reported in the consolidated financial statements?

Exercises and Problems

1. Which of the following items is normally translated the same way under both current rate and temporal methods of translation?
   a. Inventory
   b. Equipment
   c. Sales revenue
   d. Depreciation expense

2. In translating the financial statements of a foreign subsidiary into the parent's reporting currency under the current rate method, which of the following statements is true?
   a. Expenses are translated using a combination of current and historical exchange rates.
   b. Intangible assets are translated at the historical exchange rates in effect on the date the assets are purchased.
   c. The translation adjustment is a function of the foreign subsidiary's net assets
   d. The translation adjustment is a function of the relative amount of monetary assets and monetary liabilities held by the foreign subsidiary.

3. A foreign subsidiary of Wampoa Ltd. has one asset (inventory) and no liabilities. The subsidiary operates with a significant degree of autonomy from Wampoa and primarily uses the local currency (the won) in carrying out its transactions. Since the date the inventory was acquired, the won has decreased in value in relation to Wampoa's reporting currency. In translating the foreign subsidiary's peso financial statements into the parent's reporting currency, which of the following is true?
   a. A translation gain must be reported in net income.
   b. A positive translation adjustment must be reported in stockholders' equity.
   c. A negative translation adjustment must be reported in stockholders' equity.
   d. A translation loss must be reported in net income.

4. Which of the following best explains how a translation loss arises when the temporal method of translation is used to translate the foreign currency financial statements of a foreign subsidiary?
   a. The foreign subsidiary has more monetary assets than monetary liabilities, and the foreign currency appreciates in value.
   b. The foreign subsidiary has more monetary liabilities than monetary assets, and the foreign currency depreciates in value.
   c. The foreign subsidiary has more monetary assets than monetary liabilities, and the foreign currency depreciates in value.
   d. The foreign subsidiary has more total assets than total liabilities, and the foreign currency appreciates in value.

5. Which method of translation maintains, in the translated financial statements, the underlying valuation methods used in the foreign currency financial statements?
   a. Current rate method; income statement translated at average exchange rate for the year.
   b. Current rate method; income statement translated at exchange rate at the balance sheet date.
   c. Temporal method.
   d. Monetary/nonmonetary method.

6. In accordance with U.S. generally accepted accounting principles (GAAP), which translation combination would be appropriate for a foreign operation whose functional currency is the U.S. dollar?

	Method	Treatment of Translation Adjustment
a.	Temporal	Separate component of stockholders' equity
b.	Temporal	Gain or loss in income statement
c.	Current rate	Separate component of stockholders' equity
d.	Current rate	Gain or loss in income statement

7. The functional currency of Garland Inc.'s Japanese subsidiary is the Japanese yen. Garland borrowed Japanese yen as a partial hedge of its investment in the subsidiary. How should the transaction gain on the foreign currency borrowing be reported in Garland's consolidated financial statements?
   a. The transaction gain is reported as an adjustment to interest expense in the income statement.
   b. The transaction gain is reported as an extraordinary item in the income statement.
   c. The transaction gain is offset against the negative translation adjustment related to the Japanese subsidiary in the stockholders' equity section of the balance sheet.
   d. The transaction gain is offset against the negative translation adjustment related to the Japanese subsidiary on the income statement.

8. Selected balance sheet accounts of a foreign subsidiary of the Pacter Company have been translated into parent currency (₣) as follows:

	Translated at	
	Current Rates	**Historical Rates**
Accounts receivable	₣100,000	₣120,000
Marketable securities, at cost	200,000	240,000
Prepaid insurance	120,000	130,000
Goodwill	250,000	300,000
	₣670,000	₣790,000

Required:

a. Assuming that the foreign subsidiary is determined to have the foreign currency as its functional currency in accordance with IAS 21, determine the total amount that should be included in Pacter's consolidated balance sheet for the assets listed in accordance with International Financial Reporting Standards (IFRSs).

b. Assuming that the foreign subsidiary is determined to have Pacter's reporting currency as its functional currency in accordance with IAS 21, determine the total amount that should be included in Pacter's consolidated balance sheet for the assets listed in accordance with IFRSs.

9. The Year 1 financial statements of the Brazilian subsidiary of Artemis Corporation (a Canadian company) revealed the following:

	Brazilian Reals (BRL)
Beginning inventory	100,000
Purchases.	500,000
Ending inventory	150,000
Cost of goods sold	450,000

Canadian dollar (C$) exchange rates for 1 BRL as follows:

January 1, Year 1	C$0.45
Average, Year 1	0.42
December 31, Year 1	0.38

The beginning inventory was acquired in the last quarter of the previous year when the exchange rate was C$0.50 = BRL 1; ending inventory was acquired in the last quarter of the current year when the exchange rate was C$0.40 = BRL 1.

Required:
a. Assuming that the current rate method is the appropriate method of translation, determine the amounts at which the Brazilian subsidiary's ending inventory and cost of goods sold should be included in Artemis's Year 1 consolidated financial statements.
b. Assuming that the temporal method is the appropriate method of translation, determine the amounts at which the Brazilian subsidiary's ending inventory and cost of goods sold should be included in Artemis's Year 1 consolidated financial statements.

10. Simga Company's Turkish subsidiary reported the following amounts in Turkish lire (TL) on its December 31, Year 4, balance sheet:

Equipment	TL 100,000,000,000
Accumulated depreciation (straight-line)	32,000,000,000

Additional information related to the equipment is as follows:

Date	Amount Purchased	Useful Life	US$/TL Exchange Rate
1/1/Y1	TL 60,000,000,000	10 years	$0.0000070 = TL 1
1/1/Y3	TL 40,000,000,000	10 years	$0.0000020 = TL 1

U.S.-dollar exchange rates for the Turkish lira for Year 4 are as follows:

January 1, Year 4	$0.0000010
December 31, Year 4	0.0000006

Required:

a. Turkey is a highly inflationary economy. Determine the amounts at which the Turkish subsidiary's equipment and accumulated depreciation should be reported on Simga Company's December 31, Year 4, consolidated balance sheet in accordance with U.S. GAAP. Determine the net book value for equipment.

b. Now assume that Turkey is not a highly inflationary economy and that the Turkish subsidiary primarily uses Turkish lire in conducting its operations. Determine the amounts at which the Turkish subsidiary's equipment and accumulated depreciation should be reported on Simga Company's December 31, Year 4, consolidated balance sheet in accordance with U.S. GAAP. Determine the net book value for equipment.

11. Alliance Corporation (an Australian company) invests 1,000,000 marks in a foreign subsidiary on January 1, Year 1. The subsidiary commences operations on that date, and generates net income of 200,000 marks during its first year of operations. No dividends are sent to the parent this year. Relevant exchange rates between Alliance's reporting currency (A$) and the mark are as follows:

January 1, Year 1	A$0.15
Average, Year 1	0.17
December 31, 1997	0.21

Required:

Determine the amount of translation adjustment that Alliance will report on its December 31, Year 1, balance sheet.

12. Zesto Company (a U.S. company) establishes a subsidiary in Mexico on January 1, Year 1. The subsidiary begins the year with 1,000,000 Mexican pesos (Mex$) in cash and no other assets or liabilities. It immediately uses Mex$600,000 to acquire equipment. Inventory costing Mex$300,000 is acquired evenly throughout the year and sold for Mex$500,000 cash. A dividend of Mex$100,000 is paid to the parent on October 1, Year 1. Depreciation on the equipment for the year is Mex$60,000. Currency exchange rates for Year 1 are as follows:

January 1	$0.090
October 1	0.080
December 31	0.078
Average for the year	0.085

Required:

Determine the amount of remeasurement loss under the temporal method to be recognized in the Year 1 consolidated income statement.

13. Alexander Corporation (a U.S.-based company) acquired 100 percent of a Swiss company for 8.2 million Swiss francs on December 20, Year 1. At the date

of acquisition, the exchange rate was $0.70 per franc. The acquisition price is attributable to the following assets and liabilities denominated in Swiss francs:

Cash.	1,000,000
Inventory	2,000,000
Fixed assets.	7,000,000
Notes payable.	(1,800,000)

Alexander Corporation prepares consolidated financial statements on December 31, Year 1. By that date, the Swiss franc appreciated to $0.75. Because of the year-end holidays, no transactions took place between the date of acquisition and the end of the year.

Required:
a. Determine the translation adjustment to be reported on Alexander's December 31, Year 1, consolidated balance sheet assuming that the Swiss franc is the Swiss subsidiary's functional currency? What is the economic relevance of this translation adjustment?
b. Determine the remeasurement gain or loss to be reported in Alexander's Year 1 consolidated income assuming that the U.S. dollar is the functional currency? What is the economic relevance of this remeasurement gain or loss?

14. Gramado Company was created as a wholly owned subsidiary of Porto Alegre Corporation on January 1, Year 1. On that date, Porto Alegre invested $42,000 in Gramado's capital stock. Given the exchange on that date of $0.84 per cruzeiro, the initial investment of $42,000 was converted into 50,000 cruzeiros (Cz). Other than the capital investment on January 1, there were no transactions involving stockholders' equity in Year 1. Gramado's cruzeiro-denominated financial statements for Year 2 are as follows:

Income Statement
Year 2

	Cz
Sales.	540,000
Cost of goods sold	(310,000)
Gross profit	230,000
Operating expenses	(108,000)
Income before tax.	122,000
Income taxes	(40,000)
Net income.	82,000

Statement of Retained Earnings
Year 2

	Cz
Retained earnings, 1/1/Y2	154,000
Net income	82,000
Dividends (paid on 12/1/Y2).	(20,000)
Retained earnings, 12/31/Y2	216,000

Balance Sheet
December 31, Year 2

	Cz
Cash	50,000
Receivables	100,000
Inventory.	72,000
Plant and equipment (net)	300,000
Less: accumulated depreciation	(70,000)
Total assets	452,000
Liabilities	186,000
Capital stock	50,000
Retained earnings, 12/31/Y2	216,000
Total liabilities and stockholders' equity	452,000

The cruzeiro is the primary currency that Gramado uses in its day-to-day operations. The cruzeiro has steadily fallen in value against the dollar since Porto Alegre made the investment in Gramado on January 1, Year 1. Relevant exchange rates for the cruzeiro for Years 1 and 2 are as follows:

January 1, Year 1.	$0.84
Average for Year 1.	0.80
December 31, Year 1.	0.75
Average for Year 2.	0.72
December 1, Year 2.	0.71
December 31, Year 2.	0.70

Required:

a. Translate Gramado Company's Year 2 financial statements into dollars.

b. Compute the translation adjustment for Year 1 and for Year 2 and reconcile these amounts to the cumulative translation adjustment reported on the translated balance sheet at December 31, Year 2.

15. Brookhurst Company (a U.S.-based company) established a subsidiary in South Africa on January 1, Year 1, by investing 300,000 South African rand (ZAR) when the exchange rate was US$0.09/ZAR 1. On that date, the foreign subsidiary borrowed ZAR 500,000 from local banks on a 10-year note to finance the acquisition of plant and equipment. The subsidiary's opening balance sheet (in ZAR) was as follows:

Balance Sheet
January 1, Year 1

Cash	300,000	Long-term debt.	500,000
Plant and equipment	500,000	Capital stock.	300,000
Total.	800,000	Total	800,000

During Year 1, the foreign subsidiary generated sales of ZAR 1,000,000 and net income of ZAR 110,000. Dividends in the amount of ZAR 20,000 were paid to the parent on June 1 and December 1. Inventory was acquired evenly throughout the year, with ending inventory acquired on November 15, Year 1. The subsidiary's ZAR financial statements for the year ended December 31, Year 1, are presented below:

Income Statement
Year 1

	ZAR
Sales	1,000,000
Cost of goods sold	(600,000)
Gross profit	400,000
Depreciation expense.	(50,000)
Other operating expenses	(150,000)
Income before tax	200,000
Income taxes	(90,000)
Net income	110,000

Statement of Retained Earnings
Year 1

	ZAR
Retained earnings, 1/1/Y1	0
Net income	110,000
Dividends	(40,000)
Retained earnings, 12/31/Y1	70,000

Balance Sheet
December 31, Year 1

	ZAR
Cash	80,000
Receivables	150,000
Inventory	270,000
Plant and equipment (net)	450,000
Total assets	950,000
Accounts payable	80,000
Long-term debt	500,000
Common stock	300,000
Retained earnings, 12/31/Y1	70,000
Total liabilities and stockholders' equity	950,000

Relevant exchange rates for Year 1 are as follows (US$ per ZAR):

January 1, Year 1	$0.090
June 1, Year 1	0.095
Average for Year 1	0.096
November 15, Year 1	0.100
December 1, Year 1	0.105
December 31, Year 1	0.110

Required:
a. Translate the South African subsidiary's financial statements into U.S. dollars assuming that the South African rand is the functional currency. Compute

the translation adjustment by considering the impact of exchange rate changes on the subsidiary's net assets.

b. Translate (remeasure) the South African subsidiary's financial statements into U.S. dollars assuming that the U.S. dollar is the functional currency. Compute the translation adjustment (remeasurement gain or loss) by considering the impact of exchange rate changes on the subsidiary's net monetary asset or liability position.

16. Access the most recent annual report for a U.S.-based multinational company with which you are familiar to complete the requirements of this exercise.

Required:

a. Determine whether the company's foreign operations have a predominant functional currency.

b. If possible, determine the amount of remeasurement gain or loss, if any, reported in net income in each of the three most recent years.

c. Determine the amount of translation adjustment, if any, reported in other comprehensive income in each of the three most recent years. Explain the sign (positive or negative) of the translation adjustment in each of the three most recent years.

d. Determine whether the company hedges net investments in foreign operations. If so, determine the type(s) of hedging instrument(s) used.

17. To complete the requirements of this exercise, access the most recent annual reports for both Hewlett-Packard and IBM.

Required:

a. Determine whether each company's foreign operations have a predominant functional currency. Discuss the implication this has for the comparability of financial statements between the two companies.

b. Determine the amount of translation adjustment, if any, reported in other comprehensive income in each of the three most recent years. Explain the sign (positive or negative) of the translation adjustment in each of the three most recent years. Compare the relative magnitude of the translation adjustments between the two companies.

c. Determine whether each company hedges the net investment in foreign operations. If so, determine the type(s) of hedging instrument(s) used.

d. Prepare a brief report comparing and contrasting the foreign currency translation and foreign currency hedging policies of these two companies.

Case 7-1

Columbia Corporation

Columbia Corporation, a U.S.-based company, acquired a 100 percent interest in Swoboda Company in Lodz, Poland, on January 1, Year 1, when the exchange rate for the Polish zloty (PLN) was $0.25. The financial statements of Swoboda as of

December 31, Year 2, two years later, are as follows:

Balance Sheet
December 31, Year 2

Assets

Cash	PLN	1,000,000
Accounts receivable (net)		1,650,000
Inventory		4,250,000
Equipment		12,500,000
Less: Accumulated depreciation		(4,250,000)
Building		36,000,000
Less: Accumulated depreciation		(15,150,000)
Land		3,000,000
Total assets	PLN	39,000,000

Liabilities and Stockholders' Equity

Accounts payable	PLN	1,250,000
Long-term debt		25,000,000
Common stock		2,500,000
Additional paid-in capital		7,500,000
Retained earnings		2,750,000
Total liabilities and stockholders' equity	PLN	39,000,000

Statement of Income and Retained Earnings
For the Year Ending December 31, Year 2

Sales	PLN	12,500,000
Cost of goods sold		(6,000,000)
Depreciation expense—equipment		(1,250,000)
Depreciation expense—building		(900,000)
Research and development expense		(600,000)
Other expenses (including taxes)		(500,000)
Net income	PLN	3,250,000
Plus: Retained earnings, 1/1/Y2		250,000
Less: Dividends, Year 2		(750,000)
Retained earnings, 12/31/Y2	PLN	2,750,000

Additional information:

- The January 1, Year 2, beginning inventory of PLN 3,000,000 was acquired on December 15, Year 1, when the exchange rate was $0.215. Purchases of inventory during Year 2 were acquired uniformly throughout the year. The December 31, Year 2, ending inventory of PLN 4,250,000 was acquired evenly throughout the fourth quarter of Year 2 when the exchange rate was $0.16.

- All fixed assets were on the books when the subsidiary was acquired except for PLN 2,500,000 of equipment which was acquired on January 3, Year 2 when the exchange rate was $0.18 and PLN 6,000,000 in buildings which was acquired on August 5, Year 2 when the exchange rate was $0.17. Equipment is depreciated on a straight-line basis over 10 years. Buildings are depreciated on a straight-line basis over 40 years. A full year's depreciation is taken in the year of acquisition.

- Dividends were declared and paid on December 15, Year 2, when the exchange rate was $0.155.
- Other exchange rates for Year 2 are:

January 1.	$0.20
Average for the year	0.175
December 31.	0.150

Required:

1. Translate Swoboda's financial statements into U.S. dollars in accordance with U.S. GAAP at December 31, Year 2:

   a. Assuming the Polish zloty is the functional currency. (The December 31, Year 1, retained earnings that appeared in Swoboda's translated financial statements was $56,250. The December 31, Year 1, cumulative translation adjustment that appeared in Swoboda's translated balance sheet was negative $506,250.)

   b. Assuming the U.S. dollar is the functional currency. (The December 31, Year 1, retained earnings that appeared in Swoboda's remeasured financial statements was $882,500.)

   c. The same as (b) except Swoboda has no long-term debt. Instead, Swoboda has common stock of PLN 10,000,000 and additional paid-in capital of PLN 25,000,000. The December 31, Year 1, retained earnings that appeared in Swoboda's remeasured financial statements was negative $367,500.

2. Explain why the sign of the translation adjustments in (1*a*), (1*b*), and (1*c*) is positive or negative.

Case 7-2

Palmerstown Company

Palmerstown Company established a subsidiary in a foreign country on January 1, Year 1, by investing 8,000,000 pounds when the exchange rate was $1.00/pound. Palmerstown negotiated a bank loan of 4,000,000 pounds on January 5, Year 1, and purchased plant and equipment in the amount of 10,000,000 pounds January 8, Year 1. Plant and equipment is depreciated on a straight-line basis over a 10-year useful life. Beginning inventory of 1,000,000 pounds was purchased on January 10, Year 1. Additional inventory of 12,000,000 pounds was acquired at three points in time during the year at an average exchange rate of $0.86/pound. Ending inventory was acquired when the exchange rate was $0.83/pound. The first-in, first-out (FIFO) method is used to determine cost of goods sold. Additional exchange rates for the pound during Year 1 are as follows:

January 1–31, Year 1	$1.00
Average Year 1	0.90
December 31, Year 1	0.80

The foreign subsidiary's income statement for Year 1 and balance sheet at December 31, Year 1, are as follows:

Income Statement
For the Year Ended December 31, Year 1

	Pounds (in thousands)
Sales	15,000
Cost of goods sold	9,000
Gross profit	6,000
Selling and administrative expenses	3,000
Depreciation expense	1,000
Income before tax	2,000
Income taxes	600
Net income	1,400
Retained earnings, 1/1/Y1	0
Retained earnings, 12/31/Y1	1,400

Balance Sheet
At December 31, Year 1

	Pounds (in thousands)
Cash	2,400
Inventory	4,000
Fixed assets	10,000
Less: Accumulated depreciation	(1,000)
Total assets	15,400
Current liabilities	2,000
Long-term debt	4,000
Contributed capital	8,000
Retained earnings	1,400
Total liabilities and stockholders' equity	8,400

As the controller for Palmerstown Company, you have evaluated the characteristics of the foreign subsidiary to determine that the pound is the subsidiary's functional currency.

Required:

1. Use an electronic spreadsheet to translate the foreign subsidiary's financial statements into U.S. dollars at December 31, Year 1, in accordance with U.S. GAAP. Insert a row in the spreadsheet after retained earnings and before total liabilities and stockholders' equity for the cumulative translation adjustment. Calculate the translation adjustment separately to verify the amount obtained as a balancing figure in the translation worksheet.

2. Use an electronic spreadsheet to remeasure the foreign subsidiary's financial statements into U.S. dollars at December 31, Year 1, assuming that the U.S. dollar is the subsidiary's functional currency. Insert a row in the spreadsheet after depreciation expense and before income before taxes for the remeasurement gain (loss).

3. Prepare a report for the chief executive officer of Palmerstown Company summarizing the differences that will be reported in the Year 1 consolidated

financial statements because the pound, rather than the U.S. dollar, is the foreign subsidiary's functional currency. In your report, discuss the relationship between the current ratio, the debt to equity ratio, and profit margin calculated from the foreign currency financial statements and from the translated U.S.-dollar financial statements. Also, include a discussion of the meaning of the translated U.S.-dollar amounts for inventory and for fixed assets.

Case 7-3

BellSouth Corporation

BellSouth Corporation invested in two wireless communications operations in Brazil in the mid-1990s that are being accounted for under the equity method. The following note is taken from BellSouth Corporation's interim report for the quarter ended March 31, 1999.

Note E—Devaluation of Brazilian Currency

We hold equity interests in two wireless communications operations in Brazil. During January 1999, the government of Brazil allowed its currency to trade freely against other currencies. As a result, the Brazilian Real experienced a devaluation against the U.S. Dollar. The devaluation resulted in the entities recording exchange losses related to their net U.S. Dollar-denominated liabilities. Our share of the foreign exchange rate losses for the first quarter was $280.

These exchange losses are subject to further upward or downward adjustment based on fluctuations in the exchange rates between the U.S. Dollar and the Brazilian Real.

In a press release announcing first quarter 1999 results, BellSouth Corporation provided the following information (as found on the company's Web site):

BellSouth Corporation (NYSE: BLS) reported a 15-percent increase in first quarter earnings per share (EPS) before special items. EPS was 46 cents before a non-cash expense of 14 cents related to Brazil's currency devaluation.

BELLSOUTH CORPORATION
Normalized Earnings Summary ($ in millions, except per share amounts)
(unaudited)

	Quarter Ended		
	3/31/99	**3/31/98**	**%Change**
Reported Net Income	$615	$892	(31.1%)
Foreign currency loss (a)	280	—	
Gain on sale of ITT World Directories (b). . .	—	(96)	
Normalized Net Income	$895	$796	12.4%
Reported Diluted Earnings per Share	$0.32	$0.45	(28.9%)
Foreign currency loss (a)	0.14	—	
Gain on sale of ITT World Directories (b). . .	—	(0.05)	
Normalized Diluted Earnings per Share	$0.46	$0.40	15.0%

(a)Represents our share of foreign currency losses recorded during first quarter 1999 as a result of the devaluation of the Brazilian Real during January 1999.
(b)Represents the after-tax gain associated with additional proceeds received in first quarter 1998 on the July 1997 sale of ITT World Directories.

Required:

Given the disclosure provided by BellSouth Corporation, answer the following questions:

1. Why did the company report a foreign currency loss as a result of the devaluation of the Brazilian real?

2. What does the company mean when it states: "These exchange losses are subject to further upward or downward adjustment based on fluctuations in the exchange rates between the U.S. Dollar and the Brazilian Real"?

3. What is the company's objective in reporting "Normalized Net Income"? Do you agree with the company's assessment that it had a 15 percent increase in first-quarter earnings per share?

References

Arnold, Jerry L., and William W. Holder. *Impact of Statement 52 on Decisions, Financial Reports and Attitudes.* Morristown, NJ: Financial Executives Research Foundation, 1986.

Doupnik, Timothy S., and Thomas G. Evans. "Functional Currency as a Strategy to Smooth Income." *Advances in International Accounting,* 1988.

Hepworth, Samuel R. *Reporting Foreign Operations.* Ann Arbor: University of Michigan, Bureau of Business Research, 1956.

Chapter **Eight**

Additional Financial Reporting Issues

Learning Objectives

After reading this chapter, you should be able to

- Explain the concepts underlying two methods of accounting for changing prices (inflation)—general purchasing power accounting and current cost accounting.
- Describe attempts to account for inflation in different countries, as well as the rules found in International Financial Reporting Standards (IFRSs) related to this issue.
- Discuss the various issues related to the accounting for business combinations and the preparation of consolidated financial statements (group accounting).
- Present the approaches used internationally to address the issues related to group accounting, focusing on IFRSs.
- Describe segment reporting requirements in IFRSs and followed in countries around the world.

INTRODUCTION

Chapters 6 and 7 focused on accounting for foreign currency. Chapter 6 discussed foreign currency transactions and hedging activities, and Chapter 7 discussed the translation of foreign currency financial statements. These are two of the most important accounting issues for multinational corporations (MNCs).

This chapter covers three additional financial reporting topics of importance to MNCs. We describe the various alternatives available worldwide to deal with each issue, focusing on the guidance and requirements found in International Financial Reporting Standards (IFRSs). The first section deals with the accounting for changing prices (inflation). Companies operating in countries experiencing high rates of inflation, including MNCs with foreign subsidiaries in such countries, must address changing prices. The second section of this chapter covers consolidations, or group accounting, and includes the accounting for business combinations. There are several approaches followed worldwide in accounting for investments in subsidiaries, joint ventures, affiliates, and the like. Whereas consolidation involves the aggregation of assets, liabilities, revenues, and expenses of all companies in a group, segment reporting does the opposite. Segment reporting, the third major topic covered in this chapter, involves the disaggregation of consolidated totals by segment for separate reporting. Geographic segment reporting is an issue that affects only those companies with foreign operations.

ACCOUNTING FOR CHANGING PRICES (INFLATION ACCOUNTING)

Conventional accounting results in a mix of attributes being reflected in the asset section of the balance sheet. Accounts receivable are reported at the net amount expected to be received in the future; short-term investments are reported at either cost or current market value; inventory is carried at the lower of cost or market value; and property, plant, and equipment is reported at cost less accumulated depreciation. Prices of most assets fluctuate, often increasing. Reporting assets on the balance sheet at their historical cost during a period of price changes can make the balance sheet information irrelevant. For example, reporting land that was purchased in 1925 at its historical cost of $1,000 is unlikely to provide financial statement readers with useful information in the 21st century.

When the prices of goods and services in an economy increase in general, we say that inflation has occurred. Economists often measure inflation by determining the current price for a "basket" of goods and services and then compare the current price with the price for the same basket of goods and services at an earlier time. For example, if a basket of goods and services costs $120 at the end of Year 1 and the same basket costs $132 at the end of Year 2, then inflation in Year 2 was 10 percent ([$132 − $120]/$120).

In this case we have measured the increase in the general price level, or the rate of inflation. The general inflation rate also reflects the decrease in the purchasing power of the currency. In our example, it takes $132 at the end of Year 2 to purchase as much as $120 could purchase at the end of Year 1. The dollar has lost 10 percent of its purchasing power during Year 2.

Not all goods and services increase in price by 10 percent when the average rate of inflation is 10 percent. The price of a new machine might increase by 15 percent, the price of component parts might increase by 12 percent, the price of janitorial services might increase by 5 percent, and the price of raw materials might actually decrease by 4 percent. These are measures of changes in specific prices. However, the changes in specific prices throughout the economy average out to 10 percent.

Impact of Inflation on Financial Statements

During a period of inflation, assets reported on the balance sheet at historical cost are understated in terms of their current value. Having understated assets results in understated expenses (especially depreciation and cost of goods sold), which in turn results in overstated net income and overstated retained earnings. Ignoring changes in the prices of assets can lead to a number of problems:

1. Understated asset values could have a negative impact on a company's ability to borrow, because the collateral is understated. Understated asset values also can invite a hostile takeover to the extent that the current market price of a company's stock does not reflect the current value of assets.

2. Overstated income results in more taxes being paid to the government than would otherwise be paid and could lead stockholders to demand a higher level of dividend than would otherwise be expected. Through the payment of taxes on inflated income and the payment of dividends out of inflated net income, both of which result in cash outflows, a company may find itself experiencing liquidity problems.

3. To the extent that companies are exposed to different rates of inflation, the understatement of assets and overstatement of income will differ across

companies; this can distort comparisons across companies. For example, a company with older fixed assets will report a higher return on assets than a company with newer assets, because income is more overstated and assets are more understated than for the comparison company. Because inflation rates tend to vary across countries, comparisons made by a parent company across its subsidiaries located in different countries can be distorted.

Purchasing Power Gains and Losses

In addition to ignoring changes in the values of nonmonetary assets, historical cost accounting also ignores the purchasing power gains and losses that arise from holding monetary assets (cash and receivables) and monetary liabilities (payables) during a period of inflation. Holding cash and receivables during inflation results in a purchasing power loss, whereas holding payables during inflation results in a purchasing power gain.

For example, when the general price level index is 120, $120 in cash can purchase one whole basket of goods and services. One year later, when the general price level index stands at 132 (10 percent inflation), the same $120 in cash can now purchase only 90.9 percent of a basket of goods and services. It now takes $132 to purchase the same amount of goods and services as at the beginning of the year. The difference between the $132 needed to maintain purchasing power and the $120 in cash actually held results in a $12 purchasing power loss. This can be computed by multiplying the amount of cash at the beginning of the year by the inflation rate of 10 percent ($120 × 10% = $12).

Borrowing money during a period of inflation results in a purchasing power gain. Assume a company expects to receive $120 in cash at the end of the current year. If it waits until the cash is received, it will be able to acquire 90.9 percent of the market basket of goods at that time when the general price level index is 132. Instead, if the company borrows $120 at the beginning of the year and repays that amount with the cash received at the end of the year, it will be able to acquire 100 percent of the basket of goods and services at the beginning of the year when the general price level index is 120. Holding a $120 liability during a period of 10 percent inflation results in a purchasing power gain of $12 ($120 × 10%). A net purchasing power gain will result when an entity maintains monetary liabilities in excess of monetary assets during inflation, and a net purchasing power loss will result when the opposite situation exists.

Methods of Accounting for Changing Prices

Two solutions have been developed to deal with the distortions caused by historical cost (HC) accounting in a period of changing prices. The first solution is to *account for changes in the general price level*. This approach makes adjustments to the historical costs of assets to update for changes in the purchasing power of the currency and therefore is referred to as general price-level-adjusted historical cost (GPLAHC) accounting or, more simply, general purchasing power (GPP) accounting. The alternative solution is to *account for specific price changes* by updating the values of assets from historical cost to the current cost to replace those assets. This is known as current replacement cost (CRC) or, simply, current cost (CC) accounting. In addition to adjusting asset values for changes in the general price level and determining expenses from GPLAHC amounts, GPP accounting also requires that purchasing power gains and losses be included in the determination of net income.

Net Income and Capital Maintenance

Application of each of the three methods of asset valuation—HC, GPP, and CC—results in a different amount of net income. Each measure of net income relates to a specific concept of capital maintenance. Much of the debate surrounding the appropriate method for asset valuation relates to determining which concept of capital maintenance is most important. The following example demonstrates the difference in net income that results from the three different accounting models.

Example

Assume that HIE Company is formed on January 1, Year 1, by investors contributing $200 in cash. The general price index (GPI) on that date is 100. HIE Company's opening balance sheet on January 1, Year 1, appears as follows:

Cash	$200	Contributed capital	$200

With the initial equity investment, one unit of inventory is purchased on January 2 at a cost of $100 and $100 remains in cash, resulting in the following financial position:

Cash	$100	Contributed capital	$200
Inventory	100		
	$200		

On January 2, Year 1, the managers of HIE Company go on vacation, returning on December 31, Year 1, at which time the inventory is sold for $150 in cash. At December 31, Year 1, the general price index is 120 (20 percent annual inflation during Year 1) and the inventory has a current replacement cost of $150. The HC income statement for Year 1 appears as follows (ignoring income taxes):

Sales	$150
Cost of sales	100
Income	$ 50

The balance sheet at December 31, Year 1, prior to any distribution of dividends is:

Cash	$250	Contributed capital	$200
		Retained earnings	50
			$250

The economic definition of income is that it is the amount that can be distributed to owners after making sure that the company is as well off at the end of the year as it was at the beginning of the year. If HIE Company were to distribute a dividend of $50 equal to Year 1 net income, the resulting balance sheet would be exactly the same as it was at the beginning of the year:

Cash	$200	Contributed capital	$200

Thus, HC income is the amount that can be distributed to owners while maintaining the "nominal" amount of contributed capital at the beginning of the year. Note, however, that in terms of purchasing power, the company is not as well off at the end of the year as it was at the beginning of the year—$200 in cash at January 1, Year 1, when the GPI was 100, could purchase two baskets of goods and services. At December 31, Year 1, when the GPI has risen to 120, $200 in cash can purchase only $1\frac{2}{3}$ baskets of goods. The conventional HC model of accounting ignores the loss in purchasing power of the beginning of year amount of capital. GPP accounting explicitly takes the change in purchasing power of the currency into account.

General Purchasing Power (GPP) Accounting

Under GPP accounting, nonmonetary assets and liabilities, stockholders' equity, and all income statement items are restated from the GPI at the transaction date to the GPI at the end of the current period. Because inventory was acquired on January 1, Year 1, when the GPI was 100, and the GPI at December 31, Year 1, is 120, the cost of sales (inventory) is restated using the ratio 120/100. Fixed assets and intangible assets and the related depreciation and amortization would also be restated for changes in general purchasing power.

Because the sale occurred on December 31, Year 1, when the GPI was 120, there is no need to restate sales (or the restatement ratio can be expressed as 120/120). In addition to restating sales and cost of sales, GPP accounting also requires that a net purchasing power gain or loss be included in income. At January 1, Year 1, HIE Company has monetary assets of $100 (cash) and no monetary liabilities, yielding a net monetary asset position of $100. Because HIE Company holds this cash for the entire year, a net purchasing power loss (PPL) of $20 arises. In addition, HIE Company receives $150 in cash on December 31, Year 1, from the sale of inventory. Because this cash is received on December 31, there is no loss in purchasing power by the end of the year. The PPL is calculated as follows:

Cash, 1/1/Y1	$100 × (120/100) = $120	(amount of cash needed at 12/31/Y1 to maintain the purchasing power of $100 at 1/1/Y1)	
Plus: Increase in cash, Year 1 . . .	$150 × (120/120) = $150	(amount of cash needed at 12/31/Y1 to maintain the purchasing power of $150 received on 12/31/Y1)	
Subtotal	270		
Less: Cash, 12/31/Y1	(250)	(amount of cash held, prior to distribution of dividend)	
Purchasing power loss	$ 20		

Combining the restatement of the income statement items with the PPL, GPP income is calculated as follows:

	HC	Restatement Ratio	GPP
Sales	$150	× (120/120) =	$150
Cost of sales	100	× (120/100) =	120
Subtotal	$ 50		$ 30
Purchasing power loss			20
Income			$ 10

Contributed capital must also be restated for Year 1 inflation, as follows:

	HC	Restatement Ratio	GPP
Contributed capital	$200	× (120/100) =	$240

The journal entry needed to account for GPP adjustments is as follows:

Dr. Inventory (Cost of Sales) 20	
Purchasing Power Loss 20	
Cr. Contributed Capital	40

GPP income represents the amount that can be distributed to owners while maintaining the purchasing power of capital at the beginning of the year. After paying a dividend of $10, HIE Company's balance sheet at December 31, Year 1, appears as follows:

Cash	$240	Contributed capital	$240

$240 in cash at December 31, Year 1, when the GPI is 120, can purchase two baskets of goods and services, just as $200 in cash could have at January 1, Year 1, when the GPI was 100. The owners are just as well off in terms of the purchasing power of their contributed capital at the end of the year as they were at the beginning of the year.

Current Cost (CC) Accounting

Maintaining the purchasing power of equity does not necessarily ensure that the company is able to continue to operate at its existing level of capacity, because the prices of specific goods and services purchased by an individual company do not necessarily increase at the rate of average inflation. To determine the amount of income that can be distributed to owners while maintaining the company's productive capacity or physical capital, current cost (CC) accounting must be applied.

Under CC accounting, historical costs of nonmonetary assets are replaced with current replacement costs and expenses are based on these current costs. Assume that, on December 31, Year 1, the cost to replace the unit of inventory acquired at the beginning of the year is $150. In other words, this particular item has experienced a specific rate of inflation of 50 percent ([$150 − $100]/$100). The following journal entry would be made:

Dr. Inventory (Cost of Sales) 50	
Cr. Holding Gain (Equity)	50

The CC accounting income statement would be as follows:

Sales	$150
Current cost of sales	150
Income	$ 0

There is no income to distribute as a dividend. After adding the holding gain to the beginning balance in capital, the ending balance sheet at December 31, Year 1, is as follows:

Cash	$250	Contributed capital	$200
		Holding gain	50
		Total	$250

With $250 in cash at December 31, Year 1, HIE Company can replace the inventory that was sold at its current cost of $150 and still will have $100 in cash. The company can end the year with the same physical assets as it had at the beginning of the year—$100 cash plus one unit of inventory.

Comparing the amounts of income that would be reported under GPP and CC accounting with HC income shows the potential problems that can arise if changing prices are ignored.

	HC	GPP	CC
Income	50	10	0

If HC accounting is used as the basis for taxation and dividend distribution, there is a good chance that the company will not be as well off at the end of the year in terms of either purchasing power or productive capacity at it was at the beginning of the year.

Inflation Accounting Internationally

Inflation Accounting in the United States and United Kingdom

In 1979, the Financial Accounting Standards Board (FASB) in the United States issued SFAS 33, *Financial Reporting and Changing Prices,* requiring the largest U.S. companies to provide both GPP and CC information in the notes to the financial statements. SFAS 33 was intended to be a five-year experiment to see whether financial analysts would find the supplementary information useful. In 1984, the FASB discontinued the requirement for disclosure of supplemental GPP information, citing lack of usefulness and cost to comply as reasons. Two years later, in 1986, the FASB issued SFAS 89, making optional the disclosure of CC information. Few U.S. companies continue to voluntarily provide CC information in the notes to their financial statements.

Inflation accounting was introduced in the United Kingdom in 1980 through Statement of Standard Accounting Practice (SSAP) 16. This statement required presentation of CC financial statements as either primary or supplementary statements. In either case, HC financial statements also were required to be presented. As in the United States, inflation accounting in the United Kingdom was short-lived. As a result of declining inflation rates and company complaints, SSAP 16 was rescinded in 1988.

GPP Accounting in Latin America

The countries of Latin America, from Mexico in the north to Argentina in the south, historically have experienced more inflation than any other region in the world. As a result, several countries in this region have employed or continue to use a system of inflation accounting. For years, Brazil was a leader in the use of inflation accounting. However, as a result of recent successful efforts to tame inflation, Brazil has abandoned inflation accounting. Other countries, such as Chile and Mexico, continue to require financial statements to be adjusted for inflation. Next we describe Mexico's requirements to provide inflation adjustments.

The Mexican Institute of Public Accountants issued Bulletin B-10, *Recognition of the Inflation Effects in Financial Information,* effective in 1984. Bulletin B-10 requires all nonmonetary assets and nonmonetary liabilities to be restated using the general price level index published by the Central Bank. Initially, replacement cost accounting was allowed for inventory and property, plant, and equipment, but an amendment to Bulletin B-10 in 1997 eliminated this option. However, inventory (and the related cost of sales) may be valued at current replacement cost. In practice, this is similar to reporting inventory on a first-in, first-out (FIFO) basis and determining cost of Sales on a last-in, first-out (LIFO) basis. For imported machinery and equipment, an index comprised of the inflation rate of the country of origin coupled with the change in exchange rate between the foreign currency and the Mexican peso may be used. All other fixed assets must be restated using the general price index.

Equity must be restated with the general price index to show paid-in capital at constant purchasing power. A purchasing power gain or loss on the net monetary asset or liability position must be calculated and presented in income as a part of total financial cost, which also includes nominal interest expense and foreign exchange gains and losses. Finally, for comparative purposes, the financial statements of previous years must be restated in terms of the purchasing power of the peso at the latest balance sheet date presented. Exhibit 8.1 provides an excerpt from Industrias Peñoles's 2003 annual report that details the procedures followed by the company to comply with Bulletin B-10.

EXHIBIT 8.1

INDUSTRIAS PEÑOLES, SA DE CV AND SUBSIDIARIES
Annual Report
2003

Notes to Consolidated Financial Statements

Excerpts from Note 3 Significant Accounting Policies

A) Recognition of the Effects of Inflation in the Financial Information

Grupo Peñoles restates all of its financial statements in terms of the purchasing power of the Mexican peso as of the end of the latest period, thereby comprehensively recognizing the effect of inflation. The financial statements of the prior year have been restated in terms of Mexican pesos of the latest period. The prior year amounts presented herein differ from those originally reported in terms of Mexican pesos of the corresponding year. Consequently, all financial statement amounts are comparable, both for the current and the prior year, since all are stated in terms of Mexican pesos of the same purchasing power.

Inflation was determined based on the National Consumer Price Index (NCPI) for the years ended December 31, 2003 and 2002, which was 3.98% and 5.7%, respectively.

To recognize the effects of inflation in terms of Mexican pesos with purchasing power as of year-end, the procedures were as follows:

—Balance Sheet

Minerals inventories are recorded at acquisition and/or extraction cost. Metal inventories and chemical products are recognized at production cost. Such inventories are restated to reflect replacement cost, not in excess of market value.

Investments in associated companies have been recorded under the equity method.

The acquisition cost of property, plant and equipment (except for certain fixed assets that are valued at recovery value, as well as mining concessions and construction works and preoperating expenses) is restated as follows:

—The net value of property, plant and equipment of Mexican origin is based on factors derived from the NCPI.
—Production machinery and equipment, computer and transportation equipment that are identified when acquired as of foreign origin, are controlled in the currency of the country of origin, which is restated by using the consumer price index of such country and translated to pesos at the prevailing exchange rate at year-end. Below is a list of inflation and exchange rates of the principal countries as the origin of imported machinery and equipment:

COUNTRY	ANNUAL RATE OF INFLATION		EXCHANGE RATE AT DECEMBER 31 (NOMINAL MEXICAN PESOS)	
	2003	**2002**	**2003**	**2002**
United States of America (U.S. Dollar)	2.2	2.4	Ps. 11.24	Ps. 10.31
Germany (Euro)	1.0	1.0	14.05	10.71
Canada (Canadian dollar)	1.9	4.5	8.57	6.56
England (Pound Sterling)	2.8	2.7	19.93	16.31

The cost of mining concessions and works and preoperating expenses were restated based on factors derived from the NCPI.

Depreciation and depletion are calculated based on the restated value (net of salvage value) of property, plant and equipment as follows:

—Metallurgical, chemical and industrial plants, using the straight-line method, at annual rates determined on the bases of the useful lives of the related assets.

—Mining concessions and works, preoperating expenses, facilities and milling plants, on the basis of tonnage of ore extracted during the year, over the life of the mine (depletion method).

—Other equipment, using the straight-line method, at annual rates of 10% and 20%.

—Grupo Peñoles periodically evaluates its property to determine if there are differences between market value and book value.

The goodwill is restated based on the NCPI and is amortized based on its restated value.

The restatement of capital contributions, capitalized reserves, retained earnings and cumulative effect of deferred taxes is determined by applying the NCPI from the time the contributions were made, the reserves were capitalized or the earnings were generated. It represents the amount needed to maintain the investment of stockholders in terms of its original purchasing power.

—Statement of Income

Revenues and expenses that are associated with a monetary item (trade receivables, cash, liabilities, etc.) are restated from the month in which they arise through yearend, based on factors derived from the NCPI.

Cost of sales represents replacement costs at the time inventories were sold, expressed in constant year-end pesos.

—Other Statements

The statement of changes in financial position identifies the origin and use of resources that represent the differences in beginning and ending balances expressed in constant pesos. The result of monetary position and exchange differences area not treated as a part of resources provided by or used in operations.

The deficit from restatement of stockholders' equity consists basically of the accumulated result of monetary position and the accumulated result from holding nonmonetary assets, which represents the difference between the replacement value of fixed assets, inventories and the equity investment in affiliated companies compared to restated value determined on the basis of the NCPI.

H) Integral Result of Financing

The integral result of financing consists of interest income and expense, foreign exchange gains or losses and the gain or loss from monetary position. The gain or loss from monetary position is determined by applying the NCPI to the net monetary position at the beginning of each month.

Replacement Cost Accounting in the Netherlands

No country requires companies to use current replacement cost accounting to prepare primary financial statements. However, prior to the introduction of IFRSs in Europe in 2005, the Netherlands allowed companies to use replacement cost accounting in lieu of historical cost accounting in preparing financial statements. Over the years a limited number of Dutch companies, including Philips Electronics NV and Heineken NV, elected to do so. In 2003 Heineken was the only Dutch company that continued to employ replacement cost accounting. Excerpts from Heineken's 2003 annual report describing its use of replacement cost accounting are provided in Exhibit 8.2.

Heineken carried inventories (stocks) and fixed assets on the balance sheet at replacement cost, with the counterpart to the asset revaluation reflected in equity. Cost of sales (reported on Heineken's income statement as raw materials, consumables and services) and depreciation expense (included in amortization/ depreciation and value adjustments) were based on current replacement costs. The schedule of changes in tangible fixed assets reported in the notes shows that €575 million (11.5 percent) of the book value of total fixed assets of €4,995 million is the result of upward revaluation to replacement cost. Of the aggregate amount of revaluation, €39 million is attributable to the year 2003 alone.

EXHIBIT 8.2

HEINEKEN NV
Annual Report
2003

Excerpts from Notes to the Consolidated Balance Sheet, Profit and Loss Account and Cash Flow Statement

Valuation of Assets and Liabilities

Tangible fixed assets

Except for land, which is not depreciated, tangible fixed assets are stated at replacement cost less accumulated depreciation. The following useful lives are used for depreciation purposes:

Buildings 30–40 years

Plant and equipment 10–30 years

Other fixed assets 5–10 years

The replacement cost is based on appraisals by internal and external experts, taking into account technical and economic developments. Other factors taken into account include the experience gained in the construction of breweries around the world. Grants received in respect of investments in tangible fixed assets are deducted from the amount of the investment. Projects under construction are included at cost.

Current assets

Stocks bought in from third parties are stated at replacement cost, arrive at on the basis of prices from current purchase contracts and latest prices as at balance sheet date. Finished products and work in progress are stated at manufactured cost based on replacement cost and taking into account the production stage reached.

Stocks of spare parts are depreciated on a straight-line basis taking account of obsolescence. If the recoverable amount or net realizable value of stocks is less than their replacement cost, provisions are formed in respect of the difference.

Revaluations

Differences in carrying amounts due to revaluations are credited or debited to group equity, less an amount in respect of deferred tax liabilities where applicable.

Determination of results

Raw materials and consumables are stated at replacement cost in the profit and loss account. Depreciation charges based on replacement cost are calculated on a straight-line basis according to useful lives of the assets concerned.

Tangible fixed assets	Total	Land and buildings	Plant and equipment	Other fixed assets	Projects under construction
Position as at 1 January 2003	4,094	1,250	1,817	815	212
Changes in the consolidation	1,074	553	314	191	16
Investments less disposals	611	71	192	212	136
Completed projects	—	27	86	40	−153
Exchange differences	−263	−64	−134	−45	−20
Revaluation	39	7	23	9	—
Depreciation and value adjustments	−560	−72	−248	−240	—
Position as at 31 December 2003	4,995	1,772	2,050	982	191
This book value is made up as follows:					
Replacement cost	11,678	3,406	5,470	2,611	191
Accumulated depreciation	−6,683	−1,634	−3,420	−1,629	—
	4,995	1,772	2,050	982	191
The aggregate amount of revaluations included in the book value as at 31 December 2003 is:	575	236	306	33	—

Heineken reported net profit of €798 million in 2003. This amount is based on replacement cost of sales and replacement cost depreciation expense. The company does not disclose the amount of historical cost profit that would have been recognized if replacement costs had not been used. Replacement cost profit is used in the calculation of net profit per share and is the basis for distributing dividends.

With the introduction of IFRSs in the European Union in 2005, Heineken was required to implement a number of accounting and reporting changes. Two of the main changes for the company related to the valuation of tangible fixed assets and inventories. Under IFRSs, Heineken now carries fixed assets at historical cost less accumulated depreciation, and inventories are carried at weighted average historical cost.

International Financial Reporting Standards

Several standards issued by the International Accounting Standards Board (IASB) deal with the issue of accounting for price changes. International Accounting Standard (IAS) 15, *Information Reflecting the Effects of Changing Prices,* issued in 1981, required supplementary disclosure of the following items reflecting the effects of changing prices:

1. The amount of adjustment to depreciation expense.
2. The amount of adjustment to cost of sales.
3. The amount of purchasing power gain or loss on monetary items.
4. The aggregate of all adjustments reflecting the effects of changing prices.
5. If current cost accounting is used, the current cost of property, plant, and equipment.

The standard applied only to enterprises "whose levels of revenues, profits, assets or employment are significant in the economic environment in which they operate" (paragraph 3) and allowed those enterprises to choose between making adjustments on a GPP or a CC basis. Because of a lack of international support for inflation accounting disclosures, the International Accounting Standards Committee (IASC) decided to make IAS 15 optional in 1989 and the IASB completely withdrew IAS 15 in 2003.

In 1989, the IASB issued IAS 29, *Financial Reporting in Hyperinflationary Economies,* which applies to the primary financial statements of any company that reports in a currency of a hyperinflationary economy. IAS 29 does not establish an absolute definition for hyperinflation, instead leaving this determination to individual companies. However, the standard does provide a list of characteristics indicative of hyperinflation:

1. The general population keeps its wealth in nonmonetary assets or in a stable foreign currency; receipts of local currency are immediately invested to maintain purchasing power.
2. The general population thinks about prices in terms of a stable foreign currency, and prices may actually be quoted in that currency.
3. Prices for credit sales and purchases include an amount to compensate for the expected loss in purchasing power during the credit period.
4. Interest rates, wages, and prices are linked to a price index.
5. The cumulative inflation rate over a three-year period is 100 percent or higher.

The procedures required by IAS 29 for the restatement of financial statements are summarized as follows:

Balance Sheet

- Monetary assets and monetary liabilities are not restated because they are already expressed in terms of the monetary unit current at the balance sheet date. Monetary items are cash, receivables, and payables.
- Nonmonetary assets and nonmonetary liabilities are restated for changes in the general purchasing power of the monetary unit. Most nonmonetary items are carried at historical cost. In these cases, the restated cost is determined by applying to the historical cost the change in general price index from the date of acquisition to the balance sheet date. Some nonmonetary items are carried at revalued amounts, for example, property, plant, and equipment revalued according to the allowed alternative treatment in IAS 16, *Property, Plant and Equipment*. These items are restated from the date of the revaluation.
- All components of owners' equity are restated by applying the change in the general price index from the beginning of the period or the date of contribution, if later, to the balance sheet date.

Income Statement

- All income statement items are restated by applying the change in the general price index from the dates when the items were originally recorded to the balance sheet date.
- The gain or loss on net monetary position (purchasing power gain or loss) is included in net income.

Comparative Information

- Information for the previous reporting period is restated in terms of the current purchasing power of the monetary unit by applying the change in general price index during the current period to each corresponding figure.

The procedures followed by the Turkish conglomerate Koç Holding AŞ, in complying with IAS 29 are described in Exhibit 8.3. Application of IAS 29 was triggered by the fact that the three-year cumulative inflation in Turkey at the end of 2003 was 181.1 percent. Koç Holding reported operating profit of 832,612 billion Turkish lira (TL) in 2003. A "loss on net monetary position" of TL 34,890 million was subtracted from operating profit to determine income before taxes and minority interest. The size of this purchasing power loss was equal to 4.2 percent of operating profit and 9.1 percent of net income.

If a parent company has a foreign operation located in a hyperinflationary economy, IAS 21, *The Effects of Changes in Foreign Exchange Rates*, requires application of IAS 29 to restate the foreign operation's financial statements to a GPP basis. The GPP-adjusted financial statements are then translated into the parent company's reporting currency using the current rate method of translation. This approach is referred to as the restate/translate method.

IAS 16, *Property, Plant and Equipment*, also deals with the issue of changing prices by allowing companies to revalue property, plant, and equipment to current fair value subsequent to initial recognition. If a company chooses to revalue its fixed assets, depreciation should be based on revalued amounts. In effect, IAS 16 allows companies to apply current cost accounting to fixed assets if they so choose. Revaluation of fixed assets, coupled with the use of last-in, first-out (LIFO) for inventory valuation results in a measure of net income that approximates income under CC accounting.

EXHIBIT 8.3

KOÇ HOLDING AS
Annual Report
2003

Notes to the Consolidated Financial Statements

Excerpt from Note 2—Basis of Preparation

a) Turkish Lira financial statements

The consolidated financial statements have been prepared in accordance with International Financial Reporting Standards ("IFRS") including the International Accounting Standards ("IAS") and Interpretations issued by the International Accounting Standards Board ("IASB"). Koç Holding and its Subsidiaries and Joint Ventures registered in Turkey maintain their books of account and prepare their statutory financial statements ("Statutory Financial Statements") in TL in accordance with the Turkish Commerical Code (the "TCC"), tax legislation, and the Uniform Chart of Accounts issued by the Ministry of Finance, applicable Turkish insurance laws for insurance companies and Banking law and accounting principles promulgated by the Banking Regulation and Supervising Agency for banks and for listed companies; accounting principles issued by the CMB of Turkey ("CMB Principles"). The foreign Subsidiaries and Joint Ventures maintain their books of account in accordance with the laws and regulations in force in the countries in which they are registered. These consolidated financial statements are based on the statutory records, which are maintained under the historical cost convention (except for the statutory revaluation of property, plant and equipment as discussed in Note 15), with the required adjustments and reclassifications reflected for the purpose of fair presentation in accordance with IFRS (including the restatement of the TL to match the purchasing power at the balance sheet date).

The restatement for the changes in the general purchasing power of the TL at 31 December 2003 is based on IAS 29 ("Financial Reporting in Hyperinflationary Economies"). IAS 29 requires that financial statements prepared in the currency of a hyperinflationary economy be stated in terms of the measuring unit current at the balance sheet date, and that corresponding figures for previous periods be restated in the same terms. One characteristic that necessitates the application of IAS 29 is a cumulative three-year inflation rate approaching or exceeding 100%. The restatement was calculated by means of conversion factors derived from the Turkish nationwide wholesale price index ("WPI") published by the State Institute of Statistics ("SIS"). Such indices and conversion factors used to restate the financial statements at 31 December are given below:

Dates	Index	Conversion factors	Cumulative 3-year %
31 December 2003	**7,382.1**	**1.000**	**181.1**
31 December 2002	6,478.8	1.139	227.3
31 December 2001	4,951.7	1.491	307.5

The main procedures for the above-mentioned restatement are as follows:

—Financial statements prepared in the currency of a hyperinflationary economy are stated in terms of the measuring unit current at the balance sheet date, and corresponding figures for previous periods are restated in the same terms.

—Monetary assets and liabilities that are carried at amounts current at the balance sheet date are not restated because they are already expressed in terms of the monetary unit current at the balance sheet date.

—Non-monetary assets and liabilities that are not carried at amounts current at the balance sheet date and components of shareholders' equity are restated by applying the relevant conversion factors.

—Comparative financial statements are restated using general inflation indices at the currency purchasing power at the latest balance sheet date.

—All items in the statements of income are restated by applying the relevant (monthly) conversion factors.

—The effect of inflation on the net monetary asset position of Koç Holding, the Subsidiaries and Joint Ventures is included in the statements of income as loss on net monetary position in the consolidated financial statements.

BUSINESS COMBINATIONS AND CONSOLIDATED FINANCIAL STATEMENTS

Business combinations are the major vehicle through which MNCs expand their international business operations. Businesses can combine their operations in a number of different ways. In many cases, the company being acquired in a business combination is legally dissolved as a separate legal entity. Either the acquired company goes out of existence and is merged into the acquiring company, or both parties to the combination are legally dissolved with a new company formed to take their place. In yet a third method of combination, one company gains control over another company by acquiring a majority of its voting shares, but the acquired company continues its separate legal existence. In this case the acquirer becomes the parent company and the acquiree becomes the subsidiary company. Here no company goes out of existence, and both the parent and the subsidiary continue to operate as separate legal entities, maintaining their own accounting records and preparing their own financial statements.

The concept of a "group" applies to this third type of business combination. IAS 27, *Consolidated and Separate Financial Statements,* defines a *group* as a parent and all its subsidiaries, and it requires parents to present consolidated financial statements. In this section, we discuss the following issues related to the accounting for business combinations and the preparation of consolidated financial statements, focusing on IFRSs:

1. Determination of control.
2. Scope of consolidation.
3. Full consolidation, including the purchase and pooling of interests methods, and the accounting for goodwill.
4. Proportionate consolidation.
5. Equity method.

The manner in which several consolidation issues are resolved in selected countries and under IFRSs is summarized in Exhibit 8.4.

Determination of Control

The concept of a group is often based on *legal control,* which is usually reflected through the ownership of more than 50 percent of the shares and voting rights of another company. The ownership of shares reflecting control may be direct or indirect (through other controlled subsidiaries). Legal control also can be obtained through a contract whereby one company places itself under the legal control of another, which might not have 50 percent of the voting shares. Company legislation in Germany, for example, allows for such control contracts.

A company can effectively control another company through means other than majority ownership. Effective control also can be achieved through representation on the board of directors or because of widely distributed stock ownership. For example, if Company A owns 45 percent of the voting shares of Company B, and the other 55 percent of Company B is owned by thousands of small stockholders who do not exercise their votes, then Company A will be able to control Company B. In such cases, it might be appropriate to consolidate the investee's financial statements with those of the investor even though the latter does not own more than 50 percent of the investee's shares. For example, it is common for

EXHIBIT 8.4 Summary of Consolidation Procedures in Selected Countries

Country	Consolidated Financials Required	Reasons to Exclude Subsidiaries from Consolidation	Treatment of Goodwill	Goodwill Amortization	Pooling Method	Equity Method
European Union (IFRSs)	Yes	Sold in near future and buyer being sought	Asset	Impairment test	No	Yes, 20%
United States	Yes	Bankrupt Control impaired by foreign exchange restrictions	Asset	Impairment test	No	Yes, 20%
Canada	Yes	Sold in near future Control impaired Dissimilar activities	Asset	Impairment test	No	Yes, 20%
Mexico	Yes	Bankrupt Control impaired by foreign exchange restrictions	Asset	0–40 years	No	Yes, 10%
Brazil	Yes, if subsidiaries comprise >30% of total equity	Sold in near future Bankrupt Dissimilar activities	Asset, based on book values (not fair values)	0–20 years	No	Yes, 10%
Japan	Yes, since 1992	Sold in near future Control impaired Dissimilar activities Immaterial Information not available on time	Asset or expense	0–5 years, if asset	No	Yes, 20%
South Korea	Yes, unaudited only	Sold in near future Control impaired	Asset	5 years	No, unless regulation requires	Yes, 20%

companies in South Korea to consolidate investees when the investor company owns more than 30 percent of the outstanding voting stock and is the largest single shareholder.

IAS 27 requires all subsidiaries to be consolidated and defines a *subsidiary* as an enterprise controlled by another enterprise, known as the parent. *Control* is defined as "the power to govern the financial and operating policies of an entity so as to obtain benefits from its activities" (paragraph 4). In essence, IAS 27 takes a substance-over-form approach to the concept of control. It recognizes that an investor owning less than 50 percent of the stock of another company nevertheless may have control when the investor has power

- Over more than half of the voting rights through agreements with other shareholders.
- To set the company's financial and operating policies because of existing statutes or agreements.
- To appoint or remove majority of the members of the governing body (board of directors or equivalent group).
- To cast the majority of votes at meetings of the company's governing body.

U.S. GAAP (Accounting Research Bulletin 51) uses *controlling financial interest* as its criterion for consolidation without specifically defining what *controlling* means. Historically, U.S. companies have relied on majority stock ownership as evidence of control. More recently, however, in the case of so-called special purpose entities, the concept of control has been expanded by FASB Interpretation 46, *Consolidation of Variable Interest Entities*, to one based on effective control.[1] A controlling financial interest in a variable interest (special purpose) entity is evidenced by one or more of the following:

- The direct or indirect ability to make decisions about the entity's activities.
- The obligation to absorb the expected losses of the entity if they occur.
- The right to receive the expected residual returns of the entity if they occur.

The level of ownership is irrelevant in determining control for this type of entity.

Applying the concept of legal control to identify subsidiaries may not be suitable in some countries due to their traditional business structures. For example, given Japan's extensive cross-ownership of companies, identifying legal ownership patterns of Japanese company groups (*keiretsu*) can be extremely difficult. As Radebaugh and Gray explain:

> These groups are known as keiretsu (i.e., headless combinations). Legal relationships are not the critical factor here. Relationships concerning the supply of raw materials and technology, market outlets, sources of debt finance, and interlocking directorships are also very important. Group consciousness is the key, built on a system of cooperation based on mutual trust and loyalty. Hence, Japanese consolidated accounts are not necessarily an accurate reflection of group results—both earnings and assets may be seriously understated. Many companies may report compliance with U.S. GAAP for U.S. listing purposes, but they are not strictly comparable with U.S. consolidated accounts.[2]

[1] FASB Interpretation 46, *Consolidation of Variable Interest Entities*, January 2003.
[2] Lee H. Radebaugh and Sidney J. Gray, *International Accounting and Multinational Enterprises*, 5th ed. (New York: Wiley, 2002), pp. 167–68.

Scope of Consolidation

Consolidated financial statements are the financial statements of a group presented as those of a single enterprise incorporating both the parent and its subsidiaries. The preparation of consolidated financial statements can be a highly complex task given that some MNCs have a large number of subsidiaries. For example, the Swedish home appliances group Electrolux AB has approximately 350 operating subsidiaries worldwide.

IAS 27 requires a parent to consolidate all subsidiaries, foreign and domestic, unless (1) the subsidiary was acquired with the intention to be disposed of within 12 months and (2) management is actively seeking a buyer. The only other situation in which a parent might be able to exclude a subsidiary from consolidation is when the subsidiary is dormant and its operations are insignificant to the company as a whole. This is demonstrated in Exhibit 8.5, which contains an excerpt from Volkswagen AG's annual report describing the company's consolidation procedures.

IAS 27 no longer allows a subsidiary to be excluded from consolidation when it operates under severe long-term restrictions that significantly affect its ability to send funds to its parent. It also does not allow a subsidiary to be excluded from consolidated financial statements solely because its operations are dissimilar to those of the other companies that comprise the group. A subsidiary ceases to be consolidated when the parent loses the control to govern its financial and operating policies. Loss of control by the parent can occur, for example, when a bankrupt subsidiary becomes subject to the control of a bankruptcy court, when a foreign government takes control of a foreign subsidiary, or when a contractual agreement cedes control to another party.

U.S. GAAP also requires all subsidiaries to be consolidated unless the parent has lost control as a result of bankruptcy or severe restrictions imposed by a foreign government. U.S. GAAP does not allow a subsidiary to be excluded from consolidation simply because it is being held for sale.

Full Consolidation

Full consolidation refers to the line-by-line aggregation of 100 percent of a subsidiary's assets, liabilities, revenues, and expenses even if the group owns less than 100 percent of the subsidiary's stock. The proportion of income and equity in the subsidiary that is not owned by the group is reported in the consolidated financial statements in a separate item as minority interest. As explained earlier, only those affiliates controlled by the parent are consolidated. Unconsolidated affiliates are reflected in the consolidated statements by the corresponding investment accounts. The impact that the consolidation of a subsidiary's financial statements has on the resulting consolidated financial statements depends on the method used to account for the business combination at the date of acquisition. The two methods used internationally are the purchase method and the pooling of interests methods. We briefly describe these methods next.

Purchase Method

Under the purchase method, when a company acquires a majority of the voting shares of another company, assets and liabilities of the acquired company (subsidiary) are revalued to fair value as of the date of acquisition. If the purchase price exceeds the revalued net assets, the excess is described as goodwill on acquisition. With this method, the acquired company contributes to group profits only after the date of acquisition.

EXHIBIT 8.5

VOLKSWAGEN AG
Annual Report
2004

Excerpts from Notes to the Consolidated Financial Statements of the Volkswagen Group for the Fiscal Year Ended December 31, 2004

Scope of Consolidation

In addition to Volkswagen AG, which is domiciled in Wolfsburg and registered in the Wolfsburg commercial register under the number HRB 1200, the consolidated financial statements include all significant companies at which Volkswagen AG is able, directly or indirectly, to control the financial and operating policies in such a way that the Group companies obtain benefits from the activities of these companies (subsidiaries). Consolidation begins at the first date on which control is possible, and ends when such control is no longer possible.

Subsidiaries whose business is dormant or of low volume and that are insignificant for the presentation of a true and fair view of the net assets, financial position and earnings performance of the Volkswagen Group are not consolidated. They are recognized in the consolidated financial statements at the lower of cost or fair value. The aggregate equity of these subsidiaries amounts to 0.8% (previous year: 0.8%) of Group equity. The aggregate profit after tax of these companies amounts to –0.2% (previous year: 0.6%) of the profit after tax of the Volkswagen Group.

Companies where Volkswagen AG is able, directly or indirectly, to significantly influence financial and operating policy decisions (associates), as well as joint ventures, are accounted for using the equity method. Joint ventures also include companies in which the Volkswagen Group holds the majority of voting rights, but whose articles of association or partnership agreements stipulate that important decisions may only be resolved unanimously (minority protection).

The following carrying amounts are attributable to the Group from its proportionate interest in joint ventures:

€ million	2004	2003
Noncurrent assets	5,459	840
Current assets	4,659	4,257
Liabilities	6,352	3,199
Expenses	4,136	5,042
Income	4,402	5,648

The composition of the Volkswagen Group is shown in the following table:

	2004	2003
Volkswagen AG and fully consolidated subsidiaries		
Germany	50	49
Abroad	149	149
Subsidiaries carried at cost		
Germany	43	40
Abroad	85	90
Associates and joint ventures		
Germany	37	34
Abroad	50	45
	414	**406**

The number of fully consolidated subsidiaries changed in the year under review due to the initial consolidation of a German company. Four foreign companies were also consolidated for the first time, and four were deconsolidated. The change in the consolidated group had no material effect on the comparability of the consolidated financial statements.

The consolidated financial statements also include investment funds and other special purpose entities whose net assets are attributable to the Group under the principle of substance over form.

Initial Carrying Value of Acquired Net Assets   When less than 100 percent of a subsidiary is acquired, two major alternatives exist for determining the initial amount at which the subsidiary's assets and liabilities are measured and carried on the consolidated balance sheet. One approach is to initially measure the acquired assets and liabilities at book value plus the parent's ownership percentage of the difference between fair value and book value at the date of acquisition. This is sometimes known as the parent company concept. For example, assume Poinsett Company acquires 80 percent of the voting stock of Sumter Company. At the date of acquisition, Sumter has land with a book value of $100,000 that is appraised to have a fair value of $150,000. Under the parent company concept, the land would be carried on Poinsett Company's consolidated balance sheet at the date of acquisition at $140,000 ($100,000 + 80% [$150,000 − $100,000]). Under this approach, the outside shareholders' interest in Sumter Company would be reported as minority interest on Poinsett Company's consolidated balance sheet in an amount equal to 20 percent of the *book value* of Sumter Company net assets.

The alternative treatment is to initially measure the acquired assets and liabilities on the parent's consolidated balance sheet at 100 percent of their fair value at the date of acquisition. Under this treatment, also known as the economic unit or entity concept, Sumter Company's land would appear on Poinsett Company's consolidated balance sheet at date of acquisition at $150,000, and the minority interest would be reported in an amount equal to 20 percent of the *fair value* of Sumter Company's net assets.

Under IAS 22, *Business Combinations,* each of these two approaches was acceptable. IFRS 3, *Business Combinations,* issued in 2004, supersedes IAS 22. With the issuance of IFRS 3, the first alternative has been eliminated. The assets acquired and liabilities assumed in a business combination now must be initially measured at fair value in accordance with the economic unit concept. Although U.S. GAAP continued to allow the use of the parent company concept at the time this book was written, the FASB indicated that a change to the economic unit concept was likely in the near future.

Goodwill   Considerable variation exists in the accounting treatment of goodwill across countries. Most of the countries represented in Exhibit 8.4 require goodwill to be capitalized as an asset. However, Japan allows goodwill to be expensed immediately. In the case of Brazil, goodwill is based on the excess of purchase price over the book value, not fair value, of acquired net assets.

Most countries require the systematic amortization of goodwill to expense over a specified period of time. The maximum number of years over which goodwill can be amortized ranges from 5 to 40. Systematic amortization of goodwill is no longer required in Canada and the United States. Instead, goodwill must be subjected to an annual impairment test and written down when goodwill's implied fair value falls below its carrying value.

Under the original IAS 22, *Business Combinations* (issued in 1983), goodwill arising from application of the purchase method could be recognized as an asset or, alternatively, could be written off immediately against equity. In a revision to IAS 22 in 1993, the immediate write-off of goodwill against equity was eliminated as an acceptable alternative. IAS 22 (revised 1993) required goodwill to be recognized as an asset and amortized on a systematic basis over its useful life, which was assumed to be no longer than five years. A subsequent revision to IAS 22 in 1998 established the rebuttable presumption that the useful life of goodwill does not exceed 20 years.

IFRS 3 substantially changed the rules, prohibiting the amortization of goodwill on a systematic basis over its useful life. Instead, consistent with earlier changes in the United States and Canada, IFRSs now require goodwill to be tested annually for impairment.

The term *negative goodwill* often is used to refer to the excess of the acquirer's interest in the acquiree's net assets over the acquirer's purchase price. IAS 22 adopted the view that negative goodwill could arise from expectations of future losses and expenses and, to the extent that this is the case, the negative goodwill must be deferred and recognized as income when the future losses and expenses are recognized. IFRS 3 changed this treatment, requiring negative goodwill to be recognized immediately in the income statement as a gain. This serves to converge IFRSs with North American practice. Current U.S. treatment of negative goodwill is reflected in the following excerpt taken from California-based Sempra Energy's 2004 Form 10-K (page 51):

Extraordinary Gain

During 2002, Sempra Commodities acquired two businesses for amounts less than the fair value of the business' net assets. In accordance with *SFAS 141*, "Business Combinations," those differences were recorded as extraordinary income.

Pooling of Interests Method

Two companies can join together by mutual agreement and on a more or less equal basis. In this situation, a pooling of interests is said to have occurred. The pooling of interests method of accounting was created to deal with this type of business combination. Several large cross-border mergers in the 1990s were treated as pooling of interests for accounting purposes. For example, the Daimler-Benz (Germany) and Chrysler (United States) combination was treated as a pooling of interests under German GAAP, as was the BP (United Kingdom) and Amoco (United States) combination under UK accounting.

Unlike with the purchase method, in a pooling of interests there is no revaluation of assets to fair values at the date of acquisition, and no goodwill on acquisition emerges (book values are used instead). The investment in the subsidiary in the acquiring company's books is carried at the acquired company's book value of net assets. Consolidated retained earnings are simply the sum of the retained earnings of the separate companies. No distinction is drawn between pre- and post-acquisition profits, and the subsidiary's profits are included in consolidated income as from the first day of the year of acquisition. Under a pooling of interests, because depreciation is calculated on historical cost (not revalued amounts) and there is no goodwill to be amortized, reported expenses are likely to be lower, resulting in higher reported annual earnings per share than under the purchase method.

In the United States, until recently, the pooling of interests method was allowed when a set of restrictive criteria was satisfied. In July 2001, however, the FASB issued SFAS 141, *Business Combinations*, which requires that all business combinations be accounted for under the purchase method. Use of the pooling of interests method is no longer permitted in the United States. The pooling method also has been eliminated in Canada and is not allowed in Brazil and Mexico.

IAS 22 allowed the use of the pooling of interests method in those rare cases where it is impossible to identify an acquirer. However, with the enactment of IFRS 3 in 2004, that has changed. IFRS 3 requires all business combinations to be accounted for using the purchase method; the pooling of interest method is no longer acceptable under IFRSs.

Proportionate Consolidation

In some cases, two companies will jointly control another entity as a joint venture. IAS 31, *Financial Reporting of Interests in Joint Ventures,* defines *joint venture* as "a contractual arrangement whereby two or more parties undertake an activity which is subject to joint control" (paragraph 2). IAS 31 prefers proportionate consolidation for joint ventures (benchmark treatment), while equity accounting is allowed as an alternative. Proportionate consolidation is prohibited in the United States. Instead, the equity method is used to account for investments in joint ventures.

Proportionate Consolidation of a Joint Venture—Example

Assume that Alpha Company acquires 50 percent of the common shares of JV Company for cash on December 31, Year 1, at a price of $1.40 per share. (Beta Company acquires the other 50 percent of JV's shares at the same price.) The respective balance sheets for Alpha Company and JV Company at December 31, Year 1, were as follows:

<table>
<tr><td colspan="3" align="center">**ALPHA COMPANY AND JV COMPANY**
Balance Sheets
December 31, Year 1</td></tr>
<tr><td></td><td align="center">**Alpha**</td><td align="center">**JV**</td></tr>
<tr><td>Current assets ....</td><td>$ 57,200</td><td>$12,200</td></tr>
<tr><td>Fixed Assets ....</td><td>100,000</td><td>8,000</td></tr>
<tr><td>Investment in JV (16,000 shares × 50% × $1.40) ......</td><td>11,200</td><td></td></tr>
<tr><td></td><td>$168,400</td><td>$20,200</td></tr>
<tr><td>Liabilities ....</td><td>$ 88,400</td><td>$ 4,200</td></tr>
<tr><td>Common stock ($1 par) ....</td><td>80,000</td><td>16,000</td></tr>
<tr><td></td><td>$168,400</td><td>$20,200</td></tr>
</table>

The effect of the proportionate consolidation method is to remove the "Investment in JV" account from Alpha's balance sheet and replace it with the proportion of all the individual items that it represents. Assuming that JV's assets and liabilities are reported on its December 31, Year 1 balance sheet at fair values, the consolidated balance sheet is as follows:

<table>
<tr><td colspan="2" align="center">**ALPHA COMPANY**
Consolidated Balance Sheet
December 31, Year 1</td></tr>
<tr><td>Current assets ....</td><td>$ 63,300[a]</td></tr>
<tr><td>Fixed assets ....</td><td>104,000[b]</td></tr>
<tr><td>Goodwill ....</td><td>3,200[d]</td></tr>
<tr><td></td><td>$170,500</td></tr>
<tr><td>Liabilities ....</td><td>$ 90,500[c]</td></tr>
<tr><td>Common Stock ....</td><td>80,000</td></tr>
<tr><td></td><td>$170,500</td></tr>
</table>

[a]$57,200 + (50% × $12,200) = $63,300

[b]$100,000 + (50% × $8,000) = $104,000

[c]$88,400 + (50% × $4,200) = $90,500

[d]Cost of investment $11,200
50% of JV's net assets (50% × $16,000) 8,000
Goodwill .... $ 3,200

Equity Method

Many investments in the stock of another company do not provide the investor with effective control of the investee but do allow the investor to exert significant influence over the investee's operating activities. An *associate* is an enterprise in which the investor has significant influence and that is neither a subsidiary nor a joint venture. Most countries require use of the equity method to account for the investment in an associate. All countries represented in Exhibit 8.4 require its use.

The key element in identifying investments that are associates is determination of *significant influence.* The international norm is to assume that holding 20 percent or more of the voting shares is evidence of significant influence. This arbitrary level was first adopted in the United States and the United Kingdom in 1971 and then in the European Union's Seventh Directive in 1983. Although the use of 20 percent ownership is widely adopted as the threshold for determining significant influence, there does not seem to be any strong argument in its favor. On the contrary, Nobes points out that "the consensus about the threshold (20 per cent shareholding) connected to the use of the equity method seems to have arisen by accident."[3] Countries that deviate from this norm include Brazil, Mexico, and Italy, which use a 10 percent threshold; Hungary, which uses 25 percent (10 percent for banks); and Spain, which uses 3 percent.

IAS 28, *Accounting for Investments in Associates,* establishes a presumption of significant influence when the investor owns shares, directly or indirectly through subsidiaries, equivalent to 20 percent or more of the investee's voting power. Conversely, significant influence is assumed not to exist when less than 20 percent of voting shares are held, unless such influence can be clearly demonstrated.

The equity method is often known as a one-line consolidation. The procedure used in applying it to determine the carrying amount of the investment on the balance sheet is as follows: The investment is (1) initially recorded at cost; (2) increased (or decreased) for the investor's share of the associate's profit (or loss) after the date of acquisition (adjusted to eliminate the profit or loss on transactions between the investor and the associate); (3) reduced for distributions (dividends) received from the associate; (4) reduced for deprecation of the difference between fair value and book value of the investor's share of the associate's depreciable assets at the date of acquisition; and (5) adjusted for changes in the associate's equity not included in income, such as revaluation of assets and foreign exchange translation differences.

Additionally, the investor's share of the associate's profit (or loss) after the date of acquisition is treated as income (or loss). Adjustments are made to this amount to

- Eliminate the profit or loss on transactions between the investor and the associate to the extent of the investor's ownership interest in the associate.
- Depreciate the difference between fair value and book value of the investor's share of the associate's depreciable assets.

IAS 28 requires use of the equity method in accounting for investments in associates and IAS 31 allows the use of the equity method in accounting for jointly controlled entities. Exhibit 8.6 shows how the Volkswagen Group reports its share of profits and losses of group companies, including joint ventures, accounted for using the equity method in accordance with IFRSs.

---

[3] Christopher W. Nobes, "An Analysis of the International Development of the Equity Method," *Abacus* 38, no. 1 (2002), p. 16.

EXHIBIT 8.6

VOLKSWAGEN AG
Annual Report
2004

Notes to the Consolidated Financial Statements of the Volkswagen Group for the Fiscal Year Ended December 31, 2004

5. Share of Profits and Losses of Group Companies Accounted for Using the Equity Method

Million €	2004	2003
Share of the profits of Group companies accounted for using the equity method	345	626
of which from: Joint Ventures	(260)	(551)
Associates	(85)	(75)
Share of the losses of Group companies accounted for using the equity method	90	115
of which from: Joint Ventures	(83)	(23)
Associates	(7)	(92)
	255	511

In the United States, the equity method is required for investments in both associates and joint ventures and is to be applied for these types of investment in both consolidated financial statements as well as in any parent company financial statements that are prepared. Because revaluations are not allowed under U.S. GAAP, a U.S. investor with a foreign associate that carries assets at revalued amounts cannot reflect in its investment account any revaluation of the foreign investee's assets.

When an investor exerts less than significant influence over the investee, both IFRSs and U.S. GAAP require the investment to be carried on the investor's balance sheet at fair value. The fair value method is also appropriate for nonconsolidated subsidiaries.

SEGMENT REPORTING

As companies diversify internationally or in the lines of business in which they operate, the usefulness of consolidated financial statements diminishes. There are different risks and growth potential associated with different parts of the world, just as there are different risks and opportunities associated with different lines of business. The aggregation of all of a company's revenues, expenses, assets, and liabilities into consolidated totals masks these differences. Altria Group, parent company of Phillip Morris (tobacco) and Kraft (food), reported consolidated revenues of $90 billion and pretax income of $14 billion in 2004. Analysts and others might find it useful to know how much of that total was generated from each of the company's major lines of business, as there are different risks and growth prospects associated with each. In 2004, Coca-Cola Company reported consolidated revenues of $22 billion and operating income of $6 billion. Financial analysts and other financial statements users might want to know how much of this revenue was generated in North America, and how much was generated in Latin America, Africa, and other parts of the world where risks are higher.

To facilitate the analysis and evaluation of financial statements, in the 1960s several groups began to request that consolidated amounts be disaggregated and disclosed on a segment basis. Required line-of-business disclosures were introduced in the United Kingdom in 1965, and in the United States in 1969. The European Union's Fourth Directive on accounting, issued in 1978, requires both line-of-business and geographic disclosures, as does IAS 14, *Segment Reporting,* which was originally issued in 1981. Thus, segment reporting has been a part of the international accounting landscape for many years.

Notwithstanding the apparent usefulness of segment disclosures, financial analysts have consistently requested that information be disaggregated to an even greater extent than was being done in practice. Both the American Institute of Certified Public Accountants (AICPA) and the Association of Investment Management and Research (AIMR) issued reports in the 1990s recommending that segment reporting be aligned with internal reporting, with segments defined on the basis of how a company is organized and managed.

In 1992, the FASB in the United States and the Accounting Standards Board (AcSB) in Canada decided to jointly reconsider segment reporting with the objective of developing a common standard that would apply in both countries. Subsequently, the IASC began to reconsider its standard on segment reporting, IAS 14. Members of the FASB and AcSB participated in IASC meetings on segment reporting to exchange views. In 1996, all three organizations issued exposure drafts of proposed standards that were very similar. The FASB, however, made a number of changes in writing a final standard (SFAS 131), which is substantially different from what emerged in Canada and from the IASC.

International Financial Reporting Standards

IAS 14, *Segment Reporting,* requires publicly traded companies to report information along product and service lines (by business segment) and along geographic lines (by geographic segment). An enterprise must determine which of these two types of segments is its primary reporting format by determining whether its risks and rates of return are more related to its products and services or to the geographic areas in which it operates. The other type of segment represents an enterprise's secondary reporting format. The internal financial reporting to the board of directors or chief executive officer will normally reflect the primary reporting format.

IAS 14 defines *business segment* as a distinguishable component of a company that is engaged in providing an individual product or service or groups of related products or services and that is subject to risks and returns that are different from those of other business segments. A *geographic segment* is a distinguishable component of a company that is engaged in providing products or services within a particular economic environment and is subject to risks and returns that differ from those of components operating in other economic environments. Geographic segments can be a single country or groups of countries. Factors to consider in identifying geographic segments include the following:

- Similarity of economic and political conditions.
- Geographic proximity.
- Special risk associated with operations in a particular area.
- Exchange control regulations.
- Currency risks.

A business segment or a geographic segment is a reportable segment if (1) a majority of its revenue is generated from external customers and (2) it meets any one of the following three significance tests:

1. *Revenue test:* Segment revenues, both external and intersegment, are 10 percent or more of the combined revenue, internal and external, of all segments.
2. *Profit or loss test:* Segment result (profit or loss) is 10 percent or more of the greater (in absolute value terms) of the combined profit of segments with a profit or combined loss of segments with a loss.
3. *Asset test:* Segment assets are 10 percent or more of the combined assets of all segments.

In applying these tests, *segment result* is defined as segment revenue less segment expense. *Segment revenue* includes revenue directly attributable to a segment and a portion of enterprise revenue that can be allocated on a reasonable basis to a segment. *Segment expense* includes expenses directly attributable to a segment and a portion of enterprise expense that can be allocated on a reasonable basis to a segment. IAS 14 defines *segment assets* as those operating assets that are employed by a segment in its operating activities and that either are directly attributable to the segment or can be allocated to the segment on a reasonable basis.

If total external revenue attributable to reportable segments constitutes less than 75 percent of the total consolidated revenue, additional segments should be reported even if they do not meet the 10 percent threshold. All segments that are neither separately reported nor combined should be included in the segment reporting disclosures as an unallocated reconciliation item or in an "all other" category.

Segment information should be prepared in conformity with the accounting policies adopted in preparing the company's financial statements. The following example demonstrates the procedures that must be followed to determine reportable business segments.

Example: Application of IAS 14 Significance Tests

Diversified Printing Inc. consists of five business segments: Books, Cards, Magazines, Maps, and Finance. The following table presents information about each of the segments for Year 1 as reported to the chief executive officer:

	Books	Cards	Magazines	Maps	Finance
Revenues:					
External sales	$65.2	$13.8	$11.6	$3.1	—
Intersegment sales	13.2	2.4	—	1.6	—
Interest revenue—external	4.6	1.8	0.4	0.3	$4.2
Interest revenue—intersegment	—	—	—	—	1.8
Total revenues	$83.0	$18.0	$12.0	$5.0	$6.0
Expenses:					
Operating—external	$34.1	$7.2	$14.6	$3.6	$1.1
Operating—intersegment	9.6	2.0	—	—	0.3
Interest expense	4.2	2.0	4.4	—	3.0
Income taxes	12.1	2.8	(3.0)	0.4	0.1
Total expense	$60.0	$14.0	$16.0	$4.0	$4.5
Assets:					
Tangible	$19.2	$2.2	$1.6	$1.0	$4.6
Intangible	3.8	0.4	1.4	—	—
Intersegment loans	—	—	—	—	3.4
Total assets	$23.0	$2.6	$3.0	$1.0	$8.0

The first step is to determine the percentage of total revenues generated from external sources as follows:

Segment	External Revenues	Total Revenues	External Revenues as % of Total Revenues
Books	$65.2	$78.4	83.2%
Cards	13.8	16.2	85.2
Magazines . . .	11.6	11.6	100.0
Maps	3.1	4.7	65.9
Finance	4.2	6.0	70.0

Each segment generates a majority of its revenues from external customers and therefore meets the first criterion of a reportable segment. The company next applies the three significance tests to determine whether the second criterion for a reportable segment is met.

Revenue Test

The combined revenue of all segments is $124.0 ($83.0 + $18.0 + $12.0 + $5.0 + $6.0). Based on the 10 percent significance level, any segment with revenues of more than $12.4 is a reportable segment. Books and Cards meet this test and should be reported separately.

Profit or Loss Test

The profit or loss (result) for each business segment is determined by subtracting segment expenses from total segment revenues. According to IAS 14, segment revenues do not include interest revenue unless the segment is of a financial nature. Also, segment expenses do not include interest expense (unless the segment is of a financial nature) and income taxes. Profit or loss from each segment is determined as follows:

Segment	Segment Revenues	Segment Expenses	Segment Result Profit	Segment Result Loss
Books	$78.4	$43.7	$34.5	—
Cards	16.2	9.2	7.0	—
Magazines	11.6	14.6	—	$3.0
Maps	4.7	3.6	1.1	—
Finance	6.0	4.4	1.6	—
Total	$116.7	$75.5	$44.2	$3.0

The $44.2 from the four profitable segments is greater in absolute value than the $3.0 loss from the Magazines segment. Therefore, any segment with a profit or loss greater than $4.42 ($44.2 × 10%) is a reportable segment. Only Books and Cards qualify as reportable segments under the profit or loss test.

Asset Test

The final test is based on the business segments' combined total assets of $37.6 ($23.0 + $2.6 + $3.0 + $1.0 + $8.0). According to this test, any segment with assets exceeding 10 percent of combined total assets is a separately reportable segment.

Two segments, Books and Finance, meet this test as each of these segments has total assets exceeding $3.76 ($37.6 × 10%).

Although each of the five segments meets the criterion of having a majority of revenues from external sources, only three segments meet at least one of the significance tests. Magazines and Maps do not meet any of the tests. However, if total external revenue attributable to reportable segments is less than 75 percent of the total consolidated revenue, additional segments should be reported even if they do not meet the 10 percent threshold. To determine whether the 75 percent minimum is met, the percentage of consolidated revenues generated by reportable segments is determined as follows:

	Percentage of Total	
Segment	External Revenues*	Consolidated Revenues
Books	$ 69.8	66.5%
Cards	15.6	14.9
Magazines	12.0	n/a
Maps	3.4	n/a
Finance	4.2	4.0
Total consolidated revenues ...	$105.0	85.4%

*Only external revenues are considered because intersegment revenues are eliminated in the process of preparing consolidated financial statements.

Because the Books, Cards, and Finance segments, in aggregate, comprise more than 75 percent of total consolidated revenues, the Magazines and Maps segments will be combined and reported as "All Other."

Required Disclosures

Primary Reporting Format

The amount of information to be disclosed for each reportable segment differs between the primary reporting format segments and the secondary reporting format segments, with considerably more information required for primary segments. The following information must be provided for each reportable primary reporting format segment:

- Segment revenue.
- Segment profit or loss.
- Carrying amount of segment assets.
- Segment liabilities.
- Cost during the period to acquire property, plant, and equipment, and intangible assets (capital expenditures).
- Depreciation and amortization.
- Significant noncash expenses, other than depreciation and amortization.
- Aggregate share of profit or loss and aggregate investment in equity method associates and joint ventures.

A reconciliation between the information disclosed for primary segments and the aggregate information in the consolidated financial statements also must be presented.

Secondary Reporting Format

The specific disclosures made with regard to the secondary reporting format depend on whether business or geographic segments constitute the primary reporting format. When business segments are the primary reporting format, the following geographic segment information also should be provided:

- Revenue from external customers for each geographic segment whose revenue from sales to external customers is 10 percent or more of total external revenue.
- Carrying amount of segment assets for each geographic segment whose assets are 10 percent or more of total assets of all geographic segments.
- Capital expenditures for each geographic segment whose assets are 10 percent or more of total assets of all geographic segments.

If the primary reporting format is geographic segments, the following information should be provided for each business segment whose external revenues are 10 percent of total external revenues or whose segment assets are 10 percent or more of total segment assets:

- Revenue from external customers.
- Carrying amount of segment assets.
- Capital expenditures.

Additional Geographic Information

Geographic segments can be determined on the basis of where assets are located or on the basis of where customers are located. If the primary reporting format is geographic segments based on location of assets and customer location is different from asset location, the company should disclose revenues from external customers for each customer-based geographic segment that has 10 percent or more of total external revenues. If the primary reporting format instead is geographic segments based on customer location and assets are located in geographic areas different from customers, the company should disclose both of the following:

- The carrying amount of segment assets for each asset-based geographic segment that has 10 percent or more of total external revenues.
- Capital expenditures during the period for each asset-based geographic segment that has 10 percent or more of total capital expenditures.

Exhibit 8.7 presents segment information provided by the German firm Schering AG in accordance with IAS 14. Schering's primary reporting format is based on geography.

Segment Reporting in the United States

SFAS 131, *Disclosures about Segments of an Enterprise and Related Information*, requires extensive disclosures to be made for operating segments. *Operating segments* are those business activities (1) that earn revenues and incur expenses, (2) for which discrete information is available, and (3) whose operating results are regularly reviewed by the chief operating officer to assess performance and make resource allocation decisions. Operating segments can be based on product lines or geographic regions. In a matrix organization where segment managers exist

EXHIBIT 8.7

SCHERING AG
Annual Report
2004
Segment Reporting

Notes on the Consolidated Financial Statements 2004

Excerpt from Note 31. Segment reporting

	Segment net sales	Internal net sales	External net sales	Change from last year
2004				
Europe Region*	3,433	961	2,472	+ 4%
United States Region	1,247	5	1,242	+ 3%
Japan Region	468	—	468	− 10%
Latin America/Canada Region	471	60	411	+ 7%
Asia/Pacific Region	244	10	234	+ 9%
Other Activities	111	31	80	− 42%
Segment total	**5,974**	**1,067**	**4,907**	**+ 2%**
Other	—	—	—	—
Schering AG Group	**5,974**	**1,067**	**4,907**	**+ 2%**

*As of January 1, 2004 we have reassigned certain countries between the Europe Region and the Asia/Middle East Region and have renamed the Asia/Middle East Region the Asia/Pacific Region. Among others, the countries of the Middle East are now part of the Europe Region, while Australia and New Zealand are now part of the Asia/Pacific Region. The previous year's figures in our segment reporting have been adjusted accordingly.

Our primary segment reporting format is geographic, based on the location of the customers. This reflects the management structure of our sales organization, our system of internal financial reporting, and the predominant source of risks and returns in our business. Segment reporting is therefore divided into five geographic segments. Other Activities (mainly our pharmaceutical chemicals business) are managed on a worldwide basis and are therefore also presented as a separate segment.

Segment net sales include both sales to third parties (external net sales) and sales to Group companies belonging to a different region (internal net sales). Inter-segment sales are determined at arm's length prices.

Information on external net sales is generally based on the location of the customer. However, based on our management reporting format, net sales figures of the Europe Region also include the net sales of the subsidiaries Schering Oy, Jenapharm, CIS bio international, and Justesa Imagen Group that are generated outside Europe. Net sales reported for the United States Region also include net sales of the Medrad Group generated outside the United States.

	Segment performance	Central production overhead/ variances	Research and development expenses	Segment result
2004				
Europe Region	1,116	−77	−459	580
United States Region	446	−18	−274	154
Japan Region	133	−12	−79	42
Latin America/Canada Region	155	−11	−62	82
Asia/Pacific Region	90	−12	−38	40
Other Activities	39	−23	−7	9
Segment total	**1,979**	**−153**	**−919**	**907**
Other	−1,218	153	919	−146
Schering AG Group	**741**	—	—	**761**

Segment performance and Segment result are presented on a consolidated basis to ensure comparability with external net sales. Segment performance is an internal financial reporting measurement utilized by our management. Under this approach, transfers from our centralized production facilities in Europe are charged to the segments at standard production cost. Research and development expenses are not included, as this function is managed on a worldwide basis.

(Continued)

EXHIBIT 8.7   (*Continued*)

The Segment result comprises Segment performance less an allocation of research and development expenses and central production overhead and production variances. Research and development expenses specifically attributable to individual segments are allocated directly, while all other expenses incurred by our corporate research and development organization (such as general research, global development activities, and infrastructure) are allocated to the segments on the basis of sales. Central production overhead and production variances are allocated on the basis of the production supplied from our central production facilities to the individual segments.

Total segment results are reconciled to the consolidated Operating profit as follows:

	2004
Total of segment results	**907**
Cost of corporate functions	−171
Other income/expenses	25
Total other	−146
Operating profit	**761**

	Depreciation	Other significant non-cash expenses	Segment assets	Segment liabilities	Investments in intangibles and property, plant and equipment	Segment assets by geographical location	Investments by geographical location
2004							
Europe Region*	98	10	2,035	802	193	2,429	386
United States Region	85	5	927	263	287	719	162
Japan Region	28	—	441	53	31	383	9
Latin America/Canada Region	17	—	168	31	42	135	29
Asia/Pacific Region	11	—	115	7	16	83	5
Other Activities	9	—	134	6	28	71	6
Segment total	**248**	**15**	**3,820**	**1,162**	**597**	**3,820**	**597**
Other	51	4	1,572	1,281	49	1,572	49
Schering AG Group ...	**299**	**19**	**5,392**	**2,443**	**646**	**5,392**	**646**

Depreciation by segment includes amortization of intangible assets and depreciation of property, plant and equipment. Other significant non-cash expenses principally contain pension expenses for unfunded pension obligations reported within Operating profit. Segment assets include all assets with the exception of assets relating to corporate functions, marketable securities and other financial assets, other receivables and other assets, and cash and cash equivalents. Segment liabilities include all liabilities with the exception of liabilities allocated to corporate functions, financial liabilities, and tax liabilities, which are included under Other. Financial liabilities mainly consist of €439m (December 31, 2001: €911 m) pension obligations from German retirement benefit plans. The corresponding €44m (2001: €76 m) in interest costs is included in the Financial result.

Our secondary segment reporting format is based on the Business Areas:

	External net sales	Segment assets	Investments in intangibles and property, plant, and equipment
2004			
Gynecology & Andrology	1,768	1,268	68
Specialized Therapeutics	1,542	1,184	85
Diagnostics & Radiopharmaceuticals	1,308	1,026	59
Dermatology	20	167	9
Other Sources	82	70	8
Segment total	**4,907**	**3,715**	**229**
Other	—	1,875	36
Schering AG Group	**4,907**	**5,390**	**265**

for two or more overlapping sets of organizational units, units based on products and services constitute the operating segments.

After a company has identified its operating segments based on its internal reporting system, management must decide which of these segments should be reported separately. As in IAS 14, *reportable segments* are those whose revenues, profit, or assets are 10 percent or more of consolidated totals. Also as in to IAS 14, a sufficient number of segments must be separately reported to disclose at least 75 percent of consolidated revenues.

Items disclosed by operating segment under U.S. GAAP are the same as those items required to be disclosed for the primary reporting format under IAS 14, with a few exceptions. U.S. GAAP does not require disclosure of liabilities by segment, but it does require disclosure of interest, taxes, and unusual items (discontinued operations and extraordinary items). Whereas IAS 14 requires segment information to be presented in accordance with the company's accounting policies, SFAS 131 requires segment disclosures to be the same as what is reported internally even if this is on a non-GAAP basis.

Enterprise-Wide Disclosures

Unlike IAS 14, which requires disclosures for both business and geographic segments, SFAS 131 requires disclosures for operating segments only. In addition, however, SFAS 131 also requires certain enterprise-wide disclosures. Some companies define operating segments on a geographic basis or have only one operating segment yet provide a range of different products and services. SFAS 131 requires disclosure of *revenues derived from transactions with outsiders from each product or service* if operating segments have not been determined according to differences in those products and services.

Lowes Companies Inc. is an example of a company that operates in only one segment: home improvement products and equipment. In accordance with the enterprise-wide disclosure requirements of SFAS 131, Lowes reports "sales by product category" in the notes to the financial statements. In 2002, for example, Lowes reported that 11 percent of total revenues were generated from the sale of appliances and 8 percent from the sale of lumber, the two largest product categories for the company.

Information about Foreign Operations

If operating segments are not based on geography, then companies must also provide information about their foreign operations. Companies must disclose *revenues* and *long-lived assets* for the following:

1. The domestic country.
2. All foreign countries in which the company derives revenues or holds assets.
3. Each foreign country in which a material amount of revenues is derived or long-lived assets are held.

Requiring country-specific disclosures is a significant departure from previous U.S. segment reporting and from IAS 14. The FASB believes that disclosures by individual country should be more useful in assessing risk than disclosures by aggregated geographic areas. SFAS 131 does not specify a quantitative threshold for determining materiality but instead leaves this determination to management judgment.

A study of geographic area disclosures made by the 500 largest U.S. companies in 1998 found that only 52 percent reported having revenues in foreign countries and, of those, only 45 percent provided information for one or more material countries.[4] The six countries for which disclosures were most commonly provided, in order, were Canada, the United Kingdom, Japan, Germany, France, and Brazil. Although SFAS 131 requires only individual country disclosures, many companies voluntarily continue to provide information by geographic region. To illustrate the range of detail provided by companies in complying with the geographic area disclosure requirement of SFAS 131, Exhibit 8.8 presents the foreign operation revenues disclosures provided in the annual report of three companies.

International Business Machines Corporation (IBM) disclosed the fact that 37 percent of its 2004 revenue was generated in the United States, with an additional 13 percent generated in Japan, but there is no disclosure of the location of the remaining 50 percent of revenues attributable to "other countries." Johnson & Johnson also discloses the amount of sales made in the United States but provides no information with respect to any other individual country. Instead, foreign sales are reported by three broad geographic regions—Europe, Western Hemisphere excluding the United States, and Asia-Pacific and Africa (the rest of the world). General Motors provides the most detailed information of the three companies, specifically reporting the amount of sales and revenue generated in five countries other than the United States. These five countries (four European countries and Brazil) account for 52 percent of General Motors' sales outside of North America.

[4] Timothy S. Doupnik and Larry P. Seese, "Geographic Area Disclosures Under SFAS 131: Materiality and Fineness," *Journal of International Accounting, Auditing & Taxation* 10 (2001), pp. 117–38.

EXHIBIT 8.8   Geographic Area Information for Three U.S. Companies

INTERNATIONAL BUSINESS MACHINES CORPORATION
Annual Report
2004
Excerpt from Note X. Segment Information

Geographic Information

(Dollars in millions)

FOR THE YEAR ENDED DECEMBER 31	Revenue*			Long-Lived Assets**[+]		
	2004	2003	2002	2004	2003[++]	2002[++]
United States	$35,637	$33,762	$32,759	$29,780	$29,929	$28,064
Japan	12,295	11,694	10,939	2,701	2,738	2,814
Other countries	48,361	43,675	37,488	20,600	16,373	13,027
Total	$96,293	$89,131	$81,186	$53,081	$49,040	$43,905

*Revenues are attributed to countries based on location of client and are for continuing operations.

**Includes all non-current assets except non-current financial instruments and deferred tax assets.

[+]At December 31

[++]Reclassified to conform with 2004 presentation.

JOHNSON & JOHNSON
Annual Report
2004
Excerpt from Segments of Business and Geographic Areas

Geographic Areas

(Dollars in millions)	Sales to Customers			Long-lived Assets		
	2004	**2003**	**2002**	**2004**	**2003**	**2002**
United States	$27,770	25,274	22,455	$14,324	14,367	11,822
Europe	11,151	9,483	7,636	6,142	5,193	4,613
Western Hemisphere excluding U.S.	2,589	2,236	2,018	748	772	583
Asia-Pacific, Africa	5,838	4,869	4,189	620	605	555
Segments total	47,348	41,862	36,298	21,834	20,937	17,573
General corporate				444	448	383
Other non long-lived assets				31,039	26,878	22,600
Worldwide total	$47,348	41,862	36,298	$53,317	48,263	40,556

GENERAL MOTORS CORPORATION
Form 10-K
2004
Excerpt from Note 24. Segment Reporting

Information concerning principal geographic areas was as follows (dollars in millions):

	2004		2003		2002	
	Net Sales & Revenues	**Long Lived Assets(1)**	**Net Sales & Revenues**	**Long Lived Assets(1)**	**Net Sales & Revenue**	**Long Lived Assets(1)**
North America						
United States	$134,380	$46,712	$133,955	$47,354	$130,552	$45,964
Canada and Mexico	15,484	10,443	14,667	8,530	15,049	6,897
Total North America	149,864	57,155	148,622	55,884	145,601	52,861
Europe						
France	2,669	262	2,429	216	2,073	183
Germany	6,710	4,479	5,945	3,996	5,363	3,244
Spain	2,661	1,181	2,143	1,256	1,721	1,076
United Kingdom	7,563	2,273	6,480	2,244	5,513	2,096
Other	13,622	3,805	12,356	3,537	10,450	2,953
Total Europe	33,225	12,000	29,353	11,249	25,120	9,552
Latin America						
Brazil	2,987	609	2,328	584	2,487	619
Other Latin America	2,611	180	1,685	186	2,287	185
Total Latin America	5,598	789	4,013	770	4,774	804
All Other	4,830	3,290	3,849	2,820	2,372	2,404
Total	$193,517	$73,234	$185,837	$70,723	$177,867	$65,621

(1) Consists of property (Note 11), equipment on operating leases (Note 9), net of accumulated depreciation.

EXHIBIT 8.9
Survey Results Related to Compliance with IAS 14

Source: Christopher W. Nobes, ed., *GAAP 2001: A Survey of National Accounting Practices Benchmarked against International Accounting Standards* (published jointly by Andersen, BDO, Deloitte Touche Tohmatsu, Ernst & Young, Grant Thornton, KPMG, and PricewaterhouseCoopers, 2001); available at www.ifad.net.

No Specific Rules Requiring Segment Disclosures		
Argentina	India	Philippines
Brazil	Iran	Saudi Arabia
Egypt	Israel	Spain
Estonia	Luxembourg	Turkey
Iceland	Morocco	

Specific Rules for Sales Only		
Austria	Denmark	Poland
Belgium	Greece	Portugal
Czech Republic	Hungary	Switzerland

Primary/Secondary Reporting Format Not Used		
Australia	New Zealand	Thailand
Ireland	Sweden	United Kingdom
Japan	Taiwan	United States

No Significant Departures from IAS 14 Identified		
Canada	Mexico	Singapore
Cyprus	Norway	South Africa
Germany	Pakistan	Venezuela
Italy	Peru	

Segment Reporting Not Required if Prejudicial to Company	
France	Netherlands
Ireland	Poland

Disclosure of Segment Liabilities Not Required		
China	Japan	Taiwan
Finland	Korea	Thailand
Hong Kong	Malaysia	United Kingdom
Indonesia	New Zealand	United States
Ireland	Sweden	

Segment Reporting Internationally

In a 2001 survey of national accounting rules benchmarked against IFRSs, segment reporting was identified as one of the major areas in which there is a lack of convergence internationally.[5] Exhibit 8.9 shows the extent to which national accounting rules in 54 countries conform to IAS 14, *Segment Reporting*. Fourteen countries included in the survey had no specific rules requiring segment disclosure; consistent with the European Union's Fourth Directive, another 9 European countries had requirements related to segment sales only. Of the remaining 31 countries, 9 did not use the primary/secondary reporting format found in IAS 14. There were only 11 countries surveyed for which no significant departures from IAS 14 were identified.

[5] Christopher W. Nobes, ed., *GAAP 2001: A Survey of National Accounting Rules Benchmarked against International Accounting Standards* (published jointly by Andersen, BDO, Deloitte Touche Tohmatsu, Ernst & Young, Grant Thornton, KPMG, and PricewaterhouseCoopers, 2001); available at www.ifad.net.

It is interesting to note that in several countries, segment reporting requirements may be ignored if a company's board of directors determines that such disclosures could be detrimental to the company.

IASB-FASB Convergence

In January 2005, as part of the short-term project to converge with FASB standards, the IASB indicated its intention to amend IAS 14 to converge with U.S. GAAP. Specifically, the IASB intends to adopt the management approach of SFAS 131.

Summary

1. Preparing financial statements using historical cost accounting in a period of inflation results in a number of problems. Assets are understated, and income generally is overstated; using historical cost income as the basis for taxation and dividend distributions can result in cash flow difficulties; and comparing the performance of foreign operations exposed to different rates of inflation can be misleading.

2. Two methods of accounting for changing prices (inflation) have been used in different countries: general purchasing power (GPP) accounting and current cost (CC) accounting. Under GPP accounting, nonmonetary assets and stockholders' equity accounts are restated for changes in the general price level. Cost of goods sold and depreciation/amortization are based on restated asset values, and the net purchasing power gain/loss on the net monetary liability/asset position is included in income. GPP income is the amount that can be paid as a dividend while maintaining the purchasing power of capital. Under CC accounting, nonmonetary assets are revalued to current cost, and cost of goods sold and depreciation/amortization are based on revalued amounts. CC income is the amount that can be paid as a dividend while maintaining physical capital.

3. Several Latin American countries have used or continue to use GPP accounting to overcome the limitations of historical cost accounting. Prior to the introduction of IFRSs, the Netherlands allowed, but did not require, the use of CC accounting. IAS 29 requires the use of GPP accounting by firms that report in the currency of a hyperinflationary economy. IAS 21 requires the financial statements of a foreign operation located in a hyperinflationary economy to first be adjusted for inflation in accordance with IAS 29 before translation into the parent company's reporting currency.

4. Multinational corporations (MNCs) often operate as groups, and there is a need for consolidated financial statements reflecting their financial position and performance. IFRS 3 defines *group* as a parent and its subsidiaries, and requires groups to prepare consolidated financial statements. IAS 27 requires a parent to consolidate all subsidiaries, foreign and domestic, unless the subsidiary was acquired with the intention to be disposed of within 12 months and management is actively seeking a buyer.

5. The definition of *subsidiary* is based on the concept of control, which is often defined in terms of legal control through majority ownership of shares. IAS 27 also recognizes that there can be effective control without legal control, for example, through contractual agreement. Subsidiaries that are effectively controlled must be consolidated.

6. Consistent with North American practice, IFRS 3 requires the exclusive use of the purchase method in accounting for business combinations, requiring any goodwill to be recognized as an asset. Goodwill is not amortized on a systematic basis but is subjected to an annual impairment test. Negative goodwill is recognized immediately as a gain in the income statement.

7. The aggregation of all of a company's activities into consolidated totals masks the differences in risk and potential existing across different lines of business and in different parts of the world. To provide information that can be used to evaluate these risks and potentials, companies disaggregate consolidated totals and provide disclosures on a segment basis. Segment reporting is an area in which considerable diversity exists internationally.

8. IAS 14, which was originally issued in 1981, requires disclosures by both business segment and geographic segment, one of which is designated as the primary reporting format. A business segment or a geographic segment is reportable if a majority of its revenues are generated from external customers and it meets any one of three significance tests. Considerably more information is required to be disclosed for primary reporting segments than for secondary segments.

9. SFAS 131 requires extensive disclosures to be made for operating segments, which can be based on product lines or geographic regions. If operating segments are not based on geography, revenues and long-lived assets must be disclosed for the domestic country, all foreign countries in which the company operates, and each individual country in which a material amount of revenues or assets is located. Requiring country specific disclosures is a major difference between U.S. segment reporting and IAS 14. However, the IASB intends to converge IAS 14 with SFAS 131 as part of its short-term convergence project.

Questions

1. Why is it important that, in countries with high inflation, financial statements be adjusted for inflation?

2. What are the major differences in the calculation of income between the historical cost (HC) model and the general purchasing power (GPP) model of accounting?

3. Which balance sheet accounts give rise to purchasing power gains, and which accounts give rise to purchasing power losses?

4. What are the major differences in the calculation of income between the historical cost (HC) model and the current cost (CC) model of accounting?

5. Why is return on assets (net income/total assets) generally smaller under current cost accounting than under historical cost accounting?

6. In what ways do International Financial Reporting Standards (IFRSs) address the issue of accounting for changing prices (inflation)?

7. What is a group? Compare and contrast the different concepts of a group.

8. To which specific type of business combination does the concept of a group relate?

9. Define *control*. When does control exist in accordance with IAS 27?

10. Explain why the legal concept of control may be appropriate in some countries, such as Japan.

11. What are the circumstances under which a subsidiary could, and perhaps should, be excluded from consolidation?

12. What is proportionate consolidation? Under what circumstances are companies likely to use this method?

13. In accordance with IAS 14, how does a company determine which segments to report separately?

14. What are the major differences in the geographic area information required to be reported in accordance with IAS 14 and in accordance with SFAS 131?

15. In several countries, companies need not provide required segment disclosures if their board of directors determines that providing such disclosures could be detrimental to the company. How might the disclosure of segment information harm a company?

Exercises and Problems

1. Sorocaba Company is located in a highly inflationary country and in accordance with IAS 29 prepares financial statements on a general purchasing power (inflation-adjusted) basis through reference to changes in the general price index (GPI). The company had the following transactions involving machinery and equipment in its first two years of operations:

Date	Transaction	Cost	Useful Life	GPI
January 15, Year 1	Purchase Machine X	$ 20,000	4 years	100
March 20, Year 1	Purchase Machine Y	55,000	5 years	110
October 10, Year 1	Purchase Machine Z	130,000	10 years	130
December 31, Year 1		56,00	4yr	140
April 15, Year 2	Sold Machine X		5yr	160
December 31, Year 2		180,000	10yr	180

Required:
Determine the amount that would be reported as machinery and equipment in accordance with IAS 29 on the December 31, Year 1, and December 31, Year 2, balance sheets.

2. Antalya Company borrows 1,000,000 Turkish lira (TL) on January 1, Year 1, at an annual interest rate of 60 percent by signing a two-year note payable. During Year 1, the Turkish inflation index changed from 250 at January 1 to 387.5 at December 31.

Required:
Related to this note payable, determine the following amounts for Antalya Company for Year 1:
a. Nominal interest expense.
b. Purchasing power gain on the borrowing.
c. Real interest expense (nominal interest expense less purchasing power gain). What is the real rate of interest paid by Antalya Company in Year 1 on its note payable?

3. Doner Company Inc. begins operations on January 1, Year 1. The company's unadjusted financial statements for the year ended December 31, Year 1, appear as follows:

Balance Sheets	1/1/Y1	12/31/Y1
Cash and receivables	$20,000	$35,000
Fixed assets, net	50,000	45,000
Total	$70,000	$80,000
Payables	$15,000	$15,000
Contributed capital	55,000	55,000
Retained earnings	—	10,000
Total	$70,000	$80,000

Income Statement, Year 1	
Revenues	$50,000
Depreciation	(5,000)
Other expenses	(35,000)
Income	$10,000

Revenues and expenses occur evenly throughout the year; revenues and other expenses are realized in terms of monetary assets (cash and receivables).

General price indexes for Year 1 are as follows:

1/1/Y1	100
Average Y1	120
12/31/Y1	150

Required:
a. Calculate Doner Company's Year 1 purchasing power gain or loss on net monetary items.
b. Determine Doner Company's Year 1 income on a general purchasing power basis (ignore income taxes).

4. Petrodat Company provides data processing services for companies operating in the petroleum extraction business. On January 1, Year 1, Petrodat established two foreign subsidiaries—one in Mexico and the other in Venezuela—by investing $100,000 worth of data processing equipment in each. The opening balance sheets for the two subsidiaries in local currency appear as follows:

	Mexico (pesos)	Venezuela (bolivars)
Machinery and equipment	1,000,000	150,000,000
Total assets	1,000,000	150,000,000
Contributed capital	1,000,000	150,000,000
Total owners' equity	1,000,000	150,000,000

The equipment is depreciated on a straight-line basis over a five-year useful life with no residual value.

The Year 1 income statement for each subsidiary appears as follows:

	Mexico (pesos)	Venezuela (bolivars)
Revenues	400,000	60,000,000 2
Depreciation expense	(200,000)	(30,000,000)
Other expenses	(150,000)	(22,500,000)
Net income	50,000	7,500,000

Revenues and other expenses occurred evenly throughout the year and were realized in cash by year-end. As a result, the balance sheets for the two companies at December 31, Year 1, appear as follows:

	Mexico (pesos)	Venezuela (bolivars)
Cash	250,000	37,500,000
Machinery and equipment	1,000,000	150,000,000
Less: Accumulated depreciation	(200,000)	(30,000,000)
Total assets	1,050,000	157,500,000
Contributed capital	1,000,000	150,000,000
Retained earnings	50,000	7,500,000
Total equity	1,050,000	157,500,000

For Year 1, the two subsidiaries reported the following measures of profitability:

	Mexico	Venezuela
Profit margin (net income/revenues)	12.5%	12.5%
Return on equity (net income/average total stockholders' equity)	4.88%	4.88%

Values for the general price index in Mexico and Venezuela during Year 1 were as follows:

	Mexico	Venezuela
January 1	100	100
Average	105	110
December 31	110	120

Required:
a. For each subsidiary, restate Year 1 income for changes in the general price index. Include a purchasing power gain or loss. Ignore income taxes.
b. Calculate Year 1 profit margin and return on assets for each subsidiary on an inflation-adjusted basis.
c. Comment on the impact of inflation on the comparison of profitability measures across operations located in countries with different levels of inflation.

5. Auroral Company had the following investments in shares of other companies on December 31, Year 1:

Name of Company	Country	% Voting Rights	Comments
Accurcast	Domestic	100%	Operations are dissimilar from those of the parent and other subsidiaries.
Bonello	Domestic	45	No other shareholder owns more than 0.1% of voting shares.
Cromos	Foreign	30	Cromos has incurred a net operating loss three years in a row.
Fidelis	Domestic	100	Fidelis is under jurisdiction of bankruptcy court.
Jenna	Domestic	100	Operations are immaterial to those of the parent.
Marek	Domestic	40	Management control contract provides Auroral with effective control.
Phenix	Domestic	90	Parent intends to sell one-half of its investment in the company but is not yet actively seeking a buyer.
Regulus	Foreign	50	Regulus is jointly owned with Coronal Company.
Synkron	Foreign	15	No other shareholder owns more than 10% of voting shares.
Tiksed	Foreign	70	Foreign government no longer allows dividends to be repatriated to foreign parent.
Ypsilon	Domestic	51	Remaining 49% is owned by Borealis Inc.

Required:

Determine the appropriate method for including each of these investments in Auroral Company's consolidated financial statements:

a. In accordance with IFRSs.

b. In accordance with U.S. GAAP.

6. Sandestino Company contributes cash of $170,000 and Costa Grande Company contributes net assets of $170,000 to create Grand Sand Company on January 1, Year 1. Sandestino and Costa Grande each receive a 50 percent equity interest in Grand Sand. Grand Sand's financial statements for its first year of operations are as follows:

GRAND SAND COMPANY
Income Statement
Year 1

Revenues	$80,000
Expenses	50,000
Income before tax	30,000
Tax expense	10,000
Net income	$20,000

GRAND SAND COMPANY
Balance Sheet
December 31, Year 1

Cash	$ 40,000	Liabilities	$ 60,000
Inventory	60,000	Common stock	340,000
Property, plant, and equipment (net)	320,000	Retained earnings	20,000
Total	$420,000	Total	$420,000

Before making any accounting entries related to its investment in Grand Sand Company, Sandestino Company's financial statements for the year ended December 31, Year 1, are as follows:

SANDESTINO COMPANY
Income Statement
Year 1

Revenues	$800,000
Expenses	450,000
Income before tax	350,000
Tax expense	100,000
Net income	$250,000

SANDESTINO COMPANY
Balance Sheet
December 31, Year 1

Cash	$ 130,000	Liabilities	$ 250,000
Inventory	200,000	Common stock	600,000
Property, plant, and equipment (net) . . .	650,000	Retained earnings . . .	300,000
Investment in Grand Sand (at cost) . . .	170,000		
Total	$1,150,000	Total	$1,150,000

Required:

a. Restate Sandestino's Year 1 financial statements to properly account for its investment in Grand Sand Company under (1) the proportionate consolidation method, and (2) the equity method.

b. Calculate and compare the following ratios for Sandestino Company under the two different methods of accounting for its investment in Grand Sand Company: (1) profit margin (net income/revenues), and (2) debt to equity (total liabilities/total stockholders' equity).

7. Horace Jones Company consists of six business segments. The consolidated income statement as well as information about each of the segments for Year 1 as reported to the chief executive officer is as follows:

HORACE JONES COMPANY
Consolidated Income Statement
Year 1

Revenues	$ 1,790
Cost of goods sold	(1,060)
Depreciation and amortization	(230)
Other operating expenses	(380)
Operating income	120
Interest expense	(30)
Income before tax	90
Income tax	(30)
Net income	$ 60

Summary of business segment and general corporate activity for Year 1:

	General Corporate	Segment A	B	C	D	E	F
Revenues:							
External sales revenue	—	1,030	350	20	140	130	120
Intersegment sales revenue	—	30	20	200	10	0	0
Expenses:							
Cost of goods sold	—	600	300	130	90	60	80
Depreciation and amortization	10	80	100	10	20	5	5
Other operating expenses	50	120	150	10	30	5	15
Interest expense	—	10	5	5	0	5	5
Income taxes	—	20	−40	20	5	20	5
Assets:							
Current assets	10	450	150	100	80	150	70
Property, plant and equipment (net)	90	1,200	500	400	200	150	50
Purchases of property, plant and equipment	10	200	50	50	25	20	30
Liabilities	—	750	300	250	170	140	90

Additional information:

At December 31, Year 1, consolidated total assets were $3,600 and consolidated total liabilities were $1,700. Intersegment sales are made at cost plus a 30 percent markup on cost. General corporate expenses can be reasonably allocated to each business segment on the basis of its relative share of total property, plant, and equipment (net). There were no significant noncash expenses other than depreciation. There were no investments in equity method associates or joint ventures.

Required:

The company uses International Financial Reporting Standards (IFRSs) to prepare its financial statements. Prepare the note to financial statements in accordance with IAS 14 *Segment Reporting*. Business segments comprise the company's primary reporting format in compliance with IAS 14.

8. Many European companies prepare consolidated financial statements in accordance with International Financial Reporting Standards (IFRSs). You have recently been hired by one of the international public accounting firms as a staff auditor. Your first audit assignment involves Schering AG, a German pharmaceutical company.

Required:

Refer to the segment information provided by Schering AG in Exhibit 8.7 and evaluate whether the company is in compliance with IAS 14, *Segment Reporting*.

9. Geographic segment information can be used to determine how multinational a company is and the extent to which a company is diversified internationally. Refer to the geographic segment information provided by three U.S. companies in Exhibit 8.8.

Required:

a. Develop a measure of each company's degree of multinationality.
b. Evaluate the extent to which each company is diversified internationally.

10. The following geographic segment information is provided in the 2004 annual report by two German automakers, BMW and Volkswagen:

BMW AG
Annual Report
2004

Segment information by region

in euro million	External sales		Capital expenditure		Assets	
	2004	2003	2004	2003	2004	2003
Germany	11,961	10,590	3,637	3,492	24,905	21,510
Rest of Europe	15,823	13,389	515	549	15,618	14,390
America	10,648	11,620	92	143	15,949	15,263
Africa, Asia, Oceania . . .	5,903	5,926	103	61	6,877	6,142
Reconciliations	—	—	—	—	4,066	4,170
Group	44,335	41,525	4,347	51,259	67,415	61,475

Source: BMW AG, 2004 annual report, p. 101.

VOLKSWAGEN AG
Annual Report
2004

Segmental Reporting by Market 2004

€ million	Germany	Rest of Europe	North America	South America	Africa	Asia/ Oceania	Consolidation	Total
Sales to third parties	24,504	39,755	13,308	3,949	1,582	5,865	—	88,963
Investments in property, plant and equipment, and other intangible assets	3,541	1,376	417	120	71	14	11	5,550
Segment assets	72,022	43,606	17,444	3,652	686	2,693	−20,635	119,468

Segmental Reporting by Market 2003

€ million	Germany	Rest of Europe	North America	South America	Africa	Asia/ Oceania	Consolidation	Total
Sales to third parties	23,298	35,723	15,011	3,073	1,133	6,575	—	84,813
Investments in property, plant and equipment and other intangible assets	4,391	1,559	501	166	81	12	17	6,727
Segment assets	66,336	38,734	18,011	3,218	459	2,255	−16,417	112,596

Source: Volkswagen AG, 2004 annual report, p. 65.

Required:

Use the 2004 segment information provided by BMW and Volkswagen to answer the following questions:

a. Which company is more multinational?

b. Which company is more internationally diversified?

c. In which region(s) of the world did each company experience the greatest growth? greatest decline?

References

American Institute of Certified Public Accountants. *Accounting Trends and Techniques*, 55th ed. New York: AICPA, 2002.

———. Accounting Research Bulletin (ARB) 51, *Consolidated Financial Statements*, 1959.

Doupnik, Timothy S., and Larry P. Seese. "Geographic Area Disclosures Under SFAS 131: Materiality and Fineness." *Journal of International Accounting, Auditing & Taxation* 10 (2001), pp. 117–38.

Mexican Institute of Public Accountants. Bulletin B-10, *Recognition of the Inflation Effects in Financial Information*.

Nobes, Christopher W., ed. *GAAP 2001: A Survey of National Accounting Rules Benchmarked against International Accounting Standards*. Published jointly by Andersen, BDO, Deloitte Touche Tohmatsu, Ernst & Young, Grant Thornton, KPMG, and PricewaterhouseCoopers, 2001. Available at www.ifad.net.

———. "An Analysis of the International Development of the Equity Method." *Abacus* 38, no. 1 (2002), pp. 16–45.

Pacter, Paul. *Reporting Disaggregated Information*. Stamford, CT: FASB, February 1993.

Radebaugh, Lee H., and Sidney J. Gray. *International Accounting and Multinational Enterprises*, 5th ed. New York: Wiley, 2002.

Chapter **Nine**

Analysis of Foreign Financial Statements

Learning Objectives

After reading this chapter, you should be able to

- Discuss reasons to analyze financial statements of foreign companies.
- Describe potential problems in analyzing foreign financial statements.
- Provide possible solutions to problems associated with analyzing foreign financial statements.
- Demonstrate an approach for restating foreign financial statements to U.S. generally accepted accounting principles (GAAP).

INTRODUCTION.

There are more than 400 foreign companies listed on the New York Stock Exchange,[1] and a similar number are listed on the London Stock Exchange. All of the major mutual fund companies—including American Century, Fidelity, and Vanguard—offer international stock funds that focus on non-U.S. firms. In making decisions to invest in the stock of foreign companies, investors generally find financial statements to be useful.

This chapter deals with the analysis of financial statements prepared by foreign companies. The first section describes several reasons for analyzing foreign financial statements. The second section describes potential problems associated with analyzing foreign financial statements and discusses possible solutions to those problems. The final section demonstrates an approach that can be used to restate a set of foreign financial statements prepared in accordance with local accounting practice to a format and generally accepted accounting principles (GAAP) more familiar to the reader.

REASONS TO ANALYZE FOREIGN FINANCIAL STATEMENTS

Many users of financial statements might find it necessary to read and analyze the statements of foreign companies. Some common reasons for doing so are described in this section.

---

[1] A list of foreign companies listed on U.S. stock exchanges is available at www.sec.gov/divisions/corpfin/internatl/alphabetical.htm.

Foreign Portfolio Investment

Investors can reduce portfolio risks by diversifying internationally. Research shows that stock market returns across countries are not highly correlated.[2] During the period 1971–1994, the correlation of U.S. stock returns with returns on European stock exchanges ranged from 0.23 (Italy) to 0.58 (Netherlands). Even the largest correlation, at 0.68 with Canada, was far from unity. The high degree of independence across capital markets leaves substantial room for risk diversification.

Since the mid-1980s, U.S. investment firms have created a plethora of international and country-specific mutual funds. For example, Fidelity Investments offers the following targeted-country or regional stock funds: Canada, China Region, Europe, Europe Capital Appreciation, Japan, Japan Smaller Companies, Nordic, Pacific Basin, Latin America, and Southeast Asia. Fidelity's Emerging Markets Funds invest in companies located in 17 different countries, including Brazil, Hungary, and Thailand. T. Rowe Price's New Asia Fund invests in stocks of non-Japanese Asian companies, and its International Stock Fund invests in stocks and bonds of non-U.S. companies all over the world. The latter fund includes shares of companies from more than 25 different countries. The manager of each of these funds must decide which non-U.S. companies' stock to add to the fund's portfolio. Individual investors can invest in these funds and thereby diversify their personal portfolios internationally without incurring the costs of investing in foreign stocks directly.

International Mergers and Acquisitions

Interest in foreign financial statements has also grown with the increase in international mergers and acquisitions. Some of the largest mergers in the United States in recent years have involved foreign companies acquiring U.S. firms. The Daimler/Chrysler and BP/Amoco mergers are two examples. Over the last decade, Ford Motor Company has acquired an equity interest in companies located in Great Britain (Jaguar, Land Rover, Aston Martin); Sweden (Volvo); and Japan (Mazda). As a part of the due diligence process leading to an acquisition, financial analysts from the acquiring firm will use the financial statements of the target company as a starting point for determining how much to pay.

After the economic opening of Eastern Europe in 1989, one of the early impediments to Western investment in that region was a lack of economically meaningful financial statements for existing enterprises. Soviet-style accounting statements were prepared for national planning purposes, not for determining enterprise value. Potential buyers of privatized state-owned enterprises often found it necessary to engage one of the international public accounting firms to develop a set of financial statements based on U.S. GAAP or some other set of accounting rules that provide a more realistic picture of the company's assets and profitability.

Other Reasons

Other reasons to evaluate foreign company financial statements include

1. Making credit decisions about foreign customers.
2. Evaluating the financial health of foreign suppliers.
3. Benchmarking against global competitors.

---

[2] Bruno Solnik, *International Investments,* 3rd ed. (Addison-Wesley, 1996), pp. 94–95.

The next section of this chapter describes potential problems in evaluating foreign financial statements and discusses possible solutions. We focus on analyzing foreign financial statements for the purpose of making equity investment decisions.

POTENTIAL PROBLEMS IN ANALYZING FOREIGN FINANCIAL STATEMENTS

Given the information provided in earlier chapters, it should be obvious that diversity in accounting principles is one of the most significant problems in analyzing foreign financial statements. Other problems, however, may be more difficult to overcome. To appreciate the various potential problems, assume that you have taken a job with the Vanguard Group, headquartered in Valley Forge, Pennsylvania. You have been hired to assist the manager of the International Stock Fund. Your boss has decided that a certain percentage of the fund's assets should be invested in the publicly traded shares of European companies. Your job is to recommend specific companies to invest in. At least one source of information you would like to use in making your recommendations is corporate financial statements. What are the potential problems that might arise as you conduct your analysis?

Data Accessibility

Financial data for foreign companies may not be as easy to obtain as that for domestic companies. However, as international investment in equities has become more prevalent, several companies have gotten into the business of developing databases that provide financial information on foreign companies. For example, Standard & Poor's Compustat Global database provides data for 13,000 international companies in more than 80 countries. Worldscope and Global Access, provided by Thomson Research, also provide financial statement data for non-U.S. firms. In addition to providing balance sheet and income statement information, most data sources provide additional information such as financial ratios and stock prices.

There are several limitations in using commercial databases to analyze foreign companies. The first is the potential for errors when the data are entered into the database. A more serious potential problem relates to the use of a common balance sheet and income statement format for all companies in the database. Formats of financial statements differ across countries. In fact, some financial statement line items are unique to a particular country. Analysts who force all financial statements into a common format can lose information. The third, and probably greatest, limitation relates to the loss of information provided in the notes to the financial statements. None of the commercial databases provides a complete set of notes. Notes often provide important qualitative as well as quantitative information that is not available if the analyst does not have access to the actual annual report.

There are several avenues an analyst might use to obtain a copy of a foreign company's annual report. One way would be to write or call the company and request a copy. Of course, the analyst would have to know the company's address or telephone number and would have to expect some delay in receiving the report. A second way would be to use the Internet. Many companies, both domestic and foreign, maintain a Web site on which they post financial statements or through which an analyst may request an annual report. The following are Internet resources that can be helpful in obtaining financial information on foreign companies:

- Hoover's (www.hoovers.com) provides capsule information for U.S. and foreign companies, as well as links to company home pages. Access to more in-depth company profiles requires a subscription.
- The U.S. Securities and Exchange Commission (SEC; www.sec.gov) maintains a database known as Electronic Data Gathering, Analysis, and Retrieval (EDGAR), which contains the full text of reports filed electronically with the SEC, including some foreign companies listed on U.S. stock exchanges. Unfortunately, many foreign companies file annual reports with the SEC only on paper, so an electronic version is not available.
- Company Annual Reports On Line (CAROL; www.carol.co.uk) provides links to the investor relations section of European and U.S. company home pages. It is necessary to register in advance for this free service.
- The Annual Report Gallery (www.reportgallery.com) is a Web site with links to CAROL and annual reports of Japanese companies.

Language

Even if an analyst can obtain financial statements from foreign companies, he or she must realize that those statements will be in the local language. Exhibit 9.1 presents a page from the 2004 annual report of Metso OY, a Finnish company that provides equipment and services to the paper, mining, and process industries. Although the excerpt presented in Exhibit 9.1 appears to be an accounting report, anyone who is not relatively fluent in Finnish will find it difficult to know with certainty what information is being provided. There are two possible solutions to the language problem:

1. Hire a professional translator to translate the annual report.
2. Develop a multilingual capability, possibly using a team approach in which each member of the team is fluent in a different foreign language.

The least costly solution to the language problem for the analyst would be for the foreign company to prepare a "convenience translation" of the report in a language that the analyst can read. Many large foreign companies translate their annual reports into foreign languages (especially English) for the convenience of foreign audiences of interest. Exhibit 9.2 shows the extent to which companies in a number of foreign countries provide financial statements in English.

The information in Exhibit 9.2 is based on an analysis of the largest international companies in 1981. Given the globalization of capital markets that has occurred in the last 25 years, the percentage of companies not providing English-language reports is probably much smaller today. In many cases, companies with securities registered in a foreign country are required to translate the annual report into the language of that country. Foreign companies listed on U.S. stock exchanges, for example, must file an English-language annual report with the SEC. However, quarterly reports may be filed in a foreign language.

Few U.S.-based companies prepare convenience translations. During the 1980s, International Business Machines (IBM) prepared a translation of its annual report in French and Japanese. The French version might be explained by the fact that IBM's European headquarters were in Paris. The Japanese version probably resulted from IBM's having a large operation in Japan. IBM no longer prepares a convenience translation in either language.

EXHIBIT 9.1

METSO OY
Annual Report (in Finnish)
2004

Konsernin tuloslaskelma

		31.12. päättynyt tilikausi		
	Liitetieto	2002 Milj. E	2003 Milj. E	**2004 Milj. E**
Liikevaihto		4 691	4 250	**3 976**
Hankinnan ja valmistuksen kulut	3), 5)	−3 425	−3 211	**−2 959**
Bruttokate		1 266	1 039	**1 017**
Myynnin ja hallinnon yleiskustannukset	2), 3) ,5)	−1 015	−906	**−844**
Liikevoitto ennen kertaluonteisia eriä ja liikearvon poistoa		251	133	**173**
% liikevaihdosta		5.3%	3.1%	**4.4%**
Liiketoiminnan kertaluonteiset tuotot ja kulut, netto. . . .	4), 9)	−27	−106	**−25**
Liikearvon alaskirjaus	11)	—	−205	**—**
Liikearvon poisto	5), 11)	−57	−51	**−37**
Liikevoitto (-tappio)		167	−229	**111**
% liikevaihdosta		3.6%	−5.4%	**2.8%**
Rahoitustuotot ja—kulut, netto	6)	−74	−74	**−62**
Osuus osakkuusyhtiöiden tuloksista	7)	0	0	**0**
Tulos ennen satunnaiseriä ja veroja		93	−303	**49**
Satunnaiset tuotot ja kulut, netto		—	—	**—**
Tulos ennen veroja		93	−303	**49**
Tuloverot	8)	−26	44	**21**
Vähemmistöosuus tilikauden tuloksesta		−2	1	**−1**
Tilikauden tulos		65	−258	**69**
Tulos per osake, euro	10)	0.48	−1.89	**0.51**

EXHIBIT 9.2
Extent of English-Language Annual Reports

Source: Business International, *Analyzing Financial Ratios of the World's 1,000 Leading Industrial Corporations* (New York: Business International, 1981).

Percentage of Companies that Do Not Provide Financial Statements in English		
0–10%	**10–50%**	**50% or more**
Australia	Belgium	Austria
Canada	Brazil	France
Denmark	Italy	Mexico
Finland	Germany	South Korea
India		Spain
Ireland		
Japan		
Malaysia		
Netherlands		
Norway		
South Africa		
Sweden		
Switzerland		
United Kingdom		

EXHIBIT 9.3

METSO OY
Annual Report (in English)
2004

Consolidated Statements of Income

		Year ended December 31,		
(In millions, except for per share amounts)	Note	2002 EUR	2003 EUR	**2004 EUR**
Net sales		4 691	4 250	**3 976**
Cost of goods sold	3), 5)	(3 425)	(3 211)	**(2 959)**
Gross profit		1 266	1 039	**1 017**
Selling, general and administrative expenses	2), 3), 5)	(1 015)	(906)	**(844)**
Operating profit before nonrecurring operating items and amortization of goodwill		251	133	**173**
% of net sales		5.3%	3.1%	**4.4%**
Nonrecurring operating income and expenses, net	4), 9)	(27)	(106)	**(25)**
Goodwill impairment	11)	—	(205)	**—**
Amortization of goodwill	5), 11)	(57)	(51)	**(37)**
Operating profit (loss)		167	(229)	**111**
% of net sales		3.6%	(5.4)%	**2.8%**
Financial income and expenses, net	6)	(74)	(74)	**(62)**
Share of profits of associated companies	7)	0	0	**0**
Income (loss) before extraordinary items and income taxes . . .		93	(303)	**49**
Extraordinary income and expenses, net		—	—	**—**
Income (loss) before taxes		93	(303)	**49**
Income taxes	8)	(26)	44	**21**
Minority interests		(2)	1	**(1)**
Net income (loss)		65	(258)	**69**
Earnings per share	10)	0.48	(1.89)	**0.51**

Currency

Exhibit 9.3 presents the English-language version of the excerpt from Metso OY's annual report presented in Exhibit 9.1. Non-Finnish readers now can see that this is an income statement. The amounts are reported in euros. An analyst might like to have these amounts in, say, U.S. dollars to be able to compare with non-European companies. This requires translation from one currency to another. In translating financial statement amounts for the sake of convenience, all financial statement items, including stockholders' equity, should be translated at the current exchange rate. This avoids a translation adjustment. The analyst must be careful to translate previous years' comparative information using the exchange rate for the current year, not the current rate at the end of each year. The following example demonstrates the problem that arises when trend analysis is conducted using currency amounts translated using each year's ending exchange rate.

Assume that a European company has sales of €1,000 in Year 1 and €1,100 in Year 2, an increase of 10 percent. Assume further that the exchange rates were $1.00 per euro at the end of Year 1 and $1.10 per euro at the end of Year 2.

Translation of the euro amounts using the exchange rate at the end of each year results in the following:

	Year 1	Year 2	% Change
Sales in €......	€1,000	€1,100	+10%
	×$ 1.00	×$ 1.10	
Sales in $......	$1,000	$1,210	+21%

Using different exchange rates to translate sales for the two years distorts the actual change in sales from Year 1 to Year 2.

Translation at the current exchange rate at the end of Year 2 maintains the percentage change in sales in terms of euros:

	Year 1	Year 2	% Change
Sales in €	€1,000	€1,100	+10%
	×$ 1.10	×$ 1.10	
Sales in $	$1,100	$1,210	+10%

In addition to translating the language, some foreign companies will also translate the currency of their financial statements in their convenience translations. This is especially true for Japanese companies that routinely translate financial statements into U.S. dollars. However, only the current-year Japanese yen amounts are translated into dollars, thus avoiding the potential problem just demonstrated. It is uncommon for European companies to translate the currency in their English-language convenience reports, perhaps because most European multinationals share a common currency, the euro.

The fact that foreign financial statements are prepared in a foreign currency is really not a problem in analyzing those statements. Much financial statement analysis is conducted using ratios. Ratios are not expressed in any currency but instead in percentage terms. For example, a company with net income of €100 and sales of €1,000 has a profit margin of 10 percent, not €10. The profit margin of a company in, say, Brazil can be compared directly with that of a company in, say, Mexico regardless of the currencies in which sales and profit are expressed. Additionally, year-to-year changes within a company also are expressed in percentage terms, thus removing the currency issue.

Terminology

Even if a foreign company has translated its financial statements into English for the convenience of English-speaking analysts, confusion can arise because of the terminology used. Differences in terminology between British and American companies are well-known and at first may cause some problems. However, it should not require much effort for an analyst in one country to become fluent in the terminology of the other country. It is interesting to see that some non-English-language companies translate their annual report using British terms whereas others use American terms.

The use of nonstandard terminology is less easy to deal with. Esker SA, a French software firm, includes the line item "Commercial charges" as one of its operating expenses in the income statement. Even though this item is the single largest expense, there is nothing in the notes that enlightens the English-language reader as to its contents. From Esker's annual report it is impossible to determine whether this is simply a bad translation or whether this represents a type of cost unfamiliar to English speakers. The point made earlier regarding standardized databases can be demonstrated here. The data-entry person at Standard & Poor's Compustat responsible for entering Esker SA into the database must decide into which of the standard line items common to all companies—for example, selling expense, administrative expense, or interest expense—this item should be placed.

Additional anecdotal examples of financial statement items that might lead to interpretation problems include the following:

- "Items affecting comparability"—reported as an operating expense in Holmen AB's (Sweden) income statement.
- "Write-backs on intangible and tangible fixed assets and consolidation differences"—included in the "Extraordinary income" section of Union Miniere's (France) income statement.
- "Reversal of provisions and expense transfers"—included in total operating income in Picogica's (France) income statement.
- "Revenue reserves"—reported as a positive item in the stockholders' equity section of Degussa AG's (Germany) balance sheet.
- "Other liable capital"—placed between stockholders' equity and liabilities in Fielmann AG's (Germany) balance sheet.
- "Guarantee funds"—shown as a memorandum item in Geveke NV's (Netherlands) balance sheet.[3]

Familiarity with the business environment and accounting practices in each of these countries can help alleviate problems in understanding what might appear to be odd terminology.

Format

The format of financial statements varies considerably across countries. Most format differences should not present much of a problem to the financial analyst. Often financial statements can be reformatted to allow for comparisons across countries. For example, whether or not interest expense is treated as an operating expense and subtracted from operating income is a trivial issue so long as it is disclosed as a separate line item. But some format differences lead to different amounts of information being provided in the financial statements. For example, the type of expense format income statement commonly found in Europe does not report the amount of cost of goods sold. An example of this format is presented in Exhibit 9.4 for the Swiss company Swatch Group Ltd. It is not possible to calculate gross profit or a gross profit margin (Gross profit/Net sales) for companies that use this format.

As another example, the first line item in the Chinese glass manufacturer Fujian Yaohua's income statement is "Operating Income from Major Businesses." A line item for sales revenue is not presented. It might be possible to work backward to a sales amount by adding "Operating Costs" to "Operating Income," but this is unclear. Analysts would have less than complete confidence in their calculation of profit margin (Net income/Net sales) without an unequivocal measure of sales.

One more example of the potential problem presented by format differences is found in German company balance sheets where liabilities are not classified as

[3] Geveke attempts to explain in the notes what is meant by "guarantee funds" in the following way: "By guarantee funds is meant the amount that fulfills a buffer function between the value of total assets on the one hand and the obligations to preferential and unsecured creditors on the other hand" (Geveke NV, 2000 annual report, p. 83). This explanation may shed little light on the nature of this item to those unfamiliar with Dutch business practice.

EXHIBIT 9.4

SWATCH GROUP LTD
Annual Report
2003

Consolidated Income Statement

	2003		2002	
	million CHF	**%**	million CHF	%
Gross sales	**3 983**	**100.0**	4 063	100.0
Sales reductions	**−138**	**−3.5**	−130	−3.2
Net sales.	**3 845**	**96.5**	3 933	96.8
Other operating income	**28**	**0.7**	37	0.9
Changes in inventories and work in progress	**433**	**1.1**	157	3.9
Capitalized expenditures.	**24**	**0.6**	36	0.9
Material purchases	**−806**	**−20.2**	−953	−23.5
Staff costs	**−1 262**	**−31.7**	−1 269	−31.2
Other operating expenses.	**−1 062**	**−26.7**	−1 099	−27.1
Operating result before depreciation &				
amortization (EBITDA)	**810**	**20.3**	842	20.7
Depreciation of fixed assets (excluding goodwill) . . .	**−202**	**−5.1**	−198	−4.8
Amortization of goodwill	**−14**	**−0.3**	−12	−0.3
Operating result (EBIT)	**594**	**14.9**	632	15.6
Net financial result	**−1**	**0.0**	−22	−0.6
Result before taxes	**593**	**14.9**	610	15.0
Income taxes	**−96**	**−2.4**	−110	−2.7
Group result before minority interest	**497**	**12.5**	500	12.3
Minority interest.	**−5**	**−0.1**	−6	−0.1
Net income.	**492**	**12.4**	494	12.2

current and noncurrent but as "Accruals" and "Liabilities" (both current and long-term). See the balance sheet for Fielmann AG in Exhibit 9.5 for an example. Because current liabilities are not reported on the balance sheet, it is not possible to easily calculate a current ratio even though a subtotal for current assets is reported. The presentation of current assets presents an additional problem, however, as it does not include the short-term portion of prepaid expenses. Both short-term and long-term prepaids are reported in a single line item. Problems associated with financial statement format differences can be overcome if sufficient additional information is provided in the notes to the financial statements.

Extent of Disclosure

Amounts and types of disclosure differ across countries. While full disclosure is one of the fundamental principles of U.S. GAAP, some countries might not require enough disclosure for the analyst to be able to make well-informed decisions. In a survey of financial analysts conducted by Choi and Levich, the disclosure items most frequently mentioned as important but missing were related to segment information, methods of asset valuation, foreign operations disclosures, frequency and completeness of interim information, description of capital expenditures, hidden reserves, and off-balance-sheet items.[4]

---

[4] Frederick D. S. Choi and Richard M. Levich, "Behavioral Effects of International Accounting Diversity," *Accounting Horizons*, June 1991, p. 6.

EXHIBIT 9.5

FIELMANN AG
Annual Report
2003

Consolidated Balance Sheet

Assets	Ref. no. in notes	Position as at 31.12.03 €'000	Position as at 31.12.02 €'000
A. Fixed assets			
I. Intangible assets	(1)	34,431	43,582
II. Tangible assets	(2)	148,791	158,298
III. Financial assets	(3)	1,488	953
		184,710	202,833
B. Current assets			
I. Inventories	(4)	74,126	78,951
II. Receivables and other assets	(5)	88,567	49,381
III. Securities	(6)	102,033	5,315
IV. Cash and cash equivalents	(7)	56,581	42,029
		321,307	175,676
C. Prepaid expenses	(8)	31,401	1,184
		537,418	379,693

Equity and liabilities	Ref. no. in notes	Position as at 31.12.03 €'000	Position as at 31.12.02 €'000
A. Equity capital			
I. Subscribed capital	(9)	54,600	54,600
II. Capital reserves	(10)	92,652	92,652
III. Profit reserves	(11)	143,975	85,082
IV. Consolidated balance sheet profit	(12)	33,600	26,250
V. Minority interests	(11)	1,387	1,190
		326,214	259,774
B. Other liable capital	(13)	128	128
C. Special reserves	(13)	0	123
D. Accruals	(14)	109,666	32,267
E. Liabilities	(15)	100,631	87,077
F. Deferred income		779	324
		537,418	379,693
G. Contingent liabilities	(16)	10,092	10,107

An analyst's ability to reformat foreign financial statements will partially depend on whether adequate information is disclosed to allow reformatting. For example, although German companies do not classify liabilities as short-term and long-term on the balance sheet, they are required to disclose short-term liabilities in the notes. Indeed, German companies generally report not only the amount of liabilities due within one year but also the amount not due until five years in the future. Exhibit 9.6 presents the additional information related to the maturity of liabilities provided in the notes of Fielmann AG. Combining the amount of current assets provided on the balance sheet (from Exhibit 9.5) with the amount of

EXHIBIT 9.6

FIELMANN AG
Annual Report
2003

Note 15, Liabilities

15) Liabilities   The maturity dates of the liabilities shown in the consolidated balance sheet and that of FIELMANN Aktiengesellschaft are shown in the following liability tables.

Liabilities FIELMANN Group	31.12.03			31.12.02		
	Total €'000	Remaining term up to 1 year €'000	Remaining term more than 5 years €'000	Total €'000	Remaining term up to 1 year €'000	Remaining term more than 5 years €'000
Liabilities						
—to banks.	15,615	6,422	5,174	32,251	7,182	7,575
—trade creditors	43,143	43,143	0	31,963	31,963	0
—to companies in which participations are held	1,122	1,122	0	0	0	0
Other liabilities	40,751	39,494	0	22,863	21,519	186
—of which taxes: T€ 19,123 (previous year: T€ 8,950)						
—of which for social security: T€ 6,191 (previous year: T€ 5,053)						
	100,631	**90,181**	**5,174**	**87,077**	**60,664**	**7,761**

---

liabilities with remaining term up to one year provided by Fielmann in Note 15, analysts can calculate a current ratio for the company at December 31, 2003, as 3.56 (€321,307/€90,181). Of course, this ignores the possibility that some portion of the "Accruals" reported on the balance sheet are current in nature.

Historically, German companies have used provisions (accrued liabilities) to conceal profits and create hidden reserves. In profitable years, provisions are created for items such as deferred maintenance and uncertain liabilities. The counterpart to the accrual on the balance sheet is an expense reported in income. In years in which profits are below expectations, these "cookie jar" reserves are released with an offsetting increase in income.[5] One of the most dramatic examples of the use of hidden reserves was carried out by Daimler-Benz in 1989 when, through the reversal of a provision for pensions, income was reported as DM 6.8 billion rather than DM 1.9 billion. Disclosures related to provisions allow analysts to assess the impact provisions have on income.

Exhibit 9.7 presents an excerpt from Südzucker AG's note related to provisions and accrued liabilities. From this note one can see that total provisions at the beginning of the 2003/2004 fiscal year were €1,318.8 million. During the year, €371.7 million of that amount was used, resulting in a reduction in assets with an offsetting

---

[5] The term *cookie jar reserves* was made popular by former SEC chairman Arthur Levitt in describing earnings management practices by U.S. companies. See, for example, Arthur Levitt, "A Public Partnership to Battle Earnings Management," *Accounting Today*, May 24–June 6, 1999, p. 36.

EXHIBIT 9.7

SÜDZUCKER AG
Annual Report
2003/2004

Note 1.7 Movements in Provisions and Accrued Liabilities

€ million	01.03.2003	Change in companies consolidated	Additions	Use	Release	29.02.2004
Provisions for pensions and similar obligations	369.1	0.0	31.0	21.0	0.0	379.1
Deferred tax liabilities	342.7	5.1	10.7	0.0	25.5	333.0
Other provisions and accrued liabilities						
Tax liabilities	109.4	7.7	80.8	52.4	5.2	140.3
EU levies for financing the sugar market ordinance	122.5	0.0	143.8	119.9	2.2	144.2
Personnel expenses	121.2	18.1	121.6	108.7	4.1	148.1
Other provisions	253.9	14.5	58.4	69.7	51.7	205.4
Total other provisions and accrued liabilities . . .	607.0	40.3	404.6	350.7	63.2	638.0
Total provisions and accrued liabilities	1,318.8	45.4	446.3	371.7	88.7	1,350.1

decrease in provisions. An additional €88.7 million was released, resulting in a €88.7 million increase in pretax income. Pretax income was reduced, however, by additions to provisions in the amount of €446.3 million. Including the increase in provisions due to the change in companies consolidated, the movement in provisions during the year served to decrease pretax income by €402.9 million (€45.3 million + €446.3 million − €88.7 million), an amount equal to 102 percent of reported earnings before income taxes.

Many large companies interested in attracting foreign portfolio investors or entering foreign capital markets voluntarily provide disclosures that exceed local requirements.[6] For example, although European Union rules prior to 2005 did not require presentation of a statement of cash flows, it was common for multinational firms located in the EU to provide a statement of cash flows in their annual report prior to being required to do so under IFRSs.

Timeliness

The usefulness of accounting information is in part a function of its timeliness, that is, how soon after the end of the fiscal year the information is made available to the public. The time lag between the end of the year and the publication of financial statements varies considerably across countries. The variance is partly attributable to the length of time allowed by the stock market regulator in each country. U.S. companies must file their annual report with the SEC within 60 days of the end of the year. Publicly traded British companies, in contrast, are allowed six months to file

---

[6] S. J. Gray, G. K. Meek, and C. B. Roberts, "International Capital Market Pressures and Voluntary Annual Report Disclosures by US and UK Multinationals," *Journal of International Financial Management and Accounting* 6, no. 1 (1995), pp. 43–68.

their reports. Clearly, an analyst would prefer to receive financial information sooner rather than later. The usefulness of information received in June 2007 related to the period ended December 31, 2006, is questionable. The average number of days between year-end and the date auditors sign the audit report (and the annual report is ready to publish) for seven economically important countries is as follows:[7]

Average Number of Days	Countries
31–60 days	Canada, United States
61–90 days	Japan, United Kingdom
91–120 days	France, Germany, Italy

Even the timeliness of earnings announcements varies considerably across countries. On average, U.S. companies announce earnings 26 days after the end of the period, whereas French companies take 73 days and German companies announce 82 days after the period is over.[8]

The frequency of reporting also differs across countries. Quarterly reports are required in the United States, the United Kingdom, and Canada. European Union directives require semiannual reports. Many countries require only an annual report. In a country with only annual reports where the stock exchange authority allows a six-month time lag in publishing financial statements, there can be a 15-month period between the end of the first quarter of the fiscal year and the publication of reports related to that period. There is virtually nothing an individual analyst can do about the timeliness and frequency of reporting issues.

Differences in Accounting Principles

Differences in accounting principles for recognizing and measuring assets, liabilities, revenues, and expenses can have a significant impact on the amounts reported by companies in their financial statements. In a study conducted in France in 1990, the activities of a hypothetical company were accounted for using the accounting principles in six different countries.[9] The resulting amounts of profit are as follows:

Profit of Hypothetical Company Using Accounting Principles in Six Countries			
Belgium	+460	Netherlands	+520
France	+840	United Kingdom	−160
Germany	−520	United States	−235

Profit for the hypothetical company ranged from −520 to +840 depending on which country's accounting principles were followed.

---

[7] This information was obtained from V. B. Bavishi, ed., *International Accounting and Auditing Trends, vol. 2,* 4th ed. (Princeton, NJ: CIFAR Publications, 1995).

[8] Carol A. Frost, "Characteristics and Information Value of Corporate Disclosures of Forward-Looking Information in Global Equity Markets," Dartmouth College Working Paper, February 1998, as reported in Frederick D. S. Choi, Carol Ann Frost, and Gary K. Meek, *International Accounting,* 4th ed. Upper Saddle River, NJ: Prentice Hall, 2002, p. 368.

[9] "Profits Ici Pertes Au-Dela," *L'Enterprise* No. 63, December 1990, pp. 78–79.

EXHIBIT 9.8
Percentage
Differences in Net
Income and
Stockholders'
Equity between
Local GAAP and
U.S. GAAP for
Selected
Biotechnology
Companies

Source: 2001 Form 20-F filed
with the U.S. SEC obtained
through the SEC's EDGAR
(www.sec.gov).

Country/Company	Reconciliation from Local GAAP to U.S. GAAP	
	% Difference in Net Income	% Difference in Stockholders' Equity
United Kingdom		
Acambis	−19%	−44%
Amersham	−10%	+83%
Cambridge Antibody Technology	−11%	−2%
Celltech	−31%	+25%
Oxford Glycosciences	0%	−2%
Netherlands		
Crucell	−85%	+28%
Australia		
Prana Biotech	+13%	−60%
Ireland		
Trinity Biotech	−80%	+13%
Switzerland		
Serono	−8%	+1%

Non-U.S. companies' listed on U.S. stock exchanges are required to reconcile net income and total stockholders' equity in terms of U.S. GAAP. Exhibit 9.8 presents the percentage difference in net income and stockholders' equity determined under local GAAP and U.S. GAAP for a group of non-U.S. biotechnology companies.

Across the nine companies presented in Exhibit 9.8, converting to U.S. GAAP resulted in a smaller amount of net income (or larger amount of net loss) being reported by seven companies, a larger amount of net income (or smaller amount of net loss) for one company, and virtually no change for one company. The adjustments ranged from −85 percent to +13 percent. The effect on stockholders' equity was even larger, ranging from −60 percent to +83 percent. For five companies the negative change in net income is accompanied by a positive change in stockholders' equity, but the opposite is true for the other companies.

The percentages reported in Exhibit 9.8 show that differences in accounting principles can have a significant impact on the amount of income and equity reported by a company. More importantly, the *magnitude* of the change differs significantly across companies as does the *direction* of the change. There is no simple rule of thumb, such as, "Add 10 percent," that can be used to restate earnings for these companies to the common denominator of U.S. GAAP. For example, increasing Acambis's reported net loss by 10 percent would still understate the company's net loss in U.S. GAAP terms, whereas increasing Prana Biotechnology's reported net loss by 10 percent, which already overstates U.S. GAAP net loss by 13 percent, would only distort matters further.

The important question is whether differences in accounting principles actually affect investment decisions. Choi and Levich addressed this question through interviews with 16 institutional investors in Japan, Switzerland, the United Kingdom, and the United States.[10] Their major findings are summarized

[10] F. D. S. Choi and R. M. Levich, "Behavioral Effects of International Accounting Diversity," *Accounting Horizons*, June 1991, pp. 1–13.

as follows:

1. Nine of 16 investors indicated that accounting diversity hindered the measurement of their decision variables and ultimately affected their investment decisions. The effects of accounting diversity included limiting the geographic spread of investments and precluding certain types of companies from analysis.

2. Seven of the nine investors who found accounting diversity to be a problem attempted to cope by restating foreign financial statements to an accounting framework familiar to the analyst, such as U.S. GAAP. Two coped by adopting specific investment strategies. One invested only in government bonds. The other used a "top-down" investment approach in which investors use macroeconomic data to decide how much of the investment portfolio to allocate to a particular country. Once they decide how much to invest in a given country, the investors acquire a diversified portfolio of stocks in that country.

3. Of the seven investors who said accounting diversity did not hinder their decision making, four had developed a "multiple principles capability," in which investors use a local perspective when analyzing foreign financial statements. The idea is to use foreign GAAP statements and a well-developed knowledge of foreign accounting principles and foreign financial market conditions to make decisions. Three investors attempted to deal with the problem by using information less sensitive to accounting diversity. For example, one investor valued securities by using a discounted dividends model rather than a discounted earnings approach.

4. Countries most often mentioned as a source of concern for analysts were Japan, Switzerland, and Germany.

5. The most troublesome areas in which accounting differences existed were consolidations, valuation and depreciation of fixed assets, deferred income taxes, pensions, marketable securities, discretionary reserves, foreign currency transactions and translation, leases, goodwill, long-term construction contracts, inventory valuation, and provisions.

6. Areas in which lack of disclosure is a hindrance included segment information, method of asset valuation, information about foreign operations, frequency and completeness of interim financial statements, description of capital expenditures, hidden reserves, and off-balance-sheet items. Several investors indicated overcoming the lack-of-disclosure problem by making visits to the companies being analyzed.

A significant number of investors interviewed by Choi and Levich said that they attempt to restate foreign financial statements to a familiar GAAP, focusing on restatement of earnings. One of the most sophisticated attempts to restate financial statements has been carried out by Morgan Stanley Dean Witter in its so-called Apples-to-Apples project. The appendix to this chapter describes this project.

Another mechanism for dealing with accounting differences is to use a measure of earnings from which many accounting issues are removed. Sherman and Todd recommend using operating income before depreciation (OIBD) as the relevant earnings measure for evaluating company performance.[11] The logic

---

[11] R. Sherman and R. Todd, "International Financial Statement Analysis," in *International Accounting and Finance Handbook*, 2nd ed., ed. F. D. S. Choi (New York: John Wiley & Sons, 1997), pp. 8.1–8.61.

of this approach can be seen by considering the following typical income statement:

Sales
  Less: Operating expenses (cost of goods sold; general,
  selling, and administrative expenses)
Operating income
  Less: Interest expense
Income before taxes
  Less: Income tax expense
Net income

OIBD is measured by adding the depreciation included in operating expenses back to operating income. Basing analysis on OIBD removes the effect of depreciation, interest, and income taxes from the relevant measure of earnings, and any differences in the way these items are accounted for become irrelevant. Amortization of intangibles often is also added back to OIBD. The resulting measure is more commonly referred to as earnings before interest, taxes, depreciation, and amortization (EBITDA).

Additional adjustments can be made to EBITDA to further isolate the effects of accounting diversity. For example, because the determination of pension expense can vary greatly across countries, adding back the pension expense included in operating expenses to EBITDA would result in a more comparable measure of income across countries. The potential problem with this approach is that each item removed may have implications for determining the value of the firm. Removing interest expense from the earnings measure may make companies' financial statements more comparable, but it makes the earnings measure less representative of future cash flows. Carried to its logical extreme, EBITDA could be adjusted to the point where sales is the measure of performance used to analyze companies. While sales are important, they represent only one part of what determines a firm's value.

Some companies resolve the analyst's accounting diversity problem in their convenience translations by

1. Using nonlocal GAAP or IFRSs to prepare their financial statements. For example, DaimlerChrysler uses U.S. GAAP; BMW uses IFRSs).

2. Presenting two sets of financial statements in their annual report. For example, China Petroleum and Chemical Corporation (Sinopec) provides financial statements in accordance with both Chinese GAAP and IFRSs.

3. Providing a reconciliation to non-local GAAP or IFRS in the notes to their local GAAP financial statements. For example, BASF voluntarily provides a reconciliation to U.S. GAAP; as an SEC registrant, Sinopec provides a reconciliation to U.S. GAAP in addition to its IFRS-based financial statements.

As the use of IFRSs becomes more widespread across countries, the problems associated with accounting diversity should become smaller. However, in the meantime, the analyst must develop methods for coping with the potentially harmful effects of accounting diversity.

EXHIBIT 9.9
Mean Financial
Ratios in Japan,
Korea, and the
United States, 1978

Source: F. D. S. Choi, H.
Hino, S. K. Min, S. O. Nam,
J. Ujiie, and A. I. Stonehill.
"Analyzing Foreign
Financial Statements: The
Use and Misuse of
International Ratio
Analysis," *Journal of
International Business
Studies,* Spring/Summer
1983, p. 116.

	Current Ratio	Quick Ratio	Debt Ratio	Times Interest Earned	Inventory Turnover
Japan (*n* = 976)	1.15	0.80	0.84	1.60	5.00
Korea (*n* = 354)	1.13	0.46	0.78	1.80	6.60
United States (*n* = 902)	1.94	1.10	0.47	6.50	6.80

	Average Collection Period	Fixed Asset Turnover	Total Asset Turnover	Profit Margin	Return on Assets	Return on Equity
Japan (*n* = 976)	86	3.10	0.93	0.013	0.012	0.071
Korea (*n* = 354)	33	2.80	1.20	0.023	0.028	0.131
United States (*n* = 902)	43	3.90	1.40	0.054	0.074	0.139

International Ratio Analysis

Even if an analyst has foreign financial statements that are restated to a common set of accounting principles, the use of ratio analysis can be misleading because of environmental differences across countries.

Through a comparison of financial ratios in Japan, Korea, and the United States, Choi and colleagues show that substantial differences exist that are not attributable solely to differences in accounting methods.[12] Ratios are different across these three countries also because of significant differences in economic and social environments.

Exhibit 9.9 presents the means for a number of important financial ratios for a broad cross-section of companies in Japan, Korea, and the United States in 1978. Comparing these ratios, an analyst might have concluded that Japanese and Korean firms were less liquid, less profitable, and less efficient in managing their assets than U.S. companies. Although a portion of the differences in ratios is due to accounting diversity, Choi and colleagues explain that much of the difference across the three countries can be explained by differences in economic and business environments. To demonstrate the effect that environmental differences can have on financial ratios, we discuss differences in the mean current ratio, debt ratio, and profit margin across the three countries:[13]

- *Current ratio:* The current ratio (Current assets/Current liabilities) is a measure of liquidity that is used in assessing the ability of a company to pay its short-term obligations. This ratio indicates that Japanese and Korean firms appear to

[12] F. D. S. Choi, H. Hino, S. K. Min, S. O. Nam, J. Ujiie, and A. I. Stonehill, "Analyzing Foreign Financial Statements: The Use and Misuse of International Ratio Analysis," *Journal of International Business Studies,* Spring/Summer 1983, pp. 113–31.

[13] The ratios reported in Exhibit 9.9 are for the year 1978; the discussion is based on the economic and business environment in Japan, Korea, and the United States at that time. Significant changes have occurred in these countries in the intervening years. The differences in ratios found in 1978 might or might not exist today; no recent study investigating differences in ratios across these three countries has been conducted.

have been significantly less likely to meet their short-term obligations than U.S. firms. Choi and colleagues explain that the differences in this ratio can be explained partly by the fact that Japanese and Korean companies often used short-term debt to finance fixed assets. They would borrow on a short-term basis, repay the borrowing when it came due, and then negotiate a new short-term loan at that point. By successive rollovers of short-term debt, a series of 20 three-month loans, for example, became five-year financing. Renegotiation of loans was not a problem because of close relationships between companies and banks. Companies preferred short-term loans because interest rates were lower than on long-term financing, and banks preferred short-term loans because they could adjust interest rates more frequently. Excluding short-term debt from current liabilities might have resulted in a more meaningful current ratio for these firms.

- *Debt ratio:* The debt ratio (Total liabilities/Total assets) provides a measure of financial leverage, that is, the extent to which assets are financed by liabilities. It is used to assess the risk that a firm might not be able to repay its obligations, both short-term and long-term, on time. As Choi and colleagues explain, high debt ratios in Japan resulted from the reliance on bank financing that was partly a function of low levels of personal savings at the end of World War II. In addition, relatively low interest rates on bank loans made debt financing attractive. In Korea, bank loans tended to be influenced by the government. Given the limited amount of financing available, the government directed funds to companies that the government wanted to promote. A high debt ratio, therefore, was a sign of government support.

- *Profit margin:* The profit margin (Net income/Net sales) is one measure of a firm's profitability. The relatively low average profit margin in Japan in 1978 can be explained in part by the fact that Japanese companies focused on sales rather than profit. To gain market share, especially in foreign markets, Japanese companies would often compete by lowering prices, thereby reducing profits. Profit margins are probably higher today, as Japanese companies have driven competitors out of the market and can therefore raise prices and, perhaps more important, as they have become more cost-efficient. Another explanation for lower profit margins for Japanese companies is that higher amounts of debt causes a higher amount of interest expense, thereby lowering net income. Korean firms also have higher levels of interest expense as a result of higher debt financing. In addition, Korean firms in 1978 tended to have newer assets purchased at higher prices than U.S. firms. As a result, depreciation expense was larger. To obtain more comparable measures of profit margin across these countries, it might have been useful to treat dividends as an expense in the United States or add back interest expense to net income in Japan and Korea.

The important point is that analysts must be careful in comparing ratios across countries. Rules of thumb that apply in one country may not apply in another country. A U.S.-based analyst blindly relying on the ratios presented in Exhibit 9.9 might have decided not to invest in or lend to Japanese or Korean companies in the 1980s. Some very respectable investment returns would have been forgone in the process. One solution to the problem is to develop a good understanding of the local business environment and learn how to identify the best companies in that environment.

RESTATING FINANCIAL STATEMENTS

As noted earlier, foreign companies registered on U.S. stock exchanges are required to provide a reconciliation of net income and stockholders' equity to U.S. GAAP in the Form 20-F annual report they file with the U.S. Securities and Exchange Commission. Foreign SEC registrants are not required to provide a complete set of financial statements on a U.S. GAAP basis. As such, the information provided is of limited usefulness in calculating financial ratios used to assess the company's financial position and profitability on a U.S. GAAP basis. The reconciliation of income and equity does allow analysts to calculate return on equity (Net income/Average stockholders' equity) on a U.S. GAAP basis. But because of a lack of detail related to the items that comprise net income and the absence of U.S. GAAP amounts for assets and liabilities, insufficient information is provided to calculate ratios such as operating profit margin (Operating profit/Net sales), total asset turnover (Net sales/Average total assets), the debt-to-equity ratio (Total liabilities/Total stockholders' equity), and the current ratio (Current assets/Current liabilities). To calculate these and other ratios, analysts must restate financial statements. In the final section of this chapter, we use information available in the 1998 annual report of Imperial Chemical Industries (ICI) to demonstrate an approach that can be used restate financial statements to a U.S. GAAP basis.

Exhibit 9.10 provides ICI's consolidated profit and loss account, statement of recognized gains and losses, and balance sheet for the year ended December 31, 1998. Two steps are required to restate these statements to a U.S. GAAP basis. The first step is to transform the financial statements to a U.S. format. The process of preparing U.S.-format financial statements involves making adjustments for three types of differences:

1. *Terminology differences.* For example, "stocks" on a British balance sheet are "inventories" on a U.S. balance sheet.
2. *Presentation differences.* For example, the operating profit and gain on disposal of discontinued operations are reported in a separate column in ICI's income statement, but would be reported as separate line items on a U.S. income statement.
3. *Definition/classification differences.* For example, the definition of "cash at bank" on a British balance sheet is different from the definition of "cash and cash equivalents" that appears on a U.S. balance sheet. ICI's "investments and short-term deposits" must be reclassified between "cash equivalents" and "short-term investments" in the U.S.-format balance sheet.

Once financial statements have been reformatted, the second step involves restating the UK GAAP amounts to a U.S. GAAP basis. For ICI, restatement to U.S. GAAP is made easier because the company has determined the major differences between UK and U.S. GAAP that affect the company's financial statements and has quantified the effects of those differences. Additional information provided in the notes also will be needed to complete the second step.

The most efficient approach to complete these two steps is to use a worksheet in which the first column contains the reformatted financial statements. Debit and credit accounting entries are then prepared and entered in worksheet columns 2 and 3 to restate each line item to a U.S. GAAP basis. The balances that would be reported on U.S. format/U.S. GAAP financial statements are then determined in column 4 of the worksheet.

EXHIBIT 9.10

ICI
Annual Report
1998
Profit and Loss Account, Statement of Recognised Gains and Losses and Balance Sheets

---

Group profit and loss account for the year ended 31 December 1998

		1998			
		Continuing operations		Discontinued operations	Total
		Before exceptional items	Exceptional items		
	Notes	£m	£m	£m	£m
Turnover	4, 5	9,095		191	9,286
Operating costs	3, 5	(8,591)	(164)	(161)	(8,916)
Other operating income	5	86	—	7	93
Trading profit (loss)	3, 4, 5	590	(164)	37	463
After deducting goodwill amortization		*(23)*			*(23)*
Share of profits less losses of associated undertakings	7	3			3
		593	(164)	37	466
Profits less losses on sale or closure of operations	3		11	179	190
Profits less losses on disposals of fixed assets	3		3		3
Amounts written off investments	3		(34)		(34)
Profit (loss) on ordinary activities before interest	4	593	(184)	216	625
Net interest payable	3, 8	(332)			(332)
Profit (loss) on ordinary activities before taxation		261	(184)	216	293
Tax on profit (loss) on ordinary activities	9	(69)	34	(77)	(112)
Profit (loss) on ordinary activities after taxation		192	(150)	139	181
Attributable to minorities		8	4		12
Net profit (loss) for the financial year		200	(146)	139	193
Dividends	10				(232)
Profit (loss) retained for the year	25				(39)
Earnings (loss) per £1 Ordinary Share	11				
Basic		27.6p	(20.1)p	19.2p	26.7p
Diluted		27.5p	(20.1)p	19.1p	26.5p

Statement of Group total recognised gains and losses for the year ended 31 December 1998

	1998
	£m
Net profit for the financial year	193
Currency translation differences on foreign currency net investments and related loans	(59)
Taxation on foreign currency loans	16
	(43)
Other items	—
Total gains and losses recognised since last annual report	150

Balance sheets at 31 December 1998

	Notes	Group 1998 £m	Group 1997 £m	Company 1998 £m	Company 1997 £m
Assets employed					
Fixed assets					
Intangible assets—goodwill	12	**652**			
Tangible assets	4, 13	**3,816**	3,956	320	431
Investments					
Subsidiary undertakings	14	**—**	—	10,025	10,093
Participating and other interests	15	**170**	254	24	68
		4,638	4,210	10,369	10,592
Current assets					
Stocks	16	**1,213**	1,319	62	75
Debtors	17	**2,360**	2,457	2,834	3,065
Investments and short-term deposits	18	**455**	935	—	1
Cash at bank	34	**367**	340	25	22
		4,395	5,051	2,921	3,163
Total assets		**9,033**	9,261	13,290	13,755
Creditors due within one year					
Short-term borrowings	19	**(1,445)**	(1,105)	—	(1)
Current instalments on loans	21	**(585)**	(950)	(493)	(807)
Other creditors	20	**(2,356)**	(2,583)	(7,421)	(6,683)
		(4,386)	(4,638)	(7,914)	(7,491)
Net current assets (liabilities)		**9**	413	(4,993)	(4,328)
Total assets less current liabilities	4	**4,647**	4,623	5,376	6,264
Financed by					
Creditors due after more than one year					
Loans	21	**2,954**	2,975	360	694
Other creditors	20	**55**	67	2,784	3,262
		3,009	3,042	3,144	3,956
Provisions for liabilities and charges	22	**1,429**	1,342	210	218
Deferred income: Grants not yet credited to profit		**11**	14	—	—
Minority interests—equity		**49**	79	—	—
Shareholders' funds—equity					
Called-up share capital	24	**728**	727	728	727
Reserves					
Share premium account		**587**	581	587	581
Associated undertakings' reserves		**15**	26	—	—
Profit and loss account		**(1,181)**	(1,188)	707	782
Total reserves	25	**(579)**	(581)	1,294	1,363
Total shareholders' funds		**149**	146	2,022	2,090
		4,647	4,623	5,376	6,264

Included within Group net current assets are debtors of £406m (1997 £405m) which fall due after more than one year. Included within the Company net current assets are debtors of £247m (1997 £313m) which fall due after more than one year.

EXHIBIT 9.11

ICI
Annual Report
1998
Glossary

Term used in annual report	US equivalent or brief description
Accounts	Financial statements
Acquisition accounting	Purchase accounting
Advance corporation tax	No direct US equivalent. Tax paid on company distribution recoverable from UK taxes due on income
Allotted	Issued
Associated undertaking	20–50% owned investee
Called-up share capital	Ordinary shares, issued and fully paid
Capital allowances	Tax term equivalent to US tax depreciation allowances
Class of business	Industry segment
Closing rate method	Current rate method
Creditors	Accounts payable/payables
Creditors: Amounts falling due after more than one year	Long-term debt liabilities
Creditors: Amounts falling due within one year	Current liabilities
Debtors	Accounts receivable/receivables
Depreciation	Amortisation
Finance lease	Capital lease
Financial year	Fiscal year
Fixed tangible assets	Property, plant and equipment
Freehold	Ownership with absolute rights in perpetuity
Freehold land	Land owned
Gearing	Leverage
Group, or consolidated accounts	Consolidated financial statements
Interest receivable	Interest income
Interest payable	Interest expense
Loan capital	Long-term debt
Net asset value	Book value
Nominal value	Par value
Pension scheme	Pension plan
Profit	Income (or earnings)
Profit and loss account (reserve)	Retained earnings
Profit and loss account	Income statement
Profit attributable to ordinary shareholders	Net income
Reconciliation of movements in shareholders' funds	Statement of changes in stockholders' equity
Reserves	Stockholders' equity other than capital stock
Share capital	Ordinary shares, capital stock or common stock issued and fully paid
Share premium account	Additional paid-in capital relating to proceeds of sale of stock in excess of par value or paid-in surplus (not distributable)
Shares in issue	Shares outstanding
Shareholders' funds	Stockholders' equity
Stocks	Inventories
Tangible fixed assets	Property, plant and equipment
Turnover	Revenues (or sales)

Step 1: Reformatting the Financial Statements

ICI provides a glossary (presented in Exhibit 9.11) showing the U.S. equivalent for terms used in the annual report that may be unfamiliar to American readers. The glossary of accounting terms and information found in selected notes to the financial statements is used to reformat each of ICI's financial statements to a U.S. basis.

Income Statement

The group profit and loss account (refer to Exhibit 9.10) is the equivalent of an income statement in the United States. Other terminology differences that must be adjusted include turnover (sales), trading profit (operating profit), and interest payable (interest expense). Much of the difficulty in reformatting the income statement stems from the fact that ICI uses a horizontal presentation for displaying exceptional items and discontinued operations. Under U.S. GAAP, the income generated by discontinued operations is aggregated and reported on a net-of-tax basis immediately preceding net income. There is no equivalent concept of exceptional items under U.S. GAAP. These items must be included in the line-item amounts reported on the U.S.-format income statement. Note 3 in Exhibit 9.12 provides detailed information regarding exceptional items.

ICI reports operating costs as an aggregate amount with no detail on the face of the profit and loss account. It is customary in the United States for operating costs to be broken out into cost of sales, administrative expenses, research and development, and so on. Note 5 (in Exhibit 9.13) presents information for both continuing and discontinued operations with regard to operating costs and other operating income.

Column 1 of Exhibit 9.14 presents ICI's U.S.-format income statement. Note that there are several variations of a U.S.-format income statement that would have been equally acceptable. For example, administrative and other expenses could have been combined with selling expense in one line item. The U.S.-format presentation provided in Exhibit 9.14 facilitates subsequent reconciliation to U.S. GAAP.

The following is an explanation of each item that appears on the U.S.-format income statement (Column 1 of Exhibit 9.14):

Sales. This is the amount of "turnover" reported in the profit and loss account (P&L).

Cost of sales. This is the "cost of sales" component of operating costs detailed in Note 5 (see Exhibit 9.13).

Selling expense. This is the "distribution costs" component of operating costs detailed in Note 5.

Research and development expense. This is the "research and development" component of operating costs detailed in Note 5.

Administrative and other expenses. This is the "administration and other expenses" component of operating costs detailed in Note 5.

Restructuring charges. Note 3 (see Exhibit 9.12) indicates that exceptional items charged in arriving at trading profit (£164 million) relate to "rationalisation of operations." Rationalisation of operations is generally referred to as restructuring in the United States, where it is common practice to report a separate restructuring charge in the income statement.

Other income. Note 3 indicates that, under U.S. GAAP, exceptional items would be included in operating income unless they relate to discontinued operations.

EXHIBIT 9.12

ICI
Annual Report
1998
Note 3, Exceptional Items before Tax

3 Exceptional items before tax

	1998 £m	1997 £m	1996 £m
Charged in arriving at trading profit (loss)			
Continuing operations			
Rationalisation of operations			
Industrial Chemicals, including severance costs of £28m (1997 £28m), asset write downs of £42m (1997 £100m) and site clearance costs of £nil (1997 £21m)	**(70)**	(141)	
Coatings, principally severance costs of £26m (1996 £36m) and asset write downs of £27m (1996 £7m)	**(71)**		(44)
Industrial Specialties, principally severance costs of £14m (1997 £15m)	**(23)**	(37)	
Quest, principally severance costs of £20m		(24)	
Acrylics, principally severance costs of £15m			(28)
Explosives, principally severance costs of £35m and asset write downs of £18m			(53)
	(164)	(202)	(125)
Discontinued operations			
Explosives			(12)
	(164)	(202)	(137)
Credited (charged) after trading profit (loss)			
Continuing operations			
Profits less losses on sale or closure of operations			
Profits	**11**		7
Losses		(12)	(6)
Provision for losses on future sale or closure of operations		(342)	
	11	(354)	1
Profits less losses on disposal of fixed assets	**3**	35	31
Amounts written off investments	**(34)**		
Loan arrangement fee written off following loan refinancing			(31)
Discontinued operations			
Profits on sale of operations			
Profits	**244**	777	—
Losses	**(65)**	(92)	—
	179	685	—
Exceptional items within profit (loss) on ordinary activities before taxation	**(5)**	133	(105)

Under US GAAP, exceptional items would be included in operating income, unless they relate to discontinued operations.

EXHIBIT 9.13

ICI
Annual Report
1998
Note 5, Trading Profit

5 Trading profit

	1998		
	Continuing operations £m	Discontinued operations £m	Total £m
Trading profit before exceptional items			
Turnover	9,095	191	9286
Operating costs			
Cost of sales	(6,384)	(124)	(6,508)
Distribution costs	(754)	(6)	(760)
Research and development	(220)	(3)	(223)
Administrative and other expenses	(1,233)	(28)	(1,261)
	(8,591)	(161)	(8,752)
Other operating income			
Government grants	2	—	2
Royalties	15	—	15
Other income	69	7	76
	86	7	93
Trading profit	**590**	**37**	**627**
Total charge for depreciation and amortisation of goodwill included above	(336)	(14)	(350)
Gross profit, as defined by Companies Act 1985	2,711	67	2,778
Trading profit after exceptional items			
Turnover	9,095	191	9,286
Operating costs			
Cost of sales	(6,453)	(124)	(6,577)
Distribution costs	(754)	(6)	(760)
Research and development	(220)	(3)	(223)
Administrative and other expenses	(1,328)	(28)	(1,356)
	(8,755)	(161)	(8,916)
Other operating income			
Government grants	2	—	2
Royalties	15	—	15
Other income	69	7	76
	86	7	93
Trading profit	**426**	**37**	**463**
Total charge for depreciation and amortisation of goodwill included above	(372)	(14)	(386)
Gross profit, as defined by Companies Act 1985	2,642	67	2,709

EXHIBIT 9.14

IMPERIAL CHEMICAL INDUSTRIES PLC
Reformatted Income Statement and
Worksheet for Restatement to U.S. GAAP
for the year ended December 31, 1998
(amounts in £ millions)

	(1)	(2)	(3)	(4)
		Reconciling Adjustments		
U.S. Format	**U.K. GAAP**	**Debit**	**Credit**	**U.S. GAAP**
Sales	**9,095**			**9,095**
Cost of sales	(6,384)			(6,384)
Gross profit	**2,711**			**2,711**
Selling expense	(754)			(754)
Research and development expense	(220)			(220)
Administrative and other expenses	(1,233)	10 [1]		(1,292)
		25 [2]		
		24 [5]		
Restructuring charges	(164)	81 [6]		(245)
Other income	66	28 [3]	3 [10]	41
Operating income	**406**			**241**
Interest expense (net)	(332)			(332)
Equity in net income of affiliated companies	3			3
Income from continuing operations before income taxes............................	**77**			**(88)**
Income tax expense...............................	(35)		29 [(8)]	(6)
Minority interest	12			12
Income from continuing operations................	**54**			**(82)**
Income of discontinued operations (net of tax)	24	109 [2]		(85)
Gain on disposal of discontinued operations (net of tax)...........................	115		8 [7]	123
Net income......................................	193			(44)

Accordingly, the remaining exceptional items are included in "other income" as follows:

	£m
Other operating income.......................	£86
Profits less losses on sale or closure of operations . . .	11
Profits less losses on disposals of fixed assets	3
Amounts written off investments	(34)
Other income................................	£66

Interest expense (net). This is "Net interest payable" in the P&L.

Equity in net income of affiliated companies. This is "Share of profits less losses of associated undertakings" in the P&L.

Income tax expense. This consists of the following items that appear in the P&L:

	£m
Tax on profit (loss) on ordinary activities	
— continuing operations before exceptional items . . .	£(69)
— exceptional items.	34
Income tax expense	£(35)

Minority interest. This is the amount "attributable to minorities" in the P&L.

Discontinued operations. In accordance with U.S. GAAP, the income generated by discontinued operations and the gain on disposal of discontinued operations must be reported separately and net of tax. Income of discontinued operations is the amount reported as "trading profit" in the "discontinued operations" column in the P&L (£37 million). The net gain on disposal of discontinued operations is reported as "profits less losses on sale or closure of operations" in the "discontinued operations" column in the P&L (£179 million). These amounts are reported before deducting related taxes. The aggregate tax expense related to both items is reported in the "discontinued operations" column in the P&L account (£77 million). There is insufficient information to determine the amount of tax expense attributable to each item separately, so total tax expense is allocated on the basis of relative values as follows (£ millions):

	Gross	Tax	Net
Income of discontinued operations	£ 37 / £216 × £77 = £13		£ 24
Gain (loss) on disposal	179 / £216 × £77 = 64		£115
Total	£216	£77	

Statement of Retained Earnings and Statement of Other Comprehensive Income

Information to prepare the statements of retained earnings and other comprehensive income is located primarily in Note 25, Reserves (shown in Exhibit 9.15) and in the statement of group total recognised gains and losses (included in Exhibit 9.10).

Retained earnings are split into two columns in Note 25: "associated undertakings" and "profit and loss account." These columns indicate that exchange adjustments of £(43) million were taken directly to retained earnings in 1998. The last paragraph in Note 25 further explains that the cumulative exchange gains and losses on the translation of foreign currency financial statements are included in retained earnings. The amount included in beginning of year 1998 retained earnings was £(230) million. Under U.S. GAAP (SFAS 130), the cumulative translation adjustment is reported as a component of "other comprehensive income" and is not included in retained earnings. The major adjustment in preparing a statement of retained earnings on a U.S. basis is the reclassification of the cumulative translation adjustment from retained earnings to other

EXHIBIT 9.15

ICI
Annual Report
1998
Note 25, Reserves

---

25 Reserves

	Share premium account £m	Retained earnings Associated undertakings £m	Profit and loss account £m	Total £m	Total £m
Group					
Reserves attributed to parent company					
At beginning of 1998.............	581	26	(1,188)	(1,162)	(581)
Net (loss) profit for the financial year		(10)	203	193	193
Dividends (note 10)		(232)	(232)	(232)	
Transfer of goodwill on disposals			126	126	126
Amounts taken direct to reserves					
Share premiums—share option schemes......	6				6
Goodwill relating to 1997 acquisitions			(48)	(48)	(48)
Exchange adjustments		(1)	(42)	(43)	(43)
At end of 1998....................	**587**	**15**	**(1,181)**	**(1,166)**	**(579)**

Goodwill arising on acquisitions prior to 31 December 1997 was eliminated against reserves and was previously disclosed separately as a goodwill write-off reserve in the Group balance sheet and in the notes relating to the accounts. In compliance with FRS No. 10 *Goodwill and Intangible Assets*, this reserve has now been offset against the profit and loss account reserve. Comparative data have been restated.

The cumulative exchange gains and losses on the translation of foreign currency financial statements into pounds sterling are taken into account in the above statement of Group reserves. US GAAP—SFAS No. 52, *Foreign Currency Translation*, requires separate disclosure of the cumulative amount of the foreign currency translation effects on shareholders' funds, as follows:

	1998 £m	1997 £m	1996 £m
At beginning of year	**(230)**	29	218
Exchange adjustments	**(43)**	(259)	(189)
At end of year	**(273)**	**(230)**	**29**

comprehensive income. The reformatted statement is presented in Column 1 of Exhibit 9.16.

The items found in Column 1 of Exhibit 9.16 are explained as follows:

Retained earnings, 1/1/98. Based on information in Note 25, this is calculated as follows:

	£m
Retained earnings at beginning of 1998	
— associated undertakings	£ 26
— profit and loss account	(1,188)
Subtotal	(1,162)
Less: Cumulative translation adjustment, at beginning of year	230
Retained earnings, 1/1/98 (adjusted)	£ (932)

EXHIBIT 9.16

IMPERIAL CHEMICAL INDUSTRIES PLC
Reformatted Statements of Retained Earnings and Other Comprehensive Income and
Worksheet for Restatement to U.S. GAAP
for the year ended December 31, 1998
(amounts in £ million)

U.S. Format	(1) U.K. GAAP	(2) Debit	(3) Credit	(4) U.S. GAAP
Statement of Retained Earnings		Reconciling Adjustments		
Retained earnings, 1/1/98	**(932)**	281 [1]		**2,775**
			3,752 [2]	
			3 [3]	
			152 [5]	
			137 [6]	
		8 [7]		
		176 [8]		
		13 [9]		
			141 [11]	
Net income, 1998	193			(44)
Dividends	(232)			(232)
Transfer of goodwill on disposals	126			126
Goodwill relating to 1997 acquisitions	(48)			(48)
Retained earnings, 12/31/98	**(893)**			**2,577**
Statement of Other Comprehensive Income				
Other comprehensive income, 1/1/98	**(230)**			**(230)**
Translation adjustments, 1998	(43)			(43)
Other comprehensive income, 12/31/98	**(273)**			**(273)**

Net income, 1998. This is the amount reported in the income statement.

Dividends. This is the amount reported in Note 25.

Transfer of goodwill on disposals. This is the amount reported in Note 25.[14]

Goodwill relating to 1997 acquisitions. This is the amount reported in Note 25.

Statement of Other Comprehensive Income

In accordance with SFAS 130, "other comprehensive income" consists of unrealized gains and losses that are not included in net income. For ICI, the only item of

[14] "Transfer of goodwill on disposals" and "goodwill relating to 1997 acquisitions" would not be found in a U.S. statement of retained earnings. These items exist because, prior to 1998, under UK GAAP, goodwill was written off directly to shareholders' equity at the date of purchase. As described in Note 25, Reserves, the goodwill write-off was reported in a "goodwill reserve" account, and in 1998 this was transferred to retained earnings. This explains the adjustment for "goodwill relating to 1997 acquisitions." The "transfer of goodwill on disposals" is not explained but presumably arises because goodwill previously written off has been recaptured through disposal of the entity for which goodwill was originally paid. These two items should be reported in the U.S.-format statement of retained earnings just as they are found in Note 25.

EXHIBIT 9.17

IMPERIAL CHEMICAL INDUSTRIES PLC
Reformatted Balance Sheet and
Worksheet for Restatement to U.S. GAAP
at December 31, 1998
(amounts in £ million)

U.S. Format	(1) U.K. GAAP	(2) Reconciling Adjustments Debit	(3) Reconciling Adjustments Credit	(4) U.S. GAAP
Assets				
Current assets				
Cash and cash equivalents	609			609
Short-term investments	213			213
Accounts receivable (net)	1,386			1,386
Other receivables	423			423
Inventories	1,213			1,213
Prepaid expenses and other current assets	145			145
Total current assets	**3,989**			**3,989**
Non-current assets				
Property, plant and equipment	3,816	128 [5]	25 [3]	3,919
Investments	170		62 [10]	108
Goodwill	652	3,618 [2]		4,270
Other non-current assets	406			406
Total non-current assets	**5,044**			**8,703**
Total assets	**9,033**			**12,692**
Liabilities and shareholders' equity				
Current liabilities				
Short-term debt	1,445			1,445
Current portion of long-term debt	585			585
Accounts payable	1,070			1,070
Dividends payable	141	141 [11]		0
Other current liabilities	1,145			1,145
Total current liabilities	**4,386**			**4,245**
Long-term liabilities				
Long-term debt	2,954			2,954
Deferred income taxes	34		147 [8]	181
Pension liability	256		291 [1]	547
Restructuring liability	176	56 [6]		120
Other long-term liabilities	1,029		10 [10]	1,039
Total long-term liabilities	**4,449**			**4,841**
Total liabilities	**8,835**			**9,086**
Minority interest	**49**			**49**
Shareholders' equity				
Capital stock	728			728
Paid-in capital in excess of par value	587			587
Retained earnings	(893)			2,577
Other comprehensive income	(273)			(273)
Treasury stock	—	62 [10]		(62)
Total shareholders' equity	**149**			**3,557**
Total liabilities and shareholders' equity	**9,033**			**12,692**

other comprehensive income is the translation adjustment that results from translating the financial statements of foreign subsidiaries and related loans.

> *Other comprehensive income, 1/1/98.* This is the amount reported in Note 25 as the 1998 beginning of year amount of "cumulative exchange gains and losses on the translation of foreign currency financial statements into pounds."
>
> *Translation adjustments, 1998.* This is the amount reported in Note 25 as "exchange adjustments."

Balance Sheet

Major differences from a U.S.-format balance sheet include assets being listed in reverse order of liquidity, current liabilities being subtracted directly from current assets to arrive at a measure of net current assets, and differences in terminology. In addition, classifications of certain items such as cash and cash equivalents differ between British and U.S. GAAP. Information needed to reformat the balance sheet is found in Notes 17, 18, 20, and 22. There are several variations of U.S. format that would have been equally acceptable. For example, there is no requirement to separate accounts receivable from other receivables on the face of the balance sheet. The specific U.S. format presented in Column 1 of Exhibit 9.17 was selected to facilitate subsequent reconciliation to U.S. GAAP.

Assets

> *Cash and cash equivalents.* Note 18 (presented in Exhibit 9.18) indicates that £242 million of "investments and short-term deposits" are included in cash and cash equivalents. This amount must be added to "cash at bank" to determine the amount that would be reported as cash and cash equivalents under U.S. GAAP: £367 million + £242 million = £609 million.
>
> *Short-term investments.* This is the amount reported as "investments and short-term deposits" on the balance sheet less the amount that has been reclassified as cash and cash equivalents: £455 million − £242 million = £213 million.
>
> *Accounts receivable.* "Debtors" are the equivalent of receivables in the United Kingdom. Note 17 (shown in Exhibit 9.19) details the composition of debtors. "Trade debtors" are trade accounts receivable.
>
> *Other receivables.* This is the amount of debtors due within one year in Note 17 that is not reported separately as accounts receivable or prepaid expenses and other current assets, calculated as follows:

	£m
Debtors due within one year	£1,954
Less: Accounts receivable (net)	(1,386)
Other prepayments and accrued income	(145)
Other receivables	£ 423

Alternatively, the amount of other receivables can be determined as follows:

	£m
Amounts owed by associated undertakings	£ 5
Taxation recoverable	122
Other debtors	296
Other receivables	£ 423

EXHIBIT 9.18

ICI
Annual Report
1998
Note 18, Current Asset Investments and Short-term Deposits

18 Current asset investments and short-term deposits

	1998 £m	1997 £m
Listed investments	48	48
Unlisted investments and short-term deposits.	407	887
	455	935
Included in cash and cash equivalents	242	263
Market value of listed investments	48	56

Included in unlisted investments and short-term deposits and cash are amounts totaling £188m (1997 £206m) held by the Group's insurance subsidiaries. In 1998 £36m (1997 £24m) was readily available for the general purposes of the Group.

EXHIBIT 9.19

ICI
Annual Report
1998
Note 17, Debtors

17 Debtors

	Group		Nonoperating debtors included in Group	
	1998 £m	1997 £m	1998 £m	1997 £m
Amounts due within one year				
Trade debtors.	1,473	1,666		
Less: amounts set aside for doubtful accounts	(87)	(71)		
	(1,386)	(1,595)		
Amounts owed by associated undertakings	5	5		
Prepaid pension costs.	—	1		
Taxation recoverable	122	82	122	82
Other prepayments and accrued income	145	124	15	15
Other debtors	296	245	—	1
	1,954	2,052	137	98
Amounts due after more than one year				
Advance corporation tax recoverable	—	36	—	36
Prepaid pension costs.	281	243	—	—
Other debtors	125	126	—	—
	406	405	—	36
	2,360	2,457	137	134

Inventories. The amount reported as "stocks" on the balance sheet.

Prepaid expenses and other current assets. This is the amount reported as "other prepayments and accrued income" in Note 17, Debtors.

Property, plant, and equipment. This is the amount shown as "tangible assets" in the "fixed assets" category on the balance sheet.

Investments. This is the amount shown as "investments—participating and other interests" in the "fixed assets" category on the balance sheet.

Goodwill. This is the amount reported as "intangible assets—goodwill" in the "fixed assets" category on the balance sheet.

Other non-current assets. This is the amount of debtors "due after more than one year" as detailed in Note 17, Debtors.

Liabilities

Short-term debt. The amount of "short-term borrowings" reported under the heading "creditors due within one year" on the balance sheet. "Creditors due within one year" is the equivalent of current liabilities in U.S. terminology.

Current portion of long-term debt. The amount of "current instalments of loans" reported on the balance sheet.

Accounts payable. Exhibit 9.20 presents Note 20, which details "other creditors" found on the balance sheet. "Trade creditors" under the heading "amounts due within one year" are current accounts payable.

Dividends payable. The amount reported in Note 20 as "dividends to ordinary shareholders."

Other current liabilities. This is the amount of "other creditors" due within one year in Note 20 not reported separately as accounts payable or dividends payable: £2,356 million − £1,070 million − £141 million = £1,145 million. It

EXHIBIT 9.20

ICI
Annual Report
1998
Note 20, Other Creditors

20 Other creditors

	Group		Nonoperating creditors included in Group	
	1998 **£m**	1997 £m	1998 £m	1997 £m
Amounts due within one year				
Trade creditors	**1,070**	1,142		
Amounts owed to associated undertakings	**6**	4		
Corporate taxation	**223**	273	*223*	*273*
Value added and payroll taxes and social security	**25**	54		
Dividends to Ordinary Shareholders	**141**	141	*141*	*141*
Environmental liabilities	**12**	20	*2*	*—*
Pension liabilities	**—**	24	*—*	*—*
Accruals	**376**	341	*91*	*96*
. . . .	**503**	584	*29*	*7*
	2,356	2,583	*486*	*517*
Amounts due after more than one year				
Corporate taxation	**1**	1		
Environmental liabilities	**8**	9		
Pension liabilities	**14**	14		
Other creditors*	**32**	43		
	55	67		

*Includes obligations under finance lease (note 36).

Under US GAAP, provisions for liabilities and charges (note 22) would be shown under other creditors—amounts due after more than one year.

EXHIBIT 9.21

ICI
Annual Report
1998
Note 22, Provisions for Liabilities and Charges

22 Provisions for liabilities and charges

Group	Deferred taxation £m	Advance corporation tax £m	Unfunded pensions (note 38) £m	Employee benefits £m	Environmental provisions £m	Disposal provisions £m	Restructuring provisions £m	Other provisions £m	Total £m
At the beginning of 1998	143	(22)	261	249	101	263	122	225	1,342
Profit and loss account	(103)	—	24	22	3	305	108	—	359
Net amounts paid or becoming current	—	22	(20)	(13)	(15)	(156)	(51)	(51)	(284)
Movements due to acquisitions and disposals	(4)	—	(19)	(4)	—	—	—	27	—
Exchange and other movements . . .	(2)	—	10	(6)	(7)	9	(3)	11	12
At end of 1998	**34**	**—**	**256**	**248**	**82**	**421**	**176**	**212**	**1,429**

No provision has been released or applied for any purpose other than that for which it was established.

Under US GAAP provisions for liabilities and charges would be shown under other creditors (note 20).

includes a variety of items including amounts owed associated undertakings, taxes payable, environmental liabilities, accruals, and other creditors.

Long-term debt. This is the amount of "loans" listed among "creditors due after more than one year" on the balance sheet. "Creditors due after more than one year" is the equivalent of long-term liabilities in U.S. terminology.

Deferred income taxes. Exhibit 9.21 shows Note 22, which details the items included in "provisions for liabilities and charges" reported on the balance sheet. Deferred income taxes is the amount of provision for "deferred taxation" at end of 1998 disclosed in Note 22.

Pension liability. This is the amount disclosed in Note 22 as provision for "unfunded pensions" at end of 1998.

Restructuring liability. This is the amount of "restructuring provisions" at end of 1998 reported in Note 22.

Other long-term liabilities. This is comprised of three components: "provisions for liabilities and charges" not reported separately, "other creditors due after more than one year," and "deferred income—grants not yet credited to profit." These latter two items are reported separately on the UK-format balance sheet. The calculation is as follows:

	£m
Provisions for liabilities and charges.	£1,429
Less: Deferred income taxes	34
Pension liability.	256
Restructuring liability.	176
	£ 963
Other creditors	55
Deferred income.	11
Other long-term liabilities	£1,029

Minority Interest

Minority interest. The amount reported as "minority interests—equity" on the balance sheet.

Shareholders' Equity

Capital stock. The amount reported on the balance sheet as "called-up share capital."

Paid-in capital in excess of par value. The "share premium account" reported on the balance sheet.

Retained earnings. This is the 12/31/98 amount from the U.S.-format statement of retained earnings (see Exhibit 9.16).

Other comprehensive income. This is the 12/31/98 amount from the U.S.-format statement of other comprehensive income (see Exhibit 9.16).

Step 2: Restating the Financial Statements to U.S. GAAP

Once the financial statements have been transformed to a U.S. format, the second step is to convert the amounts to a U.S. GAAP basis. ICI describes differences between UK and U.S. accounting principles and provides a reconciliation of income and shareholders' equity to U.S. GAAP in Note 43 to the financial statements. The description of differences in reproduced in Exhibit 9.22 and the reconciliation to U.S. GAAP is presented in Exhibit 9.23.

ICI made 9 adjustments to conform net income to U.S. GAAP and 11 adjustments to restate shareholders' equity (see Exhibit 9.22). All income adjustments also affect shareholders' equity through retained earnings, and two adjustments affect shareholders' equity alone. We have numbered the adjustments 1–11. The most effective approach for restating the financial statements to U.S. GAAP is to construct debit/credit adjusting entries for each reconciliation item, and then post these entries to columns 2 and 3 in the worksheets in Exhibits 9.14 (Income), 9.16 (Retained Earnings), and 9.17 (Balance Sheet).

[1] *Pension expense.* There are several differences between UK and U.S. GAAP in the accounting for pension costs that affect both the periodic pension expense as well as the pension liability reported on the balance sheet. The reconciliation schedules in Exhibit 9.23 show a pension expense adjustment of £(10) million to reconcile to U.S. GAAP income and an adjustment of £(291) million to reconcile to U.S. GAAP shareholders' equity. Under U.S. GAAP, pension expense in 1998 would have been £10 million larger. The cumulative effect of recording larger pension expense over the years results in retained earnings at December 31, 1998, being smaller by £291 million. The larger accrual for pension expense under U.S. GAAP would have been offset by a larger pension liability. The entry to adjust from UK to U.S. GAAP is as follows (£ millions):

Dr. Administrative and other expense	£ 10		(Exhibit 9.14)
Retained earnings, 1/1/98 (−)	281		(Exhibit 9.16)
Cr. Pension liability..................		£291	(Exhibit 9.17)

Note that the adjustment to the beginning balance in retained earnings is only £281 million. When the additional pension expense of £10 million for 1998 is closed to retained earnings at the end of the period, the net adjustment to retained earnings at December 31, 1998, will be £291 million.

EXHIBIT 9.22

ICI
Annual Report
1998
Note 43, Differences between UK and US Accounting Principles

---

43 Differences between UK and US accounting principles

The accompanying Group financial statements included in this report are prepared in accordance with United Kingdom Generally Accepted Accounting Principles (UK GAAP). The significant differences between UK GAAP and US Generally Accepted Accounting Principles (US GAAP) which affect the Group's net income and shareholders' equity are set out below:

(a) *Accounting for pension costs*

There are four significant differences between UK GAAP and US GAAP in accounting for pension costs:

(i) SFAS No. 87, "Employers' Accounting for Pensions", requires that pension plan assets are valued by reference to their fair or market related values, whereas UK GAAP permits an alternative measurement of assets, which, in the case of the main UK retirement plans, is on the basis of the discounted present value of expected future income streams from the pension plan assets.

(ii) SFAS No. 87, requires measurements of plan assets and obligations to be made as at the date of financial statements or a date not more than three months prior to that date. Under UK GAAP calculations may be based on the results of the latest actuarial valuation.

(iii) SFAS No. 87, mandates a particular actuarial method—the projected unit credit method—and requires that each significant assumption necessary to determine annual pension cost reflects best estimates solely with regard to that individual assumption. UK GAAP does not mandate a particular method, but requires that the method and assumptions, taken as a whole, should be compatible and lead to the actuary's best estimate of the cost of providing the benefits promised.

(iv) Under SFAS No. 87, a negative pension cost may arise where a significant unrecognized net asset or gain exists at the time of implementation. This is required to be amortised on a straight-line basis over the average remaining service period of employees. Under UK GAAP the Group's policy is not to recognize pension credits in its financial statements unless a refund of, or reduction in, contributions is likely.

(b) *Purchase accounting adjustments, including* the amortisation *and* impairment *of goodwill and intangibles*

In the Group's financial statements, prepared in accordance with UK GAAP, goodwill arising on acquisitions accounted for under the purchase method after 1 January 1998, is capitalised and amortised, as it would be in accordance with US GAAP. Prior to that date such goodwill arising on acquisitions was and remains eliminated against retained earnings. Values were not placed on intangible assets. Additionally, UK GAAP requires that on subsequent disposal or closure of a previously acquired asset, any goodwill previously taken directly to shareholders' equity is then charged in the income statement against the income or loss on disposal or closure. Under US GAAP all goodwill would be capitalised in the Group balance sheet and amortised through the income statement over its estimated life not exceeding 40 years. Also, under US GAAP, it is normal practice to ascribe fair values to identifiable intangibles. For the purpose of the adjustments to US GAAP, included below, identifiable intangible assets are amortised to income over the lower of their estimated lives or 40 years. Provision is made where there is a permanent impairment to the carrying value of capitalised goodwill and intangible assets based on a projection of future undiscounted cash flows.

(c) *Capitalisation of interest*

There is no accounting standard in the UK regarding the capitalisation of interest and the Group does not capitalise interest in its Group financial statements, Under US GAAP, SFAS No. 34 "Capitalization of Interest Cost", requires interest incurred as part of the cost of constructing fixed assets to be capitalised and amortised over the life of the asset.

(d) *Restructuring costs*

US GAAP requires a number of specific criteria to be met before restructuring costs can be recognised as an expense. Among these criteria is the requirement that all the significant actions arising from the restructuring plan and their completion dates must be identified by the balance sheet date. Under UK GAAP, prior to the publication of FRS 12, when a decision was taken to restructure, the necessary provisions were made for severance and other costs. Accordingly, timing differences, between UK GAAP and US GAAP, arise on the recognition of such costs.

(e) *Foreign exchange*

Under UK GAAP foreign currency differences arising on foreign currency loans are taken to reserves and offset against differences arising on net investments (if they act as a hedge). US GAAP is more restrictive in that currency loans may only hedge net investments in the same currency, if currency loans exceed net investment in any particular currency then the exchange differences arising are included in the income statement.

(f) *Discontinued operations*

US and UK GAAP have different criteria for determining discontinued operations. As a result the Canadian based Forest Products business, the UK fertiliser business, the 'Propafilm' business and the Teesside Utilities and Services business which are discontinued operations for UK GAAP would qualify as continuing operations for US GAAP. In addition, UK GAAP only allows discontinued accounting treatment for operations which either ceased or left the Group prior to the approval of the financial statements. Under US GAAP discontinued operations also include those operations where management have committed to a formal plan of disposal, therefore under US GAAP the Tioxide business qualifies as discontinued operations. For the purpose of the US GAAP reconciliation net income has been allocated between continuing operations and discontinued operations based on the classification described in note 1 after taking into account the above differences.

At the end of 1997, the Group changed the classification of the remaining businesses within Industrial Chemicals to discontinued operations for US GAAP purposes. This included all businesses within Industrial Chemicals except for those businesses which were being sold to DuPont as these were classified as discontinued operations under US GAAP earlier in that year. In the fourth quarter of 1998 it became apparent that these businesses no longer qualified as discontinued operations under US GAAP. As a result, the 1997 and 1996 US GAAP net income reconciliations have been adjusted to reclassify the results of the remaining businesses in Industrial Chemicals as part of continuing operations. The portion of the previously recognised reserve for loss on disposal which would not be recognised for continuing operations in 1997 has been reversed in 1998. There is no change to the previously reported total US GAAP net income as a result of this change.

(g) *Employee share trust arrangements*

An employee share trust has been established in order to hedge obligations in respect of options issued under certain employee share option schemes, Under UK GAAP the Company's ordinary shares held by the employee share trust are included at historic net book value in fixed asset investments. Under US GAAP, such shares are treated as treasury stock and included in shareholders' equity.

(h) *Ordinary Dividends*

Under UK GAAP, the proposed dividends on ordinary shares, as recommended by the directors, are deducted from shareholders' equity and shown as a liability in the balance sheet at the end of the period to which they relate. Under US GAAP, such dividends are only deducted from shareholders' equity at the date of declaration of the dividend. The Group has not adjusted US GAAP shareholders' equity for this difference in prior years. As a result, 1997 US GAAP shareholders' equity has been restated to take account of this difference.

(i) *Deferred taxation*

Deferred taxation is provided on a full provision basis under US GAAP. Under UK GAAP no provision is made for taxation deferred by reliefs unless there is reasonable evidence that such deferred taxation will be payable in the foreseeable future.

---

[2] *Amortization of goodwill and intangibles.* Item (b) in Note 43 (see Exhibit 9.22) indicates that prior to 1998, goodwill was written off directly to retained earnings. Thus, under UK GAAP, goodwill and retained earnings are understated. In addition, amortization expense is understated because goodwill was not capitalized and amortized. The required adjusting entry to convert to U.S. GAAP must therefore increase goodwill and retained earnings and record amortization expense for the year 1998. Additional information provided in the notes suggests that £109 million of the 1998 amortization expense relates to operations discontinued in 1998; the portion related to continuing operations, £25 million, is included in administrative and other expenses. The reconciling entry is as follows (£ millions):

Dr. Goodwill	£3,618		(Exhibit 9.17)
Administrative and other expenses	25		(Exhibit 9.14)
Income of discontinued operations (net of tax)	109		(Exhibit 9.14)
Cr. Retained earnings, 1/1/98 (+)		£3,752	(Exhibit 9.16)

When the amortization expense of £134 million is closed to retained earnings at year-end, the net effect of this entry on December 31, 1998, retained earnings is a net increase of £3,618 million.

[3] *Disposals and other adjustments* and [4] *Other disposal adjustments.* The narrative in Note 43 (Exhibit 9.22) sheds little light on the cause of these two adjustments. Their combined effect is to decrease U.S. GAAP income by

EXHIBIT 9.23

ICI
Annual Report
1998
Reconciliation from UK GAAP to U.S. GAAP

The following is a summary of the material adjustments to net income and shareholders' equity which would have been required if US GAAP had been applied instead of UK GAAP:

	1998 £m	1997 £m	1996 £m
Net income after exceptional items—UK GAAP	193	259	275
Continuing operations	54	(331)	128
Discontinued operations	139	590	147
Adjustments to conform to US GAAP			
Pension expense [1]	(10)	(41)	(5)
Purchase accounting adjustments			
Amortisation of goodwill and intangibles [2]	(134)	(83)	(25)
Disposals and other adjustments [3]	31	112	5
Other disposal adjustments [4]	(59)	(114)	—
Capitalisation of interest less amortisation and disposals [5]	(24)	(113)	28
Restructuring costs [6]	(81)	58	2
Foreign exchange	—	12	73
Discontinued operations [7]	8	(8)	—
Deferred taxation [8]			
Arising on UK GAAP results	(16)	(12)	(29)
Arising on other US GAAP adjustments	45	54	10
Others [9]	3	17	2
Total US GAAP adjustments	(237)	(118)	61
Net income—US GAAP	(44)	141	336
Continuing operations	(82)	103	295
Discontinued operations	38	38	41

	1998 £m	1997 £m
Shareholders' equity, as shown in the Group Balance sheets—UK GAAP	149	146
Adjustments to conform with US GAAP		
Purchase accounting adjustments, including goodwill and intangibles [2]	3,618	3,985
Disposal accounting adjustments [3], [4]	(25)	33
Capitalisation of interest less amortisation and disposals [5]	128	152
Restructuring provision [6]	56	105
Pension expense [1]	(291)	(281)
Discontinued operations [7]	—	(8)
Employee share trust agreements [10]	(62)	—
Ordinary dividends [11]	141	141
Deferred taxation [8]	(147)	(156)
Other [9]	(10)	(19)
Total US GAAP adjustments	3,408	3,952
Shareholders' equity in accordance with US GAAP	3,557	4,098

£28 million (£31 million − £59 million) and decrease shareholders' equity by £25 million. Because there is a separate adjustment for discontinued operations, it can be assumed that these disposal adjustments relate to the "sale or closure of operations" and/or "disposal of fixed assets," the effects of which are reported separately on the UK-format income statement. Both of these are included in "other income" in the U.S.-format income statement. It is also reasonable to assume that the adjustments relate to disposals of property, plant, and equipment. Therefore, based on these assumptions, the adjusting entry is as follows (£ millions):

Dr. Other income	£28		(Exhibit 9.14)
Cr. Property, plant, and equipment		£25	(Exhibit 9.17)
Retained earnings, 1/1/98 (+)		3	(Exhibit 9.16)

The net effect of this entry is to reduce U.S. GAAP income by £28 and, after other income is closed to retained earnings, to reduce shareholders' equity (retained earnings) by only £25.

[5] *Capitalization of interest less amortization and disposals.* Item (c) in Note 43 (Exhibit 9.22) indicates that ICI does not capitalize interest as is required under U.S. GAAP in certain situations. To adjust to a U.S. GAAP basis (1) previously expensed interest must be capitalized in property, plant, and equipment; (2) retained earnings must be adjusted for previously expensed interest that should have been capitalized; and (3) the newly capitalized interest included in property, plant, and equipment must be depreciated. Assuming that there is no interest that should be capitalized for the year 1998, the decrease in U.S. GAAP income of £24 million is attributable solely to the depreciation of the interest that would have been capitalized under U.S. GAAP in prior years, and the entire amount can be adjusted to administrative and other expenses. The entry to effect these adjustments is as follows (£ millions):

Dr. Property, plant, and equipment (net)	£128		(Exhibit 9.17)
Administrative and other expenses	24		(Exhibit 9.14)
Cr. Retained earnings, 1/1/98 (+)		£152	(Exhibit 9.16)

Note that if there were interest incurred in 1998 that should be capitalized, a portion of the £24 million income adjustment would be a decrease in interest expense with an increase in administrative and other expenses exceeding £24 million. Also, if any capitalized interest were included in manufacturing fixed assets, part of the depreciation adjustment would be taken to cost of sales. There is insufficient information provided by the company to determine exactly which expenses are affected and in what amount.

[6] *Restructuring costs.* The accounting for a restructuring results in an increase in an expense (restructuring charge) and an offsetting increase in a restructuring liability. Item (d) in Exhibit 9.22 reports that the timing of recognition of these elements differs between UK and U.S. GAAP. The restructuring charge in 1998 under U.S. GAAP would result in a decrease in income of £81 million, but the reconciliation of shareholders' equity indicates an increase of £56 million. Apparently, the restructuring liability under UK GAAP is greater than it would be using U.S. rules. The adjusting entry is as follows (£ millions):

Dr. Restructuring charge	£81		(Exhibit 9.14)
Restructuring liability	56		(Exhibit 9.17)
Cr. Retained earnings, 1/1/98 (+)		£137	(Exhibit 9.16)

After the restructuring charge is closed to retained earnings at the end of the period, the net effect of this entry on December 31, 1998, retained earnings is an increase of only £56 million (£137 million − £81 million).

[7] *Discontinued operations.* Note 43, item (f), indicates that a loss on disposal of discontinued operations that would have been recognized in 1997 under U.S. GAAP was not recognized until 1998 under UK GAAP. In other words, a timing difference exists in the recognition of the loss. The loss recognized in 1998 must be reversed and beginning retained earnings must be reduced for the loss that should have been recognized in 1997. The net effect on retained earnings at December 31, 1998, is nil. The adjusting entry is as follows (£ millions):

Dr. Retained earnings, 1/1/98 (−)	£8		(Exhibit 9.16)
Cr. Gain on disposal of discontinued operations (net of tax) . . .		£8	(Exhibit 9.14)

[8] *Deferred taxation.* Two adjustments are made to income tax expense and deferred income taxes (liability). The first adjustment arises because of differences in deferred income tax accounting between UK GAAP and U.S. GAAP. The second adjustment arises because deferred income taxes must be recognized on the adjustments to income made in converting to U.S. GAAP. The net effect of both types of adjustment is to increase U.S. GAAP income in 1998 by £29 million (£45 million − £16 million) and reduce shareholders' equity at December 31, 1998, by £147 million. The reduction in shareholders' equity is offset by an increase in deferred income taxes (liability). Both types of adjustment can be handled in one adjusting entry (£ millions):

Dr. Retained earnings, 1/1/98 (−)	£176		(Exhibit 9.16)
Cr. Income tax expense		£ 29	(Exhibit 9.14)
Deferred income taxes (liability)		147	(Exhibit 9.17)

After closing the adjustment decreasing income tax expense, the net effect of this entry is to reduce retained earnings by £147 million.

[9] *Others.* Other, nonspecified adjustments result in an increase in 1998 income of £3 million and a decrease in shareholders' equity of £10 million. Assuming that these adjustments related to "other income" and "other long-term liabilities," the adjusting entry is as follows (£ millions):

Dr. Retained earnings, 1/1/98 (−)	£13		(Exhibit 9.16)
Cr. Other income		£ 3	(Exhibit 9.14)
Other long-term liabilities		10	(Exhibit 9.17)

[10] *Employee share trust arrangements.* Item (g) in Note 43 indicates that the company's own shares held in an employee trust are included in long-term investments under UK GAAP, but should be classified as treasury stock (contra stockholders' equity) in accordance with U.S. GAAP. The entry to reclassify this item, which has no effect on income, is as follows (£ millions):

Dr. Treasury stock	£62		(Exhibit 9.17)
Cr. Investments		£62	(Exhibit 9.17)

[11] *Ordinary dividends.* Note 43, item (h), states that a timing difference can exist in the recognition of dividends (which reduces retained earnings) and dividends payable under U.S. and UK GAAP. The reconciliation item for "ordinary dividends" indicates an increase in U.S. shareholders' equity in both 1997 and 1998 of £141 million. Apparently, dividends proposed in 1997 and recognized as a liability under UK GAAP had not yet been officially declared by year-end 1998. Retained earnings must be increased and dividends payable decreased by £141 million to reconcile to U.S. GAAP (£ millions):

Dr. Dividends payable £141		(Exhibit 9.17)
Cr. Retained earnings, 1/1/98 (+)	£141	(Exhibit 9.16)

Comparison of UK GAAP and U.S. GAAP Amounts

The adjusted U.S. GAAP amounts reported in Column 4 of Exhibits 9.14, 9.16, and 9.17 now can be used to evaluate and compare the profitability and financial position of ICI with other companies that use U.S. accounting principles. A comparison of the amounts reported in accordance with U.S. GAAP (Column 4) with the UK GAAP amounts (Column 1) shows that significant differences exist for some line items but that there are no differences under the two sets of accounting rules for other items.

The procedures demonstrated here for restating ICI's financial statements could be used to transform any company's financial statements to whatever set of accounting procedures the analyst desires. For companies that do not provide a reconciliation to the analyst's target GAAP, an additional step would involve determining the major differences between the company's GAAP and the analyst's preferred GAAP and then quantifying the effect of these differences for the specific company under analysis. This requires extensive knowledge of the two sets of standards being adjusted as well as adequate disclosure provided by the company, especially with respect to the accounting principles followed.

Summary

1. There are many reasons why one would want to analyze financial statements of foreign companies. The most important reasons relate to making investment decisions, portfolio investments by individuals and mutual fund managers, and acquisition investments by multinational companies.

2. The following are some of the problems an analyst might encounter in analyzing foreign financial statements:

   - Difficulty in finding and obtaining financial information about a foreign company.
   - An inability to read the language in which the financial statements are presented.
   - The currency used in presenting monetary amounts.
   - Terminology differences that result in uncertainty as to the information provided.
   - Differences in format that lead to confusion and missing information.
   - Lack of adequate disclosures.
   - Financial statements not being made available on a timely basis.
   - Accounting differences that hinder cross-country comparisons.
   - Differences in business environments that might make ratio comparisons meaningless even if accounting differences are eliminated.

3. Some of the potential problems can be removed by companies through their preparation of convenience translations in which language, currency, and perhaps even accounting principles have been restated for the convenience of foreign readers. Companies interested in attracting interest globally have an incentive to provide more disclosure and issue their financial statements on a more timely basis than is required by their home country.

4. A significant number of investors find that differences in accounting practices across countries hinder their financial analysis and affect their investment decisions. Some analysts cope with this problem by restating foreign financial statements to a familiar basis, such as U.S. GAAP.

5. Foreign companies listed on U.S. securities markets must reconcile net income and stockholders' equity to a U.S. GAAP basis. However, there is no requirement to reconcile assets and liabilities or to provide complete financial statements in terms of U.S. GAAP. Reconciliations of net income and stockholders' equity only are of limited usefulness in analyzing a company's financial position and profitability.

6. Foreign GAAP financial statements can be restated to a U.S. GAAP basis through a two-step process. First, financial statements are reformatted to a U.S. basis and, second, foreign GAAP amounts are restated in terms of U.S. GAAP. A restatement worksheet facilitates completion of these two steps.

7. Analysts should be careful in interpreting ratios calculated for foreign companies, even if the ratios are developed from restated financial statements. Financial ratios can differ across countries as a result of differences in business and economic environments. Optimally, an analyst will develop an understanding of the accounting and business environments of the countries whose companies they wish to analyze.

8. Foreign-company financial statements can be restated in terms of a preferred format and GAAP through a two-step process. First, financial statements are reformatted, if necessary. Second, through the use of reconciling entries in a restatement worksheet, the reformatted statements are restated to the preferred GAAP.

Appendix to Chapter 9

Morgan Stanley Dean Witter *Apples to Apples*

One way to avoid the distortions to comparability caused by differences in accounting rules is to focus analysis within a country, making comparisons across companies only in that country. Using an analysis of macroeconomic variables such as expected real growth in GDP, an investor first determines how much of his or her portfolio to allocate to a specific country. The investor then makes comparisons across companies in that country to identify the best investments. International equity investing traditionally was carried out using such a "country analysis" approach.

More recently, investment advisers have moved away from country analysis to industry analysis, in which they analyze and compare the major companies within an industry worldwide. Rather than first deciding to invest 10 percent of the portfolio in Japanese stocks, the investor might decide to invest 10 percent of the portfolio in food products companies. The task then becomes one of identifying the food companies that offer the best future returns regardless of nationality. This necessitates making comparisons across companies in different countries.

In the late 1990s, analysts at Morgan Stanley Dean Witter (MSDW) embarked on a project called Apples to Apples to identify the types of adjustments to financial statement figures needed to make information within an industry more comparable and at the same time more useful. Rather than simply adjusting foreign companies' financial statements to a U.S. GAAP basis to improve comparability, they use a cash flow and value-driver orientation to make adjustments for all companies within an industry, including those located in the United States. Some of the global industries for which the MSDW analysts have completed this project include airlines, beverage, food products, and imaging.

MSDW analysts begin by identifying the key value drivers in a particular industry and then proceed to determine how different accounting practices affect the data related to these value drivers. The scope of the analysis is limited to those items that are relevant to stock valuation—primarily earnings and stockholders' equity. The analysts do not reconcile all accounts to a single set of rules such as IFRSs or U.S. GAAP. In fact, they do not presume that U.S. GAAP provides correct data for valuing investments. Instead they make adjustments to figures reported under various GAAP to develop data that they believe more closely reflect the underlying economics. The goal is to look through the accounting rules that hinder global comparability to understand the true economics of the business. The remainder of this appendix describes the Apples to Apples process with regard to the airline industry.

GLOBAL AIRLINES

Two of the major value drivers in the airline industry are the size of a carrier's fleet of aircraft and the true cost of operations. The major accounting issues that affect the ability to value firms in this industry are capacity, capacity cost (depreciation), staff costs, taxation, and foreign currency fluctuations. The accounting problem related to each of these issues and what the MSDW analysts did to deal with them are summarized here.

Capacity

Most airlines lease a substantial portion of their fleet. Rules for capitalizing leases (reporting an asset and liability) on the balance sheet vary from country to country. MSDW believes that all leases should be capitalized and therefore made adjustments to capitalize all leases that were accounted for as operating (noncapitalized) leases. This involved removing operating lease expense (rental payments) from earnings and then adding to reported expenses depreciation on the leased asset and interest expense for the financing of the leased asset. The net effect these adjustments had on earnings ranged from +4 percent of reported earnings for KLM Royal Dutch Airlines to −59 percent of reported earnings for Japan Airlines, with the average adjustment about −10 percent. The increase in liabilities resulting from the capitalization of leases ranged from +5 percent for China Eastern to +671 percent for Delta Airlines. The change in equity was +4 percent for Southwest Airlines and −70 percent for Northwest Airlines (both are U.S. carriers). The impact on equity and pretax income was more negative for U.S. airlines than for most non-U.S. airlines, partly because U.S. airlines use more leased assets than other airlines but also because they pay higher interest rates.

Capacity Cost (Depreciation)

Depreciation is based on the historical cost of capitalized fixed assets. The analysts at MSDW believe this understates the true cost of capacity—the cost that must be incurred to maintain the revenues generated by the airline's current fleet capacity. They estimated the economic cost to sustain the current capacity by considering historical expenditures, fleet utilization, age of assets, fuel-burn rate, asset replacement policy, and the airline's market resale policy. The following steps were taken:

- Identify each airline's fleet including leased planes, and each aircraft's characteristics such as make and age.
- Estimate expenditures required to refurbish older aircraft and the amount and timing of spending on replacement aircraft.
- Estimate differences in expenses for maintenance and fuel consumption of the future fleet.
- Estimate the resulting cost outflows at present value to obtain an annual cost of capacity figure.

Reported depreciation expense was then replaced by the annual cost of capacity figure for each airline to develop a more relevant measure of earnings. For most airlines, reported depreciation undercharged for the cost of capacity. The largest adjustment resulted in a decrease in Northwest's reported income of 46 percent. Because of its aggressive depreciation policy and a relatively young fleet, China Eastern's reported income was adjusted upward by 39 percent.

Staff Costs

The major issue related to staff costs involves deferred compensation—pension and other retirement (e.g., medical) benefits promised to employees. The relevant amount for valuation is the net cash flow, on a present value basis, related to the plans. Net cash flow is the difference between cash inflows on plan assets and cash outflows to beneficiaries. In addition, an interest charge should be recognized on the underfunded portion of the benefit obligation. The extent to which benefit plans are funded and the manner in which benefit expenses are calculated varies by country. For some airlines, especially in Asia, lack of disclosures related to pension plans posed the greatest difficulty in estimating the true obligation and expense. However, the analysts were able to make assumptions and estimations to be able to develop adjustments for all airlines. The largest adjustment was a 301 percent decrease in reported income for Japan Airlines. The magnitude of this adjustment results from the fact that Japanese companies do not accrue currently an expense related to future benefit payments, which results in a large understatement of retirement benefit expense. In addition, benefits plans tend to be only partially funded so that a large interest charge must be added. Among the U.S. airlines, the cumulative adjustment for benefit obligations ranged from +23 percent (Delta) to −72 percent (Northwest) of reported equity.

Taxation

Deferred taxes are the difference between the tax expense based on accounting income and the actual taxes payable based on taxable income. For companies that use accelerated depreciation for taxes and straight-line depreciation for accounting, taxes payable are less than tax expense and a deferred tax liability will be reported on the balance sheet. Through the replacement of depreciable assets, the deferred tax liability can be deferred indefinitely. The analysts at MSDW believe the deferred tax liability reported on the balance sheet should reflect the likely amount of taxes to be paid in the future discounted to their present value. Working on the basis of certain assumptions regarding the pattern of future capital expenditures at each airline, they developed an adjustment for the present value of the deferred tax liability. This resulted in a reduction in liabilities for most companies with an offsetting increase in equity and an increase in earnings. For the U.S. airlines, the increase in income averages 15 percent and the increase in equity was greater than 20 percent in all cases. Because accounting and taxable income are closely linked in most European countries, the adjustments for the European airlines were minimal.

Foreign Currency Exposure

Airplanes and fuel are priced in U.S. dollars, so non-U.S. companies are exposed to foreign exchange risk on these items. Revenues tend to be in a variety of currencies, so net exposures to foreign exchange risk exist. The analysts attempted to determine the net exposures for the companies in the airline industry, but disclosures were inadequate to allow for a clear estimate. They believe that U.S. carriers have less risk because costs and revenues are primarily in U.S. dollars. The only adjustments that they could make were gains/losses on the local currency value of the existing fleet (used airplanes are sold for U.S. dollars) and reporting any deferred foreign exchange gains/losses in income.

Other Issues

Frequent-flyer programs represent a contingent liability for airlines. MSDW considered whether the cost of frequent-flyer programs is underreported. They concluded that giving away a seat that would otherwise not have been occupied had little if any cost, and no adjustments to reported earnings were deemed to be needed. Routes and airport slots purchased from another airline are reported as intangible assets. Routes and slots given directly to an airline are not recognized as assets but they may have value. Given the lack of disclosure by airlines about their routes and slots and the differences in regulations related to them, no direct adjustments to reported information were made.

Questions

1. Why might individual investors wish to include foreign companies in their investment portfolio?
2. Which companies might Ford Motor Company include in a benchmarking study of the automobile industry, and in which countries are those companies located?
3. What are potential problems in using commercial databases as the source of financial statement information for foreign companies?
4. How might an analyst obtain the most recent financial statements for a foreign company in which he or she is interested?
5. Why should the fact that a foreign company presents its financial statements in a foreign currency present no significant problems in analyzing those statements?
6. A foreign company prepares its financial statements in a foreign language and does not provide any convenience translations. How might this affect an analyst's decision to invest in this company?

7. As noted in the chapter, Degussa AG reports "revenue reserves" as a positive item in stockholders' equity. What do you assume this item represents? How confident are you in your assumption?

8. How can more disclosure in the notes to the financial statements facilitate the analysis of foreign financial statements?

9. In what ways does the timeliness of the publication of financial information differ across countries?

10. What are the advantages and disadvantages in using measures such as operating income before depreciation (OIBD) or earnings before interest, taxes, depreciation and amortization (EBITDA) rather than net income in comparing profitability across foreign companies?

11. What are the different features of financial statements that a foreign company might "translate" in a convenience translation?

12. Why should analysts be careful in comparing financial ratios across companies in different countries?

13. How might differences in the extent to which countries apply the accounting concept of conservatism (some countries are more conservative than others) affect profit margins, debt-to-equity ratios, and returns on equity?

14. How might differences across countries in the extent to which debt versus equity is the major source of financing affect profit margins, debt-to-equity ratios, and return on equity?

15. For what types of differences must adjustments be made in transforming UK financial statements to a U.S. format?

16. A foreign company did not capitalize any interest in the current or past years, although such capitalization is required under U.S. GAAP. Why does an adjustment to reconcile this item to U.S. GAAP affect assets, expenses, and beginning retained earnings?

Exercises and Problems

1. Refer to the worksheets in Exhibits 9.14, 9.16, and 9.17 in which the financial statements of Imperial Chemical Industries (ICI) have been reformatted and restated to U.S. GAAP.

Required:
a. Calculate each of the ratios listed below using (1) the UK GAAP (U.S.-format) amounts in Column 1, and (2) the U.S. GAAP amounts in Column 4.
b. Determine the percentage difference in each of these ratios using the formula: (U.S. GAAP ratio − UK GAAP ratio)/UK GAAP ratio.
c. Determine which ratios appear to be most and least affected by differences in the two sets of accounting principles.

Ratios

Current ratio (Current assets/Current liabilities)

Total asset turnover (Net sales/Average total assets)

Debt-to-equity ratio (Total liabilities/Total stockholders' equity)

Times interest earned ([Income from continuing operations before income taxes + Interest expense]/Interest expense)

Profit margin (Net income/Net sales)

Return on equity (Net income/Average total stockholders' equity)

Operating profit margin (Operating profit/Net sales)

Operating income as a percentage of total stockholders' equity (Operating profit/Total stockholders' equity)

2. China Petroleum & Chemical Corporation (Sinopec) provides two sets of financial statements in its annual report. One set of financial statements is prepared in accordance with Chinese (PRC) Accounting Regulations and another is prepared in accordance with IFRSs. The company also provides a reconciliation of IFRS net income and net assets to U.S. GAAP. Sinopec reported the following amounts under three different sets of accounting rules in its 2003 annual report:

	Accounting Rules		
RMB millions	PRC	IFRSs	U.S. GAAP
Consolidated profit attributable to shareholders—2003	19,011	21,593	25,577
Consolidated net assets—December 31, 2003 . . .	162,946	167,899	158,216
Consolidated net assets—December 31, 2002 . . .	151,717	163,823	150,167

Required:
a. Determine the percentage difference in profit attributable to shareholders and average net assets for 2003 under the three different sets of accounting rules.
b. Calculate return on net assets (Profit attributable to shareholders/Average net assets) for 2003 under the three different sets of accounting rules.
c. Determine the percentage difference in return on net assets under the three sets of rules.
d. Which of the three measures of return on net assets is most useful in assessing Sinopec's profitability?

3. SABMiller PLC was formed when U.S.-based Miller Brewing Company merged with South African Breweries in 2002. SABMiller uses South African GAAP in preparing its financial statements. The following is taken from the March 31, 2004, consolidated balance sheet of SABMiller PLC:

Capital and Reserves	2004 US$m	2003 US$m
Share capital	127	127
Share premium	1,383	1,373
Merger relief reserve	3,395	3,395
Revaluation and other reserves	20	20
Profit and loss reserve	1,240	657
Shareholders' funds.	6,165	5,572
Equity minority interests	819	778
Capital employed	6,984	6,350

Required:
Describe the content of each of the line items presented using accounting terminology common to the United States.

4. The consolidated balance sheet for Babcock International Group PLC at March 31, 2004, is presented in the following table:

Group Balance Sheet
As at 31 March 2004

	Notes	2004 £m	2004 £m	2003 £m	2003 £m
Fixed assets					
Intangible assets	12				
Development costs			0.7		1.0
Goodwill					
—Goodwill		81.5		84.0	
—Negative goodwill		(4.7)		(6.5)	
			76.8		77.5
			77.5		78.5
Tangible assets	13		12.2		16.5
Investments	15				
Investments in joint ventures					
Share of gross assets		2.4		1.4	
Share of gross liabilities		(2.7)		(1.8)	
Loans to joint ventures		0.9		0.8	
		0.6		0.4	
Other investments		4.1		3.9	
			4.7		4.3
			94.4		99.3
Current assets					
Stocks	16		29.7		23.4
Debtors—due within one year	17	75.2		88.7	
Debtors—due after more than one year	17	64.0		69.6	
			139.2		158.3
Cash and bank balances			17.5		12.7
			186.4		194.4
Creditors—amounts due within one year	18		(134.7)		(159.9)
Net current assets			51.7		34.5
Total assets less current liabilities			146.1		133.8
Creditors—amounts due after more than one year	19		(16.0)		(19.0)
Provisions for liabilities and charges	22		(29.0)		(27.4)
Net assets			101.1		87.4
Capital and reserves					
Called up share capital	25		90.1		88.9
Share premium account	26		38.6		38.1
Capital redemption reserve	26		30.6		30.6
Profit and loss account	26		(58.2)		(70.3)
Equity interests			101.1		87.3
Non-equity interests			—		—
Shareholders' funds			101.1		87.3
Equity minority interests	27		—		0.1
			101.1		87.4

Required:
a. Transform Babcock's March 31, 2004, balance sheet to a U.S. format.
b. Identify items for which you are unsure as to how they should be reported in a U.S.-format balance sheet.

5. China Eastern Airlines (CEA) Corporation Limited presents two sets of financial statements in its annual report; one set is prepared in accordance with Chinese (PRC) accounting regulations and one set is prepared in accordance with International Financial Reporting Standards (IFRSs). The company also

provides a reconciliation of net income and net assets from PRC GAAP to IFRSs. The following excerpts were taken from a recent annual report:

Significant differences between International Accounting Standards ("IAS") and PRC <u>Accounting Regulations</u>

(a) Under IAS, other flight equipment is accounted for as fixed assets and depreciation charges are calculated over the expected useful lives of 20 years to residual value of 5% of cost/revalued amounts. Under PRC Accounting Regulations, such flight equipment is classified as current assets and the costs are amortised on a straight-line basis over a period of 5 years.

(b) This represents the difference on gain on disposal arising from different useful lives adopted on depreciation under IAS and PRC Accounting Regulations.

Consolidated profit attributable to shareholders	RMB'000
As stated in accordance with PRC audited statutory accounts	132,919
Impact of IAS and other adjustments:	
Adjustment (1).	150,794
Adjustment (2).	(13,296)
Other adjustments	271,296
As stated in accordance with IAS.	541,713

Required:

a. Determine which adjustment, (1) or (2), relates to which item, (a) or (b), described in the excerpt. Explain your answer.

b. What impact would items (a) and (b) have on the reconciliation of net assets (stockholders' equity) from PRC GAAP to IFRSs?

6. China Eastern Airlines (CEA) Corporation Limited prepares a set of financial statements in accordance with IFRSs (in Chinese renminbi—RMB). The company also provides a reconciliation of IFRS net income and net assets to U.S. GAAP. The following excerpt was taken from a recent annual report:

Significant Differences between IFRS and U.S. GAAP

Differences between IFRS and U.S. GAAP which have significant effects on the consolidated profits/(loss) attributable to shareholders and consolidated owners' equity of the Group are summarized as follows:

Consolidated profit/(loss) attributable to shareholders

(Amounts in thousands except per share data)

	Note	Year Ended December 31, 2001 RMB	2002 RMB	2003 RMB	2003 US$ (note 2a)
As stated under IFRS		541,713	83,369	(949,816)	(114,758)
U.S. GAAP adjustments:					
Reversal of difference in depreciation charges arising from revaluation of fixed assets	(a)	94,140	20,370	63,895	7,720
Reversal of revaluation deficit of fixed assets	(a)	—	171,753	—	—
Gain/(loss) on disposal of aircraft and related assets . . .	(b)	5,791	(26,046)	(10,083)	(1,218)
Others	(c)	(11,295)	23,767	6,860	829
Deferred tax effect on U.S. GAAP adjustments	(d)	(155,877)	(28,477)	(9,101)	(1,100)
As stated under U.S. GAAP		474,472	247,736	(892,245)	(108,527)
Basic and fully diluted earnings/(loss) per share under U.S. GAAP		RMB0.097	RMB0.051	(RMB0.185)	(US$0.022)
Basic and fully diluted earnings/(loss) per American Depository Share ("ADS") under U.S. GAAP		RMB9.75	RMB5.09	(RMB18.46)	(US$2.23)

Consolidated owners' equity

(Amounts in thousands)

	Note	December 31, 2002 RMB	2003 RMB	2003 US$ (note 2a)
As stated under IFRS		7,379,103	6,382,151	771,099
U.S. GAAP adjustments:				
Reversal of net revaluation surplus of fixed assets	(a)	(908,873)	(908,873)	(109,811)
Reversal of difference in depreciation charges and accumulated depreciation and loss on disposals arising from the revaluation of fixed assets	(a), (b)	637,423	691,235	83,516
Others	(c)	29,111	35,971	4,346
Deferred tax effect on U.S. GAAP adjustments	(d)	20,844	9,225	1,115
As stated under U.S. GAAP		7,157,608	6,209,709	750,264

Notes:

(a) Revaluation of fixed assets

Under IFRS, fixed assets of the Group are initially recorded at cost and are subsequently restated at revalued amounts less accumulated depreciation. Fixed assets of the Group were revalued as of June 30, 1996 as part of the restructuring of the Group for the purpose of listing. In addition, as of December 31, 2002, a revaluation of the Group's aircraft and engines was carried out and difference between the valuation and carrying amount was recognized. Under U.S. GAAP, the revaluation surplus or deficit and the related difference in depreciation are reversed since fixed assets are required to be stated at cost.

Required:

a. Explain the difference between (1) IFRS net income and U.S. GAAP net income and (2) IFRS net assets (owners' equity) and U.S. GAAP net assets that results from the accounting difference related to "revaluation of fixed assets."

b. Determine the directional impact (increase, decrease, no effect) the accounting difference described above would have on the following ratios calculated under IFRS and U.S. GAAP:

Current ratio (Current assets/Current liabilities)
Debt-to-equity ratio (Total liabilities/Total owners' equity)
Total asset turnover (Net sales/Average total assets)
Profit margin (Net income/Net sales)
Return on equity (Net income/Average total owners' equity)

7. The following excerpts were taken from the notes to consolidated financial statements in the 2004 annual report of the Swiss pharmaceutical company Novartis Group:

Note 32 Significant Differences Between IFRS and United States Generally Accepted Accounting Principles (US GAAP)

The Group's consolidated financial statements have been prepared in accordance with IFRS, which as applied by the Group, differs in certain significant respects from U.S. GAAP.

f) Share-based compensation

The Group does not account for share-based compensation, as it is not required under IFRS. Under US GAAP, the Group applies Accounting Principles Board Opinion No. 25 (APB 25) Accounting for Stock Issued to Employees and related interpretations in accounting for its plans. As described in Note 26, the Group has several plans that are subject to measurement under APB 25.

In 2004, to reconcile IFRS net income to a U.S. GAAP basis, Novartis recognized additional compensation expense related to share-based plans totaling $326 million.

Required:

a. Determine whether 2004 net income and stockholders' equity at December 31, 2004, would be greater under IFRSs or U.S. GAAP.

b. Determine the directional impact (increase, decrease, no effect) the difference in accounting for share-based compensation in 2004 under IFRSs and U.S. GAAP would have on the following ratios:

Current ratio (Current assets/Current liabilities)

Debt-to-equity ratio (Total liabilities/Total stockholders' equity)

Total asset turnover (Net sales/Average total assets)

Profit margin (Net income/Net sales)

Return on equity (Net income/Average total stockholders' equity)

8. Wienerberger AG is an Austrian manufacturer of bricks and roof tiles that uses IFRSs in preparing its consolidated financial statements. A condensed balance sheet for Wienerberger AG at December 31, 2003, along with excerpts from Notes 17, 19, and 21, is presented in the following table:

Balance Sheet (in TEUR)

Notes		31.12.2003
	ASSETS	
	Fixed and financial assets	1,601,870
(17)	Current assets (incl. receivables)	906,996
	Deferred tax assets	39,672
	Total assets	2,548,538
	EQUITY AND LIABILITIES	
	Equity	956,680
	Minority interest	26,326
(19)	Provisions	307,016
(21)	Liabilities	1,258,516
	Total equity and liabilities	2,548,538

(handwritten annotations: "Total Equity" bracket by Equity/Minority interest; "Total Liabilities" bracket by Provisions/Liabilities)

17. Receivables and Other Assets

Development of receivables

in TEUR	2003		
	Total	Thereof remaining term under 1 year	Thereof remaining term over 1 year
1. Trade receivables	163,816	160,302	3,514
2. Receivables due from subsidiaries	28,822	19,189	9,633
3. Receivables due from affiliates	89,182	3,558	85,624
4. Other receivables and assets	87,951	81,392	6,559
Receivables	**369,771**	**264,441**	**105,330**

19. Provisions *Liabilities*

in TEUR	31.12.2003
1. Provisions for severance payments	12,415
2. Provisions for pensions	36,024
3. Provisions for deferred taxes	92,970
4. Other non-current provisions	
a) Warranties	21,962
b) Service anniversary bonuses	3,423
c) Site restoration	24,057
Non-current provisions	**190,851**
5. Provisions for current taxes	7,619
6. Other current provisions	
a) Vacations	15,157
b) Miscellaneous	93,389
Current provisions	**116,165**
Provisions	**307,016**

21. Liabilities

The remaining terms of the various categories of liabilities are shown below:

2003

in TEUR	Total	Thereof remaining term under 1 year	Thereof remaining term between 1 and 5 years	Thereof remaining term over 5 years	Thereof remaining term over 1 year and secured by collateral
1. Interest-bearing loans	1,000,836	288,837	509,123	202,876	41
2. Trade payables.	117,651	115,913	1,738	0	0
3. Finance leases	32,054	7,696	20,533	3,825	0
4. Prepayments received on orders. . . .	1,104	1,104	0	0	0
5. Liabilities from bills of exchange. . . .	623	623	0	0	0
6. Amounts owed to subsidiaries	2,252	2,252	0	0	0
7. Amounts owed to affiliates	1,939	1,939	0	0	0
8. Other liabilities	102,057	80,340	14,376	7,341	0
Liabilities as per balance sheet	**1,258,516**	**498,704**	**545,770**	**214,042**	**41**

Required:

a. Calculate the following ratios based on the condensed balance sheet provided:
   Current ratio (Current assets/Current liabilities) 7.81
   Debt-to-equity ratio (Total liabilities/Total equity)
b. Use information provided in Notes 17, 19, and 21 to reclassify assets and liabilities (current/noncurrent).
c. Calculate the ratios in (a) above on the basis of the reclassified assets and liabilities.

9. Gamma Holding NV, a Dutch textile company, presented the following calculation of operating profit in its 2003 consolidated income statement:

	2003
Net turnover.	903,865
Change in finished products and work in progress	(997)
Total operating income	902,868
Costs of raw materials and consumables.	(324,276)
Contracted work and other external costs.	(55,531)
Added value	523,061
Personnel costs	(290,006)
Amortisation of intangible fixed assets	(1,367)
Depreciation of tangible fixed assets	(38,885)
Other operating costs	(122,492)
Total operating expenses	(452,750)
Operating Result	70,311

Required:

a. Determine whether finished products and work in progress inventory in total increased or decreased during the year.
b. Identify the additional information that would be needed to calculate cost of goods sold for the company in 2003.

c. Given the following assumptions with respect to the percentage of operating expenses related to manufacturing activities and nonmanufacturing activities, provide an estimate of cost of goods sold:

	% Manufacturing	% Nonmanufacturing
Costs of raw materials and consumables	90%	10%
Contracted work and other external costs	100	0
Personnel costs	50	50
Amortisation of intangible fixed assets . . .	80	20
Depreciation of tangible fixed assets	75	25
Other operating costs	10	90

d. Given estimated cost of goods sold from part c., determine the company's gross profit margin for 2003.

10. Neopost SA is a French company operating mainly in Europe and the United States that sells and leases mailroom equipment. The following information was extracted from the company's annual report (in millions of euros):

	At 31 January		
	2004	2003	2002
Consolidated Balance Sheet			
Provisions for risk and contingencies			
Provisions for risks	10.1	15.4	4.8
Provisions for contingencies	39.3	53.6	22.9
	49.4	69.0	27.7
Consolidated Income Statement			
Net income	83.5	69.7	38.1
Note 13 Provision for risks and contingencies			
For risks			
Commercial litigation	2.0	2.9	1.6
Employee litigation	1.3	1.0	0.9
Warranties	0.2	0.2	0.2
Other	6.6	11.3	2.1
Total	**10.1**	**15.4**	**4.8**
Provisions for contingencies			
Retirement liabilities	3.1	3.0	1.9
Reorganization and restructuring	1.9	1.0	3.2
Decertification of mailroom equipment	0.0	0.0	1.7
Loop One earn-out.	0.0	3.7	15.4
Purchase accounting	29.3	39.7	0.0
Other.	5.0	6.2	0.7
Total	**39.3**	**53.6**	**22.9**

Required:
a. Determine the percentage growth in net income from 2002 to 2003 and from 2003 to 2004.
b. What impact do "provisions" have on "net income"?
c. What can cause the ending balance in provisions to change from one year to the next?

    d. What would net income have been for the years ended January 31, 2003, and January 31, 2004, if there had been no change in the ending balance of provisions? Assume an effective tax rate of 30 percent. What would the percentage growth in net income have been in this case?

    e. What additional information might you like to have with respect to Neopost's provisions for the time period presented in the excerpt.

11. The following statement of value added was presented in the 2003 annual report of Companhia Vale do Rio Doce (CVRD), a Brazilian mineral products company:

Years ended December 31

				In millions of reais				
	Parent Company				Consolidated			
	2003	**%**	**2002**	**%**	**2003**	**%**	**2002**	**%**
Generation of Value Added								
Sales revenue	10,367	100	8,570	100	20,219	100	15,267	100
Less: Acquisition of products	(1,192)	(12)	(1,039)	(12)	(2,214)	(11)	(1,401)	(9)
Outsourced services	(1,279)	(12)	(854)	(10)	(2,702)	(13)	(1,832)	(12)
Materials	(880)	(9)	(641)	(7)	(1,752)	(9)	(1,216)	(8)
Fuel oil and gas	(636)	(6)	(393)	(5)	(1,401)	(7)	(850)	(6)
Research and development commercial and administrative	(397)	(4)	(372)	(4)	(939)	(5)	(849)	(6)
Other operating expenses	(232)	(2)	(293)	(3)	(1,163)	(6)	(499)	(3)
Gross Value Added	5,751	55	4.978	59	10,048	49	8,620	56
Depreciation and depletion	(593)	(6)	(650)	(8)	(1,102)	(5)	(1,016)	(7)
Amortization of goodwill	(166)	(2)	(98)	(1)	(166)	(1)	(101)	(1)
Net Value Added	4,992	47	4,328	(51)	8,780	43	7,503	48
Received from third parties								
Financial revenue	53	1	597	7	196	1	360	2
Result of equity investments	1,122	11	1,564	18	(540)	(3)	(473)	(3)
Discontinued operations	—	—	—	—	174	1	—	—
Total Value Added to be Distributed	6,167	59	6,489	76	8,610	42	7,390	47
Distribution of Value Added								
Employees	770	12	699	11	1,213	15	1,153	16
Government	1,301	21	101	2	2,185	26	554	7
Creditors (interest and exchange rate differences, net)	(413)	(7)	3,646	56	351	4	3,761	51
Stockholders	2,254	37	1,029	16	2,254	26	1,029	14
Minority participation	—	—	—	—	253	3	(121)	(2)
Retained earnings	2,255	37	1,014	15	2,255	26	1,014	14
Total Distribution of Value Added	6,167	100	6,489	100	8,610	100	7,390	100

Required:

    a. Identify the external parties who might be interested in the information provided in CVRD's statement of value added.

    b. In what ways does the calculation of "Total Value Added" appear to differ from a calculation of net income?

    c. Prepare a brief report summarizing the story being told in CVRD's statement of value added.

Case 9-1

Swisscom AG

Swisscom AG, the principal provider of telecommunications in Switzerland, prepares consolidated financial statements in accordance with International Financial Reporting Standards (IFRSs). In addition, as a foreign company listed on the New York Stock Exchange, Swisscom also reconciles its net income and stockholders' equity to U.S. GAAP. Swisscom's consolidated financial statements for 1997 are presented in their original format in Column 1 of the following worksheet. Note 27, "Differences between International Accounting Standards and U.S. Generally Accepted Accounting Principles," which includes Swisscom's U.S. GAAP reconciliation, is also provided.

Required:

1. Use the information in Note 27 to restate Swisscom's consolidated financial statements for 1997 in accordance with U.S. GAAP. Begin by constructing debit/credit entries for each reconciliation item, and then post these entries to columns 2 and 3 in the worksheets provided.

2. Calculate each of the following ratios under both IAS and U.S. GAAP and determine the percentage differences between them using IAS ratios as the base:

   Net income/Net revenues
   Operating income/Net revenues
   Operating income/Total assets
   Net income/Total shareholders' equity
   Operating income/Total shareholders' equity
   Current assets/Current liabilities
   Total liabilities/Total shareholders' equity
   Which of these ratios is most (least) affected by the accounting standards used?

Worksheet for the Restatement of Swisscom's Financial Statements from IAS to U.S. GAAP

	(1) IAS	(2) Reconciling Debit	(3) Adjustments Credit	(4) U.S. GAAP
Consolidated Statement of Operations				
Net revenues	**9,842**			
Capitalized cost and changes in inventories	277			
Total	**10,119**			
Goods and services purchased	1,666			
Personnel expenses	2,584			
Other operating expenses	2,090			
Depreciation and amortization	1,739			
Restructuring charges	1,726			
Total operating expenses	**9,805**			
Operating income	**314**			
Interest expense	(428)			
Financial income	25			
Income (loss) before income taxes and equity in net loss of affiliated companies.	**(89)**			
Income tax expense	1			
Income (loss) before equity in net loss of affiliated companies	**(90)**			
Equity in net loss of affiliated companies	(325)			
Net income (loss).	**(415)**			

	(1)	(2) *Reconciling* Debit	(3) *Adjustments* Credit	(4) U.S. GAAP
	IAS			
Consolidated Retained Earnings Statement				
Retained earnings, 1/1	**(151)**			
Net loss	(415)			
Profit distribution declared	(1,282)			
Conversion of loan payable to equity	3,200			
Retained earnings, 12/31	**1,352**			
Consolidated Balance Sheet				
Assets				
Current assets				
Cash and cash equivalents	256			
Securities available for sale	51			
Trade accounts receivable	2,052			
Inventories	169			
Other current assets	34			
Total current assets	**2,562**			
Non-current assets				
Property, plant and equipment	11,453			
Investments	1,238			
Other non-current assets	220			
Total non-current assets	**12,911**			
Total assets	**15,473**			
Liabilities and shareholders' equity				
Current liabilities				
Short-term debt	1,178			
Trade accounts payable	889			
Accrued pension cost	789			
Other current liabilities	2,213			
Total current liabilities	**5,069**			
Long-term liabilities				
Long-term debt	6,200			
Finance lease obligation	439			
Accrued pension cost	1,488			
Accrued liabilities	709			
Other long-term liabilities	338			
Total long-term liabilities	**9,174**			
Total liabilities	**14,243**			
Shareholders' equity				
Retained earnings	1,352			
Unrealized market value adjustment on securities available for sale	39			
Cumulative translation adjustment	(161)			
Total shareholders' equity	**1,230**			
Total liabilities and shareholders' equity	**15,473**			

27. Differences between International Accounting Standards and U.S. Generally Accepted Accounting Principles

The consolidated financial statements of Swisscom have been prepared in accordance with International Accounting Standards (IAS), which differ in certain respects from generally accepted accounting principles in the United States (U.S. GAAP). Application of U.S. GAAP would have affected the balance sheet as of December 31, 1996 and 1997 and net income (loss) for each of the years in the two-year period ended December 31, 1997 to the extent described below. A description of the material differences between IAS and U.S. GAAP as they relate to Swisscom are discussed in further detail below.

Reconciliation of net income (loss) from IAS to U.S. GAAP

The following schedule illustrates the significant adjustments to reconcile net income (loss) in accordance with U.S. GAAP to the amounts determined under IAS, for the year ended December 31, 1997.

(CHF in millions)	Year ended December 31, 1997
Net income (loss) according to IAS............................	**(415)**
U.S. GAAP adjustments	
a) Capitalization of interest cost	8
c) Restructuring charges	205
c) Depreciation expense	(5)
d) Capitalization of software....................................	182
e) Restructuring charges by affiliates.............................	50
Net income according to U.S. GAAP............................	**25**

Reconciliation of shareholders' equity from IAS to U.S. GAAP

The following is a reconciliation of the significant adjustments necessary to reconcile shareholders' equity in accordance with U.S. GAAP to the amounts determined under IAS as at December 31, 1997.

(CHF in millions)	Year ended December 31, 1997
Shareholders' equity according to IAS.........................	**1,230**
U.S. GAAP adjustments	
a) Capitalization of interest cost	54
c) Restructuring charges	205
c) Depreciation expense	(5)
d) Capitalization of software....................................	475
e) Restructuring charges by affiliates.............................	50
Shareholders' equity according to U.S. GAAP...................	**2,009**

a) Capitalization of interest cost

Swisscom expenses all interest costs as incurred. U.S. GAAP requires interest costs incurred during the construction of property, plant and equipment to be capitalized. Under U.S. GAAP Swisscom would have capitalized CHF 13 million and amortized CHF 5 million for the year ended December 31, 1997.

c) Restructuring charges

During the year ended December 31, 1997 Swisscom recognized under IAS restructuring charges totaling CHF 1,726 million. The following schedule illustrates adjustments necessary to reconcile these charges to amounts determined under U.S. GAAP.

	1997 (CHF in millions)
Restructuring charges in accordance with IAS:	
Personnel restructuring charges...................................	1,326
Write-down of long-lived assets....................................	316
Miscellaneous restructuring charges	84
Total in accordance with IAS	1,726
Adjustments to restructuring charges to accord with U.S. GAAP	(205)
Restructuring charges in accordance with U.S. GAAP....................	1,521

Reconciliation of restructuring charges

Restructuring charges according to U.S. GAAP are comprised of the following:

	1997
	(CHF in millions)
Personnel restructuring charges	1,228
Write-down of long-lived assets	209
Miscellaneous restructuring charges	84
Restructuring charges in accordance with U.S. GAAP	1,521

Note: Assume the counterpart to the personnel restructuring charge affects "other long-term liabilities."

d) Capitalization of software

Swisscom has expensed software costs as incurred. For U.S. GAAP purposes external consultant costs incurred in the development of software for internal use have been capitalized from January 1, 1995. These costs are being amortized over a three year period. The capitalization of software costs accords with common practice in the U.S. telecommunications industry.

Swisscom has capitalized, as disclosed in the reconciliation of net income (loss) and shareholders' equity to U.S. GAAP, CHF 220 million and amortized CHF 37 million for the year ended December 31, 1996 and capitalized CHF 370 million and amortized CHF 188 million for the year ended December 31, 1997.

e) Restructuring charges of affiliates

During the year ended December 31, 1997, Swisscom's share of personnel and other restructuring charges recorded by affiliates amounted to CHF 50 million. These restructuring charges do not meet all the recognition criteria contained in EITF 94-3 and therefore cannot be expensed in the year ended December 31, 1997 under U.S. GAAP.

References

Bavishi, V. B., ed. *International Accounting and Auditing Trends, vol. 2,* 4th ed. Princeton, NJ: CIFAR Publications, 1995.

Choi, F. D. S.; H. Hino; S. K. Min; S. O. Nam; J. Ujiie; and A. I. Stonehill. "Analyzing Foreign Financial Statements: The Use and Misuse of International Ratio Analysis." *Journal of International Business Studies,* Spring/Summer 1983, pp. 113–31.

Choi, F. D. S., and R. M. Levich. "Behavioral Effects of International Accounting Diversity." *Accounting Horizons,* June 1991, pp. 1–13.

Frost, Carol A. 1998. "Characteristics and Information Value of Corporate Disclosures of Forward-Looking Information in Global Equity Markets," Dartmouth College Working Paper, as reported in Frederick D. S. Choi, Carol Ann Frost, and Gary K. Meek, *International Accounting,* 4th ed. Upper Saddle River, NJ: Prentice Hall, 2002.

Gray, S. J.; G. K. Meek; and C. B. Roberts. "International Capital Market Pressures and Voluntary Annual Report Disclosures by US and UK Multinationals," *Journal of International Financial Management and Accounting* 6, no. 1 (1995), pp. 43–68.

"Profits Ici Pertes Au-Dela." *L'Enterprise* 63 (December 1990), pp. 78–79.

Levitt, Arthur. "A Public Partnership to Battle Earnings Management," *Accounting Today,* May 24–June 6, 1999, p. 36.

Sherman, R., and R. Todd. "International Financial Statement Analysis," in *International Accounting and Finance Handbook,* 2nd ed., ed. F. D. S. Choi. New York: Wiley, 1997, pp. 8.1–8.61.

Solnik, Bruno. *International Investments,* 3rd ed. Reading: Addison-Wesley, 1996. pp. 94–95.

Chapter **Ten**

International Taxation

Learning Objectives

After reading this chapter, you should be able to

- Describe differences in corporate income tax and withholding tax regimes across countries.
- Explain how overlapping tax jurisdictions cause double taxation.
- Show how foreign tax credits reduce the incidence of double taxation.
- Demonstrate how rules related to controlled foreign corporations, subpart F income, and foreign tax credit baskets affect U.S. taxation of foreign source income.
- Describe some of the benefits provided by tax treaties.
- Explain and demonstrate procedures for translating foreign currency amounts for tax purposes.
- Describe tax incentives provided by countries to attract foreign direct investment and stimulate exports.

INTRODUCTION

Taxes paid to governments are one of the most significant costs incurred by business enterprises. Taxes reduce net profits as well as cash flow. Well-managed companies attempt to minimize the taxes they pay while making sure they are in compliance with applicable tax laws. For a multinational corporation (MNC) that pays taxes in more than one country, the objective is to minimize taxes worldwide. The achievement of this objective requires expertise in the tax law of each foreign country in which the corporation operates. Knowledge of how the domestic country taxes the profits earned in foreign countries is also of great importance.

MNCs make a number of very important decisions in which taxation is an important variable. For example, tax issues are important in deciding (1) where to locate a foreign operation, (2) what legal form the operation should take, and (3) how the operation will be financed.

Investment Location Decision

The decision to make a foreign investment is based on forecasts of *after-tax* profit and cash flows. Because effective tax rates vary across countries, after-tax returns from competing investment locations could vary. The decision of whether to place an operation in either Spain or Portugal, for example, could be affected by differences in the tax systems in those two countries.

Legal Form of Operation

A foreign operation of an MNCs is organized legally either as a branch of the MNC or as a subsidiary, in which case the operation is incorporated in the foreign country. Some countries tax foreign branches' income differently from foreign subsidiaries' income. The different tax treatment for branches and subsidiaries could result in one legal form being preferable to the other because of the impact on profits and cash flows.

Method of Financing

MNCs can finance their foreign operations by making capital contributions (equity) or through loans (debt). Cash flows generated by a foreign operation can be repatriated back to the MNC either by making dividend payments (on equity financing) or interest payments (on debt financing). Countries often impose a special (withholding) tax on dividend and interest payments made to foreigners. Withholding tax rates within a country can differ by type of payment. When this is the case, the MNC may wish to use more of one type of financing than the other because of the positive impact on cash flows back to the MNC.

These examples demonstrate the importance of developing an expertise in international taxation for the management of an MNC. It is impossible (and unnecessary) for every manager of an MNC to become a true expert in international taxation. However, all managers should be familiar with the major issues in international taxation so that they know when it might be necessary to call on the experts to help make a decision.

It is not possible in this book to cover all aspects of international taxation in depth; that would require years of study and many more pages of reading than can be included here. However, there are certain issues with which international accountants and managers of MNCs should be familiar to make sure that corporate goals are being achieved. The objective of this chapter is to examine the major issues of international taxation without getting bogged down in the minutiae for which tax laws are well known. We will concentrate on taxes on income and distributions of income, ignoring other taxes such as Social Security and payroll taxes, sales and value-added taxes, and excise taxes. Although this chapter concentrates on the taxation of corporate profits, certain features of individual income taxation relevant for expatriates working overseas are described in the chapter's appendix.

TYPES OF TAXES AND TAX RATES

Corporations are subject to many different types of taxes, including property taxes, payroll taxes, and excise taxes. While it is important for managers of MNCs to be knowledgeable about these taxes, we focus on taxes on profit. The two major types of taxes imposed on profits earned by companies engaged in international business are (1) corporate income taxes and (2) withholding taxes.

Income Taxes

Most, but not all, national governments impose a direct tax on business income. Exhibit 10.1 shows that national corporate income tax rates vary substantially across countries. The corporate income tax rate in most countries is between 20 and 40 percent. Differences in corporate tax rates across countries provide MNCs with a tax-planning opportunity as they decide where to locate foreign operations.

EXHIBIT 10.1
International Corporate Tax Rates, January 2004

Source: KPMG, Corporate Tax Rate Survey, January 2004, available at www.kpmg.com.

Country	National Tax Rate (%)	Effective Tax Rate (%)
Argentina	35	35
Australia	30	30
Austria	34	34
Belgium	33.99	33.99
Brazil	25	34
Canada	22.1	36.1*
Chile	17	17
China	30	33
Czech Republic	28	28
Denmark	30	30
France	33.33	34.33
Germany	25.0	38.29
Greece	35	35
Hong Kong	17.5	17.5
Hungary	16	16
Indonesia	30	30
Ireland	12.5	12.5
Israel	36	36
Italy	33	37.25
Japan	30	42
Korea (South)	29.7	29.7
Malaysia	28	28
Mexico	33	33
Netherlands	34.5	34.5
New Zealand	33	33
Russia	24	24
Singapore	22	22
Spain	35	35
Sweden	28	28
Switzerland	8.5	24.1*
Taiwan	25	25
Thailand	30	30
Turkey	33	33
United Kingdom	30	30
United States	35	40*
Venezuela	34	34

*Individual provinces (Canada), cantons (Switzerland), and states (United States) assess different levels of local tax causing the effective tax rate to vary by location. The Canadian and U.S. rates are averages. The Swiss rate is for the city of Zurich.

In making this decision, MNCs must be careful to consider both national and local taxes in their analysis. In some countries, local governments impose a separate tax on business income in addition to that levied by the national government. For example, the national tax rate in Switzerland is 8.5 percent, but additional local taxes range anywhere from 6 to 33 percent. A company located in Zurich can expect to pay an effective tax rate of 24.1 percent to local and federal governments. Corporate income tax rates imposed by individual states in the United States vary from 0 percent (e.g., South Dakota) to 12 percent (e.g., Pennsylvania).

In a few countries, corporate income taxes can vary according to the type of activity in which a company is engaged or the nationality of the company's owners. The rate of national income tax in China is reduced from 30 percent to as low as 15 percent for foreign enterprises operating in specially designated zones or in certain industries. Canada imposes a lower tax rate on manufacturers, and India taxes foreign companies at a higher rate than domestic companies.

In making foreign investment decisions, MNCs often engage in a capital budgeting process in which the future cash flows to be generated by the foreign investment are forecasted, discounted to their present value, and then compared with the amount to be invested to determine a net present value. Taxes paid to the foreign government will have a negative impact on future cash flows and might affect the location decision. For example, assume that a Japanese musical instrument manufacturer is deciding whether to locate a new factory in Hungary or in Switzerland. Although the national tax rate in Hungary is much higher than in Switzerland, the effective tax rate in some parts of Switzerland would be higher than in Hungary because of the high local taxes that would have to be paid.

Of course, the amount of taxes paid to a government is not determined solely by the corporate tax rate. The manner in which taxable income is calculated will also greatly affect a company's tax liability. Just as tax rates vary from country to country, so does the way in which taxable income is calculated. Expenses that can be deducted for tax purposes can vary greatly from country to country. For example, in the United States, only the first $1 million of the chief executive officer's salary is tax deductible. Most other countries do not have a similar rule.

Like the United States, Germany allows companies to use the last-in, first-out (LIFO) method for inventory valuation and accelerated depreciation methods for fixed assets in determining taxable income, whereas Austria does not. All else being equal, a company with increasing inventory prices that is replacing or expanding its fixed assets will have smaller taxable income in Germany than in Austria. Germany has a higher corporate income tax rate than Austria, but because taxable income is smaller, a company in Germany may actually have a smaller amount of taxes to pay.

There has been a recent and continuing international trend to reduce corporate tax rates. The United States appears to have led the way in 1986 when the corporate tax rate was reduced from 46 percent to 34 percent (it was subsequently raised to 35 percent in 1994). The United Kingdom quickly followed suit by reducing its rate from 50 percent to 35 percent, Canada from 34 percent to 29 percent, and so on. More recently, Japan lowered its corporate tax rate from 48 percent in 1999 to 42 percent in 2000, and Belgium lowered its rate from 40.17 percent in 2002 to 33.99 percent in 2003. This follow-the-leader effect is explained by the fact that countries compete against one another in attracting foreign investment.

One way to compete for foreign investment is to offer a so-called *tax holiday*. For example, to attract foreign investment, the prime minister of the Czech Republic announced in March 2000 that foreign enterprises that invest at least $10 million may be entitled to a 10-year exemption from income taxation and customs duties.[1] Following the financial crisis in Asia in the late 1990s, several countries in that region adopted various measures including tax incentives to help their economies recover. In 1999, Indonesia established eight-year holidays for new projects in 22 categories of industries, including textiles, pharmaceuticals, and auto parts.

In 2002, China surpassed the United States as the largest recipient of foreign direct investment (FDI), partly as a result of tax incentives provided foreign investors for establishing production operations in China. To further enhance its competitive position in attracting FDI, China introduced legislation in 2003 that

---

[1] Deloitte Touche Tohmatsu, "New Tax Incentives for Foreign Investors," *World Tax News*, March 2000, available at www.tax.deloitte.com.

provides a two-plus-three-year tax holiday to any new company formed with at least 25 percent foreign investment. So-called foreign investment enterprises receive a 100 percent exemption from taxation for the first two years in which profits are earned, followed by a 50 percent exemption in the following three years.[2]

Tax Havens

There are a number of tax jurisdictions with abnormally low corporate income tax rates (or no corporate income tax at all) that companies and individuals have found useful in minimizing their worldwide income taxes. These tax jurisdictions, known as *tax havens*, include the Bahamas, which has no corporate income tax; Liechtenstein, which has tax rates ranging from 7.5 to 15 percent; and the Channel Islands of Jersey and Guernsey, which have a tax rate of 2 percent for "international business companies."

A company involved in international business might find it beneficial to establish an operation in a tax haven to avoid paying taxes in one or more countries in which the company operates. For example, assume a German company manufactures a product for $70 per unit that it exports to a customer in Mexico at a sales price of $100 per unit. The $30 of profit earned on each unit is subject to the German corporate tax rate of 38.29 percent. The German manufacturer could take advantage of the fact that there is no corporate income tax in the Bahamas by establishing a sales subsidiary there that it uses as a conduit for export sales. The German parent company would then sell the product to its Bahamian sales subsidiary at a price of, say, $80 per unit, and the Bahamian sales subsidiary would turn around and sell the product to the customer in Mexico at $100 per unit. In this way, only $10 of the total profit is earned in Germany and subject to German income tax; $20 of the $30 total profit is recorded in the Bahamas and is therefore not taxed.

The Organization for Economic Cooperation and Development (OECD) has established guidelines for tax regimes to ensure that they cannot be used to avoid taxation in other countries.[3] Since the OECD lacks enforcement power, its member countries must put pressure on tax havens in order for them to change their tax regimes. Exhibit 10.2 provides a list of criteria the OECD uses to identify tax havens and the countries meeting these criteria in 2000. Many of these countries have expressed a willingness to change their tax regimes to be removed from the OECD list and avoid any possible defensive measures by its member nations.[4]

Withholding Taxes

When a foreign citizen who invests in the shares of a U.S. company receives a dividend payment, theoretically he or she should file a tax return with the U.S. Internal Revenue Service and pay taxes on the dividend income. If the foreign investor does not file this tax return, the U.S. government has no recourse for collecting the tax. To avoid this possibility, the United States (like most other countries) will require the payer of the dividend (the U.S. company) to withhold some amount of

---

[2] Ernst & Young, "New Tax Holiday Rules," *China Update*, July 2003, pp. 1–2, available at www.ey.com/china.

[3] The OECD is a voluntary organization whose membership comprises the most developed countries in the world, located primarily in Europe and North America, but also including Japan, Korea, Australia, New Zealand, and Turkey.

[4] Organization for Economic Cooperation and Development, *The OECD's Project on Harmful Tax Practices: The 2004 Progress Report* (Paris: OECD, 2004), p. 11.

EXHIBIT 10.2
OECD Criteria and List of Tax Havens

Sources: Deloitte and Touche, "OECD Publishes List of Offending Tax Regimes," *Global Tax Executive,* July/August 2000; and Organization for Economic Cooperation and Development, "Toward Global Tax Cooperation: Progress in Identifying and Eliminating Harmful Tax Practices," June 2000, available at www.oecd.org.

OECD criteria for tax haven status:

- No or only nominal effective tax rates.
- Lack of effective exchange of information.
- Lack of transparency.
- Absence of substantial activities requirement.
- Banking secrecy and legal systems that aid in tax avoidance.

The following countries met the OECD's criteria in June 2000:

Andora	Grenada	Netherlands Antilles
Anguilla	Guernsey	Niue
Antigua	Grenadines	Panama
Aruba	Isle of Man	Samoa
Bahamas	Jersey	Seychelles
Bahrain	Liberia	St. Kitts & Nevis
Barbados	Liechtenstein	St. Lucia
Belize	Maldives	Tonga
British Virgin Islands	Marshall Islands	Turks & Caicos
Cook Islands	Monaco	U.S. Virgin Islands
Dominica	Montserrat	Vanuatu
Gibraltar	Nauru	

Six jurisdictions technically met the definition of tax haven but were removed from the list because of their commitment to comply with OECD guidelines: Bermuda, Cayman Islands, Cyprus, Malta, Mauritius, and San Marino.

taxes and remit that amount to the U.S. government. This type of tax is referred to as a *withholding tax.* The withholding tax rate on dividends in the United States is 30 percent.

To see how the withholding tax works, assume that International Business Machines Corporation (IBM), a U.S.-based company, pays a $100 dividend to a stockholder in Brazil. Under U.S. withholding tax rules, IBM would withhold $30 from the payment (which is sent to the U.S. Internal Revenue Service) and the Brazilian stockholder would be issued a check in the amount of $70.

Withholding taxes are also imposed on payments made to foreign parent companies or foreign affiliated companies. There are three types of payments typically subject to withholding tax: dividends, interest, and royalties. Withholding tax rates vary across countries, and in some countries withholding rates vary by type of payment or recipient. Exhibit 10.3 provides withholding rates generally applicable in selected countries. In many cases the rate listed will be different for some subset of activity. For example, although the U.S. withholding rate on interest payments is generally 30 percent, interest on bank deposits and on certain registered debt instruments (bonds) is exempt (0 percent tax). In addition, many of the rates listed in Exhibit 10.3 vary with tax treaties (discussed later in this chapter).

Tax-Planning Strategy

Differences in withholding rates on different types of payments in some countries provide an opportunity to reduce taxes (increase cash flow) by altering the method of financing a foreign operation. For example, a British company planning to establish a manufacturing facility in Austria would prefer that future cash payments received from the Austrian subsidiary be in the form of interest rather than dividends because of the lower withholding tax rate (0 percent on interest versus

EXHIBIT 10.3
Withholding Rates
in Selected
Countries

Source:
PricewaterhouseCoopers,
*Corporate Taxes—Worldwide
Summaries, 1999–2000*, New
York: John Wiley & Sons,
2001.

Country	Dividends	Interest	Royalties
Australia	30%	10%	30%
Austria	22	0	20
Brazil	15	25	25
Canada	25	25	25
France	25	15–35	33.3
Germany	25	25	25
Indonesia	20	20	20
Italy	32.4	15	21
Japan	20	20	20
Korea (South)	25	25	25
Mexico	0	40	40
Malaysia	0	15	10
New Zealand	30	15	15
Philippines	32	32	32
Singapore	0	15	15
Spain	25	25	25
Sweden	30	0	0
Switzerland	35	35	0
Thailand	10	15	15
United Kingdom	0	20	23
United States	30	30	30

22 percent on dividends). This objective can be achieved by the British parent using a combination of loan and equity investment in financing the Austrian subsidiary. For example, rather than the British parent investing €10 million in equity to establish the Austrian operation, €5 million is contributed in equity and €5 million is lent to the Austrian operation by the British parent. Interest on the loan, which is a cash payment to the British parent, will be exempt from Austrian withholding tax, whereas any dividends paid on the capital contribution will be taxed at 22 percent.

Many countries have a lower rate of withholding tax on interest than on dividends. In addition, interest payments are generally tax deductible whereas dividend payments are not. Thus, there is often an incentive for companies to finance their foreign operations with as much debt and as little equity capital as possible. This is known as *thin capitalization*, and several countries have set limits as to how thinly capitalized a company may be. For example, in France, interest paid to a foreign parent will not be tax deductible for the amount of the loan that exceeds 150 percent of equity capital. In other words, the ratio of debt to equity may not exceed 150 percent for tax purposes. If equity capital is €1 million, any interest paid on loans exceeding €1.5 million will not be tax deductible. Similarly, in the United States, subsidiaries of foreign parents run the risk of having some interest declared nondeductible when the debt-to-equity ratio exceeds 1.5 to 1.

Value-Added Tax

Many countries generate a significant amount of revenue through the use of a national *value-added tax (VAT)*. Standard VAT rates in the European Union, for example, range from a low of 15 percent (Luxembourg) to a high of 25 percent (Denmark and Sweden).[5] Value-added taxes are used in lieu of a sales tax and are

[5] European Commission, *VAT Rates Applied in the Member States of the European Community: Situation at 1st May 2003*, available at www.eurounion.org.

generally incorporated into the price of a product or service. This type of tax is levied on the value added at each stage in the production or distribution of a product or service. For example, if a Swedish forest products company sells lumber that it has harvested to a Swedish wholesaler at a price of €100,000, it will pay a VAT to the Swedish government of €25,000 (€100,000 × 25%). When the Swedish wholesaler, in turn, sells the lumber to its customers for €160,000, the wholesaler will pay a VAT of €15,000 (25% × €60,000 value added at the wholesale stage). The VAT concept is commonly used in countries other than the European Union, including Australia, Canada, China, Hungary, Mexico, Nigeria, Turkey, and South Africa.

TAX JURISDICTION

One of the most important issues in international taxation is determining which country has the right to tax which income. In many cases, two countries will assert the right to tax the same income, resulting in the problem of *double taxation*. For example, consider the Brazilian investor earning dividends from an investment in IBM Corporation common stock. The United States might want to tax this dividend because it was earned in the United States, and Brazil might want to tax the dividend because it was earned by a resident of Brazil. This section discusses general concepts used internationally in determining tax jurisdiction. Subsequent sections examine mechanisms used for providing relief from double taxation.

Worldwide versus Territorial Approach

One tax jurisdiction issue is related to the taxation of income earned overseas, known as *foreign source income.* There are two approaches taken on this issue:

1. *Worldwide (nationality) approach.* Under this approach, all income of a resident of a country or a company incorporated in a country is taxed by that country regardless of where the income is earned. In other words, foreign source income is taxed by the country of residence. For example, Canada imposes a tax on dividend income earned by a Canadian company from its subsidiary in Hong Kong even though that income was earned outside of Canada. Most countries exercise tax jurisdiction on the basis of nationality and impose a tax on worldwide income.

2. *Territorial approach.* Under this approach, only the income earned within the borders of the country (domestic source income) is taxed. For example, the dividend income earned by a resident of Venezuela from investments in U.S. stocks will not be taxed in Venezuela. Few countries follow this approach, and the number is decreasing. South Africa, one of the few countries using a territorial approach, moved to the worldwide basis of taxation beginning in 2000. The most economically important country that continues to use a territorial approach is France.

Source, Citizenship, and Residence

Regardless of the approach used in determining the scope of taxation, a second issue related to jurisdiction is the basis for taxation. Countries generally use source, citizenship, residence, or some combination of the three for determining jurisdictional authority.

Source of Income

In general, almost all countries assert the jurisdictional authority to tax income where it is earned—in effect, at its source—regardless of the residence or citizenship of the recipient. An example would be the United States taxing dividends paid by IBM Corporation to a stockholder in Canada because the dividend income was earned in the United States.

Citizenship

Under the citizenship basis of taxation, citizens are taxed by their country of citizenship regardless of where they reside or the source of the income being taxed. The United States is unusual among countries in that it taxes on the basis of citizenship. Thus, a U.S. citizen who lives and works overseas will be subject to U.S. income tax on his or her worldwide income regardless of where the citizen earns that income or resides.

Residence

Under the residence approach, residents of a country are taxed by the country in which they reside regardless of their citizenship or where the income was earned. For example, assume a citizen of Singapore resides permanently in the United States and earns dividends from an investment in the shares of a company in the United Kingdom. Taxing on the basis of residence, this individual will be subject to taxation in the United States on his or her foreign source income, even though he or she is a citizen of Singapore.

The United States is one country that taxes on the basis of residence. For tax purposes, a U.S. resident is any person who is a U.S. permanent resident as evidenced by holding a permanent resident permit issued by the Immigration and Naturalization Service (the "green card" test) or is physically present in the United States for 183 or more days in a year (physical presence test). Note that because the United States levies taxes using a worldwide approach, the worldwide income of an individual holding a U.S. permanent resident card is subject to U.S. taxation *even if he or she is not actually living in the United States.*

Companies created or organized in the United States are considered to be U.S. residents for tax purposes. The foreign *subsidiary* of a U.S. parent is not considered to be a U.S. resident, but a foreign *branch* is. Under the U.S. worldwide approach to taxation, a U.S. parent pays U.S. income tax currently on foreign branch income, but foreign subsidiary income is not taxed in the United States until dividends are paid to the U.S. parent.[6] Other countries have a similar rule.

For a U.S. MNC, establishing a foreign operation as a subsidiary (by legally incorporating in the foreign country) generally has the advantage that U.S. taxes on the subsidiary income are deferred until profits are repatriated back to the United States through the payment of dividends. The disadvantage is that if the foreign subsidiary incurs a net loss, this loss may not be taken as a tax deduction in the parent's tax return. However, the advantage of registering the foreign operation with the foreign country as a branch is that any losses are currently deductible on the U.S. tax return. The disadvantage is that any profits are taxed currently in the United States.

This provides an opportunity for strategic tax planning. U.S. MNCs often initially set up their foreign operations as branches when losses are expected in

---

[6] An exception exists when the foreign subsidiary is located in a tax haven country and generates Subpart F income. This issue is discussed later under "Controlled Foreign Corporations."

early years. The branch is then incorporated as a subsidiary when the operation becomes profitable. The disadvantage to this is that converting a branch into a subsidiary is generally considered to be the sale of the branch to the subsidiary, usually at a gain, which is taxable.

Double Taxation

The combination of a worldwide approach to taxation and the various bases for taxation can lead to overlapping tax jurisdictions that can in turn lead to double or even triple taxation. For example, a U.S. citizen residing in Germany with investment income in Austria might be expected to pay taxes on the investment income to the United States (on the basis of citizenship), Germany (on the basis of residence), and Austria (on the basis of source).

The same is true for corporate taxpayers with foreign source income. The most common overlap of jurisdictions for corporations is where the home country taxes on the basis of residence and the country where the foreign branch or subsidiary is located taxes on the basis of source. Without some relief, this could result in a tremendous tax burden for the parent company. For example, income earned by the Japanese branch of a U.S. company would be taxed at the effective Japanese corporate income tax rate of 42 percent and at the rate of 35 percent in the United States, for an aggregate tax rate of 77 percent. The U.S. parent has only 23 percent of the profit after taxes. At that rate, there is a disincentive to establish operations overseas. Without any relief from double taxation, all investment by the U.S. company would remain at home in the United States, where income would be taxed only at the rate of 35 percent.

An important goal of most national tax systems is neutrality; that is, the tax system should remain in the background, and business, investment, and consumption decisions should be made for nontax reasons. In an international context there are three standards for neutrality, one of which is *capital-export neutrality*. A tax system meets this standard if a taxpayer's decision whether to invest at home or overseas is not affected by taxation. Double taxation from overlapping tax jurisdictions precludes a tax system from achieving capital-export neutrality; all investment will remain at home. In order to achieve capital-export neutrality, most countries have one or more mechanisms for eliminating the problem of double taxation. One mechanism is a provision in bilateral tax treaties between countries in which foreign source income is exempt. Tax treaties are discussed later in this chapter. Another major source of relief from double taxation is the *foreign tax credit*. "For U.S. citizens and residents, including domestic corporations, perhaps the most important international tax provisions are those dealing with the foreign tax credit."[7]

FOREIGN TAX CREDITS

Double taxation of income earned by foreign operations generally arises because the country where the foreign operation is located taxes the income at its source and the parent company's home country taxes worldwide income on the basis of residence. To relieve the double taxation, the question is, Which country should give up its right to tax the income? The international norm is that source should take precedence over residence in determining tax jurisdiction. In that case, it will be up to the parent company's home country to eliminate the double taxation.

---

[7] Richard L. Doernberg, *International Taxation: In a Nutshell*, 4th ed. (St. Paul, MN: West, 1999), p. 13.

This can be accomplished in several ways. One way would be to exempt foreign source income from taxation—in effect, to adopt a territorial approach to taxation. A second approach would be to allow the parent company to deduct the taxes paid to the foreign government from its taxable income. Third would be to provide the parent company with a credit for taxes paid to the foreign government.

Some countries have decided to deal with double taxation through the first option. The mechanics of applying this option are fairly straightforward; foreign source income simply is not included in the parent's tax declaration. Most countries, in contrast, have decided to use the second and third options. As a point of reference, the specific U.S. tax rules related to foreign tax credits and deductions are described here.

Credit versus Deduction

For U.S. tax purposes, U.S. companies are allowed either to (1) deduct *all* foreign taxes paid or (2) take a credit for foreign *income* taxes paid. Income taxes include withholding taxes, as discussed above, but exclude sales, excise, and other types of taxes not based on income. Unless taxes other than income taxes are substantial, it is more advantageous for a company to take the foreign tax credit rather than a tax deduction.

Example: Deduction for Foreign Taxes Paid versus Foreign Tax Credit

Assume ASD Company's foreign branch earns income before income taxes of $100,000. Income taxes paid to the foreign government are $30,000 (30 percent). Sales and other taxes paid to the foreign government are $10,000. ASD Company must include the $100,000 of foreign branch income in its U.S. tax return in calculating U.S. taxable income. The options of taking a deduction or tax credit are as follows:

ASD Company's U.S. Tax Return		
	Deduction	**Credit**
Foreign source income	$100,000	$100,000
Deduction for all foreign taxes paid	−40,000	0
U.S. taxable income	$ 60,000	$100,000
U.S. income tax before credit (35%)	$21,000	$ 35,000
Foreign tax credit (for income taxes paid)	0	−30,000
Net U.S. tax liability	$21,000	$ 5,000

Note that ASD's foreign branch earns its income in a foreign currency that must be translated into U.S. dollars for tax purposes. Foreign currency translation for tax purposes is discussed later in this chapter.

The foreign tax credit provides a dollar-for-dollar reduction in tax liability; that is, for every dollar of income tax ASD paid to the foreign government, ASD is allowed a one-dollar reduction in the amount of income taxes to be paid to the U.S. government. In this example, the foreign tax credit results in considerably less net U.S. tax liability than the deduction for foreign taxes paid. In the case of foreign branch income, the credit allowed is known as a *direct foreign tax credit* because ASD is given a credit for the taxes it paid itself to the foreign government.

In the case of foreign subsidiary income, the foreign subsidiary (as an entity legally incorporated in the foreign country) pays its own taxes to the foreign government. Remember that foreign subsidiary income will not be taxed in the United States until dividends are paid by the foreign subsidiary to the U.S. parent. At that time, ASD will include foreign source dividend income in its U.S. tax return and will be allowed an *indirect foreign tax credit* for the foreign taxes deemed to have been paid by ASD.

Calculation of Foreign Tax Credit (FTC)

The rules governing the calculation of the foreign tax credit (FTC) in the United States are rather complex. In general, the FTC allowed is equal to the lower of (1) actual taxes paid to the foreign government, or (2) the amount of taxes that would have been paid if the income had been earned in the United States.

This latter amount, in many cases, can be calculated by multiplying the amount of foreign source income by the effective U.S. tax rate on worldwide taxable income. This is known as the *overall FTC limitation* because the United States will not allow a foreign tax credit greater than the amount of taxes that would have been paid in the United States. To allow an FTC greater than the amount of taxes that would have been paid in the United States would require the U.S. government to refund U.S. companies for higher taxes paid in foreign countries. More formally, the overall FTC limitation is calculated as follows:

$$\text{Overall FTC limitation} = \frac{\text{Foreign source taxable income}}{\text{Worldwide taxable income}} \times \text{U.S. taxes before FTC}$$

Example: Calculation of Foreign Tax Credit for Branches

Assume that two different U.S.-based companies have branches in South America, Company A in Chile and Company B in Brazil. The amount of income before tax earned by each foreign branch and the amount of income tax paid to the local government is as follows:

	Company A's Chilean Branch	Company B's Brazilian Branch
Income before taxes	$100,000	$100,000
Income tax paid	$15,000 (15%)	$37,000 (37%)

Both Company A and B will report $100,000 of foreign branch income on their U.S. tax return, and each will determine a U.S. tax liability before FTC of $35,000. For both Company A and Company B, $35,000 is the amount of U.S. taxes that would have been paid if the foreign branch income had been earned in the United States. The overall FTC limitation is $35,000 for both companies.

Company A compares the amount of income tax paid to the Chilean government of $15,000 with the limitation of $35,000 and will be allowed an FTC of $15,000, the lesser of the two. Company B compares actual taxes paid to the Brazilian government of $37,000 with the limitation of $35,000 and will be allowed an FTC of $35,000, the lesser of the two. The U.S. income tax return related to foreign branch income for Company A and Company B reflects the following:

U.S. Tax Return		
	Company A	Company B
U.S. taxable income	$100,000	$100,000
U.S. tax before FTC (35%)	$ 35,000	$ 35,000
FTC	15,000	35,000
Net U.S. tax liability	$ 20,000	$ 0

Company A has a net U.S. tax liability after foreign tax credit on its Chilean branch income of $20,000, an additional 20 percent over what has already been paid in Chile (15 percent). The United States requires Company A to pay an effective tax rate of at least 35 percent (the U.S. rate) on all of its income, both U.S. source and foreign source.

Company B has no U.S. tax liability after foreign tax credit on its Brazilian branch income. Company B has already paid more than the U.S. tax rate in Brazil, so no additional taxes will be paid in the United States. Instead, the $2,000 difference between the $37,000 in taxes paid in Brazil and the foreign tax credit of $35,000 allowed in the United States becomes an *excess foreign tax credit*.

Excess Foreign Tax Credits

Excess foreign tax credits may be used to offset additional taxes paid to the United States on foreign source income in years in which foreign tax rates are lower than the U.S. tax rate. Beginning in 2005, an excess FTC may be

1. Carried back 1 year. The company applies for a refund of additional taxes paid to the United States on foreign source income in the previous year.
2. Carried forward 10 years. The company reduces future U.S. tax liability in the event that additional U.S. taxes must be paid on foreign source income in any of the next 10 years.[8]

In effect, the excess FTC can be used only if, in the previous year or in the next 10 years, *the average foreign tax rate paid by the company is less than the U.S. tax rate.*

Example: Calculation of Excess Foreign Tax Credit (One Branch, Multiple Years)

Assume Company B's Brazilian branch had $50,000 of pretax income in Year 1, $70,000 in Year 2, and $100,000 in Year 3. The effective corporate income tax rate in Brazil in Year 1 was 34 percent. In Year 2, Brazil increased its corporate income tax rate to 37 percent. The U.S. tax rate in each year is 35 percent. Company A's U.S. income tax return would reflect the following:

	Year 1	Year 2	Year 3
Foreign source income	$50,000	$70,000	$100,000
Foreign taxes paid	$17,000 34%	$25,900 37%	$ 37,000 37%
U.S. tax before FTC	$17,500 35%	$24,500 35%	$ 35,000 35%
FTC allowed in the United States . . .	17,000	24,500	35,000
Net U.S. tax liability	$ 500	$ 0	$ 0
Excess FTC	$ 0	$ 1,400	$ 2,000

In Year 2, Company B has an excess foreign tax credit of $1,400 ($25,900 foreign taxes paid less $24,500 FTC allowed in the United States). In that year, Company B will file for a refund of $500 for the additional taxes paid on foreign source income in the previous year and will have an excess FTC to carry forward in the amount of $900. Company B is unable to use its FTC carryforward in Year 3 because its effective foreign tax rate exceeds the U.S. tax rate. If Company B is not able to use its excess FTC carryforward of $900 in any of the next 10 years, the carryforward will be lost.

---

[8] Prior to 2005, excess FTCs could be carried back two years and carried forward five years. The American Job Creations Act of 2004 changed these carryover periods.

Example: Calculation of Foreign Tax Credit (One Company, Multiple Branches)

Let us return to the example related to two branches located in Chile and Brazil, but now assume that the Chilean branch and the Brazilian branch both belong to Company C. In this case, Company C has total foreign source income in Year 3 of $200,000 and the actual amount of taxes paid to foreign governments is $52,000 ([15% × $100,000 in Chile] + [37% × $100,000 in Brazil]). Company C determines the amount of FTC allowed by the United States and its net U.S. tax liability on foreign source income as follows:

	U.S. Tax Return
	Company C
U.S. taxable income	$200,000
U.S. tax before FTC (35%)	$ 70,000
FTC allowed*	52,000
Net U.S. tax liability	$ 18,000

*Calculation of FTC allowed:
Actual tax paid   =   = $52,000
Overall FTC limitation = Foreign Source Income × U.S. Tax Rate
                              = $200,000   ×   35%   = $70,000
Lesser amount   = $52,000

In the earlier example involving Company A and Company B, Company A had an additional U.S. tax liability on its Chilean branch income of $20,000 and Company B had an excess FTC related to its Brazilian branch of $2,000. In this example, when both foreign branches belong to Company C, the otherwise excess FTC from the Brazilian branch partially offsets the additional taxes on the Chilean branch income and a net U.S. tax liability of $18,000 remains.

FTC Baskets

In the United States prior to 1986, all foreign source income was combined to determine an overall FTC allowed. The Tax Reform Act of 1986 changed that by requiring foreign source income to be classified into nine separate categories (referred to as "baskets") with an FTC computed separately for each basket of foreign source income. Companies are not allowed to net FTCs across baskets. In other words, the excess FTC from one basket may not be used to reduce additional U.S. taxes owed on other baskets. The excess FTC for one basket may only be carried back and carried forward to offset additional U.S. taxes paid on that basket of income. The net effect for U.S. companies has been a reduction in the total amount of FTC allowed.

The following are the different baskets of foreign source income:

1. Passive income.
2. High withholding tax interest.
3. Financial services income.
4. Shipping and aircraft income.
5. Dividends from a domestic international sales corporation (DISC).
6. Foreign trade income of a foreign sales corporation (FSC).

7. Dividends from an FSC.

8. Foreign oil and extraction income.

9. All other income.

The "all other income" basket includes all foreign source income that cannot be classified into one of the other baskets and includes income generated from manufacturing and from sales and distribution.

Returning to the example involving Company C, assume that the Chilean branch is a manufacturing operation and the Brazilian branch is involved in financial services. The Chilean branch income would be placed in Basket 9 (all other income) and the Brazilian branch income would be placed in Basket 3 (financial services). Company C would have an additional U.S. tax liability of $20,000 on the Chilean branch income and would have an excess FTC of $2,000 on the Brazilian branch income. Company C would not be allowed to use the excess FTC from Basket 3 to offset the additional tax from Basket 9. The Basket 3 excess FTC may be carried back and forward only to offset additional taxes paid on Basket 3 (financial services) income.

The American Jobs Creation Act of 2004 reduces the number of FTC baskets from nine to two. Beginning in 2007, U.S. companies will allocate foreign source income either to (1) a *general income* basket or (2) a *passive income* basket. This change should reduce the likelihood that a company will have excess FTCs that go unused.

Indirect Foreign Tax Credit (FTC for Subsidiaries)

A direct FTC is allowed for foreign income taxes paid directly by a U.S. taxpayer. These include taxes paid by a U.S. company on foreign branch income and withholding taxes paid on dividends, interest, and royalties.

An *indirect FTC* is allowed for foreign income taxes paid by the foreign subsidiary of a U.S. parent. The indirect FTC may not be taken until the foreign subsidiary income is taxed in the United States.

The amount of income taxable in the United States from a foreign subsidiary is the before-tax amount of the dividend. This is referred to as the "grossed-up dividend" and is equal to the dividend plus the taxes deemed to have been paid on the income from which the dividend was paid.

To qualify for an indirect FTC, the U.S. company receiving the dividend must own a minimum of 10 percent of the voting stock of the foreign company. There is no indirect FTC allowed for dividends received from an investment where the U.S. company owns less than 10 percent of the stock of the foreign company.

Example: Calculation of Indirect FTC

The Malaysian subsidiary of MNC Company (a U.S.-based company) has $500,000 of before-tax income on which it pays an income tax of $140,000 (28 percent Malaysian corporate income tax rate). MNC Company receives a dividend of $72,000 from its Malaysian subsidiary. The U.S. corporate income tax rate is 35 percent. The grossed-up dividend is calculated as follows:

Grossed-up dividend = Dividend received/(1 − Foreign tax rate)
$$\$72{,}000/(1 - 0.28) = \$100{,}000$$

In other words, the Malaysian subsidiary would have had to generate before-tax income of $100,000, on which it would pay income taxes of $28,000 (28 percent), to be able to distribute a dividend of $72,000 to its parent company. MNC

Company determines the available FTC related to this dividend in the following manner:

Actual tax paid by subsidiary on income distributed as dividend = $28,000
Overall FTC limitation = Foreign Source Income × U.S. Tax Rate
                  = $100,000   ×   35%   = $35,000
Lesser amount (FTC allowed)   = $28,000

The net U.S. tax liability on the dividend received from the Malaysian subsidiary is computed as follows:

U.S. Tax Return	
	MNC Company
U.S. taxable income (grossed-up dividend)	$100,000
U.S. tax before FTC (35%)	$ 35,000
FTC allowed	28,000
Net U.S. tax liability	$ 7,000

In this example, the indirect FTC allowed is $28,000 and an additional U.S. tax liability of $7,000 will result.

Note that the *total* income earned by the foreign subsidiary and the *total* amount of income taxes paid to the foreign government are irrelevant in determining the amount of foreign source income to report in the U.S. tax return and in calculating the indirect FTC. The amount of dividend *received* is the starting point for calculating the U.S. tax liability.

Example: Calculation of Indirect FTC Including Withholding Taxes

Caribco Inc. (a U.S.-based company) receives a $1,500,000 dividend from its wholly owned subsidiary in the Dominican Republic. The income tax rate in the Dominican Republic is 25 percent, and the withholding rate on dividends is 20 percent. The grossed-up dividend to be reported by Caribco as foreign source income on its U.S. tax return is calculated by first grossing up the dividend for the withholding tax paid and then for the income tax paid:

Grossed-up dividend
= Dividend received/(1 − Withholding tax rate)/(1 − Income tax rate)
= $1,500,000   /   (1 − 0.20)   /   (1 − 0.25)
= $1,500,000 / 0.80 / 0.75 = $2,500,000

The grossed-up dividend can be verified as follows:

Before tax income (grossed-up dividend)	$2,500,000
Income tax (25%)	(625,000)
Income after income tax	$1,875,000
Withholding tax (20%)	(375,000)
Net dividend received by Caribco	$1,500,000

Given a 25 percent income tax and a 20 percent withholding tax on dividends, the subsidiary must generate $2,500,000 in income before tax to be able to pay its parent a net dividend (after taxes) of $1,500,000.

The foreign tax credit allowed and net U.S. tax liability related to Caribco's subsidiary in the Dominican Republic are determined as follows:

$$\text{Actual taxes paid} = \$625,000 + \$375,000 = \$1,000,000$$
$$\text{Overall FTC limitation} = \$2,500,000 \times 35\% = \$875,000$$
$$\text{FTC allowed} = \$875,000$$

Grossed-up dividend	$2,500,000
US tax before FTC (35%)	$ 875,000
FTC allowed	875,000
Net U.S. tax liability	$ 0

Caribco has an excess FTC of $125,000 ($1,000,000 − $875,000) that it can carry back 1 year or carry forward 10 years.

TAX TREATIES

Tax treaties are bilateral agreements between two countries regarding how companies and individuals from one country will be taxed when earning income in the other country. Tax treaties are designed to facilitate international trade and investment by reducing tax barriers to the international flow of goods and services.

A major problem in international trade and investment is double taxation where tax jurisdictions overlap. For example, both Australia and the United States might claim tax jurisdiction over dividends earned by an Australian citizen from investments in U.S. stocks. Treaties reduce the possibility of double taxation through the clarification of tax jurisdiction. Treaties also provide for the possibility of tax reduction through a reduction in withholding tax rates. In addition, treaties generally require the exchange of information between countries to help in enforcing their domestic tax provisions.

Model Treaties

OECD Model

Most income tax treaties signed by the major industrial countries are based on a model treaty developed by the Organization for Economic Cooperation and Development (OECD). An important article in the OECD model treaty indicates that business profits may be taxed by a treaty partner country only if they are attributable to a *permanent establishment* in that country. A permanent establishment can include an office, branch, factory, construction site, mine, well, or quarry. Facilities used for storage, display, or delivery, and the maintenance of goods solely for processing by another enterprise do not constitute permanent establishments. If there is no permanent establishment, then income that otherwise would be taxable in the country in which the income is earned if there were no treaty is not taxable in that country.

One of the most important benefits afforded by tax treaties is the reduction in withholding tax rates. The OECD model treaty recommends withholding rates of

1. 5% for direct investment dividends (paid by a subsidiary to its parent).
2. 15% for portfolio dividends (paid to individuals).
3. 10% for interest.
4. Zero for royalties.

Although the OECD model might be the starting point for negotiation, countries with more outbound investment than inbound investment often try to reduce the host country's right to tax, most conspicuously seeking zero withholding on interest. A very specific deviation from the model treaty is where countries that import most of their movies and TV programming seek higher withholding rates on film royalties than on other copyright royalties.

United Nations Model

The OECD model assumes that countries are economic equals. The United Nations (UN) model treaty, designed to be used between developed and developing countries, assumes an imbalance. The UN model recognizes that the host country (often a developing country) should have more taxing rights when profit repatriation essentially is a one-way street (from the developing to the developed country).

U.S. Tax Treaties

The United States also has a model treaty it uses as the basis for negotiating bilateral tax agreements. The U.S. model exempts interest and royalties from withholding tax and establishes 15 percent as the maximum withholding rate on dividends. Withholding rates from selected U.S. tax treaties are shown in Exhibit 10.4. As that exhibit shows, neither the U.S. model nor the OECD's recommendations regarding withholding rates are always followed.

EXHIBIT 10.4
Selected U.S. Tax Treaty Withholding Tax Rates

Source: Internal Revenue Service, Publication 901, "U.S. Tax Treaties."

Country	Dividend Paid to Parent	Interest Paid to Parent	Royalties
Nontreaty	30%	30%	30%
Australia	15	10	10
Canada	10	15	10
China (PRC)	10	10	10
France	5	0	5
Germany	5	0	0
Hungary	5	0	0
Indonesia	15	15	15
Japan	10	10	10
Korea (South)	10	12	15
Mexico	5	15	10
New Zealand	15	10	10
Philippines	20	15	15
Russia	5	0	0
Spain	10	10	10
Thailand	10	15	15
United Kingdom	5	0	0
Venezuela	5	10	5

The United States has treaties with more than 50 countries, including all 25 members of the European Union; Australia and New Zealand; Ukraine and Russia; Egypt and Israel; Mexico and Canada; and India, Korea, Japan, and China. As of January 1, 2005, except for Venezuela, the United States did not have a tax treaty with any country in South America. This includes Brazil, which is one of the top 10 locations for U.S. foreign direct investment.

A reason why there is no treaty between the United States and Brazil is that there is very little Brazilian investment in the United States. The reduction in withholding taxes that would result from a tax treaty would mostly benefit U.S. investors who are receiving interest and dividends from their Brazilian investments, but there would be little benefit for taxpayers in Brazil. The Brazilian government is not interested in entering into a treaty with the United States that would reduce the withholding taxes collected on payments made to U.S. investors without much reciprocal benefit to Brazilians.

There is also very little Polish investment in the United States. However, Poland differs from Brazil in that Poland is interested in attracting new U.S. investment. The United States/Poland tax treaty allows Poland to better compete with other countries in attracting U.S. investment.

Understanding the potential benefits to be derived from a tax treaty is very important when deciding where to locate a foreign investment. For example, for every $100 of after-income-tax profit earned by a subsidiary in Venezuela, $95 would be received as a dividend by its U.S. parent (after paying a 5 percent withholding tax under the United States/Venezuela tax treaty). Because there is no treaty between the United States and Brazil, for every $100 of after-income-tax profit earned by a subsidiary in Brazil, only $85 will land in the United States (after paying a 15 percent Brazilian withholding tax). All else being equal, a U.S.-based investor would prefer to establish a subsidiary in Venezuela rather than in Brazil to reduce the amount of withholding taxes paid.

Treaty Shopping

Treaty shopping describes a process in which a resident of Country A uses a corporation in Country B to get the benefit of Country B's tax treaty with Country C. As an example, assume that a Brazilian taxpayer has investments in U.S. shares. Because the United States has no treaty with Brazil, dividend payments made to the Brazilian investor by U.S. companies will be taxed by the U.S. government at the withholding rate of 30 percent. As demonstrated here, the Brazilian investor receives only 70 percent of the dividend:

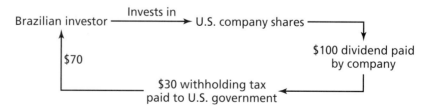

Until 1988, the Netherlands Antilles, located off the coast of South America, had a treaty with the United States that reduced the withholding rate on dividends to 10 percent. The Brazilian taxpayer could use this treaty to its advantage by establishing a wholly owned holding company in the Netherlands Antilles that in turn made investments in U.S. company shares. Dividends paid by the U.S. companies to the Netherlands Antilles (NA) stockholder would be taxed at the treaty rate of

10 percent, and income earned by the NA holding company was not taxed in the Netherlands Antilles. Dividends paid by the NA holding company to the Brazilian investor from its income, in effect, the dividend received from the U.S. companies, was not subject to NA withholding tax. In this way, the Brazilian investor was able to keep 20 percent more of the gross dividend than if the investment had been made directly from Brazil. This is demonstrated as follows:

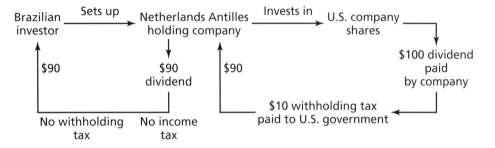

In this situation there is no incentive for Brazil to negotiate a treaty with the United States.

Since the 1980s, U.S. treaty negotiations have insisted that a "limitation of benefits" provision be included in U.S. tax treaties. A typical treaty might provide that certain treaty benefits (such as reduced withholding rates) are not available if 50 percent or more of a corporation's stock is held by third-party taxpayers (unless the stock is publicly traded). The insertion of such a limitation into the United States/Netherlands Antilles treaty would preclude the Brazilian investor from enjoying the reduced withholding rate on dividends paid by the U.S. company.

In addition to entering into new treaties, the United States has attempted to renegotiate its existing tax treaties with tax haven countries to include a limitation-of-benefits provision. In some cases negotiations have failed and the existing treaty has been canceled. This is true in the Netherlands Antilles case. The United States no longer has a double taxation treaty with the Netherlands Antilles.

The United States and Switzerland are leading the way in fighting treaty shopping. Switzerland has had a unilateral anti–treaty shopping provision in its domestic law since 1962. The OECD model treaty does not have a clause to combat treaty shopping.

CONTROLLED FOREIGN CORPORATIONS

To crack down on the use of tax havens by U.S. companies to avoid paying U.S. taxes, the U.S. Congress created *controlled foreign corporation (CFC)* rules in 1962.[9] A CFC is any foreign corporation in which U.S. shareholders hold more than 50 percent of the combined voting power or fair market value of the stock. Only those U.S. taxpayers (corporations, citizens, or tax residents) directly or indirectly owning 10 percent or more of the stock are considered U.S. shareholders in determining

[9] Other countries—including Australia, Denmark, France, Italy, Sweden, the United Kingdom, and Venezuela—have similar anti–tax haven rules. For example, France uses a territorial approach to taxation and as a result does not tax profit earned by its companies outside of France. However, under French controlled foreign corporation rules, income earned by a French company outside of France may become subject to French taxation if such income is subject to an effective tax rate in the foreign country that is less than two-thirds of the French corporate tax rate. See Ernst & Young, *Worldwide Corporate Tax Guide*, 2002, p. 217.

whether the 50 percent threshold is met. *All* majority-owned foreign subsidiaries of U.S.-based companies are CFCs.

As noted earlier in this chapter, the United States generally defers taxation of income earned by a foreign investment until a dividend is received by the U.S. investor. For CFCs, however, there is no deferral of U.S. taxation on so-called *Subpart F income*. Instead, Subpart F income is taxed currently similar to foreign branch income regardless of whether or not the investor receives a dividend. Subpart F of the U.S. Internal Revenue Code lists the income that will be treated in this fashion.

Subpart F Income

Subpart F income is income that is easily movable to a low-tax jurisdiction. There are four types of Subpart F income:

1. Income derived from insurance of U.S. risks.
2. Income from countries engaged in international boycotts.
3. Certain illegal payments.
4. Foreign base company income.

Foreign base company income is the most important category of Subpart F income and includes the following:

1. Passive income such as interest, dividends, royalties, rents, and capital gains from sales of assets. An example would be dividends received by a CFC from holding shares of stock in affiliated companies.
2. Sales income, where the CFC makes sales outside of its country of incorporation. For example, the U.S. parent manufactures a product that it sells to its CFC in Hong Kong, which in turn sells the product to customers in Japan. Sales to customers outside of Hong Kong generate Subpart F income.
3. Service income, where the CFC performs services out of its country of incorporation.
4. Air and sea transportation income.
5. Oil and gas products income.

Determination of the Amount of CFC Income Currently Taxable

The amount of CFC income currently taxable in the United States depends on the percentage of CFC income generated from Subpart F activities. Assuming that none of a CFC's income is repatriated as a dividend, the following hold true:

1. If Subpart F income is *less than 5 percent* of the CFC's total income, then none of the CFC's income will be taxed currently.
2. If Subpart F income is *between 5 percent and 70 percent* of the CFC's total income, then that percentage of the CFC's income which is Subpart F income will be taxed currently.
3. If Subpart F income is *greater than 70 percent* of the CFC's total income, then 100 percent of the CFC's income will be taxed currently.

Safe Harbor Rule

If the foreign tax rate is greater than 90 percent of the U.S. corporate income tax rate, then none of the CFC's income is considered to be Subpart F income. With the current U.S. tax rate of 35 percent, U.S. MNCs need not be concerned with the CFC rules for those foreign operations located in countries with a tax rate of 31.5 percent or higher. These countries are not considered to be tax havens for CFC purposes.

SUMMARY OF U.S. TAX TREATMENT OF FOREIGN SOURCE INCOME

Determining the appropriate U.S. tax treatment of foreign source income can be quite complicated. Factors to consider include the following:

1. Legal form of the foreign operation (branch or subsidiary).
2. Percentage level of ownership (CFC or not).
3. Foreign tax rate (tax haven or not).
4. Nature of the foreign source income (Subpart F or not) (appropriate FTC basket).

Exhibit 10.5 provides a flowchart with general guidelines for determining the amount of foreign source income to be included on the U.S. tax return, the FTC allowed, and the net U.S. tax liability on income generated by foreign operations. Use of the flowchart for determining a company's U.S. tax liability on its foreign source income is demonstrated through the following example.

EXHIBIT 10.5
Flowchart for Determining U.S. Taxation of Foreign Operations

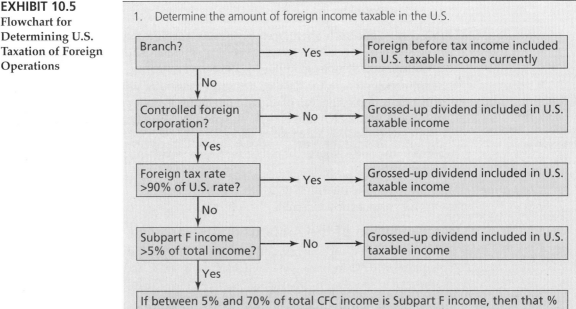

1. Determine the amount of foreign income taxable in the U.S.

| Branch? | → Yes → | Foreign before tax income included in U.S. taxable income currently |

↓ No

| Controlled foreign corporation? | → No → | Grossed-up dividend included in U.S. taxable income |

↓ Yes

| Foreign tax rate >90% of U.S. rate? | → Yes → | Grossed-up dividend included in U.S. taxable income |

↓ No

| Subpart F income >5% of total income? | → No → | Grossed-up dividend included in U.S. taxable income |

↓ Yes

If between 5% and 70% of total CFC income is Subpart F income, then that % of CFC income is included in U.S. taxable income currently.

If >70% of total CFC income is Subpart F income, then 100% of CFC income is included in U.S. taxable income currently.

2. Allocate taxable income to appropriate basket:
    Through 2006—allocate to one of nine baskets, including (*a*) passive income, (*b*) financial services income, and (*c*) overall.
    Beginning in 2007—allocate to one of two baskets: (*a*) general income or (*b*) passive income.
3. Determine (*a*) U.S. tax liability before foreign tax credit, (*b*) foreign tax credit, and (*c*) net U.S. tax liability after foreign tax credit by basket.
    Note: Step 3 is carried out separately for each basket of income.
4. Determine total net U.S. tax liability by summing across baskets.

Example: U.S. Taxation of Foreign Source Income

Assume that MNC Company (a U.S. taxpayer) has four subsidiaries located in four different foreign countries. The country location, MNC's percentage ownership, nature of activity, and income before tax for each subsidiary; the income and withholding tax rates in the host countries; and the dividend paid by each subsidiary to MNC are summarized as follows:

Foreign Entity	E	P	S	B
Country	Ecuador	Poland	Switzerland	Bahamas
Legal form	Subsidiary	Subsidiary	Subsidiary	Subsidiary
MNC's ownership	100%	51%	100%	100%
Activity	Manufacturing	Manufacturing	Investment	Shipping
Before-tax income	$100,000	$100,000	$100,000	$100,000
Income tax rate	25%	40%	8%	0%
After-tax income	$75,000	$60,000	$92,000	$100,000
Gross dividend paid to MNC	$75,000	$20,000	$20,000	$0
Withholding tax rate	0%	20%	35%	0%
Net dividend received by MNC	$75,000	$16,000	$13,000	$0

Determination of the Amount of Foreign Source Income Taxable in the United States

The amount of income from each foreign operation that will be taxable in the United States will be based on either (1) before-tax income or (2) the grossed-up dividend. Applying the flowchart in Exhibit 10.5, the first step is to determine whether the foreign operation is a branch or a subsidiary. In this example, each foreign operation is legally incorporated as a subsidiary in the country in which it resides. The next step is to determine whether the subsidiaries are controlled foreign corporations. Because MNC owns more than 50 percent of each operation, the answer to this question in each case is yes. To determine whether any of the foreign countries meets the U.S. tax law definition of a tax haven, the effective tax rate (income tax plus withholding tax) must be calculated and compared with 90 percent of the U.S. tax rate of 35 percent, or 31.5 percent. The effective tax rate is determined by adding the income tax rate plus the withholding rate applied to after-tax income:

Ecuador	25% + 0% (1 − 25%) = 25%	Tax haven
Poland	40% + 20% (1 − 40%) = 52%	Not a tax haven
Switzerland	8% + 35% (1 − 8%) = 40.2%	Not a tax haven
Bahamas	0%	Tax haven

Ecuador and the Bahamas would be considered tax havens for purposes of the controlled foreign corporation rules. Although the income tax rate in Switzerland is quite low, the withholding rate is high enough that the effective tax rate exceeds the threshold of 31.5 percent. Because neither Poland nor Switzerland is a tax haven, only the grossed-up dividend received by MNC from those subsidiaries is subject to U.S. taxation.

The next step is to determine whether the subsidiaries in Ecuador and the Bahamas had any Subpart F income. In general, Subpart F income is income that can be easily moved from one tax jurisdiction to another. Manufacturing income does not meet this definition, so subsidiary E does not have any Subpart F income. Therefore, even though Ecuador is a tax haven, only the grossed-up dividend received by MNC from subsidiary E is subject to U.S. taxation.

The Bahamian subsidiary generates its income from shipping, which is specifically included in the list of Subpart F income presented earlier. Assuming that Subsidiary B generates all of its income through shipping, 100 percent of B's before-tax income ($100,000) will be taxable in the United States.

To determine the amount of income from subsidiaries E, P, and S taxable in the United States, the net dividend received by MNC must be grossed up to a before-tax basis. The net dividend is first grossed up for withholding taxes paid, and then the before-withholding-tax dividend is grossed up for income taxes paid. The grossed-up dividend for each subsidiary is calculated as follows:

	Net Dividend		1 − Withholding Tax		Dividend Before Withholding Tax		1 − Income Tax		Grossed-up Dividend
Ecuador	$75,000	/	1 − 0.0	=	$75,000	/	1 − 0.25	=	$100,000
Poland	$16,000	/	1 − 0.20	=	$20,000	/	1 − 0.40	=	$33,333
Switzerland . .	$13,000	/	1 − 0.35	=	$20,000	/	1 − 0.08	=	$21,739

Determine Foreign Tax Credits, U.S. Tax Liability, and Excess Foreign Tax Credits, by Basket

To determine MNC's foreign tax credit, foreign taxes (both income tax and withholding tax) paid on the income taxable in the United States must be determined. For Subsidiary B, this amount is $0. For the other subsidiaries, the simplest way to determine the total amount of foreign taxes paid is to subtract the net dividend received by MNC from the grossed-up dividend—the difference between gross and net dividend is taxes deemed paid to the foreign government on the grossed-up dividend. This amount is calculated as follows:

	Ecuador	Poland	Switzerland
Grossed-up dividend	$100,000	$33,333	$21,739
Net amount received by MNC	75,000	16,000	13,000
Taxes paid to foreign government	$ 25,000	$17,333	$ 8,739

The amount of income taxable in the United States next must be allocated to the appropriate FTC basket according to each subsidiary's activity. The income of Subsidiary S is allocated to the passive income basket, Subsidiary B income is allocated to the shipping income basket, and the income of Subsidiaries E and P is allocated to the overall basket. The foreign tax credit, U.S. income tax liability, and excess FTC for each basket of income can now be calculated as follows:

	Passive	Shipping	Overall
U.S. taxable income	$21,739	$100,000	$133,333
U.S. income tax before FTC (35%)	$7,609	$35,000	$46,667
Less: FTC			
(a) Taxes paid to foreign government	$8,739	$0	$42,333
(b) Overall FTC limitation	$7,609	$35,000	$46,667
FTC allowed—lesser of (a) and (b)	7,609	0	42,333
U.S. tax liability	$ 0	$35,000	$ 4,334
Excess FTC	$1,139	$0	$0

MNC Company has a total U.S. tax liability on its foreign source income of $39,334 and an excess foreign tax credit on passive income of $1,139.

Note that beginning in 2007, foreign source income will be allocated to only two baskets: (1) passive income and (2) general income. In that case, Subsidiary S income will continue to be allocated to the passive income basket and the income of Subsidiaries B, E, and P will be combined in the general income basket. The total amount of U.S. tax liability and excess FTC in the example above will remain the same.

TRANSLATION OF FOREIGN OPERATION INCOME

In the examples presented thus far in this chapter, the income earned by foreign operations and the foreign taxes paid have been stated in terms of the parent company's domestic currency. In reality, foreign operations generate income and pay taxes in the local, foreign currency. The parent company's tax liability, however, is determined in terms of the domestic currency, for example, U.S. dollars for U.S. companies. The foreign currency income generated by a foreign operation must be translated into the parent company's currency for purposes of taxation. This section demonstrates procedures used in the United States for translating foreign currency income for U.S. tax purposes. Although we focus on U.S. tax rules, similar procedures are followed in other countries.

As is true for financial reporting, the appropriate translation procedures for determining U.S. taxable income depend on the *functional currency* of the foreign operation. The functional currency is the currency in which the foreign operation primarily conducts business and can be either a foreign currency or the U.S. dollar. For operations located in highly inflationary countries (cumulative three-year inflation exceeding 100 percent), the U.S. dollar must be used as the functional currency. Moreover, a U.S. company with a foreign branch or foreign subsidiary that primarily operates in a foreign currency can elect to use the U.S. dollar as the functional currency if it so chooses.

A foreign operation that has the U.S. dollar as its functional currency keeps its books in U.S. dollars. Any transactions that take place in a foreign currency are translated into U.S. dollars at the date of the transaction. Income of the foreign operation is directly calculated in U.S. dollars, so there is no need for translation at the end of the year.

For those foreign branches and subsidiaries that have a foreign currency as their functional currency, accounting records are kept and income is determined in the foreign currency and must be translated into U.S. dollars for U.S. tax purposes. Under U.S. tax law, foreign branch income and dividends received from foreign subsidiaries are translated into U.S. dollars differently.

Translation of Foreign Branch Income

To determine U.S. taxable income, foreign branch net income is translated into U.S. dollars using the average exchange rate for the year. Foreign branch net income is then grossed up by adding taxes paid to the foreign government translated at the exchange rate at the date of payment. When branch income is repatriated to the home office and foreign currency is actually converted into U.S. dollars, any difference in the exchange rate used to originally translate the income and the exchange rate at the date of repatriation creates a taxable foreign exchange gain or loss. The foreign tax credit is determined by translating foreign taxes at the exchange rate at the date of payment. The following example demonstrates these procedures.

Example: Translation of Foreign Branch Income

Maker Company (a U.S.-based taxpayer) establishes a branch in Mexico in January of Year 1 when the exchange rate is US$0.12 per Mexican peso (Mex$). During Year 1, the Mexican branch generates Mex$6,000,000 of pretax income. On October 15, Year 1, Mex$1,000,000 is repatriated to Maker Company and converted into U.S. dollars. The effective income tax rate in Mexico is 30 percent. Taxes were paid in Mexico on the Mexican branch income on December 31, Year 1. Relevant exchange rates for Year 1 are as follows:

	US$/Mex$
January 1	$0.125
October 15	$0.090
December 31	$0.085
Average for the year	$0.100

The amount of foreign branch income Maker Company reports on its Year 1 U.S. tax return is determined as follows:

Pretax income	Mex$6,000,000					
Taxes paid (30%)	Mex$1,800,000					
Net income × Average exchange rate	Mex$4,200,000	×	$0.100	=	$420,000	
Taxes paid × Actual exchange rate	Mex$1,800,000	×	$0.085	=	153,000	
Gain (loss) on October 15 repatriation	Mex$1,000,000	×	($0.09 − $0.100)	=	(10,000)	
U.S. taxable income					$563,000	

The foreign tax credit (FTC) allowed by the United States is determined by comparing the actual tax paid to the Mexican government (translated into US$) and the overall FTC limitation based on the U.S. tax rate of 35 percent:

(a) Foreign taxes paid (in US$)	$153,000
(b) Overall FTC limitation ($563,000 × 35%)	197,050
FTC allowed—lesser of (a) and (b)	$153,000

The U.S. tax return would include the following:

U.S. taxable income (above)	$563,000
U.S. tax before FTC (35%)	$197,050
FTC allowed (above)	153,000
Net U.S. tax liability	$ 44,050

Translation of Foreign Subsidiary Income

Unless Subpart F income is present, the income of a foreign subsidiary is not taxable until dividends are distributed to the U.S. parent. At that time, the dividend is translated into U.S. dollars using the spot rate at the date of distribution. The dividend is grossed up by adding taxes deemed paid on the dividend translated at the spot rate at the date of tax payment. The U.S. dollar–translated amount of taxes deemed paid is also used to determine the foreign tax credit. These procedures are demonstrated using the Maker Company example presented earlier.

Example: Translation of Dividends Received from Foreign Subsidiary

Assume the same facts as in the previous example except that Maker's operation in Mexico is incorporated as a subsidiary. Relevant exchange rates are:

	US$/Mex$
October 15 (date dividends are repatriated to U.S. parent)	$0.090
December 31(date taxes are paid to Mexican government)	$0.085

The amounts reported as Maker's U.S. taxable income, foreign tax credit, and net U.S. tax liability related to the Mexican subsidiary are calculated as follows:

Calculation of Grossed-up Dividend					
Dividend received	Mex$1,000,000	×	$0.090	=	$ 90,000
Tax deemed paid*	Mex$ 428,571	×	$0.085	=	36,429
Grossed-up dividend (U.S. taxable income) . . .					$126,429

*Taxes deemed paid can be calculated in two ways:

(Dividend/1 − Mexican tax rate) − Dividend =
(Mex$1,000,000/0.70 = Mex$1,428,571) − Mex$1,000,000 = Mex$428,571

(Dividend/Net income) × Taxes paid =
(Mex$1,000,000/Mex$4,200,000) × Mex$1,800,000 = Mex$428,571

Calculation of FTC	
(a) Tax deemed paid (in US$)	$36,429
(b) Overall FTC limitation ($126,429 × 35%)	44,250
FTC allowed—lesser of (a) and (b)	$36,429

Calculation of U.S. Tax Liability	
U.S. taxable income (above)	$126,429
U.S. tax before FTC (35%)	$ 44,250
FTC allowed (above)	36,429
Net U.S. tax liability	$ 7,821

Foreign Currency Transactions

U.S. taxpayers often engage in transactions denominated in foreign currency such as export sales, import purchases, and foreign currency borrowings. In general, gains or losses arising from fluctuation in exchange rates between the date of the transaction and its settlement will be taxable only when realized—in effect, at the settlement date. For tax purposes, gains and losses on forward contracts and options used to hedge foreign currency transactions and firm commitments are integrated with the underlying item being hedged. For example, if a foreign currency receivable is hedged by a forward contract that guarantees that the foreign currency can be sold for $1,000, taxable revenue of $1,000 is reported when the receivable is collected. Any gains and losses on the foreign currency receivable and forward contract recorded for financial reporting purposes are not recognized for tax purposes.

TAX INCENTIVES

Governments often use the national tax law to encourage certain types of behavior. For example, a number of countries use tax holidays to encourage investment in specific types of assets, activities, or geographical regions. To improve the national balance of trade, an incentive to export is sometimes provided by reducing the rate of taxation on export sales. Companies doing business internationally may be able to take advantage of these incentives to reduce their global tax burden. This section provides a brief description of tax holidays and then describes the history and current status of export incentives provided by the United States.

Tax Holidays

All of the countries that comprise the Association of Southeast Asian Nations (ASEAN), as well as several other Asian countries, offer tax incentive packages to attract foreign direct investment. The Philippines, for example, provides a 100 percent income tax holiday for three to eight years depending on the location and industry in which the foreigner invests. Indonesia offers tax holidays to foreign investors for up to 10 years, as does Malaysia. The country of Thailand provides a tax holiday for up to eight years for projects involving technology or human capital development, infrastructure, environmental protection, and other targeted industries. Investment projects in these industries also enjoy an exemption from import duty on machinery. Sri Lanka provides a tax holiday for 10 to 20 years for investments in "thrust" industries as defined by the national Board of Investment. Thrust industries include electronics, light engineering, ceramics, and rubber products. A preferential tax of 15 percent for 5 to 10 years follows the tax holiday. Some countries, such as Taiwan, allow investors to choose between a tax holiday and an investment tax credit.

Countries in other parts of the world also have used tax holidays in an attempt to attract foreign direct investment. For example, as a part of the process of selling off state-owned enterprises to private investors, several East European countries offered tax incentives, including tax holidays to foreign investors. Hungary, for example, offers significant tax advantages to investors. In addition to a relatively low 16 percent corporate tax rate, which is already an investment incentive, Hungary also offers tax holidays to investors that vary with the level of investment. Companies that invest at least 3 billion Hungarian forints (HUF) and create 300 new jobs in specified, underdeveloped regions of the country qualify for a five-year tax holiday. Companies that invest HUF 10 billion and create 500 new jobs are eligible for a 10-year tax holiday, regardless of the location of the investment. However, these tax holidays are unlikely to go on much longer. To become a member of the European Union, Hungary has been asked to abandon its tax holiday provisions.

Tax holidays can be of significant benefit to multinational companies as long as the income earned in the foreign country is reinvested in that country. For MNCs taxed on a worldwide basis, the benefit disappears when dividends earned in the foreign country are repatriated to the parent. At that time, the dividend is subject to home-country taxation and there is no foreign tax credit to offset the home-country liability because no income taxes were paid to the foreign government. However, some home countries grant *tax sparing* to companies that invest in developing countries. For example, Japanese companies that invest in countries with which Japan has an agreement may claim a foreign tax credit for the amount of tax that would have been paid if there were no tax holiday. This ensures that the foreign country's tax holiday provides a real incentive for investment by Japanese companies. Most of the wealthier nations provide tax sparing for investment in developing countries, but the United States does not.

U.S. Export Incentives

Prior to 1962, many U.S. companies exported through foreign base companies located in tax haven countries. By locating some of the profit earned on exports in a tax haven, companies were able to unilaterally reduce the rate of U.S. taxation on export sales. As discussed earlier in this chapter, the U.S. Congress enacted the CFC rules in 1962, which eliminated the deferral of taxation on Subpart F income and therefore the lower effective tax rate on export sales. As a result, many companies sought new legislation to create export incentives.

Domestic International Sales Corporation

In 1971, the U.S. Congress created the domestic international sales corporation (DISC) to provide companies with an incentive to export. Under the DISC provisions of the tax law, companies were able to establish export subsidiaries in the United States (DISCs) and a certain portion of the profit earned by the DISCs would be deferred from taxation until actually distributed to the parent. The U.S. parent sold goods to its DISC at a low markup, and the DISC then sold to foreign customers at higher markups, concentrating the total profit in the DISC.

The major differences from the previous use of foreign base companies in tax haven countries were that

- The DISC was located in the United States and not in a foreign country.
- The DISC was a paper company with no physical substance (the DISC did not have physical facilities or employees).
- A portion of the DISC's income was deemed to be distributed to the parent and was therefore taxed currently, even if no distribution actually took place. In the tax haven scenario, income was not taxable until actually distributed to the parent.

The DISC provisions drew immediate criticism from U.S. trading partners that were parties to the General Agreement on Tariffs and Trade (GATT), because the DISC rules violated the GATT rule against tax subsidies for exports. While not admitting any violation of GATT, the United States nevertheless withdrew the DISC and created a new export incentive in 1984—the foreign sales corporation.

Foreign Sales Corporation (FSC)

GATT did not require the taxation of export income generated from economic activity located outside of a country. Therefore, if a company funneled its exports through a foreign subsidiary that actually engaged in economic activity to earn the export income, the United States was not obligated under GATT to tax the income of the foreign subsidiary.

The U.S. Congress enacted foreign sales corporation (FSC) provisions in the Tax Reform Act of 1984. Under these provisions, a portion (generally 15 percent) of an

FSC's income was tax exempt in the United States. The nonexempt portion was taxed currently regardless of whether or not dividends were paid to the parent.

To qualify as an FSC, a foreign subsidiary had to be incorporated in a foreign country (to comply with GATT) that had an exchange of information agreement or tax treaty with the United States. There was an IRS-approved list of countries in which FSCs could be established.

The European Union believed that the FSC approach violated a rule of the World Trade Organization (WTO) that prohibits export subsidies and therefore appealed to the WTO for a ruling in the late 1990s. A WTO panel ruled that the FSC did not comply with WTO rules. To comply with a settlement with the WTO, the U.S. Congress passed the FSC Repeal and Extraterritorial Income Exclusion Act (ETI) in November 2000.

The FSC Repeal and Extraterritorial Income Exclusion Act of 2000 (ETI)

The ETI replaced the FSC regime with an income exclusion designed to more closely model European tax systems. Under the ETI rules, U.S. taxpayers may exclude income derived from export sales from their U.S. taxable income if both of the following tests are met:

1. *Sales activity test.* The company or its agent must participate outside of the United States in at least one of the following activities:
   a. Solicitation of the offer.
   b. Negotiation of the contract.
   c. Making of the contract.

   This test can be met, for example, by mailing brochures, price lists, or solicitation letters to customers from outside the United States, or by using an offshore office or agent to negotiate and/or make the contract.

2. *Direct costs test.* Direct costs associated with the export sale incurred outside of the United States must be greater than or equal to 50 percent of total direct costs in five categories of activities or 85 percent of total direct costs in any two of five categories of activities. The five categories of activities are as follows:
   a. Advertising and sales promotion.
   b. Processing of customer orders and arranging for delivery.
   c. Transportation outside of the United States.
   d. Determination and transmittal of a final invoice or statement of account.
   e. Assumption of credit risk.

   This test also can be met through the use of an offshore office or agent.

In contrast to the FSC rules, companies are not required to establish a foreign subsidiary in a qualified foreign jurisdiction to obtain ETI benefits. In addition, companies with less than $5 million of export sales are not required to meet these tests in order to exclude export income from U.S. taxable income.

The amount of extraterritorial income that may be excluded is limited to the larger of (1) 15 percent of income earned on qualifying export sales, or (2) 1.2 percent of qualifying export sales, but not to exceed 200 percent of the exclusion provided by (1).

Example: Application of the Extraterritorial Income Exclusion

Jackson Company has export sales of $10,000,000 that generate otherwise taxable income of $1,000,000. Because Jackson's export sales exceed $5 million, the company is required to meet the sales activity and direct costs tests. Jackson accomplishes this by establishing a sales office in the Cayman Islands. The sales office manager acts as Jackson's agent to negotiate and make the contracts between Jackson Company and its foreign customers, thereby satisfying the sales activity test. To meet the direct costs test, the sales office also processes all foreign customer orders, arranges all transportation on Jackson's export sales, and prepares invoices and statements of accounts for all of Jackson's foreign customers. Jackson Company determines the amount of income to exclude from U.S. taxable income as the greater of (1) $1,000,000 \times 15\% = \$150,000$, or (2) $10,000,000 \times 1.2\% = \$120,000$. In this case, Jackson Company will exclude $150,000 from U.S. taxable income.

The European Union (EU) believed that the ETI, like the FSC, violated international trade agreements and appealed to the WTO to disallow the new U.S. structure. The WTO sided with the EU, ruling that ETI is an unfair export subsidy, and authorized the EU to slap an unprecedented $4 billion of tariffs on U.S. goods in retaliation if the United States did not take substantive steps to repeal the ETI by January 1, 2004. The EU began imposing tariffs on U.S. products in March 2004. The tariffs began at a rate of 5 percent and were to increase by 1 percent per month, with a maximum tariff of 17 percent to be reached in March 2005. In October 2004, six months after retaliatory tariffs were implemented, the U.S. Congress passed the American Jobs Creation Act of 2004, which repealed the ETI.

American Jobs Creation Act of 2004

The American Jobs Creation Act of 2004 (AJCA) made the most sweeping changes in the taxation of overseas operations since the Tax Reform Act of 1986. In addition to reducing the number of FTC baskets from nine to two and changing the lengths of the carryover periods for excess FTCs, the AJCA also repealed the ETI for transactions occurring after December 31, 2004. However, to provide U.S. exporters with a soft landing, the repeal is phased in over a two-year period. For 2005, 80 percent of the ETI benefit was available, reducing to 60 percent in 2006. ETI benefits disappear completely in 2007.

To replace the phasing-out ETI benefits, the AJCA introduced a phased-in deduction for domestic manufacturing. Companies engaged in domestic manufacturing activities are able to deduct 3 percent of their qualifying production activities income from taxation in 2005 and 2006, 6 percent in 2007 through 2009, and 9 percent in 2010 and beyond. When the deduction is fully phased in, the effective corporate tax rate on manufacturing income will be 31.85 percent.[10] Manufacturing firms will be able to enjoy this deduction whether or not they export. Moreover, the AJCA defines *manufacturing* very broadly to include traditional manufacturing, construction, engineering, energy production, computer software development, film and videotape production, and processing of agricultural products. As a result, many companies that were unable to take advantage of the ETI rules will benefit from the AJCA.

One additional important feature of the AJCA for multinational corporations was a provision allowing foreign source income to be repatriated to the United States at a reduced tax rate. For one year, MNCs could elect to claim a deduction equal to 85 percent of cash dividends received from controlled foreign corporations (CFCs) in excess of a base amount. This election was available either for the year prior to enactment of the AJCA (2004) or the first year after enactment (2005).

---

[10] The 9 percent deduction means that the 35 percent corporate tax rate will be applied to only 91 percent of income: $35\% \times 91\% = 31.85\%$.

To qualify for the deduction, the repatriated dividends had to be reinvested in the United States under a domestic reinvestment plan approved by senior management. The dividend amount eligible for nontaxable treatment was limited to $500 million. The nontaxable dividend was not eligible for a foreign tax credit.

Summary

1. Taxes are a significant cost of doing business. Taxes are often an important factor to consider in making decisions related to foreign operations. Although tax returns will be prepared by tax experts, managers of multinational corporations (MNCs) should be familiar with the major issues of international taxation.

2. Most countries have a national corporate income tax rate that varies between 20 and 40 percent. Countries with no or very low corporate taxation are known as tax havens. MNCs often attempt to use operations in tax haven countries to minimize their worldwide tax burden.

3. Withholding taxes are imposed on payments made to foreigners, especially in the form of dividends, interest, and royalties. Withholding rates vary across countries and often vary by type of payment within one country. Differences in withholding rates provide tax-planning opportunities for the location or nature of a foreign operation.

4. Most countries tax income on a worldwide basis. The basis for taxation can be source of income, residence of the taxpayer, and/or citizenship of the taxpayer. The existence of overlapping bases leads to double taxation.

5. Most countries provide relief from double taxation through foreign tax credits (FTCs). FTCs are the reduction in tax liability on income in one country for the taxes already paid on that income in another country. In general, the tax credit allowed by the home country is limited to the amount of taxes that would have been paid if the income had been earned in the home country.

6. The excess of taxes paid to a foreign country over the FTC allowed by the home country is an excess FTC. In the United States, an excess FTC may be carried back 1 year and carried forward 10 years. U.S. tax law requires companies to allocate foreign source income to appropriate foreign tax credit baskets. Excess FTCs may only be applied within the basket to which they relate.

7. In general, income earned by a foreign subsidiary is taxable in the United States only when received by the parent as a dividend. Income earned by a foreign branch is taxable in the United States currently. To crack down on U.S. companies using tax havens to avoid U.S. taxation, U.S. tax law includes controlled foreign corporation (CFC) rules. Income earned by a CFC that can be moved easily from one country to another (Subpart F income) is taxed in the United States currently, regardless of whether or not it has been distributed as a dividend.

8. Tax treaties between two countries govern the way in which individuals and companies living in or doing business in the partner country are to be taxed by that country. A significant feature of most tax treaties is a reduction in withholding tax rates. The U.S. model treaty reduces withholding taxes to zero on interest and royalties and 15 percent on dividends. However, these guidelines often are not followed.

9. Foreign branch net income is translated into U.S. dollars using the average exchange rate for the year and then grossed up by adding taxes paid to the foreign government translated at the exchange rate at the date of payment. When branch income is repatriated to the home office, any difference in the

exchange rate used to originally translate the income and the exchange rate at the date of repatriation creates a taxable foreign exchange gain or loss. Dividends received from a foreign subsidiary are translated into U.S. dollars using the spot rate at the date of distribution and grossed up by adding taxes deemed paid translated at the spot rate at the date of payment.

10. Over the years, the United States has provided a variety of tax incentives to export (DISC, FSC, ETI). The Extraterritorial Income Exclusion (ETI) provisions were repealed in 2004 under pressure from the European Union and the World Trade Organization. In its place, the American Job Creation Act of 2004 allows companies engaged in domestic manufacturing activities to deduct 3 percent of their qualifying production activities income from taxation in 2005 and 2006, 6 percent in 2007 through 2009, and 9 percent in 2010 and beyond. Manufacturing firms receive this deduction whether or not they export.

Appendix to Chapter 10

U.S. Taxation of Expatriates

This chapter has concentrated on international corporate tax issues. This appendix examines several issues related to the taxation of expatriates—individuals who live and work overseas.

The United States is unusual in that it taxes its citizens on their worldwide income regardless of whether they are actually living in the United States. To make U.S. businesses more competitive by making it less expensive to use U.S. employees overseas, the U.S. Congress provides tax advantages for U.S. citizens who work abroad. These advantages are (1) a foreign earned income exclusion and (2) a foreign housing exclusion or deduction.

FOREIGN EARNED INCOME EXCLUSION

The following items of foreign earned income must be reported as income by a U.S. taxpayer:

- Wages, salaries, professional fees.
- Overseas allowance (cash payment made by employer to compensate for the "inconvenience" of living overseas).
- Housing allowance (cash payment made by employer or fair market value of housing provided by employer).
- Automobile allowance (cash allowance or fair market value).
- Cost of living allowance.
- Education allowance.
- Home leave.
- Rest and relaxation airfare.
- Tax reimbursement allowance (reimbursement for additional taxes paid to foreign government greater than what would have been paid in the home country).

If certain criteria are met, $80,000 (in 2002) of foreign earned income may be excluded from U.S. taxable income. An exclusion is allowed even if the earned income is not taxed by the foreign country (or is taxed at a lower rate than in the

United States). Since 2002, the amount of the exclusion has been indexed by the rate of inflation.

In addition, a direct foreign tax credit is allowed for foreign taxes paid on the amount of foreign earned income exceeding the amount of the exclusion. As a result, a U.S. taxpayer working in a foreign country that has a higher tax rate than the United States will pay no additional U.S. tax on his or her foreign earned income.

The real benefit of the foreign earned income exclusion arises when a U.S. taxpayer is working in a foreign country with no individual income tax or an individual tax rate less than in the United States. For example, a U.S. taxpayer working in Saudi Arabia (which has no individual income tax) would have paid no income tax at all on the first $80,000 (in 2002) of foreign earned income. Income over that amount was taxed in the United States at normal rates.

The foreign earned income exclusion is available only to U.S. taxpayers who

1. Have their *tax home* in a foreign country, and
2. Meet either (*a*) a *bona fide residence test* or (*b*) a *physical presence test*.

Tax Home

An individual's tax home is the place where he or she is permanently or indefinitely engaged to work as an employee or as a self-employed individual. An individual's tax home cannot be a foreign country if his or her abode is in the United States. *Abode* is variously defined as "home," "residence," "domicile," or "place of dwelling." It relates to where one lives rather than where one works. For your tax home to be in a foreign country, your abode must also be outside of the United States.

As an example, assume that your company transfers you to work in London for 18 months. Your home in New York is rented out and your automobile is placed in storage. In London, you purchase an automobile and you and your spouse get British driving licenses. All members of your family get a local library card and join the local golf club. You open bank accounts at the local bank. In this case, both the abode and the tax home are in London.

Bona Fide Residence Test

A bona fide residence is not necessarily the same as a domicile. A domicile is a permanent home. For example, you could have your domicile in New York and a bona fide residence in London even if you intend to return eventually to New York. Going to work in London does not necessarily mean that you have established a bona fide residence there. But if you go to London to work for an indefinite or extended period and you set up permanent quarters there for you and your family, you probably have established a bona fide residence in a foreign country, even though you intend to return to the United States eventually.

To establish a bona fide residence, you must reside in a foreign country for an uninterrupted period that includes an entire tax year. You may leave for brief trips to the United States or other foreign countries, but you must always return to the bona fide residence at the end of a trip.

The Internal Revenue Service (IRS) will determine whether you meet the bona fide residence test, given information you report in Form 2555, Foreign Earned Income.

Physical Presence Test

More objective than the bona fide residence test is the physical presence test. You meet this test if you are physically present in a foreign country or countries for

330 full days during a consecutive 12-month period. Days spent in transit to the foreign country do not count; only days in which you are in a foreign country for 24 hours count. Time spent in international waters or airspace does not count.

The minimum time requirement can be waived if you must leave a foreign country due to war, civil unrest, or similar adverse conditions. Each year, the IRS publishes a list of countries determined to have these conditions.

FOREIGN HOUSING COSTS

For those taxpayers meeting the two conditions necessary for the foreign earned income exclusion, a foreign housing exclusion (or deduction) is also available.

A housing allowance that an employer provides to an employee is taxable income in the United States. However, excess housing costs incurred by expatriates can be excluded from U.S. taxable income. *Excess housing costs* are defined as actual housing costs greater than 16 percent of the U.S. government GS-14 Step 1 pay. In 2005, that amount was $12,190 (16% × $76,193). In other words, in 2005, that portion of housing allowance provided by the employer greater than $12,190 was excluded from U.S. taxable income. If the expatriate employee does not receive a housing allowance from his or her employer, excess housing costs (as defined above) incurred directly by the expatriate employee can be deducted in calculating the employee's taxable income. For example, if you worked in Hong Kong in 2005 and paid $15,000 in apartment rent, you may deduct $2,810 ($15,000 − $12,190) as an expense in calculating your taxable income.

Expenses not eligible for the foreign housing exclusion (or deduction) include the cost of purchasing a house or apartment, mortgage interest, property taxes, wages of housekeepers and gardeners, and any costs that are lavish and extravagant.

Questions

1. How can a country's tax system affect the manner in which an operation in that country is financed by a foreign investor?
2. Why might the effective tax rate paid on income earned within a country be different from that country's national corporate income tax rate?
3. What is a tax haven? How might a company use a tax haven to reduce income taxes?
4. What is the difference between the worldwide and territorial approaches to taxation?
5. What are the different ways in which income earned in one country becomes subject to double taxation?
6. What are the mechanisms used by countries to provide relief from double taxation?
7. Under what circumstances is it advantageous to take a deduction rather than a credit for taxes paid in a foreign country?
8. How are foreign branch income and foreign subsidiary income taxed differently by a company's home country?
9. What is the maximum amount of foreign tax credit that a company will be allowed to take with respect to the income earned by a foreign operation?
10. What are excess foreign tax credits? How are they created and how can companies use them?

11. How does the foreign tax credit basket system used in the United States affect the excess foreign tax credits generated by a U.S.-based company?

12. What is a tax treaty? What is one of most important benefits provided by most tax treaties?

13. What is treaty shopping?

14. What is a controlled foreign corporation? What is Subpart F income?

15. Under what circumstances will the income earned by a foreign subsidiary of a U.S. taxpayer be taxed as if it had been earned by a foreign branch?

16. What are the four factors that will determine the manner in which income earned by a foreign operation of a U.S. taxpayer will be taxed by the U.S. government?

17. What procedures are used to translate the foreign currency income of a foreign branch into U.S. dollars for U.S. tax purposes? What procedures are used to translate the foreign currency income of a foreign subsidiary?

18. In what way did both the domestic international sales corporation and the foreign sales corporation violate international trade agreements?

The following questions relate to the appendix to this chapter:

19. What is the benefit provided to an individual taxpayer through the Foreign Earned Income Exclusion?

20. How does an individual taxpayer qualify for the Foreign Earned Income Exclusion?

Exercises and Problems

1. In deciding whether to establish a foreign operation, which factor(s) might a multinational corporation (MNC) consider?
   a. After-tax returns from competing investment locations.
   b. The tax treatments of branches versus subsidiaries.
   c. Withholding rates on dividend and interest payments.
   d. All of the above.

2. Why might a company involved in international business find it beneficial to establish an operation in a tax haven?
   a. The OECD recommends the use of tax havens for corporate income tax avoidance.
   b. Tax havens never tax corporate income.
   c. Tax havens are jurisdictions that tend to have abnormally low corporate income tax rates.
   d. Tax havens' banking systems are less secretive.

3. Which of the following item(s) might provide an MNC with a tax-planning opportunity as it decides where to locate a foreign operation?
   a. Differences in corporate tax rates across countries.
   b. Differences in local tax rates across countries.
   c. Whether a country offers a tax holiday.
   d. All of the above.

4. Why might companies have an incentive to finance their foreign operations with as much debt as possible?
   a. Interest payments are generally tax deductible.
   b. Withholding rates are lower for dividends.
   c. Withholding rates are lower for interest.
   d. Both (a) and (c).

5. Kerry is a U.S. citizen residing in Portugal. Kerry receives some investment income from Spain. Why might Kerry be expected to pay taxes on the investment income to the United States?
   a. The United States taxes its citizens on their worldwide income.
   b. The United States taxes its citizens on the basis of residency.
   c. Portugal requires all of its residents to pay taxes to the United States.
   d. None of the above.

6. Poole Corporation is a U.S. company with a branch in China. Income earned by the Chinese branch is taxed at the Chinese corporate income tax rate of 30 percent and at the rate of 35 percent in the United States. What is this an example of?
   a. Capital-export neutrality.
   b. Double taxation.
   c. A tax treaty.
   d. Taxation on the basis of consumption.

7. What are the two most common methods of eliminating the double taxation of income earned by foreign corporations?
   a. Exempting foreign source income and deducting all foreign taxes paid.
   b. Deducting all foreign taxes paid and providing a foreign tax credit.
   c. Exempting foreign source income and providing a foreign tax credit.
   d. Deducting all foreign taxes paid and tax havens.

8. Jordan Inc., a U.S. company, is required to translate the foreign income generated by its foreign operation. To determine U.S. taxable income, what must Jordan use to translate the income of its foreign branch into U.S. dollars?
   a. The exchange rate at the end of the year.
   b. The average exchange rate for the year.
   c. The exchange rate at the beginning of the year.
   d. The previous year's ending exchange rate.

9. Bush Inc. has total income of $500,000. Bush's Polish branch has foreign source income of $200,000 and paid taxes of $60,000 to the Polish government. The U.S. corporate tax rate is 35 percent. What is Bush's overall foreign tax credit limitation?
   a. $70,000.
   b. $175,000.
   c. $150,000.
   d. $60,000.

Questions 10, 11, and 12 are based on the following information:

Information for Year 1, Year 2, and Year 3 for the Dominican branch of Powell Corporation is presented in the following table. The corporate tax rate in the Dominican Republic in Year 1 was 25 percent. In Year 2, the Dominican Republic increased its corporate income tax rate to 29 percent. In Year 3, the Dominican Republic increased its corporate tax rate to 36 percent. The U.S. corporate tax rate in each year is 35 percent.

	Year 1	Year 2	Year 3
Foreign source income	$75,000	$100,000	$100,000
Foreign taxes paid	18,750	29,000	36,000
U.S. tax before FTC	26,250	35,000	35,000

10. For Year 1, Year 2, and Year 3, what is the foreign tax credit allowed in the United States?
    a. $7,500, $6,000, and $0.
    b. $18,750, $29,000, and $36,000.
    c. $75,000, $100,000, and $100,000.
    d. $18,750, $29,000, and $35,000.

11. For Year 3, what is the net U.S. tax liability?
    a. $35,000.
    b. $0.
    c. $1,000.
    d. $6,000.

12. In Year 3, how much excess foreign tax credit can Powell carry back?
    a. $7,500.
    b. $6,000.
    c. $1,000.
    d. $0.

13. Bay City Rollers Inc., a U.S. company, has a branch located in the United Kingdom and another in Ireland. The foreign source income from the UK branch is $150,000, and the foreign source income from the Irish branch is $225,000. The corporate tax rates in the United Kingdom, Ireland, and the United States are 30 percent, 24 percent, and 35 percent, respectively.

    Required:
    Determine Bay City Rollers' (*a*) U.S. foreign tax credit and (*b*) net U.S. tax liability related to these foreign sources of income.

Problems 14 and 15 are based on the following information:

Yankee Fish n' Chips, a U.S.-based company, establishes an operation in Great Britain in January of Year 1, when the exchange rate is US$1.50 per British pound (£). During Year 1, the British branch generates £5,000,000 of pretax income. On October 15, Year 1, £2,000,000 is repatriated to Yankee and converted into U.S. dollars. Assume the effective income tax rate in Great Britain is 30 percent. Taxes were paid in Great Britain on December 31, Year 1. Relevant exchange rates for Year 1 are provided below (US$ per £):

January 1	1.50
Average 30	1.45
October 15	1.35
December 31	1.30

Assume a U.S. tax rate of 35 percent.

14. Assume that Yankee's operation in Great Britain is registered with the British government as a branch.

    Required:
    Determine the amount of U.S. taxable income, U.S. foreign tax credit, and net U.S. tax liability related to the British branch (all in U.S. dollars).

15. Assume that Yankee's operation in Great Britain is incorporated as a subsidiary.

    Required:
    Determine the amount of U.S. taxable income, U.S. foreign tax credit, and net U.S. tax liability related to the British subsidiary (all in U.S. dollars).

16. Mama Corporation (a U.S. taxpayer) has a wholly owned sales subsidiary in the Bahamas (Bahamamama Ltd.) that purchases finished goods from its U.S. parent and sells those goods to customers throughout the Caribbean basin. In the most recent year, Bahamamama generated income of $100,000 and distributed 50 percent of that amount to Mama Corporation as a dividend. There are no income or withholding taxes in the Bahamas.

    Required:
    a. Determine the amount of income taxable in the United States assuming that Bahamamama makes 20 percent of its sales in the Bahamas and 80 percent in other countries.
    b. Determine the amount of income taxable in the United States assuming that Bahamamama makes 40 percent of its sales in the Bahamas and 60 percent in other countries.

17. Lionais Company has a foreign branch that earns income before income taxes of 500,000 currency units (CU). Income taxes paid to the foreign government are CU 150,000 (30 percent). Sales and other taxes paid to the foreign government are CU 50,000. Lionais Company must include the CU 500,000 of foreign branch income in determining its home country taxable income. In determining its taxable income, Lionais can choose between taking a deduction for all foreign taxes paid or a credit only for foreign income taxes paid. The corporate income tax rate in Lionais' home country is 40 percent.

    Required:
    Determine whether Lionais would be better off taking a deduction or credit for foreign taxes paid.

18. Avioco Limited has two branches located in Hong Kong and Singapore, each of which manufactures goods primarily for export to countries in the Asia-Pacific region. The corporate income tax rate in Avioco's home country is 20 percent. The amount of income before taxes and the actual tax paid (stated in terms of Avioco's home currency) are as follows:

	Hong Kong Branch	Singapore Branch
Income before taxes	100,000	100,000
Actual tax paid	17,500 (17.5%)	22,000 (22%)

    Required:
    Determine the amount of foreign tax credit Avioco will be allowed to take in determining its home country income tax liability.

19. Daisan Company is in the process of deciding where to establish a European manufacturing operation: France, Spain, or Sweden. Daisan's home country does not have a tax treaty with any of these countries. Regardless of location, the operation is expected to generate pretax income of 1 million euros annually. The operation will distribute 100 percent of its after-tax income to Daisan Company as a dividend each year.

    Required:
    a. Using the information on effective tax rates and withholding tax rates provided in Exhibits 10.1 and 10.3, determine the net amount of dividend that

Daisan would receive annually from an investment in each of these three countries.

b. With maximizing after-tax dividends as the sole criterion, in which of the three countries should Daisan locate its European operation?

20. Pendleton Company (a U.S. taxpayer) is a highly diversified company with wholly owned subsidiaries located in Singapore and Japan. The Singapore operation manufactures electric generators that are sold in the Asian market. It generated pretax income of $200,000 in the current year. The Japanese subsidiary is a finance company that provides loans to businesses for financing purchases of electric generators produced by its sister company in Singapore. The Japanese subsidiary generated pretax income of $100,000 in the current year. Both companies distribute 100 percent of after-tax income to Pendleton Company as a dividend each year. Effective income tax rates and withholding rates are provided in Exhibits 10.1, 10.3, and 10.4.

Required:
a. Determine the amount of foreign tax credit allowed by the United States in the current year, and the amount of excess foreign tax credit, if any.
b. Repeat requirement (*a*) assuming that, rather than financing purchases of electric generators, the Japanese subsidiary purchases electric generators from its Singapore sister company and distributes them in Japan.

21. Eastwood Company (a U.S.-based company) has subsidiaries in three countries: X, Y, and Z. All three subsidiaries manufacture and sell products in their host country. Corporate income tax rates in these three countries over the most recent three-year period are as follows:

Country	Year 1	Year 2	Year 3
X	50%	50%	40%
Y	25	25	25
Z	36	30	30

None of these countries imposes a withholding tax on dividends distributed to a foreign parent company. The U.S. corporate income tax rate over this period was 35 percent.

Pretax income earned by each subsidiary and the percentage of after-tax income paid to Eastwood over the most recent three-year period are as follows:

	Year 1	Year 2	Year 3
Subsidiary X			
Pretax income	$100,000	$100,000	$100,000
Dividend (% of after-tax income) ...	100%	50%	50%
Subsidiary Y			
Pretax income	$150,000	$150,000	$150,000
Dividend (% of after-tax income) ...	50%	50%	50%
Subsidiary Z			
Pretax income	$200,000	$200,000	$200,000
Dividend (% of after-tax income) ...	40%	40%	100%

Required:
a. Determine the amount of foreign source income Eastwood will include in its U.S. tax return in each of the three years.
b. Determine the amount of foreign tax credit Eastwood will be allowed to take in determining its U.S. tax liability in each of the three years.
c. Determine the amount of excess foreign tax credit, if any, Eastwood will have in each of the three years.
d. Determine Eastwood's net U.S. tax liability in each of the three years.

22. Heraklion Company (a U.S.-based company) is considering making an equity investment in an Australian manufacturing operation. The total amount of capital, in Australian dollars (A$), that Heraklion would need to invest is A$1,000,000. Heraklion has three alternatives for financing this investment:

- 100 percent equity.
- 80 percent equity and 20 percent long-term loan from Heraklion (5 percent interest rate).
- 50 percent equity and 50 percent long-term loan from Heraklion (5 percent interest rate).

Heraklion estimates that the Australian operation will generate A$200,000 of income before interest and taxes in its first year of operations. The operation will pay 100 percent of its net income to Heraklion as a dividend each year.

Required:
a. Assume there is no tax treaty between the United States and Australia. Using the information on Australian tax rates found in Exhibit 10.1 and Exhibit 10.3, determine the total amount of taxes that will be paid in Australia under each of the three financing alternatives. Which alternative results in the least amount of taxes being paid in Australia?
b. The United States/Australia tax treaty provides reduced withholding tax rates on certain payments made to a foreign parent company. Use the information on Australian tax rates found in Exhibit 10.1 and Exhibit 10.4 to determine the total amount of taxes that will be paid in Australia under each of the three financing alternatives. Which alternative results in the least amount of taxes being paid in Australia?

23. The corporate income tax rates in two countries, A and B, are 40 percent and 25 percent, respectively. Additionally, both countries impose a 30 percent withholding tax on dividends paid to foreign investors. However, a bilateral tax treaty between A and B reduces the withholding tax to 10 percent if the dividend is paid to an investor that owns more than 50 percent of the paying company's stock (parent). Both A and B use a worldwide approach to taxation but allow taxpayers take a foreign tax credit for income taxes paid on foreign earned income. The credit is limited to the amount of tax that would have been paid in the domestic country on that income. Both countries use the same currency, so foreign currency translation is not required.

Part 1.

Albemarle Company is headquartered in country A and has a wholly owned subsidiary in country B. In the current year, Albemarle's foreign subsidiary generated before tax income of 100,000 and remitted 50 percent of its net income to the parent company as a dividend.

Required:

a. Determine the amount of taxes paid in country A.

b. Determine the amount of taxes paid in country B.

Part 2.

Bostwick Company is headquartered in country B and has a wholly owned subsidiary in country A. In the current year, Bostwick's foreign subsidiary generated before tax income of 100,000 and remitted 50 percent of its net income to the parent company as a dividend.

Required:

a. Determine the amount of taxes paid in country A.

b. Determine the amount of taxes paid in country B.

24. Intec Corporation (a U.S.-based company) has a wholly owned subsidiary located in Shanghai, China that generated income before tax of 500,000 Chinese renminbi (RMB) in the current year. The Chinese subsidiary paid Chinese income taxes at the rate of 33 percent evenly throughout the year, and paid dividends of RMB 200,000 to Intec on October 1. Assume there is no withholding tax on dividends. The following exchange rates for the current year apply:

	US$ per RMB
January 1	$0.125
Average for the year	0.120
October 1	0.118
December 31	0.115

Required:

Determine the following related to the income earned by Intec's Chinese subsidiary:

a. The amount of U.S. taxable income in U.S. dollars.

b. The amount of foreign tax credited allowed in the United States.

c. The amount of net U.S. tax liability.

25. Use the information provided in problem 25. Now assume that Intec Corporation's Chinese operation is organized as a branch, and repatriates after tax profits of RMB 200,000 to Intec on October 1.

Required:

Determine the following related to the income earned by Intec's Chinese branch:

a. The amount of U.S. taxable income in U.S. dollars.

b. The amount of foreign tax credited allowed in the United States.

c. The amount of net U.S. tax liability.

26. Brown Corporation has an affiliate in France (Brun SA) that sells products manufactured at Brown's factory in Columbia, South Carolina. In the current year, Brun SA earned €10 million before tax. Assume that the effective tax rate Brun SA pays in France is 30 percent. French taxes were paid at the end of the year. Cash distributions to Brown Company were made on July 1 and December 31 in the amount of €1 million each. Relevant exchange rates for the

current year are as follows:

January 1	€1 = $1.025
July 1	€1 = $0.900
Average	€1 = $0.925
December 31	€1 = $0.980

Required:
a. Assuming that Brun SA is organized as a branch, determine the amount of branch profits in U.S. dollars that Brown Corporation must include in its U.S. taxable income and the available tax credit.
b. Assuming that Brun SA is organized as a subsidiary determine the amount of foreign source income in U.S. dollars that Brown Corporation must include in its U.S. taxable income and the available tax credit.

The following exercises and problems relate to the appendix to this chapter:

27. Which of the following items is not a tax benefit provided by Congress to U.S. citizens working abroad?
    a. Foreign earned income exclusion.
    b. Foreign tax credit.
    c. Dividend income exclusion.
    d. Foreign housing exclusion.

28. The exchange rate between the U.S. dollar (US$) and Hong Kong dollar (HK$) remained constant at HK$8.00 = US$1.00 throughout 2002. Horace Gardner (a U.S. citizen) lives and works in Hong Kong. In 2002, Gardner earned income in Hong Kong of HK$960,000, and paid taxes to the local government at the rate of 15 percent. Gardner qualifies for the foreign earned income exclusion.

    Required:
    a. Determine the amount of foreign earned income Horace Gardner included in his calculation of U.S. taxable income for the year 2002.
    b. Determine the amount of foreign tax credit Horace Gardner was allowed to take in determining his U.S. tax liability for the year 2002.
    c. Assuming Horace Gardner has a marginal U.S. tax rate of 28 percent, determine the amount of U.S. income taxes he paid on his foreign earned income in the year 2002.

29. The exchange rate between the U.S. dollar (US$) and the euro (€) remained constant at €1.00 = US$1.00 throughout 2002. Elizabeth Welch (a U.S. citizen) lives and works in France. In 2002, she earned income in France of €100,000, and paid taxes to the local government at the rate of 40 percent. Welch qualifies for the foreign earned income exclusion.

    Required:
    a. Determine the amount of foreign earned income Elizabeth Welch included in her calculation of U.S. taxable income for the year 2002.
    b. Determine the amount of foreign tax credit Elizabeth Welch was allowed to take in determining her U.S. tax liability for the year 2002.
    c. Assuming Elizabeth Welch has a marginal U.S. tax rate of 28 percent, determine the amount of U.S. income taxes she paid on her foreign earned income in the year 2002.

Case 10-1

U.S. International Corporation

U.S. International Corporation (USIC), a U.S. taxpayer, has investments in foreign entities A–G. Relevant information for these entities for the fiscal year 2006 appears in the following table:

Entity	Country	Percent Owned	Activity	Income before Tax ($ millions)	Income Tax Rate	Withholding Tax Rate	Net Amount Received by Parent ($ millions)
USIC	United States	—	Manufacturing	$10	35%	—	—
A	Argentina	100%	Manufacturing	$1	35	10%	$0.2
B	Brazil	100	Manufacturing	$2	34	15	$2.5*
C	Canada	100	Manufacturing	$3	36	5	$1.0
D	Hong Kong	100	Investment	$2	17.5	0	$1.5
E	Liechtenstein	100	Marketing	$3	10	4	$0.0
F	Japan	51	Manufacturing	$2	42	10	$0.5
G	New Zealand	60	Insurance	$4	33	15	$1.0

*Some dividends were paid out of beginning-of-year retained earnings.

Additional Information

1. USIC's $10 million income before tax is derived from the production and sale of products in the United States.
2. Each entity is legally incorporated in its host country other than entity A, which is registered with the Argentinian government as a branch.
3. Entities A, B, C, and F produce and market products in their home countries.
4. Entity D makes passive investments in stocks and bonds in the Hong Kong financial markets. Income is derived solely from dividends and interest.
5. Entity E markets goods purchased from (manufactured by) USIC. Of E's sales, 95 percent are made in Austria, Germany, and Switzerland, and 5 percent are made in Liechtenstein.
6. Entity G operates in the casualty and property insurance industry in New Zealand. It insures properties located in New Zealand only.

Required:

1. Determine the following:
   a. The amount of U.S. taxable income for each entity A–G.
   b. The foreign tax credit allowed in the United States, first by basket and then in total.
   c. The net U.S. tax liability.
   d. Any excess foreign tax credits (identify by basket).
2. Repeat the steps in (1), assuming that the information in this case pertains to fiscal year 2007, when the number of FTC baskets is reduced from nine to two.

References

Deloitte and Touche. "OECD Publishes List of Offending Tax Regimes." *The Global Tax Executive*, July/August 2000.

Deloitte Touche Tohmatsu. "New Tax Incentives for Foreign Investors." *World Tax News*, March 2000.

Doernberg, Richard L. *International Taxation: In a Nutshell*, 4th ed. St. Paul, MN: West, 1999.

Ernst & Young. "New Tax Holiday Rules." *China Update*, July 2003, pp. 1–3.

———. *Worldwide Corporate Tax Guide*, 2002, available at www.ey.com.

European Commission. *VAT Rates Applied in the Member States of the European Community: Situation at 1 May 2003*, available at www.eurounion.org.

KPMG. "Corporate Tax Rate Survey—January 2004," available at www.us.kpmg.com.

Organization for Economic Cooperation and Development. "Toward Global Tax Cooperation: Progress in Identifying and Eliminating Harmful Tax Practices," 2000, available at www.oecd.org.

———. *The OECD's Project on Harmful Tax Practices: The 2004 Progress Report*. Paris: OECD, 2004, available at www.oecd.org.

PricewaterhouseCoopers. *Corporate Taxes—Worldwide Summaries, 1999–2000*, 2001, New York: John Wiley & Sons, 2001.

U.S. Internal Revenue Service. Publication 901, "U.S. Tax Treaties," available at www.irs.gov.

Chapter **Eleven**

International Transfer Pricing

Learning Objectives

After reading this chapter, you should be able to

- Describe the importance of transfer pricing in achieving goal congruence in decentralized organizations.
- Explain how the objectives of performance evaluation and cost minimization can conflict in determining international transfer prices.
- Show how discretionary transfer pricing can be used to achieve specific cost minimization objectives.
- Describe governments' reaction to the use of discretionary transfer pricing by multinational companies.
- Discuss the transfer pricing methods used in sales of tangible property.
- Explain how advance pricing agreements can be used to create certainty in transfer pricing.
- Describe worldwide efforts to enforce transfer pricing regulations.

INTRODUCTION

Transfer pricing refers to the determination of the price at which transactions between related parties will be carried out. Transfers can be from a subsidiary to its parent (upstream), from the parent to a subsidiary (downstream), or from one subsidiary to another of the same parent. Transfers between related parties are also known as *intercompany transactions*. Intercompany transactions represent a significant portion of international trade. In 2003, intercompany transactions comprised 42 percent of U.S. total goods trade: $594 billion (48 percent) of the $1.24 trillion in U.S. imports, and $233 billion (32 percent) of the $728 billion in U.S. exports.[1] There is a wide range of types of intercompany transactions, each of which has a price associated with it. A list is provided in Exhibit 11.1. The basic question that must be addressed is, At what price should intercompany transfers be made? This chapter focuses on international transfers, that is, intercompany transactions that cross national borders.

---

[1] "U.S. Goods Trade: Imports and Exports by Related Parties, 2003," *U.S. Department of Commerce News,* April 14, 2004, p. 1.

EXHIBIT 11.1
Types of Intercompany Transactions and Their Associated Price

Transaction	Price
Sale of tangible property (e.g., raw materials, finished goods, equipment, buildings)	Sales price
Use of tangible property (leases) (e.g., land, buildings)	Rental or lease payment
Use of intangible property (e.g., patents, trademarks, copyrights)	Royalty, licensing fee
Intercompany services (e.g., research and development, management assistance)	Service charge, management fee
Intercompany loans	Interest rate

Two factors heavily influence the manner in which international transfer prices are determined. The first factor is the objective that headquarters management wishes to achieve through its transfer pricing practices. One possible objective relates to management control and performance evaluation. Another objective relates to the minimization of one or more types of costs. These two types of objectives often conflict.

The second factor affecting international transfer pricing is the law that exists in most countries governing the manner in which intercompany transactions crossing their borders may be priced. These laws were established to make sure that multinational corporations (MNCs) are not able to avoid paying their fair share of taxes, import duties, and so on by virtue of the fact that they operate in multiple jurisdictions. In establishing international transfer prices, MNCs often must walk a fine line between achieving corporate objectives and complying with applicable rules and regulations. In a recent survey, 90 percent of respondents identified transfer pricing as the most important international tax issue they face.[2]

We begin this chapter with a discussion of management accounting theory with respect to transfer pricing. We then describe various objectives that MNCs might wish to achieve through discretionary transfer pricing. Much of this chapter focuses on government response to MNCs' discretionary transfer pricing practices, emphasizing the transfer pricing regulations in the United States.

DECENTRALIZATION AND GOAL CONGRUENCE

Business enterprises often are organized by *division*. A division may be a profit center, responsible for revenues and operating expenses, or an investment center, responsible also for assets. In a company organized by division, top managers delegate or decentralize authority and responsibility to division managers. *Decentralization* has many advantages:

- Allowing local managers to respond quickly to a changing environment.
- Dividing large, complex problems into manageable pieces.
- Motivating local managers who otherwise will be frustrated if asked only to implement the decisions of others.[3]

---

[2] Ernst & Young, *Transfer Pricing 2003 Global Survey,* p. 7.

[3] Michael W. Maher, Clyde P. Stickney, and Roman L. Weil, *Managerial Accounting,* 8th ed. South-Western, 2004), p. 484.

However, decentralization is not without its potential disadvantages. The most important pitfall is that local managers who have been granted decision-making authority may make decisions that are in their self-interest but detrimental to the company as a whole. The corporate accounting and control system should be designed in such a way that it provides incentives for local managers to make decisions that are consistent with corporate goals. This is known as *goal congruence.* The system used for evaluating the performance of decentralized managers is an important component in achieving goal congruence.

The price at which an intercompany transfer is made determines the level of revenue generated by the seller, becomes a cost for the buyer, and therefore affects the operating profit and performance measurement of both related parties. Appropriate transfer prices can ensure that each division or subsidiary's profit accurately reflects its contribution to overall company profits, thus providing a basis for efficient allocation of resources. To achieve this, transfer prices should motivate local managers to make decisions that enhance corporate performance, while at the same time providing a basis for measuring, evaluating, and rewarding local manager performance in a way that managers perceive as fair.[4] If this does not happen (that is, if goal congruence is not achieved), then the potential benefits of decentralization can be lost.

Even in a purely domestic context, determining a transfer pricing policy is a complex matter for multidivision organizations, which often try to achieve several objectives through such policies. For example, they may try to use transfer pricing to ensure that it is consistent with the criteria used for performance evaluation, motivate divisional managers, achieve goal congruence, and help manage cash flows. For MNCs, there are additional factors that influence international transfer pricing policy.

TRANSFER PRICING METHODS

The methods used in setting transfer prices in an international context are essentially the same as those used in a purely domestic context. The following three methods are commonly used:

1. *Cost-based transfer price.* The transfer price is based on the cost to produce a good or service. Cost can be determined as variable production cost, variable plus fixed production cost, or full cost, based on either actual or budgeted amounts (standard costs). The transfer price often includes a profit margin for the seller (a "cost-plus" price). Cost-based systems are simple to use, but there are at least two problems associated with them. The first problem relates to the issue of which measure of cost to use. The other problem is that inefficiencies in one unit may be transferred to other units, as there is no incentive for selling divisions to control costs. The use of standard, rather than actual, costs alleviates this problem.

2. *Market-based transfer price.* The transfer price charged a related party is either based on the price that would be charged to an unrelated customer or determined by reference to sales of similar products or services by other companies to

---

[4] Robert G. Eccles, *The Transfer Pricing Problem: A Theory for Practice* (Lexington, MA: Lexington Books, 1985), p. 8.

unrelated parties. Market-based systems avoid the problem associated with cost-based systems of transferring the inefficiencies of one division or subsidiary to others. They help ensure divisional autonomy and provide a good basis for evaluating subsidiary performance. However, market-based pricing systems also have problems. The efficient working of a market-based system depends on the existence of competitive markets and dependable market quotations. For certain items, such as unfinished products, there may not be any buyers outside the organization and hence no external market price.

3. *Negotiated price.* The transfer price is the result of negotiation between buyer and seller and may be unrelated to either cost or market value. A negotiated pricing system can be useful, as it allows subsidiary managers the freedom to bargain with one another, thereby preserving the autonomy of subsidiary managers. However, for this system to work efficiently, it is important that there are external markets for the items being transferred so that the negotiating parties can have objective information as the basis for negotiation. One disadvantage of negotiated pricing is that negotiation can take a long time, particularly if the process deteriorates and the parties involved become more interested in winning arguments than in considering the issues from the corporate perspective. Another disadvantage is that the price agreed on and therefore a manager's measure of performance may be a function more of a manager's ability to negotiate than of his or her ability to control costs and generate profit.

Management accounting theory suggests that different pricing methods are appropriate in different situations. Market-based transfer prices lead to optimal decisions when (1) the market for the product is perfectly competitive, (2) interdependencies between the related parties are minimal, and (3) there is no advantage or disadvantage to buying and selling the product internally rather than externally.[5] Prices based on full cost can approximate market-based prices when the determination of market price is not feasible. Prices that have been negotiated by buyer and seller rather than being mandated by upper management have the advantage of allowing the related parties to maintain their decentralized authority.

A 1990 survey of Fortune 500 companies in the United States found that 41 percent of respondent companies relied on cost-based methods in determining international transfer prices, 46 percent used market-based methods, and 13 percent allowed transfer prices to be determined through negotiation.[6] The most widely used approach was full production cost plus a markup. Slightly less than half of the respondents reported using more than one method to determine transfer prices.

OBJECTIVES OF INTERNATIONAL TRANSFER PRICING

Broadly speaking, there are two possible objectives to consider in determining the appropriate price at which an intercompany transfer that crosses national borders should be made: (1) performance evaluation and (2) cost minimization.

[5] Charles T. Horngren, George Foster, and Srikant M. Datar, *Cost Accounting: A Managerial Emphasis,* 10th ed. (Upper Saddle River, NJ: Prentice-Hall, 2000), p. 796.

[6] Roger Y. W. Tang, "Transfer Pricing in the 1990s," *Management Accounting,* February 1992, pp. 22–26.

Performance Evaluation

To fairly evaluate the performance of both parties to an intercompany transaction, the transfer should be made at a price acceptable to both parties. An acceptable price could be determined by reference to outside market prices (e.g., the price that would be paid to an outside supplier for a component part), or it could be determined by allowing the two parties to the transaction to negotiate a price. Policies for establishing prices for domestic transfers generally should be based on an objective of generating reasonable measures for evaluating performance; otherwise, dysfunctional manager behavior can occur and goal congruence does not exist. For example, forcing the manager of one operating unit to purchase parts from a related operating unit at a price that exceeds the external market price will probably result in an unhappy manager. As a result of the additional cost, the unit's profit will be less than it otherwise would be, perhaps less than budgeted, and the manager's salary increase and annual bonus may be adversely affected. In addition, as upper management makes corporate resource allocation decisions, fewer resources may be allocated to this unit because of its lower reported profitability.

Assume that Alpha Company (a manufacturer) and Beta Company (a retailer) are both subsidiaries of Parent Company, located in the United States. Alpha produces DVD players at a cost of $100 each and sells them both to Beta and to unrelated customers. Beta purchases DVD players from Alpha and from unrelated suppliers and sells them for $160 each. The total gross profit earned by both producer and retailer is $60 per DVD player.

Alpha Company can sell DVD players to unrelated customers for $127.50 per unit, and Beta Company can purchase DVD players from unrelated suppliers at $132.50. The manager of Alpha should be happy selling DVD players to Beta for $127.50 per unit or more, and the manager of Beta should be happy purchasing DVD players from Alpha for $132.50 per unit or less. A transfer price somewhere between $127.50 and $132.50 per unit would be acceptable to both managers, as well as to Parent Company. Assuming that a transfer price of $130.00 per unit is agreed on by the managers of Alpha and Beta, the impact on income for Alpha Company, Beta Company, and Parent Company (after eliminating the intercompany transaction) is as follows:

	Alpha	Beta	Parent
Sales	$130.00	$160.00	$160.00
Cost of goods sold . . .	100.00	130.00	100.00
Gross profit	$ 30.00	$ 30.00	$ 60.00
Income tax effect	10.50 (35%)	10.50 (35%)	21.00
After-tax profit	$ 19.50	$ 19.50	$ 39.00

Now assume that Alpha Company is located in Taiwan and Beta Company is located in the United States. Because the income tax rate in Taiwan is only 25 percent, compared with a U.S. income tax rate of 35 percent, Parent Company would like as much of the $60.00 gross profit to be earned by Alpha as possible. Rather than allowing the two managers to negotiate a price based on external market values, assume that Parent Company intervenes and establishes a "discretionary" transfer price of $150.00 per unit.[7] Given this price, the impact of the intercompany transaction on income for the three companies is as follows:

	Alpha	Beta	Parent
Sales	$150.00	$160.00	$160.00
Cost of goods sold	100.00	150.00	100.00
Gross profit	$ 50.00	$ 10.00	$ 60.00
Income tax effect	12.50 (25%)	3.50 (35%)	16.00
After-tax profit	$ 37.50	$ 6.50	$ 44.00

The chief executive officer of Parent Company is pleased with this result, because consolidated income for Parent Company increases by $5.00 per unit, as will cash flow when Alpha Company and Beta Company remit their after-tax profits to Parent Company as dividends. The president of Alpha Company is also happy with this transfer price. As is true for all managers in the organization, a portion of the president's compensation is linked to profit, and this use of discretionary transfer pricing will result in a nice bonus for her at year-end. However, the president of Beta Company is less than pleased with this situation. His profit is less than if he were allowed to purchase from unrelated suppliers. He doubts he will receive a bonus for the year, and he is beginning to think about seeking employment elsewhere. Moreover, Beta Company's profit clearly is understated, which could lead top managers to make erroneous decisions with respect to Beta.

Cost Minimization

When intercompany transactions cross national borders, differences between countries might lead an MNC to attempt to achieve certain cost-minimization objectives through the use of discretionary transfer prices mandated by headquarters.

The most well-known use of discretionary transfer pricing is to minimize worldwide income taxes by recording profits in lower-tax countries. As illustrated in the preceding example, this objective can be achieved by establishing an arbitrarily high price when transferring to a higher-tax country. Conversely, this objective is also met by selling at a low price when transferring to a lower-tax country.

Conflicting Objectives

There is an inherent conflict between the performance evaluation and cost-minimization objectives of transfer pricing. To minimize costs, top managers must *dictate* a discretionary transfer price. By definition, this is not a price that has been negotiated by the two managers who are party to a transaction, nor is it necessarily based on external market prices or production costs. The benefits of decentralization can evaporate when headquarters managers assume the responsibility for determining transfer prices.

One way that companies deal with this conflict is through *dual pricing.* The official records for tax and financial reporting are based on the cost-minimizing transfer prices. When it comes time to evaluate performance, however, the actual records are adjusted to reflect prices acceptable to both parties to the transaction factoring out the effect of discretionary transfer prices. Actual transfers are invoiced so as to minimize costs, but evaluation of performance is based on simulated prices.

---

[7] The price is "discretionary" in the sense that it is not based on market value, cost, or negotiation but has been determined at Parent's discretion to reduce income taxes.

Other Cost-Minimization Objectives

In addition to the objective of minimizing worldwide income taxes, a number of other objectives can be achieved through the use of discretionary transfer prices for international transactions.

Avoidance of Withholding Taxes

A parent company might want to avoid receiving cash payments from its foreign subsidiaries in the form of dividends, interest, and royalties on which withholding taxes will be paid to the foreign government. Instead, cash can be transferred in the form of sales price for goods and services provided the foreign subsidiary by its parent or other affiliates. There is no withholding tax on payments for purchases of goods and services. The higher the price charged the foreign subsidiary, the more cash can be extracted from the foreign country without incurring withholding tax. For example, assume that the European subsidiary of Kerr Corporation purchases finished goods from its foreign parent at a price of €100 per unit; sells those goods in the local market at a price of €130 per unit; and remits 100 percent of its profit to the parent company, upon which it pays a 30 percent dividend withholding tax. Ignoring income taxes, the total cash flow received by Kerr Corporation from its European subsidiary is €121 per unit; €100 from the sale of finished goods and €21 (€30 − [€30 × 30%]) in the form of dividends after withholding tax. If Kerr Corporation were to raise the selling price to its European subsidiary to €120 per unit, the total cash flow it would receive would increase to €127 per unit; €120 in the form of transfer price plus €7 (€10 − [€10 × 30%]) in net dividends. Raising the transfer price even further to €130 per unit results in cash flow to Kerr Corporation of €130 per unit.

Selling goods and services to a foreign subsidiary (downstream sale) at a higher price reduces the amount of profit earned by the foreign subsidiary that will be subject to a dividend withholding tax. Sales of goods and services by the foreign subsidiary to its parent (upstream sale) at a lower price will achieve the same objective.

Minimization of Import Duties (Tariffs)

Countries generally assess tariffs on the value (based on invoice prices) of goods being imported into the country. These are known as ad valorem import duties. One way to reduce ad valorem import duties is to transfer goods to a foreign operation at lower prices.

Circumvent Profit Repatriation Restrictions

Some countries restrict the amount of profit that can be paid as a dividend to a foreign parent company. This is known as a profit repatriation restriction. A company might be restricted to paying a dividend equal to or less than a certain percentage of annual profit or a certain percentage of capital contributed to the company by its parent. When such restrictions exist, the parent can get around the restriction and remove "profit" indirectly by setting high transfer prices on goods and services provided the foreign operation by the parent and other affiliates. This strategy is consistent with the objective of avoiding withholding taxes.

Protect Cash Flows from Currency Devaluation

In many cases, some amount of the net cash flow generated by a subsidiary in a foreign country will be moved out of that country, if for no other reason than to distribute it as a dividend to stockholders of the parent company. As the foreign currency devalues, the parent currency value of any foreign currency cash decreases.

For operations located in countries whose currency is prone to devaluation, the parent may want to accelerate removing cash out of that country before more devaluation occurs. One method for moving more cash out of a country is to set high transfer prices for goods and services provided the foreign operation by the parent and other related companies.

Improve Competitive Position of Foreign Operation

MNCs also are able to use international transfer pricing to maintain competitiveness in international markets and to penetrate new foreign markets. To penetrate a new market, a parent company might establish a sales subsidiary in a foreign country. To capture market share, the foreign operation must compete aggressively on price, providing its customers with significant discounts. To ensure that the new operation is profitable, while at the same expecting it to compete on price, the parent company can sell finished goods to its foreign sales subsidiary at low prices. In effect, the parent company absorbs the discount.

The parent company might want to improve the credit status of a foreign operation so that it can obtain local financing at lower interest rates. This generally involves improving the balance sheet by increasing assets and retained earnings. This objective can be achieved by setting low transfer prices for inbound goods to the foreign operation and high transfer prices for outbound goods from the foreign operation, thereby improving profit and cash flow.

Exhibit 11.2 summarizes the transfer price (high or low) needed to achieve various cost-minimization objectives. High transfer prices can be used to (1) minimize worldwide income taxes when transferring to a higher-tax country, (2) reduce withholding taxes (downstream sales), (3) circumvent repatriation restrictions, and (4) protect foreign currency cash from devaluation. However, low transfer prices are necessary to (1) minimize worldwide income taxes when transferring to a lower-tax country, (2) reduce withholding taxes (upstream sales), (3) minimize import duties, and (4) improve the competitive position of a foreign operation.

It should be noted that these different cost-minimization objectives might conflict with one another. For example, charging a higher transfer price to a foreign affiliate to reduce the amount of withholding taxes paid to the foreign government will result in a higher amount of import duties paid to the foreign government. Companies can employ linear programming techniques to determine the optimum transfer price when two or more cost-minimization objectives exist. Electronic spreadsheets also can be used to conduct sensitivity analysis,

EXHIBIT 11.2
Cost Minimization Objectives and Transfer Prices

Objective	Transfer Pricing Rule
Minimize income taxes	
Transferring to a country with higher tax rate	High price
Transferring to a country with lower tax rate	Low price
Minimize withholding taxes	
Downstream transfer	High price
Upstream transfer	Low price
Minimize import duties	Low price
Protect foreign cash flows from currency devaluation	High price
Avoid repatriation restrictions	High price
Improve competitive position of foreign operation	Low price

examining the impact different transfer prices would have on consolidated profit and cash flows.

Survey Results

A survey conducted in the late 1970s found the following to be the top five factors influencing the international transfer pricing policies of U.S. MNCs:[8]

1. Overall profit to the company.
2. Repatriation restrictions on profits and dividends.
3. Competitive position of subsidiaries in foreign countries.
4. Tax and tax legislation differentials between countries.
5. Performance evaluation.

For Japanese MNCs, the top five factors were the following:

1. Overall profit to the company.
2. Competitive position of subsidiaries in foreign countries.
3. Foreign currency devaluation.
4. Repatriation restrictions on profits and dividends.
5. Performance evaluation.

Differences in income tax rates between countries ranked only 14th for the Japanese MNCs surveyed.

In an updated survey of U.S. MNCs published in 1992, the top four factors remained the same.[9] Import duty rates were the fifth most important factor influencing international transfer pricing policies. Performance evaluation dropped to the 10th position.

GOVERNMENT REACTIONS

National tax authorities are aware of the potential for MNCs to use discretionary transfer pricing to avoid paying income taxes, import duties, and so on. Most countries have guidelines regarding what will be considered an acceptable transfer price for tax purposes. Across countries, these guidelines can conflict, creating the possibility of double taxation when a price accepted by one country is disallowed by another.

The Organisation for Economic Cooperation and Development (OECD) developed transfer pricing guidelines in 1979 that have been supplemented or amended several times since then. The basic rule is that transfers must be made at arm's-length prices. The idea is that OECD member countries would adopt the OECD guidelines and thereby avoid conflicts. The OECD rules are only a model and do not have the force of law in any country. However, most developed countries have transfer pricing rules generally based on OECD guidelines with some variations. The next section of this chapter discusses the specific transfer pricing rules adopted in the United States. Although the rules we discuss are specific to the United States, similar rules can be found in many other countries.

---

[8] Roger Y. W. Tang and K. H. Chan, "Environmental Variables of International Transfer Pricing: A Japan–United States Comparison," *Abacus*, 1979, pp. 3–12.

[9] Roger Y. W. Tang, "Transfer Pricing in the 1990s," *Management Accounting*, February 1992, pp. 22–26.

SECTION 482 OF THE U.S. INTERNAL REVENUE CODE

Section 482 of the Internal Revenue Code (IRC) gives the Internal Revenue Service (IRS) the power to audit international transfer prices and adjust a company's tax liability if the price is deemed to be inappropriate. The IRS may audit and adjust transfer prices between companies controlled directly or indirectly by the same taxpayer. Thus, Section 482 applies to both upstream and downstream transfers between a U.S. parent and its foreign subsidiary, between a foreign parent and its U.S. subsidiary, or between the U.S. subsidiary and foreign subsidiary of the same parent. The IRS, of course, is primarily concerned that a proper amount of income is being recorded and taxed in the United States.

Similar to the OECD guidelines, Section 482 requires transactions between commonly controlled entities to be carried out at arm's-length prices. Arm's-length prices are defined as "the prices which would have been agreed upon between unrelated parties engaged in the same or similar transactions under the same or similar conditions in the open market." Because same or similar transactions with unrelated parties often do not exist, determination of an arm's-length price generally will involve reference to comparable transactions under comparable circumstances.

The U.S. Treasury Regulations supplementing Section 482 establish more specific guidelines for determining an arm's-length price. In general, a "best-method rule" requires taxpayers to use the transfer pricing method that under the facts and circumstances provides the most reliable measure of an arm's-length price. There is no hierarchy in application of methods, and no method always will be considered more reliable than others. In determining which method provides the most reliable measure of an arm's-length price, the two primary factors to be considered are the degree of comparability between the intercompany transaction and any comparable uncontrolled transactions, and the quality of the data and assumptions used in the analysis. Determining the degree of comparability between an intercompany transaction and an uncontrolled transaction involves a comparison of the five factors listed in Exhibit 11.3. Each of these factors must be considered in determining the degree of comparability between an intercompany transaction and an uncontrolled transaction and the extent to which adjustments must be made to establish an arm's-length price.

Treasury Regulations establish guidelines for determining an arm's-length price for various kinds of intercompany transactions, including sales of tangible property, licensing of intangible property, intercompany loans, and intercompany services. Although we focus on regulations related to the sale of tangible property because this is the most common type of international intercompany transaction, we also describe regulations related to licensing intangible assets, intercompany loans, and intercompany services.

Sale of Tangible Property

Treasury Regulations require the use of one of five specified methods to determine the arm's-length price in a sale of tangible property (inventory and fixed assets):

1. Comparable uncontrolled price method.
2. Resale price method.
3. Cost-plus method.
4. Comparable profits method.
5. Profit split method.

EXHIBIT 11.3
Factors to Be Considered in Determining the Comparability of an Intercompany Transaction and an Uncontrolled Transaction

Source: U.S. Treasury Regulations, Sec. 1.482-1(d).

1. Functions performed by the various parties in the two transactions, including
   - Research and development.
   - Product design and engineering.
   - Manufacturing, production, and process engineering.
   - Product fabrication, extraction, and assembly.
   - Purchasing and materials management.
   - Marketing and distribution functions, including inventory management, warranty administration, and advertising activities.
   - Transportation and warehousing.
   - Managerial, legal, accounting and finance, credit and collection, training, and personnel management services.

2. Contractual terms that could affect the results of the two transactions, including
   - The form of consideration charged or paid.
   - Sales or purchase volume.
   - The scope and terms of warranties provided.
   - Rights to updates, revisions, and modifications.
   - The duration of relevant license, contract, or other agreement, and termination and negotiation rights.
   - Collateral transactions or ongoing business relationships between the buyer and seller, including arrangements for the provision of ancillary or subsidiary services.
   - Extension of credit and payment terms.

3. Risks that could affect the prices that would be charged or paid, or the profit that would be earned, in the two transactions, including
   - Market risks.
   - Risks associated with the success or failure of research and development activities.
   - Financial risks, including fluctuations in foreign currency rates of exchange and interest rates.
   - Credit and collection risk.
   - Product liability risk.
   - General business risks related to the ownership of property, plant, and equipment.

4. Economic conditions that could affect the price or profit earned in the two transactions, such as
   - The similarity of geographic markets.
   - The relative size of each market, and the extent of the overall economic development in each market.
   - The level of the market (e.g., wholesale, retail).
   - The relevant market shares for the products, properties, or services transferred or provided.
   - The location-specific costs of the factors of production and distribution.
   - The extent of competition in each market with regard to the property or services under review.
   - The economic condition of the particular industry, including whether the market is in contraction or expansion.
   - The alternatives realistically available to the buyer and seller.

5. Property or services transferred in the transactions, including any intangibles that are embedded in tangible property or services being transferred.

If none of these methods is determined to be appropriate, companies are allowed to use an unspecified method, provided its use can be justified.

Comparable Uncontrolled Price Method

The *comparable uncontrolled price method* is generally considered to provide the most reliable measure of an arm's-length price when a comparable uncontrolled transaction exists. Assume that a U.S.-based parent company (Parentco) makes sales of tangible property to a foreign subsidiary (Subco). Under this method, the price for tax purposes is determined by reference to sales by Parentco of the same or similar product to unrelated customers, or purchases by Subco of the same or similar product from unrelated suppliers. Also, sales of the same product between two unrelated parties could be used to determine the transfer price.

To determine whether the comparable uncontrolled price method results in the most reliable measure of arm's-length price, a company must consider each of the factors listed in Exhibit 11.3. Section 1.482-3 of the Treasury Regulations indicates specific factors that may be particularly relevant in determining whether an uncontrolled transaction is comparable:

1. Quality of the product.
2. Contractual terms.
3. Level of the market.
4. Geographic market in which the transaction takes place.
5. Date of the transaction.
6. Intangible property associated with the sale.
7. Foreign currency risks.
8. Alternatives realistically available to the buyer and seller.

If the uncontrolled transaction is not exactly comparable, some adjustment to the uncontrolled price is permitted in order to make the transactions more comparable. For example, assume that Sorensen Company, a U.S. manufacturer, sells the same product to both controlled and uncontrolled distributors in Mexico. The price to uncontrolled distributors is $40 per unit. Sorensen affixes its trademark to the products sold to its Mexican subsidiary but not to the products sold to the uncontrolled distributor. The trademark is considered to add approximately $10 of value to the product. The transactions are not strictly comparable because the products sold to the controlled and uncontrolled parties are different (one has a trademark and the other does not). Adjusting the uncontrolled price of $40 by $10 would result in a more comparable price and $50 would be an acceptable transfer price under the comparable uncontrolled price method. If the value of the trademark could not be reasonably determined, the comparable uncontrolled price method might not result in the most reliable arm's-length price in this scenario.

Resale Price Method

The *resale price method* determines the transfer price by subtracting an appropriate gross profit from the price at which the controlled buyer resells the tangible property. In order to use this method, a company must know *the final selling price to uncontrolled parties* and be able to determine *an appropriate gross profit for the reseller.* An appropriate gross profit is determined by reference to the gross profit margin earned in comparable uncontrolled transactions. For example, assume that Odom Company manufactures and sells automobile batteries to its Canadian affiliate, which in turn sells the batteries to local retailers at a resale price of $50 per unit.

Other Canadian distributors of automobile batteries earn an average gross profit margin of 25 percent on similar sales. Applying the resale price method, Odom Company would establish an arm's-length price of $37.50 per unit for its sale of batteries to its Canadian affiliate (resale price of $50 less an appropriate gross profit of $12.50 [25 percent] to be earned by the Canadian affiliate).

In determining an appropriate gross profit, the degree of comparability between the sale made by the Canadian affiliate and sales made by uncontrolled Canadian distributors need not be as great as under the comparable uncontrolled price method. The decisive factor is the similarity of functions performed by the affiliate and uncontrolled distributors in making sales. For example, if the functions performed by the Canadian affiliate in selling batteries are similar to the functions performed by Canadian distributors of automobile parts in general, the company could use the gross profit earned by uncontrolled sellers of automobile parts in Canada in determining an acceptable transfer price. Other important factors affecting comparability might include the following:

- Inventory levels and turnover rates.
- Contractual terms (e.g., warranties, sales volume, credit terms, transport terms).
- Sales, marketing, advertising programs and services, including promotional programs, and rebates.
- Level of the market (e.g., wholesale, retail).

The resale price method is typically used when the buyer/reseller is merely a distributor of finished goods—a so-called sales subsidiary. The method is acceptable only when the buyer/reseller does not add a substantial amount of value to the product. The resale price method is not feasible in cases where the reseller adds substantial value to the goods or where the goods become part of a larger product, because there is no "final selling price to uncontrolled parties" for the goods that were transferred. Continuing with our example, if Odom Company's Canadian affiliate operates an auto assembly plant and places the batteries purchased from Odom in automobiles that are then sold for $20,000 per unit, the company cannot use the resale price method for determining an appropriate transfer price for the batteries.

Cost-Plus Method

The *cost-plus method* is most appropriate when there are no comparable uncontrolled sales and the related buyer does more than simply distribute the goods it purchases. Whereas the resale price method subtracts an appropriate gross profit from the resale price to establish the transfer price, the cost-plus method adds an appropriate gross profit to the cost of producing a product to establish an arm's-length price. This method is normally used in cases involving manufacturing, assembly, or other production of goods that are sold to related parties. Once again, the appropriate gross profit markup is determined by reference to comparable uncontrolled transactions. Physical similarity between the products transferred is not as important in determining comparability under this method as it is under the comparable uncontrolled price method. Factors to be included in determining whether an uncontrolled transaction is comparable include similarity of functions performed, risks borne, and contractual terms. Factors that may be particularly relevant in determining comparability under this method include the following:

- Complexity of the manufacturing or assembly process.
- Manufacturing, production, and process engineering.

- Procurement, purchasing, and inventory control activities.
- Testing functions.

To illustrate use of the cost-plus method, assume that Pruitt Company has a subsidiary in Taiwan that acquires materials locally to produce an electronic component. The component, which costs $4 per unit to produce, is sold only to Pruitt Company. Because the Taiwanese subsidiary does not sell this component to other, unrelated parties, the comparable uncontrolled price method is not applicable. Pruitt Company combines the electronic component imported from Taiwan with other parts to assemble electronic switches that are sold in the United States. Because Pruitt does not simply resell the electronic components in the United States, the resale price method is not available. Therefore, Pruitt must look for a comparable transaction between unrelated parties in Taiwan to determine whether the cost plus method can be used. Assume that an otherwise comparable company in Taiwan manufactures similar electronic components from its inventory of materials and sells them to unrelated buyers at an average gross profit markup on cost of 25 percent. In this case, application of the cost-plus method results in a transfer price of $5 ($4 + [$4 × 25%]) for the electronic component that Pruitt purchases from its Taiwanese subsidiary.

Now assume that Pruitt's Taiwanese subsidiary manufactures electronic components using materials provided by Pruitt on a consignment basis. To apply the cost-plus method, Pruitt would have to make a downward adjustment to the otherwise comparable gross profit markup of 25 percent, because the inventory risk assumed by the manufacturer in the comparable transaction justifies a higher gross profit markup than is appropriate for Pruitt's foreign subsidiary. If Pruitt cannot reasonably ascertain the effect of inventory procurement and handling on gross profit, the cost-plus method might not result in a reliable transfer price.

Comparable Profits Method

The *comparable profits method* is based on the assumption that similarly situated taxpayers will tend to earn similar returns over a given period.[10] Under this method, one of the two parties in a related transaction is chosen for examination. An arm's-length price is determined by referring to an objective measure of profitability earned by uncontrolled taxpayers on comparable, uncontrolled sales. Profit indicators that might be considered in applying this method include the ratio of operating income to operating assets, the ratio of gross profit to operating expenses, or the ratio of operating profit to sales. If the transfer price used results in ratios for the party being examined that are in line with those ratios for similar businesses, then the transfer price will not be challenged.

To demonstrate the comparable profits method, assume that Glassco, a U.S. manufacturer, distributes its products in a foreign country through its foreign sales subsidiary, Vidroco. Assume that Vidroco has sales of $1,000,000 and operating expenses (other than cost of goods sold) of $200,000. Over the past several years, comparable distributors in the foreign country have earned operating profits equal to 5 percent of sales. Under the comparable profits method, a transfer price that provides Vidroco an operating profit equal to 5 percent of sales would be considered arm's length. An acceptable operating profit for Vidroco is $50,000 ($1,000,000 × 5%). To achieve this amount of operating profit, cost of goods sold

---

[10] The comparable profits method is described in Treasury Regulations, Sec. 1.482-5.

must be $750,000 ($1,000,000 − $200,000 − $50,000); this is the amount that Glassco would be allowed to charge as a transfer price for its sales to Vidroco. This example demonstrates use of the ratio of operating profit to sales as the profit-level indicator under the comparable profits method. The Treasury Regulations also specifically mention use of the ratio of operating profit to operating assets and the ratio of gross profit to operating expenses as acceptable profit-level indicators in applying this method.

Profit Split Method

The *profit split method* assumes that the buyer and seller are one economic unit.[11] The total profit earned by the economic unit from sales to uncontrolled parties is allocated to the members of the economic unit based on their relative contributions in earning the profit. The relative value of each party's contribution in earning the profit is based on the functions performed, risks assumed, and resources employed in the business activity that generates the profit. There are in fact two versions of the profit split method: (1) comparable profit split method and (2) residual profit split method.

Under the *comparable profit split method,* the profit split between two related parties is determined through reference to the operating profit earned by each party in a comparable uncontrolled transaction. Each of the factors listed in Exhibit 11.3 must be considered in determining the degree of comparability between the intercompany transaction and the comparable uncontrolled transaction. The degree of similarity in the contractual terms between the controlled and comparable uncontrolled transaction is especially critical in determining whether this is the "best method." In addition, Treasury Regulations specifically state that this method "may not be used if the combined operating profit (as a percentage of the combined assets) of the uncontrolled comparables varies significantly from that earned by the controlled taxpayers."[12]

When controlled parties possess intangible assets that allow them to generate profits in excess of what is earned in otherwise comparable uncontrolled transactions, the *residual profit split method* should be used. Under this method the combined profit is allocated to each of the controlled parties following a two-step process. In the first step, profit is allocated to each party to provide a market return for its routine contributions to the relevant business activity. This step will not allocate all of the combined profit earned by the controlled parties, because it will not include a return for the intangible assets that they possess. In the second step, the residual profit attributable to intangibles is allocated to each of the controlled parties on the basis of the relative value of intangibles that each contributes to the relevant business activity. The reliability of this method hinges on the ability to measure the value of the intangibles reliably.

Licenses of Intangible Property

Treasury Regulations, Section 1.482-4, list six categories of intangible property:

- Patents, inventions, formulae, processes, designs, patterns, or know-how.
- Copyrights and literary, musical, or artistic compositions.
- Trademarks, trade names, or brand names.
- Franchises, licenses, or contracts.

---

[11] The profit split method is described in Treasury Regulations, Sec. 1.482-6.

[12] Treasury Regulations, Sec. 1.482-6 (c)(2).

- Methods, programs, systems, procedures, campaigns, surveys, studies, forecasts, estimates, customer lists, or technical data.
- Other similar items. An item is considered similar if it derives its value from its intellectual content or other intangible properties rather than from physical properties.

Four methods are available for determining the arm's-length consideration for the license of intangible property:

- Comparable uncontrolled transaction method.
- Comparable profits methods.
- Profit split method.
- Unspecified methods.

The comparable profits method and profit split method are the same methods as those available for establishing the transfer price on tangible property. The comparable uncontrolled transaction method is similar in concept to the comparable uncontrolled price method available for tangible property.

Comparable Uncontrolled Transaction (CUT) Method

The *comparable uncontrolled transaction (CUT)* method determines whether or not the amount a company charges a related party for the use of intangible property is an arm's-length price by referring to the amount it charges an unrelated party for the use of the intangible. Treasury Regulations indicate that if an uncontrolled transaction involves the license of the same intangible under the same (or substantially the same) circumstances as the controlled transaction, the results derived from applying the CUT method will generally be the most reliable measure of an arm's-length price.

The controlled and uncontrolled transactions are substantially the same if there are only minor differences that have a definite and reasonably measurable effect on the amount charged for use of the intangible. If substantially the same uncontrolled transactions do not exist, uncontrolled transactions that involve the transfer of comparable intangibles under comparable circumstances may be used in applying the CUT method.

In evaluating the comparability of an uncontrolled transaction, the following factors are particularly relevant:[13]

- The terms of the transfer, including the exploitation rights granted in the intangible, the exclusive or nonexclusive character of any rights granted, any restrictions on use or any limitation on the geographic area in which the rights may be exploited.
- The stage of development of the intangible (including, where appropriate, necessary governmental approvals, authorizations, or licenses) in the market in which the intangible is to be used.
- Rights to receive updates, revisions or modifications of the intangible.
- The uniqueness of the property and the period for which it remains unique, including the degree and duration of protection afforded to the property under the laws of the relevant countries.
- The duration of the contract or other agreement, and any termination or renegotiation rights.

---

[13] Treasury Regulations, Sec. 1.482-4 (c)(2).

- Any economic and product liability risks to be assumed by the transferee.
- The existence and extent of any collateral transactions or ongoing business relationships between the transferee and transferor.
- The functions to be performed by the transferor and transferee, including any ancillary or subsidiary services.

Furthermore, differences in economic conditions also can affect comparability and therefore the appropriateness of the CUT method. For example, if a U.S. pharmaceutical company licenses a patented drug to an uncontrolled manufacturer in Country A and licenses the same drug under the same contractual terms to its subsidiary in Country B, the two transactions are not comparable if the potential market for the drug is higher in Country B because of a higher incidence of the disease the drug is intended to combat.

Profit Split Method

Treasury Regulations provide the following example to demonstrate application of the residual profit split method to licensing intangibles. P, a U.S.-based company, manufactures and sells products for police use in the United States. P develops and obtains a patent for a bulletproof material, Nulon, for use in its protective clothing and headgear. P licenses its European subsidiary, S, to manufacture and sell Nulon in Europe. S has adapted P's products for military use and sells to European governments under brand names that S has developed and owns. S's revenues from the sale of Nulon in Year 1 are $500, and S's direct operating expenses (excluding royalties) are $300. The royalty the IRS will allow P to charge S for the license to produce Nulon is determined as follows:

1. The IRS determines that the operating assets used by S in producing Nulon are worth $200. From an examination of profit margins earned by other European companies performing similar functions, it determines that 10 percent is a fair market return on S's operating assets. Of S's operating profit of $200 (sales of $500 less direct operating expenses of $300), the IRS determines that $20 ($200 × 10%) is attributable to S's operating assets. The remaining $180 is attributable to intangibles. In the second step, the IRS determines how much of this $180 is attributable to P's intangibles and how much is attributable to S's intangibles. The amount attributable to P's intangibles is the amount the IRS will allow P to charge S for the license to produce Nulon.

2. The IRS establishes that the market values of P and S's intangibles cannot be reliably determined. Therefore, it estimates the relative values of the intangibles from Year 1 expenditures on research, development, and marketing. P's research and development expenditures relate to P's worldwide activities, so the IRS allocates these expenditures to worldwide sales. By comparing these expenditures in Year 1 with worldwide sales in Year 1, the IRS determines that the contribution to worldwide gross profit made by P's intangibles is 20 percent of sales. In contrast, S's research, development, and marketing expenditures pertain to European sales, and the IRS determines that the contribution that S's intangibles make to S's gross profit is equal to 40 percent of sales. Thus, of the portion of S's gross profit that is not attributable to a return on S's operating assets, one-third (20%/60%) is attributable to P's intangibles and two-thirds is attributable to S's intangibles (40%/60%). Under the residual profit split method, P will charge S a license fee of $60 ($180 × $\frac{1}{3}$) in Year 1.

Intercompany Loans

When one member of a controlled group makes a loan to another member of the group, Section 482 of the U.S. Internal Revenue Code requires an arm's-length rate of interest to be charged on the loan. In determining an arm's-length interest rate, all relevant factors should be considered including the principal and duration of the loan, the security involved, the credit standing of the borrower, and the interest rate prevailing for comparable loans between unrelated parties.

A safe harbor rule exists when the loan is denominated in U.S. dollars and the lender is not regularly engaged in the business of making loans to unrelated persons. Such would be the case, for example, if a U.S. manufacturing firm made a U.S.-dollar loan to its foreign subsidiary. In this situation, the stated interest rate is considered to be at arm's length if it is at a rate not less than the "applicable Federal rate" and not greater than 130 percent of the applicable Federal rate (AFR). The AFR is based on the average interest rate on obligations of the federal government with similar maturity dates. The AFR is recomputed each month. Assuming an AFR of 4 percent on one-year obligations, the U.S. manufacturing firm could charge an interest rate anywhere from 4 percent to 5.2 percent on a one-year U.S.-dollar loan to its foreign subsidiary without having to worry about a transfer pricing adjustment being made by the IRS.

Intercompany Services

When one member of a controlled group provides a service to another member of the group, the purchaser must pay an arm's-length price to the service provider. If the services provided are incidental to the business activities of the service provider, the arm's-length price is equal to the direct and indirect costs incurred in connection with providing the service. There is no need to include a profit component in the price in this case. However, if the service provided is an "integral part" of the business function of the service provider, the price charged must include profit equal to what would be earned on similar services provided to an unrelated party. For example, assume that engineers employed by Brandlin Company travel to the Czech Republic to provide technical assistance to the company's Czech subsidiary in setting up a production facility. Brandlin must charge the foreign subsidiary a fee for this service equal to the direct and indirect costs incurred. Direct costs include the cost of the engineers' travel to the Czech Republic and their salaries while on the assignment. Indirect costs might include a portion of Brandlin's overhead costs allocated to the engineering department. If Brandlin is in the business of providing this type of service to unrelated parties, it must also include an appropriate amount of profit in the technical assistance fee it charges its Czech subsidiary.

No fee is required to be charged to a related party if the service performed on its behalf merely duplicates an activity the related party has performed itself. For example, assume that engineers employed by Brandlin's Czech subsidiary design the layout of the production facility themselves and their plan is simply reviewed by Brandlin's U.S. engineers. In this case, the U.S. parent company need not charge the foreign subsidiary a fee for performing the review.

Arm's-Length Range

The IRS acknowledges that application of a specific transfer pricing method could result in a number of transfer prices thereby creating an "arm's-length range" of prices. A company will not be subject to IRS adjustment so long as its transfer price falls within this range. For example, assume that Harrell Company determines the comparable uncontrolled price method to be the "best method" for purchases of Product X from its wholly owned Chinese subsidiary. Four comparable uncontrolled transactions are identified with prices of $9.50, $9.75, $10.00, and $10.50. Harrell Company can purchase Product X from its Chinese subsidiary at a price anywhere from $9.50 to $10.50 without the risk of an adjustment being made by the IRS. The company may wish to choose that price within the arm's-length range (either the highest price or the lowest price) that would allow it to achieve one or more cost-minimization objectives.

Correlative Relief

Determination of an arm's-length transfer price acceptable to the IRS is very important. If the IRS adjusts a transfer price in the United States, there is no guarantee that the foreign government at the other end of the transaction will reciprocate by providing a correlative adjustment. If the foreign government does not provide correlative relief, the total tax liability for the MNC increases. For example, assume that Usco Inc. manufactures a product for $10 per unit that is sold to its affiliate in Brazil (Brazilco) for $12 per unit. The Brazilian affiliate sells the product at $20 per unit in the Brazilian market. In that case, the worldwide income tax paid on this sale would be $2.70 per unit, calculated as follows:

	Usco	Brazilco
Sales	$ 12	$ 20
Cost of sales	10	12
Taxable income	$ 2	$ 8
Tax liability	$.70 (35%)	$2.00 (25%)

Assume further that Usco is unable to justify its transfer price of $12 through use of one of the acceptable transfer pricing methods, and the IRS adjusts the price to $15. This results in U.S. taxable income of $5 per unit. If the Brazilian government refuses to allow Brazilco to adjust its cost of sales to $15 per unit, the worldwide income tax paid on this sale would be $3.75 per unit, determined as follows:

	Usco	Brazilco
Sales	$ 15	$ 20
Cost of sales	10	12
Taxable income	$ 5	$ 8
Tax liability	$1.75 (35%)	$2.00 (25%)

Article 9 of the U.S. Model Income Tax Treaty requires that, when the tax authority in one country makes an adjustment to a company's transfer price, the tax authority in the other country will provide correlative relief if it agrees with the adjustment. If the other country does not agree with the adjustment, the competent authorities of the two countries are required to attempt to reach a compromise. If no compromise can be reached, the company will find itself in the situation described earlier. In the absence of a tax treaty (such as in the case of the United States and Brazil), there is no compulsion for the other country to provide a correlative adjustment.

When confronted with an IRS transfer pricing adjustment, a taxpayer may request assistance from the U.S. Competent Authority through its Mutual Agreement

Procedure (MAP) to obtain correlative relief from the foreign government. In 2002, the IRS recommended $5.56 billion in transfer pricing adjustments. The MAP process resulted in a correlative adjustment in 38 percent of the adjustments.[14] In an additional 27 percent of cases, MAP resulted in the withdrawal of the adjustment by the IRS. The MAP process is not speedy. Over the period 1997–2002, the MAP process took an average of 679–948 days to secure a correlative adjustment.

Penalties

In addition to possessing the power to adjust transfer prices, the IRS has the authority to impose penalties on companies that significantly underpay taxes as a result of inappropriate transfer pricing. A penalty equal to 20 percent of the underpayment in taxes may be levied for a substantial valuation misstatement. The penalty increases to 40 percent of the underpayment on a gross valuation misstatement. A substantial valuation misstatement exists when the transfer price is 200 percent or more (50 percent or less) of the price determined under Section 482 to be the correct price. A gross valuation misstatement arises when the price is 400 percent or more (25 percent or less) than the correct price.

For example, assume Tomlington Company transfers a product to a foreign affiliate for $10 and the IRS determines the correct price should have been $50. The adjustment results in an increase in U.S. tax liability of $1,000,000. Because the original transfer price was less than 25 percent of the correct price ($50 × 25% = $12.50), the IRS levies a penalty of $400,000 (40% of $1,000,000). Tomlington Company will pay the IRS a total of $1,400,000 as a result of its gross valuation misstatement.

ADVANCE PRICING AGREEMENTS

To introduce some certainty into the transfer pricing issue, the United States originated and actively promotes the use of advance pricing agreements (APAs). An APA is an agreement between a company and the IRS to apply an agreed-on transfer pricing method to specified transactions. The IRS agrees not to seek any transfer pricing adjustments for transactions covered by the APA if the company uses the agreed-on method. A unilateral APA is an agreement between a taxpayer and the IRS establishing an approved transfer pricing method for U.S. tax purposes. Whenever possible, the IRS will also negotiate the terms of the APA with foreign tax authorities to create a bilateral APA, which is an agreement between the IRS and one or more foreign tax authorities that the transfer pricing method is correct.

The APA process consists of five phases: (1) application; (2) due diligence; (3) analysis; (4) discussion and agreement; and (5) drafting, review, and execution. The request for an APA involves the company proposing a particular transfer pricing method to be used in specific transactions. Generally, one of the methods required to be followed by Treasury Regulations will be requested, but another method can be requested if none of the methods specified in the regulations is applicable or practical. In considering the request for an APA, the IRS is likely to require the following information as part of the application:

1. An explanation of the proposed methodology.
2. A description of the company and its related party's business operations.

[14] U.S. Department of the Treasury, *Current Trends in the Administration of International Transfer Pricing by the Internal Revenue Service,* September 2003, p. 13.

3. An analysis of the company's competitors.

4. Data on the industry showing pricing practices and rates of return on comparable transactions between unrelated parties.

For most taxpayers, the APA application is a substantial document filling several binders.[15]

The clear advantage to negotiating an APA is the assurance that the prices determined using the agreed-on transfer pricing method will not be challenged by the IRS. Disadvantages of the APA are that it can be very time-consuming to negotiate and that it involves disclosing a great deal of information to the IRS. The IRS indicates that new unilateral agreements take an average of 22 months to negotiate and bilateral agreements take even longer (41 months).[16] Although thousands of companies engage in transactions that cross U.S. borders, by the end of 2002 only 434 APAs had been negotiated since the program's inception in 1991.

The first completed APA was for sales between Apple Computer Inc. and its Australian subsidiary. In 1992, Japan's largest consumer electronics firm, Matsushita (known for its Panasonic and Technics brands), announced that after two years of negotiation it had entered into an APA with both the IRS and the Japanese National Tax Administration.[17] Companies in the computer and electronics product manufacturing industry have been the greatest users of APAs.

Foreign companies with U.S. operations are as likely to request an APA as U.S. companies with foreign operations. Of a total of 58 APAs that were executed in 2003, 60 percent were between a U.S. subsidiary or branch and its foreign parent, and 40 percent involved transactions between a U.S. parent and its foreign subsidiary.[18] Through the end of 2002, almost 60 percent of all APAs were with foreign parents of U.S. companies.

In 1998, the IRS instituted an APA program for "small business taxpayers" that somewhat streamlines the process of negotiating an APA. IRS Notice 98-65 describes the special APA procedures for small businesses. In 2003, four new small-business-taxpayer APAs were completed, taking an average of 12.5 months to complete.[19]

Most APAs cover transactions that involve a number of business functions and risks. For example, manufacturing firms typically conduct research and development, design and engineer products, manufacture products, market and distribute products, and provide after-sales services. Risks include market risks, financial risks, credit risks, product liability risks, and general business risks. The IRS indicates that in the APA evaluation process "a significant amount of time and effort is devoted to understanding how the functions and risks are allocated amongst the controlled group of companies that are party to the covered transactions."[20] To facilitate this evaluation, the company must provide a functional analysis as part of the APA application. The functional analysis identifies the economic activities performed, the assets employed, the costs incurred, and risks assumed by each of

---

[15] U.S. Internal Revenue Service, "Announcement and Report Concerning Advance Pricing Agreements," *Internal Revenue Bulletin: 2004-15,* April 13, 2004.

[16] Ibid., Table 2.

[17] "Big Japan Concern Reaches an Accord on Paying U.S. Tax," *New York Times,* November 11, 1992, p. A1.

[18] U.S. Internal Revenue Service, "Announcement and Report Concerning Advance Pricing Agreements," *Internal Revenue Bulletin: 2004-15,* April 13, 2004, Table 10.

[19] Ibid., Table 7.

[20] Ibid.

the related parties. The purpose is to determine the relative value being added by each function and therefore by each related party. The IRS uses the economic theory that higher risks demand higher returns and that different functions have different opportunity costs in making its evaluation. Each IRS APA team generally includes an economist to help with this analysis.

Sales of tangible property are the type of intercompany transaction most frequently covered by an APA, and the comparable profits method is the transfer pricing method most commonly applied.[21] This is because reliable public data on comparable business activities of uncontrolled companies may be more readily available than potential comparable uncontrolled price data, ruling out the CUP method. In addition, because the comparable profits method relies on operating profit margin rather than gross profit margin (as do the resale price and cost-plus methods), the comparable profits method is not as dependent on exact comparables being available. Companies that perform different functions may have very different gross profit margins, but earn similar levels of operating profit.

A relatively large number of countries have developed their own APA programs. France introduced a procedure for APAs in 1999, and in 2000 the Ministry of Finance in Indonesia announced proposals to introduce APAs. Other countries in which APAs are available include, but are not limited to, Australia, Brazil, Canada, China, Germany, Japan, Korea, Mexico, Taiwan, the United Kingdom, and Venezuela.

REPORTING REQUIREMENTS IN THE UNITED STATES

To determine whether intercompany transactions meet the arm's-length price requirement, the IRS often must request substantial information from the company whose transfer pricing is being examined. Historically, the IRS has found it extremely difficult to obtain such information when the transaction involves a transfer from a foreign parent company to its U.S. subsidiary. The information might be held by the foreign parent, which is beyond the jurisdiction of the IRS.

To reduce this problem, U.S. tax law now requires substantial reporting and record keeping of any U.S. company that (1) has at least one foreign shareholder with a 25 percent interest in the company and (2) engages in transactions with that shareholder. Accounting and other records must be physically maintained in the United States by a U.S. company meeting this definition. In addition, Form 5472 must be filed each year for each related party with which the company had transactions during the year. Failure to keep appropriate records results in a $10,000 fine, and a fine of $10,000 is assessed for each failure to file a Form 5472. If the company does not resolve the problem within 90 days of notification by the IRS, the fine doubles and increases by $10,000 for every 30 days' delay after that. For example, a U.S. subsidiary of a foreign parent that neglects to file Form 5472 would owe the IRS $50,000 in penalties 180 days after being notified of its deficiency.

In 2001, the IRS commissioned a study to determine the cost incurred by companies in maintaining contemporaneous transfer pricing documentation as required. Of 567 companies surveyed, 4 percent indicated spending $0, 60 percent reported spending between $1 and $100,000, and 35 percent said they spent more than $100,000 in preparing transfer pricing documentation.[22] The survey also

---

[21] U.S. Department of the Treasury, *Current Trends in the Administration of International Transfer Pricing by the Internal Revenue Service,* September 2003, p. 44.

[22] U.S. Department of the Treasury, *Current Trends in the Administration of International Transfer Pricing by the Internal Revenue Service,* September 2003, p. 15.

found that 60 percent of respondents had from 1 to 10 full-time employees handling transfer pricing issues and documentation.

ENFORCEMENT OF TRANSFER PRICING REGULATIONS

The United States has made periodic attempts over the years to make sure that MNCs doing business in the United States pay their fair share of taxes. Enforcement has concentrated on foreign companies with U.S. subsidiaries, but U.S. companies with foreign operations also have been targeted. Anecdotal evidence suggests that foreign companies are using discretionary transfer pricing to waft profits out of the United States back to their home country. In one case cited in a *Newsweek* article, a foreign manufacturer was found to sell TV sets to its U.S. subsidiary for $250 each, but charged an unrelated U.S. company only $150.[23] In yet two additional cases, a foreign company was found to charge its U.S. distributor $13 a piece for razor blades, and a U.S. manufacturer sold bulldozers to its foreign parent for only $551 a piece.[24] As a result, foreign companies doing business in the United States are able to pay little or no U.S. income tax. For example, according to the IRS, "Yamaha Motor U.S.A. paid only $5,272 in corporate tax to Washington over four years. Proper accounting would have shown a profit of $500 million and taxes of $127 million."[25]

In two of its biggest victories in the 1980s, the IRS was able to make the case that Toyota and Nissan had overcharged their U.S. subsidiaries for products imported into the United States. Nissan paid $1.85 billion and Toyota paid $850 million to the U.S. government as a result of adjustments made by the IRS. In both cases, however, the competent authorities in the United States and Japan agreed on the adjustments and the Japanese government paid appropriate refunds to the companies. In effect, tax revenues previously collected by the Japanese tax authority were given to the IRS. Japanese companies are not the only ones found to violate transfer pricing regulations. In a well-publicized case, Coca-Cola Japan was found by the Japanese tax authority to overpay royalties to its parent by about $360 million. In another case, the IRS proposed an adjustment to Texaco's taxable income of some $140 million.

In his 1991 presidential campaign, candidate Bill Clinton claimed that beefed up enforcement of existing transfer pricing rules could raise about $45 billion in additional revenues over four years. In 1992, the House Ways and Means Committee introduced a bill into Congress that would have required U.S. subsidiaries of foreign parent companies to report a minimum amount of taxable income equal to at least 75 percent of the income reported by similar firms in the U.S. In addition to violating the nondiscrimination clause in U.S. tax treaties, concern was raised over the likely retaliatory effect of other countries. Not surprisingly, the bill was not passed.

In 1994, the IRS was armed with the ability to impose penalties (discussed earlier) for misstating taxable income through the use of non-arm's-length transfer prices. The administration hoped that the threat of additional penalties would provide an incentive for companies to comply with the regulations.

---

[23] "The Corporate Shell Game," *Newsweek,* April 15, 1991, pp. 48–49.

[24] "Legislators Prepare to Crack Down on Transfer Pricing," *Accounting Today,* July 13–26, 1998, pp. 10, 13.

[25] "Corporate Shell Game."

The transfer pricing saga continues. In 2004, the U.S. General Accounting Office released a report indicating that a majority of large corporations paid no U.S. income tax for the period 1996–2000.[26] During that period, from 67 percent to 73 percent of foreign-controlled corporations and from 60 to 63 percent of U.S.-controlled corporations paid no federal income tax. As a result, Congress has put renewed pressure on the IRS to enhance its enforcement of transfer pricing regulations. Discretionary transfer pricing is likely to be an issue so long as intercompany transactions exist.

Worldwide Enforcement

Over the last several years, most major countries have strengthened their transfer pricing rules, often through documentation requirements and penalties, and have stepped up enforcement. According to one of the international accounting firms, the top 10 most aggressive countries on transfer pricing are, in order, the United States, Japan, Germany, the United Kingdom, Australia, Korea, China, France, Canada, and Mexico.[27] In most of these countries, the concept of an arm's-length price is used in accordance with OECD guidelines. However, enforcement of these rules varies across countries. In Japan, for example, an adjustment made by the income tax authority is very difficult to reverse. The French tax authority is more likely to challenge technology transfers and management fees. Canada attempts to resolve disputes via advance pricing agreements and competent authority negotiations. China passed a new transfer pricing law in 1998, and enforcement is a high priority: "Unlike most of its Asian neighbors, China has explicit transfer pricing regulations and a specific audit plan. There are more than 500 tax officials in China who have been specially trained to conduct transfer pricing audits."[28]

Worldwide, there are certain types of transfers and certain industries that are more at risk for examination by tax authorities. For example, imports are more likely to be scrutinized than exports, partly for political reasons. Exports help the balance of trade; imports do not, and they compete with the local workforce. In addition, royalties paid for the use of intangible assets such as brand names, management service fees, research and development conducted for related parties, and interest on intercompany loans are all high on tax authorities' radar screen for examination. The industries most at risk are (1) petrochemicals, (2) pharmaceuticals, (3) financial services, (4) consumer electronics, (5) computers, (6) branded consumer goods, (7) media, and (8) automobiles. Each of these industries has a high volume of international intercompany transactions.[29]

There are a number of red flags that can cause a tax authority to examine a company's transfer prices. The most important of these is if the company is less profitable than the tax authority believes it should be. For example, a domestic company with a foreign parent that makes losses year after year is likely to fall under scrutiny, especially if its competitors are profitable. Price changes and royalty rate changes are another red flag. Companies that have developed a poor relationship with the tax authority are also more likely to be scrutinized. A reputation for aggressive tax planning is one way to develop a poor relationship.

[26] U.S. General Accounting Office, *Comparison of the Reported Tax Liabilities of Foreign- and U.S.-Controlled Corporations, 1996–2000,* February 2004, p. 15.

[27] Price Waterhouse, "Transfer Pricing: PW Partners Discuss Recent Developments and Planning at Hong Kong MNC Meeting," *International Tax Review 21,* no. 5 (September/October 1995), p. 1.

[28] PricewaterhouseCoopers, "China's Special Approach to Transfer Pricing," www.pwcglobal.com.

[29] Price Waterhouse, "Transfer Pricing."

As evidence of the extent to which tax authorities investigate MNCs' transfer pricing policies, a survey conducted by Ernst & Young in 2003 discovered that almost 50 percent of parent company respondents experienced a transfer pricing audit somewhere in the world in the previous three years, and 76 percent thought that an audit was likely in the next two years.[30] One-third of completed audits resulted in an adjustment being made by a tax authority, and in 40 percent of those cases no correlative adjustment was provided. Ernst & Young concludes by stating that MNCs should expect a transfer pricing audit as a rule rather than an exception.

Summary

1. Two factors heavily influence the manner in which international transfer prices are determined: (1) corporate objectives and (2) national tax laws.

2. The objective of establishing transfer prices to enhance performance evaluation and the objective of minimizing one or more types of cost through discretionary transfer pricing often conflict.

3. Cost-minimization objectives that can be achieved through discretionary transfer pricing include minimization of worldwide income tax, minimization of import duties, circumvention of repatriation restrictions, and improving the competitive position of foreign subsidiaries.

4. National tax authorities have guidelines regarding what will be considered an acceptable transfer price for tax purposes. These guidelines often rely on the concept of an arm's-length price.

5. Section 482 of the U.S. tax law gives the IRS the power to audit and adjust taxpayers' international transfer prices if they are not found to be in compliance with Treasury Department regulations. The IRS also may impose a penalty of up to 40 percent of the underpayment in the case of a gross valuation misstatement.

6. Treasury Regulations require the use of one of five specified methods to determine the arm's-length price in a sale of tangible property. The best-method rule requires taxpayers to use the method that under the facts and circumstances provides the most reliable measure of an arm's-length price. The comparable uncontrolled price method is generally considered to provide the most reliable measure of an arm's-length price when a comparable uncontrolled transaction exists.

7. Application of a particular transfer pricing method can result in an arm's-length range of prices. Companies can try to achieve cost-minimization objectives by selecting prices at the extremes of the relevant range.

8. Advance pricing agreements (APAs) are agreements between a company and a national tax authority on what is an acceptable transfer pricing method. So long as the agreed-on method is used, the company's transfer prices will not be adjusted.

9. Enforcement of transfer pricing regulations varies from country to country. Transfer pricing is the most important international tax issue faced by many U.S. multinational corporations (MNCs). The United States is especially concerned with foreign MNCs not paying their fair share of taxes in the United States.

---

[30] Ernst & Young, *Transfer Pricing 2003 Global Survey,* p. 5.

Questions	1. What are the various types of intercompany transactions for which a transfer price must be determined?

1. What are the various types of intercompany transactions for which a transfer price must be determined?
2. What are possible cost-minimization objectives that a multinational company might wish to achieve through transfer pricing?
3. What is the performance evaluation objective of transfer pricing?
4. Why is there often a conflict between the performance evaluation and cost minimization objectives of transfer pricing?
5. How can transfer pricing be used to reduce the amount of withholding taxes paid to a government on dividends remitted to a foreign stockholder?
6. According to U.S. tax regulations, what are the five methods to determine the arm's-length price in a sale of tangible property? How does the best-method rule affect the selection of transfer pricing method?
7. What is the arm's-length range of transfer pricing, and how does it affect the selection of a transfer pricing method?
8. Under what conditions would a company apply for a correlative adjustment from a foreign tax authority? What effect do tax treaties have on this process?
9. What is an advance pricing agreement?
10. What are the costs and benefits associated with entering into an advance pricing agreement?

Exercises and Problems

1. Which of the following objectives is not achieved through the use of lower transfer prices?
   a. Improving the competitive position of a foreign operation. ✓
   b. Minimizing import duties.
   c. Protecting foreign currency cash flows from currency devaluation.
   d. Minimizing income taxes when transferring to a lower-tax country. ✓

2. Which of the following methods does U.S. tax law always require to be used in pricing intercompany transfers of tangible property?
   a. Comparable uncontrolled price method.
   b. Comparable profits method.
   c. Cost-plus method.
   d. Best method.

3. Which international organization has developed transfer pricing guidelines that are used as the basis for transfer pricing laws in several countries?
   a. World Bank.
   b. Organization for Economic Cooperation and Development.
   c. United Nations.
   d. International Accounting Standards Board.

4. Which of the following countries is considered to be one of the top 10 in how strictly it enforces its transfer pricing regulations?
   a. Brazil.
   b. China.
   c. India.
   d. Russia.

5. Which of the following is not a method commonly used for establishing transfer prices?
   a. Cost-based transfer price.
   b. Negotiated price.

     c. Market-based transfer price.

     d. Industry-wide transfer price.

6. Market-based transfer prices lead to optimal decisions in which of the following situations?

     a. When interdependencies between the related parties are minimal.

     b. When there is no advantage or disadvantage to buying and selling the product internally rather than externally.

     c. When the market for the product is perfectly competitive.

     d. All of the above.

7. U.S. Treasury Regulations require the use of one of five specified methods to determine the arm's-length price in a sale of tangible property. Which of the following is not one of those methods?

     a. Cost-plus method.

     b. Market-based method.

     c. Profit split method.

     d. Resale price method.

8. Which group has negotiated the greatest number of advance pricing agreements with the U.S. Internal Revenue Service (IRS)?

     a. Foreign parent companies with branches and subsidiaries in the United States.

     b. U.S. parent companies with branches and subsidiaries in Canada and Mexico.

     c. U.S. parent companies with branches and subsidiaries in Japan.

     d. None of the above.

9. The IRS has the authority to impose penalties on companies that significantly underpay taxes as a result of inappropriate transfer pricing. Acme Company transfers a product to a foreign affiliate at $15 per unit, and the IRS determines the correct price should have been $65 per unit. The adjustment results in an increase in U.S. tax liability of $1,250,000. Due to this change in price, by what amount will Acme Company's U.S. tax liability increase?

     a. $400,000

     b. $1,250,000

     c. $1,650,000

     d. $1,750,000

Use the following information to complete Exercises 10–12:

Babcock Company manufactures fast-baking ovens in the United States at a production cost of $500 per unit and sells them to uncontrolled distributors in the United States and a wholly owned sales subsidiary in Canada. Babcock's U.S. distributors sell the ovens to restaurants at a price of $1,000, and its Canadian subsidiary sells the ovens at a price of $1,100. Other distributors of ovens to restaurants in Canada normally earn a gross profit equal to 25 percent of selling price. Babcock's main competitor in the United States sells fast-baking ovens at an average 50 percent markup on cost. Babcock's Canadian sales subsidiary incurs operating costs, other than cost of goods sold, that average $250 per oven sold. The average operating profit margin earned by Canadian distributors of fast baking ovens is 5 percent.

10. Which of the following would be an acceptable transfer price under the resale price method?

     a. $700

     b. $750

1100 − 250 − 55

c. $795

d. $825

11. Which of the following would be an acceptable transfer price under the cost-plus method?

a. $700

b. $750

c. $795

d. $825

12. Which of the following would be an acceptable transfer price under the comparable profits method?

a. $700

b. $750

c. $795

d. $825

13. Lahdekorpi OY, a Finnish corporation, owns 100 percent of Three-O Company, a subsidiary incorporated in the United States.

Required:

Given the limited information provided, determine the best transfer pricing method and the appropriate transfer price in each of the following situations:

a. Lahdekorpi manufacturers tablecloths at a cost of $20 each and sells them to unrelated distributors in Canada for $30 each. Lahdekorpi sells the same tablecloths to Three-O Company, which then sells them to retail customers in the United States.

b. Three-O Company manufactures men's flannel shirts at a cost of $10 each and sells them to Lahdekorpi, which sells the shirts in Finland at a retail price of $30 each. Lahdekorpi adds no significant value to the shirts. Finnish retailers of men's clothing normally earn a gross profit of 40 percent on sales price.

c. Lahdekorpi manufacturers wooden puzzles at a cost of $2 each and sells them to Three-O Company for distribution in the United States. Other Finnish puzzle manufacturers sell their product to unrelated customers and normally earn a gross profit equal to 50 percent of the production cost.

14. Superior Brakes Corporation manufactures truck brakes at its plant in Mansfield, Ohio, at a cost of $10 per unit. Superior sells its brakes directly to U.S. truck makers at a price of $15 per unit. It also sells its brakes to a wholly owned sales subsidiary in Brazil that, in turn, sells the brakes to Brazilian truck makers at a price of $16 per unit. Transportation cost from Ohio to Brazil is $0.20 per unit. Superior's sole competitor in Brazil is Bomfreio SA, which manufactures truck brakes at a cost of $12 per unit and sells them directly to truck makers at a price of $16 per unit. There are no substantive differences between the brakes manufactured by Superior and Bomfreio.

Required:

Given the information provided, discuss the issues related to using (*a*) the comparable uncontrolled price method, (*b*) the resale price method, and (*c*) the cost-plus method to determine an acceptable transfer price for the sale of truck brakes from Superior Brakes Corporation to its Brazilian subsidiary.

15. Akku Company imports die-cast parts from its German subsidiary that are used in the production of children's toys. Per unit, Part 169 costs the German

subsidiary $1.00 to produce and $0.20 to ship to Akku Company. Akku Company uses Part 169 to produce a toy airplane that it sells to U.S. toy stores for $4.50 per unit. The following tax rates apply:

German income tax	50%
U.S. income tax	35%
U.S. import duty	10% of invoice price

Required:

a. Determine the total amount of taxes and duties paid to the U.S. and German governments if Part 169 is sold to Akku Company at a price of $1.50 per unit.
b. Determine the total amount of taxes and duties paid to the U.S. and German governments if Part 169 is sold to Akku Company at a price of $1.80 per unit.
c. Explain why the results obtained in parts (a) and (b) differ.

16. Smith-Jones Company, a U.S.-based corporation, owns 100 percent of Joal SA, located in Guadalajara, Mexico. Joal manufactures premium leather handbags at a cost of 500 Mexican pesos each. Joal sells its handbags to Smith-Jones, which sells them under Joal's brand name in its retail stores in the United States. Joal also sells handbags to an uncontrolled wholesaler in the United States. Joal invoices all sales to U.S. customers in U.S. dollars. Because the customer is not allowed to use Joal's brand name, it affixes its own label to the handbags and sells them to retailers at a markup on cost of 30 percent. Other U.S. retailers import premium leather handbags from uncontrolled suppliers in Italy, making payment in euros, and sell them to generate gross profit margins equal to 25 percent of selling price. Imported Italian leather handbags are of similar quality to those produced by Joal. Bolsa SA also produces handbags in Mexico and sells them directly to Mexican retailers earning a gross profit equal to 60 percent of production cost. However, Bolsa's handbags are of lesser quality than Joal's due to the use of a less complex manufacturing process, and the two companies' handbags do not compete directly.

Required:

a. Given the facts presented, discuss the various factors that affect the reliability of (1) the comparable uncontrolled price method, (2) the resale price method, and (3) the cost-plus method.
b. Select the method from those listed in (a) that you believe is best, and describe any adjustment that might be necessary to develop a more reliable transfer price.

17. Guari Company, based in Melbourne, Australia, has a wholly owned subsidiary in Taiwan. The Taiwanese subsidiary manufactures bicycles at a cost equal to A$20 per bicycle, which it sells to Guari at an FOB shipping point price of A$100 each. Guari pays shipping costs of A$10 per bicycle and an import duty of 10 percent on the A$100 invoice price. Guari sells the bicycles in Australia for A$200 each. The Australian tax authority discovers that Guari's Taiwanese subsidiary also sells its bicycles to uncontrolled Australian customers at a price of A$80 each. Accordingly, the Australian tax authority makes a transfer pricing adjustment to Guari's tax return, which decreases Guari's cost of goods sold by A$20 per bicycle. An offsetting adjustment (refund) is made for the import duty previously paid. The effective income tax rate in Taiwan is 25 percent, and Guari's effective income tax rate is 36 percent.

Required:

a. Determine the total amount of income taxes and import duty paid on each bicycle (in Australian dollars) under each of the following situations:

(1) Before the Australian tax authority makes a transfer pricing adjustment.

(2) After the Australian tax authority makes a transfer pricing adjustment (assume the tax authority in Taiwan provides a correlative adjustment).

(3) After the Australian tax authority makes a transfer pricing adjustment (assume the tax authority in Taiwan does not provide a correlative adjustment).

b. Discuss Guari Company management's decision to allow its Taiwanese subsidiary to charge a higher price to Guari than to uncontrolled customers in Australia.

c. Assess the likelihood that the Taiwanese tax authority will provide a correlative adjustment to Guari Company.

18. ABC Company has subsidiaries in Countries X, Y, and Z. Each subsidiary manufactures one product at a cost of $10 per unit that it sells to each of its sister subsidiaries. Each buyer then distributes the product in its local market at a price of $15 per unit. The following information applies:

	Country X	Country Y	Country Z
Income tax rate . . .	20%	30%	40%
Import duty	20%	10%	0%

Import duties are levied on the invoice price and are deductible for income tax purposes.

Required:

Formulate a transfer pricing strategy for each of the six intercompany sales between the three subsidiaries X, Y, and Z that would minimize the amount of income taxes and import duties paid by ABC Company.

19. Denker Corporation has a wholly owned subsidiary in Sri Lanka that manufactures wooden bowls at a cost of $3 per unit. Denker imports the wooden bowls and sells them to retailers at a price of $12 per unit. The following information applies:

	United States	Sri Lanka
Income tax rate	35%	25%
Import duty	10%	—
Withholding tax rate on dividends . . .	—	30%

Import duties are levied on the invoice price and are deductible for income tax purposes. The Sri Lankan subsidiary must repatriate 100 percent of after-tax income to Denker each year. Denker has determined an arm's-length range of reliable transfer prices to be $5.00–$6.00.

Required:

a. Determine the transfer price within the arm's-length range that would maximize Denker's after-tax cash flow from the sale of wooden bowls.

b. Now assume that the withholding tax rate on dividends is 0 percent. Determine the transfer price within the arm's-length range that would maximize Denker's after-tax cash flow from the sale of wooden bowls.

20. Ranger Company, a U.S. taxpayer, manufactures and sells medical products for animals. Ranger holds the patent on Z-meal, which it sells to horse ranchers in the United States. Ranger Company licenses its Bolivian subsidiary, Yery SA, to manufacture and sell Z-meal in South America. Through extensive product development and marketing Yery has developed a South American llama market for Z-meal, which it sells under the brand name Llameal. Yery's sales of Llameal in Year 1 were $800,000 and its operating expenses related to these sales, excluding royalties, were $600,000. The IRS has determined the following:

Value of Yery's operating assets used in the production of Z-meal	$300,000
Fair market return on operating assets	20%
Percentage of Ranger's worldwide sales attributable to its intangibles	10%
Percentage of Yery's sales attributable to its intangibles	15%

Required:

Determine the amount that Ranger would charge as a license fee to Yery in Year 1 under the residual profit split method.

Case 11-1

Litchfield Corporation

Litchfield Corporation is a U.S.-based manufacturer of fashion accessories that produces umbrellas in its plant in Roanoke, Virginia, and sells directly to retailers in the United States. As chief financial officer, you are responsible for all of the company's finance, accounting, and tax-related issues.

Sarah Litchfield, chief executive officer and majority shareholder, has informed you of her plan to begin exporting to the United Kingdom, where she believes there is a substantial market for Litchfield umbrellas. Rather than selling directly to British umbrella retailers, she plans to establish a wholly owned UK sales subsidiary that would purchase umbrellas from its U.S. parent and then distribute them in the United Kingdom. Yesterday, you received the following memo from Sarah Litchfield.

Memorandum

SUBJECT: Export Sales Prices

It has come to my attention that the corporate income tax rate in Great Britain is only 30 percent, as compared to the 35 percent rate we pay here in the United States. Since our average production cost is $15.00 per unit and the price we expect to sell to UK retailers is $25.00 per unit, why don't we plan to sell to our UK subsidiary at $15.00 per unit. That way we make no profit here in the United States and $10.00 of profit in the United Kingdom, where we pay a lower tax rate. We have plans to invest in a factory in Scotland in the next few years anyway, so we can keep the profit we earn over there for that purpose. What do you think?

Required:

Draft a memo responding to Sarah Litchfield's question by explaining U.S. income tax regulations related to the export sales described in her memo. Include a discussion of any significant risks associated with her proposal. Make a recommendation with respect to how the price for these sales might be determined.

Case 11-2

Global Electronics Company

Global Electronics Company (GEC), a U.S. taxpayer, manufactures laser guitars in its Malaysian operation (LG-Malay) at a production cost of $120 per unit. LG-Malay guitars are sold to two customers in the United States—Electronic Superstores (a GEC wholly owned subsidiary) and Wal-Mart (an unaffiliated customer). The cost to transport the guitars to the United States is $15 per unit and is paid by LG-Malay. Other Malaysian manufacturers of laser guitars sell to customers in the United States at a markup on total cost (production plus transportation) of 40 percent. LG-Malay sells guitars to Wal-Mart at a landed price of $180 per unit (LG-Malay pays transportation costs). Wal-Mart pays applicable U.S. import duties of 20 percent on its purchases of laser guitars. Electronic Superstores also pays import duties on its purchases from LG-Malay. Consistent with industry practice, Wal-Mart places a 50 percent markup on laser guitars and sells them at a retail price of $324 per unit. Electronic Superstores sells LG-Malay guitars at a retail price of $333 per unit.

LG-Malay is a Malaysian taxpayer and Electronic Superstores is a U.S. taxpayer. The following tax rates apply:

U.S. ad valorem import duty	20%
U.S. corporate income tax rate	35%
Malaysian income tax rate	15%
Malaysian withholding tax rate	30%

Required:

1. Determine three possible prices for the sale of laser guitars from LG-Malay to Electronic Superstores that comply with U.S. tax regulations under (*a*) the comparable uncontrolled price method, (*b*) the resale price method, and (*c*) the cost-plus method. Assume that none of the three methods is clearly the best method and that GEC would be able to justify any of the three prices for both U.S. and Malaysian tax purposes.

2. Assume that LG-Malay's profits are *not* repatriated back to GEC in the United States as a dividend. Determine which of the three possible transfer prices maximizes GEC's consolidated after-tax net income. Show your calculation of consolidated net income for all three prices. You can assume that Electronic Superstores distributes 100 percent of its income to GEC as a dividend. However, there is a 100 percent exclusion for dividends received from a domestic subsidiary, so GEC will not pay additional taxes on dividends received from Electronic Superstores. Only Electronic Superstores pays taxes on the income it earns.

3. Assume that LG-Malay's profits *are* repatriated back to GEC in the U.S. as a dividend, and that Electronic Superstores profits are paid to GEC as a dividend. Determine which of the three possible transfer prices maximizes net after-tax cash flow to GEC. Remember that dividends repatriated back to the United States are taxable in the United States and that an indirect foreign tax credit will be allowed by the U.S. government for taxes deemed to have been paid to the Malaysian government on the repatriated dividend. Show your calculation of net after-tax cash flow for all three prices.

4. Assume the same facts as in (3) except that a United States/Malaysia income tax treaty reduces withholding taxes on dividends to 10 percent. Determine which of the three possible transfer prices maximizes net cash flow to GEC. Don't forget to consider foreign tax credits. Show your calculation of net cash flow for all three prices.

References

"Big Japan Concern Reaches an Accord on Paying U.S. Tax." *New York Times*, November 11, 1992, p. A1.

"The Corporate Shell Game." *Newsweek*, April 15, 1991, pp. 48–49.

Eccles, Robert G. *The Transfer Pricing Problem: A Theory for Practice.* Lexington, MA: Lexington Books, 1985.

Ernst & Young. *Transfer Pricing 2003 Global Survey*, 2003, available at www.ey.com.

Horngren, Charles T.; George Foster; and Srikant M. Datar. *Cost Accounting: A Managerial Emphasis*, 10th ed. Upper Saddle River, NJ: Prentice-Hall, 2000.

"Legislators Prepare to Crack Down on Transfer Pricing." *Accounting Today*, July 13–26, 1998, pp. 10, 13.

Maher, Michael W.; Clyde P. Stickney; and Roman L. Weil. *Managerial Accounting*, 8th ed. South-Western, 2004.

Price Waterhouse. "Transfer Pricing: PW Partners Discuss Recent Developments and Planning at Hong Kong MNC Meeting." *International Tax Review* 21, no. 5 (1995).

Tang, Roger Y. W. "Transfer Pricing in the 1990s." *Management Accounting*, February 1992, pp. 22–26.

———, and K. H. Chan. "Environmental Variables of International Transfer Pricing: A Japan-United States Comparison." *Abacus*, June, 1979, pp. 3–12.

U.S. Department of Commerce. "U.S. Goods Trade: Imports and Exports by Related Parties, 2003." *U.S. Department of Commerce News*, April 14, 2004.

U.S. General Accounting Office. *Comparison of the Reported Tax Liabilities of Foreign- and U.S.-Controlled Corporations, 1996–2000*, February 2004, available at www.gao.gov.

U.S. Internal Revenue Service. "Announcement and Report Concerning Advance Pricing Agreements." *Internal Revenue Bulletin: 2004-15*, April 13, 2004.

Chapter Twelve

Strategic Accounting Issues in Multinational Corporations

Learning Objectives

After reading this chapter, you should be able to

- Explain the role played by accounting in formulating multinational business strategy.
- Demonstrate an understanding of multinational capital budgeting.
- Describe the factors that influence strategy implementation within a multinational corporation.
- Discuss the role of accounting in implementing multinational business strategy.
- Identify issues involved in the design and implementation of an effective performance evaluation system within a multinational corporation.

INTRODUCTION

Strategies are grand plans that reflect the future direction of the organization as determined by senior management. A decision by a multinational corporation (MNC) to achieve at least 50 percent of the market share for one of its products in a particular foreign country within a specified period of time is an example of a strategic decision. *Strategic planning* refers to the determination of long-term goals and objectives of a firm, and the adoption of courses of action and the allocation of resources necessary for achieving these goals.[1] The strategic issues facing both domestic and multinational firms are similar in many respects and can be identified in two broad categories—strategy formulation and strategy implementation.

Strategy formulation is the process of deciding on the goals of the organization and the strategies for attaining those goals. This process involves both the revision of existing goals and plans and the adoption of new ones. At any point, therefore, an organization operates in accordance with a set of goals and strategies that it has adopted previously. The decisions made in formulating strategy have a long-term focus and include capital budgeting decision, that is, decisions related to making long-term capital investments.

---

[1] A. D. Chandler Jr. *Strategy and Structure* (Cambridge, MA: MIT Press, 1962), p. 13.

Strategy implementation refers to the process by which managers influence other members of the organization to behave in accordance with the organization's goals. Managerial influence is also known as *management control*. Two very important management control activities are preparing operating budgets and evaluating the performance of decentralized operations. Operating budgets are plans for the future expressed in quantitative terms that generally cover one year. Budgets provide a means for communicating management's plans throughout the organization. *Performance evaluation* is the task of ascertaining the extent to which organizational goals have been achieved. Identifying and rewarding good performance is important in achieving strategic goals. Performance is often evaluated by comparing actual results with expected results as summarized in the operating budget.

The accounting function within an organization plays an important role in strategy formulation and implementation through the activities of capital budgeting, operational budgeting, and performance evaluation. This chapter focuses on issues specifically related to carrying out these activities for foreign investments and foreign operations, including issues related to foreign currency fluctuations and the differences in culture and business environment that exist across countries.

STRATEGY FORMULATION

Information is the key to strategy formulation. Formulating a strategy involves analyzing information about both internal and external factors. Internal factors relate to the levels of skills and know-how available within the organization in such areas as technology, manufacturing, marketing, and distribution, whereas external factors relate to the competitors, customers, and suppliers, as well as to other regulatory, social, and political factors. The analysis allows managers to identify opportunities and match them with available competencies to determine strategies (see Exhibit 12.1).[2] The primary objective of formulating strategy is to ensure that the organization attains its goals, which are usually aimed at increasing firm value. Accounting can help in formulating strategy by quantifying opportunities and threats, as well as strengths and weaknesses, and by developing projections of costs and benefits as financial expressions of strategy.

Accounting's primary contribution to MNC strategy formulation comes through the budgeting process. Preparing a budget is the initial step in implementing change in organization. An important function of budgeting is to transfer information to decision makers. Budgeting forces managers to think about strategy because it formalizes the responsibilities for both short-term and long-term planning. Budgeting also identifies specific expectations that can be used as the basis for evaluating subsequent performance. We focus on capital budgeting in the remainder of this section.

Capital Budgeting

Multinational companies often need to commit large amounts of resources to projects with costs and benefits expected over a long period. Such projects are known as capital investments. Examples include the purchase of new equipment and the

---

[2] Robert N. Anthony and Vijay Govindarajan, *Management Control Systems*, 9th ed. (international ed.) (New York: McGraw-Hill, 1998), p. 54.

EXHIBIT 12.1
Strategy
Formulation

Source: Robert N. Anthony
and Vijay Govindarajan,
Management Control Systems,
9th ed. (international ed.)
(New York: McGraw-Hill,
1998), p. 54.

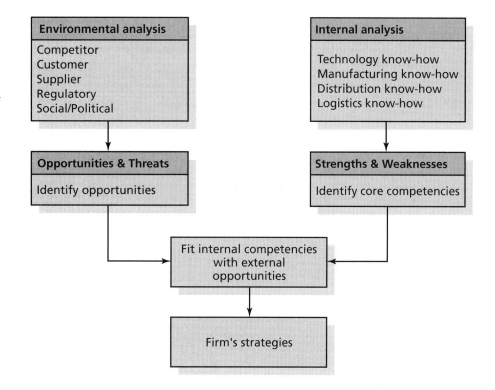

expansion into foreign territories through either greenfield investments or acquisition of existing operations. *Capital budgeting* is the process of identifying, evaluating, and selecting projects that require commitments of large sums of funds and
generate benefits stretching well into the future. Sound capital investments are
often a result of careful capital budgeting.[3] The evaluation of foreign investment
opportunities involves a more complicated set of economic, political, and strategic
considerations than those factors influencing most domestic investment decisions.
Although the decision to undertake a particular foreign investment may be determined by a mix of factors, the specific project should be subjected to traditional
investment analysis. We first explain the main features of traditional capital budgeting before considering the unique issues that need to be considered in foreign
investment analysis.

The capital budgeting process includes three steps: (1) project identification
and definition, (2) evaluation and selection, and (3) monitoring and review.[4] The
first step is critical, because without a clear definition of a proposed investment
project, it is difficult to estimate the associated revenues, expenses, and cash
flows, which is an integral part of the second step. The second step involves identifying the cash inflows and outflows expected from a specific project and then
using one or more capital budgeting techniques to determine whether the project
is acceptable. The third step becomes important during implementation of the
project. This refers to the possible need to alter the initial plan in response to
changing circumstances.

---

[3] Edward J. Blocher, Kung H. Chen, Gary Cokins, and Thomas W. Lin, *Cost Management: A Strategic
Emphasis* (New York: McGraw-Hill, 2005), p. 840.
[4] Ibid., p. 841.

EXHIBIT 12.2 Capital Investment Evaluation Techniques

Source: Adapted from Edward J. Blocher, Kung H. Chen, Gary Cokins, and Thomas W. Lin, *Cost Management: A Strategic Emphasis* (New York: McGraw-Hill, 2005), p. 881.

Technique	Definition	Computation Procedure	Advantages	Weaknesses
Payback period	Number of years to recover the initial investment	Number of years for the cumulative cash flow to equal the investment	• Simple to use and understand • Measures liquidity • Appraises risk	• Ignores timing and time value of money • Ignores cash flows beyond payback period
Book rate of return on investment (ROI)	Rate of average annual net income to the initial investment or average investment (book value)	Average net income ÷ Investment book value	• Data readily available • Consistent with other financial measures	• Ignores timing and time value of money • Uses accounting numbers rather than cash flows
Net present value (NPV)	Difference between the initial investment and the present value of subsequent net cash inflows discounted at a given interest rate	Present value of net cash inflows − Initial investment	• Consider time value of money • Uses realistic discount rate for reinvestment • Additive for combined projects	• Not meaningful for comparing projects requiring different amounts of investments • Favors large investments
Internal rate of return (IRR)	Discount rate that makes the initial investment equal the present value of subsequent net cash inflows	Solving the following equation for discount rate i: (Present value factor of i) Net cash inflows = Initial investment	• Considers time value of money • Easy for comparing projects requiring different amounts of investment	• Assumption on reinvestment rate of return could be unrealistic • Complex to compute if done manually

Capital Budgeting Techniques

There are four techniques often used in evaluating and making capital investment decisions: (1) payback period, (2) return on investment, (3) net present value, and (4) internal rate of return. The main features of these capital investment techniques are summarized in Exhibit 12.2.

Payback Period

The payback period of a project is the length of time required to recoup the initial investment. Calculation of payback period requires knowledge of the amount to be invested and an estimate of the after-tax cash flows to be received from the investment for each year of the project's life. For example, with an initial outlay of $600,000 and annual after-tax net cash inflows of $100,000, the payback period would be six years. If the decision rule is to accept only those projects with a payback period of five years or less, the company would reject an investment proposal with a payback period of six years. This is simple and straightforward. The length of payback period can be viewed as a measure of the investment's risk—the longer the payback period, the riskier the investment. The major limitations of this technique are its failure to consider the time value of money and an investment's total profitability. The use of payback period could lead to inappropriate investment decisions by rejecting investment proposals that provide larger cash inflows in the latter part of their useful lives. Payback period only considers the length of time required to recoup the initial investment regardless of the investment's total profitability.

Return on Investment

Calculation of return on investment (ROI) requires knowledge of the amount to be invested and an estimate of the average annual net income to be earned from an investment:

$$\text{ROI} = \frac{\text{Average annual net income}}{\text{Book value of investment}}$$

In using ROI for making capital budgeting decisions, a company must determine the minimum rate of return that makes an investment project worthwhile. Assume that a company requires ROI of at least 10 percent and has the following investment opportunities available:

Project	Required Investment	Average Annual Net Income
A	$800,000	$96,000
B	500,000	30,000
C	300,000	54,000

ROI for the three projects is as follows:

Project	ROI
A	12% ($96,000/$800,000)
B	6% ($30,000/$500,000)
C	18% ($54,000/$300,000)

Based on the company's decision rule, only projects A and C would be accepted because their ROI exceeds the 10 percent rate of return hurdle.

ROI is easy to compute using data from pro forma financial reports. Unlike payback period, it considers the entire period of an investment. However, it also ignores the time value of money. Further, it does not consider the possibility that a project may require other outlays such as working capital commitments in addition to the initial investment.

Discounted Cash Flow Techniques

Two discounted cash flow techniques are in common use in capital budgeting. They are (1) the net present value (NPV) method and (2) the internal rate of return (IRR) method. These techniques use present values of future cash flows in evaluating potential capital investments, using a discount rate. Usually the discount rate used is the firm's cost of capital or some other minimum rate of return. The Institute of Management Accountants defines cost of capital as "a composite of the cost of various sources of funds comprising a firm's capital structure."[5] A minimum

---

[5] Institute of Management Accountants, *Statement No. 4A: Cost of Capital* (Montvale, NJ: IMA, 1984), p. 1.

rate of return is often determined by referring to the strategic plan, the industry average rate of return, or other investment opportunities.

Net Present Value

The NPV of an investment is the difference between the initial investment and the sum of the present values of all future net cash inflows from the investment, calculated as follows:

$$\text{Present value of future net cash flows} - \text{Initial investment}$$
$$= \text{Net present value (NPV)}$$

The amount of NPV can be positive, negative, or zero. A positive NPV means that the investment is expected to provide a rate of return on the initial investment greater than the discount rate, whereas a negative NPV means the return provided would be less than the discount rate. If the NPV is zero, the project is expected to provide a rate of return exactly equal to the discount rate. The decision rule is to accept positive (or zero) NPV investment projects. Calculation of NPV requires knowledge of the amount of initial investment; estimation of future cash flows to be derived from the investment, including cash flows to be received upon the investment's liquidation (known as terminal value); and an appropriate discount rate based on the desired rate of return on investment.

Internal Rate of Return

A positive NPV implies that an investment's return exceeds the desired rate of return (discount rate), but it does not indicate the exact rate of return provided by the investment. This can be determined by calculating the internal rate of return (IRR). IRR is the discount rate that equates the present value of future net cash inflows to the initial investment. Essentially, a project's IRR is the discount rate at which NPV is equal to zero. The following example illustrates how IRR is determined.

IRR Illustration Assume that a company is considering a potential investment with a four-year life, no terminal value, and the following estimated cash flows:

Total initial investment	$5,000
Net cash inflows for each of four years	$1,750

We solve the following equation to determine the present value (PV) of an annuity factor that equates the present value of the net cash inflows to the initial investment:

$$\$5,000 = \$1,750 \times \text{Present value of annuity factor (4 periods)}$$

$$\text{PV annuity factor (4 periods)} = \frac{\$5,000}{\$1,750} = 2.857$$

From a present value of annuity table, where number of periods is equal to 4, we find 2.857 to be the present value factor at a discount rate of 15 percent. Thus, the IRR for this investment project is 15 percent, which will be compared with the firm's desired rate of return in deciding whether to invest in this particular project.

Regardless of the technique used, the quality of the capital budgeting decision rests on the accuracy with which future cash flows can be estimated. Forecasting future income to be generated by a project is often the starting point for determining future cash flows.

Research shows that preference for a particular capital budgeting technique differs across countries. Shields and colleagues found that U.S. firms commonly use discounted cash flow techniques such as net present value and internal rate of return, whereas Japanese firms prefer payback period.[6] One explanation for Japanese firms' preference for payback period is that it is consistent with their corporate strategies. Many Japanese firms have adopted a strategy of creating competitive advantage through large investments in technology, and it is necessary to recoup the investment as quickly as possible to reinvest in new technologies. Another reason is that Japanese firms are increasingly competing on the basis of short product life cycles. This requires flexibility, and short payback periods increase flexibility. Japanese firms also recognize that with innovative products in the global market it is not feasible to predict cash flows in the distant future with meaningful accuracy.

Multinational Capital Budgeting

As noted earlier, application of NPV as the capital budgeting technique requires identification of the following:

1. The amount of initial capital invested.
2. Estimated future cash flows to be derived from the project over time.
3. An appropriate discount rate for determining present values.

Calculation of NPV for a foreign investment project is more complex than for a domestic project primarily because of the additional risks that affect future cash flows. The various risks facing MNCs broadly can be described as political risk, economic risk, and financial risk.

Political risk refers to the possibility that political events within a host country can adversely affect cash flows to be derived from an investment in that country. Nationalization or expropriation of assets by the host government with or without compensation to the investor is the most extreme form of political risk. Foreign exchange controls, profit repatriation restrictions, local content laws, changes in tax or labor laws, and requirements for additional local production are additional aspects of political risk. Cross-border transactions also can be affected by special rules and regulations imposed by foreign governments. For example, companies that export products to the European Union are required to comply with International Organization for Standardization (ISO) 9000 standards and certify that their products and quality control systems meet ISO 9000 minimum quality standards.

Economic risk refers to issues concerning the condition of the host country economy. Inflation and the country's balance of payments situation are aspects of economic risk. Continuous deterioration of the balance of payments situation of a country may lead to devaluation of its currency, which may aggravate the problem of inflation. Inflation affects the cost structure in an economy and the ability of the local population to afford goods and services. High inflation also increases the cost of doing business in a foreign country as managers invest time and resources in devising strategies to cope with rapidly changing prices.

---

[6] M. D. Shields, C. W. Chow, Y. Kato, and Y. Nakagawa, "Management Accounting Practices in the U.S. and Japan: Comparative Survey Findings and Research Implications," *Journal of International Financial Management and Accounting* 3, no. 1 (1991), pp. 61–77.

Financial risk refers to the possibility of loss due to unexpected changes in currency values, interest rates, and other financial circumstances. The degree to which a firm is affected by exchange rate changes is called foreign exchange risk. As described later in this chapter, there are three types of exposure to foreign exchange risk—balance sheet exposure, transaction exposure, and economic exposure—all of which have an impact on cash flows.

The initial consideration in analyzing a potential foreign investment project is whether it should be evaluated on the basis of project cash flows (in local currency) or parent cash flows (in parent currency), taking into account the amounts, timing, and forms of transfers to the parent company. Project cash flows are especially susceptible to economic and political risk, whereas parent company cash flows can be significantly affected by political risk and foreign exchange risk. Survey results show that MNCs evaluate foreign investments from both project and parent viewpoints.[7]

Factors that vary across countries and should be considered in evaluating a potential foreign investment from a *project perspective* include the following:

1. *Taxes.* Income and other tax rates, import duties, and tax incentives directly affect cash flows.
2. *Rate of inflation.* Inflation can cause changes in a project's competitive position, cost structure, and cash flows over time.
3. *Political Risk.* Host government intervention in the business environment, for example, through the imposition of local content laws or price controls, can alter expected cash flows.

Additional factors should be considered in evaluating a foreign investment from the *parent company perspective*:

1. *The form in which cash is remitted to the parent.* Different types of payments—dividends, interest, royalties—may be subject to different withholding tax rates.
2. *Expected changes in the exchange rate over the project's life.* This will directly affect the value to the parent of local cash flows.
3. *Political risk.* Foreign exchange and/or profit repatriation restrictions imposed by the host government may limit the amount of cash flow to the parent.

Incorporating these factors into the foreign investment analysis can be accomplished in two ways:

1. The factors are incorporated into estimates of expected future cash flows.
2. The discount rate used to determine the present value of expected future cash flows is adjusted (upward) to compensate for the risk associated with changes in these various factors.

It makes sense to use a common standard in choosing among competing foreign and domestic projects. Thus, making adjustments to the expected cash flows would seem to be more appropriate than making ad hoc, country-specific adjustments to the desired rate of return. While adjusting cash flows is preferable, it also is more difficult because it involves forecasting future foreign tax rates, foreign inflation

---

[7] Vinod B. Bavishi, "Capital Budgeting Practices at Multinationals," *Management Accounting,* August 1981, pp. 32–35; and Marjorie Stanley and Stanley Block. "An Empirical Study of Management and Financial Variables Influencing Capital Budgeting Decisions for Multinational Corporations in the 1980s," *Management International Review* 3 (1983).

rates, changes in exchange rates, and changes in foreign government policy. Sensitivity analysis, in which factors are varied over a relevant range of possible values, can show how sensitive the investment decision is to a particular factor. Because of the difficulty in adjusting cash flows, many companies adjust the discount rate instead. For example, a survey conducted in 1973 found that 49 percent of responding MNCs added a risk premium to their required rate of return in making foreign investment decisions.[8]

Next we illustrate how some of the complexities associated with the evaluation of potential foreign investments can be incorporated into the multinational capital budgeting process.

Illustration: Global Paper Company

Global Paper Company (GPC), a U.S.-based firm, is considering establishing a facility in Hungary to manufacture paper products locally. GPC is attracted to Hungary because of cheaper costs and substantial tax incentives offered by the local government. However, GPC is concerned about the stability of the political situation in Hungary. GPC has gathered the following information:

Initial investment. The proposed plant will be constructed in Year 0 on a turnkey basis such that GPC incurs its entire cash outflow on December 31, Year 0. The subsidiary will begin operations on January 1, Year 1. The total investment will be 50,000,000 forints (F), of which F 24,000,000 is for fixed assets to be depreciated on a straight-line basis over three years with no salvage value. The remaining F 26,000,000 is for working capital.

Financing. The project will be financed as follows:

Forint debt (10%)		F 15,000,000
Parent loan (10%) . . .	$150,000 × F 100 =	F 15,000,000
Parent equity	$200,000 × F 100 =	F 20,000,000

The subsidiary will obtain a three-year F 15,000,000 loan from a local bank at an interest rate of 10 percent. GPC will lend the subsidiary $150,000 and make an equity investment of $200,000, for a total initial cash outlay of $350,000. The parent loan is denominated and will be repaid in U.S. dollars. Interest on the parent loan is paid at the end of each year (in U.S. dollars).

Inflation and exchange rates. Inflation in Hungary is expected to be 20 percent per year over the next three years. As a result, the forint is expected to depreciate 20 percent per year relative to the U.S. dollar. The January 1, Year 1, exchange rate is 100 forints to the dollar. Forecasted exchange rates over the next three years are as follows:

January 1, Year 1	F 100 per U.S. dollar
December 31, Year 1	F 120 per U.S. dollar
December 31, Year 2	F 144 per U.S. dollar
December 31, Year 3	F 172.8 per U.S. dollar

---

[8] J. C. Baker and L. J. Beardsley, "Multinational Companies' Use of Risk Evaluation and Profit Measurement for Capital Budgeting Decisions," *Journal of Business Finance*, Spring 1973, pp. 38–43.

Earnings. Expected earnings before interest and taxes (EBIT) is composed of the following:

- Sales—Year 1:

    Local: 200,000 units; sales price—F 50 per unit

    Export: 200,000 units; sales price—F 50 per unit

    Local sales in units are expected to increase 10 percent per year. Export sales in units are expected to increase by the rate of devaluation of the Hungarian forint (20 percent). The unit price (in forints) for both local and export sales is expected to increase by the rate of Hungarian inflation (20 percent).
- Variable costs (other than taxes)—40 percent of sales.
- Fixed costs (other than interest)—consists of depreciation on fixed assets only.

Taxes. The Hungarian corporate income tax rate is 25 percent, and the U.S. corporate tax rate is 35 percent. However, as an incentive to invest, the Hungarian government is offering a reduction in corporate income tax rates to 20 percent for the first three years. Hungarian withholding tax rates are 20 percent on interest and 30 percent on dividends and terminal value. Interest and dividends received in the United States from foreign sources are taxed as ordinary income and are allowed a foreign tax credit for foreign taxes paid. The repayment of the parent loan and receipt of terminal value is not taxed in the United States.

Political risk. Local political analysts have concluded that the Socialist Party might strengthen and beat the Government Party in the next election. GPC estimates this probability at 40 percent. If this occurs, it is possible that the new government will nationalize selected industries. With a change in government, GPC estimates that the probability that its Hungarian manufacturing facility would be nationalized is 60 percent. If the plant is nationalized, GPC expects that no terminal value will be recovered for the equity. However, the parent loan will still be repaid and local loans will not be repaid. If the plant is not nationalized, the company will receive its expected terminal value at the end of the third year. Given the timing of future elections, any change in government would take place at the end of the third year.

Terminal value. Cash flow forecasts are made for only three years. At the end of the third year the operation will be sold to local investors. The terminal value at the end of three years is expected to be equal to (1) the present value of an infinite stream of third-year cash flow from operations if no nationalization occurs and (2) zero if the project is nationalized.

Repatriation restrictions. Because of a shortage of foreign exchange, the Hungarian government allows only 50 percent of after-tax accounting income to be remitted as dividends to foreign parent corporations. This restriction is expected to exist for the foreseeable future. However, foreign exchange is readily available for interest and principal repayments on any foreign currency debt.

Weighted-average cost of capital. GPC's weighted-average cost of capital is 20 percent. In Hungary, similar projects would be expected to earn an after-tax return of 20 percent.

Present value factors. Present value factors at 20 percent are as follows:

Period	Factor
1	0.833
2	0.694
3	0.579

In making the decision whether to invest in Hungary, GPC's chief executive officer has requested that the accounting department conduct an analysis to determine the investment's expected NPV from both (1) a project perspective and (2) a parent company perspective.

Project Perspective

To calculate NPV from a project perspective, GPC begins by calculating cash flow from operations (CFO) in Hungarian forints over the three-year investment horizon using the following formula:

$$CFO = \text{Earnings (after tax)} + \text{Depreciation}$$

Depreciation is added back to after-tax earnings because it does not represent an annual cash outflow. Remember that sales volume and selling prices fluctuate each year. Export sales and the amount of Hungarian forint interest expense on the parent loan are a function of changes in the exchange rate.

GPC then calculates total annual cash flow (TACF) in Hungarian forints over the three-year investment horizon, where TACF is equal to CFO in Years 1 and 2. In year 3, TACF is equal to CFO plus terminal value minus repayment of local debt, if the project is not nationalized. If the project is nationalized, Year 3 TACF is equal to CFO only. TACF over the three-year life of the investment is determined as follows:

			Year 1			Year 2			Year 3
Calculation of Total Annual Cash Flow (in forints)									
Sales									
Local	200,000 u.	F50	F 10,000,000	220,000 u.	F60	F 13,200,000	242,000 u.	F72	F 17,424,000
Export	200,000 u.	F50	10,000,000	240,000 u.	F60	14,400,000	288,000 u.	F72	20,736,000
Total sales			20,000,000			27,600,000			38,160,000
Variable costs	40%		(8,000,000)	40%		(11,040,000)	40%		(15,264,000)
Depreciation			(8,000,000)			(8,000,000)			(8,000,000)
EBIT			4,000,000			8,560,000			14,896,000
Interest									
Local	F15,000,000	10%	(1,500,000)	F15,000,000	10%	(1,500,000)	F15,000,000	10%	(1,500,000)
Parent*	$15,000	120	(1,800,000)	$15,000	144	(2,160,000)	$15,000	172.8	(2,592,000)
Earnings before									
tax			700,000			4,900,000			10,804,000
Taxes		20%	(140,000)		20%	(980,000)		20%	(2,160,800)
Earnings after tax . . .			560,000			3,920,000			8,643,200
Add: Depreciation . .			8,000,000			8,000,000			8,000,000
CFO			F 8,560,000			F 11,920,000			F 16,643,200
Terminal value†									83,216,000
Repayment of local debt									(15,000,000)
Total annual cash flow (without									
nationalization)			F 8,560,000			F 11,920,000			F 84,859,200
Total annual cash flow (with									
nationalization)			F 8,560,000			F 11,920,000			F 16,643,200

*Annual interest on parent loan is $15,000, which is translated into a larger amount of forints each year due to the expected decline in the value of the forint.

†Terminal value is equal to the present value of an infinite stream of Year 3 CFO calculated as: $16,643,200/0.20.

GPC next calculates the net present value of the TACF in Hungarian forints over the three-year investment horizon (1) without nationalization and (2) with nationalization, as follows:

Calculation of Net Present Value (without nationalization)		
TACF	**PV Factor**	**Present Value**
Year 1 . . . . F 8,560,000	0.833	F 7,130,480
Year 2 11,920,000	0.694	8,272,480
Year 3 84,859,200	0.579	49,133,477
		F 64,536,437
Less: Initial investment		(35,000,000)
NPV		F 29,536,437

Calculation of Net Present Value (with nationalization)		
TACF	**PV Factor**	**Present Value**
Year 1 . . . . F 8,560,000	0.833	F 7,130,480
Year 2 11,920,000	0.694	8,272,480
Year 3 16,643,200	0.579	9,636,413
		F 25,039,373
Less: Initial investment		(35,000,000)
NPV		F (9,960,627)

Finally, GPC determines the project's expected value in Hungarian forints given the probability of nationalization:

Calculation of Project Expected Value		
Net Present Value	**Probability**	**Expected NPV**
• Without nationalization . . . F29,536,437	0.76	F 22,447,692
• With nationalization . . . . . . F(9,960,627)	0.24*	(2,390,551)
Project expected value		F 20,057,141

*The probability of nationalization is determined by multiplying the probability of a change in government by the probability of nationalization if the government changes: 40% × 60% = 24%.

If GPC were to base the investment decision solely on the expected value from a project perspective, the positive expected value of F 20,057,141 would result in acceptance of the project.

Parent Company Perspective

To calculate NPV from a parent company perspective, GPC begins by calculating cash flows to parent (CFP) on an after-tax basis in U.S. dollars over the three-year investment horizon where

CFP = Interest on parent loan in years 1, 2, and 3 (net of withholding taxes)
+ Dividends in years 1, 2, and 3 (net of withholding taxes)
− U.S. taxes on interest and dividends in years 1, 2, and 3 (net of foreign tax credit)
+ Repayment of parent loan in year 3
+ Terminal value in year 3 (net of withholding taxes)

Note that CFP is affected by Hungarian dividend repatriation restrictions (50 percent of accounting earnings), Hungarian withholding taxes (interest 20 percent, dividends 30 percent), and by changes in the exchange rate. In addition, CFP is reduced by the amount of U.S. income tax (net of foreign tax credit) that must be paid on the interest and dividends received from Hungary. Cash flows to parent in U.S. dollars are determined as follows:

Calculation of Cash Flows to Parent								
			Year 1			**Year 2**		**Year 3**
Foreign exchange rates			120			144		172.8
Interest on parent loan	$150,000	10%	$15,000			$15,000		$15,000
Less: Withholding tax		20%	(3,000)			(3,000)		(3,000)
Net interest (positive cash flow) . . .			$12,000			$12,000		$12,000
Dividend	F560,000	50%	$2,333	F3,920,000	50%	$13,611	F8,643,200 50%	$25,009
Less: Withholding tax		30%	(700)		30%	(4,083)	30%	(7,503)
Net dividend (positive cash flow) . . .			$1,633			$9,528		$17,506
U.S. Taxes								
Grossed up dividend*			$ 2,917			$17,014		$31,262
Grossed up interest			15,000			15,000		15,000
Taxable income			17,917			32,014		46,262
Tax before foreign tax credit		35%	6,271		35%	11,205	35%	16,192
Less: Foreign tax credit[†]			(4,283)			(10,486)		(16,192)
U.S. tax liability (negative cash flow to parent)			$ 1,988			$ 719		$ 0
Actual taxes paid in Hungary on interest and dividend:								
Interest withholding tax			3,000			3,000		3,000
Dividend withholding tax			700			4,083		7,503
Income tax (deemed paid on dividend)			583			3,403		6,252
Total			4,283			10,486		16,755
Repayment of parent loan (positive cash flow)								$150,000
Terminal value								$481,574
Less: Withholding tax							30%	(144,472)
Net terminal value (positive cash flow)								$337,102
Total cash flow to parent			$11,646			$20,809		$516,608

*The grossed-up dividend in U.S. dollars is calculated as earnings before taxes (in forints) translated into U.S. dollars at the appropriate exchange rate multiplied by the amount that may be repatriated (50%):

Year 1: F 700,000/120 = $5,833 × 50% = $2,917
Year 2: F 4,900,000/144 = $34,028 × 50% = $17,014
Year 3: F 10,804,000/172.8 = $62,524 × 50% = $31,262

[†]The foreign tax credit is limited to the amount of tax before foreign tax credit.

If the project is nationalized in Year 3, terminal value will be zero, but the parent loan still will be repaid. In that case the total cash flow to parent in Year 3 is only $179,506 ($516,608 − $337,102).

GPC then calculates the net present value of cash flows to the parent over the three-year investment horizon (1) without nationalization and (2) with nationalization, as follows:

Calculation of Net Present Value (without nationalization)			
CFP		**PV Factor**	**Present Value**
Year 1	$11,646	0.833	$ 9,701
Year 2	20,809	0.694	14,441
Year 3	516,608	0.579	299,116
			$ 323,259
Less: Initial investment			(350,000)
NPV			$ (26,741)

Calculation of Net Present Value (with nationalization)			
CFP		**PV Factor**	**Present Value**
Year 1	$11,646	0.833	$ 9,701
Year 2	20,809	0.694	14,441
Year 3	179,506	0.579	103,934
			$ 128,077
Less: Initial investment			(350,000)
NPV			$(221,923)

Finally, GPC determines the expected value from a parent company perspective given the probability of nationalization:

Calculation of Parent Company Perspective Expected Value			
Net Present Value		**Probability**	**Expected NPV**
• without nationalization	$(26,741)	0.76	$ (20,323)
• with nationalization	$(221,923)	0.24	(53,262)
Expected value			$ (73,585)

If GPC bases the investment decision solely on the expected value from a parent company perspective, the negative expected value of ($73,585) would lead to rejection of the project. Evaluation of the potential Hungarian investment from both a project perspective and a parent company perspective leads to conflicting results. GPC's accountants should conduct sensitivity analyses to determine whether the results are particularly sensitive to one or more assumptions that have been made. The result may be sensitive, for example, to the assumption regarding future fluctuations in the exchange rate. Further, the company might want to consider alternative financing arrangements or attempt to obtain additional government concessions with respect to withholding and/or income taxes that could increase the likelihood of a positive NPV from a parent company perspective. Ultimately, management will need to decide whether the parent company perspective or the project perspective should dominate the decision process.

STRATEGY IMPLEMENTATION

The function of ensuring that an organization's strategies are implemented and goals are attained is known as *management control*. Management control systems are tools designed for implementing strategies and monitoring their effectiveness. Accountants play a vital role in the management control process through the development of operating budgets and in designing performance evaluation systems. Operating budgets help express a firm's long-term strategy within shorter time frames, provide a mechanism for implementing and monitoring the implementation of strategy within that time frame, and specify criteria for evaluating performance. The implementation of strategy within an organization is influenced by a variety of factors, such as organizational structure and national culture (see Exhibit 12.3). In this section, we briefly describe these other factors in relation to MNCs' management control systems.

Management Control

Management control involves planning what the organization should do to effectively implement strategy, coordinating the activities of several parts of the organization, communicating information to organizational members, evaluating information, deciding what action should be taken, and influencing organizational members to change their behavior consistent with the organization's strategy.[9]

The extent to which decision-making authority is delegated to other members of the organization is an important issue in management control. For example, in the case of MNCs, some level of delegation to subsidiary managers is generally necessary because of the need to respond to local conditions and to provide a mechanism for motivating subsidiary managers. However, the issue of delegation is particularly complex for MNCs because of the possibility that geographically dispersed subsidiary managers may work toward parochial ends, which could conflict with the interests of the organization as a whole. Therefore, with delegation of decision-making authority to subsidiary managers, the need arises for effective control systems to ensure that subsidiary managers behave in accordance

EXHIBIT 12.3   **Framework for Strategy Implementation**

Source: Robert N. Anthony and Vijay Govindarajan, *Management Control Systems*, 9th ed. (international ed.) (New York: McGraw-Hill, 1998), p. 8.

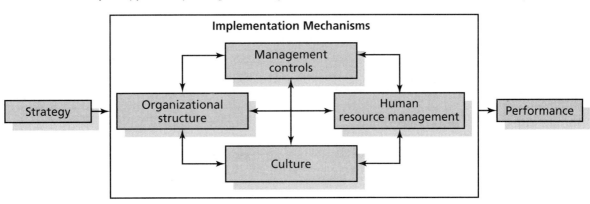

[9] Anthony and Govindarajan, *Management Control Systems*, pp. 6–7.

with organizational goals, also known as goal congruence. Determining the appropriate level of responsibility to delegate to foreign operations and designing the related control system necessary to ensure goal congruence are major issues facing MNCs in implementing strategy. Key factors that influence the design of an effective control system for an MNC include the company's organizational structure and the strategic role assigned to subsidiaries.

MNCs organize their cross-border activities in different ways depending on the main purpose of such activities. When an MNC focuses on producing products for the parent company market, its organizational structure can be described as *ethnocentric*. Firms operating on an ethnocentric principle assume that their own cultural background—including values, beliefs, language, nonverbal communication, and ways of analyzing problems—is universally applicable. In contrast, some MNCs focus on providing products to the host country with a unique product strategy. Subsidiaries in this case operate as strategic business units. The structure of such a firm can be described as *polycentric*. Polycentricism implies that the culture of the host country is important and should be adopted. Obviously, this creates the problem of adapting to multiple cultures within the overall organization. Some firms have a global networked structure, which supports both product line and geographic divisions in order to meet changing market demands. Such a structure can be described as *geocentric*. Those firms that use the principle of geocentricism believe that a synergy of ideas from different countries in which the firm operates should prevail. This, in turn, requires a common framework with enough flexibility to change when required.[10]

An MNC with a geocentric structure organizes its activities as a network of transactions in knowledge, goods, and capital among subsidiaries located in different countries. Focusing on knowledge flows, the firm can identify different roles for subsidiaries. A subsidiary that serves as the source of knowledge for other units, taking a leading role in a particular area, can be described as a *global innovator*. The Swedish company Ericsson's Italian subsidiary plays the role of a global innovator and serves as the company's global center for the development of transmission systems, while its Finnish subsidiary holds the leading global role for mobile telephones. In some cases, subsidiaries also take responsibility for creating knowledge in specific areas that other units can use. Such a subsidiary can be described as an *integrated player*. The integrator role is similar to the global innovator role. However, unlike a global innovator, which is self-sufficient in the fulfillment of its own knowledge needs, an integrated player relies on other units within the organization for some of its knowledge needs. Motorola's Chinese subsidiary is an example of an integrated player. In contrast, a unit may engage in little knowledge creation of its own and rely heavily on knowledge inflows from the parent or peer subsidiaries. Such a unit can be described as an *implementer*. Finally, a unit that has almost complete local responsibility for the creation of relevant know-how in the local context can be described as a *local innovator*. In this case, the knowledge is seen as too peculiar to be of much competitive use outside of the country in which the local innovator is located. These different subsidiary roles are shown in Exhibit 12.4.[11]

Organizational structure influences the extent to which responsibilities are delegated to individual foreign operations. Where the focus of a subsidiary's activities

[10] D. P. Rutenberg, *Multinational Management* (Boston: Little Brown, 1982).

[11] A. K. Gupta and V. Govindarajan, "Knowledge Flows and the Structure of Control within Multinational Corporations," *Academy of Management Review* 16, no. 4 (1991), pp. 773–75.

EXHIBIT 12.4
A Knowledge Flow–Based Framework of Generic Subsidiary Roles

Source: Adapted from A. K. Gupta and V. Govindarajan, "Knowledge Flows and the Structure of Control within Multinational Corporations," *Academy of Management Review* 16, no. 4 (1991), pp. 773–75.

Outflow of Knowledge† / Inflow of Knowledge*	Low	High
High	Global innovator	Integrated player
Low	Local innovator	Implementer

*From the rest of the organization to the focal subsidiary.
†From the focal subsidiary to the rest of the organization.

is on the host country (a polycentric organizational structure), the extent of delegation to the individual foreign subsidiary would be greater than in a situation in which the focus is on the synergy of activities in different countries (a geocentric organizational structure). The extent of delegation appropriate for a particular subsidiary can also depend on the specific strategic role assigned to it. For example, a subsidiary that plays the role of a local innovator may have a higher level of responsibility compared to one that plays the role of an integrated player, because of the lower level of interdependence between a local innovator and its peer units.

Two dominant control systems are available for corporate management to control subsidiaries—bureaucratic control and cultural control.[12] A bureaucratic control system makes extensive use of rules, regulations, and procedures that clearly specify subsidiary management's role and authority and set out expected performance in terms of identified targets, such as financial targets. These targets are used as the basis for evaluating performance. In contrast, in a system of cultural control, broad organizational culture plays a crucial role.[13] A cultural control system is more implicit and informal than a bureaucratic control system. Control mechanisms such as budgeting have both bureaucratic and cultural elements. The bureaucratic element of budgeting is in setting specific targets to achieve, and the cultural element is in the role budgeting plays in changing the behavior patterns within an organization.

Another important factor that influences an MNC's decision with regard to the level of control and the extent of delegation is cultural proximity, or the extent to which the host cultural ethos permits adoption of the home (parent company) organizational culture.[14] Those countries that permit easy adoption of the parent company culture would be considered high in cultural proximity. For example, a U.S. MNC might have relatively less difficulty in transmitting its organizational culture to a subsidiary in Australia than to a subsidiary in Indonesia. In this case, the cultural proximity between the United States and Indonesia would be lower compared to that between the United States and Australia. Cultural proximity

---

[12] B. R. Baliga and A. M. Jaeger, "Multinational Corporations: Control Systems and Delegation Issues," *Journal of International Business*, Fall 1984, pp. 25–40.

[13] *Organizational culture* can be defined as the common beliefs and expectations shared by the organization's members.

[14] Baliga and Jaeger, "Multinational Corporations."

becomes crucial in the selection of control systems because the lower the cultural proximity, the higher the familiarization costs. In the above example, an extra effort would be needed to familiarize the managers of the Indonesian subsidiary with the U.S. corporate culture, incurring additional costs.[15]

The effectiveness of any MNC control system depends on the quality and cooperation of management at the foreign subsidiary level. The ability and willingness of the subsidiary management to comprehend what is involved and accept what is required are crucial to the successful implementation of any control system. Furthermore, the quality of the mechanisms and process through which information is collected, processed, and transmitted at the subsidiary level will determine the quality of performance evaluation of foreign operations.

Operational Budgeting

Accounting's primary contribution to strategy implementation is operational budgeting. Whereas long-term budgets are mainly used as a strategy formulation and long-term planning device, annual operational budgets help express a firm's long-term strategy within shorter time frames. Operational budgets provide the mechanisms to translate organizational goals into financial terms, assign responsibilities and scarce resources, and monitor actual performance. Budgeted numbers become targets for managers to achieve.

Many MNCs find it necessary to translate operational budgets of foreign subsidiaries using an appropriate exchange rate. This process is complicated by exchange rate fluctuations. The next section of this chapter discusses the issues related to performance evaluation of foreign operations.

EVALUATING THE PERFORMANCE OF FOREIGN OPERATIONS

Performance evaluation is about monitoring an organization's effectiveness in fulfilling its objectives. It is a key management control task. In addition to providing measures that can be used to evaluate management performance, corporate management also expects the performance evaluation system to help assess the profitability of current operations, identify areas that need closer attention, and allocate scarce resources efficiently. Furthermore, the performance evaluation and related reward systems are expected to motivate organizational members to behave in a manner consistent with the organization's goals. Prior studies have shown that no single criterion can be used meaningfully in evaluating the performance of all subsidiaries, as no single criterion is capable of capturing all facets of performance that are of interest to corporate management. It is common for MNCs to use a mixture of measures, financial and nonfinancial, formal and informal, and formula-based and subjective to evaluate performance. For example, when there is a lower level of perceived environmental uncertainty, firms tend to use a more formula-based type of evaluation, whereas when there is a higher level of environmental uncertainty they tend to use more subjective judgment.[16] The operating environment of a foreign

---

[15] Similarly, the concept of "psychic distance" (the interaction between geographic distance and culture) has been used to explain budget control of foreign subsidiaries. See Lars G. Hassel and Gary M. Cunningham, "Psychic Distance and Budget Control of Foreign Subsidiaries," *Journal of International Accounting Research* 3, no. 2 (2004), pp. 79–93.

[16] V. Govindarajan, "Appropriateness of Accounting Data in Performance Evaluation: An Empirical Examination of Environmental Uncertainty as an Intervening Variable," *Accounting, Organizations and Society* 9, no. 2 (1984), pp. 125–35.

EXHIBIT 12.5   **Influences Affecting the Operating Environment of Subsidiaries in Foreign Countries**

Source: H. Noerreklit and H. W. Schoenfeld, "Controlling Multinational Companies: An Attempt to Analyse Some Unresolved Issues," *International Journal of Accounting* 35, no. 3 (2000), pp. 415–30.

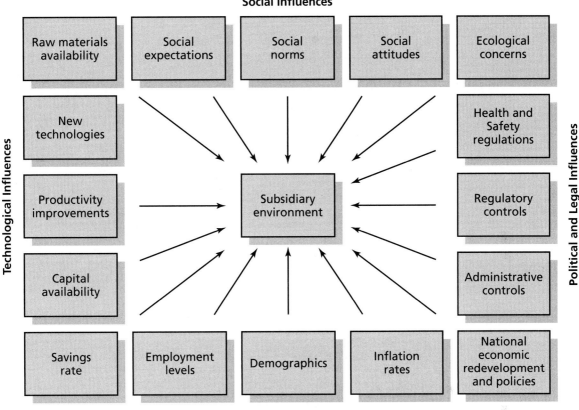

subsidiary is influenced by many factors. Exhibit 12.5 shows the social, political and legal, economic, and technological factors that are likely to influence a firm's operations in a national environment, creating a particular level of uncertainties and risks. Performance evaluation measures that attempt to capture these complexities are bound to contain a high degree of subjectivity.[17]

Further, companies do not seem to use any particular method of performance evaluation consistently. A study conducted by the Chartered Institute of Management Accountants (CIMA) in the United Kingdom found that, despite the consulting and academic literature on different approaches to performance measurement, most companies do not consistently use a particular technique.[18] For example, British companies adopt a contingency approach depending on the environment in which an organization operates, its structure and size, and the technological features of the organization. The CIMA study also points out that in the 1980s the focus of performance measurement was too historical. As a consequence, many organizations thought they were measuring the wrong things. In the 1990s,

[17] For example, S. M. Robbins and R. B. Stobaugh, "The Bent Measuring Stick for Foreign Subsidiaries," *Harvard Business Review*, September–October 1973, p. 86.

[18] Chartered Institute of Management Accountants, "Latest Trends in Corporate Performance Measurement," 2002.

companies experienced difficulties in implementing measurement frameworks and worried about having too many measures of performance. All these issues are still relevant in the new millennium.

Performance evaluation is a complex issue even in a purely domestic context. It becomes much more complex in an international context, particularly due to the issues that are unique to foreign operations, such as exchange rate fluctuations, varying rates of inflation in foreign countries, international transfer pricing, and cultural and environmental differences that exist across countries. It is important to ensure that the performance targets set for a foreign subsidiary are in line with overall corporate goals and strategies and at the same time appropriate for the local circumstances. In the remainder of this section, we discuss in some detail the issues relating to designing and implementing a system for evaluating the performance of a foreign subsidiary.

Designing an Effective Performance Evaluation System for a Foreign Subsidiary

Designing an effective performance evaluation system requires decisions with regard to the following:

1. The measure or measures on which performance will be evaluated.
2. The treatment of the foreign operation as a cost, profit, or investment center.
3. The issue of evaluating the foreign operating unit versus evaluating the manager of that unit.
4. The method of measuring profit for those foreign operations evaluated on the basis of profitability.

There are no universally right or wrong decisions with regard to these issues. There is no generically appropriate performance evaluation system, nor are there established guidelines that companies are required to follow. Each company will have a unique system tailored to its strategic objectives.

Performance Measures

Companies must decide whether to use financial criteria, nonfinancial criteria, or some combination of the two to measure and evaluate performance. Considering the diverse environments in which MNCs operate and the interdependencies among units in a multinational context, developing a global business strategy can be a highly complex task. A potential problem for MNCs in this regard is the tendency for headquarters to rely on simple financial control systems, often designed for home-country operations and extended to foreign subsidiaries. Subsidiary managers can be highly sensitive to these systems unless the systems are adapted to the local operating environment.[19] The danger here is that inappropriate performance standards may lead to dysfunctional behavior not in line with corporate goals.

Financial Measures

Financial measures are those measures of performance that are based on accounting information. They include sales growth, cost reduction, profit, and return on investment. Several surveys have asked MNCs which financial measures they use in evaluating the performance of foreign operations. The results of four surveys, three

---

[19] L. G. Hassel, "Headquarter Reliance on Accounting Performance Measures in a Multinational Context," *Journal of International Financial Management and Accounting* 3, no. 1 (1991), pp. 17–38.

EXHIBIT 12.6   Financial Measures Used by U.S. and UK MNCs to Evaluate Subsidiary Performance

Sources: [a]H. G. Moriscato, *Currency Translation and Performance Evaluation in Multinationals* (Ann Arbor, MI: UMI Press, 1980); [b]W. M. Abdallah and D. E. Keller, "Measuring the Multinational's Performance," *Management Accounting*, October 1985, pp. 26–30, 56; [c]A. Hosseini and Z. Rezaee, "Impact of SFAS No. 52 on Performance Measures of Multinationals," *International Journal of Accounting* 25 (1990), pp. 43–52; [d]I. S. Demirag, "Assessing Foreign Subsidiary Performance: The Currency Choice of U.K. MNCs," *Journal of International Business Studies*, Summer 1988, pp. 257–75.

	Ranking			
	United States			United Kingdom
Financial Measures	**1980**[a]	**1984**[b]	**1990**[c]	**1988**[d]
Profit	1	2	1	3
Return on investment (ROI)	2	3	3	2
Budget compared to actual profits	3	1	2	1

EXHIBIT 12.7   Comparison of Japanese and U.S. Performance Evaluation Measures

Source: J. C. Bailes and T. Assada, "Empirical Differences between Japanese and American Budget and Performance Evaluation Systems," *International Journal of Accounting* 26, no. 2 (1991), p. 137.

Percentage of Times Ranked in Top Three Budget Goals for Divisional Managers		
Measure	**Japan**	**United States**
Sales volume	86.3%	27.9%
Net profit	44.7	35.0
Production cost	40.7	12.4
Return on sales	30.7	30.5
Controllable profit	28.2	51.8
Sales growth	19.4	22.4
Return on investment	3.1	68.4

conducted in the United States and one conducted in the United Kingdom, are presented in Exhibit 12.6. In each survey, managers of MNCs were asked to indicate whether a particular financial measure is used in evaluating foreign subsidiary performance. In all four surveys, the top three financial measures used by both the U.S. and UK MNCs are profit, ROI, and comparison of budgeted and actual profit, although the rank order changes slightly among the four studies. Given the large percentage of companies using each measure, it is clear that MNCs use multiple financial measures in evaluating the performance of foreign operations.

By contrast, the results of a 1991 survey of U.S. and Japanese MNCs (reported in Exhibit 12.7) indicate that, compared with U.S. MNCs, Japanese MNCs are much more concerned with sales volume and production cost. In addition, Japanese MNCs are not very concerned with ROI, whereas this was the most important measure for the U.S. MNCs responding to the survey. U.S. MNCs are also more concerned with controllable profit than their Japanese counterparts. We discuss the concept of controllable profit more fully later in this chapter.

Nonfinancial Measures

Nonfinancial measures are those measures of performance that are based on information not obtained directly from financial statements. A survey of U.S. MNCs

EXHIBIT 12.8
Importance of Nonfinancial Measures in Evaluating Performance

Source: F. D. S. Choi and I. J. Czechowicz, "Assessing Foreign Subsidiary Performance: A Multinational Comparison," *Management International Review* 23 (1983), p. 17.

Nonfinancial Measure	Average Importance	
	Subsidiary	Manager
Increasing market share	1.8	1.5
Relationship with host country government	2.1	1.8
Quality control	2.2	1.9
Productivity improvement	2.2	2.1
Cooperation with parent company	2.4	2.0
Environmental compliance	2.4	2.3
Employee development	2.4	2.0
Employee safety	2.4	2.2
Labor turnover	2.7	2.5
Community service	2.9	2.8
Research and development in foreign subsidiary	3.1	3.2

Scale 1 = Very important to 4 = Not important

was conducted in 1983 to determine the use of various nonfinancial measures in evaluating the performance of foreign operations. Respondents were asked to indicate the level of importance of each measure on a scale of 1 (very important) to 4 (not important) in evaluating (1) the foreign subsidiary and (2) the manager of the foreign subsidiary. The results are reported in Exhibit 12.8.

Survey participants indicated that market share is the most important nonfinancial measure of performance. Other important measures include relationship with host country government, quality control, and productivity improvement. Nonfinancial measures such as community service and labor turnover were deemed less important. Overall, the less quantifiable and nonfinancial measures are subjective as compared with their financial counterparts.

In general, the method of evaluation depends largely on the type of subsidiary involved. It is common to use simple and straightforward criteria for evaluating a subsidiary with specific tasks, such as a sales unit. The criteria used to evaluate such affiliates include number of new customers, market share, or a combination of similar measures.

Financial versus Nonfinancial Measures

Prior studies have found national differences with respect to the prominence given to financial and nonfinancial measures in evaluating subsidiary performance. Partial results of a study of U.S. and Japanese management accounting practices that included both types of measures are reported in Exhibit 12.9. It shows that financial measures, albeit different ones, are given primary importance in both Japan and the United States. In Japan, market share is far less important than sales as a performance measure; in the United States, market share is about as important as sales, but both sales and market share are much less important than ROI in evaluating performance. In a separate study, profit-based measures also were given primary importance by European companies.[20]

A study investigated the evaluation criteria used by MNCs from four countries (Great Britain, Canada, Germany, and Japan) with regard to their operations in the United States. Some of the results are reported in Exhibit 12.10. Although

[20] Business International Corporation, "Evaluating the Performance of International Operations," New York: Author 1989, p. 174.

EXHIBIT 12.9 Comparison of Financial and Nonfinancial Measures in Japan and the United States

Source: M. D. Shields, C. W. Chow, Y. Kato, and Y. Nakagawa, "Management Accounting Practices in the U.S. and Japan: Comparative Survey Findings and Research Implications," *Journal of International Financial Management and Accounting* 3, no. 1 (1991), p. 68.

	Percentage of Time Considered Important	
Measure	**Japan**	**United States**
Sales	69%	19%
Return on investment	7	75
Market share	12	19

EXHIBIT 12.10 Ranking of Evaluation Criteria by MNCs with Operations in the United States

Source: S. C. Borkowski, "International Managerial Performance Evaluation: A Five Country Comparison," *Journal of International Business Studies*, Third Quarter 1999, pp. 533–56.

Criterion	British	Canadian	German	Japanese
Profit margin	1	1,2	1	4
Sales growth	2,3,4	1,2	2	1
Cost reduction	2,3,4	3,4	5	5
Net income	12	5	4	3
Goal attainment	5	3,4	8	2
Budget adherence	2,3,4	6	9	9
Return on sales	6	13	13	7
Return on assets	7,8	10	14	13
Technical innovation	7,8	11	7	10
Return on investment	9,10	9	11	10
Product innovation	9,10	11	6	12
Market share	11	8	3	7
Company standards	13	7	10	5
Residual income	14	14	12	13

differences exist across the four countries, the MNCs ranked several criteria highly in each. Profit margin is the number one criterion for MNCs in three of the four countries (tied with sales growth in Canada) but ranks fourth in Japan. Sales growth is the number one criterion in Japan and number two in the other three countries (with some ties). Cost reduction is a top-five criterion in each country. Net income ranks in the top five in each country other than Great Britain. Market share ranks among the top five criteria only for German MNCs.

The Balanced Scorecard: Increased Importance of Nonfinancial Measures

One of the most important achievements in the design of performance evaluation systems in recent years was the introduction of the balanced scorecard in the early 1990s.[21] A balanced scorecard combines financial measures of past performance with nonfinancial measures of the drivers of future performance to provide management with a road map for creating shareholder value. As shown

[21] For a description of this approach, see Robert S. Kaplan and David P. Norton, *The Balanced Scorecard* (Boston: Harvard University Press, 1996).

EXHIBIT 12.11
Basic Model of a Balanced Scorecard Performance System

Source: Adapted from Robert S. Kaplan and David P. Norton, "The Balanced Scorecard: Measures That Drive Performance," *Harvard Business Review*, January–February 1992, p. 72.

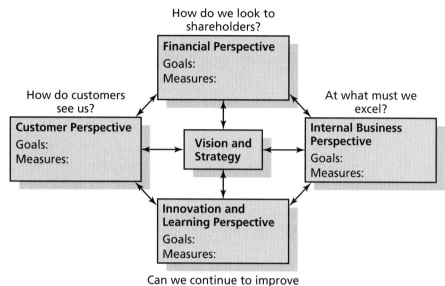

How do we look to shareholders?

Financial Perspective
Goals:
Measures:

How do customers see us?

Customer Perspective
Goals:
Measures:

Vision and Strategy

At what must we excel?

Internal Business Perspective
Goals:
Measures:

Innovation and Learning Perspective
Goals:
Measures:

Can we continue to improve and create value?

in Exhibit 12.11, a balanced scorecard focuses on an integrated relationship among the key elements of a business—vision; strategy; and four perspectives, namely, financial, customer, internal business process, and learning and growth.

Financial perspective refers to the issue of how a firm should appear to its shareholders in order to succeed financially. *Customer perspective* refers to the issue of how a firm should appear to its customers in order to succeed financially. If customers are not satisfied, they will eventually find other suppliers that will meet their needs. *Internal business process perspective* refers to the business processes at which the firm must excel in order to satisfy its shareholders and customers. This allows the managers to know how well the business is running and whether its products and services conform to customer requirements. *Learning and growth perspective* refers to how the firm will sustain its ability to change and improve in order to achieve its vision. In the current environment of rapid technological change, it is becoming necessary for both managers and other employees within a firm to be in a continuous learning mode. A balanced scorecard contains performance measures related to each of the four perspectives. Nonfinancial measures are related to three of the four perspectives included in the balanced scorecard.

A 2002 survey of 167 U.S. chief financial officers conducted by PricewaterhouseCoopers found that top executives at MNCs consider nonfinancial performance measures such as product/service quality and customer satisfaction/loyalty more important than current financial results in creating long-term shareholder value (see Exhibit 12.12). According to the survey, 69 percent of MNCs have attempted to develop a balanced scorecard combining both financial and nonfinancial measures in a comprehensive system to measure performance. While nonfinancial measures are viewed as being most important for long-term shareholder value, financial results are still viewed as a key factor in making ongoing management decisions. The major advantage of profit as a measure of performance is that it embodies all the major business functions from marketing (sales revenue) to production (cost of goods sold) to financing (interest expense).

Exhibit 12.13 shows how the senior management team of Rockwater, a worldwide leader in underwater engineering and construction, transformed its vision

EXHIBIT 12.12 CFOs' Views on Factors Contributing to Long-Term Shareholder Return

Source: PricewaterhouseCoopers, "Non-financial Measures Are Highest-Rated Determinants of Total Shareholder Value, PricewaterhouseCoopers Survey Finds," Management Barometer news release, April 22, 2002.

Measure	Importance*
Product and service quality	89%
Customer satisfaction and loyalty	83
Operating efficiency	75
Current financial results	71
Innovation	62
Employee satisfaction and turnover	47

*Percentage of respondents indicating that a particular measure is important in determining long-term shareholder value.

EXHIBIT 12.13 Rockwater's Balanced Scorecard

Source: Robert S. Kaplan and David P. Norton, "Putting the Balanced Scorecard to Work," *Harvard Business Review*, September–October 1993, p. 136.

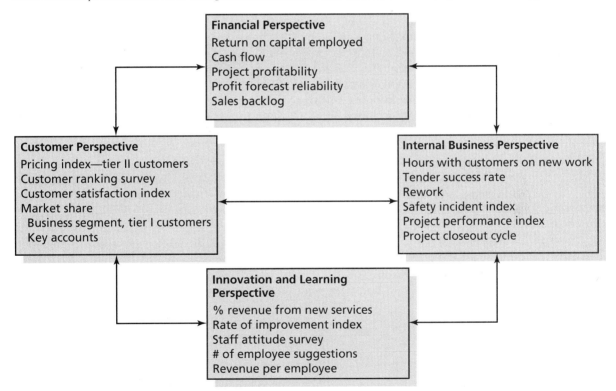

and strategy into the balanced scorecard's four sets of performance measures. Rockwater is a wholly owned subsidiary of Brown & Root/Halliburton, a global engineering and construction company. The company's vision was to be the industry leader in providing the highest standards of safety and quality to its clients.[22]

[22] Robert S. Kaplan and David P. Norton, "Putting the Balanced Scorecard to Work," *Harvard Business Review*, September–October 1993, pp. 135–40.

Responsibility Centers

A company must decide whether a foreign affiliate should be evaluated as a cost center, a profit center, or an investment center. Managers of cost centers tend to have the least amount of responsibility compared to managers of other responsibility centers within a group. They normally have no right to sell existing assets or acquire new assets. Cost centers are expected to produce as much as possible for a given amount of resources (e.g., internal service units of an organization, such as accounting, manufacturing, and research and development) or produce a given amount of output with specified quality at the lowest possible cost. Treating an operating unit as a cost center implies that responsibility is assigned only to cost control and reduction, but not to sales generation.

Evaluation as a profit center implies that profit will be used to determine whether the operating unit is achieving its objectives and that resources will be allocated according to the unit's profit. In effect, the operating unit and its management are being held responsible for generating profit. Profit center managers are given a fixed amount of assets and are ultimately responsible for both costs and revenues.

The responsibilities of an investment center manager include all the responsibilities of a profit center manager plus the responsibility for investment decisions. Return on investment is the most common investment center performance measure. If a foreign operating unit is evaluated as an investment center, the unit and its management are held responsible for generating an adequate ROI. Although identifying appropriate responsibility centers for foreign subsidiaries is a difficult task, it is also important because of the need to match the performance measure chosen to the responsibilities assigned to the responsibility center. Exhibit 12.14 summarizes major differences among the different types of responsibility centers.

Foreign Operating Unit as a Profit Center

To the extent that foreign management is not directly responsible for all of the foreign operation's activities, treating that operation as a profit center may not be useful for evaluating performance. An MNC's transfer pricing policy may not be compatible with the profit center concept. When corporate management dictates that certain transfer prices be used to achieve a specific worldwide cost-minimization objective, the local operation loses control over determination of profit. For example, it would be inappropriate to evaluate an assembly plant in a high-tax country as a profit center when it is required to purchase inputs from foreign affiliates at

EXHIBIT 12.14
Differences among Cost, Profit, and Investment Centers

Source: Adapted from Cheryl S. McWatters, Dale C. Morse, and Jerold L. Zimmerman, *Management Accounting* (New York: McGraw-Hill, 2001), p. 198.

Type of Responsibility Center	Responsibilities	Performance Measurement
Cost center	Choose output for a given cost of inputs Or Choose input mix to achieve a given output	Output (maximize given quality constraints) Or Cost (minimize given quality constraints)
Profit center	Choose inputs and outputs with a fixed level of investment	Profit (maximize)
Investment center	Choose inputs, outputs, and level of investment	Return on investment, residual income (maximize)

high prices (dictated by the parent company) in order to minimize worldwide income taxes.

Some foreign operations have strategic importance other than to generate profit. For example, a company might invest in a mining operation in a foreign country with the purpose of having a captive source of an important raw material. The original reason for making this investment was not to generate profit, and perhaps it should not be evaluated on the basis of profitability. Further, if all the output is sold (transferred) to affiliated companies, which means none is sold on the open market, then this operation may have no control over either sales volume or sales price—both are dictated by the parent or affiliated customers. For this particular type of operation, performance might be better evaluated using a measure like cost reduction or productivity, not profit. Further, if the foreign affiliate was established with the purpose to sell products produced by the parent, perhaps sales volume or market share would be a more appropriate performance measure than profit. The important point is that for some foreign operations it might not be relevant to evaluate performance on the basis of profitability. Dysfunctional behavior can occur, for example, if a parent company decides to shut down an unprofitable component-parts manufacturer when the reason it is not profitable is that the parent mandates low transfer prices. Headquarters management must decide which foreign operations should or should not be evaluated as profit centers.

In comparing the results of surveys conducted in 1978 and 1989, Business International identified a trend of companies moving away from treating individual subsidiaries as profit centers and instead treating them as cost centers. One reason for the shift is that companies have too many subsidiaries. For example, U.S.-based Cargill has 61 subsidiaries in the United Kingdom alone. Profit centers are more and more being defined at the level of strategic business unit (SBU), often product lines.[23] However, many foreign operations are legal entities in the host countries and are therefore required to maintain a complete set of accounting records and measure profit for legal and tax reasons.

Separating Managerial and Unit Performance

Intertwined with assigning levels of responsibility to foreign operating units is the question of whether the foreign operating unit and the management of that unit should be evaluated using the same performance measure. The performance of a foreign subsidiary is the result of decisions made by various parties, for example, local management, corporate management, and host governments. Local managers make most operating decisions, whereas corporate management makes transfer pricing and funds transfer decisions. Host governments may have specific rules concerning pricing and the use of foreign exchange that affect an operating unit's performance.

It is possible to have good management performance despite poor unit performance and vice versa. To properly reward and keep good managers and not inadvertently reward bad managers, the evaluation system should be able to separate subsidiary from managerial performance. The poor overall performance of the subsidiary may be largely due to the circumstances beyond the manager's control—for example, market disruption caused by terrorism—even though the manager performed well under the circumstances.

The main issue here revolves around *uncontrollable items*, that is, items that affect the performance measure over which the local manager has no control or is

[23] Business International, "Evaluating the Performance," p. 174.

not permitted to attempt to manage. The concept of *responsibility accounting* suggests that costs, revenues, assets, and liabilities should be traced to the individual manager who is responsible for them. Individual managers should not be held responsible for costs over which they have no control, nor should they be given credit for uncontrollable revenues.

Examples of Uncontrollable Items

Uncontrollable items can be classified as those that are controlled by the parent company, the host country government, and other parties. The following is a list of examples of each type:

Items Controlled by the Parent Company

- Sales revenue and cost of goods sold determined by discretionary transfer pricing.
- Allocation of corporate expenses such as the chief executive officer's salary and research and development costs to individual operating units.
- Interest expense on financing obtained from the parent (or an affiliated finance subsidiary), which sets the interest rate.

Items Controlled by the Host Government

- Restrictions on foreign exchange spending that affect the supply of imported materials and parts.
- Controls on prices that may be charged for products and services.
- Local content laws that require component parts to be sourced locally, sometimes at noncompetitive prices.

Items Controlled by Others

- Lost production due to labor strikes.
- Lost production due to power outages.
- Losses resulting from war, riots, and terrorism.
- Foreign exchange losses.

Managers normally prefer to be evaluated on the basis of controllable items because such evaluation is perceived as being fair and will make their rewards more predictable. However, costs often cannot be classified as either completely controllable or completely uncontrollable, because they are often influenced by both managerial actions and external factors.

Some companies use a measure of profit other than net profit to evaluate managers' performance. For example, using *earnings before interest and taxes (EBIT)* to measure performance does not hold the local manager responsible for interest and taxes. Likewise, the use of *operating profit* as the performance criterion avoids holding local management responsible for interest, taxes, and incidental gains and losses that are not a part of normal operations.

Business International asked survey participants what kinds of adjustments are made to the measures of profit and assets in measuring return on assets for evaluation purposes. Some of the results are reported in Exhibit 12.15. These results indicate, for example, that a majority of U.S.-based MNCs remove allocated corporate overhead costs from the measure of profit and intercompany receivables from the measure of total assets in calculating return on assets.

In evaluating the foreign operating unit, the decision of whether to adjust the performance measure for uncontrollable items should be based on whether the

EXHIBIT 12.15
Calculation of
Return on Assets
for Performance
Evaluation

Source: Rosemary Schlank,
*Evaluating the Performance of
International Operations* (New
York: Business International
Corp., 1989), p. 31.

	Percentage of MNCs	
	U.S.	European
Items Deducted from Profit		
Depreciation	68%	57%
Share of HQ administration costs	60	36
Foreign exchange gains and losses	48	50
Taxes	46	71
Interest	42	57
Share of corporate R&D	38	64
Items Included in Assets		
External receivables	80	86
Intercompany receivables	33	57
Other current assets	75	79
Fixed assets	82	71
Goodwill	44	14

item in question has any impact on cash flows to be received by the parent from the foreign operation. Generally, only those items controlled by the parent should be removed from the measurement of profit because all other items do affect cash flows. For example, although the local manager should not be fired over lost production due to power outages over which he or she has no control, the cost associated with lost production should be relevant in deciding whether to continue with this particular operation. In contrast, it would be dysfunctional to abandon a particular foreign operation located in a high-tax jurisdiction because of inadequate returns if the parent's discretionary transfer pricing policies contributed to the subpar ROI.

With regard to the issue of whether management and unit should be evaluated on the same basis, a 1990 survey of 109 U.S.-based MNCs found that most companies surveyed used the same performance measurement techniques in evaluating both managers and foreign operating units.[24]

Choice of Currency in Measuring Profit

It appears that most MNCs evaluate performance, at least partially, on some measure of profitability (net income, profit margin, return on investment, etc.). In using profit for performance evaluation, a major issue that companies must address is whether profit should be measured in local currency or parent company currency. If profit is to be measured in parent company currency, the company must select a *method of translation* and decide whether to include the *effects of exchange rate changes*.

Measurement of profit in the local currency is generally considered to be appropriate if the foreign subsidiary is not expected to generate parent currency for payment of dividends to stockholders. This would be true in the case where the operation provides a strategic benefit to the MNC other than an ability to generate parent currency dividends. An example would be a foreign operation that was established specifically to supply affiliated companies with raw materials.

[24] A. Hosseini and Z. Rezaee, "Impact of SFAS No. 52 on Performance Measures of Multinationals," *International Journal of Accounting* 25 (1990), p. 49.

EXHIBIT 12.16   Currency Used by U.S. and European MNCs for Performance Evaluation

Source: Rosemary Schlank, *Evaluating the Performance of International Operations* (New York: Business International Corporation, 1989), p. 178.

Currency	U.S. (*n* = 112)	European (*n* = 14)
Local currency	17.7%	21.1%
Parent currency	40.5	21.4
Both currencies	36.7	50.0

Measurement of profit in the parent currency is considered appropriate when the foreign subsidiary is expected to generate parent currency that could be paid as dividends to stockholders. This is true for most foreign subsidiaries.

The results of the Business International study conducted in 1989 regarding this question are shown in Exhibit 12.16. It is clear that evaluating performance on the basis of profit translated into parent currency, either alone or in conjunction with local currency results, is very popular. Only about one out of every five MNCs surveyed indicated that it evaluated the performance of foreign operations from a local currency perspective only. This study also indicates that a much greater percentage of U.S. companies than European companies evaluate the performance of foreign operations on the basis of parent currency results only.

Foreign Currency Translation

If parent currency is to be used in evaluating performance, the company must translate foreign currency profit into parent currency and decide which translation method to use. For internal purposes, a company need not use the same translation methods that it is required to use for financial reporting. A U.S.-based MNC, for example, need not use SFAS 52 rules for internal performance evaluation purposes. MNCs should consider which translation method best reflects economic reality for the particular foreign operation being evaluated.

A corollary issue is whether the *translation adjustment* should be included in the measurement of profit. Under SFAS 52, the translation adjustment that arises when the *temporal method* is used is included as a *gain or loss in net income*, whereas the translation adjustment under the *current rate method* is *deferred on the balance sheet*. Whether to include the translation adjustment in the measure of profit used for performance evaluation purposes would seem to hinge on two issues:

1. Does the translation adjustment accurately reflect the impact on parent currency cash flows resulting from a change in the exchange rate?
2. Does the foreign operation manager have authority to hedge his or her translation exposure?

If the answer to both questions is yes, then the translation adjustment should be included in the performance evaluation measure regardless of whether this is required by financial reporting rules. If the answer to either question is no, then the translation adjustment in profit may or may be included.

Choice of Currency in Operational Budgeting

As was shown in Exhibit 12.6, many MNCs evaluate annual performance by comparing actual operating performance to a budget. The company exerts management control by focusing on the variance between budgeted and actual profit.

Budgetary control allows corporate management to trace the manager or the unit responsible for the variance between budget and actual performance. In the case of an MNC, the question arises as to whether the budget should be prepared and actual profit measured in the local currency or in the parent currency. If "actual" is compared to "budget" in *local* currency, the overall budget variance will be a function of a sales volume variance and local currency price variances. If "actual" is compared to "budget" in *parent* currency, both the budget and actual results must be translated into parent currency using appropriate exchange rates. If one exchange rate is used to translate the budget (e.g., beginning-of-year exchange rate) and another exchange rate is used to translate actual results (e.g., end-of-year exchange rate), the budget variance will be a function of sales volume and local currency price variances *and the change in exchange rates.* This can be seen as follows:

$$\begin{array}{ccc} \text{Budgeted profit in} \\ \text{local currency} \end{array} \times \text{Beginning exchange rate} = \begin{array}{c} \text{Budgeted profit in} \\ \text{parent currency} \end{array}$$

$$\text{vs.} \qquad\qquad\qquad\qquad\qquad\qquad \text{vs.}$$

$$\begin{array}{c} \text{Actual profit in} \\ \text{local currency} \end{array} \times \text{Ending exchange rate} \;\; = \begin{array}{c} \text{Actual profit in} \\ \text{parent currency} \end{array}$$

Variance = f (sales volume variance and local currency price variances)   Variance = f (sales volume variance, local currency prices variances, *and exchange rate variance*)

If budget is compared to actual in parent currency, the question arises as to whether the manager of a foreign operation should be held responsible for foreign exchange risk, that is, the risk that actual results will deviate from the budget due to changes in the exchange rate. This question should be answered by determining whether foreign management has the authority to hedge, and therefore control, foreign exchange risk. If so, then it would make sense to translate the budget and actual results into parent currency and hold management responsible for the exchange rate component of the budget variance. If not, then perhaps profit measured in local currency rather than parent currency should be used for evaluation because the exchange rate variance is uncontrollable.

MNCs generally centralize their foreign exchange risk management activities and do not allow individual foreign operation managers to hedge their foreign exchange risk. Yet top management often wants to evaluate the performance of operations located in a variety of foreign countries on the basis of a common denominator—the parent currency. The question then arises as to how the local currency budget and actual results can be translated into parent currency without holding foreign management responsible for foreign exchange risk? The answer is fairly obvious: Use the same exchange rate to translate both budgeted profit and actual profit.

Conceptually, there are three possible exchange rates to use in preparing the budget and in translating actual results into parent currency:[25]

1. The actual exchange rate at the time the budget is prepared.
2. A projected future exchange rate at the time the budget is prepared.
3. The actual exchange rate at the end of the budget period.

[25] The discussion here is based on D. R. Lessard and P. Lorange, "Currency Changes and Management Control: Resolving the Centralization/Decentralization Dilemma," *Accounting Review,* July 1977, pp. 628–37.

EXHIBIT 12.17
Combinations for Translation of Budget and Actual Results

Source: D. R. Lessard and P. Lorange, "Currency Changes and Management Control: Resolving the Centralization/ Decentralization Dilemma," *Accounting Review*, July 1977, pp. 628–37.

Rate Used for Determining Budget	Rate Used to Track Actual Performance Relative to Budget		
	Actual at TOB	Projected at TOB	Actual at EOP
Actual at time of budget (TOB)	1	n/a	4
Projected at time of budget	n/a	3	5
Actual at end of period (EOP)	n/a	n/a	2

As shown in Exhibit 12.17, these three exchange rates lead to nine possible combinations, only five of which would make sense for evaluation purposes.

The five meaningful combinations of exchange rates differ as follows in the extent to which management is held responsible for fluctuations in exchange rates:

1. *Translate the budget and actual results using the spot rate that exists at the time the budget is prepared.* Under this combination, the overall budget variance is a function of sales volume and local currency price variances only. Exchange rates have no effect on evaluation. However, there is little incentive to incorporate anticipated exchange rate changes into operating decisions. This combination is equivalent to evaluating results in local currency.

2. *Translate the budget and actual results using the spot rate that exists at the end of the budget period.* The comments related to combination 1 apply equally to this combination.

3. *Translate the budget and actual results using a projected ending exchange rate (projected at the time the budget is prepared).* Under this combination, the overall budget variance also is a function of sales volume and local currency prices only. However, unlike combinations 1 and 2, the use of a projected exchange rate provides managers an incentive to incorporate expected exchange rate changes into their operating plans, but they are not held responsible for actual exchange rate changes. Because of its potential for causing local managers to consider the impact exchange rate changes will have on parent currency profit, this combination is generally favored in the literature.

4. *Translate the budget at the initial exchange rate and translate actual results using the ending exchange rate.* In this case, the overall budget variance is a function of sales volume, local currency prices, and the change in exchange rate *whether anticipated or not*. Local managers bear full responsibility for exchange rate changes. Non-economic hedging may result if foreign managers are allowed to hedge. Local managers will want to hedge their exposure even though a natural hedge may exist elsewhere in the MNC's worldwide organization.[26]

5. *Translate the budget at the projected ending exchange rate and translate actual results at the actual ending rate.* The budget variance is a function of sales volume, LC prices, and the *unanticipated* change in exchange rate. Local managers are asked to incorporate projected exchange rate changes into their operating plans. They are then held responsible for reacting to unanticipated exchange rate changes.

---

[26] A natural hedge within the MNC group exists, for example, if a subsidiary in Canada has a €1 million receivable and a subsidiary in Mexico has a €1 million payable, both due on the same date. From the group perspective, neither subsidiary should hedge its individual foreign exchange risk, because the loss (or gain) on the euro payable will be offset by a gain (or loss) on the euro receivable. If local managers are held responsible for exchange rate variances, however, there will be an incentive for both managers to hedge their specific foreign exchange exposure.

Illustration of the Combinations

To illustrate the five combinations of exchange rates in translating the budget and actual results, consider an example of a U.S.-based MNC with a subsidiary in Foreign Country. Budgeted amounts in foreign currency (FC) are as follows:

	Budget
Sales	FC100
Cost	90
Profit	FC 10

Assume that the foreign subsidiary's actual results in FC are exactly as budgeted and that exchange rates for the budget period are as follows:

Actual at time of budget preparation	$1.00/FC1
Projected ending	$0.90/FC1
Actual at end of period	$0.70/FC1

The following shows the translation of the budget and actual results into U.S. dollars under each of the five combinations:

	Combination									
	1		**2**		**3**		**4**		**5**	
	Budget	**Actual**	**Budget**	**Actual**	**Budget**	**Actual**	**Budget**	**Actual**	**Budget**	**Actual**
Exchange rate . . .	$1.00	$1.00	$0.70	$0.70	$0.90	$0.90	$1.00	$0.70	$0.90	$0.70
Sales	100	100	70	70	90	90	100	70	90	70
Costs	90	90	63	63	81	81	90	63	81	63
Profit	10	10	7	7	9	9	10	7	9	7
Variance	0		0		0		3		2	

Because the foreign subsidiary exactly met its sales volume and cost targets in terms of foreign currency, any U.S.-dollar variances are due solely to the change in the exchange rate. There is no exchange rate variance in combinations 1, 2, and 3, because the same exchange rate is used to translate both the budget and the actual figures. The exchange rate variance in combination 4 is $3, which is equal to the change in exchange rate from the beginning to the end of the period ($0.30) multiplied by the actual amount of FC profit (FC10). The exchange rate variance of $2 in combination 5 reflects the unanticipated change in the exchange rate ([$0.70 − $0.90] × FC10).

The 1989 Business International study referred to earlier in this chapter found that only about 14 percent of U.S. companies indicated using the same exchange rate to translate both the budget and actual results. In contrast, over one-third of the European companies included in the study indicated not holding anyone accountable for exchange rate variances.[27]

[27] Business International, "Evaluating the Performance," p. 178.

Incorporating Economic Exposure into the Budget Process

There are three types of exposure to foreign exchange risk: transaction exposure, translation (or balance sheet) exposure, and economic exposure. Transaction exposure refers to the risk that changes in exchange rates will have an adverse effect on cash flows related to foreign currency payables and receivables. Translation exposure refers to the risk that through the translation of foreign currency financial statements of its subsidiaries, a change in exchange rates will cause the parent company to report a negative translation adjustment in its consolidated financial statements. Chapters 6 and 7 covered financial accounting issues related to these two types of exposure to foreign exchange risk.

Economic exposure refers to the risk that changes in exchange rates will have a negative impact on an entity's cash flows. Transaction exposure is one aspect of economic exposure. However, the concept of economic exposure encompasses more than transaction exposure. Unlike transaction and translation exposures, economic exposure is not directly measured by the accounting system.

One example of economic exposure is the decrease in export sales that results from an *appreciation* of a company's home currency. For example, if the value of the British pound were to increase from US$1.50 to US$2.00, customers in the United States would have to pay a higher U.S.-dollar price for purchases denominated in British pounds and may therefore shift to non-British suppliers. An appreciation of the British pound creates economic exposure for British companies. The depreciation of a company's home currency also creates economic exposure through an increase in the home currency price paid for import purchases. The extent of economic exposure for a business enterprise is at least partially a function of its mix of imports and exports.

Transaction and translation exposures are often reduced through the use of financial instruments such as foreign currency forward contracts and options. Economic exposure is reduced by making operating and strategic decisions to make the company more competitive in the face of exchange rate changes. Shifting from the use of imported parts to locally produced parts and reducing the local currency price in the short term to shore up export sales are examples of actions that a company could take to reduce the economic exposure to exchange rate changes.

Economic exposure also provides opportunities to take advantage of exchange rate changes to increase local currency cash flows. For example, if the U.S. dollar were to decrease in value from $1.00 per euro to $1.25 per euro, a U.S.-based company could pursue a strategy to increase sales volume and market share in Europe without having to reduce its U.S.-dollar prices. Conversely, the company could pursue a skimming strategy by increasing its U.S.-dollar price such that the euro price (and therefore European demand) after the exchange rate change remains the same as before. In either case, total U.S.-dollar sales and therefore U.S.-dollar cash flows should increase.

Designing a control system that allows the parent company to evaluate the performance of its foreign subsidiary managers on their ability to manage economic exposure and at the same time motivates them to exploit opportunities afforded by exchange rate changes is not easy. Because economic exposure deals with opportunity costs, its effects are not separately measured by the normal accounting system. Let us consider what can happen if a company does not attempt to incorporate economic exposure into the evaluation system.

Assume U.S.-based Parent Company has two subsidiaries in Foreign Country: Exporter and Importer. Exporter makes export sales to the United States but sources inputs locally, and Importer imports all of its inputs from the United States but makes no export sales. Budgets in FC and US$ (using the initial exchange rate of US$1.00 = FC1) are as follows:

	Exporter		Importer	
	FC	US$	FC	US$
Sales	100	100	100	100
Costs	90	90	90	90
Profit	10	10	10	10

During the budget period the US$ appreciates 25 percent against the FC such that the ending exchange rate is US$1.00 = FC1.25 or US$.80 = FC1. Assuming that Parent Company uses the ending exchange rate to track actual performance, actual results in FC and US$ are as follows:

	Exporter		Importer	
	FC	US$	FC	US$
Sales	118	94.4	103	82.4
Costs	101	80.8	99	79.2
Profit	17	13.6	4	3.2

Actual FC sales and FC costs are larger than budgeted for both Exporter and Importer. Because the favorable sales variance is greater than the unfavorable cost variance, Exporter's actual profit exceeds the budget in both FC and US$. Although Importer outperformed the FC sales budget, FC costs rose more rapidly and Importer's actual profit is less than budgeted in both FC and US$. Given these results, should Exporter's manager, but not Importer's manager, be rewarded? Not necessarily. Incorporating the expected effect of a currency devaluation on FC sales and FC costs paints a different picture.

Exporter

Because Exporter has only export sales, a 25 percent depreciation in the FC should allow Exporter to either (1) generate 25 percent more sales volume (if FC prices are not increased), or (2) increase FC prices by 25 percent to generate higher total FC sales revenue at the same level of sale volume. In either case, Exporter's sales should have been FC125. Actual sales are only FC118 or FC7 less than they would have been if Exporter's manager had fully exploited the opportunity to increase export sales.

Because Exporter sources all inputs locally, the depreciation in the FC should not affect costs. Exporter's manager has not effectively controlled costs; costs are FC11 (FC101 − FC90) higher than they should be.

The appreciation of the U.S. dollar should have allowed Exporter to generate the following amount of FC and US$ profit:

	FC	US$
Sales	125	100
Costs	90	72
Profit	35	28

Actual profit is only $13.60, or $14.40 less than it should have been.

Importer

Because Importer imports all inputs from the United States, a 25 percent appreciation in the U.S. dollar should cause Importer's FC costs to increase by 25 percent, from FC90 to FC101.25. Actual costs are only FC99 because Importer's manager has sourced some inputs locally rather than through imports.

Because all of Importer's sales are made locally, the appreciation in the U.S. dollar should have no effect on FC sales. Nonetheless, Importer's manager was able to outperform the FC sales budget.

The appreciation of the U.S. dollar should have caused Importer to incur the following amount of FC and US$ loss:

	FC	US$
Sales	100.00	80
Costs	101.25	81
Profit (loss) . . .	(.25)	(1)

Actual profit is $3.20, or $4.20 greater than it should have been.

After incorporating the effects of economic exposure into the analysis, it would appear that the manager of Importer should be rewarded and the manager of Exporter should not be.

The accounting system does not measure the amount of profit that *should have been* earned, so information provided by that system is not helpful in measuring a manager's effectiveness in coping with economic exposure. The use of translation combinations 3 and 5 outlined earlier, in which projected rates are used to prepare the budget, is a partial solution to this problem. Using projected rates to translate the budget provides an incentive for managers to take operating and strategic actions to minimize negative effects on cash flows from changes in exchange rates and take advantage of positive effects. However, this approach is limited in that projected exchange rates may not become reality. A refinement to this process would be to periodically update the projected ending exchange rate and ask local managers to update their plans as the projection changes. This has been referred to as *contingent budgeting*.[28] Clearly, this is not an easy process, but any system that forces managers of foreign operations to consider the effect that exchange rate changes have on their operating results should help in reducing the risk associated with them.

Implementing a Performance Evaluation System

The success of a performance evaluation system will be determined by its design as well as the implementation of that system. The discussion in this section is based on a recent technical briefing published by the Chartered Institute of Management Accountants (CIMA) in the United Kingdom on the latest trends in corporate performance measurement.[29] CIMA identifies six important factors that are required for a successful performance evaluation system:

1. *Integration with the overall business strategy.* It is not possible to measure performance in a meaningful way unless it is clear what an organization is trying

---

[28] See D. Lessard and D. Sharp, "Measuring the Performance of Operations Subject to Fluctuating Exchange Rates," *Midland Corporate Finance Journal* 2 (Fall 1984), pp. 18–30.

[29] Chartered Institute of Management Accountants, "Latest trends."

to achieve. For example, if customer care has been identified as a critical success factor, then a fast response to complaints may be essential to achieve competitive advantage and a measure such as response time can be used to evaluate performance.

2. *Feedback and review.* The successful implementation of a performance evaluation system requires a continuous cycle of feedback on actual results in comparison with the original plan, feeding into the decision-making process. An important point to note here is that the original plan is based on certain assumptions about the nature of the business and what it takes to succeed. If performance falls short of what was expected in the original plan, then the company can take corrective action. This is an organizational learning process called single-loop learning. The term *single-loop* refers to the fact that the focus is for the organization to make decisions within the parameters of the original plan. In addition, a successful performance evaluation system should also include mechanisms to review performance measures over time. However, it may be appropriate to modify targets, change the activities being measured, or even modify the objectives. The action involved in this process is called double-loop learning. Here the focus extends to a consideration of the need to change aspects of the original plan. Single-loop learning is necessary to build core competencies, and double-loop learning is necessary to adapt to changes in the environment.

3. *Comprehensive measures.* The performance measurement system should reflect the range of factors that contribute to success. Financial performance, although the most important and widely used measure of performance, represents only one dimension of value and as such is inadequate in evaluating the strategic performance of an organization in its entirety. As explained earlier in this chapter, there is an increasing trend for MNCs to use nonfinancial measures in evaluating performance both at headquarters and subsidiary levels.

4. *Ownership and support throughout the organization.* It is important that employees throughout the organization understand and support the performance evaluation system. If they feel the system is imposed on them from above, without any consultation, they are less likely to cooperate with the system, and the system will not achieve its motivational objectives.

5. *Fair and achievable measures.* Performance targets should be set at a level that is achievable and at the same time should encourage high performance. Fairness is particularly important where performance measures are used to reward managers' performance. As mentioned earlier in this chapter, performance measures should include only the elements directly controlled by managers. If this is not the case, the reward system is likely to cause frustration and demotivate managers rather than encourage better performance.

6. *A simple, clear, and understandable system.* The effectiveness of a performance evaluation system depends largely on how well the people involved understand the system and the measures used to evaluate performance. There is not much point in providing complex data about performance if these data are not readily understood by those being evaluated. If the performance evaluation system is overly complex, chances are that many will not understand it. A lack of understanding will lead to a lack of cooperation and support for the system. It is best to use simple and clear measures that can be easily understood and communicated to everyone in the organization.

CULTURE AND MANAGEMENT CONTROL

For MNCs, another factor should be added to the framework developed by CIMA for the successful implementation of a performance evaluation system: the system must be sensitive to the national cultures to which local managers belong. Indeed, cultural factors should be considered in the entire strategy implementation process. Implementing a corporate strategy that will influence human behavior in the desired manner requires cultural awareness, as a given method of implementation may not produce the desired outcome across all cultures. Noerreklit and Schoenfeld explain how differences in culturally determined value systems may lead to different managerial decisions across countries:

> Different background knowledge and culturally determined value systems exist in all MNCs, because employees grow up and are educated in different national environments and thus have non-congruent value systems. Such different values may (at a minimum) place a different emphasis on specific issues. Different emphasis and values are typically placed on specific subjects during the educational process (e.g., ethics, family relationships, work, sports, art, moral contained in children stories, songs, and proverbs). . . . Each of these influences (individually or jointly) will evoke slightly or substantially different reactions in people. This applies for day-to-day life as well as for management decisions as a special dimension of life. It suggests different actions to resolve similar problems (e.g., under-utilisation of capacity may suggest lay-offs in the US, however, in Europe, due to the existing labour law and tradition, a lay-off is too costly or unacceptable socially).[30]

Due to cultural differences, MNCs may find that changes are necessary to the manner in which strategies are implemented in different countries. For example, Japanese companies assign responsibility to the group rather than to the individual, and every group member is partially responsible for the group's performance.[31] This notion of group responsibility conflicts with the way standard costs and budgets are used in the United States, in which responsibility is assigned to specific individuals within an organization.[32] This also calls into question the universal acceptability of one of the fundamental assumptions of the Western concept of management control—that the responsibility for specific tasks lies with the individual to whom the task is traceable. Research also has found differences between the United States and Japan in their use of budgets. U.S. managers tend to be more involved in the budgeting process, and budget variances are used as the basis for evaluating performance and determining rewards. Japanese managers, in contrast, tend to view budget variances as providing information that can be used to improve performance.[33]

Local managers' attitudes toward budgets also can be influenced by environmental factors. Researchers have discovered, for example, that managers in Central American countries view budgets as less critical than U.S. managers do.[34]

---

[30] Noerreklit and Schoenfeld, "Controlling Multinational Companies," p. 418.

[31] L. Kelley, A. Whatley, and R. Worthley, "Assessing the Effects of Culture on Managerial Attitudes: A Three-Country Test," *Journal of International Business Studies*, Summer 2001, p. 22.

[32] P. Miller and T. O'Leary, "Accounting and the Construction of the Governable Person," *Accounting, Organizations and Society* 12, no. 3 (1987), pp. 235–65.

[33] J. C. Bailes and T. Assada, "Empirical Differences between Japanese and American Budget and Performance Evaluation Systems," *International Journal of Accounting* 26, no. 2 (1991).

[34] R. Mandoza, F. Collins, and O. J. Holzmann, "Central American Budgeting Scorecard: Cross Cultural Insights," *Journal of International Accounting, Auditing and Taxation* 6 (1997), pp. 192–209.

Central American managers are more likely to see budgets as a source of certainty and security and as a means to protect resources amid turbulence, rather than as a performance evaluation and planning tool. The researchers argue that the differing attitudes toward budgets are due partly to the widely varying levels of environmental turbulence between the United States and Central America.

Culture also can affect management styles. Researchers have found that Mexican executives tend to use an authoritarian leadership style, do not see the need to share information with subordinates, and have little faith in participative management styles. This will have direct implications for the manner in which budgeting is applied within Mexican organizations. In particular, the idea of participative budgeting is not likely to be well received.[35]

Finally, cultural differences can influence capital budgeting decisions. For example, strong uncertainty avoidance (intolerance of uncertainty) can lead managers to require short payback periods for capital investments, because once the investment is recouped, the level of uncertainty associated with the investment is reduced significantly. This makes projects with shorter payback periods the preferred choice for some managers, even though projects with longer payback periods may produce greater longer-term benefits.

Summary

1. Accountants contribute to *strategy formulation* by providing skills to analyze customer, market, and competitor information, assess risks, develop projections as financial expressions of strategy, and prepare budgets. *Capital budgeting* is an important device used in strategy formulation.

2. *Multinational capital budgeting* is complicated by the various risks to which foreign operations are exposed. Forecasted future cash flows should be adjusted to take into account the effect of factors such as local inflation, changes in exchange rates, and changes in host government policy.

3. Accountants contribute to *strategy implementation* by providing management control tools such as operational budgets and by helping to design and implement performance evaluation systems.

4. Multinational companies (MNCs) expand across national borders for various reasons, their cross-border operations can take different forms, and they adopt a variety of organizational structures. The choices made by an MNC in these areas influence the manner in which strategies are implemented.

5. Determining *the levels of control and delegation* appropriate for foreign affiliates is an important part of implementing multinational business strategy.

6. Companies must decide on *performance evaluation measures*. Although companies often use multiple measures, both financial and nonfinancial, most focus on financial measures of performance, and profit-based measures are most commonly used.

7. Companies must decide whether a foreign operation will be evaluated as *an investment center, a profit center,* or *a cost center.* Some foreign operations may have a strategic purpose other than profit creation and should therefore be evaluated differently.

8. Companies must also decide *whether the foreign operating unit and the managers of that unit should be evaluated in the same manner,* or whether they should be

---

[35] Kelley, Whatley, and Worthley, "Assessing the Effects."

evaluated separately using different measures of performance. Responsibility accounting suggests that managers should not be held responsible for uncontrollable items. For foreign managers, this would consist of revenues and expenses controlled by the parent company, the host government, and others.

9. For those foreign operations evaluated on the basis of profitability, the company must decide whether profit will be measured in local or parent currency. Most companies evaluate the performance of foreign operations in parent currency, which necessitates *translation* from the local currency. These companies must decide whether the local manager will be *held responsible for the translation adjustment* that results.

10. If performance is evaluated by *comparing budgeted to actual results in parent currency*, exchange rate variances can be avoided by using the same exchange rate to translate the budget and actual results. Using a projected exchange rate to translate the budget provides an incentive for local management to factor the effects of expected exchange rate changes into the operating plans. Contingent budgeting involves periodic updating of operating budgets as exchange rates fluctuate during the period covered by the budget.

11. The success of a performance evaluation system is determined by its design as well as how it is implemented. To be successful, a performance evaluation system must be integrated with the overall strategy of the business; it must be comprehensive; it must be owned and supported throughout the organization; measures need to be fair and achievable; it needs to be simple, clear, and understandable; and there must be a system of feedback and review.

12. Management control systems also must be sensitive to the national cultures to which local managers belong. Cultural awareness is needed when implementing a system designed to influence human behavior in a particular, because a given method of implementation may not produce the desired outcome across all cultures.

Questions

1. What are the internal factors that influence strategy formulation within an MNC?

2. What are the external factors that influence strategy formulation within an MNC?

3. Explain the role of accounting in strategy formulation within an MNC.

4. Compare and contrast NPV and IRR as capital budgeting techniques.

5. How does the organizational structure of an MNC influence its strategy implementation?

6. How do differences in cultural values across countries influence strategy implementation within an MNC?

7. Explain the role of accounting in implementing multinational business strategy.

8. What are the main issues that need to be considered in designing and implementing a successful performance evaluation system for a foreign subsidiary?

9. What differences can you identify between performance evaluation measures adopted by Japanese and U.S. MNCs?

10. What are the nonfinancial measures available to MNCs for evaluating foreign subsidiary performance?

11. What are the factors that influence the decision regarding the manner in which a particular subsidiary should be treated for purposes of performance evaluation (e.g., as a cost center or a profit center or an investment center)?

12. Do you think it is important to separate the evaluation of the performance of a subsidiary from that of its manager? Why?

13. What issues are associated with the calculation of profit for a foreign subsidiary?

14. What are the problems caused by inflation in evaluating the performance of a foreign subsidiary?

Exercises and Problems

1. A U.S. company is considering an investment project proposal to extend its operations in Germany. As part of the proposed project, the German operation is required to pay an annual royalty of €500,000 to the parent company.

   Required:
   Explain the cash flow implications of the payment referred to above for the parent company.

2. Refer to Exhibit 12.5.

   Required:
   Briefly explain the operating environment of a developing country of your choice using the framework that identifies the social, political, economic, and technological influences.

3. On January 1, 2005, a U.S. firm made an investment in Germany that will generate $5 million annually in depreciation, converted at current spot rate. Projected annual rates of inflation in Germany and in the U.S. are 5 percent and 2 percent, respectively. The real exchange rate is expected to remain constant and the German tax rate is 50 percent.

   Required:
   Calculate the expected real value (in terms of January 1, 2005 dollars) of the depreciation charge in year 2009. Assume that the tax write-off is taken at the end of the year.

4. Sedona Electronics of Arizona exports 25,000 Disc Drive Controllers (DDCs) per year to China under an agreement that covers the period 2003–2007. In China the DDCs are sold for the RMB (Chinese currency) equivalent of $50 per unit. The total costs in the U.S. are direct manufacturing costs and shipping costs, which amount to $35 per unit. The Market for DDCs in China is stable, and Sedona holds the major portion of the market.

   In 2004, the Chinese government, adopting a policy of replacing imported DDCs with local products, invited Sedona to open an assembly plant in China. If Sedona makes the investment, it will operate the plant for five years and then sell the building and equipment to Chinese investors at net book value at the time of sale plus the current amount of any working capital. Sedona will be allowed to repatriate all net income and depreciation funds to the U.S. each year.

   Sedona's anticipated outlay in 2004 would be $1,500,000 (buildings and equipment $750,000 and working capital $750,000). Building and Equipment will be depreciated over five years on a straight-line basis (no salvage value). At the end of the fifth year, the $750,000 of working capital may also be repatriated to the U.S.

Locally assembled DDCs will be sold for the RMB equivalent of $50 each. Operating expenses per unit of DDC are as follows:

Materials purchased in China (dollar equivalent of RMB cost)	$15
Components imported from U.S. parent	$ 8
Variable costs per unit	$23

The $8 transfer price per unit for components sold by Sedona to its Chinese subsidiary consists of $4 of direct costs incurred in the U.S. and $4 of pre-tax profit to Sedona. There are no other operating costs in either China or the U.S.

In both China and the U.S., corporate income tax rate is 40 percent.

Sedona uses a 15 percent discount rate to evaluate all its investment projects.

Assume the investment is made at the end of 2004, and all operating cash flows occur at the end of 2005 through 2009. The RMB/dollar exchange rate is expected to remain constant over the five year period.

Required:
a. Do you recommend that Sedona make the investment?
b. Sedona learns that if it decides not to invest in China, a Japanese company will probably make an investment similar to that being considered by Sedona. The Japanese investment would be protected by the Chinese government against imports. How would this information affect your analysis and recommendation?
c. Assume the conditions of Question (b). China reduces income tax charged to foreign firms from 40% to 20% in order to attract foreign investors. How would this information affect your analysis and recommendation?

5. Visit the Web site of Nokia Company (www.Nokia.com).

Required:
Comment on Nokia's risk management activities as reported in the company's 2004 annual report.

6. According to Exhibit 12.7, the top three budget goals for divisional managers of Japanese companies are sales volume, net profit, and production cost, in that order, whereas those of U.S. companies are return on investment, controllable profit, and net profit, in that order.

Required:
Explain the possible reasons for differences in budget goals of Japanese and U.S. companies.

7. The concept of the balanced scorecard is becoming increasingly popular among firms internationally.

Required:
Explain the possible reasons for the popularity of the balanced scorecard.

8. It is impossible to separate the performance of a foreign subsidiary from that of its managers, and there is no need for it.

Required:
Critically comment on the preceding statement.

9. Sometimes an MNC may decide to use local currency to evaluate a foreign subsidiary.

Required:
Explain the circumstances under which it may be appropriate for an MNC to use local currency to evaluate a foreign subsidiary.

10. Developing a global business strategy for an MNC is a highly complex task.

Required:
Briefly discuss the complexities referred to in the preceding statement.

11. Globalization has made cultural values irrelevant as a factor influencing multinational business and accounting.

Required:
State whether or not you agree with the preceding statement, and develop an argument to support the position you have taken.

Case 12-1

Canyon Power Company

Late in 2004, Canyon Power Company (CPC) management was considering expansion of the company's international business activities. CPC was an Arizona manufacturer of specialist electric motors for use in industrial equipment. All of the company's sales were to other manufacturers in the industrial equipment industry. CPC's worldwide market was supplied from subsidiaries in Germany, Mexico, and Malaysia as well as the United States. The company was particularly successful in Asia mainly due to the high quality of its products, its technical expertise, excellent after-sale service, and of course the continued rapid economic growth in many Asian countries. This success led corporate management to consider seriously the feasibility of further expansion of its business in the Asian region.

The Malaysian subsidiary of CPC distributed and assembled electric motors. It also had limited manufacturing facilities so that it could undertake special adaptations required. With the maturing of the Asian market, particularly in the industrial sector, an expansion of capacity in that market was of strategic importance. The Malaysian subsidiary had been urging corporate management to expand its capacity since the beginning of 2004. However, an alternative scenario appeared more promising. The Indian economy, with its liberalized economic policies, was growing at annual rates higher much than those of many industrialized countries. Further, India had considerably lower labor costs and certain government incentives that were not available in Malaysia. Therefore, the company chose India for its Asian expansion project, and had a four-year investment project proposal prepared by the treasurer's staff.

The proposal was to establish a wholly owned subsidiary in India producing electric motors for the Indian domestic market as well as for export to other Asian countries. The initial equity investment would be $1.5 million, equivalent to 67.5 million Indian rupees (Rs) at the exchange rate of Rs 45 to the U.S. dollar. (Assume that the Indian rupee is freely convertible, and there are no restrictions on transfers of foreign exchange out of India.) An additional Rs 27 million would be raised by borrowing from a commercial bank in India at an interest rate of 10 percent per annum. The principal amount of the bank loan would be payable in full at the end of the fourth year. The combined capital would be sufficient to purchase plant of $1.8 million and other initial expenses including working capital. The cost of installation would be $15,000, with another $5,000 for testing. No new working capital would be required during the four-year period. The plant will have a salvage value of Rs 10 million at the end of four years. Straight-line depreciation would be applied to the original cost of the plant.

The firm's overall marginal after-tax cost of capital was about 12 percent. However, because of the higher risks associated with an Indian venture, CPC decided that a 16 percent discount rate would be applied to the project.

Present value factors at 16 percent are as follows:

Period	Factor
1	0.862
2	0.743
3	0.641
4	0.552

Sales forecasts are as follows:

Year	Sales (units)	
	(Domestic)	(Export)
1	5,000	10,000
2	6,000	12,000
3	7,000	14,000
4	8,000	16,000

The initial selling price of an electric motor was to be Rs 4,500 for Indian domestic sales and export sales in the Asian region, and the selling price in both cases was to increase at an annual rate of 10 percent. The exchange rate between the Indian rupee and the U.S. dollar was expected to vary as follows:

January 1, Year 1	Rs 45 per U.S. dollar
December 31, Year 1	Rs 45 per U.S. dollar
December 31, Year 2	Rs 43 per U.S. dollar
December 31, Year 3	Rs 40 per U.S. dollar
December 31, Year 4	Rs 38 per U.S. dollar

The annual cash expenditure for operating expenses, excluding interest payments, would be Rs 40 million. The Indian subsidiary is expected to pay a royalty of Rs 20 million to the parent company at the end of each of the four years. The company would be in the 35 percent bracket for U.S. income tax purposes. For convenience, ignore Indian local taxation.

Required:

Using the information provided, you are required to

1. Calculate net present value from both a project and a parent company perspective.
2. Recommend to CPC corporate management whether or not to accept the proposal.

EXHIBIT C3
Partnership with Kirin Breweries

Source: Lesley Springall, *The Independent*, May 30, 2001, p. 5.

Lion Seeks Foreign Fizz for Its China Operations

Lion Nathan yesterday quashed rumours that its majority shareholder, Japan's largest brewer Kirin Breweries, might take its loss-making Chinese operations off its hands. But Lion is looking for a buyer—or at least a partner—to help stem losses in China.

Lion's losses in China were reduced to $A12.9 million during the period compared to the previous half year loss of $A15.7 million.

Despite five-year prediction to the contrary, the operation has reported only bad news since Lion entered the market in 1995.

Kirin bought 46% of Lion in 1998 for about $1.4 billion. At the time, it said one of the reasons for its purchase was Lion's toe-hold in China which accounts for about 5% of Lion's overall business.

Since this "partnership agreement" lapsed last month, speculation has been rife about Kirin's long-term plans.

Lockey (Paul Lockey is Lion's Chief Financial Officer) says Kirin is not interested in Lion's Chinese operation and that it was not the key driver to the company's investment. "It is supportive of the process we're going through and has stated it has no intention to change or operate any differently as a result of the expiry of the partnership principles". Lockey denied there was a link between Friday's resignation of Lion director Mike Smith, who was instrumental in the setting-up of the Chinese operations and negotiations with Kirin, and the problems in China. After 30 years with Lion, 15 as director, Smith said it was simply time to move on. He has been a key contributor to Lion's progress from a small New Zealand brewer to a multinational of considerable clout.

In 2001, Lion's Chinese brewing operations in the Yangzte River Delta showed some improvement. While volume grew 5 percent to 83.7 million liters, revenue increased 8.6 percent with improved pricing and mix shift. In local currency, the loss of RMB 83.8 million was a 32 percent improvement on the comparable 12-month period in the prior year. In Australian dollars, the loss improved by 21 percent. Despite these improvements, the company's Chinese breweries continued to run below capacity.

In a media release on July 5, 2001, Lion announced that it had terminated all discussions with two of China's largest brewers. Commenting on this decision, Lion CEO, Gordon Cains said

> As well as successfully progressing a range of initiatives to improve the financial and operating performance of our Chinese business, we have, over the last twelve months been looking at the options available to us to participate in the consolidation of the Chinese beer market. Having patiently negotiated in good faith with a number of major brewers, we have now reached a point where we do not believe that a sensible outcome can be achieved in the foreseeable future. As a result, we have advised these two parties that we do not believe their proposals are realistic options for Lion Nathan and its shareholders. While this is disappointing, we are keen to bring an end to the uncertainty that is not helpful from an operating perspective.[2]

Opportunities are currently being investigated to address this issue.

In August 2001, following the retirement of Douglas Myers from the board and chairmanship, the board appointed GT Ricketts as the new chairman.

---

[2] www.lion-nathan.co.nz.

THE MARKET IN CHINA

The Chinese beer market is highly fragmented, with a large number of breweries comprising regional and subregional markets. Although it has experienced some consolidation in recent years, the competitive environment is expected to remain difficult, with most brewers having real difficulty achieving adequate returns. In early 1998, there were around 860 breweries of any significant size in China. They included 40 with foreign joint-venture participation by a roll call of brewing giants: Heineken, Carlsberg, Guinness, Anheuser-Busch, Suntory, Fosters, San Miguel, Asahi.

Lion was wrestling with a number of problems in the China side of its business. Transport in the region was expensive and unreliable, with a series of canals of varying depth, width, and height clearance. To negotiate the waterways barges can be no larger than 60 tons. However, to get beer to the distribution hub in Shanghai in sufficient volume to make the trip worthwhile requires much larger vessels. Lion was spending a lot of money to recruit and train local executives with little knowledge of Western marketing and management techniques. The task is not an easy one and, at least in the initial stages, means a heavy commitment of expatriate resources to create a corporate culture. Getting well-educated, well-trained staff is difficult, and keeping them is worse in a market full of foreign companies desperate for well-qualified locals. Many Chinese employees don't have great loyalty to their company and will move firms for as little as an extra $20 a month.[3]

The key challenge is to adapt the Chinese *guanxi* (relationship) way of doing business to Western minds, particularly those that emphasize selling. Lion's human resources director in China, Shane Slipais, says, "Relationship building is vital to all success in China, either personal or in business. . . . Chinese spend more time on and off the job with each other than in Australia or New Zealand. . . . The secret of doing business in China is to be rigid in what you want to achieve but be flexible in the way you get there."[4] *Guanxi* works in both formal and informal ways. Outright confrontation in the workplace is generally a no-no, and employer/employee disputes are dealt with through intermediaries.

Compliance with regulations, such as paying taxes and not polluting the environment, is far less obvious. The pecking order puts multinational companies at the top of the compliance list, Chinese state-owned enterprises at the bottom and overseas-Chinese-run businesses in the middle. Corruption is endemic in any system where a form of authority, in this case the Communist Party, is above the law. It is a day-to-day reality.[5] From a Western perspective, the main problem may be the need to understand different business philosophies and practices. Failure to do so can be expensive. As one commentator states, "There is a rule of thumb about China—do your homework before you get here. Take your worst-case scenario for cost and time, multiply it by two and you have the full cost estimate."

The desire for short-term profits and/or high rates of return did not bring much success for foreign investors in China. Chinese partners emphasized long-term relationships with reasonable returns and mutual benefits. Only half of China's

---

[3] Nikki Mandow, "Doing Business in China: Not for the Ethnocentric," *The Independent*, January 28, 1997, p. 18.

[4] N. Gibson, "Foreigners Still Find Breaking into China a Delicate Business," *National Business Review*, August 15, 1997, p. 37.

[5] Ibid.

EXHIBIT C4
Lion Determination

Source: Michele Simpson, "Brewers Hit Big Trouble in China but Lion Decides to Tough It Out," *National Business Review*, April 14, 2000.

Brewers Hit Big Trouble in China but Lion Decides to Tough It Out
Brewer Lion Nathan is not going to follow competitors choosing to flee the red-ink generating Chinese market.

Despite year-upon year of huge losses since it first set up in China, Lion Nathan is ploughing on with its Asian venture as other big name brewers suddenly quit the market. British brewer Bass has decided to pull the plug on its $80 million joint venture in China, the world's second-largest market.

"There is an overcapacity in China," Lion Nathan's managing director of the Chinese operation, Jim O'Mahony said. "The industry needs consolidation and we're not overly concerned whether that process is by people exiting or folding."

Bass said talks had begun to sell its 55% share in a joint venture after it fell out with its local partner in China. Foster's last year grew tired of the much hyped potential of the 1.3 billion strong Chinese market. It sold its breweries in Tianjin and Guangzhou.

The losses for Lion's Chinese venture have risen sharply in the past three years. In 1997 it was $8.8 million, in 1998 it tripled to nearly $30 million and for the financial year ended August 31, 1999, the loss before interest and tax was $32.6 million.

. . . Bass has pulled out over problems with its local partner. "The gaps between our cultures have led to different views and even clashes, as the foreign party felt it didn't get what it wanted," a Bass spokeswoman said.

---

breweries make money, and the foreigners' track record so far has not been conspicuously better than the locals'. Both Lion's Australian archrival, Foster's, whose three loss-making breweries together notched up a deficit of $29 million in 1997, and British brewer Bass decided to quit. However, Lion appeared determined to stay back (see Exhibit C4).

LION'S BRANDS

In New Zealand, Lion is one major listed company that uses Interbrand to value its beer brands. David Wethey states, "Often a company would look only at brand equity when it was thinking of buying or selling the brand. But establishing the value of a brand was important right throughout its life in a company."[6]

Lion's brands, not the beer, are worth $2.2 billion according to Lion's balance sheet (see Exhibit C5). Unlike the beer, the brand is an intangible asset and, as such, hard to pin a price tag on. However, Lion's 2001 annual report says that its brands are revalued annually and the valuations are supported by independent valuations. Furthermore, it is claimed that the company's policy in this matter is in compliance with the applicable Australian accounting standards (see Exhibit C6).

Warwick Bryan, Lion's manager of investor relations, commented that if New Zealand's proposed accounting standard (ED 87, a photocopy of IAS 38) were to be adopted, that would mean two-thirds of the brands would have to be immediately removed from Lion's balance sheet and the remainder would have to be removed over 20 years through amortization.[7]

The Advertising Agencies Association says that, in 1998, tangible assets represented only approximately 29 percent of the market value of Britain's FTSE 100 companies. They also say the idea that only brands valued through a buy-and-sell

---

[6] Michele Simpson, "Love Your Brand, Get a Do-It-Yourself Valuation," *National Business Review*, July 7, 2000.

[7] Felicity Anderson, "When Is an Asset Not an Asset?" *The Independent*, December 1, 1999, p. 32.

EXHIBIT C5
Financial Position

LION NATHAN LIMITED AND ITS CONTROLLED ENTITIES
Statement of Financial Position
As at 30 September 2001

		consolidated	
	note	30 sep $m01	30 sep $m00
Current assets			
Cash	7	10.4	5.0
Receivables	8	239.0	263.4
Inventories	9	116.0	117.6
Other	11	48.5	37.0
Total current assets		413.9	423.0
Non-current assets			
Receivables	8	27.9	16.3
Equity accounted investments	12	22.0	130.4
Other financial assets	10	12.0	1.3
Property, plant and equipment	13	821.9	776.7
Deferred tax assets	14	31.3	27.4
Intangibles	15	2,136.9	1,978.7
Other	11	28.8	51.3
Total non-current assets		3,080.8	2,982.1
Total assets		3,494.7	3,405.1
Current liabilities			
Payables	16	280.6	264.1
Interest bearing liabilities	17	7.8	10.4
Current tax liabilities	19	2.5	7.3
Provisions	20	101.3	105.4
Total current liabilities		392.2	387.2
Non-current liabilities			
Interest bearing liabilities	17	1,070.2	1,291.5
Deferred tax liabilities	19	95.8	56.9
Provisions	20	12.8	3.2
Total non-current liabilities		1,178.8	1,351.6
Total liabilities		1,571.0	1,738.8
Net assets		1,923.7	1,666.3
Equity			
Parent entity interest			
Contributed equity	22	436.1	436.1
Reserves	23	861.0	677.1
Retained profits	24	619.0	552.7
Total parent equity		1,916.1	1,665.9
Outside equity interests in controlled entities	25	7.6	0.4
Total equity		1,923.7	1,666.3

State owned, State credit was always by definition "good," and bad debt provisions were/are generally unnecessary. There seems to be a "go-slow" attitude toward change that is reflected in the broadening of the Chinese principles to accommodate the expectations of business partners from more advanced nations.[15]

The various environmental factors affecting auditing issues can be identified in terms of a broad concept often referred to as the accounting infrastructure, which includes producers of information; final users of information; information intermediaries; laws and regulations that govern the production, transmission, and usage of information; and legal entities that monitor and implement the laws and regulations.[16]

In less developed countries, in particular, creditors and investors play a minimal role in the accounting infrastructure and so a less developed auditing profession, compared to that in a developed country, would be expected. Further, the primary source of finance in a country may influence the degree to which the audit profession in that country has evolved. Countries in which the primary source of capital is absentee owners (stockholders) and creditors such as the United States, the United Kingdom, and Australia may have a much greater need for audit services and more sophisticated audit procedures compared to those countries in which state-controlled banks or commercial banks are the primary source of capital. In a debt-financing country such as Japan, for example, there may be a much reduced need for audited information or reliance on public financial information.

Different legal systems are also likely to influence auditing in different countries. For example, a codified Roman law system that exists in countries such as Germany and France may require more reliance on the stated legal objectives of the auditing profession. Countries with a common law system, such as the United Kingdom, Canada, or New Zealand, may allow audit characteristics to develop more freely or rely more on the auditing profession to set a general tone for the profession.[17]

The differences in the environment in which auditing operates can have implications for the transfer of auditing technology among countries. The international diversity in accounting and securities market regulations and practices, economic and political systems, patterns of business ownership, size and complexity of business firms, and stages of economic development would affect the nature of the demand for audit services and the complexity of the audit task. Therefore, audit technologies which are cost-beneficial in one national setting can be ineffective, or even dysfunctional, in a different setting.[18]

Further, audit quality is also likely to vary across different audit environments. *Audit quality* can be defined as the probability that an error or irregularity is detected and reported.[19] The detection probability is affected by the actual work done by auditors to reach their opinion. This in turn is influenced by the level of

[15] Graham, "Setting a Research Agenda," p. 30.

[16] C. J. Lee, "Accounting Infrastructure and Economic Development," *Journal of Accounting and Public Policy,* Summer 1987, pp. 75–86.

[17] R. A. Wood, "Global Audit Characteristics across Cultures and Environments: An Empirical Examination," *Journal of International Accounting, Auditing, and Taxation* 5, no. 2 (1996), pp. 215–29.

[18] See C. W. Chow and R. N. Hwang, "The Cross-Border Transferability of Audit Technology: An Exploratory Study in the U.S.-Taiwan Context," *Advances in International Accounting* 7 (1994), pp. 217–29.

[19] L. DeAngelo, "Auditor Size and Audit Quality," *Journal of Accounting and Economics* 3 (1981), pp. 183–200.

competence of the auditors (eligibility and qualifications), the requirements regarding the conduct of the audit (quality review and monitoring), and the reporting requirements. The reporting probability is affected by the auditor's independence. High independence implies a high probability of publicly reporting a detected material error or irregularity. We further discuss the issue of auditor independence later in this chapter.

Audit quality is also affected by the nature of the legal liability regime that exists in a country (we also discuss auditor liability later in this chapter). A strong liability regime will provide incentives for auditors to be independent and produce high-quality audits. In some Asian countries, for example, this is an unlikely scenario, because (due to cultural and other reasons) the liability regimes may not be strong and violations of professional conduct may go unpunished. This creates audit markets of uneven quality. In some countries, such as Indonesia, Malaysia, and Thailand, fraud and irregularities are required to be reported to the board of directors, not in the audit report.[20]

Regulation of Auditors and Audit Firms

The approaches taken to regulate auditing in different countries range from those that leave the task largely in the hands of the profession to those that rely heavily on the government. In Anglo-Saxon countries, mechanisms are put in place to regulate auditors within the framework of professional self-regulation. In the United States, the Public Company Accounting Oversight Board (PCAOB), composed of five independent members (not more than two of whom may be professional accountants), was established in 2002 by the SEC pursuant to the Sarbanes-Oxley Act. This act reaffirms the necessity for the auditor to be independent of management, in fact and appearance, and expands the auditor's reporting responsibility. Section 404 of the Sarbanes-Oxley Act, "Management Assessment of Internal Controls," requires public companies to include in their annual report an assessment by management of the effectiveness of the internal control structure and procedures for financial reporting. The external auditor must attest to and report on that assessment. Accordingly, the PCAOB issued an audit standard, "An Audit of Internal Control over Financial Reporting Performed in Conjunction with an Audit of Financial Statements" (PCAOB Release No.2004-003), which was approved by the SEC in June 2004.[21] The new standard requires two audit opinions: one on internal control over financial reporting and one on the financial statements.

Auditors of SEC-registered companies are required to be members of the PCAOB. This also includes non-U.S. audit firms that audit the accounts of a company or subsidiary (domestic or foreign) listed on a U.S. stock exchange. The PCAOB has the authority (1) to establish or adopt auditing standards, quality control standards, and ethical rules in relation to the conduct of audits of public companies and (2) to inspect audit firms. It also has the power to require cooperation with quality control reviews and disciplinary proceedings, and it may impose a broad range of disciplinary sanctions against auditing firms and individual

---

[20] M. Favere-Marchesi, "Audit Quality in ASEAN," *International Journal of Accounting* 35, no. 1 (2000), pp. 121–49.

[21] This is effective for audits of companies with fiscal years ending on or after November 15, 2004, for accelerated filers (an accelerated filer is, generally, a U.S. company that has equity market capitalization over $75 million as of the last business day of its most recently completed second fiscal quarter and have filed an annual report with the SEC), or July 15, 2005, for other companies. More information can be obtained at www.sec.gov/news/press/2004-83.htm.

members. Large firms that undertake audits of more than 100 public companies will be inspected annually. The requirement for non-U.S. audit firms to become members of PCAOB has caused some concern among the large European audit firms. Although at first the PCAOB said it should regulate both U.S. and non-U.S. accounting firms, in July 2004 announced that, for some non-U.S. audit firms that audit companies registered with the SEC (e.g., audit firms in Canada, Japan, and many European countries, including the Unied Kingdom), it would be willing to rely on the auditor's home-country regulators.[22]

In the United Kingdom, the word *accountant* is not defined in statute and there is no qualification requirement in order for someone to practice as an accountant. However, most accountants choose to qualify under the auspices of one of the professional bodies. The situation for *auditor* is different. The Companies Act of 1985 prescribes a statutory scheme for the regulation of auditors, under which the Department of Trade and Industries (DTI) recognizes certain accountancy bodies for the training and supervision of auditors. The Companies Act of 1985 states that every company shall appoint an auditor or auditors (except for most small companies or dormant companies). The Companies Act of 1989, which implemented the European Union's Eighth Directive, introduced stronger statutory arrangements for the regulation of auditors. It restricts qualifications for appointment as a statutory auditor to those who hold a recognized professional qualification and are subject to the requirements of a recognized supervisory body. It makes specific provision for the independence of company auditors. An officer or employee of a company being audited, for example, may not act as auditor for that company.

Under the regulatory structure for the accounting profession introduced in 1998, an independent body, the Accountancy Foundation, with a non-accountant board of trustees, was established in 2000. With the establishment of the Foundation, a strong lay and independent element was introduced into the regulatory framework. This element involves oversight arrangements concerning the regulatory activities undertaken by the principal professional accountancy bodies. The Foundation is funded by the Consultative Committee of Accountancy Bodies (CCAB).

The Foundation[23] and its related bodies[24] are responsible for the nonstatutory independent regulation of the six chartered accountancy bodies of the CCAB. This framework was developed in light of a growing recognition in the profession of the need for the regulatory arrangements to reflect the wider public interest. The regulatory functions of the Foundation include monitoring the work of accountants and auditors, handling complaints and disciplinary violations, and conducting investigations. The new regulatory structure proposes to provide an increased level of public oversight regarding statutory auditors, while essentially retaining the self-regulatory nature of the profession.[25] Accordingly, the responsibility for

---

[22] *Accountancy Magazine*, July 2004.

[23] The documents issued by the Accountancy Foundation and its related bodies are available at www.frc.org.uk.

[24] The structure of the Foundation comprises five limited companies: the Accountancy Foundation Ltd.: The Review Board Ltd. (to monitor the operation of the regulatory system to ensure that it serves the public interest); The Auditing Practices Board Ltd. (to establish and develop auditing standards): The Ethics Standards Board Ltd. (to secure the development of ethical standards for all accountants); and the Investigation and Discipline Board Ltd. (to investigate disciplinary cases of public interest).

[25] Department of Trade and Industry, *A Framework of Independent Regulation for the Accountancy Profession: A Consultation Document.* London: Department of Trade and Industry of Her Majesty's Government, 1998.

determining who may be recognized as a statutory auditor has been delegated primarily to four CCAB members: the Association of Chartered Corporate Accountants (ACCA), the Institute of Chartered Accountants in England and Wales (ICAEW), the Institute of Chartered Accountants in Ireland (ICAI), and the Institute of Chartered Accountants in Scotland (ICAS). Each of the four recognized professional bodies has its own examinations to assess the technical competence of the entry-level registered auditor (the term used in the United Kingdom for statutory auditor). In order to become a registered auditor in the United Kingdom, the professional accountant must be listed in a register maintained for that purpose by a recognized professional body.

The Auditing Practices Board (APB) is responsible for setting and developing auditing standards in the United Kingdom. The APB, as constituted under the Accountancy Foundation arrangements, continues the work of its predecessor body, which was established in 1991 under the auspices of the CCAB. Failure to abide by the professional standards issued by the APB may be grounds for disciplinary action. According to a report on audit regulation in the United Kingdom made public by the Department of Trade and Industry in July 2004, the ICAEW, ICAS, and ICAI undertook 1,030 monitoring visits during 2003. Of the firms visited, 88 percent required no action at all or, by the conclusion of the visit, had suitable plans in place to improve their audit work, and 14 firms had their registration as auditors withdrawn following a monitoring visit, compared with 11 in 2002.[26]

The Companies (Audit, Investigation and Community Enterprises) Act of 2004 provided the Financial Reporting Review Panel with statutory power to require companies, directors, and auditors to provide documents, information and explanations if it appears that accounts do not comply with relevant reporting requirements.

Under the new regime the Financial Reporting Council (FRC) is the United Kingdom's unified, independent regulator for corporate reporting and governance. Its functions, which are relevant to auditing, include the following:

- Setting, monitoring, and enforcing auditing standards, statutory oversight, and regulation of auditors.
- Operating an independent investigation and discipline scheme for public interest cases involving professional accountants.
- Overseeing the regulatory activities of the professional accountancy bodies.

Similar bodies have been established in the United States, Canada, Australia, Japan, France, Germany, and several other countries in the European Union.

The requirements for becoming an auditor may vary in different countries. For example, unlike in the United States, there is no uniform system of examination in the United Kingdom where four professional bodies conduct their own examinations. On the other hand, in Germany, the examinations for the prospective auditors are set by the Ministry of Economics, and self-regulation of the auditing profession takes place within the strict boundaries of the law.[27] Unlike in the United Kingdom, instead of the professional bodies, quasi-governmental agencies play a major role in the regulatory functions in Germany. The Auditors' Regulation specifies the admission requirements to become an statutory auditor and defines, among other things, the rights and duties of the auditor, the organization of the Chamber of Auditors, or *Wirtschaftsprüferkammer (WPK)*, and the disciplinary

---

[26] Details are available at http://accountingeducation.com/news/news5279.html.
[27] Baker, Mikol, and Quick, "Regulation of the Statutory Auditor."

measures for breeches of professional duties. The WPK is supervised by the Ministry of Economics. Statutory auditors, including audit corporations, must be members of the WPK, a public law body created in 1961. The WPK also participates in disciplining auditors who violate standards.[28]

In China, the government is heavily involved in the regulation of the auditing profession. China's accounting and auditing profession is sanctioned and regulated by the state. All certified public accounting (CPA) firms, both state owned and privately owned, are under the supervision of the local Audit Bureau, which is itself supervised by the state. The CPA firms must be approved by the state in order to be able to audit foreign owned or joint venture companies or Chinese companies listed on the stock exchange, as required by law. The state may also intervene in the allocation of audit assignments among CPA firms.

Audit Reports

There are significant differences in the audit reports across different countries and sometimes across different companies within the same country. In this section we describe some of these differences. The appendix to this chapter provides examples of audit reports from MNCs located in Japan, Germany, the Netherlands, and China. They include an audit conducted on the basis of a set of standards that is different from local standards (Toshiba); an audit conducted on the basis of local standards (Sumitomo Metal Industries); an audit conducted on the basis of both local and international standards of auditing (Bayer AG); an audit conducted on the basis of three sets of standards, the audit opinion expressed in three statements, differently worded for three audiences (Unilever); and an audit conducted on the basis of local standards and the audit opinion expressed in terms of local requirements (China Southern Airlines).

In Japan, Toshiba Corporation's audit report on its financial statements for the years ended March 31, 2004, and March 31, 2003, states that the audit was conducted in accordance with auditing standards generally accepted in the United States. But the company had not presented segment information as required by the U.S. standard SFAS 131. In their opinion, auditors state that, except for segment information, the financial statements present fairly, in all material respects, in conformity with accounting principles generally accepted in the United States. In the case of Sumitomo Metal Industries Ltd., the audit was conducted in accordance with the Japanese auditing standards.

In Germany, the independent auditors' report of the financial statements of Bayer AG for the year ended December 31, 2004, states that it is the responsibility of the board of management of Bayer AG to prepare the consolidated financial statements according to the International Financial Reporting Standards (IFRSs). The audit was conducted in accordance with German auditing standards and also extends to the group management report. The audit opinion is expressed in terms of IFRSs.

As mentioned earlier, a special feature in the corporate structure in some European countries, including Germany, is the two-tiered structure with a management board and a supervisory board. The report of the supervisory board of Volswagen AG, dated February 25, 2005, states:

> The documentation relating to the financial statements and the auditor's reports were made available to all members in good time prior to the meeting of the Audit Committee on Februry 21, 2005, and the Supervisory Board on February 25, 2005.

---

[28] Ibid.

The auditors were also present at both meetings. They reported extensively on the principal findings of their audit and were available to provide additional information if required.

Our own review of the dependent company report did not give rise to any objections to the declaration of the Board of Management at the end of the report. In addition, the Supervisory Board noted and approved the findings of the report review submitted by the auditors. (annual report 2004, p. 6)

In the auditors' report on the annual financial statements of DaimlerChrysler AG for the business years from January 1 to December 31, 2004 and 2003, audit opinion is expressed in terms of U.S. generally accepted accounting principles (GAAP).

The annual report of Unilever NV and Unilever PLC contains three auditors' reports for stockholders in the United Kingdom (conducted in accordance with the UK auditing standards), in the Netherlands (conducted in accordance with auditing standards generally accepted in the Netherlands), and in the United States (conducted in accordance with the U.S. standards). The UK auditors' report states that the auditors are not required to consider whether the directors' statements on internal control cover all risks and controls or to form an opinion on the effectiveness of the group's corporate governance procedures or its risk and control procedures (p. 94). The U.S. audit report states that the accounting principles applied in preparing the financial statements vary significantly from those generally accepted in the United States, and it notes that information relating to the nature and effect of such differences is presented in the determination of net profit and capital and reserves.

The auditors' report of the financial statements of China Southern Airlines Company Limited for the period ending December 31, 2003, states that audit was conducted in accordance with China's Independent Auditing Standards of the Certified Public Accountants. The audit opinion states that the financial statements are in compliance with the requirements of the Accounting Standards for Business Enterprises and the Accounting Regulations for Business Enterprises issued by the Ministry of Finance.

INTERNATIONAL HARMONIZATION OF AUDITING STANDARDS

The audit report is the primary tool auditors use to communicate with financial statement users about the results of the audit function. The globalization of capital markets and the growth of international capital flows have heightened the significance of cross-national understanding of corporate financial reports and the associated audit reports.[29] For MNCs the ideal situation would be for both the parent company and its foreign subsidiaries to adopt one set of accounting standards, and for the auditors in both cases to use one set of auditing standards in providing their opinion on the financial statements. However, as explained in the previous sections, the audit environments and the mechanisms for audit regulation can vary significantly among different countries, and this could affect the form, content, and quality of the audit report.

International harmonization of auditing standards is important mainly to assure the international capital markets that the audit process has been consistent

---

[29] J. S. Gangolly, M. E. Hussein, G. S. Seow, and K. Tam, "Harmonization of the Auditor's Report," *International Journal of Accounting* 37 (2002), pp. 327–46.

across companies, and in particular that one set of high quality standards has been applied in auditing both the parent and its subsidiary companies. This enhances the credibility of the information in corporate financial reports. This would lead to a more efficient and effective allocation of resources in international capital markets. In addition, harmonization of auditing standards would enable audit firms to increase the efficiency and effectiveness of the audit process globally. However, efforts to harmonize auditing standards internationally have met with limited success.

The responsibility for developing international auditing standards rests mainly with IFAC through its International Auditing and Assurance Standards Board (IAASB).[30] As a condition of IFAC membership, a professional accountancy body is obliged to support the work of IFAC by informing its members of every pronouncement developed by IFAC; to work toward implementation, to the extent possible under local circumstances, of those pronouncements; and specifically to incorporate IFAC's International Standards on Auditing (ISAs) into national auditing pronouncements.[31]

The IAASB develops ISAs and International Auditing Practice Statements (IAPSs). These standards and statements outline basic principles and essential procedures for auditors, and serve as the benchmark for high-quality auditing standards and statements worldwide. The IAASB also develops quality control standards for firms and engagement teams in the practice areas of audit, assurance, and related services. Exhibit 13.2 provides a list of ISAs issued by IFAC.[32]

IFAC's international regulatory and compliance regime consists of the Forum of Firms (FoF) and the Compliance Committee, with participation from outside the accounting profession. Firms that carry out transnational audit work are eligible for membership in the FoF. Membership obligations include compliance with ISAs and the IFAC Code of Ethics for Professional Accountants, and submission to periodic quality control review. The Compliance Committee monitors and encourages compliance with international standards and other measures designed to enhance the reliability of financial information and professional standards around the world.

The International Organization of Securities Commissions (IOSCO) supports IFAC's efforts in this area. IOSCO's Technical and Emerging Markets Committees participate in the discussions that take place between the IFAC and the international regulatory community regarding processes for the development of international auditing standards. In October 1992, IOSCO recommended that its members endorse ISAs and accept audits of financial statements from other countries audited in accordance with ISAs.

The issuance of ISA 13 in October 1983 by the International Auditing Practices Committee (IAPC) was an important landmark in international efforts to harmonize the audit report. The purpose of ISA 13 was to "provide guidance to auditors on the form and content of the auditor's report issued in connection with the independent audit of the financial statements of any entity" (paragraph 2). ISA 13 has been revised several times since 1983. ISA 700, *The Auditor's Report on Financial Statements,* establishes standards and provides guidance on the form and content of the auditor's report. It requires the auditor to express an opinion about whether the financial statements "give a true and fair view" or "present fairly," which in turn requires the auditor to conduct the necessary auditing procedures to support

---

[30] The IAASB was formerly known as the International Auditing Practices Committee (IAPC).

[31] Preface to International Standards on Auditing and Related Services.

[32] International Standards on Auditing are available at www.ifac.org.

EXHIBIT 13.2
International
Standards on
Auditing

ISA Number	Title
100–199	Introductory Matters
100	Preface to ISAs and Related Services Standards
110	Glossary of Terms
120	Framework of ISAs
200–299	Responsibilities
200	Objective and General Principles Governing as Audit of Financial Statements
210	Terms of Audit Engagements
220	Quality Control for Audit Work
230	Documentation
240	Fraud and Error
250	Consolidation of Laws and Regulations in an Audit of Financial Statements
300–399	Planning
300	Planning
310	Knowledge of the Business
320	Audit Materiality
400–499	Internal Control
400	Risk Assessments and Internal Control
401	Auditing in a Computer Information Systems Environment
402	Audit Considerations Relating to Entities Using Service Organizations
500–599	Audit Evidence
500	Audit Evidence
501	Audit Evidence—Additional Consideration for Specific Items
510	Initial Engagements—Opening Balances
520	Analytical Procedures
530	Audit Sampling
540	Audit of Accounting Estimates
550	Related Parties
560	Subsequent Events
570	Going Concern
580	Management Representations
600–699	Using Work of Others
600	Using Work of Another Auditor
610	Considering the Work of Internal Auditing
620	Using the Work of an Expert
621	Co-operation between Auditors and Actuaries in the Auditing of Insurance Companies
700–799	Audit Conclusions and Reporting
700	The Auditor's Report on Financial Statements
710	Comparatives
720	Other Information in Documents Containing Audited Financial Statements
800–899	Specialized Areas
800	The Auditor's Report on Special Purpose Audit Engagements
810	The Examination of Prospective Financial Information
900–999	Related Services
910	Engagements to Review Financial Statements
920	Engagements to Perform Agreed-Upon Procedures Regarding Financial Information
930	Engagements to Compile Financial Information

his or her expressed opinion. The requirement also helps ensure that the information satisfies the need of the international users of financial statements.

ISA 700 describes four types of audit opinion that can be expressed by the auditor: unqualified, qualified, adverse, and disclaimer of opinion. It also discusses circumstances that may result in other than an unqualified opinion, which include limitation of scope, disagreement with management, and uncertainty. The appendixes to the standard include suggested expressions for the different types of opinion. For example, Exhibit 13.3 provides an illustration of an unqualified opinion that incorporates the basic requirements.

ISA 700 points out that although the auditor's opinion enhances the credibility of the financial statements, the user cannot assume that the opinion is an assurance as to the future viability of the entity or the efficiency or effectiveness with which management has conducted the affairs of the entity.

In December 2004, the IAASB issued a revised ISA 700, *The Independent Auditor's Report on a Complete Set of General Purpose Financial Statements* (effective for auditors' reports dated on or after December 31, 2006), aiming at enhancing the transparency and comparability of auditors' reports across international borders. It sets out guidelines to the auditor when the audit is conducted in accordance with both ISAs and the auditing standards of a specific jurisdiction. For example, Appendix 3 of the report shows that according to the 2004 annual report of German company Bayer AG, the audit was conducted on the basis of both local standards and international standards.

ISA 200, *Objectives and General Principles Governing an Audit of Financial Statements*, states that the objective of an audit of financial statements is to enable the auditor to express an opinion whether the financial statements are prepared, in all

EXHIBIT 13.3
ISA 700 Illustrative Audit Report

Source: ISA 700, *The Auditor's Report on Financial Statements.*

AUDITOR'S REPORT

(Appropriate Address)

We have audited the accompanying (the reference can be by page numbers) balance sheet of the ABC Company as of December 31, 20x1, and the related statements on income, and cash flows for the year then ended. These financial statements are the responsibility of the company's management. Our responsibility is to express an opinion on these financial statements based on our audit.

We conducted our audit in accordance with International Standards on Auditing (or refer to relevant national standards or practices). Those standards require that we plan and perform the audit to obtain reasonable assurance about whether the financial statements are free of material misstatement. An audit includes examining, on a test basis, evidence supporting the amounts and disclosures in the financial statements. An audit also includes assessing the accounting principles used and significant estimates made by management, as well as evaluating the overall financial statements presentation. We believe that our audit provides a reasonable basis for our opinion.

In our opinion, the financial statements give a true and fair view of (or "present fairly" in all material respects) the financial position of the company as of December 31, 20x1, and of the results of its operations and its cash flows for the year then ended in accordance with International Accounting Standards (or [title of financial reporting framework with reference to the country of origin]*) (and comply with. . . .†)

---

*In some circumstances it also may be necessary to refer to a particular jurisdiction within the country of origin to identify clearly the financial reporting framework used.

†Refer to relevant statutes or law.

material respects in accordance with an identified financial reporting framework. However, this could be a problem in some cases; for example, the European Union has endorsed a modified version of IAS 39, and selecting an appropriate text for such identification may not be easy.

Auditors are expected to comply with IFAC's Code of Ethics for Professional Accountants (IFAC Handbook) and to consider the activities of internal auditing and their effect, if any, on external audit procedures (ISA 610, *Considering the Work of Internal Auditing*).

In June 2003, IFAC issued an IAPS providing guidance on expressing an audit opinion when the financial statements are asserted by management to have been prepared (1) solely in accordance with IFRSs, (2) in accordance with IFRSs and a national financial reporting framework, or (3) in accordance with a national financial reporting framework with disclosure of the extent of compliance with IFRSs.[33]

In accordance with IAS 1, the IAPC specifies that financial statements should not be described as complying with IFRSs unless they comply with all the requirements of each applicable standard and each applicable interpretation of the International Financial Reporting Interpretations Committee (IFRIC). An unqualified opinion may be expressed only when the auditor is able to conclude that the financial statements give a true and fair view (or are presented fairly, in all material respects) in accordance with the identified financial reporting framework. In all other circumstances, the auditor is required to disclaim an opinion or to issue a qualified or adverse opinion depending on the circumstances. An opinion paragraph that indicates that "the financial statements give a true and fair view and are in substantial compliance with International Financial Reporting Standards" does not meet the requirements of ISA 700. Further, financial statements claimed to have complied with more than one financial reporting framework must comply with each of the indicated frameworks individually.

There have been efforts at harmonizing auditing standards at the regional level, particularly within the European Union. For example, the Fourth Directive of the European Commission requires that the auditor's report include whether the financial statements present a "true and fair view." The Eighth Directive aimed at harmonizing the educational and training prerequisites necessary to become a statutory auditor. Many EU member countries, including the United Kingdom, modified their company laws and regulations to comply with the provisions of the Eighth Directive. As a result, the UK professional bodies amended their entry requirements to include a rule that new members must have a university degree in any area. In addition, a prospective candidate for membership of one of the professional bodies would also be required to undergo a three-year training period under the supervision of a practicing member of that professional body. Recently, the representative body for the accountancy profession in Europe, the *Federation des Experts Comptables Europeens (FEE)*, conducted a survey and found that fundamental requirements to be recognized as a professional accountant and auditor largely have converged across Europe.[34]

The UK Auditing Practices Board, one of the FRC's operating bodies, taking a big-bang approach, has recently issued a revised suite of auditing standards that very closely reflect the ISAs.

---

[33] IFAC, International Auditing and Assurance Standards Board, "Reporting by Auditors on Compliance with International Financial Reporting Standards," International Auditing Practice Statement 1014, June 1, 2003.

[34] Full survey results are available at: www.fee.be.

The IAASB has issued a series of key questions and answers in a publication titled "First-time Adoption of IFRSs, Guidance for Auditors on Reporting Issues" as well as a glossary incorporating terms used in ISAs issued as of October 31, 2004.[35] Further, in April 2005 the IFAC Education Committee issued an exposure draft on educational requirements for audit professionals proposing an International Education Standard (IES) titled "Competence Requirements for Audit Professionals."

ADDITIONAL INTERNATIONAL AUDITING ISSUES

As a result of the renewed interest in restoring investor confidence internationally, the issues of auditor's liability, auditor independence, and the role of audit committees have figured prominently in discussion and debate. The fact that there is no international agreement on how to deal with any of these issues is of particular interest to MNCs, because they have to operate under different regulatory regimes in different countries.

Auditor's Liability

In general, auditors can be subject to three kinds of liability—civil liability, criminal liability, and professional sanctions. Civil liability arises when auditors break contractual or civil obligations or both, and criminal liability arises when they engage in criminal acts, such as intentionally providing misleading information. Professional sanctions (warnings and exclusions by professional bodies) are imposed when auditors violate the rules of the professional bodies to which they belong.[36] In terms of civil liability, the auditor may be exposed to litigation initiated by (1) the client company (the other party to the engagement contract) or (2) a third party (a party not involved in the original contract, such as a shareholder). In certain national jurisdictions, auditors are not liable to third parties. This was the case in Germany prior to 1998, but the situation changed as a consequence of a court decision in that year. Statutory auditors in Germany currently are liable to third parties in cases of negligent behavior. In the United Kingdom, under the Companies Act, the auditor reports to the members of the company but enters into a contract with the company as a corporate entity. Accordingly, the auditor's primary duty of care is to the company and its shareholders as a group, not necessarily to individual shareholders. To be liable in negligence, the auditor must owe a "duty of care" to a third-party claimant. It is relatively difficult for individual shareholders to successfully assert claims against statutory auditors under British law.[37]

In China, the concept of legal liability extending beyond the firm to its owners does not appear to exist. This is due to the flexibility in the ownership structure of CPA firms, and the lack of a developed legal environment. A unique feature in the ownership structure of the Chinese CPA firms is that other entities, such as universities, may also have ownership interests in them. For example, Shanghai University has an ownership interest in Da Hua CPAs, one of the larger CPA firms in China.[38]

---

[35] Both publications are available at www.ifac.org/store.

[36] Favere-Marchesi, "Audit Quality."

[37] Baker, Mikol, and Quick, "Regulation of the Statutory Auditor," p. 769.

[38] Graham, "Setting a Research Agenda."

Limiting Auditor's Liability

Prompted by the collapse of Arthur Andersen, the UK government conducted a public consultation on whether it should initiate legislation to limit auditors' liability. In its response, one of the Big Four firms pointed out that the risks involved in auditing are uninsurable, unquantifiable, unmanageable, and could at any time destroy the firm or any of its competitors.[39] This should be of concern to MNCs, given that further reduction in the number of global accounting firms could seriously affect MNCs' ability to obtain the necessary professional services at reasonable prices. The remainder of this section describes some of the alternatives available for limiting auditor's liability.

Change the Ownership Structure

Audit firms, particularly in the UK tradition, are often organized as partnerships in which the principle of "joint and several liability" applies. Under this principle, each audit partner of the firm against whom a claim is made for negligence may be held liable for the whole amount of the claim. However, the joint and several liability feature is seen as a weakness of the partnership form of ownership. An effective way to limit auditor's liability would be to change the ownership structure of audit firms. Under the U.S. model of limited liability partnerships, "innocent" partners are able to protect their personal wealth from legal action. The Big Four firms are using limited liability partnerships, where permitted by law, to reduce their exposure to litigation. For example, Deloitte & Touche LLP became a limited liability partnership in August 2003.

Under UK law, limited partnerships are effective only if the limited partners are simply passive investors and take no role in the firm's professional work. Consequently, for many audit firms in the United Kingdom, the principle of joint and several liability applies to audit partners, as the firms are organized as partnerships. However, it is possible in the United Kingdom for audits to be carried out by limited liability companies.[40] In 1995, KPMG announced the formation of a new company, KPMG Audit PLC, to audit its top 700 clients worldwide.[41] It was reported recently that of the United Kingdom's top 60 accountancy firms, the majority had turned to limited liability.[42] In Germany also, statutory audits can be performed by audit corporations with limited liability. However, in other countries, such as New Zealand, an audit firm cannot be incorporated.

Proportionate Liability

Another approach that has been suggested to limit auditor's liability is to apply the concept of proportionate liability, by which the claim against each auditor would be restricted to the proportion of the loss for which he or she was responsible. However, this is not a widely adopted approach. For example, in September 1998, the New Zealand Law Commission declined a proposal by the Institute of Chartered Accountants of New Zealand (ICANZ) for changing auditors' liability from "joint and several liability" to "proportionate liability." In doing so the Law Commission stated that fairness among defendants was not relevant to fairness to the injured party. German regulators seem to have taken a different view on this

[39] Andrew Parker, "PwC Steps Up Litigation Fight," *Financial Times*, April 19, 2004, p. 18.

[40] Among the ASEAN countries, in Thailand and Vietnam, auditing firms may be organized as limited liability companies. Favere-Marchesi, "Audit Quality."

[41] *Accountancy Age*, October 5, 1995, p. 1.

[42] Liz Fisher, "Firms on the Defensive," *Accountancy,* July 2004, pp. 24–26.

issue. Although German law specifies the disciplinary procedures against auditors, they are not always strictly implemented due to an overall tendency to focus on damage to the reputation of the profession rather than on the extent of the individual culpability of the auditor. Australia and Canada have recently introduced systems that recognize proportionate liability for auditors. In a white paper on company law reform published in March 2005, the United Kingdom's Department of Trade and Industries proposes to change the current auditor liability regime (unlimited liability) and to introduce proportionality ensuring that the liability is in proportion to the level of wrongdoing.[43]

Statutory Cap

The use of a statutory cap is yet another approach that has been suggested to limit auditor's liability. The purpose of statutory cap is to reduce the amount of money that an audit firm would have to pay if found liable for negligence. In Germany, this has been the practice for many decades. In 1931, an explicit limit on auditors' maximum exposure to legal liability damages was introduced to relieve the auditor of an overwhelming worry of unlimited liability, and to limit the premiums for liability insurance.[44] In the United Kingdom, the auditors are legally prevented from limiting their liability to their client company arising from negligence, default, breach of duty, and breach of trust.[45] As an example of the extent to which auditors may be expected to pay, damages of £65 million were awarded against the accounting firm Binder Hamlyn in 1995. The case involved a careless acknowledgement of responsibility for a set of audited accounts made to a takeover bidder by the firm's senior partner.[46]

Disclaimer

UK auditors often include disclaimers of liability in their audit opinions to protect themselves from unintended liability. In March 2003, in response to a proposal put forward by the ICAEW to promote the capping of unintended auditor liability by changing the wording in audit opinions to illustrate to whom an opinion is given, the U.S. SEC clearly stated that this would not be acceptable in the United States and that disclaimers of liability placed in audit opinions by UK auditors would have no validity if placed on U.S. financial reports.

Auditor Independence

One of the main principles governing auditors' professional responsibilities is independence, in particular independence from management. However, reports of independence rule violations by major international accounting firms have appeared with increasing frequency. As an example, in January 2000, the SEC made public the report by an independent consultant who reviewed possible independence rule violations by one of the Big Four firms arising from ownership of client-issued securities. The report revealed significant violations of the firm's, the profession's, and the SEC's auditor independence rules.[47] Following the recent corporate collapses in many countries, a series of such reports appeared and auditor independence became the subject of much debate at the international level. The remainder of this section reviews various attempts to strengthen auditors' independence.

---

[43] This white paper (Cm 6456) is available at www.dti.gov.uk/cld/review.htm.

[44] Baker, Mikol, and Quick, "Regulation of the Statutory Auditor."

[45] C. J. Napier, "Intersections of Law and Accountancy: Unlimited Auditor Liability in the United Kingdom," *Accounting, Organizations and Society* 23, no. 1 (1998), pp. 105–28.

[46] *Financial Times*, December 7, 1995, p. 1.

[47] The full report is available at www.sec.gov/pdf/pwclaw.pdf.

Auditor Appointment

Having stockholders involved in the auditor appointment process is expected to strengthen the independence of auditors from management and to improve audit quality. Generally, the law, for example the UK Companies Act of 1989 (Section 384), requires that the registered (or statutory) auditor be appointed by the shareholders in an annual general meeting. However, in practice, it is the company's managers who actually select the auditor, after negotiating fees and other arrangements. The auditor often considers the managing directors of the company as the client, and hence the auditor's contractual arrangement is with the management of the company, not with the individual shareholders.

Restricted or Prohibited Activities

Another issue related to auditor independence is restricted or prohibited activities, including relationships with client companies. Mandated activities such as communication between auditors could also strengthen auditor independence. On the issue of the auditor's relationship with client companies, the Sarbanes-Oxley Act has specific provisions prohibiting certain non-audit services provided by external auditors. However, the large audit firms point out that certain consulting work in fact helps improve audit quality. For example, they argue that consulting on information systems and e-commerce puts them on the cutting edge of business, and as a result, they can (1) start to measure items, such as a company's customer service quality, that are not on balance sheets even though investors consider them to be crucial assets, (2) develop continuous financial statements that provide real-time information instead of historical snapshots, and (3) explore ways to audit other measures of value that investors use, such as Web site traffic and market share locked up by being first with a new technology.

Regulatory Oversight

In many countries, the regulation and oversight of auditors have expanded to incorporate external monitoring and oversight of auditor competence and independence. The PCAOB in the United States and the Professional Oversight Board for Accountancy (POBA) in the United Kingdom are two examples. IOSCO has issued a document titled *Statement of Principles for Auditor Oversight*, which requires that "within a jurisdiction auditors should be subject to oversight by a body that acts and is seen to act in the public interest." In its *Statement of Principles of Corporate Governance and Financial Reporting*, IOSCO recommends the following:

- Auditors should be independent, in line with international best practice.
- Auditors should make a statement to the board concerning their independence at the time the audit report is issued.
- The audit committee should monitor the auditor's appointment, remuneration and scope of services, and any retention of the auditor to provide non-audit services.
- The board should disclose the scope of the audit, the nature of any non-audit services provided by the auditors, and the remuneration for these.
- The board should disclose how auditor independence has been maintained where the auditor has been approved to provide any non-audit services.
- An independent oversight body should monitor issues of audit quality and auditor independence.

At the international level, the Public Interest Oversight Board (PIOB) was formed in early 2005 mainly to oversee the work of IFAC committees on auditing, ethics, and education standard setting.

Mandatory Rotation

Mandatory rotation of audit firms often has been advocated as a means of strengthening auditor independence, ensuring that potential conflicts of interest are avoided. A recent government inquiry into auditor independence in the United Kingdom resulted in a recommendation for mandatory auditor rotation as a way to restore investor confidence in the market in response to investor and public concerns in the wake of corporate scandals like the one involving Enron. However, the United Kingdom's largest audit firms have overwhelmingly rejected the notion that auditors should face mandatory rotation.[48] They argue that such a change would only serve to bring down the quality of the audit and that there is no evidence that rotation will prevent corporate collapse.[49]

In revising its code of ethics for professional accountants, IFAC has specified that, for audits of listed entities, the lead engagement partner should be rotated after a predefined period, normally no more than seven years, and that a partner rotating after a predefined period should not participate in the audit engagement until a further period of time, normally two years, has elapsed.[50] This requirement may be of particular concern in countries where there may be few partners with a sufficient understanding of the particular industry involved or a particular set of accounting rules (such as U.S. GAAP or SEC regulations).

Splitting Operations

To address the independence issue, the large accounting firms have taken more drastic action, splitting into separate entities, each dealing with a specific operational area. This allows auditing and consulting arms to deal with the same customer. In 2000, Ernst & Young announced the sale of its management-consulting business to CAP Gemini Group SA for around $11 billion. One reason was to reduce SEC concerns about lack of independence. Also in 2000, Pricewaterhouse-Coopers decided to separate its audit and business advisory services from its other businesses (e.g., e-commerce consulting) in a decision that was "encouraged" by the SEC. In February 2000, KPMG announced the incorporation of KPMG Consulting, to be owned by KPMG LLP and its partners (80.1 percent), and Cisco Systems Inc. (19.9 percent), which in August 1999 agreed to invest $1 billion in the new company.

Stringent Admission Criteria

In the United Kingdom, the Companies Act of 1989, which implemented the EU Eighth Directive, introduced stronger statutory arrangements for the regulation of auditors. It restricts qualifications for appointment as a statutory auditor to those who hold a recognized professional qualification and are subject to the requirements of a recognized supervisory body. It makes specific provision for the independence of company auditors; for example, an officer or employee of the company being audited may not act as auditor.

---

[48] Details are available at www.accountingeducation.com.news/news3659.html.

[49] By contrast, in Singapore, the law requires the rotation of audit partners for publicly listed companies.

[50] IFAC Ethics Committee, *Revision to Paragraph 8.151 Code of Ethics for Professional Accountants* (New York: IFAC, June 2004).

A Principles-Based Approach to Auditor Independence

In a recent auditor independence standard, the Canadian Institute of Chartered Accountants (CICA) makes a shift to a more rigorous "principles-based" approach.[51] The standard reflects features of the relevant requirements included in IFAC, the U.S. Sarbanes-Oxley Act, and the SEC for public companies. Its applicability goes beyond any specific situation and mandates a proactive approach based on clearly articulated principles. The core principle of the CICA standard is that every effort must be made to eliminate all real or perceived threats to the auditor's independence. It requires auditors to ensure that their independence is not impaired in any way. In a set of specific rules for auditors of listed entities, the standard

- Prohibits certain non-audit services (bookkeeping, valuations, actuarial, internal audit outsourcing, information technology system design or implementation, human resource functions, corporate finance activities, legal services, and certain expert services).
- Requires rotation of audit partners (lead and concurring partners after five years with a five-year time-out period, partners who provide more than 10 hours of audit services to the client and lead partners on significant subsidiaries after seven years with a two-year time-out period).
- Prohibits members of engagement team from working for the client in a senior accounting capacity until one year has passed from the time when they were on the engagement team.
- Prohibits compensation of audit partners for cross-selling non-audit services to their audit clients.
- Requires audit committee prior approval for any service provided by the auditor.
- Stipulates that the rules for listed entities apply only to those listed entities with market capitalization or total assets in excess of $10 million.

A Conceptual Approach to Auditor Independence

In Europe, the *Federation des Experts Comptables Europeens* describes its approach to auditor independence as a conceptual approach.[52] By focusing on the underlying aim rather than detailed prohibitions, it combines flexibility with rigor in a way that is unavailable with a rule-based approach. It is argued that this approach

- Allows for the almost infinite variations in circumstances that arise in practice.
- Can cope with the rapid changes of the modern business environment.
- Prevents the use of legalistic devices to avoid compliance.
- Requires auditors to consider actively and to be ready to demonstrate the efficiency of arrangements for safeguarding independence.

An example of this approach would be the two-tiered corporate governance structure that exists in many continental European countries, such as Germany, France, and the Netherlands, and its perceived impact on auditor independence. Under

---

[51] CICA, "Chartered Accountants Adopt New Auditor Independence Standard," news release, December 4, 2003.

[52] Federation des Experts Comptables Europeens, *The Conceptual Approach to Protecting Auditor Independence* (Brussels: FEE, February 2001).

that structure, since the supervisory board monitors the activities of the management board, and the auditors report to the supervisory board, the auditors may be more independent compared to their counterparts in the United Kingdom or the United States.

The main difference between the last two approaches is that, whereas the former uses a list of specific prohibitions, the latter avoids making such a list.

Audit Committees

An audit committee is a committee of the board of directors that oversees the financial reporting process including auditing. The subject of audit committees has drawn increased attention in recent years.[53] In a 1999 report, the U.S. Blue Ribbon Committee, which made recommendations on improving the effectiveness of audit committees, describes the role of the audit committee as first among equals in supporting responsible financial disclosure and active and participatory oversight.[54] It defines the oversight role as "ensuring that quality accounting policies, internal controls, and independent and objective outside auditors are in place to deter fraud, anticipate financial risks, and promote accurate, high quality and timely disclosure of financial and other material information to the board, to the public markets, and to shareholders."[55]

In general, the audit committee responsibilities are to

- Monitor the financial reporting process.
- Oversee the internal control systems.
- Oversee the internal audit and independent public accounting function.

The Sarbanes-Oxley Act contains specific provisions dealing with issues related to audit committees, expanding their role and responsibilities. It requires the audit committee to be responsible for the outside auditor relationship, including the responsibility for the appointment, compensation, and oversight of a company's outside auditor. It also requires that members of the audit committee be independent from company management. Further, the requirements cover audit committee's authority to engage advisors, funding for the audit committee to pay the independent auditor, and any outside advisers it engages, and procedures for handling complaints about accounting, internal control, and auditing matters (whistleblower communication).

In January 2003, responding to Section 301 of the Sarbanes-Oxley Act, the SEC proposed new rules for audit committees to prohibit the listing of companies that fail to comply with the Sarbanes-Oxley Act's and SEC's requirements.[56] The SEC's requirements relate to the independence of audit committee members, the audit committee's responsibility to select and oversee the issuer's independent accountant, procedures for handling complaints regarding the issuer's accounting practices,

---

[53] Each of the Big Four firms has issued audit committee guidance. See, for example, Pricewaterhouse-Coopers, *Audit Committee Effectiveness: What Works Best,* 2nd ed. (Altamonte Springs, FL: Institute of Internal Auditors Research Foundation, 2000); Blue Ribbon Committee, *Report and Recommendations of the Blue Ribbon Committee on Improving the Effectiveness of Corporate Audit Committees* (New York: New York Stock Exchange and National Association of Securities Dealers, 1999); American Institute of Certified Public Accountants, *Audit Committee Communications,* SAS No. 90 (New York: AICPA, 2000).

[54] Blue Ribbon Committee, *Report and Recommendations,* p. 7.

[55] Ibid., p. 20.

[56] Securities and Exchange Commission, *Standards Relating to Listed Company Audit Committees,* SEC Release No. 33-8173, January 8, 2003. This is available at www.SEC.gov/rules/proposed/34-47137.htm.

the authority of the audit committee to engage advisers, and funding for the independent auditor and any outside advisers engaged by the audit committee.

One of the key responsibilities of an audit committee is oversight of the external auditor. It is now widely accepted that the external auditor works for and is accountable to the audit committee and board of directors (in some cases, the supervisory board). The regulatory bodies in many countries now require listed companies to establish audit committees. For example, under the ASX Corporate Governance Guidelines, listed companies in Australia are required to set up an independent audit committee made up completely of non-executive directors. All of the audit committee members are required to be financially literate, and at least one must have financial expertise. Among the ASEAN countries, audit committees for publicly listed companies are required in Malaysia and Singapore.[57]

Understanding how the accountability relationship through audit committees is supposed to work effectively is very important for all parties interested in corporate reporting in an international context. One of the potential problems, at least in some countries, would be the unavailability of individuals with the desired skills to be independent directors. Another concern is that as a result of the expanded responsibilities given to audit committees, suitable individuals may now be reluctant to take on the position of audit committee member. KPMG reported that 65 percent of a sample of UK audit committee members in 2003 believed the enhanced role and responsibilities would discourage individuals from taking on such positions.[58]

INTERNAL AUDITING

Internal auditing is a segment of accounting that uses the basic techniques and methods of auditing, and functions as an appraisal activity established within an entity. The Institute of Internal Auditors (IIA)[59] defines *internal auditing* as "an independent, objective assurance and consulting activity designed to add value and improve an organization's operations."[60] The internal auditor is a person within the organization and is expected to have a vital interest in a wide range of company operations. The Sarbanes-Oxley Act specifically recognizes the importance of internal auditing in restoring credibility to the systems of business reporting, internal control, and ethical behavior. The SEC requires listed companies to have an internal audit function. The IIA is a main source of feedback to the SEC regarding implementation of the internal control provisions of the Sarbanes-Oxley Act.

The role of internal auditing is determined by management, and its scope and objectives vary depending on the size and structure of the firm and the requirements of its management. In general, the objectives of internal auditing differ from

---

[57] Favere-Marchesi, "Audit Quality," p. 142.

[58] This research was carried out among 118 members of FTSE 350 audit committees at the recent Audit Committee Institute Round Table. (The UK Audit Committee Institute is wholly sponsored by KPMG.) Details available at http://acountingeducation.com.news/news3892.html.

[59] The Institute of Internal Auditors (IIA) was founded in the United States in 1941. For more details, see S. Ramamoorti, *Internal Auditing: History, Evolution, and Prospects* (Altamonte Springs, FL: IIA Research Foundation, 2003).

[60] The Institute of Internal Auditors, *Internal Auditing's Role in Sections 302 and 404 of the U.S. Sarbanes-Oxley Act of 2002* (Altamonte Springs, FL: IIA, May 2004).

those of external auditing. As stated in ISA 610, internal auditing activities include the following:

- *Review of the accounting and internal control systems.* The establishment of adequate accounting and internal control systems is a responsibility of management that continuously demands proper attention. Internal auditing is an ordinarily assigned specific responsibility by management for reviewing these systems, monitoring their operations, and recommending improvements thereto.

- *Examination of financial and operating information.* This may include review of the means used to identify, measure, classify and report such information and specific inquiry into individual items including detailed testing of transactions, balances and procedures.

- *Review of the economy, efficiency, and effectiveness of operations.* These operations include nonfinancial controls of an entity.

- *Review of compliance with laws, regulations, and other external requirements, as well as with management policies and directives and other internal requirements.*

Risk management is directly related to corporate governance and is an area in which internal auditing can make a significant contribution. Monitoring risks and providing assurance regarding controls are among the main internal audit functions (refer back to Exhibit 13.1). IFAC defines an internal control system as follows:

> An internal control system consists of all the policies and procedures (internal controls) adopted by the management of an entity to assist in achieving management's objective of ensuring, as far as practicable, the orderly and efficient conduct of its business, including adherence to management policies, the safeguarding of assets, the prevention and detection of fraud and error, the accuracy and completeness of the accounting records, and the timely preparation of reliable financial information. The internal control system extends beyond these matters which relate directly to the fairness of the accounting system.[61]

Recently, the IIA published a paper on internal auditing's role in enterprise risk management (ERM).[62] As shown in Exhibit 13.4, there are competing demands on internal audits from corporate management and audit committees. On the one hand, corporate management requests, among other things, assistance in designing controls, self-assessment of risk and control, and preparing reports on controls. On the other hand, audit committee requests assurance regarding controls and independent evaluation of accounting practices and processes.

The Demand for Internal Auditing in MNCs

In a global competitive environment, internal auditing has become an integral part of managing MNCs. There is a growing demand for risk management skills as MNCs face an increasing array of risks due to the fact that their control landscape is more extensive and complicated compared to purely domestic enterprises. Further, the demand for internal auditing has been growing internationally during the past three decades, particularly due to regulatory and legislative requirements in many countries, for example, the U.S. Foreign Corrupt Practices Act.

---

[61] IFAC, *Handbook of International Auditing, Assurance, and Ethics Pronouncements*, p. 122.

[62] This is available at www.theiia.org.

EXHIBIT 13.4
Competing
Demands on
Internal Audit
Function

Source: A. D. Bailey, A. A.
Gramling, and S.
Ramamoorti, *Research
Opportunities in Internal
Auditing* (Altamonte Springs,
FL: IIA Research Foundation,
2003).

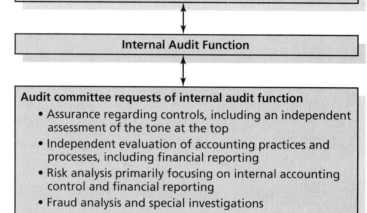

Management requests of internal audit function
- Independent evaluation of controls
- Assistance in preparing report on controls
- Evaluation of efficiency of processes
- Assistance in designing controls
- Risk analysis
- Risk assurance
- Facilitation of risk and control self-assessment

Internal Audit Function

Audit committee requests of internal audit function
- Assurance regarding controls, including an independent assessment of the tone at the top
- Independent evaluation of accounting practices and processes, including financial reporting
- Risk analysis primarily focusing on internal accounting control and financial reporting
- Fraud analysis and special investigations

The Foreign Corrupt Practices Act of 1977 (FCPA)

The Foreign Corrupt Practices Act (FCPA), which became law in December 1977, requires companies to establish and maintain appropriate internal control systems so that corporate funds are not improperly used for illegal purposes. Following the FCPA internal control requirement, the SEC Act of 1934 was amended and, as a result, all the registrants of the SEC are required to install internal control systems to prevent or detect the use of firm assets for illegal activities.

The FCPA makes it illegal for U.S. companies to pay bribes to foreign government officials or political parties in order to secure or maintain business transactions or secure another type of improper advantage. Violation of the FCPA could result in large fines being levied against the corporation, and the executives, employees, and other individuals involved could also be fined or jailed or both. U.S. companies may be subject to liability for FCPA violations by their foreign subsidiaries or joint venture partners.

The FCPA grew out of the revelations of widespread bribery of senior officials of foreign governments by American companies. In particular, the Lockheed and Watergate scandals in the mid-1970s triggered the enactment of the FCPA. The Lockheed scandal involved kickbacks and political donations paid by Lockheed, the American aircraft manufacturer, to Japanese politicians in return for aid in selling planes to All-Nippon Airlines. The scandal forced Tanaka Kakuei to resign as prime minister and as member of the ruling Liberal Democratic Party. Lockheed had paid a total of $22 million to Japanese and other government officials.

In an investigation launched by the Securities and Exchange Commission following the Watergate scandal in the 1970s, it was discovered that American companies were engaged in large-scale bribery overseas. According to the report from that investigation, by 1976 over 450 American companies had paid bribes to foreign government officials, made contributions to political parties, or made other questionable payments. A considerable amount of "slush funds" were generated for this purpose by falsifying their accounting records. Thus, the original intention behind the enactment of the FCPA was to improve corporate accountability and transparency.

The FCPA has two main components—accounting provisions and antibribery provisions. The SEC plays the main role in enforcing the accounting provisions, which require a company to maintain books, records, and accounts fairly reflecting the transactions and dispositions of the assets. In addition, a company must devise and maintain an appropriate internal accounting controls system, execute transactions in accordance with the management's authorization, prepare financial statements in conformity with accounting principles, and record transactions to maintain accountability for assets. These requirements apply to SEC-regulated public companies—both U.S. and foreign companies—including their overseas branches.

The FCPA's accounting provisions require that a company holding a majority of a subsidiary's voting securities must cause that entity to comply with the FCPA accounting requirements. With regard to cases in which the parent holds less than a majority interest, the act requires a parent entity to "proceed in good faith to use its influence, to the extent reasonable under the circumstances" to cause compliance.

The Report of the National Commission on Fraudulent Financial Reporting in the U.S. (Treadway Commission Report, 1987), and the Report of the Committee of Sponsoring Organizations (COSO) of the Treadway Commission, 1992, also placed particular emphasis on internal controls. The 1987 Treadway Report made several recommendations designed to reduce financial statement fraud by improving control and governance. The report made it clear that the responsibility for reliable financial reporting "resides first and foremost at the corporate level, in particular at the top management level." Top management "sets the tone and establishes the financial reporting environment." The idea is that good record keeping and internal control would make it more difficult to conceal illegal activities.

The International Anti-Bribery and Fair Competition Act of 1998 expanded the scope of the FCPA for application to foreign companies (other than those regulated by the SEC) and foreign nationals, if their corrupt activity occurs within the United States. A U.S. company can be prosecuted not only when it directly authorizes an illegal payment by its foreign affiliate but also when it provides funds to that affiliate while knowing or having reason to know that the affiliate will use those funds to make a corrupt payment.

In December 1997, 33 countries signed the OECD Convention on Combating Bribery of Foreign Public Officials in International Business Transactions and are required to make offshore bribery a crime under domestic law.

In the United Kingdom, the Cadbury Committee, which was set up by the FRC, the London Stock Exchange, and the accounting profession to address the financial aspects of corporate governance, presented internal control frameworks in its report published in December 1992.[63] The sponsors were concerned at the perceived low level of confidence both in financial reporting and in the ability of auditors to provide the safeguards, which the users of corporate reports sought and

[63] *Report of the Committee on the Financial Aspects of Corporate Governance* (Cadbury Report) (London: Gee, December 1, 1992).

expected. These concerns were heightened by some unexpected failures of major companies such as Polly Peck.[64] The report developed recommendations for the control and reporting functions of the board, and on the role of auditors. The main output of the committee was a Code of Best Practice for companies. It emphasized openness, integrity, and accountability, and was implemented by the London Stock Exchange. Similar proposals were made by the Criteria of Control Committee of Canada (CoCo Report) and by the OECD Convention.

The Sarbanes-Oxley Act of 2002, Section 404(a), and the SEC's related implementing rules require the management of a public company to assess the effectiveness of the company's internal control over financial reporting, and include in the company's annual report management's conclusion about whether the company's internal control is effective, as of the end of the company's most recent fiscal year. Following these requirements, the PCAOB issued an audit standard, and in June 2004 the SEC approved the PCAOB Release No.2004-003: "An Audit of Internal Control over Financial Reporting Performed in Conjunction with an Audit of Financial Statements." Accordingly, the integrated audit results in two audit opinions: one on internal control over financial reporting and one on the financial statements.[65]

For an MNC, an important task of monitoring risks is to develop a plan to systematically assess risk across multinational activities within the organization. In addition, the MNC needs to assess existing risk of audited area and reporting of that assessment to management, the audit committee, or both; lead the risk management activities when a void has occurred within the organization; facilitate the use of risk self-assessment techniques; evaluate risks associated with the use of new technology; and assist management in implementing a risk model across the organization covering operations in different countries. Exhibit 13.5 shows several evaluative frameworks that have been proposed for internal control.

However, in regard to internal controls, a question remains: What if the top management was involved in the illegal transaction? After all, the top management is responsible for internal control and has discretionary power to override or restructure the internal control system. Managers can commit fraud by overriding internal controls, and audits conducted in accordance with auditing standards do not always distinguish between errors and fraud.[66] Evidence suggests that, although better internal controls would prevent or discourage fraudulent conduct on the part of employees, it would be more difficult to prevent fraud at the top level:

- In 1992, General Electric (GE) allegedly misappropriated $26.5 million from the U.S. government by falsifying accounting records in conjunction with a sale of weapons to Israel. GE was accused of violating not only the FCPA but also the Money Laundering Control Act, among other laws, and was ordered to pay $69 million in fines.

- In 1995, Lockheed was prosecuted for violating the FCPA based on its alleged payment of a bribe of $1 million to a member of the Egyptian parliament in order to sell its military jets to Egypt's armed forces. The company paid a

[64] For details, see David Gwilliam and Tim Russell, "Polly Peck: Where Were the Analysts?" *Accountancy*, January 1991, pp. 25–26.

[65] Details are available at www.sec.gov/news/press/2004-83.htm.

[66] D. Capalan, "Internal Controls and the Detection of Management Fraud," *Journal of Accounting Research* 37, no. 1 (1999), p. 101.

EXHIBIT 13.5
Evaluative
Frameworks for
Internal Control

Source: Deloitte & Touche,
"Moving-forward: A Guide
to Improving Corporate
Governance through
Effective Internal Control—
A Response to Sarbanes-
Oxley," January 2003.

- *COSO—Internal Control—Integrated Framework.* Developed by the Committee of Sponsoring Organizations (COSO) of the Treadway Commission and sponsored by the AICPA, the FEI, the IIA and others, COSO is the dominant framework in the United States. The guidelines were first published in 1991, with anticipated revisions and updates forthcoming. This is believed to be the framework chosen by the vast majority of the U.S.-based public companies.
- *CoCo—The Control Model.* Developed by the Criteria of Control Committee (CoCo) of the CICA. The CoCo focuses on behavioral values rather than control structure and procedures as the fundamental basis for internal control in a company.
- *Turnbull Report—Internal Control.* Developed by the ICAEW, in conjunction with the London Stock Exchange, the guide was published in 1999. Turnbull requires companies to identify, evaluate, and manage their significant risks and to assess the effectiveness of the related internal control systems.
- *Australian Criteria of Control (ACC).* Issued in 1998 by the Institute of Internal Auditors—Australia, the ACC emphasizes the competency of management and employees to develop and operate the internal control framework. Self-committed control, which includes such attributes as attitudes, behaviors, and competency, is promoted as the most cost-effective approach to internal control.
- *The King Report.* The King Report, released by the King Committee on Corporate Governance in 1994, promotes high standards of corporate governance in South Africa. The King Report goes beyond the usual financial and regulatory aspects of corporate governance by addressing social, ethical, and environmental concerns.

$24.8 million fine. In this case, a fine of $20,000 was also imposed on the responsible manager, and the vice president of Middle East and North Africa marketing was fined $125,000 and sentenced to 18 months in prison.

- In 1998, a large U.S. oil company, Saybolt, was prosecuted for violating the FCPA when it allegedly paid $50,000 to a Panamanian government official to obtain a lease for a site near the Panama canal, and paid a fine of $4.9 million.
- In 1996, Montedison, a major Italian company listed on the New York Stock Exchange, allegedly concealed hundreds of millions of dollars in losses by falsifying its books, and paid bribes to Italian politicians and others. The SEC filed a civil suit alleging violations of FCPA accounting standards. In response, the company reformed its internal controls and settled the case with the SEC for $300,000.

According to the results of the Management Barometer Survey 2004, referred to earlier in this chapter, 79 percent of senior executives of U.S. MNCs stated that their company needed improvements in order to comply with Section 404 of Sarbanes-Oxley Act, which requires companies to file a management assertion and auditor attestation on the effectiveness of internal controls over financial reporting. They also mentioned the areas needing remedies, which included the following:

Financial processes	55%
Computer controls	48
Internal audit effectiveness	37
Security controls	35
Audit committee oversight	26
Fraud programs	24

For effective governance, the ultimate responsibility for internal control should be vested in the board, which represents shareholders. The board is responsible for achieving corporate objectives by providing guidance for corporate strategy and monitoring management. The board is effective only if it is reasonably independent from management. Board independence usually requires a sufficient number of outsiders; an adequate time devoted by the members; and access to accurate, relevant, and timely information.

Since the board is usually not engaged in its work on a full-time basis, it needs to rely on experts for necessary information, such as the internal auditor and the external auditor. Being employees of the company, internal auditors are faced with a built-in conflict in regard to their allegiance. This makes the role of the external auditor crucial. External auditors are normally required to make an assessment of the internal control. If the external auditors are to attest to the "fair representation" or "true and fair view" of the financial position of the firm, they need to be able to form their opinion independent of the board and management. However, the issue of auditor independence is complicated by the facts that auditors are paid by the auditee company—more specifically, its management—and often the auditors provide consultancy services to the auditee company.

FUTURE DIRECTIONS

So far in this chapter we have discussed the current status with regard to various auditing issues that are important to MNCs. In this section, we provide some thoughts on the likely future developments. We identify them in terms of consumer demand for auditing, increased competition in the audit market, Big Four firms' continued high interest in the audit market, increased exposure of Big Four firms, a tendency toward a checklist approach, and the possibility that audit may not be the external auditor's exclusive domain.

Building robust corporate governance systems and processes, managing risk on a global scale, and complying with an increasingly vast web of regulatory requirements is difficult, costly, and time-consuming for MNCs.

The Sarbanes-Oxley Act has had a noticeable effect on corporate behavior, particularly in regard to disclosure of information. For example, a recent survey of 2,588 global companies found that 95 percent of U.S. companies (versus 65 percent in 2002) now report having a qualified financial expert on the audit committee.[67] However, in November 2004, a study of audit firm performance, based on interviews with 1,007 audit committee chairs and 944 CFOs, indicated that there was a significant angst among them. Top management was concerned about the costs, in terms of money and time, of implementing the extensive requirements of Sarbanes-Oxley Act. Audit committee chairs were feeling the pressure of increased accountability of the required financial reporting process.[68] Further, a survey conducted by Financial Executives International (FEI) found that the cost of complying with Sarbanes-Oxley Section 404 requirements was much more than companies expected. The Year 1 cost averaged $4.36 million, up

---

[67] More details about rating of companies from different countries can be obtained at www.Gmiratings.com.

[68] J. D. Power and Associates, *2004 Audit Firm Performance Study Report.*

39 percent from the $3.14 million they expected to pay based on FEI's July 2004 cost survey.

Consumer Demand

Historically, the assurance opinion of the statutory auditor has been led by legislation rather than by consumer demand. In the future, however, there will be increasing demand to meet the needs of consumers at a global level.[69] For example, with the disclosure of corporate information on the Internet, auditors will be expected to find new ways of giving assurance on that information, which would not be limited to financial information, and on a real-time basis. A report published by the IASC in November 1999 concluded that there was a need for a generic code of conduct for Internet-based business reporting.[70] The report suggested that such a code should include conditions clearly setting out the information that is consistent with the printed annual report, which contains the audited financial statements. It also pointed out that the users of Internet-based reports are likely to be confused as to which part of the Web site relates to the audit report, signed off by an auditor. From the auditor's point of view, there is a risk involved when the financial report issued by the entity (on which the auditor provides an audit report) is materially misstated due to unauthorized tampering. This could put auditors at risk of legal action.

Attempts are being made to find solutions to some of these problems on a national basis. For example, according to recent legislation in Australia, stockholders are allowed to put questions in writing to auditors in advance of the annual general meeting. However, it appears that governments have now realized the importance of collective action at the international level in this area.

Reporting on the Internet

The AICPA and the CICA have developed a set of principles and criteria to provide assurance services in the area of electronic business. Accordingly, public accounting firms and practitioners, who have a Web Trust business license from an authorized professional accounting body, can provide assurance services to evaluate and test whether a particular Web site meets these principles and criteria. The AICPA/CICA initiative has received international recognition as a major development.[71]

Increased Competition in the Audit Market

In the current global environment, auditor independence in the traditional sense is becoming increasingly problematic as both the audit firms and their clients grow in size and complexity. While the Sarbanes-Oxley Act has proposed more stringent independence standards, including some restrictions on the delivery of audit and non-audit services to the same client, the Big Four international auditing firms need to ensure that they are independent both in fact and in perception. This is

---

[69] J. P. Percy, "Assurance Services: Visions for the Future," *International Journal of Auditing* 3 (1999), pp. 81–87.

[70] A. Lymer, R. Debreceny, G. Gray, and A. Rahman, *Business Reporting on the Internet* (London: IASC, 1999).

[71] For example, the third version of CICA/AICPA Web Trust principles is available at www.accountingeducation.com/news/news497.html.

critical because the perception of a lack of independence will reduce the quality premium the Big Four firms are able to charge their clients and will open the audit market to more competition.

The whole area of systems, particularly technological systems, demands an assurance of their effectiveness. In addition, there is an increasing demand for assurance on the effectiveness and quality of management arrangements and corporate governance. These new demands will require new skills. This will also encourage those not trained in accountancy, but trained in investigative matters in other areas, such as the environment and technology, to develop into a competitive force. In other words, nonaccounting groups may enter the audit market, which traditionally has been the domain of the accounting profession, protected by statutory franchise.

Continued High Interest in the Audit Market

Because they have a virtual monopoly of the large-firm audit market, the Big Four have been able to use this market to build their brands.[72] The audit market will remain central to the Big Four firms' operations because it helps them to maintain their brands. This will continue to be the case in the future, as it will be more difficult for the large firms to develop a reputation for perceived quality and build brands in the non-audit market given that they are competing against recognized competitors with their own brands, such as McKinsey and Boston Consulting Group. Thus, even though the audit market is not extremely profitable, it will be in the interest of the Big Four to protect this market from the encroachment of competitors.

Increased Exposure of the International Auditing Firms

Becoming more global also means becoming more visible. The Big Four international auditing firms audit MNCs listed in numerous jurisdictions, and as these companies grow and become more globalized, the Big Four are increasingly coming under the watchful eye of global financiers and regulatory institutions.

Tendency Toward a Checklist Approach

The advent of litigation and the need for efficiency and effectiveness has driven the audit in some cases to be led more by process than by judgment. Given the various codes of corporate governance, regulations, and auditing standards and guidelines, there is a tendency for auditors to use a checklist approach in order to protect themselves from litigation.[73]

Auditing No Longer Only the Domain of the External Auditor

Given the increased attention on corporate governance and the resulting changes to corporate structures in recent years, no longer is auditing only the domain of the external auditor. The audit function is increasingly becoming a process that involves a partnership between the audit committee, internal auditors, and external auditors.

---

[72] They audit the world's largest 100 companies, with market capitalization ranging from US$31 billion to $273 billion (see www.iasc.org.uk/frame/cen1_9.htm).

[73] Percy, "Assurance Services."

Summary

1. Recent corporate disasters, particularly in the United States, have prompted regulatory measures that emphasize the importance of assurance services as an essential ingredient in establishing and maintaining investor confidence in markets through corporate governance.

2. Over the years, the international aspects of auditing have received relatively less attention among policymakers and researchers, compared to the issues concerning international harmonization of accounting standards.

3. MNCs are realizing the need to pay attention to corporate governance issues in their efforts to succeed in increasingly competitive global markets.

4. The role of the external auditor can vary in different countries. For example, the role of the statutory auditors in Germany is much broader than that of their counterparts in the United Kingdom or the United States.

5. Corporate structure is an important factor that determines the purpose of external audit. For example, some European countries have a two-tiered corporate structure, with a supervisory board and a management board. The supervisory board has general oversight function over the performance of the management board and the basic function of the statutory auditor is to assist the supervisory board. This is different from the situation that exists in Anglo-Saxon countries.

6. Audit quality is likely to vary in different audit environments, and the audit environments in different countries are determined by cultural, legal, financing, and infrastructural factors.

7. The approaches taken to regulate the audit function in different countries range from heavy reliance on the profession, for example, in the United Kingdom, to heavy reliance on the government, for example, in China.

8. The nature of the audit report varies depending largely on the legal requirements in a particular country and the listing status of the company concerned.

9. The responsibility for harmonizing auditing standards internationally rests mainly with the International Federation of Accountants (IFAC).

10. Auditors are subject to civil liability, criminal liability, and professional sanctions.

11. Different approaches have been taken in different countries to deal with the issues concerning the auditor's liability to third parties, and the principle of joint and several liability.

12. Recently many countries have turned increased attention to audit committees as an important instrument of corporate governance.

13. Currently, regulators in the United Kingdom, the United States, and some other countries have placed emphasis on public oversight bodies to monitor issues of auditor independence.

14. Large auditing firms have adopted a policy of splitting the auditing and non-auditing work into separate entities as a way of demonstrating independence.

15. Internal auditing is an integral part of multinational business management, as it helps restore/maintain credibility of the business reporting system. The demand for internal auditing has grown during the past three decades, particularly due to regulatory and legislative requirements in many countries.

Appendix to Chapter 13

Examples of Audit Reports from Multinational Corporations

TOSHIBA CORPORATION
Report of Independent Auditors

The Board of Directors and Shareholders

Toshiba Corporation

We have audited the accompanying consolidated balance sheet of Toshiba Corporation (the "Company") as of March 31, 2004 and 2003, and the related consolidated statements of income, shareholders' equity and cash flows for the years then ended, all expressed in Japanese yen. These financial statements are the responsibility of the Company's management. Our responsibility is to express an opinion on these financial statements based on our audit.

We conducted our audit in accordance with auditing standards generally accepted in the United States of America. Those standards require that we plan and perform the audit to obtain reasonable assurance about whether the financial statements are free of material misstatement. An audit includes examining, on a test basis, evidence supporting the amounts and disclosures in the financial statements. An audit also includes assessing the accounting principles used and significant estimates made by management, as well as evaluating the overall financial statement presentation. We believe that our audit provides a reasonable basis for our opinion.

The Company has not presented segment information required to be disclosed in accordance with Statement of Financial Accounting Standards No. 131, "Disclosures about Segments of an Enterprise and Related Information" for the years ended March 31, 2004 and 2003. In our opinion, presentation of segment information is required under accounting principles generally accepted in the United States of America for a complete presentation of the Company's consolidated financial statements.

In our opinion, except for the omission of segment information discussed in the preceding paragraph, the financial statements referred to above present fairly, in all material respects, the consolidated financial position of the Company at March 31, 2004 and 2003, and the consolidated results of there operations and their cash flows for the years ended in conformity with accounting principles generally accepted in the United States of America.

We have also reviewed the translation of the financial statements mentioned above into United States dollars on the basis described in Note 3. In our opinion, such statements have been translated on such basis.

April 27, 2004

Ernst & Young

Source: Toshiba Corporation, 2003 annual report, p. 67.

SUMITOMO METAL INDUSTRIES LTD.
Independent Auditors' Report

To the Board of Directors and Shareholders of
    Sumitomo Metal Industries, Ltd:

We have audited the accompanying consolidated balance sheets of Sumitomo Metal Industries, Ltd ("SMI") and consolidated subsidiaries as of March 31, 2004 and 2003, and the related consolidated statements of income, shareholders' equity, and cash flows for the years then ended, all expressed in Japanese yen. These consolidated financial statements are the responsibility of SMI's management. Our responsibility is to express an opinion on these consolidated financial statements based on our audits.

We conducted our audits in accordance with auditing standards generally accepted in Japan. Those standards require that we plan and perform the audit to obtain reasonable assurance about whether the statements are free of material misstatement. An audit includes examining, on a test basis, evidence supporting the amounts and disclosures in the financial statements. An audit also includes assessing the accounting principles used and significant estimates made by management, as well as evaluating the overall financial statement presentation. We believe that our audits provide a reasonable basis for our opinion.

In our opinion, the consolidated financial statements referred to above present fairly, in all material respects, the consolidated financial position of SMI and consolidated subsidiaries as of march 31, 2004 and 2003, and the consolidated results of their operations and their cash flows for the years then ended in conformity with accounting principles generally accepted in Japan.

Our audit also comprehended the translation of Japanese yen amounts into U.S. dollar amounts and, in our opinion, such translation has been made in conformity with the basis stated in Note 1. Such U.S. dollar amounts are presented solely for the convenience of readers outside Japan.

Deloitte Touche Tohmatsu

June 29, 2004

Source: Sumimoto Metal Industries Ltd., 2003 annual report, p. 58.

BAYER AG
Independent Auditors' Report

We have audited the consolidated financial statements of the Bayer Group, established by Bayer Aktiengesellschaft, Leverkusen, Germany and comprising the income statement, the balance sheet, the statement of changes in stockholders' equity and the statement of cash flows as well as the notes to the financial statements for the financial year from January 1 through December 31, 2004. The preparation and the content of the financial statements according to the International Financial Reporting Standards (IFRS) of the IASB are the responsibility of the Board of Management of Bayer AG. Our responsibility is to express an opinion, based on our audit, about whether the consolidated financial statements are in accordance with IFRS.

We conducted our audit of the consolidated financial statements in accordance with German auditing regulations, generally accepted standards for audit of financial statements promulgated by the Institut der Wirtschaftsprüfer in Deutschland (IDW) (German Institute of Certified Public Accountants), and additionally observed the International Standards on Auditing (ISA). Those standards require that we plan and perform the audit to obtain reasonable assurance about whether the consolidated financial statements are free of material misstatements. Knowledge of business activities and the economic and legal environment of the Group and evaluations of possible misstatements are taken into account in the determination of audit procedures. The evidence supporting the amounts and disclosures in the consolidated financial statements is examined on a test basis within the framework of the audit. The audit includes assessing the accounting principles used and significant estimates made by the Board of Management, a well as evaluating the overall presentation of the consolidated financial statements. We believe that our audit provides a reasonable basis for our opinion.

In our opinion, the consolidated financial statements as of December 31, 2004 give a true and fair view of the net assets, financial position, results of operations and cash flows of the Bayer Group for the financial year in accordance with IFRS.

Our audit, which—according to German auditing regulations—also extends to the Group management report prepared by the Board of Management for the financial year from January 1 through December 31, 2004, has not led to any reservations. In our opinion, on the whole Group management report, together with the other information in the consolidated financial statements, Provides a suitable understanding of the Group's position and adequately presents the risks related to its future development. In addition, we confirm that the consolidated financial statements of the Bayer Group and the Group management report for the financial year from January 1 through December 31, 2004 satisfy the conditions required for the company's exemption from its duty to prepare the consolidated financial statements and the Group management report in accordance with the German accounting law.

Essen, March 3, 2005

PwC Deutsche Revision
Aktiengesselschaft
Wirtschaftsprüfungsgesellschaft

Source: Bayer AG, 2004 annual report, p. 67.

DAIMLERCHRYSLER
Report of Independent Registered Public Accounting Firm

The Supervisory Board DaimlerChrysler AG:

We have audited the accompanying consolidated balance sheets of DaimlerChrysler AG and subsidiaries ("DaimlerChrysler") as of December 31, 2004 and 2003, and the related consolidated statements of income, changes in stockholders' equity, and cash flows for each of the years in the three-year period ended December 31, 2004. These consolidated financial statements are the responsibility of DaimlerChrysler's management. Our responsibility is to express an opinion on these consolidated financial statements based on our audits.

We conducted our audits in accordance with the Public Company Accounting Oversight Board (United States). Those standards require that we plan and perform the audit to obtain reasonable assurance about whether the financial statements are free of material misstatement. An audit includes examining, on a test basis, evidence supporting the amounts and disclosures in the financial statements. An audit also includes assessing the accounting principles used and significant estimates made by management, as well as evaluating the overall financial statement presentation. We believe that our audits provide a reasonable basis for our opinion.

In our opinion, the consolidated financial statements referred to above present fairly, in all material respects, the financial position of DaimlerChrysler as of December 31, 2004 and 2003, and the results of their operations and their cash flows for each of the years in the three-year period ended December 31, 2004, in conformity with generally accepted accounting principles in the United States of America.

As described in Note 1 to the consolidated financial statements, DaimlerChrysler changed its method of accounting for stock-based compensation in 2003. As described in Notes 3 and 11 to the consolidated financial statements, DaimlerChrysler also adopted the required portions of FASB Interpretations No. 46 (revised December 2003), "Consolidation of Variable Interest Entities—an interpretation of APB No. 51", in 2003. As described in Note 11 to the consolidated financial statements, DaimlerChrysler adopted Statement of Financial Accounting Standards No. 142, "Goodwill and Other Intangible Assets," in 2002.

Stuttgart, Germany
February 21, 2005

KPMG Deutsche Treuhand-Gesellschaft
Aktiengessellschaft
Wirtschaftsprüfungsgesellschaft

Source: DaimlerChrysler, 2004 annual report, p. 99.

UNILEVER PLC
Auditors' Report (United Kingdom)

Report of the independent auditors to the shareholders of Unilevel PLC

We have audited the accounts of the Unilever Group and Unilever PLC which have been prepared under the historical cost convention, set out on pages 96 to 148 and 172 to173. We have also audited the auditable part of the Directors' Remuneration Report as set out on page 89.

Respective responsibilities of directors and auditors

As described on page 92, the Directors are responsible for preparing the Annual Report and Accounts. This includes responsibility for preparing the accounts in accordance with applicable United Kingdom law and United Kingdom accounting standards. The Directors are also responsible for preparing the directors' Remuneration Report.

Our responsibility is to audit the accounts and the auditable part of the Directors' Remuneration Report in accordance with

relevant legal and regulatory requirements and United Kingdom Auditing Standards issued by the Auditing Practices Board. This report, including the opinion, has been prepared for and only for the shareholders of Unilevel PLC, as a body in accordance with Section 235 of the United Kingdom Companies Act 1985 and for no other purpose. We do not, in giving this opinion, accept or assume responsibility for any other purpose or to any other person to whom this report is shown or into whose hands it may come save where expressly agreed by our prior consent in writing.

We report to you our opinion as to whether the accounts give a true and fair view and are properly prepared in accordance with the United Kingdom Companies Act 1985. We also report to you whether the auditable part of the Directors' Remuneration Report is properly prepared in accordance with the applicable requirements in the United Kingdom. We would also report to you if, in our opinion, the Directors' Report is not consistent with the accounts, if proper accounting records have not been kept, if we have not received all the information and explanations we require for our audit, or if information specified by United Kingdom law regarding Directors' remuneration and transactions is not disclosed.

We read the other information contained in the Annual Report and Accounts and consider the implications for our audit report if we become aware of any apparent misstatements or material inconsistencies with the accounts.

We review whether the corporate governance statement on page 64 reflects the Group's compliance with the nine provisions of the 2003 FRC Combined Code specified for our review by the Listing Rules of the United Kingdom's Financial Services Authority and we report if it does not. We are not required to consider whether the Directors' statements on internal control cover all risks and controls or to form an opinion on the effectiveness of the Group's corporate governance procedures or its risk and control procedures.

Basis of audit opinion

We conducted our audit in accordance with auditing standards issued by Auditing Practices Board. An audit includes an examination, on a test basis, of evidence relevant to the amounts and disclosures in the accounts and the auditable part of the Directors' Remuneration Report. It also includes an assessment of the significant estimates and judgements made by the Directors in the preparation of the accounts, and of whether

the accounting policies are appropriate to the Group's circumstances, consistently applied and adequately disclosed.

We planned and performed our audit so as to obtain all the information and explanations which we considered necessary in order to provide us with sufficient evidence to give reasonable assurance that the accounts and the auditable part of the Directors' Remuneration Report are free from material misstatement, whether caused by fraud or other irregularity or error. In forming our opinion we also evaluated the overall adequacy of the presentation of information in the accounts and the Auditable part of the Directors' Remuneration Report.

Opinion

In our opinion, the accounts give a true and fair view of the state of affairs of the Unilever Group, and Unilever PLC at 31 December 2004 and of the profit and cash flows of the Group for the year then ended. In our opinion the accounts of the Unilever Group and Unilever PLC have been properly prepared in accordance with the United Kingdom Companies Act 1985. In our opinion, the auditable part of the Directors' Remuneration Report has been properly prepared in accordance with the applicable requirements in the United Kingdom.

PricewaterhouseCoopers

Chartered Accountants and Registered Auditors

London, United Kingdom

1 March 2005

Source: Unilever PLC, 2004 annual report, p. 94.

UNILEVER NV AND UNILEVER PLC
Auditors' Report (United States)

Report of the independent registered public accounting firms to the shareholders of Unilever N.V. and Unilevel PLC

We have audited the accompanying consolidated balance sheets of the Unilever Group, Unilever N.V. and Unilever PLC as of 31 December 2004 and 2003, and the related consolidated profit and loss accounts, cash flow statements of total recognised gains and losses for each of the three years in the period ended December 31, 2004. These financial statements are the responsibility of the companies' management. Our responsibility is to express an opinion on these financial statements based on our audits.

We conducted our audits in accordance with the standards of the Public Company Accounting Oversight Board (United States). Those standards require that we plan and perform the audit to obtain reasonable assurance about whether the financial statements are free of material misstatement. An audit includes examining, on a test basis, evidence supporting the amounts and disclosures in the financial statements. An audit also includes assessing the accounting principles used and significant estimates made by management, as well as evaluating the overall financial statement presentation. We believe that our audits provide a reasonable basis for our opinion.

In our opinion, the consolidated financial statements referred to above present fairly, in all material respects, the financial position of the Unilever Group, Unilever N.V. and Unilever PLC at 31 December 2004 and 2003, and the results of their operations and their cash flows for each of the three years in the period ended 31 December 2004, in conformity with applicable Netherlands and United Kingdom accounting standards.

Applicable Netherlands and United Kingdom law and United Kingdom accounting standards vary in certain significant respects from accounting principles generally accepted in the United States of America. Information relating to the nature and effect of such differences is presented in the determination of net profit and capital and reserves as shown on pages 154 and 155.

PricewaterhouseCoopers Accountants N.V.

Rotterdam, The Netherlands

As auditors of Unilever N.V.

PricewaterhouseCoopers LLP

London, United Kingdom

As auditors of Unilever PLC

1 March 2005

Source: Unilever NV and Unilever PLC, 2004 annual report, p. 95.

UNILEVER N.V.
Auditors' Report (Netherlands)

Audit report of the independent auditors to the shareholders of Unilever N.V.

We have audited the accounts of the Unilever Group and Unilever N.V. set out on pages 96 to 148 and 154 to 170.

Respective responsibilities of Directors and auditors

These accounts are the responsibility of the company's Directors. Our responsibility is to express an opinion on these accounts based on our audit.

Basis of audit opinion

We conducted our audit in accordance with auditing standards generally accepted in the Netherlands. These standards require that we plan and perform the audit to obtain reasonable assurance about whether the accounts are free of material misstatement. An audit includes examining, on a test basis,

evidence supporting the amounts and disclosures in the accounts. An audit also includes assessing the accounting principles used and significant estimates made by management, as well as evaluating the overall presentation of the accounts. We believe that our audit provides a reasonable basis for our opinion.

Opinion

In our opinion, the accounts give a true and fair view of the financial position of the Unilever Group and Unilever N.V. as at 31 December 2004 and of the results for the year then ended in accordance with United Kingdom accounting standards and comply with the financial reporting requirements included in Part 9 of Book 2 of the Netherlands Civil Code.

PricewaterhouseCoopers Accountants N.V.

Rotterdam, The Netherlands

1 March 2005

Source: Unilever NV, 2004 annual report, p. 93.

CHINA SOUTHERN AIRLINES COMPANY LTD.
Report of the Auditors

TO THE SHAREHOLDERS OF CHINA AIRLINES COMPANY LIMITED:

We have audited the accompanying Company's consolidated balance sheet and balance sheet at 31 December, 2003, and the consolidated income and profit appropriation statement, income and profit appropriation statement, consolidated cash flow statement and cash flow statement for the year then ended. The preparation of these financial statements is the responsibility of the Company's management. Our responsibility is to express an audit opinion on these financial statements based on our audit.

We conducted our audit in accordance with China's Independent Auditing Standards of the Certified Public Accountants. These standards require that we plan and perform the audit to obtain reasonable assurance as to whether the financial statements are free from material misstatement. An audit includes examination, on a test basis, of evidence supporting the amounts and disclosures in the financial statements, an assessment of the accounting policies used and significant estimates made by the Company's management in the preparation of the financial statements, as well as evaluating the overall financial statements presentation. We believe that our audit provides a reasonable basis for our opinion.

In our opinion, the above-mentioned financial Statements comply with the requirements of the Accounting Standards for Business Enterprises and the Accounting Regulations for Business Enterprises issued by the Ministry of Finance of the People's Republic of China and present fairly, in all material respects, the Company's consolidated financial position and financial position at 31 December, 2003, and the consolidated results of operations, results of operations, and consolidated cash flows and cash floes for the year ended.

KPMG Huazhen

Certified Public Accountants

Registered in the People's Republic of China

23 April, 2004

Source: China Southern Airlines Company, Ltd., 2003 annual report, p. 99.

Questions

1. Why should MNCs be concerned about auditing issues?
2. What are the main differences between the OECD Principles of Corporate Governance issued in 1999 and the revised version issued in 2004?

3. What are the provisions in the Sarbanes-Oxley Act 2002 and the New York Stock Exchange listing requirements that are aimed at improving corporate governance and are directly related to audit committees?

4. What determines the primary role of external auditing in a particular country?

5. What is audit quality? What determines audit quality in a given country?

6. What is the PCAOB? What is its role in audit regulation?

7. What is the PIOB? What is its role in audit regulation?

8. What was the impact of the European Union's Eighth Directive on the regulation of auditing in the United Kingdom?

9. In what ways do company audit reports vary in different countries?

10. What are the main benefits of international harmonization of auditing standards?

11. What determines whether or not to issue an unqualified audit opinion on the compliance of a set of financial statements with IFRSs?

12. What are some of the strategies adopted internationally to limit the auditor's liability?

13. What are the main factors that complicate the issue of auditor independence?

14. What is the oversight role of an audit committee?

15. What are the main differences between internal auditing and external auditing within an MNC?

Exercises and Problems

1. Refer to the Report of Independent Auditors of Unilever NV and Unilever PLC, signed on 1 March 2005 (see the appendix to this chapter).

   Required:
   Identify the features in the above audit report that are unique to an MNC.

2. ISA 700 describes three types of audit opinions that can be expressed by the auditor when an unqualified opinion is not appropriate: qualified, adverse, and disclaimer of opinion.

   Required:
   What are the circumstances under which each of the above three opinions should be expressed? ISA 700 is accessible form the IFAC Web site (www.ifac.org).

3. In June 2003, IFAC issued an IAPS providing additional guidance for auditors internationally when they express an opinion on financial statements that are asserted by management to be prepared in either of the following ways:
   • Solely in accordance with IFRSs.
   • In accordance with IFRSs and a national financial reporting framework.
   • In accordance with a national financial reporting framework with disclosure of the extent of compliance with IFRSs.

   Required:
   Identify the additional guidelines under each of the three categories of audit opinion.

4. In June 2004, the IFAC Ethics Committee issued its "Revision to Paragraph 8.151 Code of Ethics for Professional Accountants." Accordingly, for the audit of listed entities,
   a. The lead engagement partner should be rotated after a predefined period, normally no more than seven years.
   b. A partner rotating after a predefined period should not participate in the audit engagement until a further period of time, normally two years, has elapsed.

Required:

How does the revised version differ from the previous version of the paragraph mentioned in Exercise 3?

5. Internationally, legislators and professional bodies have focused on corporate governance issues in making recommendations for restoring investor confidence, and auditing is an essential part of corporate governance.

Required:

Explain the link between auditing and corporate governance.

6. Some commentators argue that the two-tiered corporate structure, with a management board and a supervisory board, prevalent in many Continental European countries, is better suited for addressing corporate governance issues, including the issue of auditor independence, compared to that with one board of directors prevalent in Anglo-Saxon countries.

Required:

Evaluate the merits of the above argument.

7. This chapter refers to a unique ownership structure of many former state-owned enterprises in China, which have been redefined to create new economic entities.

Required:

Describe the uniqueness of the ownership structure of the entities mentioned above, and explain its implications for auditing.

8. This chapter refers to the concept of accounting infrastructure, which encompasses the various environmental factors affecting the issues concerning auditing in a particular country.

Required:

Explain the environmental factors that affect the issues concerning auditing in your own country.

9. The establishment of the Public Company Accounting Oversight Board (PCAOB) in 2002 was a major step toward strengthening the auditing function in the United States.

Required:

What can the PCAOB do to strengthen the auditing function in the United States? Provide examples of two key steps it has taken so far to achieve this.

10. In Anglo-Saxon countries, mechanisms are put in place to regulate auditors within the framework of professional self-regulation, whereas in many Continental European countries, quasi-governmental agencies play a major role in this area.

Required:

a. Briefly describe the main differences between the audit regulation mechanisms in the United States and Germany.

b. Compare the audit regulation mechanisms in the United States and the United Kingdom.

11. The responsibility for harmonizing auditing standards across countries rests with IFAC.

Required:

Comment on some of the problems faced by IFAC in achieving the above goal.

12. There is no agreement internationally on how to address the issue of auditor liability.

Required:

Describe the approach taken in your own country in addressing the issue of auditor liability, and explain the rationale behind that approach.

Case 13-1

Honda Motor Company

Following is the independent auditor's report on the financial statements of Honda Motor Company, signed on April 25, 2003:

> We have audited the accompanying consolidated balance sheets of Honda Motor Co., Ltd. and subsidiaries as of March 31, 2002 and 2003, and the related consolidated statements of income, stockholders' equity and cash flows for each of the years in the three-year period ended March 31, 2003. These consolidated financial statements are the responsibility of the Company's management. Our responsibility is to express an opinion on these consolidated financial statements based on our audits.
>
> We conducted our audits in accordance with auditing standards generally accepted in the United States of America. Those standards require that we plan and perform the audit to obtain reasonable assurance about whether the financial statements are free of material misstatement. An audit includes examining, on a test basis, evidence supporting the amounts and disclosures in the financial statements. An audit also includes assessing the accounting principles used and significant estimates made by management, as well as evaluating the overall financial statement presentation. We believe that our audits provide a reasonable basis for our opinion.
>
> The segment information required to be disclosed in financial statements under accounting principles generally accepted in the United States of America is not presented in the accompanying consolidated financial statements. Foreign issuers are presently exempted from such disclosure requirement in Securities Exchange Act filings with the Securities and Exchange Commission of the United States of America.
>
> In our opinion, except for the omission of the segment information referred to in the preceding paragraph, the consolidated financial statements referred to above present fairly, in all material respects, the financial position of Honda Motor Co., Ltd. and subsidiaries as of March 31, 2002 and 2003, and the results of their operations and their cash flows for each of the years in the three-year period ended March 31, 2003 in conformity with accounting principles generally accepted in the United States of America.
>
> The accompanying consolidated financial statements as of and for the year ended March 31, 2003 have been translated into United States dollars solely for the convenience of the reader. We have recomputed the translation and, in our opinion, the consolidated financial statements expressed in yen have been translated into dollars on the basis set forth in note 2 to the consolidated financial statements.

Required:

Comment on whether or not the above audit report is in conformity with the audit report requirements approved by the U.S. SEC.

Case 13-2

Harmonization of the Audit Report and the Big Four

The following are audit reports of three companies—one each company from the United Kingdom, Germany, and Japan—listed on the New York Stock Exchange and audited by the same Big Four firm.

Independent Auditors' Report to Members of Cadbury Schweppes Plc—United Kingdom

---

We have audited the financial statements of Cadbury Schweppes Plc for the year ended 28 December 2003, which comprise the Group and Company Balance Sheets as at 28 December 2003, and 29 December 2002, the Group Profit and Loss Accounts, the Group Cash Flow Statements, the Statements of Total Recognised Gains and Losses and the Reconciliation of Movements in Shareholders' Funds for the years ended 28 December 2003, 29 December 2002 and 30 December 2001, the related Geographical Analysis and Notes 1 to 32. These financial statements have been prepared under the accounting policies set out therein. We have also audited the information in the part of the Report on Directors' Remuneration that is described as having been audited.

Respective responsibilities of Directors and auditors

As described in the Statement of Directors' responsibilities, the Company's Directors are responsible for the preparation of the financial statements in accordance with applicable United Kingdom law and accounting standards. They are also responsible for the preparation of the other information contained in the Report & Accounts and Form 20-F including the Report on Directors' Remuneration. Our responsibility is to audit the financial statements and the part of the Report on Directors' Remuneration described as having been audited in accordance with relevant United Kingdom legal and regulatory requirements and auditing standards.

We report to you our opinion as to whether the financial statements give a true and fair view and whether the financial statements and the part of the Report on Directors' Remuneration described as having been audited have been properly prepared in accordance with the Companies Act 1985. We also report to you if, in our opinion, the Report of the Directors is not consistent with the financial statements, if the Company has not kept proper accounting records, if we have not received all the information and explanations we require for our audit, or if information specified by law regarding Directors' remuneration and transactions with the Company and other members of the Group is not disclosed.

We review whether the corporate governance statement reflects the Company's compliance with the seven provisions of the Combined Code specified for our review by the Listing Rules of the Financial Services Authority, and we report if it does not. We are not required to consider whether the Board's statements on internal control cover all risks and controls, or form an opinion on the effectiveness of the Group's corporate governance procedures or its risk and control procedures.

We read the Report of the Directors and the other information contained in the Report & Accounts and Form 20-F for the year ended 28 December 2003 as described in the contents section, including the unaudited part of the Report on Directors' Remuneration, and consider the implications for our report if we become aware of any apparent misstatements or material inconsistencies with the financial statements.

Basis of audit opinion

We conducted our audit in accordance with United Kingdom auditing standards issued by the Auditing Practices Board and with generally accepted auditing standards in the United States of America. An audit includes examination, on a test basis, of evidence relevant to the amounts and disclosures in the financial statements and the part of the Report on Directors' Remuneration described as having been audited. It also includes an assessment of the significant estimates and judgements made by the Directors in the preparation of the financial statements and of whether the accounting policies are appropriate to the circumstances of the Company and the Group, consistently applied and adequately disclosed.

We planned and performed our audit so as to obtain all the information and explanations which we considered necessary in order to provide us with sufficient evidence to give reasonable assurance that the financial statements and the part of the Report on Directors' Remuneration described as having been audited are free from material misstament, whether caused by fraud or other irregularity or error. In forming our opinion, we also evaluate the overall adequacy of the presentation of information in the financial statements and the part of the Report on Directors' Remuneration described as having been audited.

UK Opinion

In our opinion:

- The financial statements give a true and fair view of the state of affairs of the Company and the Group at 28 December 2003 and of the profit of the Group for the year then ended; and
- The financial statements and that part of the report on Directors' Remuneration described as having been audited have been properly prepared in accordance with the Companies Act 1985.

US Opinion

In our opinion the financial statements present fairly, in all material respects, the consolidated financial position of the Group at 28 December 2003 and 29 December 2002 and the consolidated results of its operations and cash flows for the years ended 28 December 2003, 29 December 2002 and 30 December 2001 inconformity with accounting principles generally accepted in the United Kingdom.

Accounting principles generally accepted in the United Kingdom vary in significant respects from accounting principles generally accepted in the United States of America. The application of the latter would have affected the determination of net income for the years ended 28 December 2003, 29 December 2002 and 30 December 2001 and the determination of shareholders equity at 28 December 2003 and 29 December 2002, to the extent summarised in Note 31 to the consolidated financial statements.

Deloitte & Touche LLP
Chartered Accountants and Registered Auditors
London, England
15 March 2004.

Source: Cadbury Schweppes, Report & Accounts and Form 20-F, 2003, pp. 86–87.

Report of Independent Auditors—BASF AG, Germany

We have audited the Consolidated Financial Statements prepared by BASF Aktiengesellschaft as well as the Management's Analysis of BASF Aktiengesellschaft and BASF Group for the business year from January 1 to December 31, 2003. The Board of Executive Directors of BASF Aktiengesellschaft is responsible for preparing the Consolidated Financial Statements and Management's Analysis in accordance with German commercial Law. It is our task, on the basis of the audit we have carried out, to give an assessment of the Consolidated Financial Statements and Management's Analysis.

Pursuant to Section 317 of the German Commercial Code, we have audited the Consolidated Financial Statements of BASF Group in accordance with the generally accepted standards of auditing laid down by the German Institute of Auditors. According to these principles, the audit is to be planned and carried out in such a way that inaccuracies and violations are recognized with reasonable certainty that could have a major effect on the view of the net assets, financial position and results of operations covered by the Consolidated Financial Statements—taking into consideration generally accepted accounting principles—and Management Analysis. The determination of the action for this audit takes into account knowledge of the business and BASF's economic and legal environment as well as expectations of possible errors. In the audit, the effectiveness of the internal checking system and proof of the details provided in the Consolidated Financial Statements and Management's Analysis are assessed predominantly on the basis of spot checks. The audit encompasses an assessment of the financial statements of the companies in the Consolidated Financial Statements, a definition of the scope of consolidation, a review of the accounting and consolidation principles employed, the main judgments made by the Board of Executive Directors, and an appreciation of the overall presentation of the Consolidated Financial Statements and Management's Analysis. In our opinion, we believe that our audit provides a reasonable basis for our assessment.

Our audit has not given rise to any reservations. It is our opinion that these Consolidated Financial Statements, taking into consideration generally accepted accounting principles, convey a true and fair view of the assets, financial position and results of operations of BASF Group. Management's Analysis of BASF Aktiengesellschaft and BASF Group conveys in all an accurate presentation of the situation of BASF and accurately shows the risks to future development.

Frankfurt, March 2, 2004.

Deloitte & Touche GmbH
Wirtschaftsprufungsgesellschaft

Source: BASF, 2003 annual report, p. 77.

Report of Independent Registered Public Accounting Firm—Kubota Corporation, Japan

To the Board of Directors and Shareholders of Kubota Corporation:

We have audited the accompanying consolidated balance sheets of Kubota Corporation and subsidiaries (the "Company") as of March 31, 2004 and 2003, and the related consolidated statements of income, comprehensive income (loss), shareholders' equity, and cash flows for each of the three years in the period ended March 31, 2004, all expressed in Japanese yen. These financial statements are the responsibility of the Company's management. Our responsibility is to express an opinion on these financial statements based on our audits.

We conducted our audits in accordance with the standards of the Public Company Accounting Oversight Board (United States). Those standards require that we plan and perform the audit to obtain reasonable assurance about whether the financial statements are free of material misstatement. An audit includes examining, on a test basis, evidence supporting the amounts and disclosures in the financial statements. An audit also includes assessing the accounting principles used and significant estimates made by management, as well as evaluating the overall financial statement presentation. We believe that our audits provide a reasonable basis for our opinion.

Certain information required by Statement of Financial Accounting Standards ("SFAS") No. 131, "Disclosures about Segments of an Enterprise and Related Information" has not been presented in the accompanying consolidated financial statements. In our opinion, presentation concerning operating segments and other information is required for a complete presentation of the Company's consolidated financial statements.

The Company has not accounted for a nonmonetary security transaction, that occurred during the year ended March 31, 1997, in accordance with accounting principles generally accepted in the United States of America. In our opinion, the recognition of the nonmonetary exchange gain, and the related impact in subsequent periods, is required by accounting principles generally accepted in the United States of America. The Company has disclosed the effects of the departure and other relevant information in Note 1 to the consolidated financial statements.

In our opinion, except for the omission of segment and other information required by SFAS No. 131 and the effect of not properly recording a nonmonetary security exchange transaction, as discussed in the preceding paragraph, such consolidated financial statements present fairly, in all material respects, the financial position of Kubota Corporation and subsidiaries as of March 31, 2004 and 2003, and the results of their operations and their cash flows for each of the three years in the period ended March 31, 2004 in conformity with accounting principles generally accepted in the United States of America.

Our audits also comprehended the translation of Japanese yen amounts into U.S. dollar amounts and, in our opinion, such translation has been made in conformity with the basis stated in Note 1. Such U.S. dollar amounts are presented solely for the convenience of readers outside Japan.

Deloitte Touche Tohmatsu
June 3, 2004.

Source: Kubota Corporation, 2004 annual report, p. 50.

Required:

Assuming that you are a member of a research team conducting a study on international harmonization of auditing, write a short essay based on the three audit reports in this case, identifying

1. The similarities and differences in the manner in which the audit reports from the United Kingdom, Germany, and Japan are presented.
2. Any issues that might be of interest to the International Federation of Accountants.

References

American Accounting Association, Committee on Basic Auditing Concepts. "A Statement of Basic Auditing Concepts," 1973.

American Institute of Certified Public Accountants. *Audit committee Communications*, SAS No. 90, New York: AICPA, 2000.

Baker, C. R.; A. Mikol; and R. Quick. "Regulation of the Statutory Auditor in the European Union: A Comparative Survey of the United Kingdom, France and Germany." *European Accounting Review* 10, no. 4 (2001), pp. 763–86.

Blue Ribbon Committee. *Report and Recommendations of the Blue Ribbon Committee on Improving the Effectiveness of Corporate Audit Committees.* New York: New York Stock Exchange and National Association of Securities Dealers, 1999.

Canadian Institute of Chartered Accountants. "Chartered Accountants Adopt New Auditor Independence Standard." News release, December 4, 2003.

Capalan, D. "Internal Controls and the Detection of Management Fraud, *Journal of Accounting Research* 37, no. 1 (1999), pp. 101–17.

Chow, C. W., and R. N. Hwang. "The Cross-Border Transferability of Audit Technology: An Exploratory Study in the U.S.–Taiwan Context." *Advances in International Accounting* 7 (1994), pp. 217–29.

Committee of Sponsoring Organizations. *Internal Control—Integrated Framework.* COSO, 1992.

DeAngelo, L. "Auditor Size and Audit Quality." *Journal of Accounting and Economics* 3 (1981), pp. 183–200.

Deloitte & Touche. "Moving Forward: A Guide to Improving Corporate Governance through Effective Internal Control—A Response to Sarbanes-Oxley." Deloitte & Touche, January 2003.

Department of Trade and Industry. *A Framework of Independent Regulation for the Accountancy Profession: A Consultation Document.* London: DTI, 1998.

Federation des Experts Comptables Europeens. "The Role of Accounting and Auditing in Europe." FEE position paper, May 2002.

———. "The Conceptual Approach to Protecting Auditor Independence," February 2001.

Favere-Marchesi, M. "Audit Quality in ASEAN." *International Journal of Accounting* 35, no. 1 (2000), pp. 121–49.

Fisher, Liz. "Firms on the Defensive." *Accountancy,* July 2004, pp. 24–26.

Gangolly, J. S.; M. E. Hussein; G. S. Seow; and K. Tam. "Harmonization of the Auditor's Report." *International Journal of Accounting* 37 (2002), pp. 327–46.

Graham, L. E. "Setting a Research Agenda for Auditing Issues in the People's Republic of China." *International Journal of Accounting* 31, no. 1 (1996), pp. 19–37.

Gwilliam, David, and Tim Russell. "Polly Peck: Where Were the Analysts?" *Accountancy,* January 1991, pp. 25–26.

Institute of Internal Auditors. *Internal Auditing's Role in Sections 302 and 404 of the U.S. Sarbanes-Oxley Act of 2002*. Altamonte Springs, FL: IIA, May 2004.

International Federation of Accountants. "Reporting by Auditors on Compliance with International Financial Reporting Standards." International Auditing Practice Statement 1014. New York: International Auditing and Assuarance Standards Board, IFAC, June 2003.

———. "Revision to Paragraph 8.151 Code of Ethics for Professional Accountants." New York: IFAC Ethics Committee, June 2004.

Lee, C. J. "Accounting Infrastructure and Economic Development." *Journal of Accounting and Public Policy,* Summer 1987, pp. 75–86.

Lymer, A.; R. Debreceny; G. Gray; and A. Rahman. *Business Reporting on the Internet*. London: IASC, 1999.

McKinnon, J. "The Accounting Profession in Japan." *Australian Accountant*, July 1983, pp. 406–10.

Mueller, G. G. "Is Accounting Culturally Determined?" Paper presented at the EIASM Workshop on Accounting and Culture, Amsterdam, June 1985.

Napier, C. J. "Intersections of Law and Accountancy: Unlimited Auditor Liability in the United Kingdom. *Accounting, Organizations and Society* 23, no. 1 (1998), pp. 105–28.

Organization for Economic Corporation and Development. *OECD Principles of Corporate Governance*. Paris: OECD 1999. (Available at www.oecd.org.)

Parker, Andrew. "PwC Steps Up Litigation Fight." *Financial Times*, April 19, 2004, p. 18.

Percy, J. P. "Assurance Services: Visions for the Future." *International Journal of Auditing* 3 (1999), pp. 81–87.

PricewaterhouseCoopers. *Audit Committee Effectiveness: What Works Best*, 2nd ed. Altamonte Springs, FL: The Institute of Internal Auditors Research Foundation, 2000.

Ramamoorti, S. *Internal Auditing: History, Evolution, and Prospects*. Altamonte Springs, FL: The Institute of Internal Auditors Research Foundation, 2003.

Report of the Committee on the Financial Aspects of Corporate Governance (Cadbury Report), December 1, 1992, London: Gee (a division of Professional Publishing Ltd.)

Roussey, R. S. "New Focus for the International Standards on Auditing." *Journal of International Accounting, Auditing and Taxation* 5, no. 1 (1996), pp. 133–46.

Securities and Exchange Commission. "Standards Relating to Listed Company Audit Committees." SEC Release No. 33-8173, January 8, 2003. (Available at www.SEC.gov/rules/proposed/34-47137.htm.)

Soeters, J., and H. Schreuder. "The Interaction between National and Organizational Cultures in Accounting Firms." *Accounting, Organizations and Society* 13, no. 1 (1988), pp. 75–85.

Treadway Commission. *Report of the National Commission on Fraudulent Financial Reporting*. Washington, DC: National Commission on Fraudulent Financial Reporting, 1987.

Turner, L. "The 'Best of Breed' Standards: Globalising Accounting Standards Challenges the Profession to Fulfil Its Obligation to Investors." *Financial Times*, March 8, 2001.

Wood, R. A. "Global Audit Characteristics across Cultures and Environments: An Empirical Examination." *Journal of International Accounting, Auditing, and Taxation* 5, no. 2 (1996), pp. 215–29.

List of Some Useful Web Sites

1. Big-Four Accounting Firms

Deloitte Touche	www.deloitte.com
Ernst & Young	www.ey.com
KPMG	www.kpmg.com
PricewaterhouseCoopers	www.pwcglobal.com

2. International Organizations Dealing with International Accounting Issues

For IFRSs and information about international accounting harmonization/convergence efforts:
International Accounting Standards Board (IASB) www.iasb.org.uk

For ISAs and information about international auditing harmonization efforts, and other developments in regard to ethics, accounting education and professional development at international level:
International Federation of Accountants (IFAC): www.ifac.org

For harmonized standards for business processes in the exchange industry, particularly in the realm of cross-border initiatives:
World Federation of Exchanges: www.world-exchanges.org

For GAAP Convergence 2002:
International Forum for Accountancy Development (IFAD): www.ifad.net

For information about global financial markets:
International Monetary Fund: www.imf.org

For information about securities regulation around the world:
International Organization of Securities Commissions (IOSCO): www.iosco.org

For guidelines on corporate governance and financial statistics for different countries:
Organization of Economic Corporation and Development (OECD): www.oecd.org

For information about country profiles on economic and accounting issues:
World Bank: www.worldbank.org

For information about the rules of trade in services, including accounting, between nations:
World Trade Organization: www.wto.org

For information about various issues related to international trade:
United Nations Conference on Trade and Development (UNCTAD): www.unctad.org

3. Regional Organizations Dealing with Accounting Issues

Asia-Pacific Economic Cooperation (APEC): www.apecsec.org.sg

Association of Southeast Asian Nations (ASEAN): www.aseansec.org

Confederation of Asian and Pacific Accountants (CAPA): www.capa.com.my

European Federation of Accountants: www.fee.be

European Union (EU): www.europa.eu.int

Federation of European Stock Exchanges: www.fese.be

4. National Accounting Standard-Setting Bodies

Australia:	Australian Accounting Standards Board (AASB) www.aasb.com.au
China:	China Accounting Standards Committee (CASC) www.casc.gov.cn/internet/internet/en.html
Germany:	German Accounting Standards Board (GASB) www.drse.de
Japan:	Accounting Standards Board of Japan (ASBJ) www.asb.or.jp
Malaysia:	Malaysian Accounting Standards Board (MASB) www.masb.org.my

United Kingdom: Accounting Standards Board (ASB): www.asb.org.uk

United States: Financial Accounting Standards Board (FASB): www.fasb.org

5. Government Agencies Influencing Accounting Standards

Australia: Australian Securities and Investment Commission (ASIC): www.asic.gov.au

China: China Ministry of Finance: www.mof.gov.cn

China Securities Regulatory Commission: www.csrc.gov.cn

Germany: The Federal Ministry of Justice www.ejtn.net/www/en/html/ nodes_main/4_1949_208/ 5_1585_11.htm

Japan: The Ministry of Justice www.moj.jp/ENGLISH/ preface.html

United Kingdom: Financial Services Authority (FSA): www.fsa.gov.uk

Department of Trade and Industry (DTI) www.dti.gov.uk

United States: Securities and Exchange Commission (SEC): www.sec.gov

6. Professional Bodies and Other Agencies Dealing with Accounting Standards

United Kingdom: Accountancy Foundation www.accountancyfoundation.com

Financial Reporting Council (FRC) www.frc.org.uk

Professional Oversight Board for Accountancy www.frc.org.uk/poba/index.cfm

United States: Public Company Accounting Oversight Board (PCAOB) www.pcaobus.org

International: Public Interest Oversight Board (PIOB) www.ifac.org/Downloads/ inauguration_of_piob.pdf

7. Other Useful Web Sites for Information about International Accounting Issues

For information about international accounting issues:

http://accountingedcuation.com

Deloitte Touche Tohmatsu IAS Plus Web site: www.iasplus.com

For information about foreign companies listed on U.S. stock exchanges:

U.S. SEC Electronic Data Gathering, Analysis, and Retrieval (EDGAR): www.sec.gov/edgarhp.htm

For information about surveys of global companies:

The Governance Metrics International (GMI) www.Gmiratings.com

8. National Professional Accounting Bodies

Australia: CPA Australia: www.cpaonline.com.au

Institute of Chartered Accountants in Australia (ICAA): www.icaa.org.au

Canada: Canadian Institute of Chartered Accountants (CICA): www.cica.ca

Certified General Accountants' Association of Canada: www.cga-canada.org

CMA Canada: www.cma-canada.org

China: Chinese Institute of Certified Public Accountants: www.cicpa.org.cn

Germany: Institute der Wirtschaftsprüfer: www.wpk.de

Hong Kong: Hong Kong Society of Accountants: www.hksa.org.hk

India: Institute of Chartered Accountants of India: www.icai.org

Japan: Japanese Institute of Certified Public Accountants (JICPA): www.jicpa.org.jp

Malaysia: Malaysian Institute of Accountants: www.mia.org.my

New Zealand: Institute of Chartered Accountants of New Zealand www.icanz.co.nz

Singapore: Institute of Certified Public Accountants of Singapore: www.accountants.org.sg

United Kingdom: Association of Chartered Certified Accountants (ACCA): www.acca.org.uk

Chartered Institute of Management Accountants (CIMA): www.cima.org.uk

Institute of Chartered Accountants in England and Wales (ICAEW): www.icaew.co.uk

Chartered Institute of Public Finance and Accountancy (CIPFA): www.cipfa.org.uk

Institute of Chartered Accountants of Scotland (ICAS): www.icas.org.uk

Association of Accounting Technicians (AAT): www.aat.co.uk

United States: American Institute of Certified Public Accountants (AICPA): www.aicpa.org

Institute of Management Accountants (IMA): www.imanet.org

Institute of Internal Auditors (IIA): www.theiia.org

9. Stock Exchanges

Australia: Australian Stock Exchange: www.asx.com.au

Canada: Toronto Stock Exchange: www.tse.com

China: Shanghai Stock Exchange: www.sse.com.cn

Shenzhen Stock Exchange: www.cninfo.com.cn.

Finland: Helsinki Stock Exchange: www.hexgroup.com

Germany: Frankfurt Stock Exchange: www.deutsche-borse.com

Hong Kong: Hong Kong Exchange: www.hkex.com.hk

India: Mumbai Stock Exchange: www.bseindia.com

Japan: Tokyo Stock Exchange: www.tse.or.jp

Osaka Stock Exchange: www.ose.or.jp

Malaysia: Kuala Lumpur Stock Exchange: www.klse.com.my

Mexico: Mexican Stock Exchange: www.bmy.com.mx

New Zealand: New Zealand Exchange: www.nzx.co.nz

Singapore: Singapore Exchange: www.singaporeexchange.com

United Kingdom: London Stock Exchange: www.londonstockexchange.com

United States: New York Stock Exchange: www.nyse.com

Chicago Stock Exchange: www.chicagostockex.com

National Association of Security Dealers Automated Quotations: www.nasdaq.com

American Exchange: www.amex.com

10. Financial Press

Asian Wall Street Journal: www.dowjones.com/awsjweekly

Financial Times: www.ft.com

Wall Street Journal Interactive Edition: www.wsj.com

11. Other Useful Sites

Business Week Magazine: www.businessweek.com

Far Eastern Economic Review: www.feer.com

Index